D1472053

Adolescent Development

Readings in Research and Theory

MARTIN GOLD and ELIZABETH DOUVAN

The University of Michigan

Allyn and Bacon, Inc.
Boston, Mass.

TO OUR PARENTS:

Authors of our adolescences

Library of Congress Catalog Card Number:
74–86835

Printed in the United States of America

Cover photograph by David Attie — DPI.

Second printing . . . July, 1970

Preface

This collection of readings grew out of the editors' experiences teaching their own classes in the psychology of adolescence. We were eager to afford our students direct access to the best of the primary materials in the field, by which we meant the most cogent and clear theoretical discussions and the most thorough and systematic empirical studies. Furthermore, we wanted to present these in a structure which would help the student grasp the pieces because they fit into a recognizable pattern.

We are hopeful that our organization will not only make the separate selections more meaningful but also will stand as a contribution in itself to the psychology of adolescence. We have intended it to demonstrate how and in what way adolescence is a special phenomenon warranting the attention of serious students of psychology.

Acknowledgments

This book has benefited in both selection and focus from the critical comments of successive groups of students. We acknowledge our indebtedness to them for this and for the continuing stimulation we find in our academic encounters.

Rebecca F. Williams assumed the work of editing, collating, and securing permissions for use of the various articles. Thelma Whecler typed the manuscript. Both she and Mrs. Williams returned smiles and fine work in exchange for hard tasks and bad handwriting. Authors can hardly ask for more.

MARTIN GOLD and
ELIZABETH DOUVAN

Contents

1

Adolescence as a Developmental Concept

Were we content simply to describe human development as it proceeds from conception to death, it would be sufficient to segment the human life span arbitrarily, making smaller segments of those years of greatest change for the purpose of containing our discussion. If, however, we aspire beyond description to a theoretical understanding of development, then we must conceive of the life span as an integrated flow of crucial changes, and let these crucial changes determine how we will segment development for the purpose of discussion. This is the value of Piaget's conceptions of the development of cognition and of morality; of Freud's conception of the psychosexual stages; and of Erikson's conception of the developmental tasks upon which we lean heavily in this review. Each of these and other similar theoretical frameworks help us organize the data on development in a way that explains as well as describes.

One change which distinguishes adolescence as a phenomenon in human development is the growth spurt, and particularly the rapid maturation of the reproductive system. This accelerated dash into adulthood and the acquisition of potent sexuality, in turn, invoke changes in the way individuals are expected to behave, particularly in social interaction. These interlocked events, the biological change within and the social change without, characterize the bio-social phenomenon of adolescence.

While changes in the pattern of growth are humorously, painfully, beautifully obvious in the gangling figures of boys and the rounding figures of girls, changes in social expectations are more subtle—and we should not go on before discussing the concept of role as it will be used here. "Role" is a way of summarizing the fact that groups of people who interact with one another come to agree after a time on how they should behave, particularly in relation to one another. These prescriptions about behavior consist of rights and obligations; some are quite specific and rigid, others are broad and flexible; some explicit, some implicit. Not everyone has the same rights and obligations: in groups where people may be differentiated according to their age or sex or family background or wealth or length of membership or some other characteristic, behavior prescribed for each subgroup may differ. The role is the set of prescriptions for proper behavior and it often bears a title like "father," "friend," "saleslady," "boy."

At successive stages of our lives we are cast into different roles by our group, and at each stage we are called upon to play many roles at once. One of the central features of adolescence is that role demands are changing rapidly, in the process requiring changes in some long-standing and heavily invested behavior as well. For example, a subtle change takes place in the roles of "son" and "daughter": the role of "child" fades out of them. When once the hurt boy could cry and be cuddled, this is no longer legitimate for the adolescent son; the adolescent daughter now finds her father vaguely uncomfortable when she snuggles with him. So some warmth and comfort fade with the role of child.

These rapid and fundamental changes generate the central developmental problem of the adolescent. Finding that he is looking different and feeling different, and that others are responding to him differently and expecting him to act differently, an adolescent must wonder whether there is anyone who is really "him." Erikson (1950) has conceptualized this problem as the crisis of identity. That is, the adolescent must find ways to integrate what he feels he is with what his society allows him to be, at a time when he is not altogether sure what he is or what he is allowed to be. And in order that he may thrive psychologically, the adolescent's integration of self with society must finally present a personality that is essentially the same—whether viewed from within by himself or from without as reflected to him by important others—and essentially respectable to those who matter.

This view of the nature of adolescence and its developmental task has led us to organize our materials around the two elements of changing body and changing roles. We begin with a description of the maturation of sexuality by which we define the adolescent phase. Then we trace this theme of growth through a series of important roles which adolescents are called upon to play— son/daughter, friend-peer, student, worker, citizen, and believer. Finally, we discuss overall integration as a problem in the development of the self-concept.

Each section begins with a review* of the theory and data on that topic, followed by those selections which we have judged to cover the relevant range of research while adhering to high standards of scientific workmanship. Where we had to choose between articles, we favored more recent ones which summarized prior literature and pieces which were not already easily available in other compendia.

The review sections and indeed the nature of the overall organization of this collection clearly stamp the editors as the social psychologists we are. But the history of psychological attention to adolescence has really, until recently, been touched only lightly by social psychology, and we have amplified its influence in our selections.

As a special interest within psychology, adolescence has a long history. G. Stanley Hall introduced the topic into the scientific literature in 1899 and published his monumental two-volume work in 1904, about the time that sensory discrimination and the unconscious were emerging as areas of special concern. Yet it is only in the last two decades that our knowledge of adolescent

* Our reviews are taken with only minor revisions from our summary of research on adolescence which appeared in the Hoffmans' two-volume *Review of Child Development Research* (1967). We are grateful to the publisher, the Russell Sage Foundation, for permission to reprint.

processes has begun to take on the quality of understanding that occurs when theory enters a field. Anna Freud's insights about the special dilemmas and defensive strategies of the period (1937) represent a theoretical claimstake in the territory of adolescence. The last twenty years have brought considerable conceptual charting and a marked advance in knowledge.

This lag between interest and theory seems to us an accident of history. Hall himself, despite the fact that he structured his thought around the idea that individual development followed the pattern of species development, was supremely atheoretical. He was an observer and cataloguer. As Dennis noted (1946), Hall's work was more vigorous, inspired, and lofty than it was theoretically relevant. Hall was a penetrating observer, and indeed he established the areas of observation (sexual development, body growth, periodicity, delinquency, religious conversion, and so on) which to this day serve as organizing concepts in textbooks on adolescent psychology. But he did not pose the questions about interrelationships among changes and causes of the organization of changes which might have advanced systematic thinking and research.

At the same time, psychoanalysis, the theory most relevant to understanding adolescence, was developing on a course that reduced late childhood and the adolescent transition to a distinctly secondary interest. The early emphasis of psychoanalysis on the instincts and their vicissitudes led to a view of adolescence as primarily, if not entirely, a recapitulation of earlier Oedipal conflict and resolution. Both clinically and theoretically, psychoanalysis probed to the earliest presentation of a problem, for it was here that misadventure generally occurred, that anxieties, defenses, and symptoms were anchored in maldistributions and peculiar transformations of drive.

Furthermore, having demonstrated the existence of infantile sexuality, psychoanalysis could then dismiss those academic theories which had concerned themselves with adolescence in the erroneous belief that it marked the entrance of sex into the individual's life history. Consequently, insofar as the proper study of psychology was drive, according to the early psychoanalysts, there was nothing about adolescence to recommend it for special theoretical concern.

Just as the concepts of drive and instinct deflected early psychoanalysts from the study of adolescence, the recent reorientation of psychoanalytic theory to the broad area of ego development has brought adolescence at long last into its own. And that same reorientation has made social psychological considerations crucial, for the ego is that psychological process which interacts directly with the environment, and especially with the social environment.

One outcome of our social psychological orientation is a much fuller discussion of the normal and modal patterns in adolescence, compared to the more prevalent clinical discussions. This, coupled with our emphasis on systematic empirical work, has produced an image of adolescence which is bland compared to most of the literature on the subject. Where are the tensions, the crises, the muddled, befuddled, struggling, exasperating personalities lurching spasmodically through the teen years? When we contemplate the systematic empirical literature we find that most adolescents really don't go through all that, and a good deal of the fervid romance is gone.

Part of this blandness is a result of what is omitted from our review. We have not included any literature on psychopathology among adolescents and only an appropriate amount on juvenile delinquency, which is certainly an adolescent phenomenon. These two subjects have contributed most to the *Sturm und Drang* image of adolescence, though together the two groups make up only a small portion of American adolescents. We have attempted a description which more or less fits the great majority. (Delinquency among adolescents is itself a subject of collections of readings. Glueck, S., 1959; Giallombardo, R., 1966.)

It should not be surprising that most adolescents manage to survive comfortably and that we survive with them. Erikson (1950) spells out the requirements a social system must meet to accommodate human development:

> . . . it gives specific meanings to early bodily and interpersonal experience so as to create the right combination of organ modes and social modalities; it carefully and systematically channelizes throughout the intricate pattern of its daily life the energies thus provoked and deflected; and it gives consistent supernatural meaning to the infantile anxieties which it has exploited by such provocation.
> In doing all this, a society cannot afford to be arbitrary and anarchic. . . . [It] cannot afford to create a community of wild eccentrics, of infantile characters, or of neurotics. In order to create people who will function effectively as the bulk of the people, as energetic leaders, or as useful deviants, even the most "savage" culture must strive for what we vaguely call a "strong ego" in its majority or at least in its dominant minority—i.e., an individual core firm and flexible enough to reconcile the necessary contradictions in any human organization, to integrate individual differences, and above all to emerge from a long and unavoidably fearful infancy with a sense of identity and an idea of integrity (p. 160).

Barring cataclysmic change and disorganization, most social systems provide for some form of adequate human development, American society no less than others and for our adolescents no less than for the rest of us.

Like the rest of us, all adolescents have problems sometimes and make problems other times. Like some of us, some adolescents have problems and make problems more of the time than not. And, for adolescents as well as the rest of us, the quality of living could be better, and hopefully we can make it so. If this contemplative look at the scientific literature robs adolescence of most of its frenetic quality, perhaps it may contribute to understanding the quiet romance between social organization and youngsters in the midst of great change.

1

A Review of Contributions to a

Psychoanalytic Theory of Adolescence*

Individual Aspects

Leo A. Spieg⸱ l

In *The Three Contributions to a Theory of Sex* Freud (1918) delineated the basic psychological changes of adolescence. These consist in the full attainment of genital primacy over pregenital sexual drives. Under normal conditions, pregenital sexuality remains confined to providing forepleasure, thus contributing greater forcefulness to the genital act. Furthermore, the process of nonincestuous object finding, initiated by the reanimation of the oedipus complex in perpuberty and puberty, comes to a completion during adolescence.

Since 1904 a number of psychoanalytic papers have dealt with adolescence mainly as with a new edition of the oedipus complex. They fail to consider that the reanimated oedipal strivings now impinge on an ego which has "dimensions, contents, capacities, dependencies different from those of childhood" (A. Freud, 1946). Yet this very interaction between the oedipal strivings and the now matured and developed ego is the source of the manifold new but unclassified manifestations of the adolescent personality. The viewpoint that equates the origin with the ultimate manifestations has been, in part, responsible for the relative lack of psychoanalytic investigations of the problems of adolescence. Yet, there is no doubt that the development of personality continues beyond the period of the original oeidipal conflict. Thus Hartmann, Kris and Loewenstein (1946) point out: We feel that the potentialities of its transformation [personality] throughout adolescence have for some time been underrated in psychoanalytic writings."

Adolescence is not a simple repetition of the oedipal and post-oedipal period. For the first time, the psychic apparatus has at its disposal genital sexuality with adequate discharge for sexual ten-

sion.[1] The complete meaning of this change is unknown, but it alone is sufficient to stamp the phase of adolescence as something new and not a duplicate of an earlier age.

After the child has passed through the oedipal phase, he enters a latency period, whereas the puberty child is to become sexually active and competent. At this time, a sharp separation of masculine and feminine takes place and through the detachment from incestuous objects, the categories of older and newer generation begin to receive their full psychosocial significance. Problems of "ego identity" (Erikson, 1946; Hoffer, 1946) with intricate social and unconscious reverberations become of acute importance. Social mobility in connection with adequate instinctual gratification and defense becomes significant (Buxbaum, 1945; Deutsch, 1944).

The intellectual scope of the adolescent is to be enormously widened.[2] The precision of rigid art forms, built up during latency, often dissolves. Creativity receives a massive stimulus and daydreams occupy a greater area in mental activity.

In general, the plenitude, scope and variety of adolescent personality, achievement and interest, contrast impressively with the "expectedness" of earlier times. Even the psychosis of the adolescent is atypical and difficult to diagnose, for he has not yet "learned" to limit his illness to well-recognized psychiatric syndromes.

As the years pass, the adolescent hardens into a "type" more or less recognizable. One gets the im-

---

[1] I neglect here Kinsey's (and others') description (1948) of a number of cases of apparently adequate orgasm from infancy on through preadolescence. This type of dissociation of orgasm from ejaculation, although of great interest, is of such rarity that it cannot be considered here. In general, adequate sexual discharge is coupled to ejaculation.

[2] Piaget's illuminating research on the intellectual development up to prepuberty has not been carried forward into adolescence.

* From *The Psychoanalytic Study of the Child*, 1951, **6**, 375–393.

pression that in adolescence, the personality is melted down, becomes molten and fluid, and ultimately hardens again into what is to remain as the characterological core. Before that hardening, it appears that the ego's habitual relations to superego, id and external reality are frequently overthrown. If this process does not take place to some extent, if the ego remains rigid in the face of the new demands of the id, a premature setting of the personality mold with subsequent impoverishment of the emotional life will result (A. Freud, 1946).

Classifications of Adolescent Phenomenology

In describing the great variety of phenomena, usually attributed to adolescence, one wishes for a focal point, a point of orientation. However, to quote Bernfeld (1923):

Adolescence is less well understood from the viewpoint of psychological and sexual development than childhood. One of the reasons for the insufficiency of scientific literature on this period of life is to be found in the *great multiplicity* of phenomena in this age. Adolescence manifests itself in various areas: physiological, psychological and sociological. Confronted by the enormous varity of individual, social, cultural, historical and physical differences in the group, one is tempted to question the validity of classifying all these manifestations under the one heading of adolescence.

In our search for a frame of reference, our first automatic reaction is to turn to the already established psychoanalytic characterology. Its usefulness in actual clinical practice appears limited to precisely those adolescents who make a prematurely mature impression; for example those who are already frozen into a compulsive type of personality.

To meet this difficulty, Wittels (1949) has developed a schema of adolescent ego development or evolution. He postulates a second phallic phase, a second latency period, and finally the stage of the mature ego. Experience will show how much this schema corresponds to observed data, and how helpful it is for surveying adolescent phenomenology.

Bernfeld has grappled with the same problem in a series of illuminating papers (1923, 1935, 1938), which unfortunately do not seem to have found sufficient recognition by other investigators of adolescence. In the first two papers, he attempts to describe two types of adolescents among the manifold forms. He bases his classification on their different reactions to the libidinal changes of puberty. An excerpt will make his view clear:

The responses to puberty are varied. One group of boys tries to deny the pubertal changes and to live as if nothing new has occurred. Anxiety and defense against anxiety characterize this group, and produce many forms which account for the innumerable phenomena of adolescence—a fact which makes a unified description of this period of life so difficult. However, we know that anxiety is the central feature of this group, and that the universal causes for this anxiety is to be found in the early years of childhood when barriers against sexuality are first erected. The signs of beginning sexual maturity threaten these barriers, and the fear of their dissolution determines the course of puberty in this group, which is called the neurotic group.

In contrast, the second group takes a positive and affirmative attitude to the first signs of sexual maturity. These adolescents behave as if they had desired and yearned for sexual maturity for a long time. This is the group of simple or uncomplicated puberty.

The contrast between the neurotic and this simple puberty is based on one condition: namely that the ideal of being grown up has remained unbroken throughout childhood. To this group, the latency period is a period of impatient waiting. The first signs of puberty are greeted with a wave of increased self-esteem. The appearance of sexual maturity is appreciated and welcomed as a sign of the fulfillment of the ancient wish to be grown up. Society, however, opposes this wish; the adolescent on his part attempts to assert himself. The *external* conflict is the basic and determining situation for this type and permeates his entire adolescence (Bernfeld, 1935).

The "neurotic type," whose conflicts are primarily inner ones, is frequently described as the typical adolescent, interested in cultural pursuits and steered by idealistic considerations. Social changes since World War I have tended to produce a mixture of "neurotic" and dissocial behavior, often limited to the sexual sphere (Bernfeld, 1935).

The second group is characterized by pronounced coarsening of the sexual life, by stunting of the tender strivings or by their attachment to objects of the same sex. Bernfeld points out that hitherto psychoanalysis has only studied this splitting of sensual and tender strivings in terms of a result of the oedipal conflict. Yet, this type of youth is also forced into such splitting as a consequence of social pressures (Bernfeld, 1935). The author discusses some critical junctures at which the "uncomplicated adolescent" may change into the "neurotic adolescent":

> Since external circumstances play a decisive role in this development, the length of their duration is important. Perhaps it is this factor which is responsible for the frequency with which youths in their eighteenth or nineteenth year, after having had sexual intercourse from the twelfth year on, suddenly give up their companions and their usual way of life and go through a period of inner deepening. They may experience a religious conversion or join a political party. This development corresponds to a retarded setting in of neurotic adolescence. Thus years of difficulties, interferences and narcissistic injuries (to which the uncomplicated type of puberty is exposed) finally bring about the same result as that childhood development which, with widespread repression of infantile sexuality and thereby the repression of the sexual aspect of the ideal to be grown up, responded to the inner dangers precipitated by the appearance of puberty, by a neurotic adolescence. Youths, who in the course of puberty switch in one of these many ways into the neurotic group, are of a special type both because of their early history and because of the special qualities of the environment in which their adolescence was passed (Bernfeld, 1935).

In comparing this group with the dissocial group, Bernfeld points out that the abstinence which society attempts to impose tends to produce "actual-neurotic" symptoms such as irritability and anxiety. Both of these reactions may add to the sum of aggression naturally present and bring this type of adolescent close to the dissocial group.

In a later paper, Bernfeld attempts to develop a more comprehensive schema for adolescent phenomenology (1938). By emphasizing the shifting nature of the ego-superego relation in adolescence, he attempts to capture and to classify the transient phenomena of adolescence. Adolescents may be divided into three groups in terms of their attitude toward sexuality. One is extremely compliant to the wishes of the environment, one is extremely rebellious, and the third is the mixed group. This typology is further subdivided by introducing the idea of compliance to or defiance of the internalized past milieu (the superego). Bearing in mind that adolescence is a process, not a state, and that in the course of several years, an adolescent may pass from one subvariety to another, this classification has the merit of considerable elasticity.

Yet it seems questionable whether compliance and defiance, as used by Bernfeld, are adequately

exhaustive criteria for a description of an evolving ego-superego relation. For example, humor, as described by Freud, is another indication of a shifting ego-superego relation and already makes its appearance in preadolescence.

More information is needed on the development of the superego at this time of life. "Less clearly has it been realized that at this stage a new set of ideals is frequently chosen . . . during adolescence, identifications gain a new impact; they become more compelling and the need for support from outside is greater" (Hartmann *et al.*, 1946). Perhaps the shifting values of our times, with their influence on superego formation in adolescence and their tendency to "maximize compliance" (Kinsey *et al.*, 1948), are responsible for the frequent appearance of the pseudomature adolescent and later the pseudomature adult who, although he complies with the serious demands of present-day society, is nevertheless emotionally very close to blind revolt against these demands. On the other hand, it seems questionable whether we find as frequently in our era the revolutionary type of adolescent described in earlier studies. A description of the ego-superego relation is not enough to describe exhaustively the changes in adolescence. Obviously, the genital changes, apart from creating problems in ego defense against id and superego, offer stimuli for ego synthesis and organization. The catalytic and organizing effect of the adolescent genital drives toward object relations, toward intellectual activities and interests, the effect of adequate sexual discharge on the total psychic tension[3]—all these phenomena require an adequate framework for their classification.

Object Relations in Adolescence

A consideration of the more individual aspects[4] of adolescence may well begin with the nature of its object relations. Changes in this area are its outstanding feature (A. Freud, 1946). The function of adolescence in the life history of the individual is the

---

[3] Bernfeld reminds us that in a sense actual neuroses are a normal part of adolescence.
[4] Problems of social organization, of group formation, of shifting social and ethical values, of special aspects of therapy, bulk large in studies of adolescence and require an approach different from the one in this paper. Therefore, important works by Reik, Róheim, Bernfeld, Daly, Redl, Erikson, and many others, must be reserved for separate discussion. As a result, certain important social and sociological aspects of adolescence receive inadequate treatment here.

attainment of genital primacy and the definitive completion of the process of nonincestuous object finding. Thus adolescence begins with the anatomical and physiological genital changes which constitute a necessary precondition for the discharge of sexual excitement via the genital apparatus (Bernfeld, 1923). Adolescence ends when the individual finds a nonincestuous love object, and tender as well as sexual drives are directed toward this same object with the goal of genital sexual gratification, i.e., when sexuality is fully integrated into the personality (Bernfeld, 1923; Fenichel, 1945; E. Jones, 1923). It is obvious that this upper limit of the adolescent phase is an indefinite one, and this accounts for the fact that many adult neurotics give the impression of adolescents (Fenichel, 1945). The indefiniteness of the upper limit has led to the description of a special adolescent, a variety of the "neurotic" type, the so-called "elongated" adolescent.[5]

While stressing the central role of the reanimated oedipus complex in the process of object finding, it is maintained that in many cases it may not appear in the clear form described by Freud for early childhood. In healthier adolescents there is at first a clear expression of the oedipus complex which then gradually diminishes. Parent substitutes who have less and less in common with the original parent images are chosen with increasing frequency as maturation continues. Healthy adolescents choose these parent substitutes on the basis of important traits, while in pathological cases trivial similarities and dissimilarities with their own parents may be decisive in their choices (Katan-Angel, 1937; Landauer, 1935). A dichotomous splitting of the parent imago into one idealized, revered and one hated, despised, also occurs in adolescence (Klein, 1946).

In the process of object finding and in the development of sexuality, adolescent masturbation has a very important place. The primacy of the genital is achieved, uniting in one act all object-directed strivings. The fantasies, accompanying the masturbatory act, are, with few exceptions, directed toward an object (Balint, 1934).

The defense mechanisms are directed against the incestuous fantasies of preadolescence. The adolescent turns away from his childhood objects with consequent transformation of significant amounts of object libido into narcissistic libido, and a feeling of isolation. This, in turn, leads to his attempts at re-

[5] Bernfeld (1923) points to the possibility that this type of adolescence may be typical for the artist.

gaining contact on a narcissistic basis (Fenichel, 1938).

In place of the childhood objects, innumerable new relationships are formed in part with contemporaries, and in part with older people, who are obviously substitutes for the renounced parents. These relationships are stormy, exclusive, and brief, and are repeated each time in identical form. They represent identifications of so primitive a type that the adolescent may change his beliefs, his style of clothing, his writing, with each new friend. In this way he temporarily resembles the "as if" type of Deutsch (1944). Friendship becomes highly idealized. This aspect of friendship is a response to the fragility of the newly acquired relationship (A. Freud, 1946). The narcissistic nature of adolescent friendship becomes evident in the functions of the somewhat younger and somewhat older friend. In the older friend, the adolescent finds the kindly, understanding father; in the younger one, he sees his recent self toward whom he acts as the forgiving father, thus relieving his own guilt (Landauer, 1935). Consequently, masturbation, telling of sexual stories, become group experiences. A certain type of "neurotic adolescent" displays contemptuous attitudes toward most contemporaries and those in authority, while exempting a selected few to love and admire. There is a tendency to make friends only with those who think and feel as he does. Problems of ego identity, delimitation of the self, homosexuality, group formation, enter here (Buxbaum, 1945; Erikson, 1946; Hoffer, 1946).

In general it may be said that adolescent object relations bear the character of restitution phenomena: they are narcissistic attempts at regaining contact with objects following the renunciation of incestuous ones. It is likely that these identification relationships also have the defensive purpose of insuring against the "return of the repressed." How these identifications are further transformed, in late adolescence and early adulthood, into aim-inhibited object relations seems not to have been studied.

Deutsch says that preadolescent girls make a homosexual object choice, those of early adolescence, a bisexual one, and finally, as adolescence advances, the heterosexual choice emerges. The homosexual relation has at times a sadomasochistic quality. Often, and perhaps regularly, the first heterosexual steps are taken in conjunction with the girl friend. A common love of two girls for a teacher may be the first model of such a constellation. A triangular situation with dynamic role changes, as the triangle evolves, is thus created (Deutsch, 1944). This constellation also involves problems of ego growth and delimitation.

Deutsch points out that the growth of object relations in adolescent girls may be seriously hampered by an excessive prepubertal attachment to the mother who constitutes a greater danger in this respect than the father. Adolescence then lacks its normal, revolutionary impetus and the object relations of such women express infantile dependence rather than love and friendship (Deutsch, 1944).

Defense Mechanisms in Adolescence

A consideration of the instinctual situation at prepuberty can best introduce the problem of defense mechanisms in adolescence. The end of the oedipal period finds the child in an equilibrium which changes little during latency. The ego now has certain favored mechanisms of defense; it has become accustomed to a given ratio of instinctual gratification to instinctual renunciation, and to a given postponement of gratification (A. Freud, 1946). However, in prepuberty an increase in instinctual energy occurs without a qualitative change. Aggressive tendencies and pregenital drives alike are reactivated, reaction formations threatened, oedipal fantasies reappear, and the castration complex in boys and penis envy in girls again occupy the center of the stage (A. Freud, 1946).

A different view of the prepuberty period in girls is presented by Deutsch who maintains that it is the period of greatest freedom from infantile sexuality and from aggression. It is marked by a thrust of activity which represents not an aggression but an intensive process of adaptation to reality and of mastery of the environment. This thrust of activity precedes the passivity of the female pubertal period (Deutsch, 1944). It is difficult to reconcile this supposed freedom from infantile sexuality with material the author gives demonstrating the strongest interest in the function of the sexual organs, the preoccupation with prostitution fantasies, and sadomasochistic interpretations of intercourse. Furthermore, the prepubertal girl is described as being full of rage and hatred as well as of dependent, clinging feelings toward the mother. Finally, the comparison between prepuberty and the preoedipal phase is presented (Deutsch, 1944).

The ego, subjected to the increased instinctual drives, knows only one wish: to regain the equilibrium of the latency period. To achieve its aims, it uses indiscriminately all the defense mechanisms that it used in early childhood and latency (A. Freud, 1946).[6] Greenacre has recently described the "prepuberty trauma" which consists of a sexual act at the hands of an adult. The prepubertal girl provokes, or co-operates in, this sexual act, shifting the resulting feelings of guilt to the adult. The experience remains in consciousness and is used as a "real" defense against the demands of puberty (Greenacre, 1950). From this investigation it becomes evident that external reality may be primarily used for defensive purposes.[7]

With the arrival of puberty the instinctual equilibrium changes.[8] Threatened by the increase of instinctual pressure the ego makes special use of two defense mechanisms: asceticism and intellectualization. These mechanisms are, of course, at the disposal of the ego in earlier periods, but they become particularly dominant during adolescence. Asceticism consists of an attempt at total suppression of all instinctual gratification. Relief from this massive attack on any form of instinctual gratification as such is obtained by sudden periods of intense instinctual indulgence so that alternating periods of asceticism and indulgence dominate the adolescent picture (A. Freud, 1946). Asceticism becomes particularly prominent as a defense mechanism during puberty because of the ego's primary antagonism to instincts (A. Freud, 1946); it is a response to the quantity, not the quality, of the instinctual drive. It is a response to the ego's fear of being overwhelmed, of losing its organization—a fear which probably originated at the time of separation of ego from id (A. Freud, 1946).

Rather than assuming a primary antagonism of the ego to instincts, Fenichel (1938) argues that "it is precisely in order to avoid such 'traumatic situations' [the overwhelming of the ego by instincts] that the ego develops its capacity to give the danger

---

[6] The various break-throughs of pregenital tendencies, while representing a failure in defense, may also be considered a regressive protection against delinquency (Lander, 1942).

[7] In this connection it is interesting to note a comment by Berta Bornstein (1949) that prepubertal experiences may be decisive for the formation of psychopathic personality—a type particularly prone to become entangled with the environment.

[8] Fenichel writes: "If it were possible finally to liquidate the Oedipus complex by satisfactory sexual experiences with non-incestuous objects, adjustment [in adolescence] would be easier. The fact that this is difficult to achieve under present-day conditions leads to the intensification of the Oedipus complex and therefore to the intensification of sexual anxieties" (1945).

signal and that the intention of the ego to make instinctual gratifications possible is underestimated." Asceticism may be the response of the ego to a situation in which it cannot master great quantities of excitation through discharge according to the pleasure principle. One must inquire whether cultural conditions make adequate gratification possible during adolescence (Bernfeld, 1935; Fenichel, 1938) and whether mechanisms of gratification themselves require time to become functionally adequate during adolescence.

On the other hand, it has also been pointed out that the differentiation of the ego from the id presupposes a certain degree of repudiation of instinct (Kris, 1938). Still, it remains debatable whether the primary inhibitory function of the ego should be offered as evidence of a primary antagonism of the ego to instincts as is apparently meant.

The defensive role of the intellect is, of course, also at the disposal of the ego from early years but it rises to special prominence during adolescence as a response to the quantitative change in instinctual drive (A. Freud, 1946). It manifests itself in endless discussions on abstract, political and philosophical themes (Bernfeld, 1923; A. Freud, 1946). The level of thinking may be high and the viewpoint may be astonishingly broad, but a close connection between this intellectual activity and its application to life is characteristically absent. Discussions exist for their own sake. This is in contrast to the attitude of the latency child whose interests are centered on concrete problems and on activity (A. Freud, 1946).

Many of the concepts of adolescents simply mirror inner instinctual processes. Intellectualization as a defense consists of an extreme attentiveness and alertness to the instinctual drive and an attempt to master it on the level of thought (A. Freud, 1946).

Creativity in Adolescence

Many adolescents experience the urge toward creativity.[9] Some of the conditions for adolescent creativity have been described under the heading of severe narcissistic injury at the time of the oedipal conflict, the early ideal formation with a compulsion toward such a formation, and a severe superego with

a pronounced mother identification (Bernfeld, 1923, 1924).

The wish to produce does not begin in adolescence but goes back to earliest childhood, representing the desire to produce a child during all phases of development. In adolescence, with the re-enactment of the oedipal conflict, this desire is also mobilized and expressed in the urge to creativity (Bernfeld, 1924).

According to Bernfeld, the instinctual conflict finds the following characteristic solution in the creative adolescent: the incestuous libidinal drives are deflected to other permissible objects, fantasies, values, ideas, which may be called "also-objects." Creativity itself, in this form of adolescence, is approved by the ego ideal (Bernfeld, 1924). Rank showed that dramas written in adolescence concern themselves, without exception, with problems of incest. He explains the sudden cessation of creative activity, which occurs so frequently toward the end of adolescence, as a result of the inability to master the incest conflict (Bernfeld, 1924).

The problem of the transformation, in adolescence, of the defensive function of artistic creativity into one that is more truly creative and progressive has also been studied. The solution that has been found is the one generally valid for all art forms. When the adolescent sacrifices his private needs to the demands of communicability, he thereby finds his way back from fantasy to reality (A. Freud, 1922). The transformation consists primarily in a modification of the *form* of art products (Bernfeld, 1924). The motor for the renunciation of gratification derived from private daydreams (as recorded in diaries) is to be found in the ambitious strivings of the adolescent for the fame and power to be gained from impressing a wide audience (Bernfeld, 1924).[10] The genetic history of a true art product, a short story written by an adolescent girl has been traced from a beginning in masochistic beating fantasies to happy daydreams, and from there to the short story itself. The beating fantasy represented the fulfillment of the sensual, sexual drives of the anal-sadistic level; the happy daydreams, the fulfillment of the aim-inhibited tender tendencies of the oedipal period. The short story, however, sacrificed these private libidinal gratifications to the needs of public communication to an audience (A. Freud, 1922).

[9] The diary is probably the most usual creative activity and in it are recorded not only objective events but reflections, plans and recollections (Deutsch, 1944). The writing of poetry and other literary efforts in adolescence have been especially studied (Bernfeld, 1924; Deutsch, 1944; A. Freud, 1928).

[10] In this transformation of the defensive function of artistic activity, the emphasis on communication contains links with Piaget's work on the changes in egocentric thinking which have not yet received analytic attention.

The hero of those literary products that are closely related to daydreams represents the author's ego ideal, for which he pleads in order to obtain sympathy, recognition and love. Particularly in late puberty, "when the erection of the ego ideal and the ego's conflict with the ego ideal play the central role, are there many motives for the production of such works" (Bernfeld, 1924).

Sexual Activity in Adolescence

Except for the previously quoted comments by Fenichel, psychoanalytic literature lacks any explicit discussion of the problem of whether sexual intercourse in adolescence is healthy or unhealthy and of whether it could alleviate the enormous tension of that period. Bernfeld has pointed out that those adolescents who determinedly seek sexual intercourse must face the strong opposition of society[11] and consequently their sexuality becomes significantly coarsened (Bernfeld, 1935). Deutsch (1944) claims the same in respect to girls. Federn (1912) suggests that adolescent sexual intercourse in itself may have a coarsening effect; that some degree of asceticism is necessary for the development of a finer understanding of the erotic life. He adds, however, that one should not push this demand at the cost of health. "Comparative pubertal research" (Fenichel, 1945) will be of value here.

Despite the great attention given to the problem of adolescent masturbation in analysis, there have been few reports in the literature which are specific contributions to this topic. It is generally accepted today that masturbation is not harmful if moderately employed, with full awareness of the action, its associated fantasies, and with attainment of orgasm. Its excessive use may be harmful, for psychological reasons rather than physiological factors. When masturbation is overfrequent it is an indication of psychopathology. Instead of attempting to modify the external world for purposes of ultimate gratification, these "masturbation characters" (Balint, 1934) turn more and more frequently to their own genital.

Considerations of chemical and physiological changes, of neurasthenia and anxiety neurosis following excessive masturbation and abstinence, which were so frequent in older analytic writings, have

disappeared today (Cf. Reich, 1951, p. 80; Kris, 1951, p. 95). Still, it is worthwhile recalling that Freud firmly retained the idea in 1912, and did not renounce it later on, that "at times" adolescent masturbation is harmful. Furthermore, he mentions that it also results "at times" in a permanent diminution of potency, but adds dryly that that is not necessarily undesirable since "virtue with full potency would be a heavy task" (Freud, 1912).

Ferenczi (1912) maintains that masturbation is both psychologically and physiologically different from coitus and points out that forepleasure is missing and fantasy tremendously increased in the masturbatory act. Forepleasure brings many parts of the central nervous system into a state of excitation and its absence must be of significance. Freud (1912) seems to be thinking along the same lines when he says that it may be the differences between masturbation and intercourse which are the bearers of the pathogenic action of masturbation (Cf. Lampl-de Groot, 1950).

The struggle against masturbation which plays so prominent a role in adolescence is, of course, of such violence because of the associated oedipal fantasies. The conflict may be solved in specifically neurotic ways, as for instance by the dissociation of the masturbatory activity from the fantasies, a solution which is frequently found in obsessive-compulsive types. This constellation is frequently preceded by a phase during which the masturbatory fantasies contain either anonymous objects or objects vague in outline. Often the masturbatory fantasies are completely repressed but may manifest themselves in hysterical conversion symptoms, especially in female adolescents. According to Deutsch, masturbation in girls may either begin or stop in connection with the menarche. The task that has to be achieved by the adolescent girl in order to attain full femininity is a twofold one: Firstly, there has to be a shift of cathexis from the clitoris to the vagina; and secondly, a shift from activity to passivity. The first menstruation, as a sign of biological maturity, may play an important role in this process, either by supporting the feminine tendencies with all the fantasies concerning passive-masochistic gratification, pregnancy and childbirth; or, on the contrary, leading to a rejection of femininity by increasing penis envy and the castration complex. Unconsciously, the first menstruation is experienced as an injury to the genital, as a castration, and as a punishment for masturbation (Buxbaum, 1933).

Helene Deutsch (1944) emphasizes the double

---

[11] Because of the much higher rate of adolescent intercourse among "lower-class" males, one must consider the likelihood of "class" variations in the attitudes toward early sexual intercourse (Hollingshead, 1949; Kinsey *et al.*, 1948).

sexual role of womanhood, namely that of mother and lover. Characteristic of the young girl's erotic longing is the expectation of sexual experience as distinct from motherhood. Only later and gradually, perhaps not until the actual sexual experience has taken place, do the two tendencies become closely interwoven, either mutually supportive or in conflict with one another.

Aspects of Ego Functioning

A study of the differences between adolescence and early childhood is expected to throw much light on problems of ego development, just as the study of similarities between the two periods has thrown light on libidinal development (A. Freud, 1946). The massive lidibinization of the ego, the counterpart to the withdrawal of object cathexes, makes adolescence a period of prolonged and frequently painful narcissism. A number of contradictory traits, often considered characteristic of adolescence, are probably subsumed under this heading, such as altruism and selfishness, gregariousness and solitariness, indulgence and asceticism. It is also maintained that the contradictory attitudes are due to newly strengthened drives and defenses against them (Fenichel, 1945). However, it does seem necessary to assume some dysfunction of the ego to explain the toleration of these contradictions.

An increased sensitivity to inner changes both of a somatic and of a psychological nature are, of course, consequences of the increase in narcissistic libido. The working over of the inner psychological changes on a mental level constitutes the defense described as intellectualization. The numerous friendships on the basis of identifications, likewise attributable to the narcissism of that period, are obviously akin to restitution phenomena. The need to experience the self as a separate entity (the "individualism" of adolescence) becomes acute at this time and appears to be another aspect of the same restitution process. Hoffer (1946) studied the process in a hebephrenic boy in whom a concurrently increasing megalomania kept step with increasingly desperate attempts to attach himself to his fellows and yet not lose his identity.

These manifestations of significant ego dysfunctions make the comparison to the initial phases of a psychosis an instructive one (A. Freud, 1946). The attempts at contact, the increased awareness of so-matic processes, the understanding of inner changes, all these appear to be points of similarity between the two states. The increase in instinctual tension and the increased defensive procedures of the ego in both cases are the common agents. But the particular similarity between adolescence and the psychotic episode lies in the emergence of primitive defensive procedures, belonging to the ego's fear of the strength of instincts—a fear older than superego anxiety or real anxiety (A. Freud, 1946).

Specific changes in the narcissistic libido occur at puberty and are quantitatively different in the sexes. The male retains the narcissistic estimation of his own penis to a great extent throughout his life, while the woman, on reaching maturity at puberty, is obliged to renounce this high valuation and instead to prize the beauty of her figure and face. Or to express the same thing in a formula: in men, the genital continues to be the center of their narcissism, while in women there is a secondary narcissism, which becomes attached to the body as a whole—the whole body becomes a genital (Hárnik, 1924). The basis for the libidinal shift from the genital to the body as a whole is found in the wave of repression, occurring at puberty, which relates especially to the sexuality associated with the clitoris (Hárnik, 1924).

A similar libidinal shift occurs in the male sex, but less powerfully, as it seems. "Men cannot continue, any more than women, to center their narcissism upon the genitals without some sacrifice. Under the pressure of the castration complex, they are obliged—in a manner analogous to the processes which characterize puberty in females—to effect a secondary cathexis of the whole body with a part of the narcissistic libido and to bring about a displacement of libido on to interests, the aim of which is to increase their bodily strength. With this conclusion we touch upon the process which may be called the formation of the ego-ideal of 'manliness'" (Hárnik, 1924). This view of the process at puberty has been summarized as a tendency toward a secondary reactivation of the prenatal diffused sexuality, the stage of primary narcissism (Hárnik, 1924). An increase in the "libidinal cathexis of the body ego" is also found at puberty as a result of characteristic pains arising from the sexual changes. Thus the boy often experiences painful sensations in the vas deferens due to inadequate discharge; the girl often has pain at the introitus and breasts. Both suffer from various cramps and low back pain (Landauer, 1935).

The integration of the maturing genitals and of

the secondary sexual characteristic into the body image is a gradual and at times conflict-ridden process. The pubic and axillary hair and the breasts become the source of conflict, and the question as to whether to be a man or a woman may be displaced from genital to breast (Landauer, 1935). The acceptance of the sexually competent penis may also be a gradual affair. The loss of control, manifested in the involuntary erections and emissions of this period of life, is a severe blow to the narcissism of the male adolescent. Particularly the nocturnal emissions reactivate the early conflicts centering on enuresis. After the defeat represented by the first involuntary emission, competition in this field (whose penis is the biggest, the hardest, who can have an orgasm most quickly, who can keep it back the longest, who can spurt the furthest?) may lead to a complete transformation of the "penis urinator" into the "penis phallus" (Landauer, 1935).

A number of other characteristic ego dysfunctions for the age will be mentioned here: fainting, excessive sleepiness, feelings of unreality (often a result of repression of orgastic sensations as well as the result of repression of sensations derived from accidental contact with the genitals) and various disturbances in motility (Landauer, 1935).

Decisive and permanent changes of character may occur as a result of impairment of the ego-superego relation at this time. The superego may be treated as an incestuous object in so far as it is still invested with libido stemming from the parental relationships. The adolescent experiences this estrangement of his superego as a severe blow and this in turn increases the danger from the instinctual drives (A. Freud, 1946). Now the ego, deserted by the super-ego in its struggle with the rising tide of instinctual need, may succumb more readily to the id and then the conditions are present for the development of an "impulsive character" (Fenichel, 1945). On the other hand, the ego may be able to retain a completely rigid control of the id at the cost of a permanent impoverishment of the emotional life (A. Freud, 1946). Because of the incapacity to tolerate and synthesize the polarities of love and hate, the weak ego of many adolescents falls apart repeatedly and "the whole period of adolescence becomes a series of psychoses and neuroses" (Landauer, 1935).

2

Adolescent Personality

as Self-Other Systems*

Orville G. Brim, Jr.

For the past several years, the author and his colleagues have been formulating some ideas about personality development and organization which emphasize the distinctive point of view of the sociologist. In most previous work in child development and personality theory, the sociologist's traditional concerns with role learning, social interaction, and the influence of reference groups have not been included. One of the objectives is to introduce such sociological materials into the analysis of personality.

The stimulus for this is really a point of view, rather than a theory, a point of view which insists that there are some materials from sociology which should be included in any comprehensive theory of personality. This paper will sketch these concepts and hypotheses and discuss several of them in detail.

Most of what is learned in childhood, and indeed throughout life—that we call personality—is a series of complex interpersonal relationships. The net result is that the personality of the individual is constituted in largest measure by these learned interpersonal relationships and in fact should be described and understood in these terms. Personality can be viewed as a set of learned self-other relationships or systems, each of these built up from thousands of remembered expectations of others, from the appraisals of one's behavior both by these others and by himself, from the perceived success or failure of the action, and from the rewards and punishments given by society through its agents—parents, teachers, peers, etc. It follows that we should attempt to describe personality by reference to the individual's perceptions of himself and his behavior, and of the social organization in which he lives.[1]

We should be interested in the kinds of people he says are of greatest significance to him, and interested in what he thinks others expect him to do, and in what they think about his performances. We should also know whether or not he accepts what others prescribe for him as right and legitimate or whether he thinks their expectations are unfair; we should know about his relationships, as he sees them, to these significant others—whether he likes them, trusts them, thinks they are consistent in their behavior, whether the relationship is of long or short duration, and so on. We should find out how he seeks to resolve conflicts between himself and others, and whether his attempts at resolution actually work or whether he continues in a state of conflicting demands. All of these—and more—are significant components of his personality and describe the important aspects of his relationships to other people.

Some familiar personality components and processes are intentionally missing in the work of the author and his colleagues. The research is not dealing with biological processes of the individual, learning processes, cognition, or problem solving. Moreover, at this time the research deals only with that part of the individual's personality which he is able and willing to tell about himself—his own self-descriptions—his voluntarily revealed self-image. This is not to doubt repression, or that there are components of the personality which are uncon-

* From *Journal of Marriage and the Family*, 1965, 27, 156–162.

[1] The data in these studies are the respondents' perceptions both of themselves, i.e., their own personalities, and of other persons, i.e., the structure of the social environment in which they are involved. In one sense, the latter data may be treated as more or less veridical descriptions of the world. In this view, each respondent can be regarded as a participant observer in the social order, permitting analysis of the total set of data by a scheme which relates personality, i.e., the data the respondents report about themselves, to social organizations, i.e., the data they report about their world. In another sense, however, since the data are perceptual, it is possible to treat *all* the data, including the reports on the social environment, as personality data. With this approach, the analytic problem concerns the interrelations of personality components, some of which are traditional—i.e., the descriptions of one's self, and some of which are not—i.e., the descriptions of the social order. Heuristically, it seems valuable to explore the advantages of both points of view. The descriptions of the social environment are assumed here to be components of personality.

scious and inaccessible to the individual's self-report. It is just that the present studies concentrate on this one particular set of materials about personality and one's own self-report information as a body of data. This is justified on the grounds that this one thing, done well, will contribute to fuller understanding at a later date.

The subjects of the adolescent study constituted the whole population of one public and one private secondary school in the eastern United States. Sophomores, juniors, and seniors were included, and in the public school, both male and female students were involved. The total number of students for whom complete results were obtained is 1,305. A wide range of variation appears in social class, intelligence, and other characteristics among these students.

The data on personality were obtained from the students by means of an especially developed four-booklet questionnaire. Each booklet was administered during a separate one-hour period scheduled about a week apart during the fall or winter of the school year.

Adolescent Role Prescriptions

Of the personality variables studied, this paper will examine two in detail. The first is the adolescent's view of the prescriptions for his behavior that other people hold for him. The "perceived role prescriptions" really are a basic part of the adolescent's view of the world surrounding him.

Content of the Prescriptions

Each adolescent was asked for his perception of the role prescriptions held for him by his father, mother, friends, and best-liked teacher. These prescriptions were sought with reference to the three main social contexts or roles in the adolescent's life, namely, the roles of family member, peer group member, and student.

For each of these three roles, 12 different items were used to describe how one might behave in that role. These items were such things as "get along well with brothers and sisters"; "always live up to my family's good name"; "take part in class discussions"; "be known as an outstanding student"; "have social poise and self-confidence"; "be popular with girls"; and so on, there being 36 items in all, 12 for each of the three roles.

The adolescent was asked how each of these significant persons (that is, parents, friends, and teachers) felt about each of these items. (The one exception was that only teacher prescriptions were requested with reference to the student role.) To illustrate, the respondent was asked to state whether he thought his father strongly agreed, agreed, did not care, disagreed, or strongly disagreed with each item such as "be known as an outstanding student." Thus, for each significant person, for each role, it was found whether the adolescent believed that the other prescribed or proscribed the behavior in question. The adolescent's answers give a picture of the most salient role prescriptions which bound his day-to-day activities.

In writing the actual items, the researchers emphasized the general theme of achievement, which has a specific manifestation in each role in the following way: in the student role, since achievement is manifested in scholarship and achieving good grades, the items for this role centered around scholastic performance; in the peer group, since leadership and popularity are the criteria of achievement, items were concerned with these; in the family, being responsible for carrying out one's duties, maintaining the family's good reputation, and being supportive, seemed to be the kind of items which best indicated adequacy of role performance.

Factor Structure of the Prescriptions

How do these various role prescriptions—involving several significant people, several kinds of behavior and attitudes, and three basic social roles—fit together? In the adolescent personality, are these prescriptions ordered or organized in terms of specific roles so that the adolescent thinks of himself as a student one time, a friend another time, and a son or daughter at still another time? Or are these prescriptions centered on persons, so that he thinks of himself in specific interpersonal relationships, one at a time; e.g., "What would my father want me to do in this situation?" or "What would my friends want me to do in this situation?" Or, thirdly, is the adolescent personality organized around actual themes in behavior, regardless of which role it is, or who is the significant other; for example, is one oriented toward achievement at all times, rather than toward people or social contexts?

To answer this question, the researchers turned to the use of factor analysis. What are the basic elements which stem from the correlations between these 150 role prescriptions, taken from different roles and different people? If the adolescent reports that his father strongly agrees with a particular item in the peer role, such as "be popular with girls," what else is correlated with this particular response, what other item, prescribed by what person, and for what role?

The factor analysis resulted in certain clusterings of role prescription items, i.e., "factors." The first of these clearly referred to the pressures of friends to do well academically in the student role. Thus the respondent, if he said that his friends prescribed that he study hard as a student, also said that they wanted him to take part in class discussions, get along well with teachers, do outside work for credit, get good grades, etc.

The second factor is different. Where the first was role specific, person specific, and, one might say, theme specific, the second factor cuts across roles, cuts across people, and cuts across themes or content. It appears to be what at the Ivy League colleges used to be called the "gentleman C" factor. The items forming the factor include: "work below my capacity," "act less smart than I really am," "belong to a definite crowd or social club," and "go steady." These items come from both the peer and student role, and all of the significant others are involved in prescribing or proscribing the behavior—fathers, teachers, friends, and mothers. To clarify this interesting cluster, the following example shows that the items are correlated with each other in the cluster. If the adolescent reports that his friends prescribe for him in his student role that he should work below his capacity, he also reports that his father prescribes for him that in his peer role he act less smart than he really is. Here, then, are dual themes derived from the prescriptions of all of these significant others and regulating both the peer and student roles. Again, an interesting insight into the organization of the adolescent personality.

The third factor involves just the father as the significant other, but his prescriptions cut across all three roles (home, student, and peer) and involve responsibility in the home, being a good student, and not being socially frivolous. It is a Jack Armstrong or Eagle Scout component of personality, in which the father is the sole point of reference. Examples of items are "be respectful to my parents," "be serious about things with my friends," "get along well with teachers."

In the fourth factor, the peer group is the sole source of prescriptions. The only role involved is the adolescent's home role, and the content has to do with being a good responsible family member. In this respect, this fourth factor is like the first, involving one significant other, one role, and one behavioral theme.

The fifth factor is like the third, only here the mother is the sole prescriber. Once again the prescriptions cut across roles and across areas of behavior, and might be summarized by the concept of the all-American boy (or girl).

In the next factor, the prescriptions concern the single theme of popularity in the role of the adolescent with his peers. Surprisingly, though, one's friends and one's mother are the prescribers; if the adolescent reports that his friends say he should be popular, he reports that his mother also expects this of him. Friends and mothers join in this particular aspect of adolescent personality. It is interesting that this push toward popularity in the peer role does not emanate from the father.

The seventh factor is like the first and the fourth, for it too involves one significant other (the teacher), one role (the student role), and one theme (in this case, academic achievement). This is to be expected, of course, since the relationship with the teacher is restricted for most adolescents to the classroom relationship and is oriented to academic achievement.

The last four factors are sharply defined by specific content areas and have fewer items involved in the cluster. Each of these, however, is of particular interest because it picks up some predictable areas of adolescent concern. The first of these final four factors includes a single item, namely, making one's own decisions about such things as smoking and late hours in the peer group role; but the adolescent reports that his mother, his father, and his friends all have this prescription; or to put it more precisely, if one of the triumvirate is reported as having this prescription, he also perceives the other two as holding it.

The second of these final four factors is a generalized prescription for leadership, which involves going out for athletics, being popular with boys and girls, having social poise, taking part in many extracurricular activities. In this instance, both the mother and the father are the role prescribers, and the focal points of behavior are both the student and peer group roles.

The third of the remaining four factors is defined by the single item, "be nonconformist," in relation to others in the peer group; and like the factor involving making one's own decisions, this too is prescribed by mother, father, and friends.

The final factor clusters items related to creativity and originality, namely, doing outside work for credit, studying something just because it interests me, and being creative and original regardless of grades; here the student role is the focus, and it is the mother and father who are the role prescribers.

Prescriptions and Motivation

This information about how role prescriptions are organized in the adolescent personality is of considerable significance because it leads directly to an understanding of the sources of motivation in the adolescent. Motivation is generated from interpersonal relationships. The individual, because of his prior learned desire to conform to others' expectations, to their role prescriptions, is motivated to live up to them now; his sense of well-being or satisfaction depends on perceived conformity. Any self-other relationship leads to an individual's appraisal of himself as being good or bad according to the degree to which he lives up to the other's prescriptions. Of course, the importance of the self-appraisal to the adolescent varies according to the significance of the other person to him, which in turn is based on the history of his relationship. The present study has dealt with persons in the adolescent's world who in most cases would be highly salient figures. His appraisal of whether or not he is living up to the expectations of these others thus should increase or decrease his self-esteem.

In any given instance of motivation, then, what triggers off activity is the adolescent's perception of discrepancies between his own role performance and others' prescriptions (or frequently, a perception of a possible discrepancy in the future which now he seeks to avoid). Thus, for example, where achievement is concerned, the expression of behavior coming from an "achievement motive" depends really on the existence of a set of reference figures whose expectations for performance (in a given context such as the school) are for the adolescent to reach a high level of success.

This does not mean that the source of motivation necessarily lies in the prescriptions of significant, nearby other persons such as fathers. The adolescent's set of reference figures is diverse and complex. As has already been suggested, it is not just parents, teachers, and friends who are valued, but other adult groups, distant relatives, and, for some of the re-

spondents, figures from the world's religions and literature. The sources of motivation in the form of role prescriptions may lie far beyond the immediate, face-to-face social system in which the adolescent is engaged. The adolescent is motivated by the expectations of powerful, not readily apparent figures, by attention to the desires of significant persons removed from direct interaction but nevertheless of influence in setting standards and ideals.

Nevertheless, directing the adolescent's behavior in considerable part are the prescriptions of the important people in his immediate environment. Individual differences between adolescents on these particular factors of prescriptions are of the utmost importance in describing their personalities. There are two important facets of the analysis leading to a description of personality. One is the degree to which any one of the particular clusters of role prescriptions characterizes that particular adolescent. One adolescent, or a group of them, such as girls as contrasted with boys, may score much higher on one of them, e.g., they may report that the others do in fact prescribe a high academic performance in their student role. Other adolescents may score low on this factor. These adolescents' scores on the role prescription factors are fundamental, descriptive, and theoretically important characteristics of their personalities.

There also is another more abstract way of characterizing the adolescent personality which can be derived from these factors. Some, for example, may score high on a factor representing what a particular significant other thinks. For example, the same adolescents may score high on the factor where the father is the major or sole prescriber, and low on those factors where mothers and peers are the significant others. These adolescents could be described as "person-oriented."

Another adolescent might score high on those factors which are role-specific in nature, so that his personality might best be described in terms of its compartmentalization into his role activities as a student, a peer group member, or at home. This person then would score low on other factors which involve behavior across different roles.

Still a third type of adolescent might be oriented to behavioral themes and score high on the factors which cut across roles and across people, but lower on these where some specific person is making reference to some specific role.

This analysis of the adolescents' perceptions of role prescriptions thus gives insight into the structure of their personalities and leads to appraising individual and group differences. In turn, this leads to typologies of personality, and eventually to the prediction of other aspects of adolescent behavior.

In conclusion, some of the social structural components of adolescent personality have been reviewed. A fully developed theory of personality incorporating the contributions that the sociologist can make is an ultimate objective. This point of view should be better represented in the arena of competing concepts, hypotheses, and theories about personality.

3

The Problem of Ego Identity*

Erik H. Erikson

Genetic: Identification and Identity

I

The autobiographies of extraordinary (and extraordinarily self-perceptive) individuals are a suggestive source of insight into the development of identity. In order to find an anchor point for the discussion of the universal genetics of identity, however, it would be well to trace its development through the life histories or through significant life episodes of "ordinary" individuals—individuals whose lives have neither become professional autobiographies (as did Shaw's) nor case histories such as will be discussed. I will not be able to present such material here; I must, instead, rely on impressions from daily life, from participation in one of the rare "longitudinal" studies of the personality development of children, and from guidance work with mildly disturbed young people.

Adolescence is the last and the concluding stage of childhood. The adolescent process, however, is conclusively complete only when the individual has subordinated his childhood identifications to a new kind of identification, achieved in absorbing sociability and in competitive apprenticeship with and among his age-mates. These new identifications are no longer characterized by the playfulness of childhood and the experimental zest of youth: with dire urgency they force the young individual into choices and decisions which will, with increasing immediacy, lead to a more final self-definition, to irreversible role pattern, and thus to commitments "for life." The task to be performed here by the young person and by his society is formidable; it necessitates, in different individuals and in different societies, great variations in the duration, in the intensity, and in the ritualization of adolescence. Societies offer, as individuals require, more or less sanctioned intermediary periods between childhood and adulthood, institutionalized *psychosocial moratoria*, during which a

*In *Identity and the Life Cycle* (New York: International Universities Press, 1959), pp. 110-164. This material has been revised and reformulated in *Identity: Use and Crisis*, © copyright 1968 by W. W. Norton & Company, Inc., New York.

lasting pattern of "inner identity" is scheduled for relative completion.

In postulating a "latency period" which precedes puberty, psychoanalysis has given recognition to some kind of *psychosexual moratorium* in human development—a period of delay which permits the future mate and parent first to "go to school" (i.e., to undergo whatever schooling is provided for in his technology) and to learn the technical and social rudiments of a work situation. It is not within the confines of the libido theory, however, to give an adequate account of a second period of delay, namely, adolescence. Here the sexually matured individual is more or less retarded in his psychosexual capacity for intimacy and in the psychosocial readiness for parenthood. The period can be viewed as a *psychosocial moratorium* during which the individual through free role experimentation may find a niche in some section of his society, a niche which is firmly defined and yet seems to be uniquely made for him. In finding it the young adult gains an assured sense of inner continuity and social sameness which will bridge what he *was* as a child and what he is *about to become*, and will reconcile his *conception of himself* and his *community's recognition* of him.

Where, in the following, we speak of the community's response to the young individual's need to be "recognized" by those around him, we mean something beyond a mere recognition of achievement; for it is of great relevance to the young individual's identity formation that he be responded to, and be given function and status as a person whose gradual growth and transformation make sense to those who begin to make sense to him. It has not been sufficiently recognized in psychoanalysis that such recognition provides an entirely indispensable support to the ego in the specific tasks of adolescing, which are: to maintain the most important ego defenses against the vastly growing intensity of impulses (now invested in a matured genital apparatus and a powerful muscle system); to learn to consolidate the most important "conflict-free" achievements in line with work opportunities; and to resynthesize all childhood identifications in some unique way, and yet in concordance with the roles offered by some wider section of society—be that section the neighborhood block, an anticipated occupational field, an association of kindred minds, or, perhaps (as in Shaw's case) the "mighty dead."

II

Linguistically as well as psychologically, identity and identification have common roots. Is identity, then, the mere sum of earlier identifications, or is it merely an additional set of identifications?

The limited usefulness of the *mechanism of identification* becomes at once obvious if we consider the fact that none of the identifications of childhood (which in our patients stand out in such morbid elaboration and mutual contradiction) could, if merely added up, result in a functioning personality. True, we usually believe that the task of psychotherapy is the replacement of morbid and excessive identifications by more desirable ones. But as every cure attests, "more desirable" identifications tend to be quietly subordinated to a new, a unique Gestalt which is more than the sum of its parts. The fact is that identification as a mechanism is of limited usefulness. Children, at different stages of their development, identify with those *part aspects* of people by which they themselves are most immediately affected, whether in reality or fantasy. Their identifications with parents, for example, center in certain overvalued and ill-understood body parts, capacities, and role appearances. These part aspects, furthermore, are favored not because of their social acceptability (they often are everything but the parents' most adjusted attributes) but by the nature of infantile fantasy which only gradually gives way to a more realistic anticipation of social reality. The final identity, then, as fixed at the end of adolescence is superordinated to any single identification with individuals of the past: it includes all significant identifications, but it also alters them in order to make a unique and a reasonably coherent whole of them.

If we, roughly speaking, consider introjection-projection, identification, and identity formation to be the steps by which the ego grows in ever more mature interplay with the identities of the child's models, the following psychosocial schedule suggests itself:

The mechanisms of *introjection and projection*, which prepare the basis for later identifications, depend for their relative integration on the satisfactory mutuality (Erikson, 1950a) between the *mothering adult(s) and the mothered child*. Only the experience of such mutuality provides a safe pole of self-feeling from which the child can reach out for the other pole: his first love "objects."

The fate of *childhood identifications*, in turn, depends on the child's satisfactory interaction with a trustworthy and meaningful hierarchy of roles as provided by the generations living together in some form of *family*.

Identity formation, finally, begins where the usefulness of identification ends. It arises from the selective repudiation and mutual assimilation of childhood identifications, and their absorption in a new configuration, which in turn, is dependent on the process by which a *society* (often through subsocieties) *identifies the young individual*, recognizing him as somebody who had to become the way he is, and who, being the way he is, is taken for granted. The community, often not without some initial mistrust, gives such recognition with a (more or less institutionalized) display of surprise and pleasure in making the acquaintance of a newly emerging individual. For the community, in turn, feels "recognized" by the individual who cares to ask for recognition; it can, by the same token, feel deeply—and vengefully—rejected by the individual who does not seem to care.

III

While the end of adolescence thus is the stage of an overt identity *crisis*, identity *formation* neither begins nor ends with adolescence: it is a lifelong development largely unconscious to the individual and to his society. Its roots go back all the way to the first self-recognition: in the baby's earliest exchange of smiles there is something of a *self-realization coupled with a mutual recognition*.

All through childhood tentative crystallizations take place which make the individual feel and believe (to begin with the most conscious aspect of the matter) as if he approximately knew who he was— only to find that such self-certainty ever again falls prey to the discontinuities of psychosocial development (Benedict, 1938). An example would be the discontinuity between the demands made in a given milieu on a little boy and those made on a "big boy" who, in turn, may well wonder why he was first made to believe that to be little is admirable, only to be forced to exchange this effortless status for the special obligations of one who is "big now." Such discontinuities can amount to a crisis and demand a decisive and strategic repatterning of action, and with it, *compromise* which can be compensated for only by a consistently accruing sense of the social value of such increasing commitment. The cute or ferocious, or good small boy, who becomes a studious, or gentlemanly, or tough big boy must be able—and must be enabled—to combine both sets of values in a recognized identity which permits him, in work and play, and in official and in intimate behavior to be (and to let others be) a big boy *and* a little boy.

The community supports such development to the extent to which it permits the child, at each step, to orient himself toward a complete *"life plan"* with a hierarchical order of roles as represented by individuals of different age grades. Family, neighborhood, and school provide contact and experimental identification with younger and older children and with young and old adults. A child, in the multiplicity of successive and tentative identifications, thus begins early to build up expectations of what it will be like to be older and what it will feel like to have been younger—expectations which become part of an identity as they are, step by step, verified in decisive experiences of psychosocial "fittedness."

IV

The *critical phases* of life have been described in psychoanalysis primarily in terms of instincts and defenses, i.e., as "typical danger situations" (Hartmann, 1958). Psychoanalysis has concerned itself more with the encroachment of psychosexual crises on psychosocial (and other) functions than with the specific crisis created by the maturation of each function. Take for example a child who is learning to *speak*: he is acquiring one of the prime functions supporting a sense of individual autonomy and one of the prime techniques for expanding the radius of give-and-take. The mere indication of an ability to give intentional sound-signs immediately obligates the child to "*say* what he wants." It may force him to *achieve* by proper verbalization the attention which was afforded him previously in response to mere gestures of needfulness. Speech not only commits him to the kind of voice he has and to the mode of speech he develops; it also *defines him* as one responded to by those around him with changed diction and attention. They, in turn, expect henceforth to be understood by him with fewer explana-

tions or gestures. Furthermore, a spoken word is a *pact*: there is an irrevocably committing aspect to an utterance remembered by others, although the child may have to learn early that certain commitments (adult ones to a child) are subject to change without notice, while others (his) are not. This intrinsic relationship of speech, not only to the world of communicable facts, but also to the social value of verbal commitment and uttered truth is strategic among the experiences which support (or fail to support) a sound ego development. It is this psychosocial aspect of the matter which we must learn to relate to the by now better known psychosexual aspects represented, for example, in the autoerotic enjoyment of speech; the use of speech as an erotic "contact"; or in such organ-mode emphases as eliminative or intrusive sounds or uses of speech. Thus the child may come to develop, in the use of voice and word, a particular combination of whining or singing, judging or arguing, as part of a new element of the future identity, namely, the element "one who speaks and is spoken to in such-and-such-a-way." This element, in turn, will be related to other elements of the child's developing identity (he is clever and/or good-looking and/or tough) and will be compared with other people, alive or dead, judged ideal or evil.

It is the ego's function to integrate the psychosexual and psychosocial aspects on a given level of development, and, at the same time, to integrate the relation of newly added identity elements with those already in existence. For earlier crystallizations of identity can become subject to renewed conflict, when changes in the quality and quantity of drive, expansions in mental equipment, and new and often conflicting social demands all make previous adjustments appear insufficient, and, in fact, make previous opportunities and rewards suspect. Yet, such developmental and normative crises differ from imposed, traumatic, and neurotic crises in that the process of growth provides new energy as society offers new and specific opportunities (according to its dominant conception and institutionalization of the phases of life). From a genetic point of view, then, the process of identity formation emerges as an *evolving configuration*—a configuration which is gradually established by successive ego syntheses and resyntheses throughout childhood; it is a configuration gradually integrating *constitutional givens, idiosyncratic libidinal needs, favored capacities, significant identifications, effective defenses, successful sublimations, and consistent roles.*

V

The final assembly of all the converging identity elements at the end of childhood (and the abandonment of the divergent ones)[1] appears to be a formidable task: how can a stage as "abnormal" as adolescence be trusted to accomplish it? Here it is not unnecessary to call to mind again that in spite of the similarity of adolescent "symptoms" and episodes to neurotic and psychotic symptoms and episodes, adolescence is not an affliction but a *normative crisis*, i.e., a normal phase of increased conflict characterized by a seeming fluctuation in ego strength, and yet also by a high growth potential. Neurotic and psychotic crises are defined by a certain self-perpetuating propensity, by an increasing waste of defensive energy, and by a deepened psychosocial isolation; while normative crises are relatively more reversible, or, better, traversable, and are characterized by an abundance of available energy which, to be sure, revives dormant anxiety and arouses new conflict, but also supports new and expanded ego functions in the searching and playful engagement of new opportunities and associations. What under prejudiced scrutiny may appear to be the onset of a neurosis is often but an aggravated crisis which might prove to be self-liquidating and, in fact, contributive to the process of identity formation.

It is true, of course, that the adolescent, during the final stage of his identity formation, is apt to suffer more deeply than he ever did before (or ever will again) from a diffusion of roles; and it is also true that such diffusion renders many an adolescent defenseless against the sudden impact of previously latent malignant disturbances. In the meantime, it is important to emphasize that the diffused and vulnerable, aloof and uncommitted, and yet demanding and opinionated personality of the not-too-neurotic adolescent contains many necessary elements of a semideliberate role experimentation of the "I dare you" and "I dare myself" variety. Much of this apparent diffusion thus must be considered *social play* and thus the true genetic successor of childhood play. Similarly, the adolescent's ego development demands and permits playful, if daring, experimentation in fantasy and *introspection*. We are apt to be alarmed by the "closeness to consciousness" in the

adolescent's perception of dangerous id contents (such as the oedipus complex) and this primarily because of the obvious hazards created in psychotherapy, if and when we, in zealous pursuit of our task of "making conscious," push somebody over the precipice of the unconscious who is already leaning out a little too far. The adolescent's leaning out over any number of precipices is normally an experimentation with experiences which are thus becoming more amenable to ego control, provided they can be somehow communicated to other adolescents in one of those strange codes established for just such experiences—and provided they are not prematurely responded to with fatal seriousness by overeager or neurotic adults. The same must be said of the adolescent's "fluidity of defenses," which so often causes raised eyebrows on the part of the worried clinician. Much of this fluidity is anything but pathological; for adolescence is a crisis in which only fluid defense can overcome a sense of victimization by inner and outer demands, and in which only trial and error can lead to the most felicitous avenues of action and self-expression.

In general, one may say that in regard to the social play of adolescents prejudices similar to those which once concerned the nature of childhood play are not easily overcome. We alternately consider such behavior irrelevant, unnecessary, or irrational, and ascribe to it purely regressive and neurotic meanings. As in the past the study of children's spontaneous games was neglected in favor of that of solitary play,[2] so now the mutual "joinedness" of adolescent clique behavior fails to be properly assessed in our concern for the individual adolescent. Children and adolescents in their presocieties provide for one another a sanctioned moratorium and joint support for free experimentation with inner and outer dangers (including those emanating from the adult world). Whether or not a given adolescent's newly acquired capacities are drawn back into infantile conflict depends to a significant extent on the quality of the opportunities and rewards available to him in his peer clique, as well as on the more formal ways in which society at large invites a transition from social play to work experimentation, and from rituals of transit to final commitments: all of which must be based on an implicit mutual contract between the individual and society.

---

[1] William James (1896) speaks of an abandonment of "the old alternative ego," and even of "the murdered self."

[2] For a new approach see Anna Freud's and Sophie Dann's (1951) report on displaced children.

VI

Is the sense of identity conscious? At times, of course, it seems only too conscious. For between the double prongs of vital inner need and inexorable outer demand, the still experimenting individual may become the victim of a transitory extreme *identity consciousness* which is the common core of the many forms of "self-consciousness" typical for youth. Where the processes of identity formation are prolonged (a factor which can bring creative gain) such preoccupation with the "self-image" also prevails. We are thus most aware of our identity when we are just about to gain it and when we (with what motion pictures call "a double take") are somewhat surprised to make its acquaintance; or, again, when we are just about to enter a crisis and feel the encroachment of identity diffusion—a syndrome to be described presently.

An increasing sense of identity, on the other hand, is experienced preconsciously as a sense of psychosocial well-being. Its most obvious concomit-

ants are a feeling of being at home in one's body, a sense of "knowing where one is going," and an inner assuredness of anticipated recognition from those who count. Such a sense of identity, however, is never gained nor maintained once and for all. Like a "good conscience," it is constantly lost and regained, although more lasting and more economical methods of maintenance and restoration are evolved and fortified in late adolescence.

Like any aspect of well-being or, for that matter, of ego synthesis, a sense of identity has a preconscious aspect which is available to awareness; it expresses itself in behavior which is observable with the naked eye; and it has unconscious concomitants which can be fathomed only by psychological tests and by the psychoanalytic procedure. I regret that, at this point, I can bring forward only a general claim which awaits detailed demonstration. The claim advanced here concerns a whole series of criteria of psychosocial health which find their specific elaboration and relative completion in stages of development preceding and following the identity crisis. This is condensed in Figure I below.

	1.	2.	3.	4.	5.	6.	7.	8.
I. **INFANCY**	Trust vs. Mistrust				Unipolarity vs. Premature Self- Differentation			
II. **EARLY CHILDHOOD**		Autonomy vs. Shame, Doubt			Bipolarity vs. Autism			
III. **PLAY AGE**			Initiative vs. Guilt		Play Identification vs. (oedipal) Fantasy Identities			
IV. **SCHOOL AGE**				Industry vs. Inferiority	Work Identification vs. Identity Foreclosure			
V. **ADOLESCENCE**	Time Perspective vs. Time Diffusion	Self-Certainty vs. Identity Consciousness	Role Experimentation vs. Negative Identity	Anticipation of Achievement vs. Work Paralysis	Identity vs. Identity Diffusion	Sexual Identity vs. Bisexual Diffusion	Leadership Polarization vs. Authority Diffusion	Ideological Polarization vs. Diffusion of Ideals
VI. **YOUNG ADULT**					Solidarity vs. Social Isolation	Intimacy vs. Isolation		
VII. **ADULTHOOD**							Generativity vs. Self-Absorption	
VIII. **MATURE AGE**								Integrity vs. Disgust, Despair

Identity appears as only one concept within a wider conception of the human life cycle which envisages childhood as a *gradual unfolding of the personality through phase-specific psychosocial crises:* I have, on other occasions (1950a, 1950b), expressed this *epigenetic principle* by taking recourse to a diagram which, with its many empty boxes, at intervals may serve as a check on our attempts at detailing psychosocial development. (Such a diagram, however, can be recommended to the serious attention only of those who can take it *and* leave it.) The diagram (Figure I), at first, contained only the double-lined boxes along the descending diagonal (I, 1—II, 2—III, 3—IV, 4—V, 5—VI, 6—VII, 7—VIII, 8) and for the sake of initial orientation, the reader is requested to ignore all other entries for the moment. The *diagonal* shows the sequence of psychosocial crises. Each of these boxes is shared by a criterion of relative psychosocial health and the corresponding criterion of relative psychosocial ill-health: in "normal" development, the first must persistently outweigh (although it will never completely do away with) the second. The sequence of stages thus represents a successive development of the component parts of the psychosocial personality. Each part exists in some form (verticals) before the time when it becomes "phase-specific," i.e., when "its" psychosocial crisis is precipitated both by the individual's readiness and by society's pressure. But each component comes to ascendance and finds its more or less lasting solution at the conclusion of "its" stage. It is thus *systematically related* to all the others, and all depend on the proper development at the proper *time* of each; although individual make-up and the nature of society determine the rate of development of each of them, and thus the *ratio* of all of them. It is at the end of adolescence, then, that identity becomes phase-specific (V, 5), i.e., must find a certain integration as a relatively conflict-free psychosocial arrangement—or remain defective or conflict-laden.

With this chart as a blueprint before us, let me state first which aspects of this complex matter will *not* be treated in this paper: for one, we will not be able to make more definitive the now very tentative designation (in *vertical* 5) of the precursors of identity in the infantile ego. Rather we approach childhood in an untraditional manner, namely, from young adulthood backward—and this with the conviction that early development cannot be understood on its own terms alone, and that the earliest stages of childhood cannot be accounted for without a unified theory of the whole span of preadulthood. For the infant (while he is not spared the chaos of needful rage) does not and cannot build anew and out of himself the course of human life, as the reconstruction of his earliest experience ever again seems to suggest. The smallest child lives in a community of life cycles which depend on him as he depends on them, and which guide his drives as well as his sublimations with consistent feedbacks. This verity necessitates a discussion of the psychoanalytic approach to "environment" to which we shall return toward the end of this paper.

A second systematic omission concerns the psychosexual stages. Those readers who have undertaken to study the diagrams of psychosexual development in *Childhood and Society* (Erikson, 1950a) know that I am attempting to lay the ground for a detailed account of the dovetailing of psychosexual and psychosocial epigenesis, i.e., the two schedules according to which component parts, present throughout development, come to fruition in successive stages. The essential inseparability of these two schedules is implied throughout this paper, although only the psychosocial schedule, and in fact only one stage of it, is brought into focus.

What traditional source of psychoanalytic insight, then, *will* we concern ourselves with? It is: first pathography; in this case the clinical description of *identity diffusion.* Hoping thus to clarify the matter of identity from a more familiar angle, we will then return to the over-all aim of beginning to "extract," as Freud put it, "from psychopathology what may be of benefit to normal psychology."

Pathographic: The Clinical Picture of Identity Diffusion

Pathography remains the traditional source of psychoanalytic insight. In the following, I shall sketch a syndrome of disturbances in young people who can neither make use of the institutionalized moratorium provided in their society, nor create and maintain for themselves (as Shaw did) a unique moratorium all of their own. They come, instead, to psychiatrists, priests, judges, and (we must add) recruitment officers in order to be given an authorized if ever so uncomfortable place in which to wait things out.

The sources at my disposal are the case histories of a number of young patients who sought treatment following an acutely disturbed period between the ages of sixteen and twenty-four. A few were seen, and fewer treated, by me personally; a larger number were reported in supervisory interviews or seminars at the Austen Riggs Center in Stockbridge and at the Western Psychiatric Institute in Pittsburgh; the largest number are former patients now on record in the files of the Austen Riggs Center. My *composite sketch* of these case histories will remind the reader immediately of the diagnostic and technical problems encountered in adolescents in general (Blos, 1953) and especially in any number of those young borderline cases (Knight, 1953) who are customarily diagnosed as preschizophrenias, or severe character disorders with paranoid, depressive, psychopathic, or other trends. Such well-established diagnostic signposts will not be questioned here. An attempt will be made, however, to concentrate on certain common features representative of the common life crisis shared by this whole group of patients as a result of a (temporary or final) inability of their egos to establish an identity: for they all suffer from *acute identity diffusion*. Obviously, only quite detailed case presentations could convey the full necessity or advisability of such a "phase-specific" approach which emphasizes the life task shared by a group of patients as much as the diagnostic criteria which differentiate them. In the meantime, I hope that my composite sketch will convey at least a kind of impressionistic plausibility. The fact that the cases known to me were seen in a private institution in the Berkshires, and at a public clinic in industrial Pittsburgh, suggests that at least the two extremes of socioeconomic status in the United States (and thus two extreme forms of identity problems) are represented here. This could mean that the families in question, because of their extreme locations on the scale of class mobility and of Americanization, may have conveyed to these particular children a certain hopelessness regarding their chances of participating in (or of successfully defying) the dominant American manners and symbols of success (see G. H. Mead, 1934, Ch. 8, 11; Ackerman, 1951). Whether, and in what way, disturbances such as are outlined here also characterize those more comfortably placed somewhere near the middle of the socioeconomic ladder, remains, at this time, an open question.

Time of Breakdown

A state of acute identity diffusion usually becomes manifest at a time when the young individual finds himself exposed to a combination of experiences which demand his simultaneous commitment to *physical intimacy* (not by any means always overtly sexual), to decisive *occupational choice*, to energetic *competition*, and to *psychosocial self-definition*. A young college girl, previously overprotected by a conservative mother who is trying to live down a not-so-conservative past, may, on entering college, meet young people of radically different backgrounds, among whom she must choose her friends and her enemies; radically different mores especially in the relationship of the sexes which she must play along with or repudiate; and a commitment to make decisions and choices which will necessitate irreversible competitive involvement or even leadership. Often she finds among very "different" young people a comfortable display of values, manners, and symbols for which one or the other of her parents or grandparents is covertly nostalgic, while overtly despising them. Decisions and choices and, most of all, successes in any direction bring to the fore conflicting identifications and immediately threaten to narrow down the inventory of further tentative choices; and, at the very moment when time is of the essence, every move may establish a binding precedent in psychosocial self-definition, i.e., in the "type" one comes to represent in the types of the age-mates (who seem so terribly eager to type). On the other hand, any marked *avoidance of choices* (i.e., a moratorium by default) leads to a sense of outer *isolation* and to an *inner vacuum* which is wide open for old libidinal objects and with this for bewilderingly conscious incestuous feelings; for more primitive forms of identification; and (in some) for a renewed struggle with archaic introjects. This regressive pull often receives the greatest attention from workers in our field, partially because we are on more familiar ground wherever we can discern signs of regression to infantile psychosexuality. Yet the disturbances under discussion here cannot be comprehended without some insight into the specific nature of transitory adolescent regression as an attempt to postpone and to avoid, as it were, a psychosocial foreclosure. A state of paralysis may ensue, the mechanisms of which appear to be devised to maintain a state of minimal actual choice and commitment with a maximum inner conviction of still being the chooser. Of the complicated presenting pathology only a few aspects can be discussed here.

The Problem of Intimacy

The chart which accompanied the preceding section shows "Intimacy vs. Isolation" as the core conflict which follows that of "Identity vs. Identity Diffusion." That many of our patients break down at an age which is properly considered more preadult than postadolescent is explained by the fact that often only an attempt to engage in intimate fellowship and competition or in sexual intimacy fully reveals the latent weakness of identity.

True "engagement" with others is the result and the test of firm self-delineation. Where this is still missing, the young individual, when seeking tentative forms of playful intimacy in friendship and competition, in sex play and love, in argument and gossip, is apt to experience a peculiar strain, as if such tentative engagement might turn into an interpersonal fusion amounting to a loss of identity, and requiring, therefore, a tense inner reservation, a caution in commitment. Where a youth does not resolve such strain he may isolate himself and enter, at best, only stereotyped and formalized interpersonal relations; or he may, in repeated hectic attempts and repeated dismal failures, seek intimacy with the most improbable partners. For where an assured sense of identity is missing even friendships and affairs become desperate attempts at delineating the fuzzy outlines of identity by mutual narcissistic mirroring: to fall in love then often means to fall into one's mirror image, hurting oneself and damaging the mirror. During lovemaking or in sexual fantasies, a loosening of *sexual identity* threatens: it even becomes unclear whether sexual excitement is experienced by the individual or by his partner, and this in either heterosexual or homosexual encounters. The ego thus loses its flexible capacity for abandoning itself to sexual and affectual sensations, in a fusion with another individual who is both partner to the sensation and guarantor of one's continuing identity: fusion with another becomes identity loss. A sudden collapse of all capacity for mutuality threatens, and a desperate wish ensues to start all over again, with a (quasi-deliberate) regression to a stage of basic bewilderment and rage such as only the very small child knows.

It must be remembered that the counterpart of intimacy is *distantiation*, i.e., the readiness to repudiate, to ignore, or to destroy those forces and people whose essence seems dangerous to one's own. Intimacy with one set of people and ideas would not be really intimate without an efficient repudiation of another set. Thus, weakness or excess in repudiation is an intrinsic aspect of the inability to gain intimacy because of an incomplete identity: whoever is not sure of his "point of view" cannot repudiate judiciously.

Young persons often indicate in rather pathetic ways a feeling that only a merging with a "leader" can save them—an adult who is able and willing to offer himself as a safe object for experimental surrender and as a guide in the relearning of the very first steps toward an intimate mutuality, and a legitimate repudiation. To such a person the late adolescent wants to be an apprentice or a disciple, a follower, sex mate or patient. Where this fails, as it often must from its very intensity and absoluteness, the young individual recoils to a position of strenuous introspection and self-testing which, given particularly aggravating circumstances or a history of relatively strong autistic trends, can lead him into a paralyzing borderline state. Symptomatically, this state consists of a painfully heightened sense of isolation; a disintegration of the sense of inner continuity and sameness; a sense of over-all ashamedness; an inability to derive a sense of accomplishment from any kind of activity; a feeling that life is happening to the individual rather than being lived by his initiative; a radically shortened time perspective; and finally, a basic mistrust, which leaves it to the world, to society, and indeed to psychiatry to prove that the patient does exist in a psychosocial sense, i.e., can count on an invitation to become himself.

Diffusion of Time Perspective

In extreme instances of delayed and prolonged adolescence an extreme form of a disturbance in the *experience of time* appears which, in its milder form, belongs to the psychopathology of everyday adolescence. It consists of a sense of great urgency and yet also of a loss of consideration for time as a dimension of living. The young person may feel simultaneously very young, and in fact baby-like, and old beyond rejuvenation. Protests of missed greatness and of a premature and fatal loss of useful potentials are common among our patients as they are among adolescents in cultures which consider such protestations romantic; the implied malignancy, however, consists of a decided disbelief in the possibility that time may bring change, and yet also of a violent fear that it might. This contradiction often is expressed in a general slowing up which makes the patient behave, within the routine of activities (and also of therapy) as if he were moving in molasses. It is hard for him to go to bed and to face the transition into a state of sleep, and it is equally hard for him to get up and face the necessary restitution of wakefulness; it is hard to come to the hour, and hard to leave it. Such complaints as, "I don't know," "I give up," "I quit," are by no means mere habitual statements reflecting a mild depression: they are often expressions of the kind of despair which Edward Bibring (1953) has recently discussed as a wish on the part of the ego "to let itself die." The assumption that life could actually be made to end with the end of adolescence (or at tentatively planned later "dates of expiration") is by no means entirely unwelcome, and, in fact, can become the only pillar of hope on which a new beginning can be based. Some of our patients even require the feelings that the therapist does not intend to commit them to a continuation of life if (successful) treatment should fail to prove it really worthwhile; without such a conviction the moratorium would not be a real one. In the meantime, the "wish to die" is only in those rare cases a really suicidal wish, where "to be a suicide" becomes an inescapable identity choice in itself. I am thinking here of a pretty young girl, the oldest of a number of daughters of a millworker. Her mother had repeatedly expressed the thought that she would rather see her daughters dead than become prostitutes; at the same time she suspected "prostitution" in their every move toward companionship with boys. The daughters were finally forced into a kind of conspiratorial sorority of their own, obviously designed to elude the mother, to experiment with ambiguous situations, and yet probably also to give one another protection from men. They were finally caught in compromising circumstances. The authorities, too, took it for granted that they intended to prostitute themselves, and they were sent to a variety of institutions where they were forcefully impressed with the kind of "recognition" society had in store for them. No appeal was possible to a mother who, they felt, had left them no choice; and much good will and understanding of social workers was sabotaged by circumstances. At least for the oldest girl (and this, because of a number of reasons) no other future was available except that of another chance in another world. She killed herself by hanging after having dressed herself up nicely, and having written a note which ended with the cryptic words "Why I achieve honor only to discard it. . . ."

Less spectacular but not less malignant forms and origins of such "negative identities" will be taken up later.

Diffusion of Industry

Cases of severe identity diffusion regularly also suffer from an acute upset in the sense of workmanship, and this either in the form of an inability to concentrate on required or suggested tasks, or in a self-destructive preoccupation with some one-sided activities, i.e., excessive reading. The way in which such patients sometimes, under treatment, find the one activity in which they can re-employ their once lost sense of workmanship is a chapter in itself. Here, it is well to keep in mind the stage of development which precedes puberty and adolescence, namely, the elementary-school age, when the child is taught the prerequisites for participation in the particular technology of his culture and is given the opportunity and the life task of developing a sense of workmanship and work participation. The school age significantly follows the oedipal stage: the accomplishment of real (and not only playful) steps toward a place in the economic structure of society permits the child to reidentify with parents as workers and tradition bearers rather than as sexual and familial beings, thus nurturing at least one concrete and more "neutral" possibility of becoming like them. The tangible goals of elementary practice are shared by and with age-mates in places of instruction (sweathouse, prayer house, fishing hole, workshop, kitchen, schoolhouse) most of which, in turn, are geographically separated from the home, from the mother, and from infantile memories: here, however, wide differences in the treatment of the sexes exist. Work goals, then, by no means only support or exploit the suppression of infantile instinctual aims; they also enhance the functioning of the ego, in that they offer a constructive activity with actual tools and materials in a communal reality. The ego's tendency to turn passivity into activity here thus acquires a new field of manifestation, in many ways superior to the mere turning of passive into active in infantile fantasy and play; for now the inner need for activity, practice, and work completion is ready to meet the corresponding demands and opportunities in social reality (Hendrick, 1943; Ginsburg, 1954).

Because of the immediate oedipal antecedents of

the beginnings of a work identity, the diffusion of identity in our young patients reverses their gears toward oedipal competitiveness and sibling rivalry. Thus identity diffusion is accompanied not only by an inability to concentrate, but also by an excessive awareness as well as an abhorrence of competitiveness. Although the patients in question usually are intelligent and able and often have shown themselves successful in office work, in scholastic studies and in sports, they now lose the capacity for work, exercise, and sociability, and thus the most important vehicle of social play, and the most significant refuge from formless fantasy and vague anxiety. Instead infantile goals and fantasies are dangerously endowed with the energy emanating from matured sexual equipment and increased aggressive power. One parent, again, becomes the goal, the other, again, the hindrance. Yet this revived oedipal struggle is not and must not be interpreted as exclusively or even primarily a sexual one: it is a turn toward the earliest origins, an attempt to resolve a diffusion of early introjects and to rebuild shaky childhood identifications—in other words, a wish to be born again, to learn once more the very first steps toward reality and mutuality, and to acquire the renewed permission to develop again the functions of contact, activity, and competition.

A young patient, who had found himself blocked in college, during the initial phase of his treatment in a private hospital nearly read himself blind, apparently in a destructive overidentification with father and therapist, both of whom were professors. Guided by a resourceful "painter in residence" he came upon the fact that he had an original and forceful talent to paint, an activity which was prevented by advancing treatment from becoming self-destructive overactivity. As painting proved a help in the patient's gradual acquisition of a sense of identity of his own, he dreamed one night a different version of a dream which previously had always ended in panicky awakening. Now he fled, from fire and persecution, into a forest which he had sketched himself; and as he fled into it, the charcoal drawing turned into live woods, with an infinite perspective.

The Choice of the Negative Identity

The loss of a sense of identity often is expressed in a scornful and snobbish hostility toward the roles offered as proper and desirable in one's family or immediate community. Any part aspect of the re-

quired role, or all parts, be it masculinity or femininity, nationality or class membership, can become the main focus of the young person's acid disdain. Such excessive contempt for their backgrounds occurs among the oldest Anglo-Saxon and the newest Latin or Jewish families; it easily becomes a general dislike for everything American, and an irrational overestimation of everything foreign. Life and strength seem to exist only where one is not, while decay and danger threaten wherever one happens to be. This typical case fragment illustrates the superego's triumph of depreciation over a young man's faltering identity: "A voice within him which was disparaging him began to increase at about this time. It went to the point of intruding into everything he did. He said, 'if I smoke a cigarette, if I tell a girl I like her, if I make a gesture, if I listen to music, if I try to read a book—this third voice is at me all the time—"You're doing this for effect; you're a phony." ' This disparaging voice in the last year has been rather relentless. The other day on the way from home to college, getting into New York on the train, he went through some of the New Jersey swamplands and the poorer sections of the cities, and he felt that he was more congenial with people who lived there than he was with people on the campus or at home. He felt that life really existed in those places and that the campus was a sheltered, effeminate place."

In this example it is important to recognize not only an overweening superego, overclearly perceived as an inner voice, but also the acute identity diffusion, as projected on segments of society. An analogous case is that of a French-American girl from a rather prosperous mining town, who felt panicky to the point of paralysis when alone with a boy. It appeared that numerous superego injunctions and identity conflicts had, as it were, short-circuited in the obsessive idea that every boy had a right to expect from her a yielding to sexual practices popularly designated as "French."

Such estrangement from national and ethnic origins rarely leads to a complete denial of *personal identity* (G. Piers and Singer, 1953), although the angry insistence on being called by a particular given name or nickname is not uncommon among young people who try to find a refuge from diffusion in a new name label. Yet confabulatory reconstructions of one's origin do occur: a high-school girl of Middle-European descent secretly kept company with Scottish immigrants, carefully studying and easily assimilating their dialect and their social habits. With the help of history books and travel guides she reconstructed for herself a childhood in a given milieu in an actual township in Scotland, apparently convincing enough to some descendants of that country. Prevailed upon to discuss her future with me, she spoke of her (American-born) parents as "the people who brought me over here," and told me of her childhood "over there" in impressive detail. I went along with the story, implying that it had more inner truth than reality to it. The bit of reality was, as I surmised, the girl's attachment, in early childhood, to a woman neighbor who had come from the British Isles; the force behind the near-delusional "truth" was the paranoid form of a powerful death wish (latent in all severe identity crises) against her parents. The semideliberateness of the delusion was indicated when I finally asked the girl how she had managed to marshal all the details of life in Scotland. "Bless you, sir," she said in pleading Scottish brogue, "I needed a past."

On the whole, however, our patients' conflicts find expression in a more subtle way than the abrogation of personal identity: they rather choose a *negative identity*, i.e., an identity perversely based on all those identifications and roles which, at critical stages of development, had been presented to the individual as most undesirable or dangerous, and yet also as most real. For example, a mother whose firstborn son died and who (because of complicated guilt feelings) has never been able to attach to her later surviving children the same amount of religious devotion that she bestows on the memory of her dead child may well arouse in one of her sons the conviction that to be sick or dead is a better assurance of being "recognized" than to be healthy and about. A mother who is filled with unconscious ambivalence toward a brother who disintegrated into alcoholism may again and again respond selectively only to those traits in her son which seem to point to a repetition of her brother's fate, in which case this "negative" identity may take on more reality for the son than all his natural attempts at being good: he may work hard on becoming a drunkard and, lacking the necessary ingredients, may end up in a state of stubborn paralysis of choice. In other cases the negative identity is dictated by the necessity of finding and defending a niche of one's own against the excessive ideals either demanded by morbidly ambitious parents or seemingly already realized by actually superior ones: in both cases the parents' weaknesses and unexpressed wishes are recognized

by the child with catastrophic clarity. The daughter of a man of brilliant showmanship ran away from college and was arrested as a prostitute in the Negro quarter of a Southern city; while the daughter of an influential Southern Negro preacher was found among narcotic addicts in Chicago. In such cases it is of utmost importance to recognize the mockery and the vindictive pretense in such role playing; for the white girl had not really prostituted herself, and the colored girl had not really become an addict—yet. Needless to say, however, each of them had put herself into a marginal social area, leaving it to law-enforcement officers and to psychiatric agencies to decide what stamp to put on such behavior. A corresponding case is that of a boy presented to a psychiatric clinic as "the village homosexual" of a small town. On investigation, it appeared that the boy had succeeded in assuming this fame without any actual acts of homosexuality except one, much earlier in his life, when he had been raped by some older boys.

Such vindictive choices of a negative identity represent, of course, a desperate attempt at regaining some mastery in a situation in which the available positive identity elements cancel each other out. The history of such a choice reveals a set of conditions in which it is easier to derive a sense of identity out of a *total* identification with that which one is *least* supposed to be than to struggle for a feeling of reality in acceptable roles which are unattainable with the patient's inner means. The statement of a young man, "I would rather be quite insecure than a little secure," and that of a young woman, "At least in the gutter I'm a genius," circumscribe the relief following the total choice of a negative identity. Such relief is, of course, often sought collectively in cliques and gangs of young homosexuals, addicts, and social cynics.

A relevant job ahead of us is the analysis of snobbism which, in its upper-class form, permits some people to deny their identity diffusion through a recourse to something they did not earn themselves, namely, their parents' wealth, background, or fame. But there is a "lower lower" snobbism too, which is based on the pride of having achieved a semblance of nothingness. At any rate, many a late adolescent, if faced with continuing diffusion, would rather *be nobody or somebody bad, or indeed, dead —and this totally, and by free choice—than be not-quite-somebody.* The word "total" is not accidental in this connection, for I have endeavored to describe in another connection (Erikson, 1954b) a human proclivity to a "totalistic" reorientation when, at critical stages of development, reintegration into a relative "wholeness" seems impossible.[3] We will return to this problem in the last section.

Transference and Resistance

What I can say here about the therapeutic problems encountered with the patients described must be restricted to an attempt at relating to the concepts of identity and diffusion such matters of therapeutic technique as have been elaborated by workers in the field of borderline cases.[4]

On facing therapy, some of the patients under discussion here undergo a phase of particular malignancy. While the depth of regression and the danger of acting out must of course guide our diagnostic decisions, it is important to recognize, from the start, a mechanism present in such a turn for the worse: I would call it the "rock-bottom attitude." This consists of a quasi-deliberate giving in on the part of the patient to the pull of regression, a radical search for the rock-bottom—i.e., both the ultimate limit of regression and the only firm foundation for a renewed progression.[5] The assumption of such a deliberate search for the "base-line" means to carry Ernst Kris's "regression in the service of the ego" to an extreme: the fact that the recovery of our patients sometimes coincides with the discovery of previously hidden artistic gifts suggests further study of this point (Kris, 1952).

The element of deliberateness added here to "true" regression is often expressed in an all-pervasive mockery which characterizes the initial therapeutic contact with these patients; and by that strange air of sadomasochistic satisfaction, which makes it often hard to see and harder to believe that their self-depreciation and their willingness to "let the ego die" harbors a devastating sincerity. As one patient said: "That people do not know how to succeed is bad enough. But the worst is that they do not know how to fail. I have decided to fail well." This almost "deadly" sincerity is to be found in the patients' very determination to *trust nothing but mistrust*, and yet to watch from a dark corner of their minds (and indeed, often from the corner of an eye) for new experiences simple and forthright enough to permit a renewal of the most basic experiments in trustful mutuality. The therapist, manifestly faced with a mocking and defiant young adult, actually must take over the task of a mother who introduces a baby to life's trustworthiness. In the center of the treatment is the patient's need to redelineate himself, and thus to rebuild the foundations of his identity. At the beginning these delineations shift abruptly, even as violent shifts in the patient's experience of his ego boundary take place before our eyes: the patient's mobility may suddenly undergo a "catatonic" slowdown; his attentiveness may turn into overwhelming sleepiness; his vasomotor system may overreact to the point of producing sensations of fainting; his sense of reality may yield to feelings of depersonalization; or the remnants of his self-assurance may disappear in a miasmic loss of a sense of physical presence. Cautious but firm inquiry will reveal the probability that a number of contradictory impulses preceded the "attack." There is first a sudden intense impulse completely to destroy the therapist, and this, it seems, with an underlying "cannibalistic" wish to devour his essence and his identity. At the same time, or in alternation, there occur a fear and a wish to be devoured, to gain an identity by being absorbed in the therapist's essence. Both tendencies, of course, are often dis-

---

[3] *Wholeness* connotes an assembly of parts, even quite diversified parts, that enter into fruitful association and organization. This concept is most strikingly expressed in such terms as wholeheartedness, wholemindedness, wholesomeness, and the like. As a Gestalt, then, wholeness emphasizes a progressive mutuality between diversified functions and parts. *Totality*, on the contrary, evokes a Gestalt in which an absolute boundary is emphasized: given a certain arbitrary delineation, nothing that belongs inside must be left outside; nothing that must be outside should be tolerated inside. A totality must be as absolutely inclusive as it is absolutely exclusive. The dictionary uses the word "utter" in this connection. It conveys the element of force, which overrides the question whether the original category-to-be-made-absolute is a logical one, and whether the parts really have, so to speak, a yearning for one another.

There is both in individual and in group psychology a periodical need for a totality without further choice or alternation, even if it implies the abandonment of a much-desired wholeness. To say it in one sentence: Where the human being despairs of an essential wholeness, he restructures himself and the world by taking refuge in totalism.

Psychoanalysis reveals how strong and systematic are man's unconscious *proclivities and potentialities for total realignments*, often barely hidden behind one-sided predilections and convictions, and, on the other hand, how much energy is

employed in inner defenses against a threatening total reorientation in which black may turn into white and vice versa. Only the affect released in sudden conversions testifies to the quantity of this energy. (See Erikson, 1954b).

[4] I owe new insights in this field to Robert Knight (1953) and to Margaret Brenman (1952).

[5] David Rapaport's (1953) ego-psychological approach to "activity and passivity" sheds new light on the ego's role in such crises.

simulated or somatized for long periods, during which they find a manifestation (often kept secret) only after the therapeutic hour. This manifestation may be an impulsive flight into sexual promiscuity acted out without sexual satisfaction or any sense of participation; enormously absorbing rituals of masturbation or food intake; excessive drinking or wild driving; or self-destructive marathons of reading or listening to music, without food or sleep.

We see here the most extreme form of what may be called *identity resistance* which, incidentally, far from being restricted to the patients described here, is a universal form of resistance regularly experienced but often unrecognized in the course of analyses. Identity resistance is, in its milder and more usual forms, the patient's fear that the analyst, because of his particular personality, background, or philosophy, may carelessly or deliberately destroy the weak core of the patient's identity and impose instead his own. I would not hesitate to say that some of the much-discussed unsolved transference neuroses in patients, as well as in candidates in training, are the direct result of the fact that the identity resistance often is, at best, analyzed only quite unsystematically. In such cases the analysand may throughout the analysis resist any possible inroad by the analyst's identity while surrendering on all other points; or he may absorb more of the analyst's identity than is manageable within the patient's own means; or he may leave the analysis with a lifelong sense of not having been provided with some essence owed to him by the analyst.

In cases of acute identity diffusion this identity resistance becomes the core problem of the therapeutic encounter. Variations of psychoanalytic technique have in common that the dominant resistance must be accepted as the main guide to technique and that interpretation must be fitted to the patient's ability to utilize it. Here the patient sabotages communication until he has settled some basic—if contradictory—issues. The patient insists that the therapist accept his negative identity as real and necessary (which it is and was) without concluding that this negative identity is "all there is to him." If the therapist is able to fulfill both of these demands, he must prove patiently through many severe crises that he can maintain understanding and affection for the patient without either devouring him or offering himself for a totem meal. Only then can better known forms of transference, if ever so reluctantly, emerge.

These are nothing more than a few hints regarding the phenomenology of identity diffusion as reflected in the most outstanding and immediate transferences and resistances. Individual treatment, however, is only one facet of therapy in the cases under discussion. The transferences of these patients remain diffused, while their acting out remains a constant danger. Some, therefore, need to undergo treatment in a hospital environment in which their stepping out of the therapeutic relationship can be observed and limited; and in which first steps *beyond* the newly won bipolar relationship to the therapist meet with the immediate support of receptive nurses, cooperative fellow patients, and helpful instructors in a sufficiently wide choice of activities.

Specific Factors in Family and Childhood

In the discussion of patients who have a relevant pathogenic trend in common, we are apt to ask what their parents have in common. I think that one may say that a number of the mothers in our case histories have in common some outstanding traits. The first is a pronounced status awareness, of the climbing and pretentious or of the "hold-on" variety. They would at almost any time be willing to overrule matters of honest feeling and of intelligent judgment for the sake of a façade of wealth, propriety, and "happiness": they, in fact, try to coerce their sensitive children into a pretense of a "natural" and "glad-to-be-proper" sociability. They also have the special quality of a penetrating omnipresence; their very voices and their softest sobs are sharp, plaintive, or fretful, and cannot be escaped within a considerable radius. One patient, all through childhood had a repetitive dream of a pair of flapping scissors flying around a room: the scissors proved to symbolize his mother's voice, cutting, and cutting off.[6] These mothers love, but they love fearfully, plaintively, intrusively; they are themselves so hungry for approval and for recognition that they burden their young children with complicated complaints, espe-

---

[6] This example illustrates well the balance which must be found in the interpretation given to such patients between *sexual symbolism* (here castration) which, if overemphasized by the therapist, can only increase the patient's sense of being endangered; and the *representation of dangers to the ego* (here the danger of having the thread of one's autonomy cut off) the communication of which is more urgent, more immediately beneficial, and a condition for the safe discussion of sexual meanings.

cially about the father, and they plead with the children to justify by their existence their mother's existence. They are highly jealous and highly sensitive to the jealousy of others; in our context it is especially important that the mother is intensely jealous of any sign that the child may identify primarily with the father, or, worse, base his very identity on that of the father. It must be added that whatever these mothers are, they are more so toward the patient; the conclusion is inescapable that these patients, in turn, have, from the beginning, deeply hurt their mothers by shying away from them, and this because of an utter intolerance of extreme temperamental differences. These differences, however, are only extreme expressions of an essential affinity: by which I mean to imply that the patient's excessive tendency to withdraw (or to act impulsively) and the mother's excessive social intrusiveness have in common a high degree of social vulnerability. Behind the mother's persistent complaints, then, that the father failed to make a woman out of her, is the complaint, deeply perceived by both mother and child, that the patient failed to make a mother out of her.

The fathers, while usually successful, and often outstanding in their particular fields, do not stand up against their wives at home because of an excessive mother dependence on them, in consequence of which the fathers also are deeply jealous of their children. What initiative and integrity they have either surrenders to the wife's intrusiveness or tries guiltily to elude her: in consequence of which the mother becomes only the more needy, plaintive, and "sacrificial" in her demands upon all or some of her children.

Of the relationship of our patients to their brothers and sisters I can only say that it seems to be more symbiotic than most sibling relationships are. Because of an early identity hunger, our patients are apt to attach themselves to one brother or sister in a way resembling the behavior of twins (Burlingham, 1952): except that here we have one twin, as it were, trying to treat a nontwin as a twin. They seem apt to surrender to a total identification with at least one sibling in ways which go far beyond the "altruism by identification" described by Anna Freud (1946). It is as if our patients surrendered their own identity to that of a brother or sister in the hope of regaining a bigger and better one by some act of merging. For periods they succeed; the letdown which must follow the breakup of the artificial twinship is only the more traumatic. Rage and paralysis follow the sud-

den insight that there is enough identity only for one, and that the other seems to have made off with it.

The early childhood histories of our patients are, on the whole, remarkably bland. Some infantile autism is often observed early but usually rationalized by the parents. Yet one has the general impression that the degree of malignancy of the acute identity diffusion in late adolescence depends on the extent of this early autism, which will determine the depth of regression and the intensity of the encounter between new identity fragments and old introjects. As to particular traumata in childhood or youth, one item seems frequent, namely, a severe physical trauma either in the oedipal period or in early puberty—and this in connection with a separation from home. This trauma may consist of an operation or a belatedly diagnosed physical defect; it may be an accident or a severe sexual traumatization. Otherwise the early pathology conforms with that expected as typical for the dominant psychiatric diagnosis given.

Once More: the Diagram

Diagrams have a quiet coerciveness all their own. Especially does a diagram which has neither been completed nor discarded become a conceptual Harvey: one converses with it unawares. In therapeutic work, one tries to ignore the embarrassing fact that now and again the diagram looks over one's shoulder, as it were, and makes a suggestion; nor do the patients appreciate such atmospheric interferences. Only as I concluded this impressionistic survey of some of the main features of identity diffusion, did it occur to me to "locate" them on the chart: and it cannot be denied that they clarify previously vague parts of the diagram and suggest specific expansions of theory. Insisting, then, that in principle Harveys should remain expendable, we will briefly outline what this one can teach us.

The original chart showed only the diagonal, i.e., the successive achievement (or failure) of the main components of relative psychosocial health. However, it bore the legend: "Above the diagonal there is space for a future elaboration of the precursors of each of these solutions, all of which begin with the beginning; below the diagonal there is space for the designation of the derivatives of these solutions in the maturing personality."

Because all the *verticals* "begin with the beginning," one hesitates to enter even tentative terms into the top boxes. Yet, work with borderline cases (adolescent, juvenile, and infantile) suggests that the infantile frontier, to which they have all regressed, is that of a basic mistrust in their *self-delineation* and of a basic doubt in the possibility of any relationship of *mutuality*. The chart, tentatively, assumes that a successful struggle on the earliest psychosocial frontier of infancy (i.e., the trust-mistrust frontier), if well guided by a favorable maternal environment, leads to a dominant sense of Unipolarity (I, 5) by which is meant something like a dominant sense of the goodness of individual existence. This, I believe, deserves to be differentiated from the narcissistic omnipotence ascribed to this age. While still vulnerably dependent on direct, continuous, and consistent maternal support, an actual sense of the reality of "good" powers, outside and within oneself, must be assumed to arise. Its negative counterpart is a diffusion of contradictory introjects and a predominance of fantasies which pretend to coerce hostile reality with omnipotent vengeance. Once gained, however, the psychosocial foundation of unipolarity subsequently permits *Bipolarization* (II, 5) or what, in id terms, has been called the cathexis of objects. This permits an outgoing experimentation with powerful but loving individuals who retain consistent reality, even though they may go before they come, deny before they give, seem indifferent before they again become attentive. In transitory of lasting forms of autism, the child can be seen to shy away from or to despair of such bipolarization, always in search of an illusory good "oneliness."

Subsequent *Play* and *Work Identifications* (III, 5—IV, 5) with powerful adults and with older and younger age-mates need no further discussion here; the literature on the preschool and school stage amply illustrates the gains and the defeats of these more obviously psychosocial periods.

It is the horizontal (V) which contains the *derivatives of earlier relative achievements which now become part and parcel of the struggle for identity*. It is necessary to emphasize (and possible to illustrate briefly) the principle according to which early relative achievements (diagonal) when considered at a later stage (any horizontal below the diagonal) must be reviewed and renamed in terms of that later stage. Basic Trust, for example, is a good and a most fundamental thing to have, but its psychosocial quality becomes more differentiated as the ego comes into the possession of a more extensive apparatus, even as society challenges and guides such extension.

To begin, then, with the pathology just described: *Time Diffusion* (V, 1) or a loss of the ego's function of maintaining perspective and expectancy is related to the *earliest crises in life* (I, 1), and this because of the fact that the conception of temporal cycles and of time qualities is inherent in and develops from the first experience of mounting need tension, of delay of satisfaction, and final unification with the satisfying "object." As tension increases, future fulfillment is anticipated in "hallucinatory" images; as fulfillment is delayed, moments of impotent rage occur in which anticipation (and with it, future) is obliterated; the perception of an approaching potential satisfaction again gives time a highly condensed quality of intense hope and feared disappointment. All of this contributes temporal elements to the formation of basic trust, i.e., the inner conviction that—after all—sufficient satisfaction is sufficiently predictable to make waiting and "working" worthwhile. Whatever the original inventory of time qualities are, our most malignantly regressed young people are clearly possessed by general attitudes which represent something of a mistrust of time as such: every delay appears to be a deceit, every wait an experience of impotence, every hope a danger, every plan a catastrophe, every potential provider a traitor. Therefore, time must be made to stand still, if necessary by the magic means of catatonic immobility—or by death. These are the extremes which are manifest in few, and latent in many cases of identity diffusion; yet, every adolescent, I would believe, knows at least fleeting moments of being at odds with time itself. In its normal and transitory form, this new kind of mistrust quickly or gradually yields to outlooks permitting and demanding an intense investment in a future, or in a number of possible futures. If these, to us, seem often quite "utopian" (i.e., based on expectations which would call for a change in the laws of historical change as we know them), we must, for the moment, postpone any judgment of value. The adolescent—or some adolescents—may need, at all costs, an outlook with a perspective worth an investment of energy. The actual realizability of such an outlook may be a matter of later learning and adjusting, and often a matter of historical luck.

In the following, I shall let each step on the chart lead to a few suggestive *social considerations* which were only briefly touched on in the foregoing. To envisage a future, the young adult may also need that something which Shaw called "a religion" and "a clear comprehension of life in the light of an intelligible theory." I indicated at the beginning that we would call this something-between-a-theory-and-a-religion an *ideology,* a term highly conducive to misunderstanding. At this point let me stress only the *temporal* element in world views which might be called ideological: they are grouped around *a utopian simplification of historical perspective* (salvation, conquest, reform, happiness, rationality, technological mastery) in accordance with newly developing identity potentials. Whatever else ideology is (Mannheim, 1949; Schilder, 1951b), and whatever transitory or lasting social forms it takes, we will tentatively view it here and discuss it later—*as a necessity for the growing ego* which is involved in the succession of generations, and in adolescence is committed to some new synthesis of past and future: a synthesis which must include but transcend the past, even as identity does.

We proceed to *Identity Consciousness* (V, 2) the ancestors of which are *Doubt* and *Shame* (II, 2). They counteract and complicate the sense of autonomy, i.e., the acceptance of the psychosocial fact of being, once and for all, a separate individual, who actually and figuratively must stand on his own feet. Here, I beg to quote myself (1950a): "Shame is an emotion insufficiently studied,[7] because in our civilization it is so early and easily absorbed by guilt. Shame supposes that one is completely exposed and conscious of being looked at: in one word, self-conscious. One is visible and not ready to be visible; which is why we dream of shame as a situation in which we are stared at in a condition of incomplete dress. Shame is early expressed in an impulse to bury one's face, or to sink, right then and there, into the ground. But this, I think, is essentially rage turned against the self. He who is ashamed would like to force the world not to look at him, not to notice his exposure. He would like to destroy the eyes of the world. Instead he must wish for his own invisibility. . . . Doubt is the brother of shame. Where shame is dependent on the consciousness of being upright and exposed, doubt, so clinical observation leads me to believe, has much to do with a consciousness of having a front and a back—and especially a 'behind'. . . . This basic sense of doubt in whatever one has left behind forms a substratum for later and more verbal forms of compulsive doubting; which finds its adult expression in paranoiac fears concerning hidden persecutors and secret persecutions threatening from behind and from within the behind" (p. 223).

[7] See, however, G. Piers and Singer (1953).

Identity Consciousness then is a new edition of that original *doubt,* which concerned the trustworthiness of the training adults and the trustworthiness of the child himself—only that in adolescence, such self-conscious doubt concerns the reliability and reconcilability of the whole span of childhood which is now to be left behind. The obligation now to achieve an identity, not only distinct but also distinctive, is apt to arouse a painful over-all *ashamedness,* somehow comparable to the original shame (and rage) over being visible all around to all-knowing adults—only that such potential shame now adheres to one's identity as a being with a *public history,* exposed to *age-mates* and *leaders.* All of this, in the normal course of events, is outbalanced by that *Self-certainty,* which comes from the accrued sense of an ever-increased identity at the conclusion of each previous crisis, a certainty now characterized by an increasing sense of independence from the family as the matrix of childhood identifications.

Among the societal phenomena corresponding to this second conflict there is a universal trend toward some form of *uniformity* (and sometimes to special uniforms of distinctive clothing) through which incomplete self-certainty, for a time, can hide in a group certainty, such as is provided by the badges as well as the sacrifices of investitures, confirmations, and initiations. Even those who care to differ radically must evolve a certain uniformity of differing (snobs, zoot-suiters). These and less obvious uniformities are supported by the institution of comprehensive *shaming* among peers, a judgmental give-and-take and free banding together which leaves only a few "holding the bag" in painful (if sometimes creative) isolation.

The matter of the choice of a *Negative Identity* (V, 3) as against *free Role Experimentation* has been discussed. The position of these terms on the chart signifies their obvious connection with the earlier conflict (III, 3) between free *Initiative* (in reality, fantasy, and play) and oedipal guilt. Where the identity crisis breaks through to the oedipal crisis and beyond it, to a crisis of trust, the choice of a negative identity remains the only form of initiative, complete denial of guilt or complete denial of ambition the only possible ways of managing guilt. On the other hand, the normal expression of relatively guilt-free initiative at this stage is a kind of disciplined role experimentation which follows the unwritten codes of adolescent subsocieties.

Of the social institutions which undertake to channel as they encourage such initiative, and to provide atonement as they appease guilt, we may point here, again, to *initiations* and *confirmations*: they strive, within an atmosphere of mythical timelessness, to combine some form of sacrifice or submission with an energetic guidance toward sanctioned and circumscribed ways of action—a combination which assures the development in the novice of an optimum of compliance with a maximum sense of fellowship and free choice. This ego aspect of the matter (namely, the achievement of a sense of a choice as a result of ritual regimentation) still awaits study and integration with the better explored sexual aspects of initiation rites and related rituals, official or spontaneous. Armies, of course, utilize this potentiality.

As we approach the middle region of the chart, we find that a more detailed discussion of the terms used has already been offered. Extreme *Work Paralysis* (V, 4) is the logical sequence of a deep sense of inadequacy (regressed to a sense of basic mistrust) of one's general equipment. Such a sense of inadequacy, of course, does not usually reflect a true lack of potential: it may rather convey the unrealistic demands made by an ego ideal willing to settle only for omnipotence or omniscience; it may express the fact that the immediate social environment does not have a niche for the individual's true gifts; or it may reflect the paradoxical fact that an individual in early school life was seduced into a specialized precocity which early outdistanced his identity development. All of these reasons, then, may exclude the individual from that experimental competition in play and work through which he learns to find and to insist on *his* kind of achievement and work identity.

Social institutions support the strength and the distinctiveness of work identity by offering those who are still learning and experimenting a certain *status-of-the-moratorium*, an apprenticeship or discipleship characterized by defined duties, sanctioned competitions, and special freedoms, and yet potentially integrated with the hierarchies of expectable jobs and careers, castes and classes, guilds and unions.

In Box V, 5 we again meet the diagonal, and the over-all focus of this paper; crossing it we enter the area of psychosocial elements which are not derivatives but precursors of future psychosocial crises. The first such element (V, 6) is *Sexual Identity* vs. *Bisexual Diffusion*, the most immediate precursor of *Intimacy* vs. *Isolation*. Here the sexual mores of cultures and classes make for immense differences in the psychosocial differentiation of masculine and feminine (M. Mead, 1949), and in the age, kind, and ubiquity of genital activity. These differences can obscure the common fact discussed above, namely, that the development of psychosocial intimacy is not possible without a firm sense of identity. Bisexual diffusion can lead young adults toward two deceptive developments. Induced by special mores, or otherwise seduced, they may foreclose their identity development by concentrating on early genital activity without intimacy; or, on the contrary, they may concentrate on social or intellectual status values which underplay the genital element, with a resulting permanent weakness of genital polarization with the other sex. Different mores (Kinsey, Pomeroy, and Martin, 1948) demand from some the ability to postpone genital activity, and from others, the early ability to make it a "natural" part of life: in either case, special problems ensue which may well impair true heterosexual intimacy in young adulthood.

Social institutions here offer ideological rationales for a *prolongation of the psychosexual moratorium* in the form of complete sexual abstinence, in the form of genital activity without social commitment, or in the form of sexual play without genital engagement (petting). What a group's or an individual's "libido economy" will stand for depends to some extent on the identity gain which accrues from such preferred sexual behavior.

The study of horizontal V of the chart, then, reveals certain systematic consistencies in the described elements of identity diffusion, and in those of identity formation. As pointed out parenthetically, these consistencies correspond to certain social institutions, which (in ways still to be elucidated) support the ego needs and ego functions subsumed under the term identity. In fact, the two remaining boxes of horizontal V (which at any rate are marginal to this clinical section) cannot be approached at all without a discussion of social institutions. The prime institution which awaits clarification here is that system of ideals which societies present to the young individual in the explicit or implicit form of an *ideology*. To ideology we may, in tentative summary, ascribe the function of offering youth (1) an overly clear perspective of the future, encompassing all foreseeable time, and thus counteracting individual "time diffusion"; (2) an opportunity for the exhibition of some uniformity of appearance and action counteracting individual identity consciousness; (3) inducement to collective role and work experimentation which can counteract a sense of inhibition and personal guilt; (4) submission to leaders who as "big brothers" escape the ambivalence of the parent-child relation; (5) introduction into the ethos of the prevailing technology, and thus into sanctioned and regulated competition; and (6) a seeming correspondence between the internal world of ideals and evils, on the one hand, and, on the other, the outer world with its organized goals and dangers in real space and time: a geographic-historical framework for the young individual's budding identity.

I am aware of having, in the conclusion of a pathographic sketch, "sketched in" some references to phenomena which are the domain of social science. I can justify this only with the assumption that clinical work, in cutting through the immense diversity of individual pathology in order to arrive at some workable generalities, may well come upon an aspect of matters institutional which the historical and the economic approach has necessarily neglected. Here, however, we must first attempt to bring some order into the terminological household of our own field, and this especially where it overlaps with areas of social science.

Societal: Ego and Environment

I

It has not escaped the reader that the term identity covers much of what has been called the self by a variety of workers, be it in the form of a self-concept (George H. Mead, 1934), a self-system (Harry S. Sullivan, 1953), or in that of fluctuating self-experiences described by Schilder (1951a), Federn (1952), and others.[8] Within psychoanalytic ego psychology, Hartmann, above all, has circumscribed this general area more clearly when in discussing the so-called

libidinal cathexis of the ego in narcissism, he comes to the conclusion that it is rather a self which is thus being cathected. He advocates a term *"self-representation,"* as differentiated from "object representation" (Hartmann, 1950). This self-representation was, less systematically, anticipated by Freud in his occasional references to the ego's "attitudes toward the self" and to fluctuating cathexes bestowed upon this self in labile states of "self-esteem" (Freud, 1957). In this paper, we are concerned with the *genetic continuity* of such a self-representation—a continuity which must lastly be ascribed to the work of the ego. No other inner agency could accomplish the selective accentuation of significant identifications throughout childhood and the gradual integration of self-images in anticipation of an identity. It is for this reason that I have called identity, at first, ego identity. But in brashly choosing a name analogous to "ego ideal," I have opened myself to the query as to what the relationship of these two concepts is.

Freud assigned the *internalized perpetuation* of cultural influences to the functions of the "superego or ego ideal" which was to represent the commands and the prohibitions emanating from the environment and its traditions. Let us compare two statements of Freud's which are relevant here. ". . . the super-ego of the child is not really built up on the model of the parents, but on that of the parents' super-ego; it takes over the same content, it becomes the vehicle of tradition and of all the age-long values which have been handed down in this way from generation to generation. You may easily guess what great help is afforded by the recognition of the super-ego in understanding the social behavior of man, in grasping the problem of delinquency, for example, and perhaps, too, in providing us with some practical hints upon education. . . . Mankind never lives completely in the present; the *ideologies of the super-ego*[9] perpetuate the past, the traditions of the race and the people, which yield but slowly to the influence of the present and to new developments, and, so long as they work through the super-ego, play an important part in man's life" (Freud, 1933, pp. 95–96). Freud, it is to be noted here, speaks of the "ideologies of the super-ego," thus giving the super-ego ideational content; yet he also refers to it as a "vehicle," i.e., as a part of the psychic system through which ideas work. It would seem that by ideologies of the superego Freud means the super-ego's specific contributions to the archaic, to the magic in the inner coerciveness of ideologies.

[8] I am not yet able to establish the systematic convergencies and divergencies between the work of the so-called "Neo-Freudians" and that which I am trying to formulate. It will be seen, however, that in individuals as well as in groups I prefer to speak of a "sense of identity" rather than of a "character structure" or "basic character." In nations, too, my concepts would lead me to concentrate on the conditions and experiences which heighten or endanger a national sense of identity rather than on a static national character. An introduction to this subject is offered in my book, *Childhood and Society* (1950a). Here it is important to remember that each identity cultivates its own sense of freedom—wherefore a people rarely understands what makes other peoples feel free. This fact is amply exploited by totalitarian propaganda and underestimated in the Western world.

[9] My italics.

In a second statement Freud acknowledges the social side of the ego ideal. "The ego ideal opens up an important avenue for the understanding of group psychology. In addition to its individual side, this ideal has a social side; it is also the common ideal of a family, a class or a nation" (1957, p. 101).

It would seem that the terms superego and ego ideal have come to be distinguished by their different relation to phylogenetic and to ontogenetic history. The superego is conceived as a more archaic and thoroughly internalized representative of the evolutionary principle of morality, of man's *congenital proclivity* toward the development of a primitive, categorical conscience. Allied with (ontogenetically) early introjects, the superego remains a rigidly vindictive and punitive inner agency of "blind" morality. The ego ideal, however, seems to be more flexibly bound to the ideals of the particular *historical period* and thus is closer to the ego function of reality testing.

Ego identity (if we were to hold on to this term and to this level of discourse) would in comparison be even closer to *social reality* in that as a subsystem of the ego it would test, select, and integrate the self-representations derived from the psychosocial crises of childhood. It could be said to be characterized by the more or less *actually attained but forever-to-be-revised* sense of the reality of the self within social reality; while the imagery of the ego ideal could be said to represent a set of *to-be-strived-for but forever-not-quite-attainable ideal* goals for the self.

However, in using the word self in the sense of Hartmann's self-representation, one opens the whole controversy to a radical consideration. One could argue that it may be wise in matters of the ego's perceptive and regulative dealings with its self to reserve the designation "ego" for the subject, and to give the designation "self" to the object. The ego, then, as a central organizing agency, is during the course of life faced with a changing self which, in turn, demands to be synthesized with abandoned and anticipated selves. This suggestion would be applicable to the *body ego*, which could be said to be the part of the self provided by the attributes of the organism, and, therefore, might more appropriately be called the *body self*; it would also concern the ego ideal as the representative of the ideas, images, and configurations, which serve the persistent comparison with an *ideal self*; and finally, it would apply to what I have called *ego identity*. What could consequently be called the *self-identity* emerges from all those experiences in which a sense of temporary self-

diffusion was successfully contained by a renewed and ever more realistic self-definition and social recognition. *Identity formation thus can be said to have a self-aspect, and an ego aspect.* It is part of the ego in the sense that it represents the ego's synthesizing function on one of its frontiers, namely, the actual social structure of the environment and the image of reality as transmitted to the child during successive childhood crises. (The other frontiers would be the id, and the demands made on the ego by our biological history and structure; the superego and the demands of our more primitively moralistic proclivities; and the ego ideal with its idealized parent images.) Identity, in this connection, has a claim to recognition as the adolescent ego's most important support, in the task of containing the postpubertal id, and in balancing the then newly invoked superego as well as the again overly demanding ego ideal.

Until the matter of ego vs. self is sufficiently defined to permit a terminological decision, I shall use the bare term identity in order to suggest a social function of the ego which results, in adolescence, in a relative psychosocial equilibrium essential to the tasks of young adulthood.

II

The word "psychosocial" so far has had to serve as an emergency bridge between the so-called "biological" formulations of psychoanalysis and newer ones which take the cultural environment into more systematic consideration.

The so-called basic *biological* orientation of psychoanalysis has gradually become a habitual kind of *pseudo biology*, and this especially in the conceptualization (or lack thereof) of man's "environment." In psychoanalytic writings the terms "outer world" or "environment" are often used to designate an uncharted area which is said to be outside merely because it fails to be inside—inside the individual's somatic skin, or inside his psychic systems, or inside his self in the widest sense. Such a vague and yet omnipresent "outerness" by necessity assumes a number of ideological connotations, and, in fact, assumes the character of a number of world images: sometimes "the outer world" is conceived of as reality's conspiracy against the infantile wish world; sometimes as the (indifferent or annoying) fact of the existence of other people; and then again as the (at least partially benevolent) presence of maternal care. But even in the recent admission of the significance of the "mother-child relationship," a stub-born tendency persists to treat the mother-child unit as a "biological" entity more or less isolated from its cultural surroundings, which then again become an "environment" of vague supports or of blind pressures and mere "conventions." Thus, step for step, we are encumbered by the remnants of juxtapositions which were once necessary and fruitful enough: for it was important to establish the fact that moralistic and hypocritical social demands are apt to crush the adult and to exploit the child. It was important to conceptualize certain intrinsic antagonisms between the individual's and society's energy households. However, the implicit conclusion that an individual ego could exist against or without a specifically human "environment," i.e., social organization, is senseless; and, far from being "biological" in its orientation, threatens to isolate psychoanalytic theory from the rich ethological and ecological findings of modern biology.

It is again Hartmann (1958) who opens the way to new considerations. His statement that the human infant is born preadapted to an "average expectable environment" implies a more truly biological as well as an inescapably societal formulation. For not even the very best of mother-child relationships could, by themselves, account for that subtle and complex "milieu" which permits a human baby not only to survive but also to develop his potentialities for growth and uniqueness. Man's ecology includes among its dimensions constant natural, historical, and technological readjustment; which makes it at once obvious that only a perpetual social metabolism and a constant (if ever so imperceptible) restructuring of tradition can safeguard for each new generation of infants anything approaching an "average expectability" of environment. Today, when rapid technological changes have taken the lead, the matter of establishing by scientific means and of preserving in flexible forms an "average expectable" continuity in child rearing and education has, in fact, become a matter of human survival.

The specific kind of preadaptedness of the human infant (namely, the readiness to grow by predetermined steps through institutionalized psychosocial crises) calls not only for one basic environment, but for a whole chain of such successive environments. As the child "adapts" in spurts and stages, he has a claim, at any given stage reached, to the next "average expectable environment." In other words, the human environment must permit and safeguard a series of more or less discontinuous and yet culturally and psychologically consistent steps, each extending further along the radius of expanding life tasks. All of this makes man's so-called biological adaptation a matter of life cycles developing within their community's changing history. Consequently, a psychoanalytic sociology faces the task of conceptualizing man's environment as the persistent endeavor of the older and more adult egos to join in the organizational effort of providing an integrated series of average expectable environments for the young egos.

III

In a recent paper which thoughtfully yet somewhat sweepingly reviews efforts at approaching the relation of culture and personality, Hartmann, Kris, and Loewenstein (1951) state: "Cultural conditions could and should be viewed also with the question in mind which and what kind of opportunities for ego functions in a sphere free from conflict they invite or inhibit." In regard to the possibility of studying the reflection of such "cultural conditions" in the psychoanalysis of individuals, the writers seem less encouraging. They state: "Analysts, too, are aware of differences of behavior caused by cultural conditions; they are not devoid of that common sense which has always stressed these differences, but their impact on the analytic observer tends to decrease as work progresses and as available data move from the periphery to the center, that is from manifest behavior to data, part of which is accessible only to an analytic investigation." The present paper ventures to suggest that rather central problems of ego development, which are, indeed, "accessible only to an analytic investigation," demand that the psychoanalyst's awareness of cultural differences go well beyond that "common sense" which the three authors (being themselves outstanding cosmopolitans) seem to find sufficient in this particular area of observation, while they would assuredly urge a more "analyzed" common sense in other areas.

In order to approach this whole matter psychoanalytically, it may well be necessary for the individual psychoanalyst to ask himself what particular configuration of drives, defenses, capabilities, and opportunities led him into the choice of this ever-expanding field. Some search in this area may clarify the fact that some of the most heated and stubborn answers to the question of what psychoanalysis *is* or *is not* originate in another question of great urgency, namely: what psychoanalysis *must be* (or *must remain or become*) to a particular worker because a particular psychoanalytic "identity" has become a cornerstone of his existence as a man, a professional, and a citizen. I am not denying here the necessity, in a suddenly expanding and unexpectedly popular field, to define the original sources of its inspiration and the fundamentals of its specific morality. Yet, psychoanalysis, in its young history, has offered rich opportunities for a variety of identities: it gave new function and scope to such divergent endeavors as natural philosophy and Talmudic argument; medical tradition and missionary teaching; literary demonstration and the building of theory; social reform and the making of money. Psychoanalysis as a movement has harbored a variety of world images and utopias which originated in the various stages of its history in a variety of countries, and this as a result of the simple fact that man, in order to be able to interact efficiently with other human beings, must, at intervals, make *a total orientation out of a given stage of partial knowledge*. Individual students of Freud thus found their identity best suited to certain early theses of his which promised a particular sense of psychoanalytic identity, and with it, an inspiring ideology. Similarly, overstated antitheses to some of Freud's tentative and transient theses have served as bases for professional and scientific identities of other workers in the field. Such identities easily find elaboration in ideological schools and in irreversible systematizations which do not permit argument or change.

In speaking of scientific proof and scientific progress in a field which deals directly with the immediate needs of men, it is necessary to account not only for methodological, practical, and ethical factors, but also for the necessity of a professional identity backed by an ideological quasi-synthesis of the available orientations. Sooner or later, then, training analyses must encompass the varieties of professional identity formation in candidates-for-training, while theoretical teaching must throw light also on the ideological background of principal differences in what is felt to be most practical, most true, and most right at various stages of this developing field.

IV

The discussion of "professional identities" has necessarily led us beyond identity formation proper, to its derivatives in later, truly adult stages. I will make one more step into adulthood, before returning, in conclusion, to the problem of ideological polarization as an aspect of the societal processes which meets a necessity of adolescent ego development.

I have already implied a hypothesis which goes beyond that of Hartmann, Kris, and Loewenstein (1951), who state that "cultural conditions could and should be viewed *also*[10] with the question in mind which and what kind of opportunities for ego functions in a sphere free from conflict they invite or inhibit." It may well be that the relationship between the organized values and institutional efforts of societies, on the one hand, and the mechanisms of ego synthesis, on the other, is more systematic; and that, from a psychosocial point of view at any rate, basic social and cultural processes can *only* be viewed as the joint endeavor of adult egos to develop and maintain, through joint organization, a maximum of conflict-free energy in a mutually supportive psychosocial equilibrium. Only such organization is likely to give consistent support to the young egos at every step of their development.

I have characterized the psychosocial gains of adult ego development with the terms Intimacy, Generativity, and Integrity (VI, 6—VII, 7—VIII, 8 on the chart). They denote a postadolescent development of libidinal cathexes in *intimate engagements*; in parenthood or other *forms of "generating,"*[11] and, finally, in the most *integrative experiences* and values accrued from a lifetime. All of these developments have ego aspects and social aspects; in fact, their very alternatives (Isolation, VI, 6—Self-Absorption, VII, 7—and Despair, VIII, 8) can be held in check only by the individual's fitting participation in social endeavors which "invite opportunities for ego functions in spheres free from

---

[10] My italics.
[11] See the concern over personal children, patients, and germinating ideas in Freud's "Irma dream" (Erikson, 1954a). In my psychosocial interpretation of this dream I pointed out that a dream can be seen to retrace the steps of psychosocial development at the same time that it represents a psychosexual regression to a certain infantile stage of libido development. Freud's dreams (because of the strong inner structure of his personality and maybe also because of the didactic interest with which he went about dreaming them) prove to be continuously enlightening even in regard to matters not explicitly formulated by him, such as the parallelism of psychosocial and psychosexual themes. In the Irma dream, so I showed in my paper, the theme of *phallic* intrusion can be seen to be closely associated with that of *initiative*. Similarly, Freud's dream of the Three Fates clearly points to the close relationship of *oral* incorporation and the problem of *trust*; while the dream of Count Thun strongly emphasizes themes of *autonomy* and the modes of *anal* elimination. A paper comparing these three dreams is in preparation.

conflict." The older generation thus needs the younger one as much as the younger one depends on the older; and it would seem that it is in this mutuality of the development of the older and younger generations that certain basic and universal values such as love, faith, truth, justice, order, work, etc., in all of their defensive strength, compensatory power, and independent creativity become and remain important joint achievements of individual ego development and of the social process. In fact, as our clinical histories begin to reveal, these values provide indispensable support for the ego development of the growing generations, in that they give some specific superindividual consistency to parental conduct (although *kinds* of consistency—including consistent kinds of being inconsistent—vary with value systems and personality types).

The intrinsic complication and the peculiar social pathology adhering to the *verbal conventions* and *formal institutions* which communicate and perpetuate social values periodically call for special societal processes which will recreate the "average expectability" of the environments either through ceremonial rededication, or through systematic reformulation. In both cases, selected leaders and elites feel called upon to demonstrate a convincing, a "charismatic" kind of generalized generativity, i.e., a superpersonal interest in the maintenance and the rejuvenation of institutions. In recorded history, some such leaders are registered as "great"; they, it seems, are able, out of the deepest personal conflicts to derive the energy which meets their period's specific needfulness for a resynthesis of the prevalent world image. At any rate, only through constant rededication will institutions gain the active and inspired investment of new energy from their young members. More theoretically stated: only by maintaining, in its institutionalized values, meaningful correspondences to the main crises of ego development, does a society manage to have at the disposal of its particular group identity a maximum of the conflict-free energy accrued from the childhood crises of a majority of its young members.[12]

---

[12] In this paper, I cannot more than approach the possible relation of the problem of identity to ideological processes (see Erikson, 1958), and I can only parenthetically list possible analogous correspondences between stages of psychosocial development in the individual and major trends of social organization. As pointed out in "Growth and Crises of the Healthy Personality" (pp. 65–82), the problem of Autonomy (versus Shame and Doubt) has intrinsic relations with the delineation of individual rights and limitations in the basic principles of law and justice, and the problem of Initiative

Before briefly applying this general assumption to ideology, I must ask the reader to take one more look at the chart. In boxes V, 6—V, 7—and V, 8 he will find whatever indication I can give of the precursors in adolescence of what later on are Intimacy, Generativity, and Integrity. The struggle for *Sexual Identity*, V, 6, while, at first, consumed with the question as to what kind of a male or female one is, through the selective search for *Intimacy*, VI, 6, approaches the problem of a choice of a future coparent. The clarification, through a firmer identity formation, of one's status as a *follower* (of some) and a *leader* (of others), V, 7, permits the early development of a responsibility toward younger agemates which, although an important social phenomenon in its own right, is a precursor of the sense of responsibility for the next generation (*Generativity*), VII, 7. Finally, some form of *Ideological Polarization*, V, 8, some breakdown of the multiplicity of values into a few which coerce commitment, must be part and parcel of this gradual reversal of roles, through which the "identified" individual becomes a figure of identification for the young. Such polarization, however, cannot fail eventually to become a critical part of the problem of *Integrity*, VIII, 8: a matter which we saw reflected in Shaw's statement (1952): that he "succeeded only too well" in living the public identity "G.B.S.," i.e., in the polarization of his propensities for acting like an actor on the stage of life, and for acting as a reformer in social reality.

V

Shaw, of course, was a studiedly spectacular man. But, to extend a Shavianism quoted above: a clown is often not only the best but also the most sincere part of the Great Show. It is, therefore, worth while at this point to review the words chosen by Shaw to characterize the story of his "conversion": "I was *drawn into* the Socialist *revival* of the early eighties, among Englishmen *intensely serious* and *burning with indignation* at very *real* and very *fundamental evils* that affected *all the world*." The words here italicized convey to me the following implications. "Drawn into": an ideology has a compelling power. "Revival": it consists of a traditional force in the

---

(versus Guilt) with the encouragements and limitations emanating from the dominant ethos of production. The problem of workmanship critically prepares for the predominant techniques of production and their characteristic division of labor.

state of rejuvenation. "Intensely serious": it permits even the cynical to make an investment of sincerity. "Burning with indignation": it gives to the need for repudiation the sanction of righteousness. "Real": it projects a vague inner evil onto a circumscribed horror in reality. "Fundamental": it promises participation in an effort at basic reconstruction of society. "All the world": it gives structure to a totally defined world image. Here, then, are the elements by which a group identity harnesses in the service of its ideology the young individual's aggressive and discriminative energies, and encompasses, as it completes it, the individual's identity. Thus, identity and ideology are two aspects of the same process. Both provide the necessary condition for further individual maturation and, with it, for the next higher form of identification, namely, the *solidarity linking common identities*. For the need to bind irrational self-hate and irrational repudiation makes young people, on occasion, mortally compulsive and conservative even where and when they seem most anarchic and radical; the same need makes them potentially "ideological," i.e., more or less explicitly in search of a world image held together by what Shaw called "a clear comprehension of life in the light of an intelligible theory."

As far as Fabian Socialists are concerned, Shaw seems fully justified in using terms characterizing an ideology of marked intellectual brilliance. More generally, an ideological system is a coherent body of shared images, ideas, and ideals which (whether based on a formulated dogma, an implicit *Weltanschauung*, a highly structured world image, a political creed, or a "way of life") provides for the participants a coherent, if systematically simplified, over-all orientation in space and time, in means and ends.

The word "ideology" itself has somewhat of a bad name. By their very nature ideologies contradict other ideologies as "inconsistent" and hypocritical; and an over-all critique of ideology characterizes its persuasive simplifications as a systematic form of collective hypocrisy (Mannheim, 1949). For it is true that the average adult, and in fact, the average community, if not acutely engaged in some ideological polarization, are apt to consign ideology to a well-circumscribed compartment in their lives, where it remains handy for periodical rituals and rationalizations, but will do no undue harm to other business at hand. Yet, the fact that ideologies are simplified conceptions of what is to come (and thus later can serve as rationalizations for what has come about)

does not preclude the possibility that at certain stages of individual development and at certain periods in history, ideological polarization, conflict, and commitment correspond to an inescapable inner need. Youth needs to base its rejections and acceptances on ideological alternatives vitally related to the existing range of alternatives for identity formation.

Ideologies seem to provide meaningful combinations of the oldest and the newest in a group's ideals. They thus channel the forceful earnestness, the sincere asceticism, and the eager indignation of youth toward that social frontier where the struggle between conservatism and radicalism is most alive. On that frontier, fanatic ideologists do their busy work and psychopathic leaders their dirty work; but there, also, true leaders create significant solidarities. All ideologies ask for, as the prize for the promised possession of a future, uncompromising commitment to some absolute hierarchy of values and some rigid principle of conduct: be that principle total obedience to tradition, if the future is the eternalization of ancestry; total resignation, if the future is to be of another world; total martial discipline, if the future is to be reserved for some brand of armed superman; total inner reform, if the future is perceived as an advanced edition of heaven on earth; or (to mention only one of the ideological ingredients of our time) complete pragmatic abandon to the processes of production and to human teamwork, if unceasing production seems to be the thread which holds present and future together. It is in the totalism and exclusiveness of some ideologies that the superego is apt to regain its territory from identity: for when established identities become outworn or unfinished ones threaten to remain incomplete, special crises compel men to wage holy wars, by the cruelest means, against those who seem to question or threaten their unsafe ideological bases.

We may well pause to ponder briefly the fact that the technological and economic developments of our day encroach upon all traditional group identities and solidarities such as may have developed in agrarian, feudal, patrician, or mercantile ideologies. As has been shown by many writers, such over-all development seems to result in a loss of a sense of cosmic wholeness, of providential planfulness, and of heavenly sanction for the means of production (and destruction). In large parts of the world, this seems to result in a ready fascination with totalistic world views, views predicting millenniums and cataclysms, and advocating self-appointed mortal gods. Technological centralization today can give small groups of such fanatic ideologists the concrete power of totalitarian state machines (Erikson, 1954b).

Psychoanalysis has made some contributions to the understanding of these developments especially in so far as they reflect the universal anxieties, inner dependencies, and vulnerabilities adhering to the common fact of human childhood. Psychoanalysis can also help to understand the fact that even in civilized beings the superego's paternalistic-primitive simplicity may call for an irrational trust in super-police chiefs on earth, now that the heavenly discipline which encompassed earlier world images seems to have lost its convincing firmness. However, the application of the psychoanalytic instrument to the questions as to how man changes in his depth as he changes the expanses of his environment, and as to who is affected (and how, and how deeply) by technological and ideological changes (Erikson, 1954b)—these questions must await better formulations of the ego's relationship to work techniques, to the technological "environment," and to the prevalent division of labor.

VI

In a recent seminar in Jerusalem[13] I had an opportunity to discuss with Israeli scholars and clinicians the question of what the identity of an "Israeli" is, and thus to envisage one extreme of contemporary ideological orientations. Israel fascinates both her friends and her enemies. A great number of ideological fragments from European history have found their way into the consciousness of this small state; and many of the identity problems which have occupied a century and a half of American history are being faced in Israel within a few years. A new nation is established on a distant coast (which does not seem to "belong" to anybody) out of oppressed minorities from many lands, a new identity based on imported ideals which are libertarian, puritanic, and messianic. Any discussion of Israel's manifold and most immediate problems sooner or later leads to the extraordinary accomplishments and the extraordinary ideological problems posed by the pioneer Zionist settlers (now a small minority) who make up what is known as the Kibbutz movement. These European ideologists, given—as it were—a *historical*

moratorium created by the peculiar international and national status of Palestine first in the Ottoman Empire and then in the British mandate, were able to establish and to fortify a significant *utopian bridgehead* for Zionist ideology. In his "homeland," and tilling his very home soil, the "ingathered" Jew was to overcome such evil identities as result from eternal wandering, merchandising, and intellectualizing (Erikson, 1950a) and was to become *whole* again in body and mind, as well as in nationality. That the Kibbutz movement has created a hardy, responsible, and inspired type of individual, nobody could deny, although certain details of its educational system (such as the raising of children, from the very beginning, in Children's Houses, and the rooming together of boys and girls through the high-school years) are under critical scrutiny, both in Israel and abroad. The fact is, however, that in Israel a utopia was established on a frontier exposed all around, under conditions reminiscent of those faced by the Mormons. This historical fact is the only framework for judging the rationale and the rationalizations of the style of life which ensued. For no doubt, these pioneers (comparable to this country's settlers, who, in turn, utilized the historical moratorium offered by the discovery of an empty continent, for the establishment of a new "way of life") provided a new nation, sprung up overnight, with a historical ideal. A legitimate question, however, and one not too foreign to this country's historians, concerns the relationship of a revolutionary elite to those who subsequently crowd into and thrive on the lands occupied and on the gains made.[14] In Israel, the by now somewhat exclusive elite of Kibbutzniks faces that incomparably larger part of the population which represents an ideologically all but indigestible mixture: the masses of African and Oriental immigrants, powerful organized labor, the big city dwellers, the religious orthodoxy, the new state bureaucracy—and then, of course, the "good old" mercantile class of middlemen. Furthermore, the more uncompromising part of the Kibbutz movement has not failed to place itself between the two worlds to both of which Zionism maintains strong historical bonds: American and British Jewry (which bought much of the Kibbutz land from Arab absentee landlords) and Soviet Communism, to which the (shall we say) communalistic Kibbutz

[13] Organized by Professors S. Eisenstadt and C. Frankenstein of the Hebrew University. The initial impressions presented here are mine.

[14] We may state tentatively that the elites which emerge from historical change are groups which out of the deepest common identity crisis manage to create a new style of coping with the outstanding danger situations of their society.

movement[15] felt ideologically close—only to be repudiated by Moscow as another form of deviationism.

The Kibbutz movement thus is one example of a modern ideological utopia which freed unknown energies in young people who considered themselves as of one "people," and created a (more or less explicit) group ideal of pervading significance—if of quite unpredictable historical fate in an industrial world. However, Israel is, undoubtedly, one of the most ideology-conscious countries that ever existed; no "peasants" nor workmen ever argued more about the far-reaching meanings of daily decisions. The subtler meanings of ideology for identity formation can probably be fathomed best by comparing highly verbal ideologies with those transitory systems of conversion and aversion which exist in any society, in that no-man's land between childhood and adulthood more or less derisively called adolescence—exist as the most meaningful part of a young person's or a young group's life, often without the knowledge, or indeed, curiosity, of the adults around them. It must be assumed that much of the spontaneous polarization of tastes, opinions, and slogans which occupy the arguments of young people, and much of the sudden impulse to join in destructive behavior, are loose ends of identity formation waiting to be tied together by some ideology.

VII

In the pathographic section of this paper I have pointed to the *total choice* of a negative identity in individuals who could achieve such escape on the basis of autistic and regressive proclivities.

The escape of many gifted if unstable young individuals into a private utopia or, as another patient put it, a "majority of one," might not be necessary were it not for a general development to which they feel unable to submit, i.e., the increasing demand for standardization, uniformity, and conformity which characterizes the present stage of our individualist civilization. In this country, the demand for large-scale conformity has not developed into an explicit totalitarian ideology; it has associated itself with the total dogmas of churches and with the stereotypes of businesslike behavior, but, on the whole, shuns political ideology. We appreciate as we study the capacity of our youth to manage the identity diffu-

sion of an industrial democracy with simple trustfulness, with playful dissonance, with technical virtuosity, with "other-minded" solidarity (Riesman, 1950)—and with a distaste for ideological explicitness. What exactly the implicit ideology of American youth (this most technological youth in the world) is—that is a fateful question, not to be lightly approached in a paper of this kind. Nor would one dare to assess in passing the changes which may be taking place in this ideology and in its implicitness, as a result of a world struggle which makes a military identity a necessary part of young adulthood in this country.

It is easier to delineate that malignant turn toward a *negative group identity* which prevails in some of the youth especially of our large cities, where conditions of economic, ethnic, and religious marginality provide poor bases for positive identities: here negative group identities are sought in spontaneous clique formations ranging all the way from neighborhood gangs and jazz mobs, to dope rings, homosexual circles, and criminal gangs. Clinical experience can be expected to make significant contributions to this problem.[16] Yet, we may well

---

15 I.e., relative communism within the individual community, which, however, in its relation to the national economy, rather represents a capitalist cooperative.

16 We may ask, for example, what inner, unconscious gain the delinquent may derive from a total choice of delinquency as a way or as a goal of life. It is possible that his radical closing up, his provocative smugness, his utter denial of remorse, may cover and counteract the anxiety of threatening identity diffusion. Are we, in turn, exposing him to this very danger as we hammer at him, offering him a "chance" at the price of remorse—the one price that he cannot afford to pay? A glance at the components of identity diffusion (column V, p. 120) will lead to these considerations:

Juvenile delinquency saves some young individuals from *time diffusion*. In the delinquent state, any future perspective, with its demands and uncertainties, is overruled by the dominant emphasis on short-range goals serving, say, a need to "get at somebody," or to just "do something," or "go somewhere." This, of course, also constitutes a simplification of social modalities, together with a primitivization of impulse life.

Identity consciousness is escaped also; or, at any rate, it is firmly hidden by the delinquent's particular identification-with-himself-in-the-role-of-delinquent, which offers such an impenetrable façade to investigator and judge. This façade—the outward appearance of a total choice—denies any emotional response, and prevents the emergence of any sense of shame or guilt.

Work paralysis, the painful inability to enjoy the mastery of materials and of cooperative situations, is also sidetracked in delinquency. Work mastery is, in any culture, the backbone of identity formation. In delinquents (often recruited from groups who are denied a meaningful work experience) there appears, instead, a perverse but deep satisfaction in "doing a job" in the destructive sense. The legal classification of such a deed may seal a young individual's *negative identity* as a criminal once and for all. This, in turn, relieves him of the necessity to search further for a "good" identity (Erikson and Erikson, 1957).

In addition, delinquent behavior saves many individuals

warn ourselves against an uncritical transfer of clinical terms, attitudes, and methods to such public problems. Rather we may come back to a point made earlier: teachers, judges, and psychiatrists, who deal with youth, come to be significant representatives of that strategic act of "recognition" (the act through which society "identifies" its young members and thus contributes to their developing identity) which was described at the beginning of this paper. If, for simplicity's sake or in order to accommodate ingrown habits of law or psychiatry, they diagnose and treat as a criminal, as a constitutional misfit, as a derelict doomed by his upbringing, or—indeed—as a deranged patient, a young person who, for reasons of personal or social marginality, is close to choosing a negative identity, that young person may well put his energy into becoming exactly what the careless and fearful community expects him to be—and make a total job of it.

It is hoped that the theory of identity, in the long run, can contribute more to this problem than to sound a warning.

---

from *bisexual diffusion*. The exaggeration of the phallic-sadistic role on the part of the boy delinquent and the careless and loveless promiscuity on the part of the girl offer an escape either from a sense of sexual inferiority or from any commitment to true intimacy.

In this connection a development highly characteristic of our time must be emphasized: I mean the new emphasis on locomotion, as provided by the machine. There is first of all what might be called the *locomotorist intoxication* of our time—the pleasure of imagining oneself to be an immensely powerful driver, while actually being moved by powers stronger and faster than those of the human body.

The second intoxication (now conveniently combined with the first in drive-in shows) is the passive *intoxication by powerfully moving spectacles*—in which continuous motion is not only observed but experienced, while the organism "races its engine," as it were. Since youth is an eminently locomotor period, and since in adolescence perambulatory (as well as mental) exploration must take over much of sexual tension, the disbalance between increased passive stimulation provided by mechanical invention and decreased opportunities for vigorous action is probably a major contributor to such specific delinquencies as the appropriation of motorcars and

Summary

In my attempt to circumscribe the problem of identity I have been "all over the map." I do not propose to leave the matter in this condition: as far as is possible, studies taking into account the specific dynamic nature of selected media (life history, case history, dream life, ideology) will follow (Erikson, 1958). In the meantime, and in summary: identity, in outbalancing at the conclusion of childhood the potentially malignant dominance of the infantile superego, permits the individual to forgo excessive self-repudiation and the diffused repudiation of otherness. Such freedom provides a necessary condition for the ego's power to integrate matured sexuality, ripened capacities, and adult commitments. The histories of our young patients illustrate the ways in which aggravated identity crises may result from special genetic causes and from specific dynamic conditions. Such studies, in turn, throw new light on those more or less institutionalized rites and rituals, associations, and movements through which societies and subsocieties grant youth a world between childhood and adulthood: a psychosocial moratorium during which extremes of *subjective experience*, alternatives of *ideological choice*, and potentialities of *realistic commitment* can become the subject of social play and of joint mastery.

---

the urge to do physical violence, and to the widespread addiction to excessive forms of dancing.

As for *authority diffusion*, it is clear that organized delinquency clearly aligns the young person with an ingroup of equals with a defined hierarchy of leadership, and clearly circumscribes outgroups such as other gangs, or all the world outside the gang. Similarly, gang ethics protect the ingroup member from a sense of *diffusion of ideals*.

It is in this way that I would approach the problem of juvenile delinquency with concepts gained from the observation of psychiatric kinds of juvenile disturbance. Such a comparison suggests that we may learn much about the dynamics of youth by juxtaposing the delinquent joiners and the schizoid isolates (even as Freud juxtaposed perversion and neurosis as the expression and the inhibition of certain impulses) (Erikson, 1956).

4

Our Educational Problems

*in the Light of Samoan Contrasts**

Margaret Mead

. . . For many chapters we have followed the lives of Samoan girls, watched them change from babies to baby-tenders, learn to make the oven and weave fine mats, forsake the life of the gang to become more active members of the household, defer marriage through as many years of casual love-making as possible, finally marry and settle down to rearing children who will repeat the same cycle. As far as our material permitted, an experiment has been conducted to discover what the process of development was like in a society very different from our own. Because the length of human life and the complexity of our society did not permit us to make our experiment here, to choose a group of baby girls and bring them to maturity under conditions created for the experiment, it was necessary to go instead to another country where history had set the stage for us. There we found girl children passing through the same process of physical development through which our girls go, cutting their first teeth and losing them, cutting their second teeth, growing tall and ungainly, reaching puberty with their first menstruation, gradually reaching physical maturity, and becoming ready to produce the next generation. It was possible to say: Here are the proper conditions for an experiment; the developing girl is a constant factor in America and in Samoa; the civilization of America and the civilization of Samoa are different. In the course of development, the process of growth by which the girl baby becomes a grown woman, are the sudden and conspicuous bodily changes which take place at puberty accompanied by a development which is spasmodic, emotionally charged, and accompanied by an awakened religious sense, a flowering of idealism, a great desire for assertion of self against authority—or not? Is adolescence a period of mental and emotional distress for the growing girl as inevitably as teething is a period of misery for the small baby? Can we think of adolescence as a time in

the life history of every girl child which carries with it symptoms of conflict and stress as surely as it implies a change in the girl's body?

Following the Samoan girls through every aspect of their lives we have tried to answer this question, and we found throughout that we had to answer it in the negative. The adolescent girl in Samoa differed from her sister who had not reached puberty in one chief respect, that in the older girl certain bodily changes were present which were absent in the younger girl. There were no other great differences to set off the group passing through adolescence from the group which would become adolescent in two years or the group which had become adolescent two years before.

And if one girl past puberty is undersized while her cousin is tall and able to do heavier work, there will be a difference between them, due to their different physical endowment, which will be far greater than that which is due to puberty. The tall, husky girl will be isolated from her companions, forced to do longer, more adult tasks, rendered shy by a change of clothing, while her cousin, slower to attain her growth, will still be treated as a child and will have to solve only the slightly fewer problems of childhood. The precedent of educators here who recommend special tactics in the treatment of adolescent girls translated into Samoan terms would read: Tall girls are different from short girls of the same age, we must adopt a different method of educating them.

But when we have answered the question we set out to answer we have not finished with the problem. A further question presents itself. If it is proved that adolescence is not necessarily a specially difficult period in a girl's life—and proved it is if we can find any society in which that is so—then what accounts for the presence of storm and stress in American adolescents? First, we may say quite simply, that there must be something in the two civilizations to account for the difference. If the same process takes

* In *Coming of Age in Samoa* (New York: William Morrow, 1928), Pp. 195–233.

a different form in two different environments, we cannot make any explanations in terms of the process, for that is the same in both cases. But the social environment is very different and it is to it that we must look for an explanation. What is there in Samoa which is absent in America, what is there in America which is absent in Samoa, which will account for this difference?

Such a question has enormous implications and any attempt to answer it will be subject to many possibilities of error. But if we narrow our question to the way in which aspects of Samoan life which irremediably affect the life of the adolescent girl differ from the forces which influence our growing girls, it is possible to try to answer it.

The background of these differences is a broad one, with two important components; one is due to characteristics which are Samoan, the other to characteristics which are primitive.

The Samoan background which makes growing up so easy, so simple a matter, is the general casualness of the whole society. For Samoa is a place where no one plays for very high stakes, no one pays very heavy prices, no one suffers for his convictions or fights to the death for special ends. Disagreements between parent and child are settled by the child's moving across the street, between a man and his village by the man's removal to the next village, between a husband and his wife's seducer by a few fine mats. Neither poverty nor great disasters threaten the people to make them hold their lives dearly and tremble for continued existence. No implacable gods, swift to anger and strong to punish, disturb the even tenor of their days. Wars and cannibalism are long since passed away and now the greatest cause for tears, short of death itself, is a journey of a relative to another island. No one is hurried along in life or punished harshly for slowness of development. Instead the gifted, the precocious, are held back, until the slowest among them have caught the pace. And in personal relations, caring is as slight. Love and hate, jealousy and revenge, sorrow and bereavement, are all matters of weeks. From the first months of its life, when the child is handed carelessly from one woman's hands to another's, the lesson is learned of not caring for one person greatly, not setting high hopes on any one relationship.

And just as we may feel that the Occident penalises those unfortunates who are born into Western civilization with a taste for meditation and a complete distaste for activity, so we may say that Samoa is kind to those who have learned the lesson of not caring, and hard upon those few individuals who have failed to learn it. Lola and Mala and little Siva, Lola's sister, all were girls with a capacity for emotion greater than their fellows. And Lola and Mala, passionately desiring affection and too violently venting upon the community their disappointment over their lack of it, were both delinquent, unhappy misfits in a society which gave all the rewards to those who took defeat lightly and turned to some other goal with a smile.

In this casual attitude towards life, in this avoidance of conflict, of poignant situations, Samoa contrasts strongly not only with America but also with most primitive civilizations. And however much we may deplore such an attitude and feel that important personalities and great art are not born in so shallow a society, we must recognise that here is a strong factor in the painless development from childhood to womanhood. For where no one feels very strongly, the adolescent will not be tortured by poignant situations. There are no such disastrous choices as those which confronted young people who felt that the service of God demanded forswearing the world forever, as in the Middle Ages, or cutting off one's finger as a religious offering, as among the Plains Indians. So, high up in our list of explanations we must place the lack of deep feeling which the Samoans have conventionalised until it is the very framework of all their attitudes toward life.

And next there is the most striking way in which all isolated primitive civilizations and many modern ones differ from our own, in the number of choices which are permitted to each individual. Our children grow up to find a world of choices dazzling their unaccustomed eyes. In religion they may be Catholics, Protestants, Christian Scientists, Spiritualists, Agnostics, Atheists, or even pay no attention at all to religion. This is an unthinkable situation in any primitive society not exposed to foreign influence. There is one set of gods, one accepted religious practice, and if a man does not believe, his only recourse is to believe less than his fellows; he may scoff but there is no new faith to which he may turn. Present-day Manu'a approximates this condition; all are Christians of the same sect. There is no conflict in matters of belief although there is a difference in practice between Church-members and non-Church-members. And it was remarked that in the case of several of the growing girls the need for choice between these two practices may some day produce a conflict. But at present the Church makes too slight a bid for young unmarried members to force the adolescent to make any decision.

Similarly, our children are faced with half a dozen standards of morality: a double sex standard for men and women, a single standard for men and women, and groups which advocate that the single standard should be freedom while others argue that the single standard should be absolute monogamy. Trial marriage, companionate marriage, contract marriage—all these possible solutions of a social impasse are paraded before the growing children while the actual conditions in their own communities and the moving pictures and magazines inform them of mass violations of every code, violations which march under no banners of social reform.

The Samoan child faces no such dilemma. Sex is a natural, pleasurable thing; the freedom with which it may be indulged in is limited by just one consideration, social status. Chiefs' daughters and chiefs' wives should indulge in no extra-marital experiments. Responsible adults, heads of households and mothers of families should have too many important matters on hand to leave them much time for casual amorous adventures. Everyone in the community agrees about the matter, the only dissenters are the missionaries who dissent so vainly that their protests are unimportant. But as soon as a sufficient sentiment gathers about the missionary attitude with its European standard of sex behaviour, the need for choice, the forerunner of conflict, will enter into Samoan society.

Our young people are faced by a series of different groups which believe different things and advocate different practices, and to each of which some trusted friend or relative may belong. So a girl's father may be a Presbyterian, an imperialist, a vegetarian, a teetotaler, with a strong literary preference for Edmund Burke, a believer in the open shop and a high tariff, who believes that woman's place is in the home, that young girls should wear corsets, not roll their stockings, not smoke, nor go riding with young men in the evening. But her mother's father may be a Low Episcopalian, a believer in high living, a strong advocate of States' Rights and the Monroe Doctrine, who reads Rabelais, likes to go to musical shows and horse races. Her aunt is an agnostic, an ardent advocate of woman's rights, an internationalist who rests all her hopes on Esperanto, is devoted to Bernard Shaw, and spends her spare time in campaigns of anti-vivisection. Her elder brother,

whom she admires exceedingly, has just spent two years at Oxford. He is an Anglo-Catholic, an enthusiast concerning all things medieval, writes mystical poetry, reads Chesterton, and means to devote his life to seeking for the lost secret of medieval stained glass. Her mother's younger brother is an engineer, a strict materialist, who never recovered from reading Haeckel in his youth; he scorns art, believes that science will save the world, scoffs at everything that was said and thought before the nineteenth century, and ruins his health by experiments in the scientific elimination of sleep. Her mother is of a quietistic frame of mind, very much interested in Indian philosophy, a pacifist, a strict nonparticipator in life, who in spite of her daughter's devotion to her will not make any move to enlist her enthusiasms. And this may be within the girl's own household. Add to it the groups represented, defended, advocated by her friends, her teachers, and the books which she reads by accident, and the list of possible enthusiasms, of suggested allegiances, incompatible with one another, becomes appalling.

The Samoan girl's choices are far otherwise. Her father is a member of the Church and so is her uncle. Her father lives in a village where there is good fishing, her uncle in a village where there are plenty of cocoanut crabs. Her father is a good fisherman and in his house there is plenty to eat; her uncle is a talking chief and his frequent presents of bark cloth provide excellent dance dresses. Her paternal grandmother, who lives with her uncle, can teach her many secrets of healing; her maternal grandmother, who lives with her mother, is an expert weaver of fans. The boys in her uncle's village are admitted younger into the *Aumaga* and are not much fun when they come to call; but there are three boys in her own village whom she likes very much. And her great dilemma is whether to live with her father or her uncle, a frank, straightforward problem which introduces no ethical perplexities, no question of impersonal logic. Nor will her choice be taken as a personal matter, as the American girl's allegiance to the views of one relative might be interpreted by her other relatives. The Samoans will be sure she chose one residence rather than the other for perfectly good reasons, the food was better, she had a lover in one village, or she had quarrelled with a lover in the other village. In each case she was making concrete choices within one recognized pattern of behavior. She was never called upon to make choices involving an actual rejection of the standards of her social group, such as the daughter of Puritan parents, who permits indiscriminate caresses, must make in our society.

And not only are our developing children faced by a series of groups advocating different and mutually exclusive standards, but a more perplexing problem presents itself to them. Because our civilization is woven of so many diverse strands, the ideas which any one group accepts will be found to contain numerous contradictions. So if the girl has given her allegiance whole-heartedly to some one group and has accepted in good faith their asseverations that they alone are right and all other philosophies of life are Antichrist and anathema, her troubles are still not over. While the less thoughtful receives her worst blows in the discovery that what father thinks is good, grandfather thinks is bad, and that things which are permitted at home are banned at school, the more thoughtful child has subtler difficulties in store for her. If she has philosophically accepted the fact that there are several standards among which she must choose, she may still preserve a childlike faith in the coherence of her chosen philosophy. Beyond the immediate choice which was so puzzling and hard to make, which perhaps involved hurting her parents or alienating her friends, she expects peace. But she has not reckoned with the fact that each of the philosophies with which she is confronted is itself but the half-ripened fruit of compromise. If she accepts Christianity, she is immediately confused between the Gospel teachings concerning peace and the value of human life and the Church's whole-hearted acceptance of war. The compromise made seventeen centuries ago between the Roman philosophy of war and domination, and the early Church doctrine of peace and humility, is still present to confuse the modern child. If she accepts the philosophic premises upon which the Declaration of Independence of the United States was founded, she finds herself faced with the necessity of reconciling the belief in the equality of man and our institutional pledges of equality of opportunity with our treatment of the Negro and the Oriental. The diversity of standards in present-day society is so striking that the dullest, the most incurious, cannot fail to notice it. And this diversity is so old, so embodied in semi-solutions, in those compromises between different philosophies which we call Christianity, or democracy, or humanitarianism, that it baffles the most intelligent, the most curious, the most analytical.

So for the explanation of the lack of poignancy in the choices of growing girls in Samoa, we must look to the temperament of the Samoan civilization which discounts strong feeling. But for the explanation of the lack of conflict we must look principally to the difference between a simple, homogenous primitive civilization, a civilization which changes so slowly that to each generation it appears static, and a motley, diverse, heterogeneous modern civilization.

And in making the comparison there is a third consideration, the lack of neuroses among the Samoans, the great number of neuroses among ourselves. We must examine the factors in the early education of the Samoan children which have fitted them for a normal, unneurotic development. The findings of the behaviourists and of the psychoanalysts alike lay great emphasis upon the enormous role which is played by the environment of the first few years. Children who have been given a bad start are often found to function badly later on when they are faced with important choices. And we know that the more severe the choice, the more conflict; the more poignancy is attached to the demands made upon the individual, the more neuroses will result. History, in the form of the last war, provided a stupendous illustration of the great number of maimed and handicapped individuals whose defects showed only under very special and terrible stress. Without the war, there is no reason to believe that many of these shellshocked individuals might not have gone through life unremarked; the bad start, the fears, the complexes, the bad conditionings of early childhood, would never have borne positive enough fruit to attract the attention of society.

The implications of this observation are double. Samoa's lack of difficult situations, of conflicting choice, of situations in which fear or pain or anxiety are sharpened to a knife edge will probably account for a large part of the absence of psychological maladjustment. Just as a low-grade moron would not be hopelessly handicapped in Samoa, although he would be a public charge in a large American city, so individuals with slight nervous instability have a much more favourable chance in Samoa than in America. Furthermore the amount of individualization, the range of variation, is much smaller in Samoa. Within our wider limits of deviation there are inevitably found weak and nonresistant temperaments. And just as our society shows a greater development of personality, so also it shows a larger proportion of individuals who have succumbed before the complicated exactions of modern life.

Nevertheless, it is possible that there are factors

in the early environment of the Samoan child which are particularly favorable to the establishment of nervous stability. Just as a child from a better home environment in our civilization may be presumed to have a better chance under all circumstances it is conceivable that the Samoan child is not only handled more gently by its culture but that it is also better equipped for those difficulties which it does meet.

Such an assumption is given force by the fact that little Samoan children pass apparently unharmed through experiences which often have grave effects on individual development in our civilization. Our life histories are filled with the later difficulties which can be traced back to some early, highly charged experience with sex or with birth or death. And yet Samoan children are familiarized at an early age and without disaster, with all three. It is very possible that there are aspects of the life of the young child in Samoa which equip it particularly well for passing through life without nervous instability.

With this hypothesis in mind it is worth while to consider in more detail which parts of the young child's social environment are most strikingly different from ours. Most of these centre about the family situation, the environment which impinges earliest and most intensely upon the child's consciousness. The organization of a Samoan household eliminates at one stroke, in almost all cases, many of the special situations which are believed to be productive of undesirable emotional sets. The youngest, the oldest, and the only child, hardly ever occur because of the large number of children in a household, all of whom receive the same treatment. Few children are weighted down with responsibility, or rendered domineering and overbearing as eldest children so often are, or isolated, condemned to the society of adults and robbed of the socializing effect of contact with other children, as only children so often are. No child is petted and spoiled until its view of its own deserts is hopelessly distorted, as is so often the fate of the youngest child. But in the few cases where Samoan family life does approximate ours, the special attitudes incident to order of birth and to close affectional ties with the parent tend to develop.

The close relationship between parent and child, which has such a decisive influence upon so many in our civilization, that submission to the parent or defiance of the parent may become the dominating pattern of a lifetime, is not found in Samoa. Children reared in households where there are a half

dozen adult women to care for them and dry their tears, and a half dozen adult males, all of whom represent constituted authority, do not distinguish their parents as sharply as our children do. The image of the fostering, loving mother, or the admirable father, which may serve to determine affectional choices later in life, is a composite affair, composed of several aunts, cousins, older sisters and grandmothers; of chief, father, uncles, brothers and cousins. Instead of learning as its first lesson that here is a kind mother whose special and principal care is for its welfare, and a father whose authority is to be deferred to, the Samoan baby learns that its world is composed of a hierarchy of male and female adults, all of whom can be depended upon and must be deferred to.

The lack of specialized feeling which results from this diffusion of affection in the household is further reinforced by the segregation of the boys from the girls, so that a child regards the children of the opposite sex as taboo relatives, regardless of individuality, or as present enemies and future lovers, again regardless of individuality. And the substitution of relationship for preference in forming friendships completes the work. By the time she reaches puberty the Samoan girl has learned to subordinate choice in the selection of friends or lovers to an observance of certain categories. Friends must be relatives of one's own sex; lovers, non-relatives. All claim of personal attraction or congeniality between relatives of opposite sex must be flouted. All of this means that casual sex relations carry no onus of strong attachment, that the marriage of convenience dictated by economic and social considerations is easily born and casually broken without strong emotion.

Nothing could present a sharper contrast to the average American home, with its small number of children, the close, theoretically permanent tie between the parents, the drama of the entrance of each new child upon the scene and the deposition of the last baby. Here the growing girl learns to depend upon a few individuals, to expect the rewards of life from certain kinds of personalities. With this first set towards preference in personal relations she grows up playing with boys as well as with girls, learning to know well brothers and cousins and schoolmates. She does not think of boys as a class but as individuals, nice ones like the brother of whom she is fond, or disagreeable, domineering ones, like a brother with whom she is always on bad terms. Preference in physical make-up, in temperament, in character, develops and forms the foundations for a very different adult attitude in which choice plays a vivid role. The Samoan girl never tastes the rewards of romantic love as we know it, nor does she suffer as an old maid who has appealed to no lover or found no lover appealing to her, or as the frustrated wife in a marriage which has not fulfilled her high demands.

Having learned a little of the art of disciplining sex feeling into special channels approved by the whole personality, we will be inclined to account our solution better than the Samoans. To attain what we consider a more dignified standard of personal relations we are willing to pay the penalty of frigidity in marriage and a huge toll of barren, unmarried women who move in unsatisfied procession across the American and English stage. But while granting the desirability of this development of sensitive, discriminating response to personality, as a better basis for dignified human lives than an automatic, undifferentiated response to sex attraction, we may still, in the light of Samoan solutions, count our methods exceedingly expensive.

The strict segregation of related boys and girls, the institutionalized hostility between pre-adolescent children of opposite sexes in Samoa are cultural features with which we are completely out of sympathy. For the vestiges of such attitudes, expressed in our one-sex schools, we are trying to substitute coeducation, to habituate one sex to another sufficiently so that difference of sex will be lost sight of in the more important and more striking differences in personality. There are no recognizable gains in the Samoan system of taboo and segregation, of response to a group rather than response to an individual. But when we contrast the other factor of difference the conclusion is not so sure. What are the rewards of the tiny, ingrown, biological family opposing its closed circle of affection to a forbidding world, of the strong ties between parents and children, ties which imply an active personal relation from birth until death? Specialization of affection, it is true, but at the price of many individuals' preserving through life the attitudes of dependent children, of ties between parents and children which successfully defeat the children's attempts to make other adjustments, of necessary choices made unnecessarily poignant because they become issues in an intense emotional relationship. Perhaps these are too heavy prices to pay for a specialization of emotion which might be brought about in other ways, notably

through coeducation. And with such a question in our minds it is interesting to note that a larger family community, in which there are several adult men and women, seems to ensure the child against the development of the crippling attitudes which have been labelled Oedipus complexes, Electra complexes, and so on.

The Samoan picture shows that it is not necessary to channel so deeply the affection of a child for its parents and suggests that while we would reject that part of the Samoan scheme which holds no rewards for us, the segregation of the sexes before puberty, we may learn from a picture in which the home does not dominate and distort the life of the child.

The presence of many strongly held and contradictory points of view and the enormous influence of individuals in the lives of their children in our country play into each other's hands in producing situations fraught with emotion and pain. In Samoa the fact that one girl's father is a domineering, dogmatic person, her cousin's father a gentle, reasonable person, and another cousin's father a vivid, brilliant, eccentric person, will influence the three girls in only one respect, choice of residence if any one of the three fathers is the head of a household. But the attitudes of the three girls towards sex, and towards religion, will not be affected by the different temperaments of their three fathers, for the fathers play too slight a role in their lives. They are schooled not by an individual but by an army of relatives into a general conformity upon which the personality of their parents has a very slight effect. And through an endless chain of cause and effect, individual differences of standard are not perpetuated through the children's adherence to the parents' position, nor are children thrown into bizarre, untypical attitudes which might form the basis for departure and change. It is possible that where our own culture is so charged with choice, it would be desirable to mitigate, at least in some slight measure, the strong role which parents play in children's lives, and so eliminate one of the most powerful accidental factors in the choices of any individual life.

The Samoan parent would reject as unseemly and odious an ethical plea made to a child in terms of personal affection. "Be good to please mother." "Go to church for father's sake." "Don't be so disagreeable to your sister, it makes father so unhappy." Where there is one standard of conduct and only one, such undignified confusion of ethics and affection is blessedly eliminated. But where there are many standards and all adults are striving desperately to bind their own children to the particular courses which they themselves have chosen, recourse is had to devious and non-reputable means. Beliefs, practices, courses of action, are pressed upon the child in the name of filial loyalty. In our ideal picture of the freedom of the individual and the dignity of human relations it is not pleasant to realize that we have developed a form of family organization which often cripples the emotional life, and warps and confuses the growth of many individuals' power to consciously live their own lives.

The third element in the Samoan pattern of lack of personal relationships and lack of specialized affection, is the case of friendship. Here, most of all, individuals are placed in categories and the response is to the category, "relative," or "wife of my husband's talking chief," or "son of my father's talking chief," or "daughter of my father's talking chief." Consideration of congeniality, of like-mindedness, are all ironed out in favour of regimented associations. Such attitudes we would of course reject completely.

Drawing the threads of this particular discussion together, we may say that one striking difference between Samoan society and our own is the lack of the specialization of feeling, and particularly of sex feeling, among the Samoans. To this difference is undoubtedly due a part of the lack of difficulty of marital adjustments in a marriage of convenience, and the lack of frigidity or psychic impotence. This lack of specialization of feeling must be attributed to the large heterogeneous household, the segregation of the sexes before adolescence, and the regimentation of friendship—chiefly along relationship lines. And yet, although we deplore the prices in maladjusted and frustrated lives, which we must pay for the greater specialization of sex feeling in our own society, we nevertheless vote the development of specialized response as a gain which we would not relinquish. But an examination of these three causal factors suggests that we might accomplish our desired end, the development of a consciousness of personality, through coeducation and free and unregimented friendships, and possibly do away with the evils inherent in the too intimate family organization, thus eliminating a part of our penalty of maladjustment without sacrificing any of our dearly bought gains.

The next great difference between Samoa and our own culture which may be credited with a lower

production of maladjusted individuals is the difference in the attitude towards sex and the education of the children in matters pertaining to birth and death. None of the facts of sex or of birth are regarded as unfit for children, no child has to conceal its knowledge for fear of punishment or ponder painfully over little-understood occurrences. Secrecy, ignorance, guilty knowledge, faulty speculations resulting in grotesque conceptions which may have far-reaching results, a knowledge of the bare physical facts of sex without a knowledge of the accompanying excitement, of the fact of birth without the pains of labor, of the fact of death without the fact of corruption—all the chief flaws in our fatal philosophy of sparing children a knowledge of the dreadful truth—are absent in Samoa. Furthermore, the Samoan child who participates intimately in the lives of a host of relatives has many and varied experiences upon which to base its emotional attitudes. Our children, confined within one family circle (and such confinement is becoming more and more frequent with the growth of cities and the substitution of apartment houses with a transitory population for a neighborhood of householders), often owe their only experience with birth or death to the birth of a younger brother or sister or the death of a parent or grandparent. Their knowledge of sex, aside from children's gossip, comes from an accidental glimpse of parental activity. This has several very obvious disadvantages. In the first place, the child is dependent for its knowledge upon birth and death entering its own home; the youngest child in a family where there are no deaths may grow to adult life without ever having had any close knowledge of pregnancy, experience with young children, or contact with death.

A host of ill-digested fragmentary conceptions of life and death will fester in the ignorant, inexperienced mind and provide a fertile field for the later growth of unfortunate attitudes. Second, such children draw their experiences from too emotionally toned a field; one birth may be the only one with which they come in close contact for the first twenty years of their lives. And upon the accidental aspects of this particular birth their whole attitude is dependent. If the birth is that of a younger child who usurps the elder's place, if the mother dies in child birth, or if the child which is born is deformed, birth may seem a horrible thing, fraught with only unwelcome consequences. If the only death bed at which one has ever watched is the death bed of one's mother, the bare fact of death may carry all the emotion which that bereavement aroused, carry forever an effect out of all proportion to the particular deaths encountered later in life. And intercourse seen only once or twice, between relatives towards whom the child has complicated emotional attitudes, may produce any number of false assumptions. Our records of maladjusted children are full of cases where children have misunderstood the nature of the sexual act, have interpreted it as struggle accompanied by anger, or as chastisement, have recoiled in terror from one highly charged experience. So our children are dependent upon accident for their experience of life and death; and those experiences which they are vouchsafed, lie within the intimate family circle and so are the worse possible way of learning general facts about which it is important to acquire no special, distorted attitudes. One death, two births, one sex experience, is a generous total for the child brought up under living conditions which we consider consonant with an American standard of living. And considering the number of illustrations which we consider it necessary to give of how to calculate the number of square feet of paper necessary to paper a room eight feet by twelve feet by fourteen feet, or how to parse an English sentence, this is a low standard of illustration. It might be argued that these are experiences of such high emotional tone that repetition is unnecessary. It might also be argued if a child were severely beaten before being given its first lesson in calculating how to paper a room, and as a sequel to the lesson, saw its father hit its mother with the poker, it would always remember that arithmetic lesson. But what it would know about the real nature of the calculations involved in room-papering is doubtful. In one or two experiences, the child is given no perspective, no chance to relegate the grotesque and unfamiliar physical details of the life process to their proper place. False impressions, part impressions, repulsion, nausea, horror, grow up about some fact experienced only once under intense emotional stress and in an atmosphere unfavorable to the child's attaining any real understanding.

A standard of reticence which forbids the child any sort of comment upon its experiences makes for the continuance of such false impressions, such hampering emotional attitudes, questions such as, "Why were grandma's lips so blue?" are promptly hushed. In Samoa, where decomposition sets in almost at once, a frank, naïve repugnance to the odors of corruption on the part of all the participants at a funeral robs the physical aspect of death of any special significance. So, in our arrangements, the child is not allowed to repeat his experiences, and he is not permitted to discuss those which he has had and correct his mistakes.

With the Samoan child it is profoundly different. Intercourse, pregnancy, childbirth, death, are all familiar occurrences. And the Samoan child experiences them in no such ordered fashion as we, were we to decide for widening the child's experimental field, would regard as essential. In a civilization which suspects privacy, children of neighbors will be accidental and unemotional spectators in a house where the head of the household is dying or the wife is delivered of a miscarriage. The pathology of the life processes is known to them, as well as the normal. One impression corrects an earlier one until they are able, as adolescents, to think about life and death and emotion without undue preoccupation with the purely physical details.

It must not be supposed, however, that the mere exposure of children to scenes of birth and death would be a sufficient guarantee against the growth of undesirable attitudes. Probably even more influential than the facts which are so copiously presented to them, is the attitude of mind with which their elders regard the matter. To them, birth and sex and death are the natural, inevitable structure of existence, of an existence in which they expect their youngest children to share. Our so often repeated comment that "it's not natural" for children to be permitted to encounter death would seem as incongruous to them as if we were to say it was not natural for children to see other people eat or sleep. And this calm, matter-of-fact acceptance of their children's presence envelops the children in a protective atmosphere, saves them from shock and binds them closer to the common emotion which is so dignifiedly permitted them.

As in every case, it is here impossible to separate attitude from practice and say which is primary. The distinction is made only for our use in another civilization. The individual American parents, who believe in a practice like the Samoan, and permit their children to see adult human bodies and gain a wider experience of the functioning of the human body than is commonly permitted in our civilization, are building upon sand. For the child, as soon as it leaves the protecting circle of its home, is blasted by an attitude which regards such experience in children as ugly and unnatural. As likely as not, the attempt of the individual parents will have done the child more harm than good, for the necessary supporting social attitude is lacking. This is just a further example of the possibilities of maladjustment inherent in a society where each home differs from each other home; for it is in the fact of difference that the strain lies rather than in the nature of the difference.

Upon this quiet acceptance of the physical facts of life, the Samoans build, as they grow older, an acceptance of sex. Here again it is necessary to sort out which parts of their practice seem to produce results which we certainly deprecate, and which produce results which we desire. It is possible to analyse Samoan sex practice from the standpoint of development of personal relationships on the one hand, and of the obviation of specific difficulties upon the other.

We have seen that the Samoans have a low level of appreciation of personality differences, and a poverty of conception of personal relations. To such an attitude the acceptance of promiscuity undoubtedly contributes. The contemporaneousness of several experiences, their short duration, the definite avoidance of forming any affectional ties, the blithe acceptance of the dictates of a favorable occasion, as in the expectation of infidelity in any wife whose husband is long from home, all serve to make sex an end rather than a means, something which is valued in itself, and deprecated inasmuch as it tends to bind one individual to another. Whether such a disregard of personal relations is completely contingent upon the sex habits of the people is doubtful. It probably is also a reflection of a more general cultural attitude in which personality is consistently disregarded. But there is one respect in which these very practices make possible a recognition of personality which is often denied to many in our civilization, because, from the Samoans' complete knowledge of sex, its possibilities and its rewards, they are able to count it at its true value. And if they have no preference for reserving sex activity for important relationships, neither do they regard relationships as important because they are productive of sex satisfaction. The Samoan girl who shrugs her shoulder over the excellent technique of some young Lothario is nearer to the recognition of sex as an impersonal force without any intrinsic validity, than is the sheltered American girl who falls in love with the first man who kisses her. From their familiarity with the reverberations

which accompany sex excitement comes this recognition of the essential impersonality of sex attraction which we may well envy them; from the too slight, too casual practice comes the disregard of personality which seems to us unlovely.

The fashion in which their sex practice reduces the possibility of neuroses has already been discussed. By discounting our category of perversion, as applied to practice, and reserving it for the occasional psychic pervert, they legislate a whole field of neurotic possibility out of existence. Onanism, homosexuality, statistically unusual forms of heterosexual activity, are neither banned nor institutionalised. The wider range which these practices give prevents the development of obsessions of guilt which are so frequent a cause of maladjustment among us. The more varied practices permitted heterosexually preserve any individual from being penalized for special conditioning. This acceptance of a wider range as "normal" provides a cultural atmosphere in which frigidity and psychic impotence do not occur and in which a satisfactory sex adjustment in marriage can always be established. The acceptance of such an attitude without in any way accepting promiscuity would go a long way towards solving many marital impasses and emptying our park benches and our houses of prostitution.

Among the factors in the Samoan scheme of life which are influential in producing stable, well-adjusted, robust individuals, the organization of the family and the attitude towards sex are undoubtedly the most important. But it is necessary to note also the general educational concept which disapproves of precocity and coddles the slow, the laggard, the inept. In a society where the tempo of life was faster, the rewards greater, the amount of energy expended larger, the bright children might develop symptoms of boredom. But the slower pace dictated by the climate, the complacent, peaceful society, and the compensation of the dance, in its blatant precocious display of individuality which drains off some of the discontent which the bright child feels, prevent any child from becoming too bored. And the dullard is not goaded and dragged along faster than he is able until, sick with making an impossible effort, he gives up entirely. This educational policy also tends to blur individual differences and so to minimize jealousy, rivalry, emulation, those social attitudes which arise out of discrepancies of endowment and are so far-reaching in their effects upon the adult personality.

It is one way of solving the problem of differences between individuals and a method of solution exceedingly congenial to a strict adult world. The longer the child is kept in a subject, non-initiating state, the more of the general cultural attitude it will absorb, the less of a disturbing element it will become. Furthermore, if time is given them, the dull-conservatives upon whose shoulders the burden of the civilization can safely rest. Giving titles to young men would put a premium upon the exceptional; giving titles to men of forty, who have at last acquired sufficient training to hold them, assures the continuation of the usual. It also discourages the brilliant so that their social contribution is slighter than it might otherwise have been.

We are slowly feeling our way towards a solution of this problem, at least in the case of formal education. Until very recently our educational system offered only two very partial solutions of the difficulties inherent in a great discrepancy between children of different endowment and different rates of development. One solution was to allow a sufficiently long time to each educational step so that all but the mentally defective could succeed, a method similar to the Samoan one and without its compensatory dance floor. The bright child, held back, at intolerably boring tasks, unless he was fortunate enough to find some other outlet for his unused energy, was likely to expend it upon truancy and general delinquency. Our only alternative to this was "skipping" a child from one grade to another, relying upon the child's superior intelligence to bridge the gaps. This was a method congenial to American enthusiasm for meteoric careers from canal boat and log cabin to the White House. Its disadvantages in giving the child a sketchy, discontinuous background, in removing it from its age group, have been enumerated too often to need repetition here. But it is worthy of note that with a very different valuation of individual ability than that entertained by Samoan society, we used for years one solution, similar and less satisfactory than theirs, in our formal educational attempts.

The methods which experimental educators are substituting for these unsatisfactory solutions, schemes like the Dalton Plan, or the rapidly moving classes in which a group of children can move ahead at a high, even rate of speed without hurt to themselves or to their duller fellows, is a striking example of the results of applying reason to the institutions of our society. The old red school-house was almost as haphazard and accidental a phenomenon as the Samoan dance floor. It was an institution which had grown up in response to a vaguely felt, unanalyzed need. Its methods were analogous to the methods used by primitive peoples, non-rationalised solutions of pressing problems. But the institutionalization of different methods of education for children of different capacities and different rates of development is not like anything which we find in Samoa or in any other primitive society. It is the conscious, intelligent directing of human institutions in response to observed human needs.

Still another factor in Samoan education which results in different attitudes is the place of work and play in the children's lives. Samoan children do not learn to work through learning to play, as the children of many primitive peoples do. Nor are they permitted a period of lack of responsibility such as our children are allowed. From the time they are four or five years old they perform definite tasks, graded to their strength and intelligence, but still tasks which have a meaning in the structure of the whole society. This does not mean that they have less time for play than American children who are shut up in schools from nine to three o'clock every day. Before the introduction of schools to complicate the ordered routine of their lives, the time spent by the Samoan child in running errands, sweeping the house, carrying water, and taking actual care of the baby, was possibly less than that which the American school child devotes to her studies.

The difference lies not in the proportion of time in which their activities are directed and the proportion in which they are free, but rather in the difference of attitude. With the professionalization of education and the specialization of industrial tasks which has stripped the individual home of its former variety of activities, our children are not made to feel that the time they do devote to supervised activity is functionally related to the world of adult activity. Although this lack of connection is more apparent than real, it is still sufficiently vivid to be a powerful determinant in the child's attitude. The Samoan girl who tends babies, carries water, sweeps the floor; or the little boy who digs for bait, or collects cocoanuts, has no such difficulty. The necessary nature of their tasks is obvious. And the practice of giving a child a task which he can do well and never permitting a childish, inefficient tinkering with adult apparatus, such as we permit to our children, who bang aimlessly and destructively on their fathers' typewriters, results in a different attitude towards work. American children spend hours in schools learning tasks whose visible relation to their mothers' and fathers' activities is often quite impossible to recognise. Their participation in adults' activities is either in terms of toys, tea-sets and dolls and toy automobiles, or else a meaningless and harmful tampering with the electric light system. (It must be understood that here, as always, when I say American, I do not mean those Americans recently arrived from Europe, who still present a different tradition of education. Such a group would be the Southern Italians, who still expect productive work from their children.)

So our children make a false set of categories, work, play, and school; work for adults, play for children's pleasure, and schools as an inexplicable nuisance with some compensations. These false distinctions are likely to produce all sorts of strange attitudes, an apathetic treatment of a school which bears no known relation to life, a false dichotomy between work and play, which may result either in a dread of work as implying irksome responsibility or in a later contempt for play as childish.

The Samoan child's dichotomy is different. Work consists of those necessary tasks which keep the social life going: planting and harvesting and preparation of food, fishing, house-building, mat-making, care of children, collecting of property to validate marriages and births and succession to titles and to entertain strangers, these are the necessary activities of life, activities in which every member of the community, down to the smallest child, has a part. Work is not a way of acquiring leisure; where every household produces its own food and clothes and furniture, where there is no large amount of fixed capital and households of high rank are simply characterized by greater industry in the discharge of greater obligations, our whole picture of saving, of investment, of deferred enjoyment, is completely absent. (There is even a lack of clearly defined seasons of harvest, which would result in special abundance of food and consequent feasting. Food is always abundant, except in some particular village where a few weeks of scarcity may follow a period of lavish entertaining.) Rather, work is something which goes on all the time for every one; no one is exempt; few are overworked. There is social reward for the industrious, social toleration for the man who does barely enough. And there is always leisure—leisure, be it noted, which is not the result of hard work or accumulated capital at all, but is merely the result of a kindly climate, a small population, a well-integrated social system, and no social demands for spectacular expenditure. And play is what one does

with the time left over from working, a way of filling in the wide spaces in a structure of unirksome work.

Play includes dancing, singing, games, weaving necklaces of flowers, flirting, repartee, all forms of sex activity. And there are social institutions like the ceremonial inter-village visit which partake of both work and play. But the distinctions between work as something one has to do but dislikes, and play as something one wants to do; of work as the main business of adults, play as the main concern of children, are conspicuously absent. Children's play is like adults' play in kind, interest, and in its proportion to work. And the Samoan child has no desire to turn adult activities into play, to translate one sphere into the other. I had a box of white clay pipes for blowing soap bubbles sent to me. The children were familiar with soap bubbles, but their native method of blowing them was very inferior to the use of clay pipes. But after a few minutes' delight in the unusual size and beauty of the soap bubbles, one little girl after another asked me if she might please take her pipe home to her mother, for pipes were meant to smoke, not to play with. Foreign dolls did not interest them, and they have no dolls of their own, although children of other islands weave dolls from the palm leaves from which Samoan children weave balls. They never make toy houses, nor play house, nor sail toy boats. Little boys would climb into a real outrigger canoe and practise paddling it within the safety of the lagoon. This whole attitude gave a greater coherence to the children's lives than we often afford our children.

The intelligibility of a child's life among us is measured only in terms of the behavior of other children. If all the other children go to school the child who does not feels incongruous in their midst. If the little girl next door is taking music lessons, why can't Mary; or why must Mary take music lessons, if the other little girl doesn't take them. But so sharp is our sense of difference between the concerns of children and of adults that the child does not learn to judge its own behavior in relationship to adult life. So children often learn to regard play as something inherently undignified, and as adults mangle pitifully their few moments of leisure. But the Samoan child measures her every act of work or play in terms of her whole community; each item of conduct is dignified in terms of its realised relationship to the only standard she knows, the life of a Samoan village. So complex and stratified a society as ours cannot hope to develop spontaneously any such simple scheme of education.

Again we will be hard put to it to devise ways of participation for children, and means of articulating their school life with the rest of life which will give them the same dignity which Samoa affords her children.

Last among the cultural differences which may influence the emotional stability of the child is the lack of pressure to make important choices. Children are urged to learn, urged to behave, urged to work, but they are not urged to hasten in the choices which they make themselves. The first point at which this attitude makes itself felt is in the matter of the brother and sister taboo, a cardinal point of modesty and decency. Yet the exact stage at which the taboo should be observed is always left to the younger child. When it reaches a point of discretion, of understanding, it will of itself feel "ashamed" and establish the formal barrier which will last until old age. Likewise, sex activity is never urged upon the young people, nor marriage forced upon them at a tender age. Where the possibilities of deviation from the accepted standard are so slight, a few years leeway holds no threat for the society. The child who comes later to a realization of the brother and sister taboo really endangers nothing.

This laissez faire attitude has been carried over into the Samoan Christian Church. The Samoan saw no reason why young unmarried people should be pressed to make momentous decisions which would spoil part of their fun in life. Time enough for such serious matters after they were married or later still, when they were quite sure of what steps they were taking and were in less danger of falling from grace every month or so. The missionary authorities, realizing the virtues of going slowly and sorely vexed to reconcile Samoan sex ethics with a Western European code, saw the great disadvantages of unmarried Church members who were not locked up in Church schools. Consequently, far

from urging the adolescent to think upon her soul the native pastor advises her to wait until she is older, which she is only too glad to do.

But, especially in the case of our Protestant churches, there is a strong preference among us for the appeal to youth. The Reformation, with its emphasis upon individual choice, was unwilling to accept the tacit habitual Church membership which was the Catholic pattern, a membership marked by additional sacramental gifts but demanding no sudden conversion, no renewal of religious feeling. But the Protestant solution is to defer the choice only so far as necessary, and the moment the child reaches an age which may be called "years of discretion" it makes a strong, dramatic appeal. This appeal is reinforced by parental and social pressure; the child is bidden to choose now and wisely. While such a position in the churches which stem from the Reformation and its strong emphasis on individual choice was historically inevitable, it is regrettable that the convention has lasted so long. It has even been taken over by non-sectarian reform groups, all of whom regard the adolescent child as the most legitimate field of activity.

In all of these comparisons between Samoan and American culture, many points are useful only in throwing a spotlight upon our own solutions, while in others it is possible to find suggestions for change. Whether or not we envy other peoples one of their solutions, our attitude towards our own solutions must be greatly broadened and deepened by a consideration of the way in which other peoples have met the same problems. Realizing that our own ways are not humanly inevitable nor God-ordained, but are the fruit of a long and turbulent history, we may well examine in turn all of our institutions, thrown into strong relief against the history of other civilizations, and weighing them in the balance, be not afraid to find them wanting.

II

Sexual Maturation

Since changes in the sex glands are the central changes by which we will define maturational adolescence, it is necessary to consider changes separately for boys and girls. Among boys, the best hallmark of the onset of adolescence seems to be the beginning of accelerated growth of the testes. It is one of the earliest signs of puberty; it correlates well (about .55 to .75) with other criteria such as skeletal measures and the appearance of pubic hair, and it is a direct measure of sexual maturation. It is also a criterion which can be used in the midst of adolescent growth, in contrast to some of the usual criteria like the attainment of 90 percent of maximum height, which can be determined only after growth is completed.

To the casual observer the most striking and obvious sign of the onset of adolescence is the spurt in height which about 75 percent of boys experience around a year after onset of testicular growth (Tanner, 1962). Because of the comparative ease and reliability of its measurement and because of its direct comparability to growth among girls, the height spurt rather than testicular growth is often taken as the measure of adolescent onset. The most rapid gains in penis size also occur for most boys simultaneously with the spurt in height.

The end of adolescence in boys seems best indicated by the end of testicular growth. Stolz and Stolz (1951) found that measures of later stages of testicular growth, using photographs, are less reliable than measures of the end of the height spurt or of penis growth. Nevertheless, the ages at the beginning and end of accelerated testicular growth are intercorrelated .77. Testicular development almost invariably continues beyond development of the penis and in about 80 percent of boys continues for about a year following the end of the spurt in height (Stolz and Stolz, 1951, p. 344).

So far we have not mentioned chronological ages associated with adolescence. We have not in order to emphasize that adolescence is a *developmental* rather than a *chronological* phenomenon. While the development of testes, penis, height, weight, and other indicators of adolescence occurs in similar sequence for almost all boys, age at onset, rate of development, and age at end of adolescence vary widely. Reynolds and Wines (1951) provide data based on a sample of 59 boys observed over a decade at the Fels Research Institute. Onset and end of adolescence were measured by ratings of genital development from photographs, measures of onset relying heavily on observations of the scrotum and the penis.

Among the boys observed by Reynolds and Wines, the youngest adoles-

TABLE 1. ONSET AND END OF ADOLESCENCE IN BOYS[a]

ONSET

Chronological age	Percent of boys beginning maturational adolescence at each age	Percent of boys at each age who are maturational adolescents
9.5	3	3
10.0	2	5
10.5	12	17
11.0	18	35
11.5	29	64
12.0	13	77
12.5	14	91
13.0	6	97
13.5	3	100

END

Chronological age	Percent of boys entering maturational adulthood at each age	Percent of boys at each age who are maturational adults
15.5	3	3
16.0	1	4
16.5	8	12
17.0	11	23
17.5	21	44
18.0	31	75
18.5	25	100

[a] Adapted from Reynolds and Wines (1951).

cents were nine and a half years old and the oldest preadolescents thirteen and a half. The youngest adults were fifteen and a half years old and the oldest adolescents over eighteen. Nor should we assume that boys characteristically begin adolescence at a specific age and progress smoothly through to the end of adolescence. Rather, the more typical pattern is one of fits and starts, boys unevenly and erratically growing into adulthood.

In girls, the beginning of adolescence may be best denoted by the development of breast buds. This criterion recommends itself for the same reasons testicular growth is the useful criterion among boys: its early place in the sequence of adolescent growth, its reliable relationships to other measures of growth, its specifically sexual nature, and the possibility of observing it as it occurs. The height spurt among girls usually begins around the same time as the development of breast buds. The menarche, taken by most authorities as the indicator of adolescent onset in girls, follows on the average two years later (Simmons and Greulich, 1943; Tanner, 1962). Tanner finds a correlation of .86 between age of appearance of breast buds and age of menarche; Nicholson and Hanley (1953) a correlation of .74. According to Tanner, age of appearance of pubic hair is correlated .66 with breast development, appearing sometimes before breast buds, sometimes after. Development of the uterus and vagina probably begins about the time the breast buds appear (Tanner, 1962, pp. 31–32).

TABLE 2. ONSET OF ADOLESCENCE IN GIRLS, DEFINED BY BREAST BUD DEVELOPMENT[a]

Chronological age	Percent of girls beginning maturational adolescence at each age	Percent of girls at each age who are maturational adolescents
8.5	4	4
9.0	4	8
9.5	10	18
10.0	16	34
10.5	16	50
11.0	20	70
11.5	10	80
12.0	6	86
12.5	10	96
13.0	4	100

[a] Adapted from Reynolds and Wines (1948).

The youngest adolescent girl in the **Reynolds and Wines** study **(1948)** is eight and one-half years old, and the oldest preadolescent, thirteen years old.

We have not been able to determine a clear criterion for the end of adolescence among girls. The full development of breasts, the initial stage of which serves as our criterion of onset, is reached while other aspects of growth are continuing, at about the age of fourteen (Nicholson and Hanley, 1953). Other measures reported in the literature also would set adulthood at an earlier age than we believe appropriate. A promising criterion, suggested by Montagu's work on the fertility of adolescents (1957), is the regular production of fertile eggs or perhaps the stabilization of the menstrual cycle. It seems likely that these stages are reached at a modal age of sixteen to seventeen, which is the usual year or so earlier than the modal age for boys to reach adulthood and follows the termination of other aspects of growth. However, we have not been able to find any research on the ages at which any population of girls reaches these stages.

According to our criterion of adolescent onset, girls enter adolescence on the average of six months earlier than boys do. Other criteria, such as the attainment of 90 percent of maximum height, set the average boy's lag as much as a year and a half behind the average girl's. It appears that, on the average, boys begin their sexual maturation only shortly after girls but take longer to reach maturity.

5

Individual Differences in Physical Changes

*Associated with Adolescence in Girls**

Earle L. Reynolds
Janet V. Wines

It is certainly true that many of the psychologic tensions and inadequacies of the adolescent have a physical or physiologic basis, related to differentials which often exist in body size, sexual maturation and social or intellectual maturity.

> There are widely accepted behavior expectations for children of differing degrees of physical maturity. . . . The body parts and characteristics and functional properties do not mature evenly. . . . The appearance of the adolescent sometimes will not be in harmony with his physiological maturity; a mature appearing adolescent may have a child's tolerance for tobacco or alcohol, or a childish resistance to fatigue (Barker *et al.*, 1946, pp. 8–54).

There is little doubt that, in the study of the growth, development and behavior of adolescents, individual differences in sexual maturation play an important role (Jung, 1941; Stolz and Stolz, 1944).

Jung (1941) pointed out that knowledge of simple numerical facts about puberty helps to provide the data on which diagnosis and treatment of abnormalities may be based. The purpose of the present paper is to examine various types of individual variations in female sexual maturation, particularly the shape, size and maturation, particularly the shape, size and maturation of the breasts, the development of pubic hair, the advent of the menarche and certain aspects of body size and shape. Data obtained from 557 semiannual examinations of 49 girls at the Fels Research Institute provided the materials for analysis.[1]

The general order of appearance was determined for the various external physical changes accompanying pubescence in girls. The maturational sequence,

as described by Priesel and Wagner (1931) and confirmed by Pryor (1936) and others, includes rounding of the hips, beginning development of the breasts, appearance of pubic hair and appearance of axillary hair. The menarche usually occurs just before the appearance of axillary hair (Greulich and Thomas, 1944). Seckel (1946) presented in tabular form the average approximate age and sequence of appearance of normal sexual characters in both sexes, as obtained from the literature.

Greulich (1941) may be cited as giving the usual relations:

> During normal puberty, the development of the breasts is among the earliest external manifestations of beginning sexual maturation, and the breast changes are usually well under way before the pubic hair appears in any considerable quantity. The growth of axillary hair usually begins after the pubic hair is fairly well developed and is ordinarily preceded by the menarche, the first menstruation.

In many of the studies mentioned, reference was made to the wide individual differences which exist in the processes of sexual maturation. The menarche, for instance, is commonly considered to occur within a normal age range of 9 to 17 years. It may occur even earlier, accompanied with other sexual characters, in the so-called constitutional type of female precocious puberty, with no demonstrable endocrinopathic symptoms (Novak, 1944). Within much narrower limits, there are many differences between early maturing and late maturing girls, for example, in growth patterns, skeletal development, terminal size and tissue distribution. Differences among girls in sexual maturation taken as a whole constitute the commonest type of variability studied.

There are, however, other aspects of differences in sexual maturation which appear to be well worth considering. One of these relates to reversals and unconformities in the developmental patterns of

* From *American Journal of Diseases of Children*, 1948, 75, pp. 329–350.
[1] Sontag, L. W.: The Fels Research Institute for the Study of Human Development, Antioch College, Yellow Springs, Ohio, 1946; Biological and Medical Studies at the Samuel S. Fels Research Institute, Child Development. 17:81–84 (March–June) 1946.

individual girls. Thus, there are girls who do not follow the usual sequence, in which appearance of breasts precedes appearance of pubic hair, but in whom the process is reversed, so that pubic hair appears several years before the first visible signs of breast development. There are girls who at menarche show a physical development considerably less mature than that usually seen at this stage of sexual maturation, while other girls possess a mature body configuration some time before menarche occurs.

Another type of individual difference is seen in the appearance of specific sexual structures, such as pattern of distribution of pubic hair, the shape and size of the breasts and the degree of prominence of the areolar area. For example, Stratz's (1909) four stage classification of breast development, involving as one stage a temporary uplift of the papilla and areola as a separate mound above the general contour of the breast, does not seem to represent a universal phenomenon of female pubescence.

Consideration will be given in the following sections to these and other aspects of variability in female sexual maturation.

Material and Methods

The 49 girls reported on in this paper are regular participants in the long term study of growth and development conducted by the Fels Research Institute. Each of these girls has been followed since birth or early childhood, and the present report considers records beginning at the age of 8 years, a total of 557 observations. The average age of these girls is about 14, the oldest being 18, and 32 girls have reached menarche. Examinations are made at the birthday and the half-birthday and include medical examinations, menstrual record, photographs in the nude, body measurements, roentgenograms and the recording of the development of various sexual characteristics.

In order partially to objectify observations of pubescence, pictorial cues were used to record various stages of breast development and growth of pubic hair. These cues were obtained from an analysis of our own material and from the literature. For breast development the stages distinguished by Stratz (1909), and described by Greulich and associates (Greulich *et al.*, 1938) and Pryor (1936) were used, with the inclusion of an additional (stage 3) category: (1) the infantile form: elevation of papilla only; (2) the bud stage: elevation of breast and

papilla as a small mound; (3) intermediate stage: elevation of breast and areola with no distinct separation of their contours; (4) primary mamma stage: areola and papilla form a secondary mound above the level of the breast; (5) mature stage: the pappilla only projects, owing to the recession of the areola to the general contour of the breast.

The size of the breast was classified as small, medium or large and the shape of the breast as conical, hemispherical or flat. These characters will be described further in the next section of the paper.

Ratings of development of pubic hair were also made on a five point scale: (1) infantile, no pigmented pubic hair; (2) hair pigmented, straight or only slightly curled, sparse, primarily along the labia; (3) hair curled, slight spread on mons; (4) hair curled, moderate amount and spread; (5) hair tightly curled, profuse definite inverse triangular pattern extending to inguinal region, corresponding to the horizontal type described by Dupertuis and associates (Dupertuis *et al.*, 1945).

Results

Relations of First Appearance of Breasts, First Appearance of Pubic Hair and Menarche.—Figure 1 shows the percentage distribution of age at first breast development and first appearance of pubic hair in the 49 girls of the present series, and also the age at menarche of 32 girls. The mean age at bud stage of breast development was 10.8 plus or minus 1.1 years, while the mean age for first appearance of pubic hair was 11.0 plus or minus 1.1 year. Breast development began before the appearance of pubic hair in 26 girls by the following age intervals: 0.5 year, 11 girls; 1 year, 11 girls; 1.5 years, 3 girls; 2 years, 1 girl. Pubic hair appeared before the beginning of breast development in 16 girls at the following age intervals: 0.5 year, 7 girls; 1 year, 4 girls; 1.5 year, 2 girls; 2 years, 1 girl; 2.5 years, 1 girl; 3.5 years, 1 girl. In 7 girls, the two characteristics appeared at approximately the same age. Breast development thus appeared a year or more before pubic hair in 15 girls, while pubic hair appeared a year or more before the beginning of breast development in 9 girls.

The mean age at menarche was 12.9 ± 1.4 years. As judged by the coefficient of correlation (r), age at menarche appears to be more closely associated with appearance of breasts than with appearance of pubic hair: The r between age at menarche and age at appearance of breast buds was +0.86, while the r between age at menarche and first appearance of pubic hair was +0.70. The *r* between age at appearance of breast buds and age at appearance of pubic hair was +0.66.

Actually, then, breast development appears to be more closely related to a maturational event—menarche—appearing on the average over two years later, than it does to an event—the appearance of pubic hair—appearing on the average only two months later.

It is of some interest to compare beginning maturation—as it is measured by appearance of breasts or of pubic hair, whichever is earlier—with the time elapsing between that event and menarche. Based on the data now available, there appears to be no tendency for early maturing girls to reach menarche in a shorter length of time than late maturing girls. They do, of course, achieve menarche at an earlier age; however, the 5 earliest maturing girls in the series, whose maturation began at the age of 9 or before, took on the average 2.5 years to achieve menarche, while the 5 latest maturing girls whose maturation began at 12 or after, took on the average 2.3 years to achieve menarche. This problem of

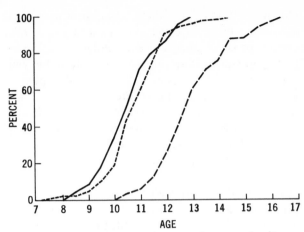

FIG. 2.   Percentage distribution of age at first breast development (indicated by solid line) and age at first appearance of pubic hair (indicated by dashes) in 49 girls and age at menarche (indicated by broken line) in 32 girls.

attained by an individual girl appears early and maintains itself through the maturational stages, unless broken down by such a factor as early obesity.

Stage	\ Age, Yr.										
	8	8.5	9	9.5	10	10.5	11	11.5	12	12.5	13
1.	49	47	45	40	33	25	15	10	7	2	0
2.	0	2	2	6	12	14	14	10	5	4	3
3.	0	0	2	2	2	6	12	11	8	6	8
4.	0	0	0	1	2	4	6	9	12	16	15
5.	0	0	0	0	0	0	0	0	0	2	3

duration of maturation will again be discussed in a later section on maturational extremes.

Breast Development: Maturation, Shape, Size and Development of the Areola.—The average ages at the various stages of breast development, as previously defined, were: bud stage, 10.8 years; intermediate stage, 11.4 years; primary mamma stage, 12.2 years; mature stage, 13.7 years. There was, of course, a high association between the stages, the *r* between any two stages being +0.90 or higher. The distribution of stages, from 8 through 13 years, at which age all girls have passed out of the infantile stage, is shown in the table above.

Breast size as such was not a factor in the determination of the maturational stage of the breast; that is, at any stage the breast size ranged from small to large.

Breast shape was also not a factor in the rating of breast development. The characteristic breast shape

In fact, definitive breast shape can be most easily determined at these early age levels, before the vicissitudes of time and circumstance have broken down the contour, as is particularly true in the case of conical breasts.

Pubic Hair: Maturation; Maturational Asymmetries.—The average ages at the various stages of maturation of the pubic hair, as previously defined, were: stage 2, 11.0 years; stage 3, 11.9 years; stage 4, 12.5 years; stage 5, 13.9 years. There were a moderate association ($r = 0.80$) between stages 2 and 3 and a high association ($r = 0.97$) between stages 3 and 4, and 4 and 5. The distribution of stages, from the ages of 8 through 14½ years, at which age all girls had passed through the infantile period, is shown in the table on page 63.

Menarche: Early and Late Menarche; Individual Differences in Maturational Status at Menarche.—The wide individual differences which exist in the timing of maturational processes are well shown in a comparison between an early maturing and a late maturing girl. The early maturing girl had menarche at 10.5 years, at which time both breasts and pubic hair were in the fourth stage of maturation and an adult body configuration was present. The late maturing girl had the menarche at 16 years, and at the age of 13.5 years was in stage 2 for breast development and appearance of pubic hair, with a body configuration still immature.

The majority of the girls in the series were in stage 4 for both breast development and appearance of pubic hair at the time of menarche, regardless of their chronologic age when this event occurred. The

istics, the age at menarche, inflections in the growth cycle, endocrine status, skeletal development and other indexes of maturation.

This section of the present paper will be concerned with only two aspects of a large problem: the relation of weight, height and the weight: height index at 8 years to age at menarche, and the growth progress in weight and height of the earliest maturing and the latest maturing girls in the series.

There is a tendency for early maturing girls to be larger and stockier at the age of 8, but it is also interesting to note that girls whose age at menarche was only slightly earlier than the average of 12.9

Age, Yr.

Stage	8	8.5	9.0	9.5	10	10.5	11	11.5	12	12.5	13	13.5	14	14.5
1.	48	48	47	44	40	28	21	12	5	3	2	1	1	0
2.	1	1	2	4	7	16	14	13	12	6	3	3	1	0
3.	0	0	0	1	1	3	8	11	8	7	3	1	2	2
4.	0	0	0	0	1	2	5	6	8	14	17	12	7	5
5.	0	0	0	0	0	0	0	1	0	1	4	6	6	7

	Weight* Lb.	Height* Cm.	Index*
Girls having menarche by 11.5 years or earlier (6 girls)	56.7	122.0	27.3
Girls having menarche between 11.6 and 12.4 years (7 girls)	64.1	126.1	28.6
Girls having menarche at 14.2 years or later (6 girls)	44.8	115.7	25.7

* Values for girls at 8 years of age.

distribution of maturational stages at menarche is as follows:

Breast Development, Stage	Appearance of Pubic Hair, Stage	Number of Girls
2	2	0
3	3	1
4	4	18
5	5	1
3	4	1
4	5	2
4	3	4
5	4	1

Other combinations 4

Height, Weight and Body Build.—Many studies have been concerned with the relation of sexual maturation to various aspects of height, weight and body build (Bayer, 1939; 1940a, 1940b; Bullen and Hardy, 1946; Bayley and Bayer, 1946). Sexual maturation has been defined in terms of such criteria as the appearance of certain secondary sexual character-

years (those girls between 11.6 and 12.4 years of age) were, in turn, larger and stockier than girls whose age at menarche was early (11.5 years or before). The relations of size and body build at the age of 8 to time of menarche appears, therefore, in the present series to be curvilinear, rather than linear, as shown in lower table above.

The average weight for the entire Fels series of 8 year old girls was 55.6 pounds and the average height, 126.9 cm.

Several differences between early and late maturing girls may be noted: the greater variability in the growth patterns of early maturing girls; the larger size of early maturing girls, when compared according to chronologic age; the smaller size of early maturing girls, when weight and height are compared in terms of menarche; the characteristic differences in growth patterns of early and late maturing girls, resulting in an eventual tendency for convergence of the growth curves. All these phenomena, and others, have been explored in great detail in the studies previously referred to, particularly in the monographs by Shuttleworth (1937, 1938, 1939).

Summary

Various aspects of individual variation in female sexual maturation are described and illustrated, based on an analysis of data obtained from 557 semiannual examinations of 49 girls who are regular participants in the longitudinal growth program of the Fels Research Institute.

Characteristics discussed include the maturation, size, shape and areolar protrusion of the breasts; the development of pubic hair; the advent of menarche, and the interrelations of these maturational features. A comparison is made of girls representing five different types of maturational extremes. The relation of body size to sexual maturation is examined briefly.

Stages of maturation for breasts and pubic hair are defined, and the average age at the attainment of the various stages is given, as well as the distribution of the stages at half-yearly age levels. The interrelations of age at first appearance of breasts, age at first appearance of pubic hair and age at menarche are described.

Individual differences in maturational status at menarche are described; examples of maturational asymmetries are shown, and individual variations in the interrelations of chronologic age, menarche and maturational status are illustrated.

Girls showing maturational extremes in breast size, breast shape, areolar development, maturational sequences and duration of maturation are compared in terms of age at various stages of sexual maturation and in terms of weight and height at age of first breast development.

Two aspects of individual differences in the association of body size with sexual maturation are examined: the relation of weight, height and weight:height index at 8 years of age to age at menarche and the growth progress of early and late maturing girls.

The observations in the present study are primarily descriptive and classificatory in nature, and the characteristics discussed represent only a portion of the data being collected and analyzed on these same girls. Additional material includes ratings of other secondary sex characters such as axillary hair, the assessment of osseous development and the study of menstrual patterns, differential tissue growth, growth of body segments, physiologic function and endocrine activity during adolescence.

The present study offers, in our opinion, preliminary materials for further research in the variability of human sexual maturation and provides a certain amount of information for the clinician interested in problems of adolescent development.

6

Physical Changes

Associated with Adolescence in Boys*

Earle L. Reynolds
Janet V. Wines

In a previous paper (Reynolds and Wines, 1948) a description was given of certain physical changes accompanying adolescence in girls. The value of such information to the pediatrician was discussed, with particular reference to the normal range of individual variation in sexual maturation. In the present study a similar report is made for boys.

The general literature on adolescent bodily changes and various studies of female adolescence were cited in the earlier publication. In addition, a number of studies have dealt specifically with male adolescent development (e.g. Stuart, 1946, 1947; Ellis, 1948). These range from concise descriptions of developmental processes to broad discussions of the relation of sexual maturation to behavior in adolescence.

Materials and Methods

The 59 boys reported on in this paper are, like the girls in the earlier study, regular participants in the long-term study of growth and development under way at the Fels Research Institute for the Study of Human Development.[1] The progress of Fels Research Institute children is being followed from birth through maturity, and the records of all boys between 9 and 21 yr. of age (706 observations) are used in this report. Each boy visits the physical growth department of the Fels Research Institute on his birthday and half-birthday, and the program includes medical examination and health history, nude photographs, body measurements, roentgenograms of various joints and parts, and a recording of the development of a number of sexual characteristics.

Pictorial cues, obtained from an analysis of our series, were used to describe various stages of maturation of external genitalia, penis size and shape, and growth of pubic hair. In the older boys the regional distribution of body hair was recorded (Reynolds, 1951).

Ratings of genitalia maturation were made on a five-point scale: (1) infantile; (2) enlargement of scrotum, first reddening and texture change; (3) first "sculpturing" and enlargement of penis; (4) pronounced sculpturing and darkening; (5) essentially adult; reddish brown color, loose penile skin, loss of sharp sculpturing.

Size of penis was rated on a seven-point scale. The standards were applied in each case without reference to other aspects of sexual maturation. That is to say, ratings of penis size were made apart from ratings of genitalia maturation, although there is, of course, a relation between the two phenomena. For instance, no boy in our normal series whose genitalia were in Stage 1 (infantile) had a penis size larger than Size 4, while no boy whose genitalia were in Stage 5 (adult) had a penis size smaller than Size 4. The relation of pictoral standards to direct measurements of penis size will be discussed in a later section.

Growth of pubic hair, as in the girls, was rated on a five-point scale: (1) infantile; (2) first appearance, pigmented, usually straight, sparse, at base of penis; (3) slight curl, slight spread, usually darker; (4) curled, moderate amount and spread, not yet extended to thighs; (5) "adult" in type, profuse, forming an inverse triangle extending to thighs corresponding to the horizontal type described by Dupertuis and co-workers (Dupertuis *et al.*, 1945).

Some comments concerning the ratings should be made. First, all the standards were derived from photographs taken under similar conditions of distance, positioning, and lighting. Second, observations were obtained from longitudinal data, an average of 12 sets of semiannual photographs (front, side, and back view) being available on each boy, with a

* From *American Journal of Diseases of Children*, 1951, 82, 529–547.
[1] Sontag, L. W.: The Fels Research Institute for the Study of Human Development, Antioch College, Yellow Springs, Ohio, 1946; Biological and Medical Studies at the Samuel S. Fels Research Institute, Child Develop. 17:81–84, 1946.

range of three to 20 sets. This permitted a check on whether a characteristic shown represented a growth or maturational change or was a transient factor induced by an immediate environmental stimulus such as temperature. It also permitted both earlier and more accurate detection of slight changes in individual boys.

Third, an attempt was made to rate each characteristic independently of other characteristics; for instance, ratings of pubic hair were made without reference to stage of maturation of genitalia. This made possible the examination of discrete elements of sexual maturation. Finally, there are differences in the reliability with which these ratings can be applied to an individual boy if he were to be seen only at a single visit. Generally speaking, ratings of genitalia maturation are somewhat more difficult to make than ratings of penis size and shape, while the stage of pubic-hair development may be determined with little difficulty.

Results

Genitalia: Maturation, Duration; Penis Size and Shape.—Table 3 shows, by age level, the percentage of boys in each stage of genitalia maturation. The number of cases at each age level are also given. Figure 1 gives the distribution in graphic form. The average age at which each stage is attained is shown in the following tabulation:

Genitalia Maturation, Stage	Mean Age, Yr.	Standard Deviation	Median Age, Yr.
2	11.5	0.9	11.3
3	12.7	0.8	12.5
4	13.4	0.7	13.2
5	17.3	0.8	17.6

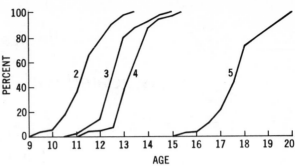

FIG. 3. Percentage distribution for stages of genitalia maturation.

Associations between the various stages, as shown by the coefficient of correlation, range from 0.34 (between Stages 4 and 5) to 0.86 (between Stages 3 and 4).

The average duration of the various stages and the range of individual cases in the present series are shown in the following tabulation:

Period Covered	Mean, Yr.	Range for Individual Boys
From Stage 2 to Stage 3	1.3	From 6 mo. to 3 yr.
From Stage 3 to Stage 4	0.6	From 3 mo. to 1.75 yr.
From Stage 4 to Stage 5	3.9	From 2.5 yr. to 5 yr.
From Stage 2 to Stage 5	5.8	From 5 yr. to 7.25 yr.

The average Fels Research Institute boy, therefore, took slightly less than six years to pass from beginning genitalia maturation to the adult stage. The boy who made the transition fastest in our series did it in five years, while the boy who made it slowest took over seven years to make a similar shift.

It will be noted that the transition from Stage 3 to Stage 4 is relatively rapid, while a much longer period generally elapses between the attainment of

TABLE 3. PERCENTAGE OF BOYS AT EACH STAGE OF GENITALIA MATURATION, BY AGE LEVEL

	Age, Yr.																			
Stage	9	9.5	10	10.5	11	11.5	12	12.5	13	13.5	14	14.5	15	15.5	16	16.5	17	17.5	18	19–21
1	100	97	95	83	65	36	23	9	3	0	0	0	0	0	0	0	0	0	0	5
2	0	3	5	17	33	55	63	42	18	13	8	3	0	0	0	0	0	0	0	0
3	0	0	0	0	2	4	9	42	41	23	5	3	3	0	0	0	0	0	0	0
4	0	0	0	0	0	4	5	7	38	64	87	94	97	97	96	88	77	56	25	0
5	0	0	0	0	0	0	0	0	0	0	0	0	0	3	4	12	23	44	75	100
No. of cases	59	59	57	52	49	47	43	43	39	39	37	35	34	31	27	26	22	16	16	5

Total no. of cases: 736

TABLE 4. PERCENTAGE OF BOYS IN EACH CATEGORY OF PENIS SIZE, BY AGE LEVEL

	Age, Yr.																	
Size	10	10.5	11	11.5	12	12.5	13	13.5	14	14.5	15	15.5	16	16.5	17	17.5	18	19–21
1	28	26	24	25	16	12	8	3	3	0	0	0	0	0	0	0	0	0
2	53	54	54	48	56	36	10	13	8	3	0	0	0	0	0	0	0	0
3	14	15	16	17	16	40	36	8	5	3	3	0	0	0	0	0	0	0
4	5	5	6	8	7	5	26	36	11	18	16	20	16	15	14	18	27	20
5	0	0	0	2	0	2	15	20	35	27	23	20	20	23	36	35	40	60
6	0	0	0	0	5	2	3	15	22	33	42	40	48	42	41	41	27	20
7	0	0	0	0	0	2	3	5	16	15	16	20	16	19	9	6	7	0
No. of cases	58	54	50	48	43	42	39	39	37	33	31	30	25	26	22	17	15	5

Total no. of cases: 614

Stage 4 and the achievement of the adult stage of genitalia maturation.

Table 4 shows, by age level, the percentage of boys in each stage of penis size. The number of cases at each age level are also shown.

There seems to be a tendency, in some boys, for penis size to be smaller in the adult stage of genitalia maturation than it was at its maximum size during Stage 4. The tabulation below illustrates this:

Genitalia Maturation, Stage	*Mean Size of Penis*
2	2.1
3	3.0
4	4.6
Maximum size reached during Stage 4	5.9
5	4.9

Thus, the average size of penis is Size 5 at the time the adult stage of genitalia maturation is reached, but the maximum size of penis reached during the period between Stages 4 and 5 of genitalia maturation is on the average almost Size 6.

All boys do not show this size reduction, but in general the larger the penis size in Stage 4 of genitalia maturation, the likelier there is to be a decrease in penis size when the adult stage of genitalia maturation is reached. Moreover, no boy who reached penis Size 7 remained in this category by the time he had reached the adult stage of genitalia maturation. The greatest size reduction noted was three size units.

Size changes ranged from as little as two units (Size 2 at beginning of genitalia maturation, Size 4 at maximum size, and Size 4 at adult stage of genitalia maturation) to as much as 5 units (Size 1 at beginning of genitalia maturation, Size 6 at maximum size, and Size 5 at adult stage of genitalia maturation).

Our continued observation on the development of Fels Research Institute boys leads us to believe that this tendency toward a reduction in penis size in later adolescence, when it occurs, is a significant developmental pattern.

Pubic Hair: Growth; Duration; Relation to Geni-

TABLE 5. PERCENTAGE OF BOYS AT EACH STAGE OF PUBIC-HAIR MATURATION, BY AGE LEVEL

	Age, Yr.																			
Stage	8.5	9	9.5	10	10.5	11	11.5	12	12.5	13	13.5	14	14.5	15	15.5	16	16.5	17	17.5	18	19–21
1	100	98	98	98	91	86	69	60	48	28	10	3	3	3	0	0	0	0	0	0	0
2	0	2	2	2	9	14	29	31	43	38	33	14	3	0	0	0	0	0	0	0	0
3	0	0	0	0	0	0	2	7	7	20	20	22	9	3	0	0	0	0	0	0	0
4	0	0	0	0	0	0	0	2	2	12	33	59	74	76	73	56	46	32	12	0	0
5	0	0	0	0	0	0	0	0	0	2	3	3	12	18	27	44	54	68	88	100	100
No. of cases	59	59	59	59	54	50	48	45	42	40	39	37	34	33	30	25	26	22	16	15	5

Total no. of cases: 797

talia Maturation.—Table 5 shows, by age level, the percentage of boys in each stage of pubic-hair development and the number of boys at each age level. Norms for each stage are shown in the following tabulation:

Pattern of Pubic Hair, Stage	Mean Age, Yr.	Standard Deviation	Median Age, Yr.
2	12.2	1.1	12.4
3	13.3	0.8	13.4
4	13.9	0.7	13.8
5	16.1	1.2	16.3

Associations between the various stages, as shown by the coefficient of correlation, range from 0.50 (between Stages 2 and 5) to 0.94 (between Stages 3 and 4).

The average duration of the various stages and the range of individual cases in the present series are shown in the following tabulation:

Period Covered	Mean, Yr.	Range for Individual Boys
From Stage 2 to Stage 3	1.1	From 3 mo. to 3.25 yr.
From Stage 3 to Stage 4	0.6	From 3 mo. to 1.25 yr.
From Stage 4 to Stage 5	2.2	From 1 yr. to 4 yr.
From Stage 2 to Stage 5	3.9	From 2 yr. to 6 yr.

The average Fels Research Institute boy thus took about four years to reach the adult pattern of pubic-hair distribution, after the first appearance of pubic hair. The fastest transition in our series was in two years, the slowest in six years.

Considering both genitalia maturation and the development of pubic hair, the following is the commonest sequence of appearance of the various stages:

Item	Approximate Age, Yr.
1. Genitalia 2 (enlargement of scrotum, etc.)	11.5
2. Pubic Hair 2 (first appearance)	12.0
3. Genitalia 3 (enlargement of penis, etc.)	12.5
4. Pubic Hair 3 (slight curl and spread) and Genitalia 4 (sculpturing and darkening)	13.5
5. Pubic Hair 4 (curled, moderate amount and spread)	14.0
6. Pubic Hair 5 (adult)	16.0
7. Genitalia 5 (adult)	17.5

The above sequence is followed exactly by only 12 boys, indicating the great range of individual variation. The commonest reversals between adjacent stages are:

Genitalia 3 before Pubic Hair 2	41%
Genitalia 4 before Pubic Hair 3	32%

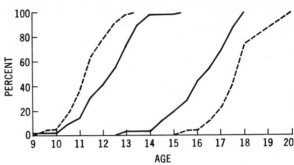

FIG. 4. Percentage distribution for Stage 2 (beginning) and Stage 5 (adult) for genitalia maturation (broken lines) and development of pubic hair (solid lines).

Genitalia maturation began before the appearance of pubic hair in 70 percent of the cases examined; in 16 percent the two processes began at approximately the same age, and in 14 percent pubic hair appeared before genitalia maturation could be observed.

Genitalia maturation, therefore, tends to begin earlier (around 11.5 yr.) and to reach the adult stage later (around 17.5 yr.) than does the development of pubic hair (beginning around 12 yr., adult around 16 yr.). This is shown graphically in Figure 2, in which the beginning and the adult stages for both characteristics are plotted on the same graph.

Comparisons of Boys Showing Various Maturational Extremes

The boys with profuse body hair at 18 yr. were somewhat earlier, both in genitalia maturation and in development of pubic hair, particularly in first appearance of pubic hair. In terms of penis size, they averaged one unit smaller at the beginning of genitalia maturation but were slightly larger at the time of maximum penis size.

Boys with a long "duration of maturation," using genitalia as a criterion, show a much earlier beginning genitalia maturation but are only slightly older at Genitalia 4. Boys with a long maturation period for genitalia have a much shorter developmental period for pubic hair, while those boys who pass from Genitalia 2 to 4 in a very short period show a long developmental span for pubic hair. There is little difference between the two groups in penis size.

Boys with a long "duration of maturation," using

pubic hair as a criterion, show little difference in genitalia maturation from boys whose comparable development of pubic hair was rapid. The longer duration seems to be chiefly a result of an earlier appearance of pubic hair, rather than of reaching Stage 4 at a much later age. There is little difference between the two groups in mean penis size at Genitalia 2, but the group with the long maturation span have a penis size at maximum averaging one unit larger.

Two other comparisons of boys showing extremes of development were made, with negative results. There was no great difference, in the items compared, between boys showing extremes of penis size at Genitalia 2, or at time of maximum growth.

Weight, Height and Body Build.—Several differences between the growth patterns of early-maturing and late-maturing boys may be noted: early-maturing boys are on the average both heavier and taller than late-maturing boys, throughout the period studied, although there is some overlapping in individual cases; late-maturing boys tend to close the gap during their period of rapid growth, but not completely so; in both groups there is an acceleration in growth between Pubic Hair 2 and 4, which is more marked during the shorter span of time covered by the late-maturing boys. In general, differences in weight and height between early-maturing and late-maturing boys are in the same direction, but are not as marked, as like comparisons in girls.

Other Maturational Items.—Information has been gathered on a number of other maturational items, on which less regular observations have been made. Our data on axillary hair are not complete, and the working out of regular stages was not attempted. In general, our observations of development of axillary hair are in line with the findings of other investigators (Greulich, Dorfman *et al.*, 1942; Schonfeld, 1943).

We have noted marked breast development during adolescence in only two boys, although a slight degree of development is rather common. In both cases there was a recession at later age levels. Since male adolescent breast development, when it appears, is often an event of fairly short duration, it is possible that our observations, made at six-month intervals, may have missed some cases.

The appearance and distribution of body hair in the older boys were recorded (Reynolds, 1951). The percentage of boys having hair in various areas of the body, at three age levels, is shown in the following tabulation:

Area	14 Yr.	16 Yr.	18 Yr.
Pubic	97	100	100
Axillary	40	97	100
Anterior leg	46	90	100
Posterior leg	38	77	95
Posterior thigh	35	40	95
Anterior thigh	30	67	95
Forearm	14	37	80
Abdomen	14	37	75
Buttocks	14	33	50
Chest	3	7	40
Lower back	3	7	20
Arms	0	0	10
Shoulders	0	0	0

Circumcision appeared to have no relation to maturational factors studied, and there were no significant differences found between the 29 uncircumcised and the 38 circumcised boys studied.

In four boys there is a history of semi-erections at a number of visits. This is noted routinely on the physical examination record, and can also be seen readily in the photographs. In all, 18 boys, at one time or another, showed a noticeable degree of erection during some phase of the program. Physically speaking, these boys cannot be distinguished from the rest of the Fels Research Institute series.

Our work to date has convinced us of the need and value of more objective measurements and more systematized observations than are usually available on adolescent children. For instance, although ratings of genitalia size from photographs provide useful information, direct measurements of penis and testicle size are preferable, whenever it is feasible to obtain them. Color photographs are more informative than the usual black and white. We have also taken a number of infrared photographs on young adolescents, which have given promising results, particularly in the study of beginning breast development.

Summary

This report is a companion article to a previously published study on girls (Reynolds and Wines, 1948). Various aspects of individual variation in male sexual maturation are described and illustrated, based on an analysis of data obtained from 706 semiannual examinations of 59 boys who are regular participants in the longitudinal growth program of the Fels Research Institute for the Study of Human Development.

Included in the discussion are maturation of external genitalia, size and shape of penis, development of pubic hair, and interrelations of these maturational features. A comparison of boys representing various types of maturational extremes is given. The relation of body build and growth progress in weight and height to sexual maturation is discussed briefly.

Standards for rating genitalia maturation and development of pubic hair are illustrated, and the average ages at which the various stages are reached are given, as well as the distribution of these stages at half-year intervals. Standards are also illustrated for rating penis size on a seven-point scale and for describing penis shape.

Individual differences in sexual maturation are described, and examples of maturational asymme-

tries are shown. Boys showing extremes in the development of body hair, in the duration of maturation, and in three types of body build are compared. Individual and group patterns of weight and height in early-maturing and in late-maturing boys are also shown.

The observations in the present study of boys, as in the previous study of girls, are chiefly descriptive and classificatory in nature, and only a portion of the data on sexual maturation now being collected are discussed.

The materials here presented were selected so as to provide information which it is hoped will be useful to the clinician interested in the growth of adolescent boys.

III

Psychic Maturation

As suggested in the way we have defined "adolescence," what is most crucial and interesting about this phase of development is the sudden surge of new drive and the reorganization of drives in the individual. The study of adolescence may usefully be regarded as the study of the impact of rapid changes in the intensity and quality of the sexual drive on the individual's mental life and on his social role. In this section, we will review research on psychic development, emphasizing those aspects which seem most closely related to sexual maturation.

Sexual Behavior

As a result of the fairly rapid maturing of sexual organs, one expects to find an increasingly intense and focused sexual drive and a greater manifestation of the sexual drive in adolescent behavior. Specifically, one expects an increase in the frequency of direct sexual behavior, in sexual interests, in sexual fantasy, and in anxiety and defensiveness about sexual matters. When one turns to the literature in search of evidence of such behaviors, one finds some surprises waiting. The evidence on sexual behavior, for example, turns up an interesting sex difference. While our image of sexual changes in adolescence includes both boys and girls, the pattern of change in direct sexual activity is markedly different in the two groups.

Kinsey and his associates (1948, 1953) present the best available data on sexual behavior, despite the fact that their samples of respondents may not be precisely representative of any identifiable population, particularly in the adolescent age range. While sexual behavior begins in infancy and continues throughout childhood, a much broader group of individuals engage in sexual behavior with greater frequency at the onset of adolescence. The curves in Figure 7 show sharp rises in sexual experiences at about the age of puberty. We are interested here especially in the portion of the curves between ten and twenty years of age.

We note that Kinsey reports far less drive expression in females at all ages, especially during adolescence. Figure 7 shows that fewer females than males achieve orgasm in any type of activity. It seems reasonable to suppose that stricter social control of girls and the force of social taboos combine to produce this difference: sexual activity in adolescent girls does not result in reinforcing tension release often enough to maintain the activity at the male level.

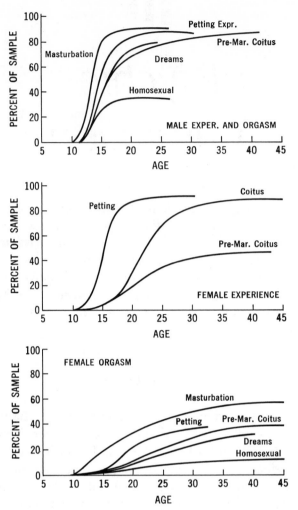

FIG. 5.   Comparison of female and male experience
          and orgasm. Accumulative incidences (Fig-
          ures 148–150 in Kinsey *et al.* 1953, p. 717).

Asayama's data, in Japanese sexual patterns (1957a) reported in one of the
selections in this section, provides interesting confirmation of Kinsey's findings
from another culture.

There is another striking detail in Figure 7. Not only does the curve of
sexual activity for boys rise more sharply, but it also begins to rise, according
to the researchers' estimates, earlier than the curve for girls. The authors
write:

> . . . we have emphasized . . . the latter development of sexual responsiveness in
> the female and its earlier development in the male. We have pointed out that the
> male's capacity to be stimulated sexually shows a marked increase with the ap-
> proach of adolescence, and that the incidences of responding males and the fre-
> quencies of response to the point of orgasm, reach their peak within three to
> four years after the onset of adolescence. On the other hand, we have pointed out
> that the maximum incidences of sexually responding females are not approached
> until some time in the late twenties and in the thirties, although more individuals
> became fully responsive at an earlier age (Kinsey *et al.*, 1953, p. 714).

In at least two ways, these data are in direct contradiction to data presented earlier. In the first place, we have seen that females as a group mature sexually earlier than males, which suggests that girls would manifest sexual behavior earlier than boys, rather than later. Second, the sharp rise in sexual activity for boys and the more gentle rise for girls precedes the ages at which puberty begins for boys and girls; perhaps these early increments are manifestations of the relatively few youngsters who are precipitated into puberty early, or of social pressures.

As to the sex differences, Kinsey and his associates (1953) write: "Nothing that we know about the anatomy or physiology of sexual response, or about the relative significance of psychological stimuli in females and males, would account for these differences in the development of sexual responsiveness and for these differences in the aging patterns of the two sexes" (p. 715). Some data on covert, emotional responses to surgent sexual drives, to be presented later, may help to illuminate these sex differences.

Figure 7 indicates that most adolescent sexual activity consists of masturbation, heterosexual petting, and heterosexual intercourse. The Kinsey data also make possible some rough estimates of changes and trends in adolescent's sexual practices over the first forty years of this century. The data for males of the youngest group studied compared with the generation who were adolescent sometime between 1910 and 1925 reveal very few generational differences. In the least educated group (grade school or less), the younger generation experienced heterosexual intercourse on the average a year or two earlier than the older generation of men did, and they report a somewhat higher incidence of petting, masturbation, and nocturnal emission than the older group. In the most educated group (college), the younger generation report a higher incidence of petting and of petting to climax than the other group. Kinsey summarizes his findings on historical trends for males in this way:

> . . . slight changes in attitudes, some increase in the frequency of masturbation among boys of the lower educational levels, more frequent nocturnal emissions, increased frequencies of pre-marital petting, earlier coitus for a portion of the male population, and the transference of the pre-marital intercourse from prostitutes to girls who are not prostitutes (Kinsey *et al.*, 1948, p. 416).

Changes in girls' sexual behavior over this same period are more marked, as we would expect from Kinsey's remark about the males' choice of partners. Among females, increases in both petting to climax and heterosexual intercourse appear in each decade since 1900 up to the group born in the 1920's (reaching adolescence in the 1930's and 1940's), where the curve levels off. Less than 20 per cent of the women born in the 1920's report petting to climax by age eighteen. About 20 per cent experienced heterosexual intercourse by this same age.

I. L. Reiss (1960), who has analyzed the attitudes and standards underlying sexual practices as well as the behaviors themselves, suggests that new standards have evolved over the last fifty years or so, and that the changes are generally away from a double standard toward a humanized single standard allowing sexual expression in the context of a strong affectional bond (i.e., when the partners are in love or plan to marry). He also concludes, however, that the change is occurring slowly, that the ideology of sexual freedom reached its peak of acceptance during the 1920's, and that strong traditional and irrational forces prevent rapid changes in either sexual standards or sexual behavior. Reiss's own research and most of the studies he reviews deal with older adolescents and young adults (i.e., college students, engaged couples, and so on) and we suspect that conservative forces, particularly parental attitudes, operate even more effectively in opposing change during adolescence proper.

Sexual Interests and Sensitivities

Interest in and sensitivity to sexual matters increase markedly at adolescence. Data from the Terman-Miles (1936) Masculinity-Femininity Test show a sharp rise in the masculinity interest scores of boys, which begins in junior high school and peaks during the high school years. The onset of adolescence marks a smaller increase in masculinity among girls as well; this trend quickly levels off among girls whose formal education ends at high school graduation or before but continues to rise to a peak among college sophomore women. Although the general trend during adolescence is toward greater masculinity of interests among girls and boys, adolescent girls as a group remain decidedly feminine compared to boys, and Terman and Miles note that the greatest differentiation of interests between the sexes occurs during adolescence.

Lessler (1962) provides a different kind of data to demonstrate that sex consciousness rises rapidly at adolescence. He had 120 males and females sort 3 by 5 cards on which were printed symbols previously judged by independent observers as symbolic of masculinity and femininity. Half of the cards displayed symbols which were masculine or feminine in their shapes (pointed versus rounded); half, in their textures (rough versus smooth). All the groups of subjects from fourth grade, ninth grade, and college successfully differentiated masculine from feminine symbols. But of special interest to us is the finding that ninth-grade and college students correctly identified more symbols than forth-graders did. **P. Cameron's** study (1967) of shape preference of boys and girls at various ages supports the Freudian theory of psychosexual stages, including specific hypotheses about the preferences of adolescents in our culture and other less male-dominant cultures.

Some of the increasing differentiation of interests revealed by the Terman-Miles M-F Test undoubtedly is a result of social rather than maturational forces, of subtle or explicit pressures on youngsters to "act like a man" or "be a lady." The activity preference list which is part of the test has obvious sex-role expectations built into choices between things like baseball and sewing. Lessler also feels that social factors are the major determinant of differentiation. He asserts that the sexuality of the textured symbols are more social in origin than the anatomically symbolic shapes. Since the textured symbols elicited stronger age differences than the anatomically symbolic shapes, Lessler concludes that social factors account for more of the age differences.

On the other hand, maturational factors should not be discounted. It seems likely that sexual maturation accounts for at least some of the differences in the word association component of the M-F Test. For example, more adolescent than preadolescent boys associate "trunk" with the extended proboscis of an elephant, while more adolescent girls think of "trunk" as something to pack for traveling.

We can agree, then, with Lessler's summary statement, ". . . cultural-biological symbol dichotomy probably does not exist." Whatever the major source of influence, the Terman-Miles and Lessler studies indicate that adolescence carries with it a greater sensitivity to the sexual connotations of words and other symbols.

Sexual Fantasy

There is no clear evidence for an increase in sexual fantasies at adolescence. There are almost no developmental data on dreams. Evidence on adolescent fantasy is largely from Rorschach and TAT protocols.

Some evidence suggests that daydreams become more infused with sexuality at puberty. Hamilton (1929) asked 200 upper-middle-class married men and women to recall their earliest sexual daydreams. Many of them recalled such daydreams occurring prior to puberty, although 32 reported that the waking fantasies became more realistic or vivid during their adolescence.

Specific references to sex appear in Rorschach protocols so infrequently that no age trends can be discerned from them. Ames, Metraux, and Walker (1959) collected 700 Rorschach records from 398 boys and girls ten to sixteen years old, about 80 per cent of them members of upper-middle or upper-class families. Only small increases over age in projections of lush, flowery images gave any evidence of increasing sexual interest and awareness. Nor was there any indication of an increase with age in instinctual drives, inasmuch as there was no increase in images of animals or objects moving. That adolescents are gaining more control over instinctual drives is perhaps reflected in the increasing balance between fantasies of human as against nonhuman movement.

Two studies employing the Thematic Apperception Test, by Sanford and associates (1943) and Symonds (1949), agree, as far as we can tell, about the course of sexual and aggressive fantasy from preadolescence into the adolescent years. Sanford's data from 55 adolescents suggest that sexual fantasy increases among boys and decreases among girls as they enter adolescence, while aggressive fantasy increases for both sexes at the age of puberty. Symonds' TAT protocols from 20 boys and 20 girls aged twelve to eighteen suggest that aggressive themes grow more frequent during adolescence, while sexual fantasy declines and general eroticism is not reliably correlated with age. However, Symonds does not present data separately for boys and girls. Taken together, studies of sex and aggression in adolescent fantasy are not clear about the course of these drives at the onset of puberty.

Perhaps the data on anxiety among adolescents will help to make more sense of Sanford's evidence concerning sex differences in sexual fantasy. Symonds' TAT data reveal marked increases in anxiety with age during adolescence: the anxiety theme increased in incidence more clearly than any other. Furthermore, those youngsters who wrote stories expressing anxiety tended not to write stories of love. Further still, those individuals who showed the least interest in the opposite sex on a questionnaire also tended to write stories rated high in anxiety. Assuming an increase in biological sex drive at adolescence, these data support the interpretation that when the drive is blocked from fantasy expression, this defensive blocking is accompanied by anxiety.

The Rorschach data confirm that adolescent fantasy is increasingly infused with anxiety. While Rorschach analysts are by no means agreed on this interpretation, attention to shading and descriptions of cloud formations and distant vistas are often taken to be indicative of pervasive and overwhelming, diffuse anxiety, (Allen, 1954). Of this indicator, Ames *et al.* (1959) write, "This is the determinant that increases most strikingly during the adolescent period" (p. 290). Further, "At every age except 11, many more girls than boys give shading responses. The difference . . . tends to increase with age" (p. 292).

Rorschach data from studies by Hertz (1942, 1943a, b) and Hertz and Baker (1943) support the proposition that adolescence generates anxiety, especially among girls. They report that the protocols of 76 boys and girls showed greater "introversiveness" at age fifteen than at age twelve. That is, the older youngsters were directed relatively more than the younger by their inner feelings—their impulses and their anxieties. Their characteristic response was to limit outward expression, and the girls appeared to grow much more introversive than boys, while boys seemed freer and less inhibited.

Powell (1955) contributes data of another sort to document heightened anxiety about increasing sexuality among adolescents, especially girls. He reports that 448 males and females aged ten to thirty years gave verbal associations to stimulus words categorized according to the area of conflict which they represented—religion, vocational outlook, heterosexual relations, and so on. An individual's anxiety in each area of conflict was measured by the average length of time it took him to announce associations to the words in that area, compared to how long it took him to respond to sets of neutral words. The sharpest increases in anxiety over the years eleven to seventeen occur in the areas of heterosexual relations and social acceptability. Girls show more anxiety than boys in both these areas at five out of the seven age levels, ages eleven and fifteen being the exceptions.

Powell's data fit neatly with the sex differences in growth rates: the sharp increase in anxiety over sex is at age eleven among girls, and not until a year later among the boys.

We are struck by the juxtaposition of data on themes of "abasement" and sexual themes in Sanford's study. The former, expressions of feelings that one needs to do penance, be condemned and be punished, rises and falls among adolescents in mirror image of sexual expression. As boys grow into adolescence, their stories contain more sexual and fewer abasement themes. Girls' stories, on the other hand, show a marked increase in themes of abasement and the incidence of sexual themes declines. These data suggest that sexual impulses generate guilt and conflict in some adolescent girls which mask direct expression of impulses even when they are elicited by projective techniques.

This interpretation gains some additional support from a recent study by Tooley (1966). Comparing high school girls, college girls, and adult women on TAT responses, she found the high school girls to be relatively flamboyant in expressive style except in the area of heterosexuality. In addition, the high school girls, more than either of the other age groups, avoid the theme of pregnancy in response to a picture that normally elicits it.

To summarize our interpretation of the psychological manifestations of adolescent sexual maturation: Increases in specifically sexual behavior at the onset of puberty indicate that sexual maturation is reflected in increasing sexual motivation. Sexual activity does not increase so markedly among girls as it does among boys, nor does it reach as high a level, probably because the increasing intensity of sexual motivation arouses more restraining anxiety among girls. Both boys and girls become more sensitive to sexual connotations in stimulus objects, but only boys seem free enough of anxiety over sex to indulge in more sexual fantasy at adolescence. It is this differential level of anxiety which, we feel, clarifies the lower incidence of direct sexual expression in girls. Of course, both boys and girls are subject to higher levels of anxiety about sex at adolescence, and even among boys, this anxiety may repress any striking increase in the level of sexual fantasy.

We should point out that nearly all the data we have cited were collected from American subjects. It is altogether possible that in cultures where norms governing sexuality are more permissive, sexual maturation would not generate so much anxiety.

Several investigators have concentrated on the effect of puberty and the pacing of physiological change on personality traits. **Stone and Barker** (1937a) first looked at this problem in their classic study of personality and intelligence in pre- and post-mencheal girls matched for chronological age. *Davidson and Gottlieb* (1955) studied the impact of the menarche on emotional maturity.

Mussen and his associates (Mussen and Jones, 1958, **Mussen and Bouterline-Young,** 1964) have extended and refined this line of investigation, asking about the impact of early and late physical maturation on the personality development of boys in different cultural settings. The selection we have included from this work (Mussen and Bouterline-Young, 1964) is a remarkable example of a sophisticated design analytically separating the effects of physical and cultural forces in personality development.

Intellectual Development

Throughout adolescence most youngsters continue to improve their intellectual performance—a growth which continues beyond adolescence into the early twenties. At least two independent studies document the fact that the peak of general intellectual performance is reached after the adolescent years. The curves in Figure 2 were generated by data from the Army Alpha Test administered by H. E. Jones and Conrad (1933) in the early 1930's and by the Wechsler-Bellevue set of tests in the 1950's (Wechsler, 1958). Both show decelerated growth through adolescence, the peak being reached in late adolescence in the 1930 data and after adolescence in the 1950 data. However, at least one study reports finding an adolescent spurt in intellectual growth (Boyne and Clark, 1959), so the problem requires further research.

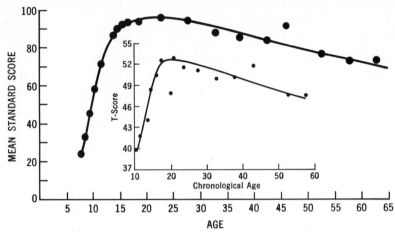

FIG. 6. Curves of General performance over the lifespan. (Insert from Jones, H. E. The growth and decline of intelligence, *Genetic Psychology Monogram*, 13, 1933. The larger curve adapted from Wechsler, D. *The Measurement of Adult Intelligence*, 4th edition. (Baltimore: Williams and Wilkins, 1938, p. 31) by Horrocks, J. E. in *The Psychology of Adolescence*, 2nd edition (Boston: Houghton-Mifflin, 1962, p. 454).

The curves for specific intellectual abilities differ only slightly from these curves of change in general ability, some peaks being reached earlier than others. For example, peak performances on common-sense items, analogies, and numerical completions are reached in the late teens, while the best performances on arithmetic problems and following oral directions are turned in at about age twenty, and vocabulary continues to improve further on into adulthood. This pattern may indicate that certain specific abilities are more closely tied to maturation, while others depend more heavily on continuing education and experience.

There is some evidence that intellectual capacity improves at least in part through maturation rather than solely because of continued training. First, youngsters who reach adolescence early are slightly brighter than those who reach adolescence late (Freeman, 1936). Second, post-menarcheal girls have been found to score higher as a group on intelligence tests than do pre-menarcheal girls of the same age (Stone and Barker, 1937a). Nevertheless, the relationship between physical growth and intellectual development is slight.

Moreover, the stability of intelligence scores is not particularly disturbed by adolescence. Bradway (1944) compared test scores gathered from 138 children, first when they were from two to six years old, and again ten years later. About three-fourths of their scores changed 10 points or less; the correlation between the two sets of scores was .67. Correlations of intelligence scores taken at the onset and at the end of adolescence range in the .70's and .80's (J. E. Anderson, 1940).

Piaget detects an important development in intellectual capacity at adolescence (**Flavell**, 1963). Whereas the preadolescent is limited to concrete thinking, tied to present time and present objects, the adolescent becomes capable of formal thinking, which may include not only the concrete and present but also the possible and future. Formal thinking is thinking with abstractions, and it recognizes structures of relationships between abstractions in the realm of the theoretical and hypothetical. According to Piaget, this basic advance in intellectual development makes possible adolescents' increasing concern with philosophical issues of life and reality, and their ability to plan and dream far into the future. It is also the root of a resurgence of egocentricism which Piaget observes among adolescents, a renewal based on a mature form of an infantile belief in the power of one's thoughts to change reality.

There are no clear sex differences in the level of intelligence or in the rate of intellectual development. However, some cultural differences in sex-roles seem to be reflected in the scores on specific abilities. "In general, girls during the adolescent years appear to excel in the more verbal type of tests, while boys appear to excel in quantitative and scientific content tests" (Horrocks, 1962, p. 467). This pattern differs from the preadolescent years, when girls seem to excel in all mental abilities (Ames and Ilg, 1964; Kagan, 1964).

7

Comparison of Sexual Development

of American and Japanese Adolescents*

Shin'ichi Asayama

In Japan, a survey of the sexual life of Japanese adolescents was started in 1922 by Senji Yamamoto, a biologist, with the cooperation of Tokutaro Yasuda. During the first four years they could get data from only 396 persons, of whom only two were female. But until 1928, they had collected data from 1,000 male volunteers, and part of their results was published in a journal of physiology (Yamamoto, 1924) in 1924; but this study was blocked from further progress by the objection of a medical doctors' group as obscene, nor was such a study supported by the popular feeling prevalent in those days. However, the writer, being deeply impressed by their research chose a career as a biologist. He tried to study the sexual life of Manchurian people when he was a professor of Hsinking Medical College but

could not complete his study because of the outbreak of the World War II. Soon after the end of the War and his return home, he made a survey of 1,482 Japanese adolescents in 1948 and published the "Sexual behavior of the Japanese students" (Asayama, 1949) in 1949, based on the data of 693 college males and 293 college females. Then he extended his survey to the younger generation and could get data on 4,888 males and 1,270 females, out of which the cases of 698 male and 936 female students of high school age were studied; and the findings were published in the writer's recent book, *Records of Sex* (1957b).

The survey was conducted with a questionnaire method instead of Kinsey's interview method. The questionnaire consists of 210 questions ranging over nineteen different problems. The writer believes by his experience that in Japan the questionnaire

* From *Psychologia*, 1957, **1**, 129–131.

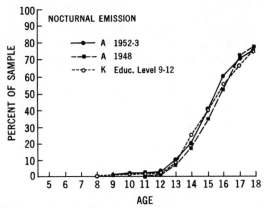

FIG. 7–A. Accumulative incidence: nocturnal emission, comparing Asayama's data (A) of high school students with Kinsey's data (K) of educational level 9–12.

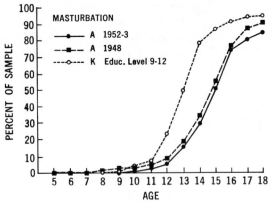

FIG. 7–D. Accumulative incidence: masturbation, comparing Asayama's data (A) with Kinsey's (K).

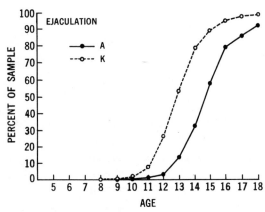

FIG. 7–B. Accumulative incidence: ejaculation, comparing Asayama's data (A) with Kinsey's (K).

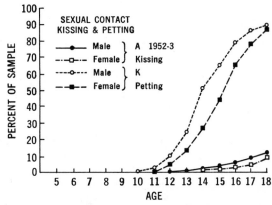

FIG. 7–E. Accumulative incidence: sexual contact, comparing Asayama's data (A) of kissing experience with Kinsey's data (K) of petting experience of educational level 9–12.

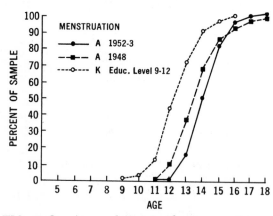

FIG. 7–C. Accumulative incidence: menstruation, comparing Asayama's data (A) with Kinsey's (K).

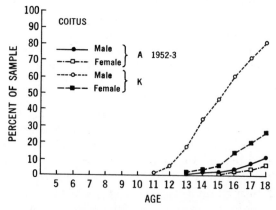

FIG. 7–F. Accumulative incidence: coitus, comparing Asayama's data (A) of high school students with Kinsey's data (K) of educational level 9–12.

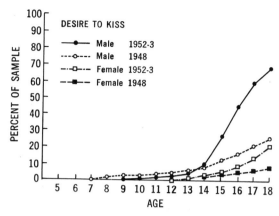

FIG. 7–G. Accumulative incidence: desire to kiss, comparing female and male in Asayama's data of 1948 and 1952–3.

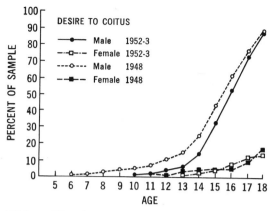

FIG. 7–H. Accumulative incidence: desire to coitus, comparing female and male in Asayama's data of 1945 and 1952–3.

method is better fitted for the study to those intimate aspects of personal life than the interview method.

The following is the comparison of Asayama's results with Kinsey's in six items, and the comparison between Japanese adolescents in 1948 and those in 1952–3.

These items were arranged according to the order of size of difference between the American and the Japanese data. We can see the coincidence of the growth curve in nocturnal emission, which belongs to the half conscious, half physiological process, but some difference in ejaculation, menstruation and masturbation, and lastly striking difference in kissing and petting, which is highly determined by social and cultural backgrounds. A similar striking difference is also found in the curve of sexual intercourse.

Fig. 8 shows little difference in the desire of sexual intercourse in Japanese students in 1948 and 1952–3, while in the desire to kiss, as to be seen in Figure 7, considerable difference is found between the curves of 1948 and 1952–3. The desire to kiss was much stimulated during these years, when many

American soldiers were still in Japan, and young people had contact with their behavior and at the same time with American films, and even with Japanese films which has been influenced by American films.

As shown in Figs. 7 and 8, there is a remarkable difference in the development of such sexual desires as kissing and sexual intercourse between the male and the female, that is, distinct retardation of growth in the female. Comparing the data of both sexes obtained in a previous study (Asayama, 1949, pp. 330–336), the writer pointed out that in the female the aforesaid desires develop after 21–22 years of age while in the male these desires reach their apex at the age of 18. A similar difference of the two sexes was ascertained by Kinsey *et al.* in their second study (1953), so that the difference seems to be ubiquitous regardless of racial differences. However, it should not simply be decided whether the factors which cause such a difference are intrinsic or extrinsic; the difference seems to the writer to have an essential significance yet to be investigated in future.

8

Aspects of Personality and Intelligence

in Post Menarcheal and Premenarcheal

Girls of the Same Chronological Ages[*]

C. P. Stone
R. G. Barker

When the organs of reproduction are nearing functional maturity there appear, in many animals, new types of behavior, the *oestrus*, with which are manifested changes in interests and in attitudes toward the material and social aspects of their external environments. Naturally, both in lay and in scientific circles the query has often been voiced as to whether in man, also, there are analogous changes which are closely correlated with the appearance of the somatic evidences of sexual maturity.

Bearing on this question are certain data showing that changes in the attitudes and interests of groups of girls actually do appear during the years when sexual maturity is being achieved. However, little is known as to individual differences in attitudes and interests within these same groups, or as to their relations to other variables, such as premenarcheal or post menarcheal status, age at the menarche, time since the menarche, or measures of physique and intelligence.

In the present paper we shall present a preliminary study on certain aspects of personality and intelligence in post and in premenarcheal girls. A paper recently published (Stone and Barker, 1937b) dealt with relationships between menarcheal age and measurements of physique in these same individuals and in others similarly selected.

Subjects

The subjects studied consisted of 770 girls varying in ages from 132 to 182 months. These girls were attending the junior high schools of San Jose, California, and the elementary and secondary schools of Redwood City, California. In the former place, all

* From *Journal of Comparative Psychology*, 1937, **23**, 439–455.

girls attending two junior high schools were studied, and in the latter place all girls in the school system between the ages of 11 and 15–3 years were studied. Five hundred seventy subjects were secured from San Jose and two hundred from Redwood City.

There was undoubtedly some selection of the subjects from San Jose for factors associated with school success, in as much as a few relatively accelerated students had passed to the senior high school and a few relatively retarded students were still in the elementary schools. Because of this, all crucial comparisons between post menarcheal and premenarcheal girls have been made within carefully restricted age groups, with the result that accelerated premenarcheal girls have been compared with accelerated post menarcheal girls and vice versa. The unavoidable selection of a part of the total group would undoubtedly operate to reduce the amount of the premenarcheal–post menarcheal differences. Hence, the present data, at best, could only establish the existence of differences. It could not determine their full amount.

All girls were American born and of middle class, North European stock. Selection was exercised to eliminate Negroes, Orientals, Hebrews, Philipinos, Mexicans, and South Europeans. The preponderant proportion of the subjects were drawn from families of tradesmen, office workers, and skilled artisans. Further details concerning economic status will be given below in connection with the discussion of the matched premenarcheal-post menarcheal groups.

Tests Administered

Intelligence level was determined by means of the Otis intelligence tests (Otis, 1922). For those under 12½ years the Intermediate Test, Form A, was used, and for those over this age the Higher Examination,

Form A, was used. The 20-minute limit was adopted. Scores for the Intermediate Test were translated into equivalent scores of the Higher Examination. All of the children were familiar with group intelligence tests, but none of them had taken the Otis tests.

The Pressey Interest-Attitude Tests (Pressey and Pressey, 1933) and the Sullivan Scale for Measuring Developmental Age in Girls (C. Sullivan, 1934) were given to all subjects. These tests can readily be administered to girls of the ages herein studied and are practically self-administering after suitable preliminary instructions are given. Our procedures incorporated the directions given by the authors of these tests; in addition, they stressed the importance of reacting to every item of each test truthfully and, as it applied to each girl personally. It was stated with emphasis that no one who knew the subjects would see the papers, and that the information would be used by people who had no connection whatever with their respective classes or schools. The examiner and monitors explained the meaning of difficult words, but carefully avoided prejudicing the subjects in their answers.

The Bernreuter Personality Inventory (Bernreuter, 1931) was administered to the girls over 12½ years of age in the Redwood City schools and to the girls in one of the junior high schools of San Jose. Preliminary tests with this inventory suggested that it was quite unsuited to still younger children because of difficulties with the terminology and concepts involved. Even with children between 12½ and 15 years it was necessary to explain the meaning of many words and phrases. As this had to be done in a manner that would insure uniformity from group to group a set of explanatory phrases and synonyms was compiled by the examiner and the present authors, on the basis of experience with preliminary tests given to children of the ages herein considered. In the preliminary verbal directions, the children were instructed to ask for aid if they did not understand a word or phrase and, on request, the agreed-upon synonyms or explanatory phrases were given by the monitors or examiners. While so doing, the latter avoided prejudicing the answer of the pupil by giving additional unauthorized explanations or examples. In many instances a lack of experiential background seemed to be the cause of difficulty; for that, no aid could be offered by the examiners.

All of the foregoing tests were administered in class rooms by a single experienced woman tester. The Otis test, being the only one with a fixed time limit, was always given first. With a few exceptions,

this was followed in the same class period by the Pressey test. The Bernreuter and the Sullivan tests were given in a second class period on the same or the following day. Sufficient seating space was allowed in the test room to safeguard the privacy of answers, and monitors studiously avoided creating an impression of eavesdropping or being interested in the answers of the subjects. Near the end of the period each group was reminded to "check back" to discover items or pages that had been overlooked. Also they were asked to attempt to answer all items temporarily skipped for any reason whatever. Finally, the examiner hurriedly checked over the test blanks as they were handed in to detect gross omissions or unnoticed pages. When such were found she tactfully encouraged the pupil to complete the task before leaving the room.

Age of Menarche

When the anthropometric measures were taken the examiner ascertained whether or not the menarche had been reached and, if so, the age at the time of first mensis. The pupil was asked to fix this occurrence as definitely as possible in relation to some well-dated event in her life so that the chronological age at the onset of the menses might be established with a minimum of error. In certain cases the mother was asked to cooperate in fixing the date. No attempt was made to deal systematically with errors in dating that might arise from irregularity of the menses at the outset.

For the purposes of this study we used the data on menarcheal age only for dividing the girls into two groups: those who reported that the menarche had been reached, and those who reported that it had not been reached. We believe that in this way we have roughly divided the subjects into those who are relatively more advanced and those who are relatively less advanced with respect to the age of sexual maturity, even though relations of the menarche to other aspects of the total process may still be somewhat obscure.

Analysis of the Data

Preliminary study of Bernreuter Personality Inventory data

All of the test data from 60 post menarcheal and 60 premenarcheal girls (matched for age and social status) were subjected to a preliminary analysis before administering the tests to all of the subjects.

These results gave no indication that post menarcheal and premenarcheal girls responded differently to the items of the Bernreuter Personality Inventory. Whether this result was due to the inadequacy of the test at these ages, or to a true absence of differences in the functions which the test measures, we are not able to say. But from purely practical considerations, in as much as our primary aim was to find post menarcheal-premenarcheal differences, if such occur, it seemed advisable to discard this inventory and to proceed with the other tests that, from preliminary analyses, did seem promising.

The Otis, Pressey, and Sullivan data

For our final study we were able to select 175 post menarcheal and 175 premenarcheal girls with equivalent chronological ages from the toal group of 770 cases. This was done by pairing post menarcheal and premenarcheal girls whose ages differed by not more than one month. The mean age of both the post menarcheal and premenarcheal groups was 159.7 months, the standard deviation of the distributions of ages was 9.1 months and the range of the ages was between 141 and 182 months. The two groups are drawn from families which are very similar in social-economic status.

Otis test data. The data respecting mean Otis intelligence scores are given in table 1. The mean score of the post menarcheal group is slightly the greater; the difference is 2.47 times its standard error. This difference is not decisive, but it is very suggestive in view of the fact mentioned above, that selection operated in such a way that superior young subjects and retarded old subjects were obtained in both premenarcheal and post menarcheal groups, thus tending to equate them at the extreme ages. It seems not improbable that in groups of post menarcheal and premenarcheal girls completely unselected for intelligence the differences might be greater.

Pressey interest attitude test data. The 360 items of the Pressey test concern interests, fears, qualities that are admired in people, and ideas of right and wrong. In this test there is no provision, such as the "?," for uncertain responses. It was standardized by weighting for maturity of interests and attitudes those responses with increasing frequencies of occurrence at each succeeding age from 8 to 22 years, and

by weighting for immaturity those responses with a decreasing frequency. A small score indicates maturity of interest or attitude; a large score, immaturity.

The results for the total scores are shown in table 7. From these data we find that the post menarcheal

TABLE 6. DATA FROM THE DISTRIBUTIONS OF THE OTIS SCORES OF POST MENARCHEAL AND PREMENARCHEAL GIRLS OF EQUIVALENT CHRONOLOGICAL AGES

	Post Menarcheal	Premenarcheal
Number	175	175
Mean	31.80	29.55
Standard deviation	8.70	8.35
Standard error, mean	0.66	0.63
Difference in means	2.25	
Difference		
σ difference	2.47	

TABLE 7. DATA FROM THE DISTRIBUTIONS OF PRESSEY SCORES OF POST MENARCHEAL AND PREMENARCHEAL GIRLS OF EQUIVALENT CHRONOLOGICAL AGES

	Post Menarcheal	Premenarcheal
Number	175	175
Mean	65.75	81.50
Standard deviation	43.75	50.92
Standard error, mean	3.30	3.85
Difference in means	15.75	
Difference		
σ difference	3.1	

girls give the mature responses more frequently than the premenarcheal girls; the difference of 15.75 points is 3.1 times its standard error. The regression of Pressey scores upon chronological age in months does not differ significantly from 1.0 for either the post menarcheal or the premenarcheal groups. Therefore it appears that the average difference between the scores of these two groups of girls of the same age is approximately equal to the average difference in the scores of either post menarcheal or premenarcheal girls differing by approximately 15 months in chronological age.

When chronological age of the post menarcheal and premenarcheal groups is not equated the maturity score of the post menarcheal girls is 58.5 and that of the premenarcheal girls is 90.5; the difference is 8.9 times its standard error. This enhanced differentiation is due primarily to the fact that the mean age of the unselected post menarcheal girls is 10.7

months greater than that of the unselected pre-menarcheal group.

The correlation between Pressey and Otis scores, with chronological age constant is −.347, and the

TABLE 8. ITEMS OF THE PRESSEY TEST WHICH DIFFER-ENTIATE BETWEEN POST MENARCHEAL AND PREMENARCHEAL GIRLS

(The plus (+) before the critical ratio means that the post menarcheal girls give the nature response in greater proportion than the premenarcheal girls, and vice versa. Only responses with a critical ratio of 1.5 or over are reported.)

Item Number	Item	Critical Ratio	Post Menarcheal Response
Test I. Things that some people think are wrong			
4	Talking back	−2.1	Wrong
15	Smoking	+1.5	Not wrong
17	Anger	+2.5	Not wrong
18	Spending money	+1.5	Not wrong
22	Peddling	+1.7	Not wrong
26	Going to dances	+1.8	Not wrong
28	Joking	+1.6	Not wrong
41	Fussiness	+3.1	Not wrong
45	Pawning jewelry	+1.5	Not wrong
64	Playing cards	+2.1	Not wrong
65	Divorce	+2.4	Not wrong
67	Fear	+1.6	Not wrong
72	Playing hookey	+3.0	Not wrong
77	Quarreling	+1.8	Not wrong
85	War	−1.7	Wrong
86	Grumbling	+1.7	Not wrong
Test II. Things people often worry about or feel fearful or anxious about			
3	Collision	+2.1	Do not worry
5	Murder	+1.5	Do not worry
8	Poison	+1.5	Do not worry
12	Smothering	+1.6	Do not worry
15	Choking	+1.6	Do not worry
20	Appearance	+1.6	Worry
29	Rackets	+2.0	Do not worry
32	Fire	+2.3	Do not worry
35	Suffocating	+1.8	Do not worry
38	Tuberculosis	−2.1	Worry
39	Movies	+1.6	Do not worry
43	Death	+1.9	Do not worry
48	Burglars	+2.3	Do not worry
49	Wickedness	+2.4	Do not worry
51	Gun	+1.9	Do not worry
57	Floods	+2.4	Do not worry
62	Danger	+1.8	Do not worry
75	Feebleness	+1.6	Do not worry
76	Flames	+3.7	Do not worry
78	Thieves	+1.5	Do not worry
79	Smoking	+2.3	Do not worry
81	Dying	+2.5	Do not worry
83	Cyclones	+3.9	Do not worry
85	Robbers	+1.5	Do not worry
90	Work	+2.3	Worry

Item Number	Item	Critical Ratio	Post Menarcheal Response
Test III. Things that people often like or are interested in			
12	Clothes	+1.6	Like
13	Business men	+1.9	Like
17	College	+1.5	Like
18	Magazines	+1.8	Like
23	Joy riding	−1.8	Like
32	Dancing	+2.0	Like
39	University	+3.0	Like
41	Chewing gum	+1.5	Do not like
43	Sailors	−1.8	Like
54	Baseball player	−2.2	Like
67	Social affairs	+2.6	Like
69	Cards	−2.1	Do not like
73	Picture puzzles	+1.5	Do not like
81	Sunday School	+1.7	Do not like
82	Candy	+3.1	Do not like
83	Swinging	+1.5	Do not like
88	Shooting	−2.1	Like

Item Number	Item	Critical Ratio	Post Menarcheal Response
Test IV. Words that describe the kind of person you like			
2	Courageous	+1.6	Like
9	Efficient	+2.3	Like
29	Dependable	+1.9	Like
30	Distinguished	+2.3	Like
34	Able	+2.1	Do not like
39	Loving	+1.5	Do not like
49	Well-informed	+2.7	Like
54	Innocent	+2.3	Do not like
55	Good-looking	−1.5	Like
62	Economical	+2.4	Like
70	Convincing	+2.0	Like

regression of Pressey scores upon Otis scores is −1.92. It is apparent that the difference of 2.25 points in Otis scores can account for but 4.3 of the 15.75 points difference between post menarcheal and pre-menarcheal girls in Pressey test scores.

In order to identify the items which differentiate the two groups most satisfactorily we have made an item analysis of the same type as that used in connection with the Bernreuter data. The items with critical ratios of 1.5 or more are given in table 3.

Sullivan test for developmental age. The Sullivan test was standardized in a manner roughly similar to the Pressey test. There are 200 items presented in six sub-tests which deal respectively with play interests, vocational interests, reading interests, things one desires to possess, things one desires to see, and things one desires to think about. In this case a large score indicates maturity of interest.

In table 9 the data concerning total scores are presented. These results indicate that the post

TABLE 9. DATA FROM THE DISTRIBUTIONS OF SULLIVAN
SCORES OF POST MENARCHEAL AND PREMENARCHEAL
GIRLS OF EQUIVALENT CHRONOLOGICAL AGES

	Post Menarcheal	Premenarcheal
Number	175	175
Mean	146.88	135.74
Standard deviation	23.25	24.06
Standard error, mean	1.76	1.82
Difference in means Difference	11.14	
σ difference	4.4	

menarcheal girls give mature responses with greater
frequency than do the premenarcheal girls; the
difference of 11.14 points is 4.4 times its standard
error. The regression of Sullivan scores upon chronological age does not differ significantly from 1.0 with
either group, hence the difference between their
mean scores is approximately equal to the difference
between the mean scores of either post menarcheal
or premenarcheal girls differing by approximately 11
months in chronological age. When chronological
age is not equated the mean score of the post
menarcheal girls is 150.0 and that of the premenarcheal girls is 132.0; the difference is 10.5 times its

TABLE 10. ITEMS OF THE SULLIVAN TEST WHICH DIF-
FERENTIATE BETWEEN POST MENARCHEAL AND
PREMENARCHEAL GIRLS

(The plus (+) before the critical ratio means that the
post menarcheal girls give the mature response in greater
proportion than the premenarcheal girls, and vice versa. The
(x) designates the post menarcheal response. Only responses
with a critical ratio of 1.5 or over are reported.)

Item	Critical Ratio
Test I. Things to Do.	
Would you rather:	
Go to a ball game, (x) or Wade in the water	+2.4
Play jacks, Drive an auto (x)	+2.5
Make silk underwear, (x) or Play "Red Rover"	+2.5
Wade in the water, or Read the newspaper (x)	+2.8
Cut out pictures, or Ride in an auto (x)	+1.9
Play "Hop Scotch," or Hear the band play (x)	+3.0
Read magazines (x), or Play "Punch and Judy"	+2.5
Go on scooter, or Play golf (x)	+2.7
Do hair dressing (x), or Play circus	+2.0
Cook a meal at camp (x), or Dress paper dolls	+3.2
Play circus, or Go to the opera (x)	+2.9
Read novels (x), or Ride the "Merry-Go-Round"	+1.6
Go to the movies (x), or Visit the zoo	+3.0

Item	Critical Ratio
Test II. Things to be When you Grow up.	
Would you rather be:	
An architect (x), or A cafeteria helper	+2.3
A cook, or An actress (x)	+2.1
A baker, or A judge (x)	+3.5
A candy-store clerk, or A buyer for a store (x)	+2.9
A lawyer (x), or A waitress	+1.8
Test III. Books to Read.	
Would you rather read:	
My Dog, Kiddo, or Monsieur Beaucaire (x)	+3.6
Little Women (x), or Peter Pan	+1.7
Green Lane Mystery (x), or Billy Whiskers	+1.5
Life of Theodore Roosevelt (x), or Alice in Wonderland	+2.2
In the Days of Giants, or Conrad's Sea Stories (x)	+2.3
The Legend of Sleepy Hollow (x), or Little Boy Lost	+1.9
The Monkey Who Would Not Kill, or The Tale of Two Cities (x)	+2.8
The Ginger-Bread Shop, or Daniel Boone (x)	+3.0
The Golden Staircase (x), or Mopsa, the Fairy	+1.9
Lorna Doone (x), or All About Peter Rabbit	+1.9
Twenty-Thousand Leagues Under the Sea (x), or Jack and the Bean Stalk	+3.0
Uncle Tom's Cabin (x), or Three Little Puppies	+1.6
Tom Thumb, or Famous Movie Stars (x)	+1.6
Life of Franklin (x), or Billy Whiskers	+3.1
A Night of Terror (x), or The Tale of Tom Tiddler	+2.5
Test IV. Things to Have.	
Is it more fun to have:	
A cedar chest (x), or Lots of ice cream	+2.2
A box of paints, or A party dress (x)	+2.0
A picture story book, or A new bedroom set (x)	+2.1
A set of doll dishes, or A set of golf clubs (x)	+2.0
A croquet set (x), or A doll party	+2.2
Some party handkerchiefs (x), or Lots of ice cream	+2.3
A doll trunk, or A bridge set (x)	+2.0
Test V. Things to See.	
Would you rather see:	
Pictures of famous women (x), or A puppet show	+2.4
A candy factory, or Soldiers marching (x)	+2.8
Animals in the zoo, or An auto race (x)	+2.0
A fancy dress ball (x), or A baby nursery	+1.5
An autumn scene (x), or A candy shop window	+2.0
A Hindu Prince (x), or A beautiful doll buggy	+2.3
A lot of candy, or A street accident (x)	+1.5
A bakery window, or Boys in uniform (x)	+4.0
A diving exhibition (x), or A class play	+2.1
Test VI. Things to Think About.	
Is it more fun to think about:	
People in far-off countries, or College life (x)	+2.0
Having a palace, or Getting ahead in life (x)	+2.5
Visiting your best friend (x), or Pet animals	+1.9
Finding a lot of money, or Going on the stage (x)	−2.0
Roller skating, or A dancing party (x)	+2.0
Playing circus, or The boys you have met (x)	+2.0
Having a palace, or Being popular (x)	+1.5

standard error. This increased difference is attributable to the fact that the post menarcheal group is 10.7 months older than the premenarcheal.

The correlation between Sullivan scores and Otis scores with chronological age constant is only +.09. It would appear, therefore, that no appreciable portion of the difference between post menarcheal and premenarcheal groups is associated with the small difference in intelligence.

The items which differentiate between the two groups to an extent indicated by a critical ratio of 1.5 are given in table 10. The plus sign means that the more mature score was given by the post menarcheal group. The minus sign denotes the reverse.

Discussion

Taking at their face value the differentiating items from the Pressey and Sullivan tests, we have at least a meager amount of evidence which indicates that significant and characteristic changes in the interests, attitudes, and preferred activities of adolescent girls run *pari passu* with changes in primary and secondary sexual characters, in physical proportions, and in physiological functions associated with the attainment of sexual maturity.

This study is, of course, subject to the well recognized limitation of the technique used; i.e., the discrepancy between the verbal report of behavior and the actual behavior. Although such a discrepancy does not vitiate the value of a study of verbal responses, *per se*, we believe that in the present case there are reasons for thinking that this discrepancy may minimize rather than magnify the true range and magnitude of actual behavior differences. This would be the case, for instance, (a) if there were a tendency to conceal responses revealing new interests, attitudes, and preferences; (b) if new tensions effective in determining behavior were not consciously recognized or were too vague to be explicitly identified; or (c) if there were a paucity of items dealing in unmistakable terms with impulses and ideology undergoing the greatest amount of alteration at the time of puberty.

Of importance in connection with the last factor mentioned is a study of the differentiating items given in tables 8 and 10. Such a study suggests that the following regions of interests and attitudes may

be important: (a) personal appearance, (b) heterosexual interests and activities, (c) avoidance of physical exertion, (d) daydreaming, and (e) home conflicts.

Summary

1. In the main part of this study 175 post menarcheal and 175 premenarcheal girls paired for chronological ages, have been compared with respect to the social-economic status of their families, their abilities upon a group intelligence test, and their responses to three personality tests of the questionnaire variety. The means of the distributions of both post menarcheal and premenarcheal ages were 159.7 months; the standard deviations, 9.1 months; and the ranges from 141 to 182 months.

2. There is no important difference in the social-economic status of the families of the two groups of girls.

3. On the Otis group intelligence test the post menarcheal girls obtained a mean score 2.25 points higher than that of the premenarcheal group; this difference is 2.47 times its standard error.

4. An analysis of responses to the items of the Pressey Interest-Attitude Test showed that the post menarcheal girls gave the mature responses significantly more frequently than the premenarcheal girls of the same chronological age. The difference in the mean scores of the two groups is equivalent to the average difference between the scores of either post menarcheal or premenarcheal girls differing by approximately 15 months in chronological age. This difference is 3.1 times its standard error.

5. Upon the Sullivan Test for Developmental Age, post menarcheal girls gave the mature responses more frequently than premenarcheal girls of equivalent chronological age. The difference in the means scores of the two groups is equal to the average difference between the scores of either post menarcheal or premenarcheal girls who differ by approximately 11 months in chronological age; the difference is 4.4 times its standard error.

6. An analysis of responses to the items of the Bernreuter Personality Inventory made by 60 post menarcheal and 60 premenarcheal girls of equivalent chronological ages revealed no significant differences between the groups.

9

Relationships Between Rate
of Physical Maturing and Personality
Among Boys of Italian Descent*

By Paul Mussen
H. Boutourline-Young

There is clear evidence from a number of systematic studies, as well as from common observation, that physique and rate of physical development may have important effects on personality structure. In one study of early- and late-maturing American adolescent boys, ratings by a staff of trained observers indicated that the latter were considered less physically attractive, less well groomed, and less matter of fact (more unrealistic) than those who were physically accelerated. The late-maturing boys were rated higher in sociability, social initiative (often of an attention-getting, immature sort) and eagerness. According to sociometric tests, their peers also regarded these boys as more attention-seeking, restless, and bossy, but less grown up and less good looking than early-maturing boys (M. C. Jones and Bayley, 1950).

Mussen and Jones (1957) analyzed the TAT responses of 16 boys who were consistently physically accelerated during adolescence and 17 who were consistently retarded in order to assess their underlying motivations, self-conceptions, and attitudes. These data showed that late-maturers were "more likely to have negative self-conceptions, feelings of inadequacy, strong feelings of being rejected and dominated, prolonged dependency needs, and rebellious attitudes toward parents. In contrast, the early maturing boys presented a much more favorable psychological picture during adolescence. Relatively few of them felt inadequate, rejected, dominated, or rebellious toward their families. More of them appeared to be self-confident, independent, and capable of playing an adult role in interpersonal relationships" (Mussen and Jones, 1957, p. 255).

These correlations between rate of physical maturing, on the one hand, and social status, person-

ality structure, and adjustment, on the other, may be attributed, at least in part, to the American cultural emphasis on motives such as competence, achievement, and competition. Consequently, personal characteristics such as "maturity," "independence," and great size and strength are highly valued, especially for males. When the boy attains mature size and strength he is likely to be regarded and treated as a young man, and if he reaches this stage earlier than most of his peers, he will enjoy some of the advantages, privileges, benefits, and rewards associated with the status of manhood before the others do. As a result, this boy is likely to become self-assured, independent, and generally better adjusted socially and emotionally. In contrast, his peers who mature slowly are more likely to lack self-confidence and to feel inadequate, dependent, and rejected.

Rate of physical growth might not have the same kinds of influence on personality structure in cultures with different values—for example, in a culture in which the child's situation is extremely comfortable and secure, where parents attempt to foster and prolong the child's dependency, and where social status has little or no relationship to physique. These have been often-described, traditional characteristics of Italian culture. Most Italian children are protected and secure, showered with warmth and affection. Independence is not such a highly esteemed characteristic as in America, and parents enjoy and encourage their children's dependency on them, doing relatively little to stimulate the development of autonomy and independence (Campisi, 1953; Ianni, 1961). Moreover, in evaluating others, Italians pay much less attention to physical size and strength than do Americans.

For these reasons, there are probably relatively few special advantages associated with early matura-

* From *Vita Humana*, 1964, **7**, 186–200.

tion in Italy, as compared with the United States. Early maturing Italian boys are less likely to be accorded superior social status or to be granted many more rights and privileges than those who mature relatively late. It may therefore be hypothesized that the personality structure and motivations would not be as closely related to rate of maturation among Italian adolescents as among Americans.

Stated in very general terms, the purpose of the present study was to demonstrate that the effects of differential physical growth rates on personality may vary with—and be modified by—the cultural context.

Data from the Harvard-Florence Project, a longitudinal study of adolescents, were used to test this hypothesis. The relationships between rates of physical maturing and aspects of personality and interpersonal attitudes among Italian boys in Florence, Rome, and Palermo and among American boys of Italian descent in Boston were examined. The last group of subjects might provide data of great interest because they are likely to have encountered two partially contradictory sets of values: from their American peers, emphasis on growth, maturity, and independence; and from their parents, Italian attitudes toward becoming mature. The data of the present study may permit us to determine how these two cultural pressures affect the relationship between physical growth rate and personality structure. In addition, comparison of the present findings with those from studies of late- and early-maturing American boys cited earlier may provide further evidence relevant to the basic hypothesis being tested.

Procedure

The subjects of this study, part of the Harvard-Florence Project, were recruited when they were between ten and thirteen years of age and were followed for four years. They came from two separate groups. In one, all the boys (approximately 300) were of the same racial background, their grandparents having come from Southern Italy regions of Sicily, Calabria, Lucania, Puglie, Campania and Abruzzo. They were resident in three urban sites, Palermo (105 boys), Rome (119 boys) and Boston (87 boys). According to objective ratings based on a five-point category system, these groups did not differ from each other in socioeconomic status or in intellectual ability as measured by the Raven Progressive Matrices Test.

The second group consisted of 150 boys chosen at random from approximately 450 boys in Florence who were subjects in the Project. According to objective ratings, the Florence group was comparable to the others in socioeconomic status, but performed better than the other groups on the Progressive Matrices Test.

Each boy was given a complete physical examination by a physician every year throughout his adolescence, beginning in most cases at age 11–12. After each examination, his degree of physical maturity was rated on an objective 6 point scale having carefully defined points. For example, a rating of 1 indicated "no evidence of any sexual maturation;" a rating of 3, the "presence of some pigmented crinkled pubic hair, enlargement of testes (to mean volume of 5 cc) and penis; perhaps some cracking or deepening of voice; marked growth spurt;" a rating of 6, "adult form, adult voice, frequent shaving, testis growth to mean volume of 20 cc; growth in body length coming to a halt." The time interval between one maturity rating and another was approximately one year.

Early- and late-maturing boys were selected in the following way. Distributions of the maturity ratings of each age group (e.g., 12, 13, etc.) were constructed separately for each research site. All boys who *at any time during adolescence* were rated above or below the modal rating for the group, i.e., who were not at the stage of maturity most characteristic of boys their own age in their own community, were considered either accelerated or retarded in development. These were the subjects of the study. The numbers of early-maturers and late-maturers in the four research sites were as follows: 35 and 22 in Florence; 17 and 28 in Rome; 17 and 16 in Palermo —a total of 69 early-maturers and 66 late-maturers in Italy; and 25 early- and 17-late-maturers in Boston.

It should be noted that, in general, early- and late-maturers within each community were of comparable socioeconomic, intelligence (Raven Progressive Matrices Test Scores) and educational levels, and did not differ in chronological age. The only exception occurred in the case of the Boston boys, the Italian-Americans, where the early-maturers were, on the average, somewhat older than the late-maturers (mean ages of 15.2 and 14.4, respectively)—and consequently further advanced in school—at the time of testing and interviews.*

* While this age difference was statistically significant, we do not believe that this can account for group differences in the major dependent variables of this study, since 14–15-year-old average maturers in Boston did *not* differ in any of these variables.

The research instruments used to evaluate personality in the present study were not the same as those of the earlier American studies of the effects of early- and late-maturing, but the studies are comparable in many ways and focused on the same variables. Personality structure and interpersonal attitudes were assessed by means of two instruments: 1. a standardized interview with the subject lasting approximately a half hour to an hour, conducted by a psychologist or a psychologically oriented social worker; and 2. the Imagination Test (essentially McClelland's test of Need Achievement). In the latter, subjects were given 8 verbal stimuli (e.g., a father and son discussing an important problem) and instructed to write a story in response to each of them.

The interviews yielded data on the boy's conscious self-concepts and his social and familial attitudes. The interviewer also made judgments about each subject's personality, rating him on 3-point rating scales on 11 characteristics such as independence, reasoning ability, and responsibility toward the community.

Interview responses were dichotomized in terms of presence or absence of a particular relevant response to an interview question (e.g., answering "more" to the question, "Do you feel more or less loved than most other boys?"). Each subject was judged to be high or low in each of the interview ratings, depending on whether he was above or below the median for all subjects in his community on this rating variable.

The stories elicited by the Imagination Test—which was given in Palermo, Rome, and Boston, but not in Florence—presumably reflected the subject's own underlying attitudes, motivations, and feelings. The test responses were scored for achievement, power, and affiliation motives, according to standard methods (see McClellan, Atkinson *et al.*, 1953; Veroff, 1957; and Shipley and Veroff, 1952).

A number of additional variables were also scored: 6 motives (e.g., aggression, sex affiliation), positive and negative self-concepts, and 3 press variables (domination, fear-worry, and nurturance). The score for each of these variables was simply the number of stories in which the variable was expressed. To avoid any bias, all scoring was done "blind," that is, without the scorer's knowledge of the subject's rate of physical maturing.

Frequency distributions for all Imagination Test scores were constructed for all subjects at each research site and these distributions were dichoto-mized as closely as possible to the median. Subjects scoring above the median were considered high in the variable; those below the median were considered low. Fisher's tests of exact probability (Fisher, 1954) were then applied to ascertain whether high (above the dichotomization point) scores on the Imagination Test and interview ratings, or relevant responses to the interview questions, occurred with greater frequency (i.e., were more characteristic) in one group than in the other.

Results and Discussion

In earlier studies, the major aspects of personality that correlated with rate of maturing among American boys were self-confidence, motivation, and interpersonal attitudes. Since the present findings on Italian boys are to be compared with these, all relevant psychological data from the Harvard-Florence Project were classified (admittedly arbitrarily in some cases) into one of these three areas. The findings are therefore presented in three major sections.

Self-concepts. In the previous study responses to the TAT indicated that American late-maturers are more likely than early-maturers to maintain negative self-concepts, and to feel inadequate, insecure, rejected, and dominated. Judging from their responses to interview questions, however, the comparable groups of Italian boys living in Italy did *not* differ significantly from each other in these respects—at least, not consciously. More specifically, the Italian early- and late-maturers did *not* differ in their answers to questions designed to assess some of these feelings: Do you usually feel calm or upset? Do you feel more or less intelligent than other boys? Do you feel more or less strong than other boys? Do you feel more or less unjustly treated than other boys? Do you feel more or less loved than other boys? (See Table 11.)

The early- and late-maturing Italian-American boys, however, seemed to resemble the Americans of the earlier study. As Table 11 shows, a significantly smaller proportion of late-maturing Italian-American boys regard themselves as strong and more of them reported that they were "unjustly treated by others." (The data from the earlier study of American boys is not in parallel form, and does not appear in Table 11.) In addition, there are some indications (differences significant at approximately $p = 0.10$ level) that relatively few of these boys viewed themselves as highly intelligent or very much loved and they reported having fewer friends. Assuming that these responses reflect feelings of rejection, it may be inferred that these late-maturing boys, having acquired many typically American attitudes toward growth and maturity, reacted as American boys to their retardation in physical development, that is, by feeling that others have little love or respect for them and, in effect, rejected them.

Analyses of the interview ratings that dealt with self-confidence and feelings of independence or dependence (specifically, ratings of degree of independence, capacity to resolve emotional problems, support given at home, responsibility toward the community) yielded some results consistent with these (see Table 11). The groups of early- and late-maturing Italian boys did not differ from each other in any of these ratings. Among the Italian-Americans, however, a significantly greater proportion of early-maturers were rated high in "responsibility toward the community" and there are indications that more of them appear to have better than average capacity to resolve emotional problems and to cooperate with others. Insofar as high ratings in these variables reflect self-confidence, feelings of personal maturity and independence, this is further evidence that Italian-American boys, like other American early-maturers, have more positive attitudes toward themselves than do their late-maturing peers.

While the interviews, and the ratings based on them, reflect the subject's conscious, reportable feelings, the Imagination Test assessed his deeper—perhaps unconscious—motives and self-concepts. Fourteen scores were derived from this test. Table 12 lists most of these variables and the number of subjects in each of the groups with high scores. Wherever possible, the comparable data from the earlier American study (Mussen and Jones, 1957) are included.

Three of the Imagination Test variables were related to self-confidence: positive self-concepts, negative self-concepts, and fear-worry (reflecting the subject's general self-confidence). Only one of these group differences in self-confidence variables approached statistical significance: Italian late-maturers tended to have more underlying negative self-concepts than the early-maturing Italian comparison group. Compared with Italian-American late-maturers, early-maturing Italian-American boys—like other American early-maturers—had more positive self-concepts, fewer negative self-concepts, and fewer fear-worry responses, but none of these differences were statistically significant.

To summarize, there is little evidence that late or early maturing affects Italian boys' self-confidence or feelings of rejection and dependency, as measured here, in the same ways that differential growth rates affect American boys' attitudes toward themselves. American boys of Italian descent seem to react, at least in some ways, as American boys do to acceleration or retardation in physical development, more of the late-maturers feeling unjustly treated and less well loved.

TABLE 11. INTERVIEW RESPONSES AND RATINGS OF EARLY- AND LATE-MATURING ITALIAN AND ITALIAN-AMERICAN BOYS

	Italians		Italian Americans	
Variable	Early-maturers (N = 69)	Late-maturers (N = 66)	Early-maturers (N = 25)	Late-maturers (N = 17)
Self reports				
Stronger	19	14	12	0*
More intelligent	10	9	21	12**
More unjustly treated	5	8	0	4*
More loved	7	9	5	1**
Have more friends	24	23	14	7**
Understood by adults	47	37**	23	14
High ratings in:				
Independence	43	39	12	10
Responsibility toward community	41	35	22	6*
Capacity to resolve emotional problems	35	40	17	9**
Capacity to cooperate with others	20	19	17	8**
Open and affectionate with family	30	24	4	7**

* Difference significant at p = 0.05 or better.
** Difference significant at p = >0.05 − <0.10.

Motivations. The major source of data on basic, underlying motivations was the Imagination Test which is in many ways similar to the TAT, the test used in earlier studies of personality structures of late- and early-maturing American boys. In the earlier studies cited above, analysis of TAT responses indicated that late-maturing American boys, compared with their early-maturing peers, have stronger dependency and autonomy (rebellious) needs and, surprisingly, stronger motivation for heterosexual affiliation.

As Table 12 shows, neither Italian nor Italian-American late-maturing boys differed from early-maturers in their own cultures in dependency motivation, as measured by the Imagination Test. Like the American groups studied, however, a significantly greater proportion of physically retarded than of physically accelerated Italian adolescent boys displayed strong autonomy needs—specifically, motivations to escape from, or defy, their parents. This cross-cultural finding may be interpreted to mean that late-maturing adolescents in both these cultures are regarded, and treated, as immature children. The boys, aware that they are becoming mature—albeit at a slow rate—probably resent these parental attitudes and kinds of treatment and, in their fantasies at least, rebel against their parents. (Incidentally, these stories of escape and defiance were often of a childish sort, probably indicative of emotional immaturity.)

Among the Italian-American subjects, the differ-ence is reversed: strong autonomy needs are manifested by more early- rather than late-maturing boys. This difference may be interpreted in terms of another difference between the two groups that will be discussed in the next section; namely, early-maturers of this cultural background tend to feel more dominated by their parents. Actually their elders, imbued with traditional Italian attitudes, probably do not allow these boys the degree of freedom and independence enjoyed by mature American boys, who undoubtedly serve as the Italian-American boys' reference group. The strong autonomy needs and rebelliousness characteristic of the early-maturing Italian-Americans may therefore be viewed as reactions against what they regard as inordinately strong parental domination. By contrast, the late-maturing Italian-American boys, comparing their situations with those of other late-maturing American boys, who tend to be restricted and treated as children, do not feel unusually strongly dominated, and consequently, they react less rebelliously.

Another difference between the two Italian-American groups, consistent with this last-mentioned difference, involves the motivation for power—to control and manipulate others. In this variable too, early maturers of this cultural background score higher than their late-maturing peers, probably again reflecting this group's resentment of being (in their view) unduly restricted, dominated and controlled by their parents, while other American boys their age are allowed greater independence. Consequently, in

TABLE 12. NUMBER OF EARLY- AND LATE-MATURERS IN AMERICAN, ITALIAN-AMERICAN, AND ITALIAN GROUPS SCORING HIGH IN IMAGINATION TEST VARIABLES

Variable	Americans[1]		Italian-Americans		Italians[2]	
	Early-maturers (N = 16)	Late-maturers (N = 17)	Early-maturers (N = 25)	Late-maturers (N = 17)	Early-maturers (N = 30)	Late-maturers (N = 43)
Negative self-concepts	5	13*	22	16	4	12**
Positive self-concepts	–	–	5	1	4	3
Fear-worry	–	–	9	7	15	19
n Succorance (dependency)	7	12**	15	10	18	24
n Autonomy	3	9*	11	3**	8	24*
n Affiliation (opposite sex)	9	14*	20	7*	11	9**
n Power	–	–	16	5*	14	22
p Dominance	4	8**	20	5*	19	16*
p Nurturance (from parents)	5	8	13	12**	16	16**

[1] American data based on TAT, from Mussen and Jones (1957) study.

[2] Subjects from Palermo and Rome only; the Imagination Test was not given to the subjects in Florence.

– Indicates variable not scored in American study.

* Difference significant at $p = 0.05$ or better.

** Difference significant at $p = <0.05 >0.10$.

their fantasies, they reverse the real situation, controlling others as they feel they have been controlled.

American late-maturers showed stronger motivations for heterosexual affiliation in their TAT (stories involving love, romance, dating, and marriage) than did their early-maturing peers. This finding was explained in terms of their stronger needs for affiliation and greater orientation toward social activity, often of an immature sort. This explanation seems reasonable in the light of other data—based on the research staff's observations of social behavior—that indicated that late-maturers had *less* overt interest in girls and probably fewer successful and rewarding experiences with them.

In contrast, more physically accelerated than late-maturing Italian and Italian-American boys give evidence of strong needs for heterosexual affiliation. Boys who are physically mature are undoubtedly, for many reasons, more responsive—and more attractive—to the opposite sex and probably have more successful relationships with girls than those who are immature. Late- and early-maturers from these two cultures—as opposed to those from middle class American culture—do *not* differ in needs for affiliation and social interaction.

Attitudes toward others. Some interpersonal attitudes and their correlates were inevitably discussed above in the paragraphs on responsibility toward the community, autonomy needs, and sex affiliation. In this section, the focus is on attitude toward "significant others" or, more specifically, parents, friends, and the community at large. This aspect of the study was centered on whether groups of early- and late-maturing boys of Italian background differ from each other in: feelings of being understood, nurtured, or dominated by adults; perceptions of the general milieu as nurturant; affection for, and aggression toward, others. The basic data for this aspect of the investigation were interview responses and ratings by interviewers (see table 11) plus the press nurturance and dominance scores derived from the Imagination Test (see table 12).

Compared with their early-maturing peers, more late-maturing American boys have negative and rebellious attitudes toward their families and more feelings of parental rejection and dominance. The direction of the difference is reversed for the Italian-American groups. According to their Imagination Test stories, more of the late-maturers regarded their parents as highly nurturant and helpful; fewer of them felt dominated or rebellious. It seems likely

that the parents of these boys have incorporated the traditional values of Italian culture, enjoy their sons' dependency on them and encourage it. Perhaps, in effect, they discourage their children's independence and infantilize them by solving their problems for them, making decisions for them, being extremely kind, helpful and supportive, and restricting their activities. Compared with other American parents, these parents would be more likely to prolong the boys' child-like status. The boy who is physically immature may be content with this treatment for he does not expect or demand independence. But the physically accelerated adolescent is more likely to view his parents as restrictive and dominating. He is likely to resist their "babying him," and their preventing him from achieving the independent status to which he feels entitled. Hence, he is more likely to become rebellious.

More of the early- than of the late-maturing Italian subjects also felt dominated by their parents whom they perceived as highly restrictive. Undoubtedly the rapidly maturing Italian boys feel that they are almost adults and should be granted some adult privileges and greater independence. Their parents may share this realization but have conflicts about it, for at the same time they wish to prolong their sons' dependence and childlike status. As a result, they may become sterner disciplinarians with their early-maturing sons who then feel dominated and restricted. In contrast, the late-maturer's parents may see him as a child, expecting little from him and handling him permissively; hence the late-maturers have relatively fewer feelings of being dominated by their parents.

In spite of the fact that Italian early-maturers feel their parents to be dominating and restrictive, they, like American early-maturers, seem to have generally good relationships and close ties with their families and positive attitudes toward them. Evidence for this statement may be found in both their Imagination Test stories and their interviews. As noted earlier, they are *not* rebellious against their parents and in fact, in their Imagination Test stories, portray them as nurturant, helpful, kindly and loving. The early-maturing Italian boy is obviously still closely tied to his family, and his warm feelings about his family may be heightened by the imminence of his adult status and the prospect of leaving the comfort and security of the parents' home.

The close ties of the Italian early-maturers to their families are also demonstrated by their responses to the interview questions. A greater proportion of early- than of late-maturing boys in this group asserted that their parents understand them, answering "yes" to the question, "Are you understood by adults?" Moreover, on the basis of their contacts with the boys, the interviewers rated more of the early-maturing than the late-maturing boys high in "openness and affection with the family."

In brief, the Italian boy who is physically accelerated may indeed feel dominated by his family but, at the same time, he regards his parents as kind and nurturant and he responds to them with warmth and affection. The Italian-American early-maturing boys, like those in Italy, feel dominated by their families but, unlike their peers in Italy, they give little evidence of generally positive feelings toward their parents. It may be hypothesized that Italian-American early-maturers are involved in particularly complicated cultural and intergenerational conflicts. On the one hand, these boys have undoubtedly acquired many of the American values and ideals about striving for independence. On the other, their parents attempt to restrict them. They see that many of their peers, from non-Italian families, are granted considerable independence. The child in this kind of conflictful situation begins to regard his parents as dominating and controlling; he reacts by rebelling.

Conclusions

The data of the present study, considered together with findings of previous studies, support the general hypothesis that the influences of acceleration or retardation in physical maturation on personality structure are conditioned by the culture in which the individual grows up. The cultural variability in these effects are assumed to result from two sets of related factors: the prevailing cultural attitudes and values toward physical size and strength, maturity, and independence; and parental and other adults' reactions to the child's striving for autonomy and independence.

1. The effects of early- and late-maturing on the self-conceptions and self-evaluations are much more marked among American than among Italian boys. American and Italian-American late-maturers are more likely to suffer from feelings of inferiority, inadequacy, and rejection than their early-maturing peers. Relative rate of maturing does not appear

noticeably to affect the personality structures of Italian boys in Italy, perhaps because physical size and strength and hence the characteristics of "maturity" and "independence" are not as highly prized in Italian culture as they are in American.

2. The relationships between rate of physical maturing and attitudes toward family vary in the different cultural groups studied. While among American boys not of Italian descent those who mature slowly feel more dominated by their families and more rebellious toward them, among the Italian-Americans and Italians it is the *early* maturers who feel dominated. In spite of this, Italian early maturers, like American early maturers, have warm, positive, accepting, and affectionate attitudes toward their families and feel accepted by them. In contrast, physically accelerated Italian-American boys view their parents as relatively lacking in nurturant qualities and, consequently, are more defiant and rebellious.

It may be inferred that the Italian-American boy's reactions to accelerated physical maturation are related in the contrasting cultural value systems to which he is exposed. From his American peers, he acquires the values and standards of the general American culture concerning physique, physical size and strength; hence he becomes more self-confident —and feels and acts more mature—because he acquires these characteristics relatively early. On the other hand, his parents encourage his dependency and discourage his autonomy. Compared with early-maturing American boys, his frame of reference, he feels he is subjected to sterner discipline and is more restricted. Hence, he views himself as highly dominated and reacts with rebellion and strong drives to control and manipulate others.

In brief, compared with late maturers, the American early maturer who is not of Italian background tends to be a self-confident, self-assured adolescent who enjoys good relationships with his family. The Italian-American early maturer also feels relatively more mature and adequate but he does not share his American peer's positive familial attitudes. Instead, he tends to see himself as dominated by his parents who are lacking in nurturance and he is rebellious toward them. The early-maturing Italian boy living in Italy is not more likely than his late-maturing peers to feel highly adequate and accepted, but he shares the American early maturer's positive and affectionate attitudes toward his parents, even though he views them as dominating.

Summary

This paper describes a study of the effects of different rates of physical development on the personality structures of Italian and Italian-American boys. It has previously been shown that physically accelerated American adolescent boys tend to be more self-confident and independent—and less rebellious toward parents—than their slow-maturing peers.

Unlike the American boys studied earlier, Italian early-maturing boys do not have more positive self-concepts, but, like the former, feel warm and affectionate toward their parents. The Italian-American early maturers resemble American early maturers in self-confidence, but they are rebellious and view their parents as restrictive, controlling, and lacking nurturance. These negative attitudes may be the result of their exposure to conflicting cultural values: those of the general American milieu and, at home, the parents' traditional Italian mores.

10

Age and Sex Differences in Degree

of Conflict Within Certain Areas

of Psychological Adjustment*

Marvin Powell

Introduction

In the American culture the period of adolescence is generally considered to be a time of many psychological changes in the individual's adjustment pattern. Increasing knowledge of the nature of these changes should be valuable to parents, counselors, and guidance workers in their attempts to understand, guide, and modify the individual adolescent's behavior.

The purpose of this investigation was to examine experimentally a number of hypotheses related to supposed psychological changes in adolescent behavior, and to determine the chronological ages at which the greatest intensity of psychological conflict is manifested in various areas of adjustment. Since it has been demonstrated that pubescence occurs earlier for females than for males, this study also represents an attempt to determine sex differences in the age at which the greatest intensity of psychological conflict in each area of adjustment is manifested.

Word-association tests were chosen for this study as an indirect, but extremely useful, measure of psychological conflict, since previous research has demonstrated that the reaction time in such tests, as well as the type of verbal response to a "conflict" word, will differ from the reaction time and type of verbal response to a "neutral" word. A number of words, each of which was believed to be associated with one of the various areas of psychological adjustment, were selected for use in this investigation, along with a large number of "neutral" words.

These lists were then administered to a population of an equal number of males and females at yearly age levels from 10 to 17 years of age, and to groups of 21- to 25-year-old and 26- to 30-year-old married adults. In the 10- to 17-year-old groups, only

* From *Psychological Monographs,* 1955, 69 (No. 387).

those individuals with IQ's of 98 or above were chosen for the experimental population. It would have been difficult to test the older groups for intelligence; therefore, only those who had graduated from high school and/or had attended college were chosen, in the expectation that they would be fairly comparable in intelligence to the younger groups.

General Hypotheses for
This Investigation

General Hypotheses Concerning Sex Differences

It was hypothesized that there are age differences in the degree of conflict which individuals experience in certain areas of psychological adjustment. Since it is generally agreed that females reach sex-social maturity at an earlier age than males, it was proposed that conflicts in certain areas of psychological adjustment will appear at an earlier age for females than for males. It was postulated on the basis of findings reported in the available research literature that these earlier conflicts for females will appear in the following adjustment areas: Parent-Child Relationships, Emotional Tendencies, Heterosexual Relations, Physical Appearance, and Social Acceptability.

Since the area of Vocational Outlook appears to be more highly related to societal demands than to sex-social maturity, it was hypothesized that the intensity of conflict in this area would be found to be greater, and appear at an earlier age, in males than in females.

Since Religious interests appear to be more closely related to general intellectual development than to sexual maturity, it was postulated that no sex differences in intensity, and age of onset, of conflict in this area would be found.

General Hypotheses Concerning Age Trends

It was hypothesized that intensity of conflict in psychological adjustment would be at a maximum during the adolescent years, as contrasted with the pre-adolescent or early maturity years in the following areas of psychological adjustment: Parent-Child Relationships, Emotional Tendencies, Heterosexual Relations, Physical Appearance, Religion, and Social Acceptability.

It was postulated that Vocational Outlook would become a conflict area through early maturity.

Since in our society marriage affords an opportunity for the individual to satisfy certain human needs that appear in intense forms during adolescence, it was postulated that married individuals, in early maturity, would experience less intense conflicts in the following areas of psychological adjustment: Parent-Child Relationships, Emotional Tendencies, and Heterosexual Relations.

However, it was hypothesized that married individuals, during early maturity, would experience as great or greater intensity of conflict in the following areas of psychological adjustment: Vocational Outlook, and Social Acceptability to individuals and/or groups.

Major Assumptions Concerning the Word-Association Test

It was assumed that intensity of psychological adjustment is related to reaction time and to type of verbal response to certain word-symbols which stand as surrogates for actual experience in a given area of psychological adjustment.

Specifically it was assumed that (*a*) there will be a longer reaction time to words in the areas in which the individual is experiencing the more intense conflict, and (*b*) the type of verbal response given to a "conflict" word will differ from the type of verbal response to a "neutral" word.

Experimental Procedures

A total of 448 individuals (224 males and 224 females) ranging in age from 10 to 30 years participated in this study. An extensive analysis of this population with respect to age, sex, education, and religion is presented in Powell (1952). The popula-

tions studied in the age range from 10 to 17 years were white children attending elementary school, junior high school, and high school, having IQ scores of 98 and above on either the 1937 Revision of the Stanford-Binet or the California Test of Mental Maturity. A child was placed in the age bracket which was within six months of his nearest birthday. The adult populations were composed of married white subjects who had completed high school and/or were attending college.

Derivation of the Word Lists Employed in This Study

The areas of psychological adjustment examined in this study concerned Parent-Child Relationships, Emotional Tendencies, Heterosexual Relations, Physical Appearance, Religion, Vocational Outlook, and Social Acceptability. Lists of stimulus words having emotional association with each of the above areas were selected. These lists of words were then checked against Rinsland's Word List (1945), and only those words appearing in the first 6,000 for fifth graders were selected for the revised list. This revised list of 250 words was presented to a group of judges (nine graduate students in the field of psychology, five college sophomores, and fifteen high school sophomores, the latter to determine whether these words had similar connotations at the younger age levels). Judges were instructed as follows:

Place one of the following symbols before each word to indicate the area with which it has the highest degree of association in an emotional sense.

P   Parent-child relationships and home life
E   Emotional tendencies
H   Heterosexual relations
PA Physical appearance
R   Religion
V   Vocational outlook
S   Social acceptability

A list of neutral words (N) having no apparent emotional connotations to the experimenter and previous investigators was also judged in this manner. The words finally selected to represent each critical area were those on which there was 87 per cent agreement or greater among all the judges; in the neutral series only those words on which there was 91 per cent agreement or better among the judges were chosen.

In its final form for experimental use each critical list of five words was followed by a neutral list of four words. The neutral series were inserted to act as a partial control for the "generalization" effect which has been noted in previous studies (the emotional tone aroused by the critical stimulus words may extend to the subsequent reaction, thus causing the appearance of "disturbance" where no disturbance really exists).

The critical-word series and the intervening neutral-word series are presented in Table 13, together with the initial word series presented to each subject to determine his average reaction time. The practice series presented in Table 13 was presented to each subject at the beginning of the study to familiarize him with the technique.

To control for any position effect in the experimental situation, seven different "total" lists (con-

TABLE 13. THE VARIOUS WORD SERIES EMPLOYED IN THE PRESENT STUDY

Word Series for Each Area of Conflict

Series A	Series B	Series C	Series D	Series E	Series F	Series G
Parent-Child Relationships	Emotional Tendencies	Hetero-sexual Relations	Physical Appearance	Religion	Vocational Outlook	Social Acceptability
Father	Worry	Dance	Handsome	Church	Wages	Popular
Children	Afraid	Kissing	Shabby	God	Money	Friend
Home	Unhappy	Marriage	Neat	Heaven	Employed	Lonely
Mother	Restless	Dates	Beautiful	Worship	Hire	Party
Parents	Anxious	Hugging	Ugly	Prayer	Job	Unfriendly

Word Series for the Intervening Neutral Groups

Group 1	Group 2	Group 3	Group 4	Group 5	Group 6	Group 7
Sleep	Apple	Second	Lamp	Leaves	Daylight	Cardboard
Carpet	Window	Tree	Elevator	Fender	Photograph	Banana
Hill	Minnow	Bench	Table	Magazine	Bean	Harmonica
Flour	Piano	Sand	Balloon	Sandwich	Monday	Door

Initial Neutral Series	Practice Series
Canary	White
Counter	Cat
Ladder	Man
Lantern	Black
Lighthouse	Girl
Shadow	
Tower	

TABLE 14. POSITION OF EACH CRITICAL SERIES AND OF THE INTERVENING NEUTRAL SERIES ON EACH OF THE SEVEN "TOTAL" LISTS

(Letters represent the critical series; numbers the neutral series)

"Total" List	Critical-Word Groups						
I	A–1	B–2	C–3	D–4	E–5	F–6	G–7
II	B–1	C–2	D–3	E–4	F–5	G–6	A–7
III	C–1	D–2	E–3	F–4	G–5	A–6	B–7
IV	D–1	E–2	F–3	G–4	A–5	B–6	C–7
V	E–1	F–2	G–3	A–4	B–5	C–6	D–7
VI	F–1	G–2	A–3	B–4	C–5	D–6	E–7
VII	G–1	A–2	B–3	C–4	D–5	E–6	F–7

sisting of the seven critical and the seven intervening neutral series) were set up in such a manner that each critical series was presented in a different position and was followed by a different neutral series, as shown in Table 14. Each of these "total" lists (I, II . . . VII) was presented to an equal number of subjects at each age (e.g., at age 11, 3 males and 3 females were tested on "total" list I, 3 males and 3 females were tested on "total" list II, etc.).

Apparatus

The subject was seated facing a large board in which there was a small door at eye level. When this door was opened by the experimenter, the stimulus word was exposed to the subject and an electric chronometer was started simultaneously. The experimenter stopped the chronometer by depressing a switch when the subject made a verbal response to the stimulus word. The apparatus is diagrammed in Powell (1952).

Procedure

Each subject was chosen from a group of volunteers of white children in the school classrooms in a large metropolitan area. Subjects were assured that the results of the experiment would have no effect on scholastic records. The experimental room was a small, well-lighted classroom containing a table or desk and two chairs, and the experimental apparatus.

The subject was seated facing the small door, and the experimenter was seated at the left of the subject. Neither the timer nor the experimenter's control key was visible to the subject. The following instructions were given:

> I am going to give you a list of words one at a time. When I open this door (experimenter points to door) you will see a word. As soon as you see the word I want you to say the first word that comes to your mind. I will say "Ready" just before I open the door.

A short list of practice words was given before the test began and any misunderstandings in the instructions were corrected during this period.

Type of Data Obtained

1. The individual's average reaction time to the "neutral" series of words.
2. The individual's reaction time to "conflict" words in each adjustment area.
3. The verbal response of the individual to each word.

Several tests were made on the accuracy of the electric chronometer and of slight changes in the experimenter's speed in manipulating the key which stopped the electric chronometer. For these purposes the experimenter was able to secure a rather specialized electronic timer used to test accuracy of chronometers. This special electric chronometer was synchronized with the timer employed in this study before each day's testing began, and was again checked for synchronization at various times during experimental progress. By the use of this mechanism it was possible to determine the speed with which the experimenter manipulated the switch to stop the chronometer when the subject responded. This test was also made at regular intervals during each of the two-hour periods of testing on a number of different occasions. It was found that the experimenter's reaction speed varied within the range of 28 to 37 milliseconds, with little or no fatigue effect apparent as a two-hour session drew to a close. Since this is an extremely narrow range, this time was treated as a constant error common to all the reaction times derived in this study.

Methodological Considerations for Analyzing Obtained Data

It seemed best to use each subject as his own control, and to derive a *difference score* for each critical area. This was arrived at for each individual by calculating (*a*) his mean reaction time to the neutral words, (*b*) his mean reaction time to the critical words in each area of adjustment, and (*c*) the *difference* between these two (*a* being subtracted from *b*); the latter is termed the subject's *difference score* in the giving area, which is used in the statistical analyses in this study.

The above-mentioned difference scores were computed for each sex at each of the various age levels. It was hypothesized that there would be a slower reaction time to "critical" words in the various areas of psychological adjustment as the degree of conflict in these areas increased. In order to determine whether the increase in reaction time was greater than could be accounted for by sampling errors from a population of such difference scores, the Fisher-Behrens *d* test (Fisher, 1939; Behrens, 1929) was employed.

Qualitative Word Analysis

For the qualitative categorization of the words given by the subjects in response to the stimulus words an attempt was first made to determine the reliability of the categorization. Five judges were presented with a list which consisted of each stimulus word followed by five sample responses to that word, and were given the following directions:

> Place the letter of the category in which you would place each word (in relation to its stimulus word) in the blank to the left of the word.

There was 93 per cent agreement among the five judges and the experimenter as to the proper categorization.

In the final analysis, these responses were classified into two categories; *normal* (equivalent plus logical) and *disturbed* (personal, perseverative, irrelevant, and no response). Any finer discrimination seemed too uncertain. The percentage of response in each of these two over-all categories was determined for each sex at each of the age levels studied.

Results

Age and Sex Differences in Average Reaction Time to Neutral Words

Before any attempt to test for differences within and between the sexes on the various areas of psychological adjustment was made, it was decided first to determine what differences, if any, existed between the sexes in terms of average reaction time per

se, that is, to "neutral" words. In general, it can be stated on the basis of the results that there are no statistically significant differences within or between the sexes during the adolescent and young adult age ranges, i.e., from age 12 to age 30 (Powell, 1952).

Age and Sex Differences in the Psychological Adjustment Area of Parent-Child Relationships

It can be seen from Table 15 that there is a fairly steady increase in difference scores, indicative of conflict, to the "critical" stimulus words pertaining to the psychological adjustment area of Parent-Child Relationships for both sexes, starting at age 12 and reaching a maximum between 15 and 17 years.

The data presented in Table 17 demonstrate that there is a statistically significant increase in differ-

TABLE 15. MEANS AND STANDARD DEVIATIONS OF THE DIFFERENCE SCORES IN THE VARIOUS AREAS OF PSYCHOLOGICAL ADJUSTMENT

Age in Years	Measure	Parent-Child Relationships		Emotional Tendencies		Hetero-sexual Relations		Physical Appearance		Religion		Vocational Outlook		Social Acceptability	
		M	F	M	F	M	F	M	F	M	F	M	F	M	F
10	Mean	.072	.029	.169	.138	.144	.156	.107	.080	.245	.201	.113	.152	.128	.167
	SD	.088	.115	.129	.105	.104	.118	.094	.110	.185	.193	.107	.113	.109	.120
11	Mean	.050	.041	.142	.105	.163	.137	.086	.075	.241	.137	.108	.074	.184	.113
	SD	.069	.054	.106	.062	.114	.083	.077	.058	.201	.074	.085	.049	.098	.070
12	Mean	.050	.082	.130	.193	.130	.281	.083	.128	.186	.283	.074	.067	.104	.198
	SD	.099	.086	.117	.106	.094	.187	.077	.064	.129	.296	.061	.053	.073	.104
13	Mean	.115	.206	.189	.564	.206	.707	.096	.335	.395	.599	.095	.135	.254	.678
	SD	.084	.140	.113	.294	.123	.403	.092	.181	.335	.288	.147	.112	.235	.434
14	Mean	.415	.365	.986	1.133	.776	1.176	.392	.477	.859	1.030	.392	.532	.790	1.623
	SD	.735	.456	.626	.693	.622	.829	.339	.574	.888	.665	.335	.471	.674	.998
15	Mean	.508	.458	.914	1.043	1.290	1.234	.525	.552	.860	1.082	.836	.569	1.605	1.478
	SD	.542	.474	.786	.814	1.008	1.021	.467	.642	.941	1.396	.894	.727	1.177	.968
16	Mean	.521	.452	1.033	1.080	1.051	1.570	.740	.882	.744	.970	.610	.629	.950	1.721
	SD	.599	.586	.732	1.026	.831	1.337	.722	.860	.433	.599	.948	.512	.703	.924
17	Mean	.498	.482	.936	1.280	.714	1.061	.555	.710	.791	.805	.699	.601	.893	1.727
	SD	.642	.651	.759	.867	.685	.635	.681	.623	.927	.484	.545	.504	.597	1.253
21–25	Mean	.131	.116	.355	.329	.235	.256	.147	.130	.204	.193	.596	.606	.306	.273
	SD	.087	.099	.116	.070	.080	.058	.085	.056	.073	.092	.305	.272	.119	.093
26–30	Mean	.134	.106	.344	.329	.230	.261	.146	.117	.192	.194	.651	.579	.321	.303
	SD	.091	.105	.098	.113	.083	.069	.081	.052	.081	.081	.221	.211	.105	.057

ence scores to the "critical" stimulus words between the ages of 12 and 13 for both sexes. It is, therefore, concluded that the psychological adjustment area of Parent-Child Relationships becomes a source of conflict[1] for both sexes between the ages of 12 and 13 years, although it would appear to be a source of greater conflict for females, since the difference for females seems to be somewhat more significant than the difference for males. It is suggested that further investigation may demonstrate that this arises as an area of conflict for females approximately one year earlier than for males.

It is further concluded, on the basis of the data presented in Table 17, that the psychological adjustment area of Parent-Child Relationships becomes a statistically significantly lesser source of conflict for both sexes in the two populations of young adults. The data presented in Table 17 indicate a statistically significant decrease in difference scores to the "critical" words in this area between the ages of 17 and 21–25 for both sexes. There is no significant difference between the 21- to 25- and the 26- to 30-year-old groups for either sex.

The data presented in Table 16 may serve to substantiate further the conclusion that this area is a source of greater conflict for females than for males at age 13. It can be noted that the only statistically significant difference between the two sexes at any of the ages studied occurs at age 13, and that this difference is in the direction of greater conflict for females.

[1] The word "conflict" will be used to mean conflict as indicated by an increase in difference scores.

Age and Sex Differences in the Psychological Adjustment Area of Emotional Tendencies

It can be noted from Table 15 that there is a steady increase in difference scores to "critical" words related to the psychological adjustment area of Emotional Tendencies. This increase reaches a peak for both sexes at 14 years of age, although there seems to be another slight increase for females at about age 17 and somewhat of a decrease for males at this same age. From the data presented in Table 5 it can be seen that there are statistically significant increases in different scores between the ages of 11 and 12, 12 and 13, and 13 and 14, for the females, while the statistically significant increase in difference scores for males occurs between the ages of 13 and 14.

These data support our hypothesis that the psychological adjustment area of Emotional Tendencies becomes a source of conflict at an earlier age for females than for males. Such conflict first begins to appear between 11 and 12 years of age for females, and between 13 and 14 years of age for males, with approximately a two-year differential between the sexes.

There is a statistically significant difference between the 17-year-old and the 21- to 25-year-old groups of both sexes, demonstrating a decrease in difference scores for the older group, but no significant difference between the two adult populations. These data tend to substantiate our postulate that the psychological area of Emotional Tendencies is no longer a source of such great conflict during the years of early maturity for either sex.

TABLE 16. *d* TEST OF STATISTICAL SIGNIFICANCE OF DIFFERENCES IN THE DIFFERENCE SCORES BETWEEN MALES AND FEMALES AT VARIOUS AGE LEVELS TO WORDS DRAWN FROM THE VARIOUS PSYCHOLOGICAL ADJUSTMENT AREAS
(Values of Fisher-Behrens *d*)

Adjustment Area	Age in Years									
	10	11	12	13	14	15	16	17	21–25	26–30
Parent-Child Relationships	1.34	.54	1.10	2.95*	.26	.36	.37	.09	.40	.98
Emotional Tendencies	.84	1.54	1.79	6.20*	.79	.59	.17	1.56	.68	.41
Heterosexual Relations	.34	.99	3.20*	6.18*	1.71	.20	1.46	1.94	.75	1.03
Physical Appearance	.57	.58	2.01	6.13*	.57	.18	.56	.87	.61	1.07
Religion	.74	2.46*	1.32	2.35*	.69	.69	1.37	.07	.34	.06
Vocational Outlook	1.11	1.79	.39	1.14	1.07	1.20	.08	.69	.01	.85
Social Acceptability	1.07	3.04*	3.31*	4.50*	3.30*	.44	2.98*	3.35*	.79	.55

* .05 level of confidence.

TABLE 17. *d* TEST OF STATISTICAL SIGNIFICANCE OF AGE DIFFERENCES IN THE DIFFERENCE SCORES IN
THE VARIOUS AREAS OF PSYCHOLOGICAL ADJUSTMENT, BY SEX
(Values of Fisher-Behrens *d*)

Stimulus Area	Sex	10 vs. 11	11 vs. 12	12 vs. 13	13 vs. 14	14 vs. 15	15 vs. 16	16 vs. 17	17 vs. 21–25	21–25 vs. 26–30	15 vs. 17
Parent-Child	Male	1.05	.00	2.53*	1.83	.47	.08	1.26	2.90*	.09	—
Relationships	Female	.43	1.87	3.75	1.51	.67	.04	.17	2.86*	.25	—
Emotional	Male	.77	.38	1.79	5.52*	.26	.53	.44	3.26*	.26	—
Tendencies	Female	1.27	3.26*	6.08*	3.45*	.41	.13	.70	5.66*	.00	—
Heterosexual	Male	.63	1.13	2.38*	4.32*	2.14	.89	1.47	3.57*	.16	2.46*
Relations	Female	.61	3.20*	4.84*	2.33*	.21	.93	1.59	6.54*	.20	—
Physical	Male	.81	.13	.52	3.79*	1.13	1.16	.88	3.02*	.03	—
Appearance	Female	.19	2.93*	5.45*	1.07	.42	1.44	.17	4.79*	.62	—
Religion	Male	.07	1.15	2.86*	2.20*	.04	.56	.23	3.28*	.40	—
	Female	1.42	2.15*	3.67*	2.78*	.17	.37	1.01	6.24*	.03	—
Vocational	Male	.21	1.62	.67	3.71*	2.40*	.83	.38	.76	.53	—
Outlook	Female	3.12*	.47	2.83*	3.64*	.21	.31	.18	.04	.28	—
Social	Male	1.81	3.20*	3.12*	3.41*	2.99*	2.37*	.29	4.89*	.34	2.80*
Acceptability	Female	1.80	3.15*	5.52*	3.97*	.47	.87	.02	6.01*	1.06	—
	M = 0	1	4	6	2	1	0	6	0	2	
	F = 1	5	7	5	0	0	0	6	0	0	

* .05 level of confidence.

The differences between males and females at various age levels in difference scores to "critical" words having reference to the psychological adjustment are of Emotional Tendencies are presented in Table 16. It can be observed that the greatest difference between the sexes occurs at age 13, with the difference indicating a significantly greater increase in difference scores for females than for males. These data further substantiate the conclusion that there is a greater intensity of conflict for females at an earlier age than for males in this area of psychological adjustment. It appears that by age 14 both sexes show the same degree of conflict, as evidenced by the fact that there are no longer any significant differences between males and females at any of the succeeding age levels beyond age 13.

Age and Sex Differences in the Psychological Adjustment Area of Heterosexual Relations

The rather sharp increase in difference scores to "critical" words related to the psychological adjustment area of Heterosexual Relations can be observed from Table 15. There is a steady increase in difference scores for both sexes reaching a maximum at 15 years of age for males, with a steady decrease from 15 to 17; and reaching a maximum at 16 years of age for females with a decrease from 16 to 17, with a still

greater decrease in difference scores apparent in the young adult populations. As indicated in Table 17 there are statistically significant differences in the increase in difference scores for females between the ages of 11 and 12, 12 and 13, and 13 and 14, and statistically significant differences for males between the ages of 12 and 13, and 13 and 14. There is also a statistically significant decrease in difference scores between the 15-year-old males and the 17-year-old males, with no difference between the 21- to 25-year-olds and the 26- to 30-year-olds of either sex.

These data support the hypothesis of earlier conflict for females than for males, demonstrating a difference in onset of conflict to this area of adjustment of about one year. For males the conflict is most apparent during the adolescent period from 12 to 17 years of age, reaching a maximum peak at 15 and declining significantly between 15 and 17. For the female population, conflict is most apparent from 11 to 17 years of age, reaching a maximum at 16 and declining from 16 to 17, although less abruptly than for the males. There seems to be relatively little conflict manifested by either of the sexes in the two adult populations.

In the comparison between the sexes at various age levels presented in Table 16 it can be noted that there are statistically significant differences between males and females in difference scores to "critical" words regarding the psychological adjustment area of Heterosexual Relations at age 12 and at age 13. At both of these age levels the females show significantly greater difference scores, indicating a greater degree of disturbance than is manifested by the males at these ages. There are no other significant differences between the sexes in degree of conflict shown in response to "critical" words in this area of adjustment, although the difference between males and females at age 17 does approach statistical significance, indicating a somewhat greater decrease in difference scores for males at that age than for females.

Age and Sex Differences in the Psychological Adjustment Area of Physical Appearance

The fairly steady increase in difference scores to "critical" words concerned with the psychological adjustment area of Physical Appearance during the age range from 12 to 16 years of age for females and 13 to 16 years of age for males can be noted from Table 15. These data seem to indicate that conflict arises approximately one year earlier for females than for males. For both sexes the peak occurs at age 16, with a slight decrease in difference scores from 16 to 17, and a statistically significant decrease in difference scores between 17 and 21–25 years of age (see Table 16). From the data presented in Table 5 it can be seen that there are statistically significant increases in difference scores between 11 and 12, and between 12 and 13 for the females, and between 13 and 14 for the males. This would seem to support the hypothesis that conflict appears earlier for females than for males in this area of psychological adjustment. The statistically significant decrease in difference scores between the 17-year-old and 21- to 25-year-old groups suggests that the psychological adjustment area of Physical Appearance is no longer a source of so much conflict for the two populations of young adults.

From the data presented in Table 16 it can be seen that the only statistically significant difference between males and females is difference scores to "critical" words regarding the psychological adjustment area of Physical Appearance occurs at the 13-year level. This, too, would demonstrate greater conflict for females at 13 years of age than for males. There seems to be some possibility that this greater degree of conflict for females than for males is present at age 12, since the tests of statistical significance closely approximate the .05 level of confi-

dence. By age 14, however, there is no longer a significant difference between the sexes in difference scores.

Age and Sex Differences in the Psychological Adjustment Area of Religion

The data presented in Table 15 demonstrate the relatively steady increase in difference scores for both sexes to "critical" words concerned with the psychological adjustment area of Religion. It appears that onset of the increase in difference scores occurs about one year earlier for the females than for the males; however, the males reach a maximum about one year earlier than the females. It can be seen from Table 15 that there is a statistically significant increase in difference scores for females between 11 and 12, a somewhat greater increase between 12 and 13, and still another increase between 13 and 14, while for the males the increase begins between 12 and 13, and is greatest between 13 and 14.

These findings are not in accord with the postulate that there would be no differences in the age of onset of conflict in this area. Here, as in the areas of psychological adjustment previously discussed, there is a one-year difference in age of onset of conflict in the direction of the female group. The statistically significant decrease in difference scores between the 17-year-old and 21- to 25-year-old groups of both sexes leads to the conclusion that little conflict is exhibited by the two young adult populations in this area of adjustment.

The data presented in Table 16 demonstrate a statistically significant difference between males and females at age 13 in difference scores to "critical" words pertaining to the psychological adjustment area of Religion. This is a further indication of the existence of a greater degree of conflict being manifested by females than by males at age 13.

Age and Sex Differences in the Psychological Adjustment Area of Vocational Outlook

From the data presented in Table 15 it can be seen that there is a steady increase in difference scores to "critical" words concerned with the psychological adjustment area of Vocational Outlook for both sexes throughout the adolescent period. It can be further noted that this increase in difference scores continues through the years of early maturity.

The data presented in Table 17 indicate significant increases in difference scores for females between the ages of 12 and 13, and between 13 and 14;

for males, between 13 and 14, and between 14 and 15.

These results are contrary to the hypothesis that onset of conflict in this area of psychological adjustment would occur earlier for males than for females. Here there was instead approximately a one-year differential between the sexes, favoring earlier onset of conflict for females.

These results do, however, substantiate the postulate that Vocational Outlook would continue as a conflict area through early maturity, since there is no significant decrease in difference scores of either sex between the 17-year olds and the 21- to 30-year olds.

It can be noted in Table 16 that no significant differences are found between the sexes at any age level in difference scores to "critical" words regarding the psychological adjustment area of Vocational Outlook. These results are also contrary to hypothesis, since it was postulated that intensity of conflict in this area would be greater for males than for females. This failure to predict may have been due to the possibility than certain of the "critical" words used in this area (e.g., money) may have had some unpleasant connotation unrelated to Vocational Outlook.

Age and Sex Differences in the Psychological Adjustment Area of Social Acceptability

The data presented in Table 15 demonstrate the sharp increase in difference scores to "critical" words concerning the psychological adjustment area of Social Acceptability from age 11 to age 14 for females, and from age 12 to age 15 for males, indicating

approximately a one-year difference in age of onset of conflict in this area. As indicated in Table 17 there are statistically significant increases for females in difference scores between the ages of 11 and 12, 12 and 13, and 13 and 14, whereas for males the statistically significant increases in difference scores occur between the ages of 12 and 13, 13 and 14, and 14 and 15.

The increased difference scores for females remain at about the same level from ages 14 to 17, with a statistically significant decrease in difference scores occuring between ages 17 and 21–25. For the male population, however, the increase in difference scores appears to reach a maximum at age 15, at which time a statistically significant decrease in difference scores between ages 15 and 16 occurs. There is a further statistically significant decrease in difference scores for males between the ages of 17 and 21–25. No significant difference appears to be present between the two young adult populations of either sex.

It can be seen in Table 16 that there are a number of statistically significant differences in difference scores between males and females at a number of the age levels considered in this study. From age 12 to age 14 females show statistically significant greater increases in difference scores to "critical" words in this area than do the males. At the 15-year age level no significant differences occur between the sexes, but at ages 16 and 17 the males are demonstrating statistically significant differences from the females in the direction of decreased difference scores. There are no significant differences between the sexes at the two young adult age levels.

TABLE 18. PERCENTAGES OF "DISTURBED" RESPONSES OF MALES AND FEMALES AT EACH AGE LEVEL TO "CRITICAL" WORDS IN THE VARIOUS AREAS OF PSYCHOLOGICAL ADJUSTMENT
(The "Disturbed" Response Percentages are the Sum of the Percentages of the Responses Categorized as "Personal," "Perseverative," "Irrelevant," and "No Response.")

Age	Parent-Child Relationships		Emotional Tendencies		Heterosexual Relations		Physical Appearance		Religion		Vocational Outlook		Social Acceptability	
	Male	Female	Male	Female	Male	Female	Male	Female	Male	Female	Male	Female	Male	Female
10	14%	11%	9%	10%	12%	15%	6%	8%	10%	9%	13%	10%	11%	10%
11	5	5	2	12	6	16	2	6	4	9	3	4	4	7
12	5	3	1	0	4	2	0	0	2	0	1	1	3	1
13	3	3	2	4	2	3	1	1	0	1	0	0	2	4
14	9	11	8	17	12	15	6	10	3	2	13	8	10	14
15	8	10	6	12	19	19	1	6	5	7	5	8	7	14
16	12	14	4	13	14	14	8	7	4	3	6	6	9	12
17	13	10	10	4	13	11	6	6	4	4	4	4	9	10
21–25	3	0	7	4	9	7	0	3	3	4	10	16	11	10
26–30	3	3	3	6	6	7	0	0	0	3	17	17	14	9

Results of the Qualitative Word Analyses

The percentages of "disturbed" responses of males and females at each age level to "critical" words in the various areas of psychological adjustment are presented in Table 18. Although certain trends may be apparent, the results of the qualitative analysis do not substantiate the hypotheses as do the results of the reaction time study presented earlier in this section. Since these percentages may have occurred purely by chance, no conclusions can be drawn from these data.

Summary

The purpose of this study was to investigate a number of the psychological changes in behavior which appear to take place during the period of adolescence; to determine the chronological ages at which the greatest intensity of psychological conflicts is manifested in the various areas of adjustment; and to determine the age differences between the sexes, and sex differences within a given age, where psychological conflict to these areas of adjustment is manifested.

The word-association test was chosen for this study as an indirect measure of psychological conflict, and a number of words, each of which was believed to be associated with one of the various areas of psychological adjustment, were selected for use in this study, along with a number of "neutral" words.

These lists were then administered to 448 subjects (224 males and 224 females ranging in age from 10 to 30 years old) in a large metropolitan area. In the 10- to 17-year-old group, only those with IQ's of 98 or above were chosen for the experimental population. The 21- to 30-year-old groups were composed of married individuals who had graduated from high school.

After the word-association test was administered to an individual, there were calculated (*a*) his mean reaction time to the neutral words, (*b*) his mean reaction time to the critical words in each area of adjustment, and (*c*) the difference between these two (*a* being subtracted from *b*). The latter is termed the subject's difference score in the given area. These difference scores of each of the psychological adjustment areas were computed for each sex at each of the age levels studied. The *d* test of statistical significance was used to determine the presence of any significant differences between or within sexes in the various areas of psychological adjustment.

A qualitative analysis of the individual's verbal responses to the stimulus words was also made. These responses were placed into one of six categories (Equivalent, Logical, Personal, Perseverative, Irrelevant, and No Response). These percentages of responses for the categories were then combined into "Disturbed" (Personal plus Perseverative plus Irrelevant plus No Response) and "Nondisturbed" (Equivalent plus Logical) categories.

In general, the results from the qualitative analysis did not yield statistically reliable differences related to the hypotheses of the present paper. On the other hand, the results from the reaction-time study in terms of difference scores indicate that conflicts appear at an earlier age for females than for males in the psychological adjustment areas of Parent-Child Relationships, Emotional Tendencies, Heterosexual Relations, Physical Appearance, and Social Acceptability. Although contrary to hypotheses, conflict also appears earlier for females than for males in the psychological adjustment areas of Religion and Vocational Outlook.

The results from the difference scores also demonstrate that intensity of conflict in psychological adjustment is at a maximum during the adolescent years, as opposed to the pre-adolescent or early maturity years, in the following areas of psychological adjustment: Parent-Child Relationships, Emotional Tendencies, Heterosexual Relations, Physical Appearance, Religion, and Social Acceptability. The psychological adjustment area of Vocational Outlook as a conflict area reaches a maximum during late adolescence and continues as an area of conflict through early maturity.

In general, it appears that married individuals experience much less conflict in the psychological adjustment areas of Parent-Child Relationships, Emotional Tendencies, Heterosexual Relations, Physical Appearance, and Religion. Somewhat greater conflict seems to be exhibited in the psychological adjustment area of Social Acceptability.

Further research in all of the areas of adjustment investigated is needed. Perhaps a study similar in design to the present one, but making use of different words to represent the various "conflict" areas would add to the results presented here. For example, it is possible that the results concerning the psychological adjustment area of Vocational Outlook which were contrary to hypothesis may have been due to the fact that certain of the words used to represent this area (e.g., money) may have had connotations unrelated to Vocational Outlook.

Although the use of reaction time without any measures of motor disturbance was justified in the present study, perhaps other valuable information might be gained by the additional use of certain other indices, such as the Luria technique, which also are measures of emotional disturbance.

In general, these findings seem to reinforce those of previous investigators who have concluded that stress is present during adolescence. It is hoped that the findings of this study may be of some use to those concerned with the guidance of adolescents (parents, teachers, counselors, etc.) in furthering their understanding of the areas of psychological adjustment investigated in the present study.

References

BEHRENS, W. U. Ein Beitrag zur Fehlerberechnung bei wenigen Beobachtungen. *Landw. Jb.*, 1929, 86, 807–837.

FISHER, R. A. The comparison of samples with possibly unequal variances. *Ann. Eugen., London*, 1939, 9, 174–180.

JOHNSON, P. O. *Statistical methods in research.* New York: Prentice-Hall, 1949.

POWELL, M. Age differences in degree of conflict within certain areas of psychological adjustment. Unpublished doctor's dissertation, Syracuse Univer., 1952.

RINSLAND, H. D. A *basic vocabulary of elementary school children.* New York: Macmillan, 1945.

SUKHATME, P. V. On Fisher and Behren's test of significance for the difference in means of two normal samples. *Sankhyā*, 1938, 4, 39–48.

11

*Confirmation of the Freudian Psychosexual Stages Utilizing Sexual Symbolism**

Paul Cameron

Interest in Freud's (1950) hypotheses that ". . . all elongated objects, sticks, tree trunks, umbrellas . . . represent the male member—small boxes, chests, cupboards and ovens correspond to the female organ" (p. 242), coupled with the contention of psychoanalysts (e.g., Fenichel, 1945; Thouless, 1947) that individuals tend to prefer shapes representative of the sexual organs of the opposite sex has recently provided the impetus for a number of investigations. One line of inquiry has attempted to establish the existence of the sexual referent in shape perception. Among adults the validity of the sexual

referent in perception seems fairly well established (A. Jones, 1956; Starer, 1955; Stennett and Thurlow, 1958; Winter and Prescott, 1957; Lessler, 1964), while L. H. Levy (1954) and Acord (1962) have found no evidence of a sexual referent in the shape perception of children. On a different tack, McElroy (1954) and Jahoda (1956) have exploited the assumed opposite-sex-shape preference to test the sexuality of pre-adolescents and adolescents.

The present study was undertaken to test the following psychoanalytic notions simultaneously: H_1: Children under the age of four, being in the oral and anal stages, will evidence little or no preference for shapes representative of either sex; children aged

* From *Psychological Reports*, 1967, **21**, 33–39.

four to six (in the phallic stage) will prefer shapes representative of the opposite sex; children aged seven to 11 or 12 will be attracted to shapes representative of the same sex; and children over the age of 12 (genital stage) will prefer shapes representative of the opposite sex (derived from Freud, 1943). H_2: As the U.S. is a male-oriented culture (McKee and Sheriffs, 1957) opposite-sex attraction will be evidenced by a greater preference by females for masculine shapes after the latency period. Further, assuming that children in the phallic stage are largely incapable of discerning ascendency of the male sex in our culture, their choice of shapes should be made according to opposite-sex-shape preference without interaction with the cultural norm of male-preference.

Method

The 12 pairs of sex-related shapes described by McElroy (1954) were reproduced on one side of a 8½-× 11-in. sheet of paper. The letters "A" or "B" were not printed under each figure as in the McElroy (1954) and Jahoda (1956) studies to avoid grade connotation or symbol-letter interaction. Considerable care was exercised in preparing the drawings to assure symmetry and good form of each figure.

Ss were 2,336 children approximately evenly distributed between the ages of three and 17 from western Wisconsin. Most of the Ss aged five or younger

were obtained via an area sample of Menomonie and its environs. The area was divided into approximately equal sections and a random-like process determined the area that each of the 42 interviewers would sample. Individual Ss were typically contacted in the yard or in the home of randomly-selected residences. Ss were given a sheet of the sex-related shapes and asked to choose the shape in each pair that they preferred or liked the best with the cover story that we were studying design preferences among children. Where possible, S drew a circle around or otherwise indicated his preferred shape for each pair, if the child was unable to mark his choice the interviewer marked it for him. Additional Ss were contacted in nursery schools. Most Ss aged six or older were sampled in class in one of three school systems. The cover story introduced the request for each pupil to indicate on his sheet of shapes the member of each pair S preferred; Ss were instructed to work alone and not to compare choices. For S above the second grade age was self-reported; most of the younger Ss' ages were reported by a teacher or parent.

Results

Hypothesis 1, that the psychosexual stages would evidence themselves in the shape preferences of children, was confirmed. Table 19 presents the sexual attraction indexed by sexual symbolism for each age for the 12 McElroy and six Jahoda items which significantly differentiated beyond the .10 level. Al-

TABLE 19. DIRECTION OF SEXUAL ATTRACTION FOR EACH AGE AS INDEXED BY SEXUAL SYMBOLISM

Age	n	12 pairs of McElroy symbols		6 pairs of Jahoda's significant symbols	
		x^2	Dir.†	x^2	Dir.
3	83	.03	S	.06	O
4	72	16.4‡	O	7.5**	O
5	227	2.63*	O	2.01	O
6	225	8.6**	O	2.23*	O
7	140	1.90	S	4.35	S
8	133	.40	S	4.19**	S
9	169	.51	O	.07	O
10	154	1.10	S	.02	S
11	135	2.03	S	12.09‡	S
12	259	.10	S	.09	S
13	246	10.3‡	O	.01	O
14	171	.37	O	1.14	O
15	104	.31	O	3.49**	O
16	122	15.6‡	O	8.37**	O
17	107	.56	O	3.95**	O

‡ $p < .01$. ** $p < .05$. * $p < .10$.
† Dir. = direction toward opposite (O) or Same (S) sex preference.

TABLE 20. BOYS' AND GIRLS' CHOICES OF M OR F SYMBOLS FOR THE STAGES OF PSYCHOSEXUAL DEVELOPMENT

McElroy Item No.	Phallic Ages 4–6; n = 514					Latency Ages 7–12; n = 965					Genital Ages 13–17; n = 761				
	Boys' choices		Girls' choices		χ^2	Boys' choices		Girls' choices		χ^2	Boys' choices		Girls' choices		χ^2
	M	F	M	F		M	F	M	F		M	F	M	F	
1	102	132	177	103	23.19	353	122	366	124	.01	221	132	266	142	.53
2	118	126	139	131	1.28	277	223	314	192	28.45	204	149	241	167	.10
3	118	125	147	133	.80	277	223	276	214	.08	186	167	249	157	2.15
4	116	128	153	127	6.38	332	158	268	222	7.58*	215	138	239	169	.40*
5	122	121	142	137	.03	302	181	331	159	2.75	318	135	285	123	.01*
6	117	116	157	123	1.98	318	182	276	214	5.45*	194	159	242	166	1.46
7	128	116	113	167	7.66*	302	197	251	239	8.64*	196	157	215	192	.53*
8	130	113	163	117	.58	302	198	266	223	2.79*	190	163	239	169	1.72
9	105	138	158	122	9.86	382	118	342	148	5.64*	242	111	316	92	8.07
10	108	135	157	120	8.16	324	176	351	139	5.45	232	121	303	105	6.84
11	104	138	127	190	2.28	143	359	126	363	.88*	76	276	89	313	.02
12	123	121	157	114	2.97	356	144	363	127	1.02	228	125	288	119	50.09
Σ	1391	1509	1790	1584	16.41†	3668	2281	3530	2364	21.05*†	2502	1833	2972	1916	8.75†

* χ^2 are in a direction opposite to that found in McElroy's (1954) study, i.e., indicate same sex preference.

† $.01 > p > .001$.

though the values of χ^2 are typically small, they are generally in a direction consonant with the prediction. Table 20 groups the data by psychosexual stages with clear confirmation of the hypothesis.

Hypothesis 2, that as the U.S. is a male-oriented culture opposite-sex attraction would evidence itself by a greater preference by females for shapes representative of the male sex after the latency period, while in the phallic stage both females and males would prefer shapes representative of the opposite sex, was confirmed. McElroy and Jahoda reported essentially equal numbers of each sex, while we had unequal numbers of boys and girls. We controlled for these unequal numbers by multiplying the total male-shape and female-shape choices of each sex by that percentage of the total sample the opposite sex represented. Thus the total number of male-representative shapes chosen by our genital stage sample was 2723 [e.g., 2502 (.53) + 2972 (.47)] and by the female-representative was 1871 [e.g., 1833 (.53) + 1916 (.47)]. We would have expected if no cultural sex-preference bias existed; an equal number of male- and female-representative shape choices (e.g., 2297); the resulting χ^2 of 156.6 ($p < .001$) clearly indicates a male preference. McElroy's Scottish data for children from nine to 16 yr. of age yields a χ^2 of 94.6 ($p < .001$), indicating male attraction. Jahoda's data for children aged 11 to 19 were obtained in Accra, Ghana, a female-oriented culture

(Murdock, 1959), e.g., the Ashanti (Murdock, Tuden, & Hammond, 1962) and Agni (Busia, 1963a and 1963b), which are among the largest subcultures of the region and utilize matrilineal descent of property and social rights. When the expectation of no sex-preference is compared with Jahoda's data, a χ^2 of 124.2 ($p < .001$), indicating *female* preference, is found.

Our phallic-stage children's male- and female-shape preferences were multiplied by the percentage of the sample represented by the opposite sex. Their male choices were 1573 [e.g., 1391 (.54) + 1790 (.46)] and female choices were 1543 [e.g., 1509 (.54) + 1584 (.46)], yielding a χ^2 of .29 (NS) which suggests equal attraction to the opposite sex.

Items 5 and 7 do not separate males from females in the phallic and/or genital stages for our sample and were among Jahoda's 3 most weakly discriminating items. But these were among McElroy's 7 most differentiating items, leading one to suspect that each item contains age- and culturally-linked attractants as well as the sexual referent [see Lessler (1964) for an elaboration of this notion].

Discussion

When one considers the rather small differences between the over-all anatomy of males and females one must be struck with the audacity of psychoanalysts in magnifying this difference into one of the major factors in our artistic (Grotz, 1930) and aesthetic (Thouless, 1947) tastes. That adults might be influenced by opposite-sex-organ appeal has not been too strenuously questioned, but that "innocent children" should be so influenced has brought many a scornful smile to the faces of laymen and has encountered no little opposition among psychologists (e.g., L. H. Levy, 1954; Acord, 1962). Three previous studies utilizing children reported mixed results regarding application of Freudian symbolism to children. Levy (1954) had fifth graders (i.e., 10 to 11 yr. old) match female and male names to sex-related shapes. Finding no correspondence between the shapes and the gender of names chosen, he concluded that he had found evidence weighing against the Freudian hypotheses. Acord (1962) had his Ss (third, sixth, and ninth graders) create generic names for symbolic designs and also observed no correlation between their matches. Lessler (1964) required fourth and ninth graders to sort symbolic shapes into piles labeled 'masculine' or 'feminine' and found the children did sort according to the Freudian hypothesis. These three studies required their Ss to *sort* according to gender, a regimen somewhat different from the choosing of "preferred" vs "non-preferred," e.g., Jahoda (1956) found that Ss were largely incapable of verbalizing why they preferred one or the other of a pair of designs; attraction is often considerably less consciously rational than sorting seems to demand. It will be noted that Lessler's study, which appears to have required less rational judgment than the other two investigations, yielded results consonant with the Freudian paradigm.

A major problem in designing the hypotheses to be tested was that of tying the Freudian psychosexual stages to age periods. The phallic stage was defined by Freud rather loosely, e.g., ". . . between the ages of three and eight . . ." (1943, p. 286), which could be construed as three to eight yr. of age or from four to seven. N. Cameron (1963) regards the lower limit as three yr. of age, while J. C. Coleman (1956), English and Pearson (1945), R. C.

Johnson and Medinnus (1965), and O'Connor and Franks (1961) regard the lower limit as four. We adopted four as representing the majority and more mature psychoanalytic opinion. The upper limit of the phallic stage is also difficult to tie down. Freud contended that from ". . . about the sixth or eighth year onward a standstill or retrogression is observed in the sexual development called a *latency period*" (1943, p. 286). R. C. Johnson and Medinnus (1965) regard latency as starting at about the age of six, N. Cameron (1963) at about the age of five, English and Pearson (1945) at the age of seven. We decided to define the beginning of latency at the midpoint of Freud's estimate (i.e., at seven yr. of age) and that left us with six as the upper limit of the phallic stage. The upper age limit of the latency period is defined as 11 or 12 by N. Cameron (1963), at 10 by English and Pearson (1945), at 11 by E. Jones (1955), until "just before adolescence" by R. C. Johnson and Medinnus (1965). We included the 12-yr.-olds in the latency period analysis for statistical convenience; however, their absence would have in no way affected the results. Thirteen was judged the clear onset of adolescence and the genital stage. We must admit to a good deal of "luck" that the data fell so neatly into our expectations. Obviously, if the data had shown the predicted pattern but at different ages, e.g., as the phallic stage being evidence as between three and five yr. of age, the essential validity of this aspect of Freudian formulation would not have been harmed thereby.

We further confess to almost complete surprise at the results. The author has not regarded himself as a Freudian and, before these results, had considered the psychosexual stages hypotheses with distrust. Our results could not have fit the Freudian paradigm better if they had been manufactured (although the strength of the relationship is small considering the large numbers of Ss employed and the relatively modest probabilities associated with the results obtained). The present study sought to "kill" two birds —the validity of Freudian sexual-symbolism and the kind of psychosexual stages in children—but confirms both.

12

Intellectual Growth of Children

as Indicated by Repeated Tests*

Frank N. Freeman

There are many problems concerning the intellectual growth of children on which marked differences of opinion exist, but on which the evidence is either scanty or conflicting. Almost any conclusion that might be drawn concerning intellectual growth is a matter of dispute. For example, there are many differences concerning the general character of the intellectual growth curve. At least three definite views have been expressed on the general form of this curve: According to the traditional view, mental growth is most rapid in early life and decreases progressively until maturity is reached. In other words, the growth curve is negatively accelerated from start to finish. According to a second view, held with some variation by Thurstone and Courtis, the rate of mental growth increases in the early years, is fairly constant for a period of years during childhood, and then diminishes during adolescence until the limit is reached at intellectual maturity. In other words, the growth curve is compound, being positively accelerated at the beginning and negatively accelerated at the end, with an inflection point somewhere between. A third view is that the rate of mental growth is fairly constant during childhood and diminishes in adolescence.

Similar divergencies of opinion exist concerning the terminus of mental growth or the age at which mental maturity is reached. Estimates vary from 13½ years to 20 years and beyond.

Differences of opinion are also to be found concerning the variations in intellectual development among different persons. The difference between the two sexes, the differences in rate and terminus of growth of bright and dull children, the relation between precocity of physiological development and intellectual growth, and the comparative variability at successive ages are all matters on which there are doubt and diversity of views.

The traditional and most widely used method of studying intellectual growth is the mass or cross-section method. By this method the characteristics of growth are inferred from a comparison of the attainments of different individuals at different ages. The most common method is to test a large number at each age, find the averages, plot these graphically, and then construct a curve by connecting the points representing the successive averages. This method has serious limitations. One is the possibility and indeed high probability that the sampling at successive ages is not comparable. The result is that the averages at some ages do not represent the total population in the same fashion as do those at other ages. Another difficulty is that the growth curve of individuals cannot safely be inferred from an average or mass curve. Individual differences may very well be concealed in the average.

A more elaborate method of constructing the growth curve for mass data is the absolute scaling method used by Thurstone. By this method the increments of growth are measured in terms of the standard deviation of successive ages used as a unit. This method is like other mass methods in not making possible the identification of individual growth curves.

The other general method is based upon repeated tests and is commonly called the longitudinal method. By this method individual growth curves may be kept separate and studied separately, or they may be combined. This method, like any method which uses raw scores, has been criticized on the ground that it may be invalidated by the lack of comparability of the units of the various parts of the scale. This difficulty may be met, as in the present investigation, by testing the comparability of the scale units. This was done in the present instance by comparing the distribution of scores of a given age group with a normal distribution. The assumption is made that if the scale units are equal the distribution of scores will coincide approximately with the expected distribution.

The data which are presented in the present

* From *Psychological Monographs*, 1936, **47**, 29–34.

paper were gathered by the longitudinal method. A composite mental test of the general type of intelligence test was applied to several hundred children annually at their birthdays. The test consists of four parts, namely, vocabulary, analogies, completion, and opposites, and is called the VACO test, from the initials of the names of the four parts. The test is given individually. The time allowance is generous, and the individual proceeds as far as he is able on the graduated scale with reasonable time allowance. There are about 280 items on the test, and it requires about an hour to give. Because the test requires reading, it is not given below the eighth year. Our curves run from age eight until later adolescence. Because of the dropping out of cases, the number of individuals from whom longer runs are available is much less than the total number who were tested. For example, there are but 21 with nine-year runs, 75 with eight-year runs, and 149 with seven-year runs. In some cases composite curves are made up of the scores of pupils whose tests do not cover the entire age range of the curve. In other cases only pupils whose tests cover the entire range are included.

Certain results have been selected for this report which bear upon more important problems of intellectual development. The first of these is the general character of the growth curve. Figure 8 is a composite curve representing the gain in scores of all the boys and girls for whom records were obtained from age eight to age 17. Two general facts are evident from this curve. The first is that the rate of increase in ability is relatively constant from 8 to 15 years, with a slight decline in rate at about 12 years of age. From 15 to 17 there is a more rapid falling off, but this may in part be due to the elimination of some of the brighter children at the ages of 16 and 17 by graduation from high school. That this is the case is shown by the fact that the pupils who graduate at these ages make considerably higher average scores than those who graduate later.

Our data do not indicate the form of the growth curve below eight years. It is possible that it is positively accelerated at this period. It is also possible that it is negatively accelerated. From the general direction of the curve, however, I am inclined to believe that it is more nearly straight than either positively or negatively accelerated.

The other main finding which is revealed by this curve is the fact that intellectual growth does not cease before 17 and probably continues well beyond this age. Other evidence on this point is furnished by a few tests that were made of students who were followed into college and given the test two or more years after they had left high school. Figure 9 gives the curves of 26 students who were thus tested at the college level. This curve is, of course, not affected by elimination as is the composite curve. The continued advance up to age 19 is uninterrupted. The rate of this advancement will doubtless surprise even those

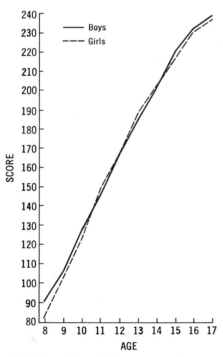

FIG. 8. Composite curves from the mean scores for boys and girls.

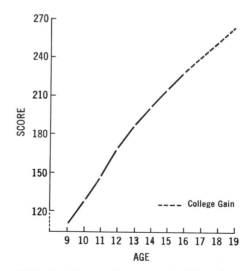

FIG. 9. Composite curves for 26 students tested at the college level.

who have believed that intellectual growth does not end at early adolescence or even at age 16. These data from repeated tests appear to indicate that the advance does not cease even at age 20.

Since the composite curve which was used to indicate the general rate of growth is somewhat affected by the addition or elimination of cases at various ages, the question may be raised whether it is any better than the ordinary curve drawn from mass data. A specimen figure in which the composite curve is compared with the curves which represent a series of continuous runs will throw light on this question. This comparison is made in Figure 10. Each of the shorter curves is based upon a group of pupils for whom five-year runs were obtained. There were no additions or eliminations in these shorter curves. It is evident that the curves representing five-year runs are almost exactly parallel to the composite curve and in several instances are almost identical with it. The curve of the first five-year run, which begins at 8 years of age, is somewhat above the other curves and shows a somewhat more rapid advance. The run beginning at age 8 evidently represents somewhat brighter pupils than the runs beginning at later ages, due to the fact that the brighter pupils at this age are in the third grade where the first tests were made. The somewhat more rapid advance from years 10 to 12 of this group will be confirmed in a later figure.

As has been remarked, one of the advantages of the longitudinal method is that it makes possible the determination of the growth of individuals. This enables us to study individual differences in growth

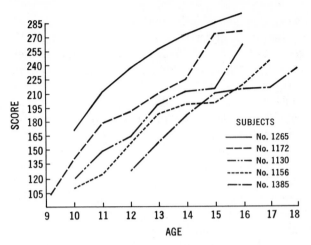

FIG. 11. Some selected individual growth curves which suggest a negatively accelerated development of intellectual abilities.

and may lay the basis for the prediction of growth. A few individual growth curves will be presented for the purpose of showing the diversity which exists and to lay the foundation for an attempt to draw generalizations concerning the relation between individual differences and the nature of intellectual growth.

In Figure 11 are shown the five growth curves which have been selected because they reveal, through at least part of their course, rather marked negative acceleration. The upper curve shows this acceleration during the first three years. From then on it approaches a straight line. Each of the other curves shows negative acceleration followed by a spurt. This is true of the lowest curve as well as of the higher ones. The later course of these curves is unfortunately missing due to the early graduation of these pupils from high school.

In Figure 12 are shown a number of curves in which there is fairly marked positive acceleration through a course of several years. This positive acceleration comes fairly late in the lowest curve and brings the curve approximately to the level of the others. This is contrary to the usual opinion that children of lesser ability reach the culmination of their mental growth early.

In Figure 13 are shown four curves which are approximately uniform in rate of advancement throughout their course. We have, then, three types of curves, all of which are represented by a number of cases. It is obviously incorrect to infer from the form of an average curve just what the form of the growth curve of each individual is. Considerable diversity exists and must be allowed for in any at-

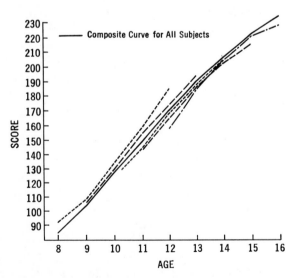

FIG. 10. Five-year runs compared with the composite curve for all subjects.

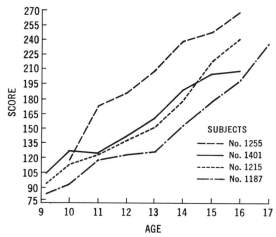

FIG. 12.   Some selected individual growth curves which suggest a positively accelerated development of intellectual abilities during at least a part of the growth period.

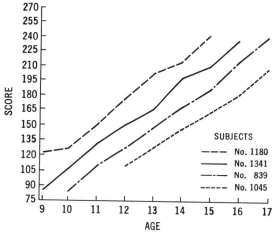

FIG. 13.   Some selected individual growth curves which suggest a relatively uniform rate of development for intellectual abilities.

tempt to interpret or predict the intellectual growth of an individual.

Making due allowance for the divergence of the growth curves of individuals from any general pattern, we may inquire whether there exists factors which bring about a difference in the growth curves of definable groups of children. We should, of course, expect the individuals of various groups to overlap, but a difference in the average growth curves of groups may be an evidence of the existence of general factors.

The first grouping we may consider is that according to sex. It has frequently been held that the mental growth curve of boys differs from that of girls. This assumed difference has sometimes been used as a basis for the interpretation of the inherent or final ability of boys and girls. Our curves, as shown in Figure 8, reveal no significant difference according to sex. The curves cross and recross, but the difference at any one age is so slight as to be negligible. The findings on this point appear to be conclusive, and we have, therefore, combined the curves for boys and girls in classifying them for the purpose of making other comparisons.

The second general factor we may consider is that of ability. We may ask whether or in what respect the growth curves of bright, average, or dull children differ from each other. The prevailing view is that bright children advance more rapidly, and that they continue to advance to a later age. They thus have a double advantage over average or dull children.

In order to compare the growth of different ability groups, 122 children were selected for whom

there were available continuous measurements from ages 11 to 16. These children were divided into three groups, based upon the mean of their scores at ages 12, 13, and 14. The division was made at certain natural breaks in the scores and this gave 35 in the upper group, 43 in the middle group, and 44 in the lower group. The average scores of the high group are all above 207, those of the middle group range from 185 to 206, and those of the lower group are all below 185. The children of these three groups can be described as bright, average, and dull only in relation to each other. The children of the Laboratory Schools have an average I.Q. of about 115. The lower group, therefore, is not actually dull in comparison with children in general, but only in comparison with the children of the Laboratory Schools. Whether a comparison of the children throughout the entire range of ability would agree with our findings is an open question. It is my opinion, however, that something like the same differences would be found if the comparison included only children of normal intelligence.

The mental growth of the three groups is presented in the form of growth curves in Figure 14 and in the form of increments in Figure 15. From Figure 14 it is clear that there is a difference in the rate of growth at different ages in the three groups. The high group exhibits more acceleration in rate, the middle group a lesser acceleration, and the lower group manifests an almost uniform rate of growth. The three curves, therefore, diverge somewhat from year nine to year 13, but from 13 to 16 they are nearly parallel. There is a hint that the upper group may slow down slightly earlier than the other two groups, but the evidence on this point is inadequate since selective elimination may be responsible for the deviation in the upper curve at year 17. In any case, there is no evidence that the lower group is slackening at all in its pace of growth at the highest age, or that its rate of growth is any less than that of the other two groups. This is quite definitely at variance with the customary view and is highly significant for the educational and vocational guidance of this group.

Figure 15 shows the same facts in a little different

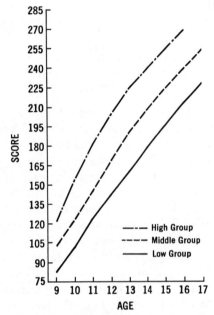

FIG. 14.   Mean scores for 3 groups of pupils with consecutive tests from 11 to 16.

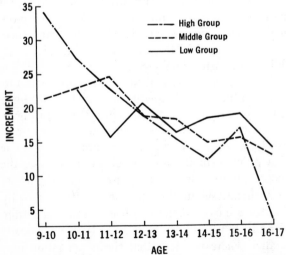

FIG. 15.   Annual increments for 3 groups of pupils with consecutive test scores.

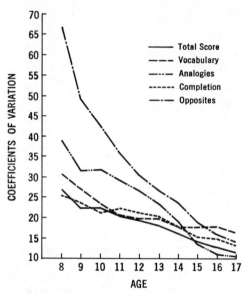

FIG. 16.   Coefficients of variation for the total score and for each test for all subjects.

form. The chief fact is that the upper group exhibits decreasing increments, whereas the lower group shows almost constant increments of growth.

The spread between the abilities of individuals at various ages is indicated in another fashion by measures of variability at succeeding ages. The usual view is that this spread increases regularly and markedly with age. The average curves of the three groups seem to contradict this view. The standard deviation and the coefficient of variation also contradict it. The coefficients of variation for the composite score as well as for the scores of the parts of the test are shown in Figure 16. It is obvious that the relative variability decreases rapidly. Even the standard deviation itself, shown in Figure 17, increases only up to age 12 for boys and age 13 for girls and decreased beyond these ages. The meaning of these facts is that abilities of a given group of individuals do not continue to diverge beyond 12 or 13 years of age.

The last factor to be considered is that of physiological maturing. Following the early work of Dr. Rotch many have maintained that mental growth is markedly affected by the rate and age of physiological maturing. To determine the effect of this factor, mental test scores for groups differing in age of maturing were tabulated. The curves for three groups are shown in Figure 18. It appears that there is a very slight difference between these groups up to age 12. Beyond that age the group maturing in the middle years advances somewhat more rapidly than

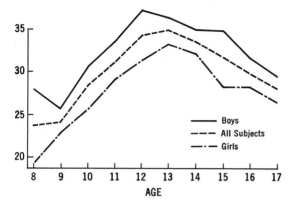

FIG. 17. The variability of the VACA tests for all subjects and for boys and girls separately.

that maturing in the early years. This is contrary to the usual view. The group maturing late develops slightly slower than the other two. These and other similar comparisons seem to indicate that if the rate of physiological maturing affects the rate of mental maturing, the influence is very slight and could hardly be taken into account in predicting the mental growth of individuals. This may explain an apparent contradiction between the fact that girls mature about two years earlier than boys, and the fact that there is no significant difference in the rate of intellectual development between boys and girls.

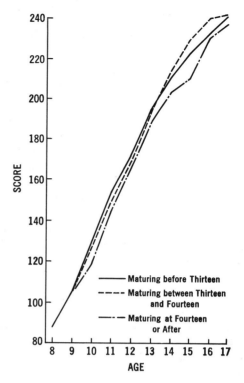

FIG. 18. Mental test scores for all girls with 5 or more consecutive tests divided into 3 groups on the basis of their pubescent development.

Summary

The chief points which are shown by our longitudinal study of mental growth are:

1. The intellectual growth curve diminishes only slightly in rate from eight years to 15 or 16 years of age.
2. Intellectual growth continues at least to 20 years and probably beyond.
3. The growth curves of individuals differ markedly in form. Comparatively few conform closely to to the average
4. The growth curves of boys and girls are practically identical.

5. The growth curves of children of different levels of ability diverge somewhat up to age 12 or 13 due to more rapid acceleration in the growth of brighter children. Beyond this age the growth rates are parallel, and it is even possible that the children of lower ability partially overtake the brighter children in later adolescence. There is, at least, no indication that they reach the terminus of growth earlier.
6. The rate of physiological maturing influences the rate of intellectual maturing slightly, if at all. It is possible that the slight effect of this factor is responsible for the early acceleration in the growth of brighter children.

13

*Formal Operations and Perception**

John H. Flavell

We are now in position to give an initial paradigm of how the adolescent thinks. He begins by organizing the various elements of the raw data with the concrete-operational techniques of middle childhood. These organized elements are then cast in the form of statements or propositions which can be combined in various ways. Through the method of combinatorial analysis he then isolates for consideration the totality of distinct combinations of these propositions. These combinations are regarded as hypotheses, some of which will be confirmed and some infirmed by subsequent investigation. Is it true that A elicits X? If so, does B also? Is it true that A produces X only when B is absent? Such are the hypothetical questions which make up the domain of the possible in such problems; and the adolescent views his task as that of determining the actual shape of things by successively putting them to empirical test.

But abstract descriptions need supplementing by concrete examples. The following problem was administered to children at both developmental levels:

In experiment I, the child is given four similar flasks containing colorless, odorless liquids which are perceptually identical. We number them: (1) diluted sulphuric acid: (2) water: (3) oxygenated water: (4) thiosulphate: we add a bottle (with a dropper) which we will call g: it contains potassium iodide. It is known that oxygenated water oxides potassium iodide in an acid medium. Thus mixture $(1 + 3 + g)$ will yield a yellow color. The water (2) is neutral, so that adding it will not change the color, whereas the thiosulphate (4) will bleach the mixture $(1 + 3 + g)$. The experimenter presents to the subject two glasses, one containing $1 + 3$, the other containing 2. In front of the subject, he pours several drops of g in each of the two glasses and notes the different reactions. Then the subject is asked simply to reproduce the color yellow, using flasks 1, 2, 3, 4, and g as he wishes (Inhelder and Piaget, 1958, pp. 108–109).

* In *The Developmental Psychology of Jean Piaget* (Princeton, N.J.: Van Nostrand, 1963), pp. 206–211.

The two behavior protocols which follow illustrate the kinds of concrete-formal differences we have been discussing:

REN (7;1) tries $4 \times g$, then $2 \times g$, and $3 \times g$: "*I think I did everything . . . I tried them all.*"—"What else could you have done?"—"*I don't know.*" We give him the glasses again: he repeats $1 \times g$, etc.—"You took each bottle separately. What else could you have done?"—"*Take two bottles at the same time*" [he tries $1 \times 4 \times g$, then $2 \times 3 \times g$, thus failing to cross over between the two sets (of bottles), for example 1×2, 1×3, 2×4, and 3×4].—When we suggest that he add others, he puts $1 \times g$ in the glass already containing 2×3 which results in the appearance of the color: "Try to make the color again." —"*Do I put in two or three?* [he tries with $2 \times 4 \times g$, then adds 3, then tries it with $1 \times 4 \times 2 \times g$]. No, I don't remember any more,*" etc. (Inhelder and Piaget, 1958, p. 111).

CHA (13;0): "*You have to try with all the bottles. I'll begin with the one at the end* [from 1 to 4 with g]. *It doesn't work any more. Maybe you have to mix them* [he tries $1 \times 2 \times g$, then $1 \times 3 \times g$]. *It turned yellow. But are there other solutions? I'll try* [$1 \times 4 \times g$; $2 \times 3 \times g$; $2 \times 4 \times g$; $3 \times 4 \times g$; with the two preceding combinations this gives the six two-by-two combinations systematically]. *It doesn't work. It only works with* [$1 \times 3 \times g$].*"*—"Yes, and what about 2 and 4?"— "*2 and 4 don't make any color together. They are negative. Perhaps you could add 4 in $1 \times 3 \times g$ to see if it would cancel out the color* [he does this]. *Liquid 4 cancels it all. You'd have to see if 2 has the same influence* [he tries it]. *No, so 2 and 4 are not alike, for 4 acts on 1×3 and 2 does not.*" —"What is there in 2 and 4?"—"*In 4 certainly water. No, the opposite, in 2 certainly water since it doesn't act on the liquids; that makes things clearer.*"—"And if I were to tell you that 4 is water?"—"*If this liquid 4 is water, when you put it with 1×3 it wouldn't completely prevent the yellow from forming. It isn't water; it's something harmful*" (Inhelder and Piaget, 1958, p. 117).

Let us first examine the younger child's behavior. Notice that it is by no means unsystematic and unorganized. He proceeds by making what is in effect a one-many multiplicative correspondence (Grouping IV) between the perceptually salient element g and the other four, yielding as product $(g \times 1) + (g \times 2) + (g \times 3) + (g \times 4)$. This systematic structuring of the data, although it happens to be inadequate to the solution of the problem, is a definite cut above preoperational behavior on a scale of genetic maturity. It turns out that preoperational children generally make a few random associations of elements (without really knowing what these associations are capable of proving) and intersperse this activity with phenomenalistic and other types of prelogical causal explanations (Inhelder and Piaget, 1958).

But the differences between this behavior and that of the adolescent are nonetheless striking for all its advances over that of the younger children. REN is capable of forming only a few of the total number of possible combinations: the four binary ones mentioned plus (after liberal suggestions and hints from the examiner) three ternaries and two quarternaries. CHA, on the other hand, seems disposed right from the outset to think in terms of all possible combinations of elements (or at least, what amounts to about the same thing, all the ones necessary to arrive at a full determination of the causal structure). Moreover, he appears to possess a systematic and orderly method for generating these combinations: $(1 \times g) \times (2 \times g)$, etc., and then $(1 \times 2 \times g) + (1 \times 3 \times g)$, etc. His language alone clearly attests to his hypothetico-deductive attitude towards the data: there are a number of statements of the "if . . . then" type (and none of this type in REN's protocol).

These statements are worth a closer look. Take for example CHA's assertion: "If this liquid 4 is water, when you put it with 1×3 it wouldn't completely prevent the yellow from forming [Therefore] it isn't water [since it does in fact prevent the yellow from forming]; it's something harmful." It is clear that the content very much concerns the possible rather than the real, since the event *4-does-not-prevent-the-yellow-from-forming* is nowhere seen in reality. In general, Piaget finds that contrary-to-fact "what if" suppositions of this kind tend to be foreign to the thought of middle childhood. Further, the total assertion consists of more than simple statements about data (whether true statements or false). Of greater developmental significance is the fact that it comprises a statement *about* these state-

ments, a proposition about propositions: namely, the assertion that one statement (liquid 4 is water) logically implies another (liquid 4 will not prevent the yellow from forming). As we said earlier, it is because adolescent cognition shows this implicative, propositions-about-propositions character that Piaget uses the expressions *interpropositional thought* and *second-degree operations* to describe it.

All the traits of formal thought we have described go to make it a very good instrument for *scientific reasoning*. As CHA's protocol shows, he is quite capable of achieving the correct solution of what is in all essential respects a genuine problem of scientific discovery. The hypothetical-deductive attitude, the combinatorial method, and the other attributes of formal thought provide him with the necessary tools for separating out the variables which might be causal, holding one factor constant in order to determine the causal action of another, and so on. He is not only able to imagine the various transformations which the data permit in order to try them out empirically: he is also capable of giving correct logical interpretation to the results of these empirical tests. If it eventuates, for instance, that the yellow color is produced by the combination $1 \times 3 \times g$ and no other, he is able to conclude that $1 \times 3 \times g$ is the necessary and sufficient cause (e.g., $1 \times 2 \times 3 \times g$ also suffice to produce the color, but 2 is not necessary to the combination), and he then knows his problem is solved. This is clearly a good imitation of how the scientist goes about his business.

How, by what route, does the subject move from concrete to formal operations? Piaget suggests that the route is similar in a general way to that by which the transition from preoperational to concrete-operational thinking was effected: as the child becomes more and more proficient at organizing and structuring problem data with concrete-operational methods, he becomes better and better able to recognize the latter's shortcomings as a device for yielding a complete and logically exhaustive solution (Inhelder and Piaget, 1958, p. 283). That is, as the child's concrete-operational analyses become sharper and more complete, they present him with gaps, uncertainties, and contradictions which a more impoverished analysis could never have brought to light. (Concrete operations themselves were similarly born out of problems raised by an increasingly differentiated preoperational analysis.)

Faced with these new problems, the child gropes for new methods of attack. The scientific-type tasks which Piaget has set for this age group have mostly required for their solution the isolation of variables, that is, an assessment of the separate causal contributions of the various factors extant in the data. It is particularly with respect to this ability to isolate variables that transitional forms show up most clearly. The younger children develop the ability to use a single experimental method to test the causal efficacy of a variable: simple *negation* or *inversion*, the literal *removal* of the variable from operation. For instance, one can determine that substance 4 in the chemical-mixture problem is important for removing the yellow color by the operations of adding (direct operation) and not adding (negation) it to $1 \times 3 \times g$: when not added, the yellow color does not clear up; when added, it does. Useful though this method is in some cases, it does not serve in all. A major step forward is made when the child can supplement the reversible operation of negation by that of *reciprocity*. Reciprocity entails not the outright elimination or negation of a factor but its *neutralization*, that is, holding its effect constant in some way while a second factor is being varied. For instance, where the problem is to study the separate effects of kind of metal and length on the flexibility of a rod (Inhelder and Piaget, 1958, Ch. 3), the younger child finds himself at an impasse; he cannot literally negate either variable, i.e., work with a rod not made of *some* metal and not possessing *some* length. The older child uses the reciprocal operation with great profit here. He takes two rods of different metals but of the same length (here length is not negated, but neutralized or controlled—not lengths *per se* but length *differences* are annulled) in order to study the effect of kind of metal, and two rods of a single metal and different lengths to study the effect of length.

The addition of the reciprocal operation to the subject's repertory in solving scientific problems brings a general advance in strategy and tactics: it disposes the subject towards the controlled experiment, that is, the nullification of one variable, not simply to study that one variable, but to study the action of some other variable free from error variance contributed by the first. The younger child negates a variable in order to study the causal efficacy *of that variable*. The older child develops a better strategy: negate or neutralize (whichever circumstances dictate; both negation and reciprocity are at his disposal) factor *A* in order to study the effects of varying factor *B*; negate or neutralize *A* and *B* in order to assess the uncontaminated action

of *C*, and so on. Once again we see that the transition from concrete to formal operations is a transition towards genuinely scientific methods of analysis.

What are the behavioral criteria for saying that one child is limited to concrete operations, whereas another child (of the same age or even younger) is at the formal level? Piaget's answer to this question is of principal interest, in the writer's opinion, not so much for whatever air of precision it may seem to lend to this segment of his work—a drop in an ocean of imprecision, surely—but because it gives added insight into what he thinks are the crucially important cognitive acquisitions of the adolescent. He says that one cannot confidently make a diagnosis of formal operations from one or two isolated bits of behavior, even when they consist of propositionlike, causal statements (Inhelder and Piaget, 1958, pp. 278–280). He offers instead two other diagnostic procedures:

> A second and more adequate method is to compare all of the statements and particularly the actions of a single subject. It then becomes clear whether he is limited to a simple registration of the raw experimental results, forming only the classifications, serial orders, and correspondences he sees as sufficient for solving the problem, or whether he tries to separate out the variables. The latter implies both hypothetico-deductive reasoning and a combinatorial system: when they appear, we have to interpret the stated judgments as propositional expressions, since the links between the successive statements (whether explicit or implicit) consist in interpropositional operations.
> But the third and surest method of differentiation (which is actually a simple specialization of the second) is to analyze the proofs employed by the subject. If they do not go beyond observation of empirical correspondences, they can be fully explained in terms of concrete operations, and nothing would warrant our assuming that more complex thought mechanisms are operating. If, on the other hand, the subject interprets a given correspondence as the result of any one of several possible combinations, and this leads him to verify his hypotheses by observing their consequences, we know that propositional operations are involved (Inhelder and Piaget, 1958, p. 279).

We see, then, that formal thought is for Piaget not so much this or that specific behavior as it is a generalized *orientation*, sometimes explicit and sometimes implicit, towards problem-solving: an orientation towards organizing data (combinatorial analysis), towards isolation and control of variables, towards the hypothetical, and towards logical justification and proof. The temptation is great to draw sharp images to better convey the salient contours of each developmental period, despite the obvious dangers of oversimplification it entails. What could be the archetypes for the three postinfantile eras? The preoperational child is the child of wonder; his cognition appears to us naive, impression-bound, and poorly organized. There is an essential lawlessness about his world without, of course, this fact in any way entering his awareness to inhibit the zest and flights of fancy with which he approaches new situations. Anything is possible because nothing is subject to lawful constraints. The child of concrete operations can be caricatured as a sober and bookkeeperish organizer of the real and a distruster of the subtle, the elusive, and the hypothetical. The adolescent has something of both: the seven–11-year-old's zeal for order and pattern coupled with a much more sophisticated version of the younger child's conceptual daring and uninhibitedness. Unlike the concrete-operational child, he can soar; but also unlike the preoperational child, it is a controlled and planned soaring, solidly grounded in a bedrock of careful analysis and painstaking accommodation to detail.

14

The Development of

Logical Problem-Solving Strategies*

Edith D. Neimark
Nan Lewis

A number of studies by a variety of investigators have shown that cognitive development in children progresses in an orderly fashion from primitive, concrete operations through progressively more abstract levels. Thinking in terms of formal logical relations normally begins to appear about 11 or 12 (Flavell, 1963, p. 265). Although this evidence is both extensive and impressive, its interpretation is open to question on two grounds, both having to do with the experimental procedures employed: (a) performance may be affected by specific school training and content knowledge (Goodnow & Bethon, 1966); (b) data typically are the child's own report and are, therefore, affected by his own verbal fluency and by E's interpretation. Moreover, most of the available research has been concerned with the development of specific concepts rather than with other aspects of the thinking process. The present experiment was designed to examine the development of logical thinking in a problem-solving task deliberately designed to (a) be relatively content free, and (b) provide objective quantitative measures of the quality of Ss performance.

The task chosen is a paradigm of the diagnostic problem-solving situation in which S is confronted with an initial state of affairs, or problem, which may have a finite number of solutions. His task is to determine a unique correct solution by gathering information with which to eliminate inappropriate alternative solutions. Medical diagnosis, trouble shooting of malfunctioning equipment, and the game of twenty questions are common examples of this type of procedure. The present task differed from them in requiring no specific knowledge; S was to identify one of a number of patterns of binary elements.

* From *Child Development*, 1967, 38, 107–117.

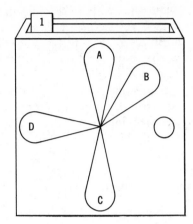 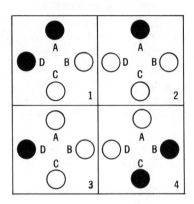

FIG. 19.   Schematic of a problem board with four shutters and an answer array containing four patterns. Shutter B has been opened revealing a white circle beneath; thus patterns 1, 2, or 3 might be the answer, but pattern 4 could not be. In this instance, gambling is not rewarded.

A simplified version of the task is shown in Figure 19. The S is given an answer sheet containing n numbered patterns each composed of k binary elements (black or white circles), and a problem board in which one of those patterns is concealed under k movable shutters, one over each element. His task is to identify the concealed pattern by uncovering as few of its elements as possible. Figure 19 shows four patterns of four elements and a board with the shutter over element B opened to reveal a white circle below.

The total information required to identify one from among n patterns is measured in terms of uncertainty, H; and $H = \log_2 n$. Thus, for the example in Figure 19, two bits of information are required for solution; for the experimental problems employed, three bits of information are required; that is, S must identify one from among eight patterns. The potential information available to S is completely determined by the structure of the patterns on his answer sheet. The information he actually does obtain may be quantitatively described in terms of expected reduction in uncertainty. For brevity, the term "strategy score" will be used to describe S's actual information-gathering behavior as expressed in terms of mean expected informational outcome (in bits) of a series of shutter openings (moves). To see how this score is obtained, consider the four patterns in Figure 19. By opening shutters A or D, S will eliminate two of the four patterns as possible answers regardless of the state of the con-

cealed information and will be called "safe moves." By opening shutter B or C, on the other hand, S will have solved the problem (and obtained two bits of information) if the concealed element is black, but will have eliminated only one alternative (gotten .415 bits of information) if it is not. A move of this sort will be called a "gamble." Its expected informational outcome, $\bar{E}$, is obtained by weighting each informational outcome by its likelihood of occurrence (assuming that patterns are equally likely to be concealed in the board): $\bar{E} = .25(2 \text{ bits}) + .75(.415) = .811$ bits. These values may be obtained directly from tables of $p \log_2 p$.

The strategy score is obtained by summing the expected informational outcome, $\bar{E}_1$, of each successive move over all i moves and dividing the sum by the number of moves. The maximal possible value is unity, which can result only from a series of safe moves; this will be called a "safe strategy." The strategy score is lowered either by gambling (and, generally, the earlier in a series of moves S gambles, the more it lowers the score) or by making noninformative (redundant) moves. An example of a redundant move in Figure 19 would arise if S opened shutter C after first having opened shutter B (or vice versa). In the experiment which follows, S was never rewarded for gambling (i.e., only those patterns which had no one-move solution were concealed in the board). The optimal solution procedure was, thus, a safe strategy, and the development of a safe strategy was investigated.

Method

Subjects

The Ss were boys and girls between the ages of nine and 14 enrolled in the public schools of Warren Township, New Jersey, whose parents had granted written permission for them to serve as Ss. This is primarily a residential community with a middle-class population. At least one (and for the older children, two) set of scores on the California Mental Maturity Scale (CMMS) was available for each child. Children were assigned to chronological age groups of eight Ss each on the basis of IQ: Those with a CMMS of 90–117 were classified as normal, while those with a CMMS of 122–145 were classified as bright. All children were white (total $N = 96$).

For purposes of extending the age comparisons, three additional groups of eight volunteers each from Highland Park, New Jersey, High School were added: one group of 16-year-olds and two groups of 14-year-olds (one bright, one normal). For the 18-year-old group, data on eight girls enrolled in an introductory psychology course at Douglass College were used.

Apparatus

The experimental series of problems consisted of eight problems, each of which was done with a different answer sheet. The answer sheet contained eight patterns of eight binary elements. Each answer sheet was so constructed that, as a first move, half of the available moves were safe moves and the remaining half were gambles. All gambles were correlated, that is, would "pay off" on the same pattern. That pattern was never concealed in the board; thus, gambling would never be successful on any problem. Each of the answer sheets was a variant of a prototype obtained by permuting (a) shutter positions within a pattern and (b) arrangement of patterns on a page. Thus they were physically different in appearance but alike in principle. Order of administration of the problems was varied in an eight-by-eight Latin square with one S of the group assigned to each order.

Eight problems, each on a tabbed cardboard square, were loaded in a nine-inch-square wooden board with eight movable shutters equally spaced around the circumference of a circle eight inches in diameter.

Procedure

The task was first demonstrated to S with an example in which there were four patterns and a problem board with three shutters. The E opened one shutter and, after asking S to eliminate the patterns which were no longer appropriate, asked him which shutter should be opened next. Of the two remaining moves, one was noninformative while the other would solve the problem; regardless of S's choice, this fact was pointed out to him. The S was then given a series of four or five practice problems to familiarize him with the details of the procedure. For the practice problems, the problem board was a standard manilla file folder with a black or white circle concealed beneath each of four shutters. The answer sheets contained six (for the first two problems) or eight (for the remaining problems) patterns of four circles. After having mastered the mechanics of the procedure, S began the series of eight experimental problems for which the procedure was as follows: On opening a shutter, S was to write the letter designating its position on the appropriate line of his answer sheet and across the face of all patterns thereby eliminated as possible solutions. On attaining a solution, he was to write its identifying number on the line labeled "answer." The E then closed all shutters and removed the problem from the board, after which S went on to the next problem and its accompanying answer sheet. Upon completion of the last problem, S was questioned about his procedure for solving and given the Kagan Conceptual Style Test (CST). He was then thanked for his participation and returned to his classroom.

Results

Group mean strategy score as a function of mental age is plotted in Figure 20. Two reference points for extremes of performance have been included: the lower line is the strategy score which would be predicted if S opened shutters at random and stopped on attaining a solution; the upper line is the theoretical optimum performance. It is evident that young Ss perform at essentially a random or nonlogical level, with increasing improvement in performance with advancing mental age. That mental age does account for a good proportion of the variance in the data is indicated by a product-moment correlation of $r = .52$ for MA (based upon total CMMS IQ) and strategy. Corresponding correlations: for

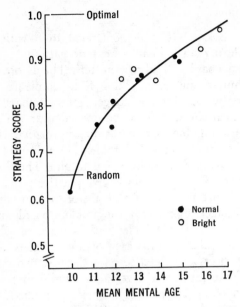

FIG. 20. Group mean strategy score (in bits) as a function of mean mental age. Groups of normal intelligence are indicated by filled circles, bright groups by open circles. Data points were fitted visually.

MA (based upon nonverbal scale IQ) and strategy, r = .54; for IQ and strategy, r = .25, further suggest that MA rather than IQ is the major factor. All correlations cited are statistically significant at or beyond the .01 level. The correlation of number of analytic responses on the Kagan CST and strategy score is .16; the correlation of CST with nonverbal MA is r = .15; neither of these values is statistically significant at the .05 level.

Although it is reassuring to find such a smooth growth curve relating MA and performance, it is of greater interest to account for the details of this development. One possible explanation is that all Ss eventually adopt an optimal strategy but that they do so at different rates, with rate being a function of developmental level. This explanation may be readily rejected after an examination of group learning curves for strategy scores over the series of eight problems. Figure 21 compares normal Ss from nine to 18, while Figure 22 compares bright with normal Ss at nine, 10, and 12. In both cases, the F for group × trials interaction (which would indicate differential slope) is less than 1. For Figure 21, differences among age groups are significant at the .001 level, F (5,42) = 7.49; and the overall trend of the learning curve

differs from horizontality, $F(7,294) = 2.40$. Comparable results obtain for the curves of Figure 21: for between-age groups $F(2,42) = 8.81$; for between bright and normal $F(1,42) = 21.00$; while the age × intelligence interaction falls just short of significance at the .05 level, $F(2,42) = 3.10$. The trials' main effect is significant at the .01 level, $F(7,294) = 3.11$; but as indicated previously none of the trial interactions even approaches statistical significance. Thus, it is clear that all groups learn at essentially the same rate; group differences stem from the fact that group curves start out at different levels and run essentially parallel throughout.

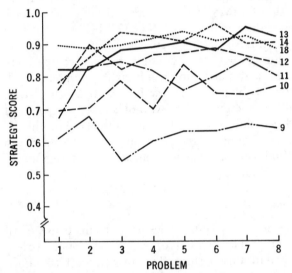

FIG. 21. Group mean strategy score on successive problems for groups of normal intelligence at 9, 10, 11, 12, 13, and 14 years of age and one college group at 18.

Differences among age and intelligence groups in initial level of strategy seem to be attributable to the number of Ss in the group who display logical information-gathering behavior at the outset. The behavior of all normal nine-year olds is accurately described by a model which assumes that S opens shutters at random until a solution is obtained. Such a model accurately describes not only group mean strategy score but also the frequency distribution of number of moves to solution and probability of first-choice move for the normal nine-year-old group. With increasing age, the relative frequency of this "random" behavior decreases. The increase in logical information-gathering behavior is reflected in a number of response measures, such as the occurrence

TABLE 21. SUMMARY OF A NUMBER OF ADDITIONAL RESPONSE MEASURES

MA Group[a] CA	Total Non-informative (1)	At Least One Non-informative (2)	More than One Non-informative (3)	Proportion Safe First Moves (4)	Total Safe Strategy (5)	One or More Safe Strategy (6)	More than One Safe Strategy (7)	N Full Correct Rules (8)	N Full or Partial Rules (9)
10.0 9N 9.49	128	8	8	.547	8	5	2	0	0
11.30 10N 10.24	73	7	7	.562	11	6	2	1	2
11.90 11N 11.10	55	4	0	.594	18	7	5	2	5
12.32 9B 9.30	35	6	4	.625	28	6	6	3	4
12.84 10B 10.29	3	3	0	.672	26	8	7	3	6
13.09 12N 12.16	33	5	4	.641	26	7	5	0	5
13.13 12N 12.26	32	5	4	.609	27	6	5	2	4
13.87 10BB 10.21	1	1	0	.703	24	7	5	3	4
13.88 13N 13.19	15	6	5	.672	23	7	6	3	7
14.68 14N 14.03	15	5	2	.766	30	7	7	2	7
15.86 12B 11.94	20	3	2	.891	42	7	7	4	8
16.65 12B 12.72	4	3	0	.781	45	7	7	5	7

Note.—See text for explanation of measures.

[a] B = bright; N = normal.

of noninformative moves and relative frequency of first-move gambles (see Table 21).

The very first move always yields information and, in general, so does the second. However, later moves are increasingly likely to be uninformative. The S had been informed of this possibility in the initial instructions, and it was always evident from the behavior of individual Ss that they were aware of their mistake after having made it.

Column (1) of Table 21 summarizes the total number of noninformative moves for each group (with groups arranged in order of increasing mental age). It is evident that the number of noninformative moves decreases sharply and systematically with some suggestion of more rapid decrease for bright than for normal Ss. Column (2) gives the number of Ss in the group of eight who made one or more noninformative moves over the total eight problems. Again, the youngest Ss show poorest performance. Column (3) gives the number of Ss in each group who made more than one noninformative move; comparison of this data with the preceding column gives an indication of the extent to which S profits from a noninformative move by eliminating that mistake on subsequent problems. It is clear that normal nine- and 10-year-olds do not immediately profit from sad experience, whereas older Ss do.

We assume that a noninformative move shows S the inefficiency of simply opening shutters. This usually happens when only two patterns remain as alternative solutions. At this point, many Ss begin to

compare the two patterns to find the move (usually there is only one) which differentiates them. At this point also, S is clearly thinking, in that he represents alternative choices at a symbolic level, examines their consequences, and "plans ahead" prior to overt action. Although the decrease in redundant moves from MA > 11.5 suggests that this is the first step toward a logical approach to the problem (and some Ss go no further), it is a simple extrapolation to see that one can "plan ahead" not only the last move but all moves. The extent to which S plans all moves is indicated by a number of response measures. One

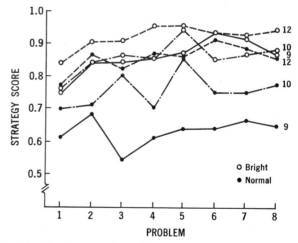

FIG. 22. Comparison of group mean strategy scores on successive problems for bright and normal children at 9, 10, and 12 years of age.

is the proportion of safe first moves over all eight problems. These data are given in the column (4) of Table 21. Since half the available first moves are safe moves and half are gambles, if Ss simply opened a shutter the probability of a safe first move would be .50; which it effectively is for normal nine-year-olds (and possibly for normal 10- and 11-years-olds as well). It is clear, however, that selection of safe first moves increases with mental age.

Columns (5), (6), and (7) summarize data on safe strategies (i.e., a sequence of three successive safe moves). Total number of instances of a safe strategy (out of a maximum possible of 64) again increases systematically with mental age. Although it is uncertain how best to estimate the likelihood of a safe strategy by chance, one defensible estimate is .071, which is slightly exceeded by the normal nine-year-olds (.125) and exceeded to an increasing extent by the older groups. Columns (6) and (7) give the number of Ss showing (a) at least one instance of a safe strategy and (b) more than one instance of a safe strategy (since one instance is within the range of chance probability). With the possible exception of the bright nine- and 10-year-olds (who perform a bit better than their normal counterparts of higher chronological age), there seems to be steep increase in safe strategies around an MA of 11 with gradual increase thereafter.

Although most older Ss seem to be adopting a consistent safe strategy, one may question whether this reflects a "conscious" logical plan on their part. At the end of the session, each S was asked if he was doing anything systematic and to describe his procedure. Some Ss, especially among the younger groups, reported that they were not doing anything special or were "just opening shutters." A number of younger Ss reported magical sequences, for example, ABC, AECG, etc. Columns (8) and (9) of Table 21 give the number of Ss reporting a logical plan (as contrasted with a magical plan or no plan). Column (8) includes only those Ss who verbalized a safe strategy (generally expressed in terms of "split them in half each time" or "look for 4:4 then 2:2 then 1:1); column (9) includes these Ss plus Ss who formulated the rule in a more limited context (generally for the last move). It would appear that Ss may employ a safe strategy before they accurately describe it (all Ss who gave an accurate description were, in fact, employing a safe strategy). Furthermore, there is some suggestion that bright Ss may be more adept at verbalizing a rule than their normal counterparts at equivalent MA levels.

Discussion

The present experiment confirms findings from a wide variety of studies of conceptual development and extends them to a content-free problem-solving task. At early stages the child's behavior is largely under control of details of the environmental stimulus; he has to push open a shutter and is then guided by the consequences of his action. In utilizing the information, however, even very young children do generate stimuli, usually in the form of self-instructions, which control their behavior. For example, many children say something like "G was black, so I must write G over all the ones that are white there." Frequently, on the early practice trials the child says this aloud; on later trials he may or may not continue saying it to himself. Older children, apparently, also generate stimuli for themselves in the form of rules, such as "Look to see where the two patterns are different," or "Count how many times it is black, and open that shutter if the answer is four [or two, or one]." Once information-gathering behavior is brought under control of a rule, then it becomes much less dependent upon changes in the structure of the answer sheet, problem, etc. This latter speculation is supported by evidence of rapid positive transfer in adults after a variety of training conditions (Neimark, 1961).

But how does the child come to bring behavior under the control of self-generated stimuli? The present results suggest that brighter children are more likely both to formulate a rule and to verbalize it (at least, that is one possible interpretation of the somewhat higher frequency of statements of a correct rule among brighter children). It is our general impression that children move to progressively higher levels of abstraction in an all-or-none fashion. That is, once a child discovers how to avoid noninformative moves, he makes no more of them although they occurred at a relatively uniform rate previously. Similarly, once a child discovers that first-move gambles do not "pay off," he avoids them thereafter (e.g., one little girl, after consistently starting each problem with a gamble, announced "no more of these big deals for me"; her behavior was already clearly under control of a rule, but she changed rules). Unfortunately, the present data are inadequate for a rigorous test of the all-or-none assumption.

15

Cognitive Growth during High School*

Marion F. Shaycoft

In the spring of 1960, Project TALENT tested nearly half a million students in grades 9, 10, 11, and 12 in schools in all parts of the country. These students were given a comprehensive two-day battery of paper-and-pencil tests and inventories developed especially for the project. Three years later some of the students who had been tested in the grade 9 group in 1960 were retested as grade 12 students. This report is concerned with some of the results of that 1963 testing. The complete report of the retest study (Shaycoft, 1967), is available at cost from the Project TALENT Office.

Purposes of the Study

The chief purposes of the study were to investigate the changes in students' abilities between grades 9 and 12 and to learn something about the factors that produced these changes.

Design of the Study

Sample. In 1963 the grade 12 students in over 100 public secondary schools that had been among the 1,353 schools included in the 1960 TALENT testing were given an abridged TALENT battery. Approximately 10,000 grade 12 students were in the group tested. About three-quarters of them had also been in the original testing as ninth-graders. These 7,500 students were the core of the retest study.

Retest batteries. The instruments used in the 1963 testing were identical with those in the original battery, with the exception that the biographical inventory (Student Information Blank) was revised and three of the original instruments (Student Activities Inventory, Memory for Sentences Test, and Preferences Test) were omitted entirely. (See Flanagan *et al.*, 1962, for a description of the original battery.) Since only one day was available for the retesting, each student could take only about half of the total battery. Therefore, the tests were reorganized into a set of six partially overlapping bat-

teries, each including about half the tests. Each school retested (except for a few vocational high schools in which a seventh battery was used) was given one of these six batteries. The overlapping of the batteries was so arranged that each pair of tests was taken by at least one-sixth of the boys and one-sixth of the girls. To provide a basis for checking on the comparability of the groups taking the various batteries, and for adjusting statistically to make them more comparable, one test, Abstract Reasoning, was included in all batteries.

Data analysis. The data analysis involved use of many statistical techniques, including canonical correlation between grade 9 and grade 12 scores, factor analysis, univariate analysis of variance among schools, multivariate analysis of variance among schools, multiple discriminant function analysis, partial and part correlation matrices, partial canonical correlation analysis, and stepwise multiple regression analysis.

Changes in Student Abilities Between Grade 9 and Grade 12

Amount of Growth

The average amount of growth in cognitive skills between grades 9 and 12 was not only statistically significant, but also large enough to be important. In general, the larger gains were associated with school-taught subjects—or areas such as vocabulary that, if not taught directly, are at least fields in which most schools would like to increase their students' mastery. Other areas in which growth in knowledge or ability was fairly large between grades 9 and 12 were information about law, accounting, business, electronics, and mechanics. All of these areas are curriculum-related (though not all are related to the *academic* curriculum). For example, information about accounting and business is imparted in commercial courses, and mechanical information and electrical-electronics information are staples of vocational curricula. Electrical-electronics information is

* Project TALENT Bulletin 6 (Pittsburgh: Project TALENT, 1967).

also an important component of physics and general science courses.

Sex Differences in Amount of Growth

The two sexes showed somewhat different patterns of mental growth between grades 9 and 12. Boys seemed to acquire significantly more information than girls in many areas, including mathematics, physical science, aeronautics and space, electricity and electronics, mechanics, and sports; they also had significantly larger score gains than girls on several aptitude tests, including Creativity, Mechanical Reasoning, Visualization in Three Dimensions, and Abstract Reasoning.

Some of the tests on which girls showed significantly larger gains than boys were Literature Information, Memory for Words, Spelling, and, of course, Home Economics Information.

For almost all of these tests, the sex showing the larger average gain between grades 9 and 12 was also the one with the higher mean score in grade 9. (Literature Information was about the only exception.)

What Produced These Changes?

The School

Having established that growth did occur in all ability areas, especially curriculum-related areas, the first question which arises is whether schools differed in producing these changes. (If it were to develop that schools did *not* differ, it would be rather hopeless to seek clues concerning what school characteristics were likely to be effective.) In answering this question, it is not sufficient to consider the school differences based on twelfth-graders and then claim these differences represent what the high school has accomplished. They don't, unless one can assume that all high schools started with student bodies having identical distributions of test scores at entrance (or grade 9 scores) and identical distributions of environmental characteristics (both home and community) that are also likely to affect the development of abilities. Of course, these aren't valid assumptions. If a high school in a prosperous suburban community has higher grade 12 scores, on the average than its counterpart in a slum neighborhood, it certainly does not mean that the suburban school is doing a better job. It is obviously possible that the better showing made by the suburban school is the result of two potent factors: (1) the students

entered the high school with higher aptitude and achievement levels than their peers from the depressed urban area, and (2) the better environmental factors provided by home, family, and community in the prosperous suburb promoted more out-of-school learning than typical in less favored situations. Therefore, to find out whether schools differed in their effects, the initial situation (as represented in the case of Project TALENT by the grade 9 scores) must be taken into account.

The results of three analyses showed that, in any area of knowledge or ability represented by the TALENT tests under consideration, students in some schools learned more, or improved their ability more, than students in other schools. But this does not imply that the schools themselves were entirely responsible; the community and the people in it must be considered, too. Of course, the schools almost certainly played an important role, especially in gains in curriculum-related subjects, such as literature, mathematics, social studies, and electrical-electronics information.

The gains in information about areas not normally part of the school curriculum, such as recreational activities and hobbies, are probably primarily a function of community and home differences rather than school practices. Boys in a rural area, for example, are much more likely than city boys to have hunting as a hobby and consequently to know a lot about it. Likewise, knowledge about legitimate theater and ballet is in part a matter of living in a community where there is live theater and partly a matter of being in a socioeconomic stratum where theater-going is customary. Information about foods is another area that is probably dependent in large part on community characteristics (and probably has a substantial correlation with socioeconomic level).

Having established that the "school-plus-community-plus-the-people-in-it" entities differed in their effectiveness, the next problem was to try to determine what there was about certain schools that made their students learn more effectively (or less effectively) than students in other schools. The only feasible approach to this problem, with the present data, was to examine school characteristics as described on the questionnaires answered by the schools participating in Project TALENT, and determine how these characteristics were related to the school differences in performance. The results, however, were inconclusive. For instance, there was no clear relation between test performance and such school characteristics as course offerings. Schools that reported a strong program in mathematics or in physical science (many courses offered and strong requirements for graduation) were not especially likely to be among the schools scoring higher than average in those areas. It seems that the lack of any readily apparent relation between these two might be due primarily to the fact that courses offered by a school are not necessarily taken by a large proportion of that school's students—or by the students who would profit most.

In summary, schools do vary in effectiveness, but the specific school characteristics that produce results are somewhat elusive. One reason they are so resistant to identification may be that they are elusive *inherently*, not just in the present context. In other words, one of the crucial differences between an effective school and an ineffective one may be something as vague as the school's atmosphere. A school may provide an atmosphere where the motivation to learn is stimulated or it may provide one that produces students whose goal is to "get by." This sort of information cannot be gathered through a questionnaire survey.

Socioeconomic Status

Insofar as achievement of the types measured in this retest study is concerned, whatever *direct* effects socioeconomic background has on achievement occur before grade 9. The damage of a poor environment has already occurred by then; the benefits from a good one have already been established. After that point, the role of socioeconomic level as a causative agent, insofar as it has a role, appears to be *indirect*, operating on achievement partly through the medium of the effects of past achievement. Other indirect ways in which socioeconomic background operates are in affecting the kind of program a student takes in high school and his plans, if any, for a career and for further education after high school. There is also some evidence that students in the lower brackets on socioeconomic status tend to have fewer contacts with a school counselor than their more privileged classmates. Whether this is because students not planning to enter college are less likely to seek such contacts or because counselors are less likely to be available in the schools attended by such students is not clear.

College Plans

Is planning to go to college accompanied by greater motivation toward achievement in high school? The answer is uncertain. Among students at the same initial ability level, there is a significant relationship between whether a student plans to go to college and his or her achievement in subjects included in a college-preparatory curriculum in high school (literature, mathematics, physical science, English, etc.). But does this better achievement represent the results of greater motivation and harder work or does it represent mere exposure to courses? There is some evidence that the latter may be the case. If planning to go to college has any motivating effects, they are apparently manifested primarily in choice of courses—insofar as the student has any option. Students planning to go to college presumably are more motivated to take college-preparatory courses than are their non-college-bound classmates.

Courses Taken in High School

Considerable evidence points towards the effects of course work on changes in test scores between grades 9 and 12. In brief, taking math courses in high school improves the student's performance on Mathematics Information, Introductory High School Math, and Advanced High School Math, but not on Arithmetic Reasoning; taking courses in physical science improves performance on the Physical Science Information test, and also, perhaps, on Biological Science Information; and studying foreign languages improves performance on the Word Functions in Sentences test.

The correlation of Word Functions in Sentences with number of foreign language courses is particularly interesting because Word Functions in Sentences is a measure of *aptitude* for foreign languages. Specifically, what it measures is knowledge of formal grammar or, in the absence of such knowledge, aptitude for *learning* grammar. Thus it appears that study of foreign languages helps students learn something about English grammar. Whether this tends to be true in all schools or only in those where English courses place little or no stress on grammar is not apparent from the available data.

Amount of Counseling in High School

The amount of counseling a student receives in high school appears to have little effect on test score gains after initial ability and socioeconomic status have been taken into account. One of the few significant relationships involving amount of counseling that shows up for both sexes is its relation with scores on Math Information and Introductory

High School Math. Perhaps this is a result of the fact that the more counseling a student receives, the more likely he is to take mathematics courses in high school. As a matter of fact, amount of counseling is associated in a positive direction with course-taking in math, physical science, and foreign languages (all college-preparatory subjects), and with planning to attend college. However, no causal relationship can be established definitely in either direction. Counseling contacts may be either a result or a cause (or both, in part) of plans to attend college.

Aptitude

Socioeconomic status, college plans, courses taken, and counseling received are of varying importance in determining grade 12 achievement levels as measured by tests. But far outweighing any of them in its effect is "initial aptitude" (as indicated by grade 9 test scores). Of course, there is no reason to think that aptitude as of grade 9 is necessarily independent of socioeconomic status. It probably isn't. After all, environmental factors had been acting on the individual for 14 or 15 years at the time the grade 9 measurements were made, and it would be strange if they had no effect at all.

Aptitude Versus Achievement: A New Viewpoint

Is it possible in studying performance at high-school age to draw a sharp distinction between ability measures called "aptitudes," which are allegedly impervious to external effects (training, education, etc.), and those called "achievement," which are very much subject to the effects of education (as well as to the effects of the "aptitudes")? Retest data provide no sound basis for making this distinction. However, there is some evidence that certain variables in the TALENT battery function more as aptitude measures and others more as achievement measures. For instance, the Memory for Words test was not significantly correlated with foreign language courses, even though foreign language study might reasonably be supposed to afford experience and practice in just the sort of memorizing tested by the Memory for Words test.

A tentative conclusion is that the following nine tests provide a sufficiently stable picture between

grades 9 and 12 that they may be regarded as aptitude measures:

> Abstract Reasoning
> Arithmetic Reasoning
> Memory for Words
> Disguised Words
> Vocabulary I
> Scientific Attitude
> Creativity
> Mechanical Reasoning
> Visualization in Two Dimensions

The first six of these are probably primarily measures of "general verbal ability" or "general mental ability." The remaining three aptitude tests probably should be regarded primarily as measures of specialized aptitudes.

Just as significant is the finding that certain other tests, which might reasonably have been surmised to be *aptitude* measures, turned out to be substantially correlated with amount of course work in certain subjects. The two most noteworthy tests in this category were Visualization in Three Dimensions and Reading Comprehension. Scores on the former were related to number of math courses. As for the Reading Comprehension test, there seemed to be a tendency for performance on it to improve more if a student planned to go to college and took college-preparatory courses than if he didn't. However the picture is not entirely clear-cut. Reading Comprehension may still be relatively independent of high-school course-work effects. Further data analysis is needed to sort out the cause-and-effect relationships.

Implications for Education

The Disadvantaged Child

The handicap that disadvantaged youngsters are under appears to have taken root firmly by the time high school is reached. In other words, whatever direct effect socioeconomic factors have on abilities of the type measured by the TALENT battery occurs before grade 9. This finding supports the idea that special efforts to help the disadvantaged child overcome the handicaps imposed by a deprived background should concentrate on younger age levels—as Project Headstart is doing, for instance. The implication of the present research findings is that postponement of remedial efforts until high school would sharply curtail the success of such efforts.

General Education versus Vocational Education

The preliminary finding that reading comprehension improves in high school somewhat more for students taking a lot of academic courses than for students taking less of this kind of classwork suggests that attention should be focused on research concerning the academic-versus-vocational-education issue. Reading is undeniably an important skill. Therefore, it would be well to find out whether the boy or girl taking a vocational program in high school will, as an indirect and unsought consequence, have less reading competence in adult life than he otherwise would. If it is found out that this is indeed the case, redesigning vocational courses in such a way as to provide more practice in reading and more motivation to read would be well worth while. Steps in this direction have already been taken in some vocational high schools. A strong research finding supporting such steps might result in other schools following suit.

Effective and Ineffective High Schools

Evidence has shown that some schools do a better job of educating their students than other schools do. It isn't just a matter of some schools having more able students than others (although this is a factor that explains *part* of the difference). Furthermore, schools differ in regard to the subject-matter areas in which they are especially successful. These are encouraging findings. If it had developed that schools don't differ in regard to the characteristics of the graduates they turn out, it would be very difficult indeed to find evidence in support of the notion that *any* schools do *anything* that is especially effective—which would be a most discouraging conclusion for those who have any stake in American schools. And that includes just about everybody.

Although the conclusion that schools do differ in effectiveness bodes well for the prospects of future improvements in education, we first have to identify the ways in which the more effective schools differ from the ineffective ones. Further research is the key to that. Even though such research is necessarily complex and difficult, it would be well worth while if it could throw some light on how schools can be improved.

IV
Family Roles

The classic statement of adolescence places biological change—the accession to sexual maturity—at the center of a larger interpersonal and social ring of effects. In this view, the child's sexual maturity brings with it a need to detach from the family and to develop, with the aid of the peer group and other supports, a set of standards and behavior controls that is distinctly the adolescent's own—in the sense that it carries its own force, aside from external reinforcement, and that it accommodates his newly acquired sexual possibilities. The need for autonomy may be cast in the language of social role changes: the adolescent, no longer within purview of the parents, and mobile in the adult world, must assume the burden of self-regulation. Or one may emphasize the intrapsychic necessities as in psychoanalytic theory: the child is driven to leave home because of the danger that old affectional relationships in the family will become tainted by the reemergence of sexuality with its incestuous implications, or because the child's sexual maturity will be endangered by the regressive pulls of old object ties. Whatever the emphasis, all theories of adolescence agree that this is the time when the child must cut and run, when he must disentangle himself from the family network and become his own man—emotionally, behaviorally, in his values and controls.

And traditionally, the autonomy issue at adolescence has been conceived as a struggle: father against son in a contest for dominance, child against mother in a softer but more difficult and enveloping struggle for self-definition and integrity, the child managing a departure only by means of a rebellion, masked or starkly staged, muted or strident.

Let us state at the outset that research findings, by and large, do not support the traditional view. In the large-scale studies of normal populations, we do not find adolescents clamoring for freedom or for release from unjust constraint. We do not find rebellious resistance to authority as a dominant theme. For the most part, the evidence bespeaks a modal pattern considerably more peaceful than much theory and most social comment would lead us to expect. "Rebellious youth" and "the conflict between generations" are phrases that ring; but, so far as we can tell, it is not the ring of truth they carry so much as the beguiling but misleading tone of drama. We think the discrepancy here—between the objective evidence and much of contemporary thought about the period—has occurred because theories about adolescence have often developed from observations of one or another of two highly visible but small and atypical segments of the adolescent population: the acting-out delinquent subgroup, and the upper-middle-class, sensitive, introspective adolescents who find the transition to adulthood unbearable and seek professional help. But the modal pattern, the way of most American youngsters, is neither to act out nor to suffer the strains and conflicts, the guilts and anxieties of neurosis. It seems, rather, that the normal, the average, the modal youngster, makes his bid for autonomy gradually and appropriately, and that his requests meet reasonable consideration and deference from parents who ally themselves (more or less gracefully) with the child's need to grow.

The role change required of the child in the family at adolescence is this: he must continue to be a son (or daughter) and meet the obligations this role imposes, while at the same time abandoning the role of dependent child and gradually assuming the position of independent, autonomous adult. This shift, with its dual implications, is obviously more complicated than many role changes. To move from nonworker to worker, or from nonvoter to fully enfranchised citizen—these changes may be problematic, may require new skills and carry the difficulties of any new learning that involves the self. But they do not make the same complicated and intricate demands to change certain aspects of role behavior while maintaining in a state of exquisite stability certain other behaviors that seem, at least, intimately tied to the things that must change. Nor does becoming a worker or voter—instrumental and realistic—imply the same regressive hazards that are a part of more expressive and emotional family role changes. Nevertheless, most adolescents do make the transition, and apparently without excessive conflict.

What does empirical research have to say about the tropic movement of adolescents toward autonomy? In this section we will look at data on changes in dependency and autonomy that occur during adolescence, the areas that crystallize autonomy concerns at various stages within the adolescent period, the response of parents to growing independence, and some of the conditions and factors that affect both the pace and pattern of this development. In considering research on the growth of autonomy during adolescence, we will need to be explicit about the particular way in which autonomy has been measured and the sense in which the term is used.

Findings from national studies (Douvan and Adelson, 1966) indicate that behavioral autonomy increases sharply during adolescence. Table 22 sum-

TABLE 22. INDICES OF BEHAVIORAL AUTONOMY FOR GIRLS AT ELEVEN AND EIGHTEEN AND FOR BOYS AND GIRLS AGED FOURTEEN TO SIXTEEN[a]

Item	Change in girls from 11 to 18		Girls 14 to 16 (N = 822) %	Boys 14 to 16 (N = 1045) %
	(N = 206) from %	(N = 148) to %		
1. S dates or goes steady	4	94	72	59
2. S has a job outside home	34	60	56	47
3. S has some independent funds	63	84	74	
4. S spends most of free time with				
a. friends	22	46	32	
b. family	68	44	56	

[a] The data for boys are incomplete because some questions asked in the study of girls were not included in the boys' study.

marizes data on dating, job-holding outside the home, access to independent funds (from work or allowance), and choice of leisure companions outside the family. The largest age change occurs in dating, but substantial shifts occur in all of the behaviors. Most American girls have money of their own even at eleven, so there is not a lot of room for age change on this item. Only one item of behavioral autonomy—primary commitment of leisure to friendship rather than family relationships—fails to show a majority by eighteen, and in this item we touch closer to emotional autonomy from the family than in any of the other behaviors.

But when we look beyond relatively superficial freedom of movement to more subtle and emotional aspects of autonomy, we find changes occurring during adolescence to be more modest. Children, and particularly girls, do not abandon emotional ties to the parents with anything like the ease with which they shift companions. Apparently adolescents are happy enough to settle for ritual signs of independence (holding jobs, having money, dating, and sharing leisure with friends) and to let the more critical problems of detachment rest and wait (Bowerman and Elder, 1962; Douvan and Adelson, 1966; *Westley and Elkin*, 1957).

In Table 23 age trends are summarized for a number of aspects of emotional autonomy. These include conscious evaluation of the importance of friendship and family relationships; choice of advisers, confidantes, and ideals from outside the family; incidence and areas of disagreements with parents. Overall, the differences reveal some growth in emotional autonomy. But the differences are in some cases small, and in many cases indicate that even at eighteen the modal pattern among girls is family oriented and compliant. A majority of eighteen-year-olds choose their adult ideals within the family; comply, on a projective question, with a parental request to give up a job and return home; and resolve another projective conflict, between a commitment to parents and pressure from peers, in a parent-oriented way. Even where a majority at eighteen take the more autonomous position, about a third of the girls indicate that the emotional bond to the parents remains preeminent (i.e., they choose parents as confidantes and accept without cavil parental restrictions in a projective situation). Where comparison is possible, we find girls slightly more advanced than boys in the transfer of emotion to extrafamily relationships, but we will see later that this does not necessarily reflect increasing independence in critical areas.

Bowerman and Kinch (1959) distinguish three aspects of the child's orientation toward parents, and find that the rate of detachment from the family depends on the aspect being considered. Between grades 4 and 10, they note, boys and girls markedly shift their *associations* from family to peer group, continue to *identify* more closely with the family, and change moderately in *normative* orientation. Increased orientation toward peers does not necessarily bring reduced orientation toward the family, even in associations, the reduction occurring only in cases where family relationships are poor in any case.

Gradual changes occur during adolescence in what has been called "moral autonomy," that is, self-government in issues of impulse control, of correct behavior, of right and wrong. Kohlberg (1958), sampling boys at ten, thirteen, and sixteen years of age, shows that thought about moral problems tends

TABLE 23. INDICES OF EMOTIONAL AUTONOMY FOR GIRLS AT ELEVEN AND EIGHTEEN
AND FOR BOYS AND GIRLS AGED FOURTEEN TO SIXTEEN

Item	Change in girls from 11 to 18		Girls 14 to 16 (N = 822) %	Boys 14 to 16 (N = 1045) %
	(N = 206) from %	(N = 148) to %		
1. S thinks friendship can be as close as family relationship	53	71	61	42
2. S disagrees with parents about:				
a. Ideas	12	46	34	
b. More than one issue out of six	54	59	56	
3. S would take advice of friends on more than one issue out of six				29
4. S chooses adult ideal				
a. outside the family	22	48	38	36
b. within the family	66	52	55	45
5. Projective: Response to request from lonely mother to give up good job and return to hometown				
a. reject request	8	26	18	
b. comply, conditionally comply	78	59	66	
6. Projective: Response to parental restriction				
a. accept, reassure parents	51	38	36	
7. Projective: Response to conflict between parent-peer pressure				
a. parent oriented	78	61	63	
8. S chooses as confidante				
a. friend	5	33	26	
b. one, both parents	67	36	45	
9. Part in rule making				
a. S has some part	45	64	58	
10. Attitude toward parental rules				
a. Right, good, fair	47	56	56	

NOTE: The data for boys are incomplete because some questions asked in the study of girls were not included in the boys' study.

to move from a premoral level to a morality based on conventional role conformity, and then to a morality based on self-accepted moral principles. Douvan and Adelson (1966) find a similar trend toward moral autonomy in boys, but not in girls. *Tuma and Livson (1960)* found a small sex difference in the same direction and a significant difference between status groups. Boys from lower middle class homes are more compliant to authority "at home, in school, (and) in the outside world" compared to boys from higher status backgrounds.

So adolescence witnesses some emotional detachment from the family. We are struck, however, by the relatively modest degree of change and wonder whether continued emotional attachment reflects parental refusal to accommodate autonomy stirrings, or whether the adolescent's urgent need for emotional escape has been overdrawn. Our search of the data leads us to consider the latter the more viable and realistic conclusion.

As the youngsters see it, certainly, parents are interested and concerned about them, and reasonable in their expectations and requirements. *Meissner* (1965) found that while boys become more distant from parents as they move through adolescence, they show increasing respect for parental authority. He reports that fathers take a more active role in guiding their sons as the boys get older, a finding also reported for girls (Douvan and Adelson, 1966). In projective stories and in responses to both projective and direct questions, the majority of boys and girls portray parents as concerned and guiding but not harsh or extremely restricting (*Maxwell, Connor, and Walters,* 1961; Douvan and Adelson, 1966; Rosenberg, 1965). Similiar results were reported when G. H. Elder (1962) assessed types of parent-adolescent interdependence by asking adolescents direct questions about their relationship to each parent. In a large sample, he found that types of interdependence ranged from extreme parental domination to a complete absence of parental control, but that the most common level of control was a democratic structure in which the adolescent was allowed considerable opportunity to make his own decisions under the final supervision of his parents.

What, then, are the conditions and forces that lead to the development of autonomy? What factors predispose a child to delay the change in family relations or to fall into one of the numerous corruptions of emotional autonomy (e.g., rebellious resistance, defensive independence covering strong but hidden dependency needs) that we hear so much about in discussions of delinquency and in therapeutic practice with neurotic youth?

The family conditions that encourage and support autonomy are parental warmth and concern, a democratic level of control, consideration and consistency in rule enforcement (Bronfenbrenner, 1961; G. H. Elder, 1965). A democratic level (or style) of parental control produces autonomy in the adolescent; autocratic or very lenient parents more often have children who are low in self-confidence and either dependent or rebellious (Douvan and Adelson, 1966; G. H. Elder, 1962). Bowerman and Elder (1962) describe democratic control as a situation in which the children are involved in making their own decisions and experience reasoning and explanations in their interaction with parents. Elder concludes that "both opportunities for learning skills of responsible independence and training for this role of self-reliance [are] essential conditions for the development of competent autonomy" (1963, p. 64).

Autonomy and self-direction are consistently found among those adolescents whose parents allow and encourage their children to detach themselves gradually from the family (Douvan and Adelson, 1966). The more autonomous children portray parents as concerned and guiding but not restrictive. According to their children's reports, these parents more often allow their children some voice in making rules that govern them, and they more often expect autonomy from their children—more than the parents of dependent or rebellious adolescents. In direct questions, children from equalitarian homes more often say they have disagreements with their parents, and in projective stories they more often picture a boy questioning a parental restriction directly. Their stance toward their parents is most clearly marked by that easy assumption of certain rights that must, we think, stem from a history of being treated like an independent person.

The dependent and rebellious—who are not entirely separate groups, by any means—say that the most important thing their parents expect is obedience, respect for authority. They rarely admit disagreements with parents at a conscious level, yet in the projective series and certain other situations, they show signs of a deeper and more corrosive hostility toward the parents. They more often say a boy would break a rule to rebel against his parents, that they do not have any adult ideal, that a boy who misbehaved would not tell his parents about it, or would not tell unless the parents asked. They are dependent but alienated, and the pattern follows a family interaction in which parents dominate heavily and harshly and regulate the child in ways that seem to the child arbitrary and mysterious.

In part, the differences between these systems of control can be conceived as differences in the nature of the cognitive signals offered the child. The democratic family, in contrast to the autocratic, emphasizes appeal to thought: the child is offered clear limits and rules which his parents formulate and verbalize for themselves and the child. The child understands what the rules are, and his parents recognize deviations and can control them consistently. The importance of rule explanations to adolescent progress in autonomy and internalization has been supported consistently by the large studies in this area (Bowerman and Elder, 1962; Douvan and Adelson, 1966; G. H. Elder, 1963; D. R. Miller and Swanson, 1958). One interesting exception to the association between rule verbalization and adolescent growth has been noted by Bowerman and Elder (1962): "Guidance and other types of verbal communication tend to produce dependency when combined with autocratic control."

Consistency of rules and rule enforcement has also held up across studies of both normal and deviant populations. More responsible autonomous adolescents think of their parents as consistent (Bowerman and Elder, 1962; Peck and Havighurst, 1960). Inconsistent rules and rule-enforcement more often characterize the families of adolescents who are nonautonomous and immature (Bowerman and Elder, 1962; Peck and Havighurst, 1960); impulse-ridden and defiant (Bandura and Walters, 1963; Bowerman and Elder, 1962; Douvan and Adelson, 1966; Rosenthal *et al.*, 1959; Rosenthal *et al.*, 1962); and delinquent (Glueck and Glueck, 1950; Martin, 1961; McCord and McCord, 1959; Nye, 1958; *Stanfield*, 1966).

While most adolescents show some movement toward greater autonomy, parental standards continue to play a dominant role in determining their ideas of right and wrong and in guiding their behavior of consequence. Boys through the age of sixteen still indicate that in personal decisions and moral conflict, their parents' standards and their own are more important than anyone else's, including those of their friends. Girls rely even more than boys on their parents' judgment, and they are more dependent on their peer group for validation of their self-concept (Douvan and Adelson, 1966; Solomon, 1961).

16

Changes in Family and Peer Orientation

of Children Between the Fourth and

Tenth Grades*

Charles E. Bowerman
John W. Kinch

There are a number of important theoretical problems which center around the transition of the child from sole membership in the family group during infancy to dual membership in the family and in a friendship group of peers. This shift involves not only an increasing orientation toward peers, but a change in relative orientation toward the family. The literature abundantly supports the view that the changing pattern of orientations toward these two primary groups with respect to affection, common interests, association, and acceptance of norms and values not only is related to the personal development of the individual, but also is an important factor in the dynamics of family relationships (e.g., Baldwin, 1955; Bossard, 1954).

It is generally accepted, for instance, that adequate socialization, as well as personal and social adjustment, requires an increasing ability of the child to get along with a group of peers as well as to maintain close relationships with members of his family. On the other hand, the nature of family interaction is affected by the decreasing participation and interest of the child in family activities as he becomes more involved in peer association; by the decline of the family as the primary source of affection with increasing attachment to peers; and by the weakening of authority and control of the parents as the child grows in independence and as norms and values of parents must compete for acceptance with those of peers. These are among the reasons why this transitional period is one of potential increase in parent-child conflict, due not only to the striving of the child to achieve status in two important primary groups with conflicting or competing interests, but also to the difficulties which parents as well as children experience in reacting to the changing situa-

tional and interactional characteristics of interpersonal relationships.

In this study, we were interested in the trend of relative orientation toward family or peers of students from the fourth through the tenth grade in school. The subjects were classified on three types of orientation: the extent to which they identified with one group or the other; the group with which they would prefer to associate; and the group which they thought of as having norms and values most like their own. For identification, subjects were asked which group (family or friends) understood them better and whether, when they grew up, they would rather be the kind of persons their parents are or the kind they think their friends would be. For association orientation, they were asked which group they most enjoyed doing things with, and which they would rather spend their time with in the evening and on weekends. The norm orientation questions asked whose ideas were most like theirs with respect to decisions of right and wrong, things that are fun to do, the importance of school, and what they would do if one group wanted them to do something that the other did not approve of. Each question, or pair of questions, provided for choice of either family or friends, and a neutral response indicating they felt the same about family and friends or would choose neither. On each of the three types of orientation, subjects were classified as neutral if there were an equal number of family and peer choices or if choices were neutral; as family oriented if there were more family than peer choices; and as peer oriented if there was a predominance of choices for friends. Using the same procedure, a combined orientation rating was made from the three separate orientation ratings.

The subjects used for the study were 686 students

* From *Social Forces*, 1959, **37**, 206–211.

from the fourth through the tenth grades from a middle-class school district north of Seattle, Washington. Questionnaires were filled out by four classrooms of students in each of the seven grades under the supervision of two school psychologists. The classes selected for study were those required of all students in a particular grade, to minimize bias in sample selection. The elementary school, junior high school, and high school from which the classes were selected drew students from the entire school district, so the basis for selection in the three schools was the same. Students who were not living with both parents at the time of the study were eliminated from the sample, and no nonwhite students were included in the sample.

Results

The data reveal the expected shift away from an orientation toward the family. (See Table 24.) On the combined index, 87.1 percent of the fourth graders were family oriented. By the eighth grade the percentage with family and peer orientation was approximately equal, and only 31.6 percent of the tenth graders were more highly oriented toward family than toward peers. The difference was made up, however, by an increase of neutral or equal orientation as well as by an increase in a greater peer than parent orientation. Those classed as neutral can be viewed not as shifting orientation away from the family, but of sharing peer and parent orientations equally.

The amount of change in orientation during this period was considerably different for the three types of orientation studied. The greatest shift from a predominant family orientation was with respect to association. By the tenth grade, only 15.2 percent indicated a preference for the family in association, although close to 30 percent were willing to share time with parents and peers equally. At the other extreme, 51.9 percent of the tenth graders still identified more closely with family than with peers, on our index, while only 26.6 percent identified more closely with peers. Trends in normative orientation were intermediate between the other two types.

Of particular interest in Table 24 is the reversing or slowing down of the trend between the eighth and ninth grades, and to a lesser extent between the fifth and sixth grades. In the school system used for this study, children moved to a junior high school for the sixth grade and to the senior high school for

TABLE 24. PERCENTAGE OF CHILDREN CLASSIFIED AS HAVING FAMILY, PEER, OR NEUTRAL ORIENTATION, BY GRADE IN SCHOOL

Orientation toward	Grade in School						
	4th	5th	6th	7th	8th	9th	10th
Combined Orientation							
Family ...	87.1	80.5	80.2	66.7	41.7	44.7	31.6
Neutral ...	6.9	12.2	11.2	9.3	18.3	22.4	20.2
Peer	5.9	7.3	8.6	24.1	40.0	32.9	48.1
Normative Orientation							
Family ...	82.2	64.6	69.8	51.9	33.0	42.4	30.4
Neutral ...	5.9	12.2	12.1	13.9	14.8	16.5	19.0
Peer	11.9	23.2	18.1	34.3	52.2	41.2	50.6
Association Orientation							
Family ...	75.2	65.9	62.1	51.9	20.9	21.2	15.2
Neutral ...	15.8	24.4	25.0	22.2	39.1	37.6	29.1
Peer	8.9	9.8	12.9	25.9	40.0	41.2	55.7
Identification							
Family ...	81.2	79.2	77.6	72.2	57.4	62.3	51.9
Neutral ...	13.8	18.3	18.1	18.5	24.3	24.7	21.5
Peer	5.0	2.4	4.3	9.2	18.2	13.0	26.6
N	101	82	116	108	115	85	79

the ninth grade. At first glance, this interruption of the trend might be attributed to sampling error, since the differences are small, and, individually, not statistically significant. However, the possibility that real differences exist is increased by the fact that the inflection occurs in each of the separate indices and in the breakdowns by sex and other background characteristics. The evidence is sufficient to suggest two hypotheses. First, a change in peer group structure will temporarily decrease or slow up peer orientation, at the same time increasing the tendency toward family orientation. In moving to a new school, the student is separated from many of the friends he had established in the previous grade. This, of course, happens to some extent between every grade, but in this case there are students from several schools put into the same new school, classes are mixed up, and the chances of a group staying together are lower. This change in association patterns, coupled with the shifting sociometric framework of a larger group, the new environment, new regulations and new expectations, may be sufficiently disturbing to many children to cause them to look to their family for support.

The second hypothesis is that the orientation of the child is a function of the perception which the family has of his status, and that moving to another school on a higher level is associated with a significant change in status. There would appear to be something like a law of perseveration in human relations, according to which we tend to react to another person in the same manner until there is some force operating, such as a status change imposed on the relationship, which modifies our perception of the other and the way in which we shall react to them. We would expect, for this reason, that parents tend to hold the same demands and expectations of their children until a change in external circumstances forces them to look at their children from a new perspective. In many societies, such transitional periods of status are built in and observed by elaborate rituals. In our society, increase in physical growth and the onset of puberty are signs that the child is growing up. Our hypothesis states that changes in school status, such as starting to high school, and to a lesser extent starting junior high, are indications of such a transitional period, visible to the family as well as to other members of the community. It may be at such periods that parental controls are somewhat relaxed, and that they change their behavior toward the child in other ways so that he comes to react to the parents in more positive terms.

Sex of child. There is abundant evidence that the socialization process differs for boys and girls in many ways (Hartley and Hartley, 1952; Lindesmith and Strauss, 1956; Newcomb, 1955). The male in our society is given more independence at an earlier age than the female, and consequently might be expected to be less limited in peer group contacts and be oriented toward peers earlier. On the other hand, an excess of parental restriction might foster a lower family orientation for girls. Ausubel (1954), for one, reports a difference both in intensity and type of conflicts with parents reported by boys and girls. Although the girls' conflicts are more intense, they are concerned with broad issues of independence, self-determination, and sex role. The boys' problems are of lower intensity and are centered around specific adolescent privileges of growing up.

The orientation trends for boys and girls in our sample are essentially similar, but there are several interesting differences. Girls in the fourth through sixth grades have a slightly higher percentage who are family oriented, but from the seventh through tenth grades there is a larger percentage of family oriented boys than girls. These differences, though small, hold for most of the comparisons with the

subindices of orientation as well as for the combined index. For example, 42 percent of the ninth and tenth grade boys had a predominant family orientation on the combined index, compared with 35 percent of the girls in those grades.

The greatest difference between the two sexes is the point at which the largest shift from family to peer orientation takes place. The year-to-year comparisons of the combined orientation ratings show that the greatest shift in orientation takes place about a year earlier for girls than for boys. The percentage of parent-oriented girls decreases from 85.7 in the sixth grade to 56.2 in the seventh, with a corresponding increase in peer orientation from 3.6 to 33.3 percent. The percentage for the boys remained relatively stable for these two years, but dropped in parent orientation from 75.0 to 41.4 percent from the seventh to the eighth grades with an increase in peer orientation from 16.7 to 43.1 percent. The same trend appears in each of the separate indices, but the change in associational orientation was more gradual for the girls, continuing on into the eighth grade.

The most obvious association to make with the difference in trends of orientation found between boys and girls is the difference in physical maturation, since it is known that such changes occur approximately a year earlier in girls. There might appear to be a logical inconsistency between the statement that changes associated with puberty are associated with an increase in peer orientation, and our previous hypothesis that status changes associated with going to a higher level of school are responsible for a retarding or inflection in the trend. However, we are dealing not only with status in the family group but also in the peer group, and it is likely that status changes attendant on puberty have greater implications for peer-group relations than for relations with the family. In addition to this, the changes in status in the family accompanying puberty may, particularly for girls, be associated with a new set of restrictions and controls which may serve to intensify the orientation toward peers and exaggerate the differences in norms and values of the parent and peer groups.

Family size and father's occupation. Due to the limited number of cases, family size was considered as a dichotomous variable with families having three or fewer children classified as small, and those with four or more children classified as large families. During the first three grades of our sample, the large

and small family orientation patterns were very similar. From the seventh grade on, however, the shift
away from a predominant family orientation was
more rapid and reached a lower point for the large-
family children than for those from smaller families.
This was true not only for the combined index, but
also for each of the three separate indices and, for
most comparisons, for both boys and girls, although
for the latter breakdown the numbers were too
small to iron out irregularities in the curves.

Father's occupation was classified as high status
(including professionals, proprietors, managers, and
officials), medium status (clerical and sales workers,
craftsmen, foremen), and low status (operatives,
service workers, and laborers). No consistent differences were found in orientations of children whose
fathers were in these three groups. This may have
been because of the small number of cases in the subgroups, but more likely is because other factors are
of greater importance in determining orientation.

Adjustment to family and peers. To get an index
of adjustment to the family, four questions were
used: (1) How well do you get along with the
members of your family? (2) Does your family give
you the attention you think they should? (3) Do
you talk over your personal problems with your
family? (4) Does your family treat you the way you
think you should be treated? The same four questions were repeated with "friends" substituted for
"family." Each scale was then dichotomized to provide four groups with respect to combined adjustment to family and to peers: Group I—high on both
scales (N = 148); Group II—high toward family,
low toward peers (N = 161); Group III—high toward peers, low toward family (N = 156); and
Group IV—low toward both (N = 221). The orientation pattern was then found for the students in
each grade who fell into these four groups. The
number of cases in some of the subgroups was very
small, with 10 of the 28 groups having fewer than 20
cases. However, certain regularities appear and, since
each of the seven grades can be considered as an
independent sample, greater confidence can be
placed on differences appearing consistently. Trends
from grade to grade are somewhat more tenuous,
although consistencies are apparent.

The relationship between family-peer adjustment
and the combined index of orientation can be seen
in Table 25. It will be noted that the over-all trend
toward a reduction of family orientation with increasing age holds for each of the four groups.

TABLE 25. PERCENTAGES OF CHILDREN CLASSIFIED AS
FAMILY, NEUTRAL, OR PEER ORIENTED, ON COMBINED
INDEX, BY ADJUSTMENT TO FAMILY AND PEERS

Level of Adjustment to family and peers*	Grade in School						
	4th	5th	6th	7th	8th	9th	10th
Percent Family Oriented							
Group I ...	93.3	92.0	89.3	77.8	75.0	55.6	52.9
Group II ...	97.3	100.0	90.6	100.0	83.3	71.4	61.5
Group III ..	54.5	46.2	52.9	50.0	21.6	25.9	16.1
Group IV ..	78.3	69.6	76.9	42.9	33.0	45.7	16.7
Percent with Neutral Orientation							
Group I ...	3.3	8.0	10.7	3.7	0.0	11.1	17.6
Group II ...	2.7	0.0	3.1	0.0	0.0	21.4	15.4
Group III ..	9.1	23.1	11.8	10.0	24.3	25.9	22.5
Group IV ..	17.4	21.7	17.9	20.0	25.0	22.9	22.0
Percent Peer Oriented							
Group I ...	3.3	0.0	0.0	18.5	25.0	33.3	29.4
Group II ...	0.0	0.0	6.2	0.0	16.7	7.1	23.1
Group III ..	36.4	30.8	35.3	40.0	54.1	48.1	61.3
Group IV ..	4.3	8.7	5.1	37.1	41.7	31.4	61.1

* Group I: High adjustment to family and peers
Group II: High with family, low with peers
Group III: High with peers, low with family
Group IV: Low with family and with peers

However, there is a striking difference in the pattern
for those who were highest on the scale of adjustment to family (Groups I and II). They are consistently higher on family orientation, with over half of
the tenth graders remaining more family than peer
oriented, and they are also lower on neutral orientation than the other two groups. The greatest difference, as would be expected, is between Groups II
and III which differ most in relative adjustment to
family and peers. Peer orientation for the Group III
children starts early, emphasizing the point that
family orientation is a function not only of age, but
also of adjustment to the group.

When we hold constant the level of adjustment
to family, the percentage of children with family
orientation is lower for those having high adjustment to peers than for those with low adjustment.
However, the differences are not too great. The
average difference for all seven grades in percentage
of family adjustment between Groups I and II is
only 9.7, and the average difference between Groups
III and IV is 13.7. On the other hand, when we
hold constant the level of adjustment to peers, family orientation is greatly affected by adjustment to

family. The average difference in percent with family orientation between Group I and Group III is 38.4, while the difference between Groups II and IV averages 34.4.

These differences, along with the high level of family orientation for Groups I and II and the much lower level of family orientation at all grade levels for children in Group III, indicate that *the pattern of family-peer orientation is much more affected by adjustment to family than by adjustment to peers.*

The temporary reversal of the orientation trend between the fifth and sixth grades and again between the eighth and ninth grades was noted earlier. It can be seen in Table 25 that this reversal holds only for children with low adjustment to family (Groups III and IV). This lends support to the explanation suggested earlier that the change in status accompanying the achievement of a new school level may affect the family interaction in such a way as to modify the orientation pattern. Any change in interaction would presumably be felt most in those families with low adjustment.

The relative differences among the four adjustment groups, reported in this section for the combined orientation rating, hold up for the three separate orientation ratings from which the combined rating was derived. The most clear-cut differences among the four adjustment groups were found for identification, where 77 percent of the tenth graders in Group II still had a predominant family orientation, compared with only 32 percent of the students in Group III. It should also be noted that by the tenth grade all four groups had fairly low percentages who were primarily oriented toward the family with respect to association. Even the Group II students in the tenth grade had only 31 percent whose association orientation was toward the family, compared with 7 percent of those in Group III. When adjustment toward the family is favorable, the family can still maintain a close relationship in terms of affection, or identification, and acceptance of family values, even though the child prefers the peer group for association.

Conclusions

The results of this study would seem to lend support to the following hypotheses. First, as children become increasingly involved in activities with peers, they become increasingly oriented toward the peer group, particularly with respect to association, and to a lesser extent in accepting the norms and values of the peer group. The degree of peer orientation is related to the level of adjustment to peers, but in most cases will be high for the adolescent regardless of the adjustment to peers.

Second, a lowered orientation toward the family during the period of adolescence is not inevitable, but takes place only when a poor adjustment is made to members of the family. We found that those students who had a high level of adjustment to the family were most likely to be oriented toward the family, particularly in identification and in acceptance of family norms and values.

Finally, although not directly suggested by our data, our findings are consistent with the hypothesis that low adjustment to the family and low family orientation are a function of the way in which the family reacts to the child during the period of increasing peer orientation. This is to say that orientation toward the family and the peer group is not an either/or matter for the adolescent, in which increasing orientation toward peers necessarily deflates his orientation toward family, but that certain ambiguities in group commitment are involved which complicate relationships both for the child and for his family and lead to types of interaction within the family group which may prevent the adolescent from maintaining strong primary relationships with both groups.

Additional investigation along these lines will require, first of all, improved measures of orientation. Rather than finding the prodominant orientation toward family *or* peers, it will be necessary to measure the degree of orientation toward each group. Also, separate measures of orientation toward mother and father, as well as toward siblings, will have to be developed. Our findings here suggest the importance of distinguishing among at least three types of orientation—affection or identification, association, and acceptance of norms and values. With improved measures of orientation, it would be of interest to relate orientation patterns to various family patterns and interactional processes in terms of which differences and trends in orientation could be explained.

17

Parental Interaction

of the Adolescent Boy[*]

W. W. Meissner, S.J.

Introduction

In the last few years, the awareness of the importance of the home environment and the pattern of interaction between the parents and the child has become central in the search for a better understanding of personality development and adjustment. The adolescent years represent a crucial period in the formation of "identity" (Erikson, 1959) and in the formation of values, ideals and attitudes; and the formation of values, ideals, and attitudes is profoundly influenced by the relations that obtain between the adolescent and his parents. Disturbances in the development of identity or the "identity diffusion" that has been thought to underlie the defective adjustment of so many adolescents (and, subsequently, adults) in American culture has been traced to the influence of inconsistencies in intrafamiliar relationships and early deprivation (Beres, Gale, and Oppenheimer, 1960). Also, evidence has been provided that seems to link delinquency, which is a major symptom of identity diffusion, with a defect in parental identification and a lack of strong and open affection (Andry, 1960).

While the importance of the parent-child interaction has been widely accepted, no clear understanding has emerged as to what factors are crucial in the parent-child interaction. The importance of the mother's role has been accepted ever since H. S. Sullivan's work (1953), but more recently the father's influence on a child's development has received emphasis. Andry's investigations (1960) seem to imply that a child's failure to identify with his father and inadequate communication with his father are central elements in the etiology of delinquency. Further, current studies in family dynamics have focused on the importance of the father's role (Bowen, Dysinger, and Basamanis, 1959; Lidz, Parker, and Cornelison, 1956; Lidz, Cornelison,

* From *The Journal of Genetic Psychology*, 1965, **107**, 225–233.

Fleck, and Terry, 1957). Undoubtedly, the significant environment within a family is compounded not only of the level of adjustment and functioning of each parent individually or not only of the pattern of the interaction of the parents with each other, but also of the manner in which both parents interact with the growing adolescent. This study is directed to the assessment of the frequency of occurrence of certain typical parent-child interactions in a population of normal adolescent boys.

Procedure

The results presented arise from a 217-item questionnaire that was given to 1278 high-school boys attending nine schools. The schools were private, denominational schools under Catholic direction and were located in the states of New York, Pennsylvania, New Jersey, and Maryland. The questionnaires were given with a standard set of instructions read to the subjects by the test administrator. The test forms were sent in a sealed envelope to each administrator, who opened the envelope in the presence of the subjects, and immediately after the questionnaries were completed resealed the forms in an envelope for delivery to the investigator.

The subjects were selected randomly according to classes in their respective schools and they represented the medium range in academic achievement in their schools. Three hundred thirty-one were freshmen; 313, sophomores; 343, juniors, and 291, seniors. Ages ranged from 13 to 18, with average ages as follows: freshmen, 14.3 years; sophomores, 15.2 years; juniors, 16.2 years; and seniors, 17.2 years.

Family Characteristics

The families from which the boys came can be described as average middle-class families, and the average family group consists of father, mother, and siblings. Only 13 percent of the subjects reported any persons living in the home other than members of the immediate family group. In six percent of the families the father was deceased; in two percent of the families the mother was deceased. Eight of the subjects lost a parent before the subject reached the age of two years; 13, between the ages of two and six; 28, between the ages of six and 10; and 41, after the age of 10. Only four percent of the boys reported divorce or separation of parents, not an unexpected figure in a predominantly Catholic population.

The families, for the most part, appear to have been financially stable; but 21 percent of the subjects reported that financial troubles were a source of difficulty at home, and 27 percent of the subjects reported a mother engaged in some form of work outside the home. The parents were predominantly native-born Americans, with only 14 percent of the fathers and 10 percent of the mothers having been born outside the United States. The proportion of Catholics in this population is strong: 91 percent of the fathers and 96 percent of the mothers profess the Catholic faith.

The only significant difference between fathers and mothers is educational level (Anastasi and Foley, 1953). Seventy percent of the fathers and 72 percent of the mothers had progressed beyond the high-school level, but 37 percent of the fathers and 54 percent of the mothers failed to finish college. Thirty-three percent of the fathers and only 17 percent of the mothers had graduated from college or had received some postgraduate training.

Not quite 13 percent of the boys indicated that illness is a source of frequent home difficulty.

Perception of Parents

Whatever may be the attitudes or behavior of parents toward their children, the effect on the children is mediated through the children's perception of them (Ausubel *et al.*, 1954) and there seem to be detectable differences between the perceptions of parents and adolescents. Hess (1959–1960), for example, has shown that (while the descriptions of teenagers of themselves tend to agree with descriptions of them by their parents) teenagers expect their parents to underrate them; and parents expect the teenagers to overestimate the maturity and ability of teenagers. Adolescents rate parents higher than parents rate themselves on every item on which adolescents were questioned. These findings can be explained easily on the basis of the high valuation

put on adult status by the adolescent who is struggling to define his own identity; but, at the same time, the explanation raises the question of the relationship between the objective situation and the adolescent's perception of it. In other words, the adolescent's perception of his home and parents is colored to a certain extent by his own needs.

The questionnaire responses suggest that certain differences exist between the perceptions of fathers and mothers and that these differences may be meaningful for understanding the interactions between adolescents and their parents. The differential parental characteristics can be listed as follows:

Father	*Mother*
Colder and more indifferent.	More friendly and interested.
More old-fashioned.	More nervous.
Less understanding.	More understanding.
More unreasonable.	More reasonable.

Thirty-five percent of the students felt that their fathers were cold or indifferent; only 13 percent thought this of their mothers. Fifty-one percent thought their fathers more or less old-fashioned; 41 percent regarded their mothers that way. Thirty-nine percent thought their fathers understood the subject's difficulties; 54 percent thought their mothers did. Thirteen percent thought their fathers "nervous"; 30 percent perceived their mothers as "nervous."

The typical relationship that emerges is decidedly more positive in regard to the mother than it is in regard to the father. Although the configuration may or may not run counter to the presumptive identification of the male child with the father figure, it raises a question about the influence of typical parental perceptions on the course of child development. Apparently the father figure becomes fixed with the role of mediator of parental authority and restriction; while the mother is perceived as responding more to emotional needs for sympathy, acceptance, and understanding. Moreover, the trends in the data, while not always significant, suggest that the foregoing perceptions become more dominant as one moves from the first year to the senior year of high school.

In general, the attitudes toward parents tapped by our questions were positive. The majority thought their parents not overly careful or concerned about them (62 percent) or overly strict (85 percent). Most felt proud of their parents and liked to have them meet their friends (74 percent).

Parent-Child Interaction

As the young boy proceeds through the adolescent period, the pattern of his interactions with his parents shifts in both positive and negative dimensions. The dimensions of interaction, in which the shifts are statistically significant ($p < .05$), can be listed as follows:

Positive

1. Increased feeling of adequate social opportunity.
2. Increased feeling of sufficient social freedom.
3. Increased acceptance of parental authority.
4. Increased valuation of father's guidance.

Negative

1. Increased dissatisfaction with home life.
2. Increased unhappiness in the home.
3. Decrease in amount of leisure time spent at home.
4. Increased conflict with parents over religion.
5. Decreased approval of parental guidance.
6. Increase in seeing friends disapproved by parents.
7. Increased feeling of the imposition of parents' ideas.
8. Decreased valuation of father's understanding of personal problems.
9. Increased feeling of being misunderstood by parents; more misunderstood by father than mother.

The overall picture is one of gradual alienation from parental influence and increasing rebelliousness against parental control. The shifts, however, are variable. As might be expected, reports of satisfaction and happiness in the home situation are high (80 percent and 89 percent respectively), and a large majority (84 percent) report that half or more of their leisure time is spent at home. Dissatisfaction and unhappiness, however, increase significantly as the boy grows older.

Religious belief does not provide a singular source of conflict. Only seven percent report that differences in the religious beliefs of their parents have ever caused them any difficulty, and only 16 percent report that they have ever come into conflict with their parents on the question of religion. There is a trend, however, toward increasing conflict as the boy grows older. This pattern coincides with the previ-

ously reported finding (Meissner, 1961b) that religious belief becomes a primary source of serious doubt for this same group in their junior and senior years. This increasing concern would be likely to express itself in conflict with the parents.

Most of the boys do not feel that their parents' demands are excessive, but 18 percent feel that their parents expect more than they can ordinarily accomplish. The large majority, however, approve of the manner in which their parents guide them (73 percent). These attitudes undergo a significant shift ($p < .01$) between the freshman year (79 percent) and the junior year (68 percent).

The adolescent period is one of increasing social and heterosexual contacts; consequently it is to be expected that the regulation of these activities provides a common source of friction between the adolescent and his parents. In general, the majority of our subjects report that their parents encourage them to bring their friends into the home (75 percent) and, to a lesser extent, that their parents approve of all their friends (54 percent). Parental approval is reported as increasing steadily until the junior year and dropping off sharply in the senior year ($p < .02$). However, when parents do not approve of particular friends, only 34 percent stop going with those friends.

Most of the parents (75 percent) have the practice of setting a time for their sons to be home at night, but the practice seems to be observed less frequently as the boys grow older (freshmen, 83 percent; sophomores, 82 percent; juniors, 76 percent; and seniors, 60 percent). The difference between seniors and each of the other groups is significant at the .01 level; that between juniors and freshmen is significant at the .05 level. Coincident with a relaxation of parental restriction, there is an increasing feeling that the boys are being treated as maturely as they should be (freshmen, 54 percent; sophomores, 64 percent; juniors, 73 percent; and seniors, 77 percent). A majority of the boys (66 percent) feel that they are given as much social freedom as other boys, and the frequency of that feeling parallels closely their feelings of being maturely treated (freshmen, 55 percent; sophomores, 65 percent; juniors, 70 percent; seniors, 74 percent). One-half of the boys (50 percent) claim that they argue for greater liberty when they feel they deserve it.

In a minority of cases, parents are listed as the first source of sex information. Fathers are given as the source of first sex information by 22 percent of the boys; mothers, by 20 percent. For the most part, parents seem to be successful in giving such information. Only 11 percent of the boys report that they lost confidence in their parents because of the way the sex issue was handled. In the majority of cases (73 percent), the parents are acquainted with the girls whom the boys date, and conflict with the parents over girlfriends is not frequent (13 percent).

A large majority of the boys (87 percent) recognize that parents exercise legitimate authority over them, but the figure fluctuates significantly between class groups. The shift that occurs between the freshman and senior years may reflect a maturing acceptance of the intellectual awareness of the grounds of parental authority or it may reflect a greater degree of identification with adult figures and adult status. In any case, parents are selected as the persons whom the boys obey more frequently than they do any other authority figure (83 percent). Ninety percent of the boys report that they understand the reason why they should obey their parents.

Parental authority, however, is not accepted without resistance. A small minority of the boys feel that the discipline in the home is too severe (10 percent), and 19 percent express the feeling that they are not treated as young men of their age should be treated. The majority, however, feel that in the exercise of responsibility their parents give them sufficient opportunity (58 percent). At the same time, 28 percent are not satisfied with the opportunities made available to them for responsible activity. Some boys (32 percent) report that they are frequently scolded by their parents, and an even larger number (42 percent) express the feeling that parents tend to impose their own ideas and customs. This latter feeling grows more frequent as the boy matures, possibly because of the increasing influence on him of opinions and attitudes derived from his peer group and because of other influences external to the home. Finally, 14 percent feel that parents exert too much authority over them.

Negative attitudes toward parental authority and discipline are damaging because the internalization of parental norms is an essential step in the development of a responsible person. The formation of a mature identity depends in part on the stable and mature use of authority on the part of the parents; so unless the adolescent maintains positive attitudes the developmental pattern is more likely to be one of rejection and rebellion than one of acceptance. More often than not the question of rebellion does not arise so much as does the question of the adoles-

cent's need and desire to establish his independence. When parental norms are presented in an authoritarian manner there is a tendency to develop negative attitudes toward them, and this tendency becomes more noticeable as the child grows older or shows better verbal intelligence. When parental restrictions are presented with rational motivations there is a tendency for positive attitudes to assert themselves (Pikas, 1961).

Perhaps the most important area of interaction between the adolescent and his parents is that of communication. It is particularly during the period of adolescence that the maturing young man needs the counsel and advice of his elders to enable him to work his way through the conflicts and turmoil characteristic of that period of development. In the present study, 33 percent of the boys claim that they do discuss difficulties and personal problems with their fathers. Almost 39 percent feel that their fathers understand their difficulties, while the rest of the subjects are divided between those who feel their fathers do not understand them (30 percent) and those who are still undecided (31 percent). There is a definite trend between the freshmen and the seniors (freshmen, 45 percent; seniors, 33 percent) to call into question the father's understanding. Fifty-three percent of the boys say that they discuss their problems with their mothers, and 54 percent feel that the mother understands the difficulties.

The father's influence regarding guidance seems to become relatively more dominant as the boy grows older. This trend presents a pattern much different from the previously observed pattern of discussing problems and difficulties. Apparently, adolescent boys turn to the father when there is a question of working out the ordinary everyday affairs; but, when immediate problems and difficulties arise, they tend to turn to the mother.

A small percent of the boys (nine percent) report that they fear their fathers rather than love them. In all age groups, there is a consistent tendency to feel more often misunderstood by the father than by the mother. The fixation of the perception of the mother establishes an expectation of continued feminine responsiveness in the future marriage relationship. The more negative fixation of the perception of the father, however, may have the effect of inhibiting the acceptance of the more masculine characteristics that depend on internalization of norms of restrictive discipline. Internalization is essential to the development of a strong sense of masculine identity. At the same time, the positive aspect of the significantly increased valuation of the father's guidance must be kept in mind.

The results of this study imply that there is a pattern of increasing alienation from parental influence and control that can be traced through the critical years of adolescence. There is a growing acceptance of the principle of parental authority and increased respect for parental judgment, especially significant because the strong Catholic influence would have been expected to have reinforced parental authority and to have stressed the value of obedience.

It is not clear, however, that the independent indications justify an identification of the visible pattern as one of rebelliousness. Analysis in terms of "rebelliousness" may reflect a prejudice dictated by a vested interest. From the point of view of the adolescent, the growing indications of decreasing parental authority may represent nothing more than a critical phase of differentiation from parental influence: an essential part of development toward mature and independent functioning.

In conclusion, the author suggests that there is a relationship between identifiable perceptions of parental figures and patterns of interaction between the adolescent and his parents, and that there is a determinable shift in these perceptions reflected in shifting patterns of interaction.

Summary

A total of 1278 high-school boys were asked to answer 217 questions on areas of interaction between themselves and their parents. The results indicate that certain typical perceptions of father and mother can be identified, and that these perceptions are significantly different. Also identified were patterns of interaction that reveal significant shifts between the early and the late years of high school. The shifts, generally, are in the direction of parental alienation and increased rebelliousness. An attempt was made to relate the boys' perceptions of parental perceptions to the developing pattern of interaction with the parents.

18

Family Member Perceptions

of Parent Role Performance *

Patricia Henderson Maxwell
Ruth Connor
James Walters

Studies of family behavior are increasingly pointing up the importance of analyses of family member perceptions of parent-child roles. Such an emphasis stems from a recognition that conflict and disagreement among family members not infrequently result from differences in the evaluation of day-to-day patterns of interaction, and that the identification of differences in perceptions of family member roles is an important step in determining the etiology of familial conflicts.

Several investigators (Duvall, 1946; R. L. Elder, 1949) in studying the perceptions of single groups of family members (fathers, mothers, adolescents) have made significant contributions concerning (a) conceptions of characteristics of "good" mother, father, and child roles and (b) actual role performance of family members. Still others (Connor, Greene, and Walters, 1958; Connor, Johannis, and Walters, 1954) have been concerned with the extent to which conceptions of one member of a family reflect the role conceptions of other members of the same family. However, because little attention has been directed to a study of the degree of personal bias which is reflected in the subject's evaluation of family member *role performance*, the present investigation has undertaken a study of the perceptions of members of the same family concerning role performance of parents.

Specifically, it was the purpose of the study (a) to determine whether the perceptions of role performance are a function of the role of the family member responding (father, mother, or adolescent); (b) to obtain indices of agreement concerning perceptions of members of the same family; and (c) to ascertain whether there is a tendency for one group to rate parental performance more favorably than the other groups.

* From *Merrill-Palmer Quarterly of Behavior and Development*, 1961, **7,** 31–37.

In one of the initial studies of parent-adolescent relationships undertaken at Florida State University (Connor et al., 1954), no significant differences were found to exist among fathers, mothers, and college-age youth with respect to their conceptions of good father, good mother, and good child roles. These findings suggest that insofar as role conceptions of what constitutes "good" family member roles are concerned, college-age youth reflect conceptions which are similar to those of their parents. A later study (Connor *et al.*, 1958) investigated role conceptions of a younger (tenth-grade) group together with the conceptions of their parents. Evidence was found to support the hypothesis that significant differences exist among fathers, mothers, and adolescents concerning their conceptions of good family member roles. Because all of the students in the initial study were university students enrolled in a course including material on marriage and the family, and thus represented a highly select sample, it is difficult to generalize from the findings of these two studies. Perhaps as adolescents mature, their conceptions may reflect greater agreement with their parents than at earlier levels of development.

The present report describes a phase of the study of the high-school youth and their parents. It should be noted that an important difference exists between the present analysis of responses of high-school youth and the study reported earlier (Connor *et al.*, 1958) which was concerned with agreement of family members' conceptions of "good" parent and child roles. Whereas the earlier study focused on differences in *role conceptions*, the present study is concerned with differences in perceptions of actual *role performance*. It is evident that an individual's role performance as a father, for example, may be deficient (by a given culture's standards), and yet his perceptions of what a "good" father is like may accurately reflect the cultural prescription. Thus, it would not necessarily follow that because family members were in agreement, or were not in agreement, as to what constituted "good" family member roles, they would necessarily agree, or disagree, on how well members performed their roles.

That differences do exist among family members in their evaluations of role performance is evidenced by the research of Hess and Goldblatt (1957) which indicated that among their subjects the adolescents evidenced a much higher opinion of the adults than did their parents while the parents anticipated that the teen-agers would evidence a tendency to undervalue the adults.

Method

A sample consisting of fifty adolescents, twenty-five males and twenty-five females, enrolled in the tenth grade of the Leon County High School, Tallahassee, Florida, and their mothers and fathers, was selected according to a table of random numbers. The sample consisted of a broad socioeconomic range of intact families, predominantly Protestant, living in the Tallahassee area. The subjects responded to selected questions concerned with parental role performance. Each participant responded individually to a questionnaire within which were 17 items concerning the mother-child relationship and 17 items concerning the father-child relationship. The adolescents completed their questionnaires during a regular class period at school, and the parents completed theirs at home. Two questionnaires with parallel items were delivered to each home with the instructions that the parents were to respond to their questionnaires independently and that they were not to alter their responses after they had compared them with their spouses'. The parents' questionnaires were reclaimed within 48 hours.

Parallel items were presented to the parents and their children. For example, the parent item, "I nag my child . . .," was presented to the youth as "My father nags me . . ."; "My mother nags me. . . ."

The subjects responded to the items on a variety of five-point continua, e.g. (a) always, almost always, usually, sometimes, seldom or never; (b) always fair, almost always fair . . .; (c) do exactly as told, do about as told . . .; (d) in all situations, in most situations. . . .

The parallel items were analyzed for the father's and child's perceptions of the father's role perfor-

mance and for the mother's and child's perceptions of the mother's role performance.

To determine whether the nature of the rating of the role performance of the parent was a function of the role of the family member responding (father, mother, or adolescent), a chi-square analysis was employed. To obtain evidence concerning the extent to which differences in ratings of role performance existed among members *of the same family*, percentages of agreement were calculated.

Results and Discussion

In general, the data fail to support the belief that the ratings of parental role performance are dependent upon the role of the family member responding. There were, however, several exceptions.

A comparison of the responses of the fathers and adolescents concerning the question of interest in what the child does revealed a relationship significant at the .001 level: The fathers' ratings indicated that they were more interested in what their children were doing than the adolescents perceived their fathers to be.

An analysis of the responses of the fathers and adolescents and the mothers and adolescents to questions concerned with the generosity with which the parent spent money on the adolescent yielded chi-square values which were statistically significant at the .01 and at the .05 levels, respectively. These results indicated that the perceptions reported were a function of the role of the family member responding. In both instances, the adolescents indicated their parents to be more generous than their parents felt themselves to be.

The responses of the mothers and adolescents concerning the question of how the mothers and adolescents "got along" revealed a relationship significant at the .05 level between rating of respondents and their roles. The responses of the adolescents revealed a more favorable evaluation of the mother-child relationship than did those of the mothers.

The data indicate that considerable similarity exists between fathers and mothers with respect to their ratings of their relationships with their adolescents. The responses, however, indicated that mothers nagged their adolescents more frequently than did fathers.

TABLE 26. PARENT-ADOLESCENT AGREEMENT ON THE RELATIONSHIP BETWEEN THEM

Parent Items[a]	Specific Agreement (%)		Nonspecific Agreement (%)	
	Fathers-Adolescents	Mothers-Adolescents	Fathers-Adolescents	Mothers-Adolescents
I am interested in what my child does	60	74	74	96
When my child asks me questions, I give him (her) honest answers	54	72	84	98
I respect my child's opinion	42	48	84	86
I consider the punishment which I give my child	48	40	80	84
I nag at my child				
Considering the amount of money I have, I consider that I spend it on my child	32	44	76	84
When I make my child do something, I tell him (her) why it is necessary	22	42	70	78
I approve of how my child behaves	44	36	92	76
When my child wants help with homework, I help him (her)	30	26	76	66
When I tell my child to do something, he (she) usually	60	66	92	86
In giving my child information about sex, I	61	58	76	84
Of the problems of young people the age of my child, I think I understand	54	54	88	90
If my child were in trouble, he (she) would tell me	48	56	80	94
I scold my child	62	56	90	96
Generally, my child and I get along	58	44	96	97
My child feels that I approve of how he (she) behaves	43	40	90	88
I discuss with my child	44	38	78	80

[a] Parallel items were given to the adolescents.

The percentages of specific and nonspecific agreement are reported in Table 26. When two family members responded identically, the agreement was designated as *specific*; however, when the responses were as much as one scale step apart, the agreement was designated as *nonspecific*.

Although it became clear in the analysis of the data that the ratings between fathers and adolescents and mothers and adolescents concerning role performances were independent of the group of subjects responding, i.e., whether fathers, mothers, or adolescents; it was deemed desirable to ascertain if there was a tendency for one group (fathers, mothers, or adolescents) to portray the relationships more favorably than the others. In Figure 23 such a comparison is made. Although it will be noted that the ratings of the mothers and adolescents and the fathers and adolescents were similar, in a greater number of instances the adolescents' ratings were more favorable than were those of either the fathers or the mothers.

The present study tends to support the conclusion of Hess and Goldblatt (1957) that adolescents evidence a "higher opinion" of adults than do their parents. More important, however, it suggests that precise descriptions of family member role performance may not be obtained through studies of the

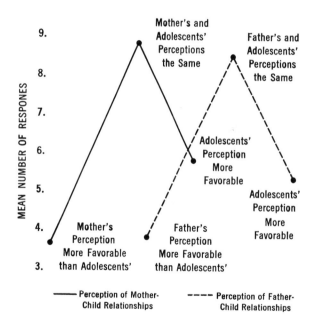

FIG. 23. Perception of parent-child relationships.

perceptions of adolescents, although it does suggest that fairly reliable *estimates* of role performance may be obtained from studies of single groups of individuals, e.g., adolescents. This may be important for the researcher since adolescent subjects are often more easily obtained than adult subjects.

Summary

It was the purpose of the study (a) to determine whether the ratings of parent role performance are dependent upon the role of the family member responding, (b) to obtain indices of agreement among members of the same family concerning role performance, and (c) to ascertain whether there is a tendency for one group (fathers, mothers, or adolescents) to rate the role performance of parents more favorably than do the other groups.

A random sample of fifty adolescents and their mothers and fathers responded to selected questions concerned with perceptions of parent-adolescent relationships.

The major findings were as follows:

1. In general, the data fail to support the belief that the perceptions of the parent-adolescent relationships are a function of the role of the family member responding.

2. In the vast majority of instances the ratings of the fathers and mothers were within one scale step of each other. Greater agreement was evidenced between the responses of the mothers and adolescents than between those of fathers and adolescents.

3. Although the ratings of the mothers and adolescents and the fathers and adolescents were similar, in the majority of instances the adolescents tended to rate parent-adolescent relationships more favorably than did either their fathers or mothers.

19

Family Socioeconomic Status

*and Adolescent Attitudes to Authority**

Elias Tuma
Norman Livson

This study explores the relationships between several indices of family socioeconomic status and adolescents' attitudes to authority in some common social contexts—in the home, in school, and with their friends. The emphasis here is not upon behavioral conformity or rebellion but, rather, upon the degree to which the adolescent—on a phenomenological level—accepts or rejects the rules and regulations set for him in a given situation. The hypotheses to be evaluated are very general ones: that the socioeconomic status of the family plays some part in determining the degree of conformity experienced by an adolescent and that the various components of this social status differ in the extent of their effects

upon his attitudes to authority. While the specific nature of these effects—and their mediation—remains an active and current research question, there is consensus on the general statement that social classes in the United States differ in their characteristic socialization values and practices and, in turn, that children exhibit corresponding differences in their attitudes and behaviors (see review by Bronfenbrenner, 1958).

There is little previous work specifically relevant to the present question and the two most informative studies are not in agreement. Dimock (1937) reports no significant relationship between adolescents' degree of *felt* emancipation from parents and the socioeconomic status of their families. Psathas (1957) finds, two decades later, that on three of four

* From *Child Development*, 1960, **31**, 387–399.

dimensions of "independence" the social class of the family is a significant correlate: the lower the social class, the more independence the adolescent *perceives* himself to have in the form of his parents' permissiveness towards him and their respect for his judgment. The apparent contradiction between the two studies may not demand reconciliation since they differ in their samples: Dimock studied boys only; Psathas, while including the two sexes, failed to differentiate between boys' and girls' reports in his data analyses. Since cultural role expectancies and socialization emphases clearly differ for the sexes (and these differences may show rather complex interactions with social class), comparison of the results from these two studies becomes difficult.

Furthermore, both studies are only of limited import to our problem since they are based solely on questionnaire data. In the present study the adolescent's self-characterization, gained from an intensive personal interview, is supplemented with evaluations of his behavior in a variety of situations in order to arrive at an inference concerning his underlying attitudes to authority. These attitudes are related, separately for boys and girls, to indices of the family social class at three age levels (14, 15, and 16 years) and in three interpersonal situations (at Home, in School, and with Peers).

Method

Sample

The sample used is a subsample of the Guidance Study group at the Institute of Human Development at the University of California in Berkeley (MacFarlane, 1938). The Guidance Study has been concerned with the investigation of the physical, mental, and personality development of a group of normal children. Observations of these children began at the age of 21 months and continued up to age 18. All of the subjects, serially selected from the birth certificate registry of Berkeley (an urban community in the San Francisco metropolitan area), were born in the years 1928 and 1929.

The Guidance Study group was, at the time that study began, a fair sampling of the Berkeley population but differed from the general United States urban population in respect to a lower rate of infant mortality, higher educational level, higher occupational level, higher percentage of home-owners, better household facilities, lower percentage of for-

eign-born parents, more Protestants and fewer Catholics and Jews, and, because they were young childbearing families, they had a lower per capita income.

A "core" group of 19 boys and 29 girls was selected from the total Guidance Study population as the sample for this study in order to permit study of changes over time for the same group of individuals. This "core" group comprises *all* the subjects available from the Guidance Study group for whom there were complete ratings of attitude to authority in all three of the interpersonal situations and at each of the three ages. In this total subsample of 48 families, 87 percent of fathers and 83 percent of mothers are native born; 81 percent and 77 percent, respectively, are Protestant. It should be noted that the children were reared during the depression years and that their adolescence, here under study, coincides with the span of World War II.

Measures

Measures of conformity. Each adolescent was rated on his attitude to authority in three situations (at Home, in School, and with his Peers) at ages 14, 15, and 16. These ratings were based upon a clinical evaluation of all information available on a child for a given situation at each age level. The sources of data included interviews with the adolescent and with his mother and, also, teacher ratings and sociometric appraisals from his school. The same five-point rating scale was employed for the three situations:

5. Hectic drive to conform.
4. Real urge to conform, to be accepted, to avoid friction, etc.
3. Occasional assertions of individuality but for the most part accepts rules, regulations, social standards without much wear and tear.
2. Tries to side-step rules and regulations to avoid conformity. Passive resistance or avoidance of situations where rules or regulations would have to be met.
1. Extremely resistive to rules, regulations, and authority. Extreme individualism and nonconformity.

Measures of socioeconomic status. A number of socioeconomic indices available for Guidance Study families permitted the assessment of the relationships between an adolescent's conformity patterns and the socioeconomic level of his family *at the time of his birth*. An over-all measurement is provided by the California Institute of Child Welfare Index which is composed of a number of socioeconomic indices (selected by H. E. Jones). It combines four elements: (a) Berkeley Social Rating Scale (to be denoted by BSRS), which covers house exterior, neighborhood, family accommodation, living room, and special equipment; (b) total family income; (c) midparent education; and (d) occupation of father. This composite index (SES) has been shown by Atherton (1958) to relate highly in the Guidance Study sample to several other socioeconomic indices, among them the Warner Index of Status Characteristics (Warner, Meeker, and Eells, 1949) with which it correlates .85. This general measure is supplemented by two additional scores intended to differentiate socioeconomic status into its "social" and "economic" components. Such a distinction seems logically tenable and is supported by the results of a factor-analytic study of all socioeconomic indices available in the Guidance Study (Atherton, 1958). In this report it is found that, although a single factor may account for the bulk of covariance among 18 individual indices, it is possible to discern two empirical clusters of indices which generally separate educational and occupational items from more directly income-related items. The best measures of the former ("social") cluster are mothers' and fathers' educational level (years of schooling); for the latter ("economic") cluster the best single measurement is provided by the previously mentioned BSRS.

Results and Discussion

Table 27 summarizes the distributions for the three conformity ratings at each of the three age levels for boys and girls separately.

Although girls show higher conformity than boys in seven out of nine comparisons, only one significant sex difference is found (age 16, Peers, $p < .01$). However, girls show a consistent tendency to increase their degree of conformity from ages 14 to 15 to 16 in all three situations, while boys show no clear age trend, except perhaps the suggestion that in school and with peers they become somewhat less conforming during the age span studied. Figure 24 illustrates these age trends. We may speculate whether these reverse trends for boys and girls in conforming behavior in school and with peers may reflect differential cultural training and values and/or the effects of differing levels and rates of physical maturation for the two sexes. Whatever the

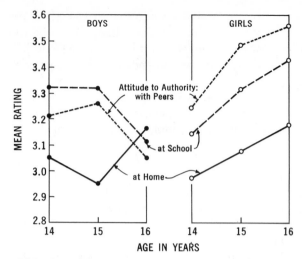

FIG. 24.   Mean ratings of degree of conformity in three situations as a function of age.

pattern of determination, there is the suggestion that, within this age range, boys are beginning to assume their "traditional" leadership and decision-making roles and girls to adopt the more conforming patterns of behavior for which they tend to be rewarded in our society.

The average ratings for both boys and girls over the three-year period fall consistently on the conformity side (above 3.0) of our scale (see Table 27). The grand means over the three age levels are 3.16 and 3.26 for boys and girls respectively. The distributions of ratings are generally skewed and, in a frequency distribution of all ratings, 33 percent of adolescents are rated "4" or "5" and only 12 percent receive ratings of "2" or "1." Over the three-year period there seems to be a considerable degree of instability in the attitude to authority in each situation. Interage correlations for boys (among the three ages over the three situations) range from .21 to .68 with a median correlation of .59. For girls, the range is .25 to .61 with a median of .43. It is possible, of course, that these low interage correlations are primarily reflections of low reliability in the ratings of conformity. However, an additional breakdown of the scores questions this interpretation: there are more changes in degree of conformity recorded for adjacent ages when the same person was responsible for both ratings than when different raters provided the data. This analysis argues that we may regard the interage correlational data as indicating that adolescent boys and girls undergo considerable fluctuations in their degree of conformity, a characteristic quite compatible with the view that the establishment of

TABLE 27. MEANS AND STANDARD DEVIATIONS OF RATINGS OF CONFORMITY AT HOME,
SCHOOL, AND WITH PEERS AT AGES 14, 15, AND 16*
(19 Boys, 29 Girls)

Age	Boys		Girls		Sex Difference in Means
	Mean	SD	Mean	SD	
Attitude to Authority in Home:					
14 years	3.05	.69	2.97	.49	−.08
15 years	2.95	.69	3.07	.58	.12
16 years	3.16	.93	3.17	.59	.01
Mean	3.05	.77	3.07	.55	.02
Attitude to Authority in School:					
14 years	3.32	.80	3.14	.57	−.18
15 years	3.32	.65	3.31	.70	−.01
16 years	3.11	.72	3.38	.61	.27
Mean	3.25	.72	3.28	.63	.03
Attitude to Authority with Peers:					
14 years	3.21	.69	3.24	.57	.03
15 years	3.26	.64	3.48	.81	.22
16 years	3.05	.69	3.55	.62	.50†
Mean	3.17	.67	3.26	.67	.09
Grand Mean	3.16	.72	3.26	.62	.10

* Above 3, conforming side of rating scale; below 3, nonconforming side.
† Significant at the .01 level by *t* test.

TABLE 28. INTERCORRELATIONS AMONG RATINGS OF CONFORMITY IN THE HOME,
SCHOOL, AND PEER SITUATIONS
(19 Boys, 29 Girls)

	Age 14			Age 15			Age 16		
	Home	Sch.	Peer	Home	Sch.	Peer	Home	Sch.	Peer
Boys:									
Home		.64	.53		.74	.51		.84	.73
School			.83			.56			.74
Girls:									
Home		.51	.53		.62	.44*		.58	.59
School			.86			.77			.63

* Only this correlation does *not* reach the .05 level of significance.

personal autonomy is a focal and wavering struggle of the adolescent period.

The interrelationships among the measures of conformity in the three situations provide a necessary background for understanding whatever differential correlation with SES variable they may show. In their own right these interrelationships permit certain inferences concerning the situational generality of conforming behavior. At age 14 both boys and girls tend to show the same degree of conformity in school and with peers, with the home situation evoking more unique behavior. The tendency to show quite different attitudes toward authority in the home than outside of it is less at age 15 than at age 14 and is no longer apparent in either sex by age 16. This age change in the meaning of the home situation, however, may be attributable to apparently opposite trends for boys and girls: for the boys, age 16 marks a period of greatly increased generality in conforming behavior; for girls, the three situations have become relatively differentiated from one another with respect to the authority attitudes they evoke.

Conformity in Relation to Socioeconomic Indices

Socioeconomic Composite (SES). Exploring the relationships between conformity of the adolescent to authority pressures at home, in school, and with

TABLE 29. CORRELATIONS BETWEEN SOCIOECONOMIC STATUS COMPOSITE (SES) AND CONFORMITY IN HOME, SCHOOL, AND PEER GROUPS

| | | Attitude to Authority in | | | | | | | | |
| | | Home | | | School | | | Peers | | |
	N	14 yrs.	15 yrs.	16 yrs.	14 yrs.	15 yrs.	16 yrs.	14 yrs.	15 yrs.	16 yrs.
Boys	19	−.22	−.51*	−.38	−.38	−.42	−.33	−.37	−.44	−.51*
Girls	29	.22	.18	−.25	.26	−.02	.19	.24	−.04	.10
Significance of Sex Difference		ns	.02	ns	.04	ns	ns	.05	ns	.04

* Significant at the .05 level.

peers and the SES of his family, we find that for boys these relationships are consistently negative (see Table 29). However, only two of the nine negative relationships are significant at the five percent level. In contrast, there are no significant relationships between the girls' conformity and SES, nor are these relationships consistent in direction.

Evaluating the sex differences in these relationships, we find that in four of the nine comparisons the differences are significant at or beyond the five percent level. It seems fair to suggest from these data that, the lower the SES of his family, the more compliant will be the boy to authority whether it occurs in the home, in school, or in the "outside" world in general. However, before attempting an interpretation of this phenomenon on the basis of the SES composite factor alone, we will proceed to explore the relationship of conformity to its more purely "economic" and more purely "social" components.

The Berkeley Social Rating Scale (BSRS). As Table 30 shows, correlations between ratings of the family on the BSRS and the adolescent's degree of conformity remain consistently negative for boys with but a single exception; however, only one correlation achieves significance. In the case of the girls

there are no significant correlations and, since the relationships fluctuate in direction, no general trend can be detected. Furthermore, there are no significant sex differences in these relationships. Since the "economic" component of the SES composite shows such low relationships, we are encouraged to expect that the "social" component (i.e., parental education) will prove more predictive.

Parents' Education in Relation to Conformity

The parents' education ranges from five to 19 years of schooling for both fathers and mothers. The mean score for mothers is 11.8 with a standard deviation of 3.4 years; for fathers the mean value is 12.1, the standard deviation is 3.7.

The relationships between parents' education and adolescents' attitudes to authority reproduce, but in a much more clear-cut fashion, those found with the SES scale. For boys, of the nine correlations with mothers' education, all are significant beyond the five percent level, and four of these beyond the one percent level. All are negative. With fathers' education, boys' attitudes to authority show consistently negative relationships, four of these significant at the five percent level (two at the one percent level). In comparison with the corresponding SES correlations,

TABLE 30. CORRELATIONS BETWEEN BERKELEY SOCIAL RATING SCALE (BSRS) AND CONFORMITY IN HOME, SCHOOL, AND PEER GROUPS

| | | Attitude to Authority in | | | | | | | | |
| | | Home | | | School | | | Peers | | |
	N	14 yrs.	15 yrs.	16 yrs.	14 yrs.	15 yrs.	16 yrs.	14 yrs.	15 yrs.	16 yrs.
Boys	19	.01	−.14	−.26	−.10	−.04	−.23	−.11	−.08	−.46*
Girls	29	.08	.16	−.12	.12	−.02	.13	.07	.00	.09
Significance of Sex Difference		ns	ns	ns	ns	ns	ns	ns	ns	.07

* Significant at the .05 level.

TABLE 31. CORRELATIONS BETWEEN PARENTS' EDUCATION AND CONFORMITY IN HOME, SCHOOL, AND PEER GROUP

| | | Attitude to Authority in | | | | | | | | |
| | | Home | | | School | | | Peers | | |
	N	14 yrs.	15 yrs.	16 yrs.	14 yrs.	15 yrs.	16 yrs.	14 yrs.	15 yrs.	16 yrs.
Mothers' Education:										
Boys	19	−.24	−.65**	−.49*	−.63**	−.55*	−.50*	−.65**	−.55*	−.58**
Girls	29	.32	.16	−.20	.17	.03	.17	.07	−.18	.18
Significance of Sex Difference		.08	.004	ns	.01	.05	.03	.01	ns	.01
Father's Education:										
Boys	19	−.29	−.58**	−.36	−.46*	−.54*	−.26	−.43	−.59**	−.37
Girls	29	.28	.15	−.08	.10	−.01	.20	.29	−.16	.24
Significance of Sex Difference		.08	.01	ns	.07	.07	ns	.02	ns	.05

* Significant at the .05 level.
** Significant at the .01 level.

mothers' education always indicates a stronger negative relationship while fathers' education is, in general, also a better predictor of attitude to authority than is the SES composite.

In contrast with boys, there are no significant relationships between either of the parental education indices and the girls' attitudes to authority.

The data clearly admit the conclusion that an inverse relationship exists between boys' degree of conformity and the socioeconomic level of their families and that this relationship most clearly resides in the "social," rather than in the "economic," component of social status. There are a number of ways in which we may account for this general finding, and it is doubtful whether any single mediating hypothesis can encompass the full range of linkages between class and conformity which occur in the present sample. Also, although we have implicitly regarded the socioeconomic indices as continuous variables (by employing correlational analyses), the concept of social classes or strata argues for the existence of discontinuities along socioeconomic dimensions. Thus, an hypothesis put forward to account for high conformity in boys from somewhat lower social positions does not necessarily find its polar opposite in—and may even be irrelevant to—the determinants of less conformity in relatively higher classes. In this instance our sample of boys is essentially middle class (14 of the 19 families are so designated by the Warner classification; the remaining five boys come from upper-lower families) so that the relationships reported here largely reflect comparisons between upper-middle and lower-middle homes.

In lower-middle families we suggest that parents are more likely to imbue their sons with the importance of "respectable" behavior and also with a greater acceptance of their social status—and thus of authority. Upper-middle families, by contrast, may be more likely to value an improvement in their social positions and to implement these strivings through the manner in which they raise their children. Recalling the specific context for this investigation, it is not difficult to attribute to a highly-educated, upper-middle class mother in the 1940's a striving for upward mobility which, in part, is manifested in a need to insure, through her childrearing "philosophy" and practices, that her son achieves highly in school, in status among his peers, and in his future vocation. Under such compelling pressures reactions of both greater independence and rebellion in her son are predictable.

The formulations for boys' conformity gain some support from the literature on social class differences in parental values and practices. However, such data are notorious for their dependence upon the particular temporal and subcultural contexts in which they were gathered so that their relevance to the present findings, which themselves are tied to an atypical social period, is at best tangential. Nevertheless, we are encouraged by Duvall's (1946) conclusion that working-class mothers, more than those from the middle class, stress the importance of children's obedience to their parents—and to adults in general.

These data were obtained in 1943–1944, a period coinciding with our own observations. More recently, Kohn reported that ". . . middle-class parents (fathers as well as mothers) are more likely to ascribe predominant importance to the child's acting on the basis of internal standards of conduct, working-class parents to the child's compliance with parental authority" (1959, p. 341). Specifically, he reports that such traits as self-control, dependability, independence, and curiosity are more valued by middle-class parents, while working-class children are more often expected by their parents to be neat, clean, and obedient. These differences hold up for breakdowns based on mothers' education, even within social classes. Coupling these observations with Bronfenbrenner's (1958) general conclusion, based upon an intensive review of studies in this area, that, in the period 1943–1953, middle-class mothers have had higher expectations for achievement for their children than did working-class mothers, we can draw some support for our interpretations of the relationship of social class variables (and particularly mothers' education) with the degree of independence shown by adolescent boys. If, indeed, more highly educated mothers are more likely to combine pressures for independence and achievement and mothers with less education to stress compliance with adult authority, then our results for boys become comprehensible.

However, since much the same class differentials in parental expectations have been found for girls, the riddle posed by their failure to show class-related variation in attitudes to authority is intensified. We can only suggest, as one contributing factor, that the expectation in the larger culture of greater conformity in girls may be equally implemented in families along the full socioeconomic range (or, at least, throughout the middle class). This is not to argue that the intentions of socialization for girls do not vary with social class; the higher-status families may be training for social poise, while lower-status families may—as we suggested for boys—value "respectability" in their daughters. We must seek elsewhere for the determinants of individual variations in conformity among girls.

Composite socioeconomic status, as measured by SES, is by itself a good predictor of boys' attitudes to authority, but more powerful indicators are the educational levels of the parents, particularly mothers' education. This is in line with the above hypotheses which assume that the mother is the primary agent mediating social class and boys' behav-ior. That the economic level shows such low relationships with the degree of conformity may be due to the fact that the sample has a relatively restricted socioeconomic range. Furthermore, the impact of economic factors upon attitudes toward authority may not yet be manifest by age 16. Somewhat later, when the adolescent has faced more directly the restraints on his educational and occupational mobility due to his economic level, then these factors possibly will come to bear a relationship to his conformity.

One further analysis may be of interest. Throughout this report there has been little systematic variation attributable to chronological age, per se, which is not surprising in view of the overriding importance of differential maturity rates during this period. For boys especially, the adolescent years 14 to 16 represent a time of great disparity in physical characteristics relatable to growth rate. Since physiological maturation is reflected in changes in bodily functioning (and in one's perception of one's own body) as well as in changes in one's social stimulus value (being seen less as a child and more as an adult), we were encouraged to examine the interaction between maturation, social status, and the adolescent's attitudes toward authority.

Physiological maturity status was measured, both for boys and girls, by a general (first) factor score evolved from a factor-analytic study of the interrelationships among a large number of physical development indices obtained on Guidance Study children throughout its span (Nicolson and Hanley, 1953). Dichotomizing on this factor score and on the socioeconomic composite (at their respective medians), four subgroups of boys were constituted: Early Maturing-High SES, Early Maturing-Low SES, Late Maturing-High SES, and Late Maturing-Low SES. While the sizes of these groups (5, 5, 5, and 4, respectively) precludes statistical tests of adequate power, one trend in their mean conformity scores is sufficiently consistent to merit mention: the Late Maturing-High SES boys are least conforming (or tied for lowest rank) in each of the nine possible intergroup comparisons (each situation at each age). We may speculate that the additional pressures for social achievement (which we postulated for higher SES homes) bear even more heavily upon the late-maturing boy who, in adolescence, is less well-equipped to meet the achievement standards set by his home and by his peer social groups. This isolated finding becomes more meaningful when considered in the context of some data on the personality correlates of maturation rate. M. C. Jones and Bayley (1950) conclude, from their study of the relationships between maturational status and social behavior in adolescent boys, that late maturers exhibit ". . . a 'natural' or 'childish' expressiveness in the earlier years of adolescence, and a more compensatory attention-seeking expressiveness in the later years" (p. 137). Working with the same sample, Mussen and Jones (1957) report that late-maturing boys show ". . . strong feelings of being rejected and dominated, prolonged dependency needs, and rebellious attitudes towards parents" (p. 255). However, they also are rated higher than are early-maturing boys on the drive for social acceptance by their peer group with the qualification, in line with the earlier study, that ". . . the late maturer's high social drives . . . are often manifested in childish, affected, attention-getting social techniques" (Mussen and Jones, 1958, p. 66). The gist of these findings suggests that the low conformity in school and with peers of the Late Maturing-High SES boy in the present study may stem primarily from the behavioral unconventionality of the social techniques he employs in order to impress and win over his schoolmates and friends while, in the home situation, low conformity denotes true rebellion against parents. The Late Maturing-Low SES boy, by contrast, is—on the average—the most conforming of the four groups. We may wonder whether this is due to a greater acceptance of, or resignation to, his physical retardation and whether, in turn, his conformity is an expediency made possible by the lesser achievement pressures of his lower-middle-class home.

Replicating this analysis for girls, for whom the effects of differential maturation should be less by this age due to their earlier maturation, we find only that Early Maturing-High SES girls are most conforming of the four groups in school and with peers: at all three ages they show the highest mean ratings in these two situations. One possible interpretation is that more mature girls from High SES families accept earlier and more rapidly internalize the standards for "good" behavior put forward by their so-

cially superior (and perhaps more socially striving) parents.

The suggestions arising from this additional analysis have, as is evident, only very fragile support from our data. At the very least, however, they do indicate the potential usefulness of regarding the adolescent's physical status as a relevant mediator of the effects of his family's social status and its accompanying values upon his attitudes toward authority, both in the home and in his social environment.

Summary

Attitudes to authority, ranging from conformity to rebelliousness, were evaluated in three interpersonal situations (at Home, in School, and with Peers) for the same sample of adolescent boys and girls at ages 14, 15, and 16 years. These inferential ratings, based on interviews with the subjects and their parents and on data provided by teachers and classmates, were analyzed for sex differences (a slight tendency toward greater acceptance of authority in girls), for generality among the three ratings at a given age (moderately positive intercorrelations), and for stability of a given attitude over the three age levels (considerable fluctuation).

Most striking is the consistently negative relationship between degree of conformity experienced by the male adolescent (in all situations and all ages) and the socioeconomic status of his family (measured separately by a composite index, by the Berkeley Social Rating Scale, and by mothers' and fathers' educational levels). No consistent trend is apparent for girls. Mothers' education is the single, most powerful predictor of boys' attitudes to authority, yielding significant negative correlations in eight of nine instances. There is a suggestion, for both sexes, of variation in degree of conformity relatable to an interaction between socioeconomic factors and the physical maturity level of the adolescent. The results are evaluated in the context of reported social class differences in parental values and practices and their corresponding socialization goals.

20

The Protective Environment

*and Adolescent Socialization**

William A. Westley
Frederick Elkin

This article presents a challenge to a popular conception of adolescence. In the literature of psychology and sociology, adolescence is generally described as a period of severe storm and stress. As a consequence of psychological and institutional pressures, the adolescent is said to experience innumerable conflicts and tensions. He must resolve discrepancies between his sexual impulses and societal restrictions. His prolonged tenure in school prevents him from "trying his wings" and discovering his own natural abilities. He has strong dependency needs in the family while at the same time he is expected to choose his goals and become a self-reliant independent adult. As a result of his uncertainties about his status and obligations, he tends to identify with a youth culture and seek the solidarity and support of a peer group, a group in turn which makes its own strong demands for conforming behavior. The following description of adolescence in the American middle class family by an anthropologist and psychiatrist is not atypical.

> The wild fluctuations between extreme dependence and disdainful or defiant independence, the gyrations from idealism to cynicism, from lush romancing to hard-bitten, stripped-down sexual aims, and from cringing conformity to last ditch non-conformity are attitudes largely unique to our own social system. Threaded through all the adolescent attitudes is the power of the gang, or the adolescent peer group with its own, unique and frequently spectacular behavior patterns (Kluckhohn and Spiegel, 1954, p. 16).

As dramatic and logical as is this explanation, the question remains—to what extent is the above adolescent pattern characteristic of all middle-class adolescents. The authors' study of one middle-class suburban community, characterized by relative social and geographical isolation, suggests a quite different

pattern. According to this pattern, the adolescent belongs to a small closely-knit family and participates with other family members in many activities. He internalizes aspirations for a professional or business career; he learns the expected patterns of language and breeding; he learns to resolve disputes by peaceable means; he learns to defer many immediate gratifications for the sake of future gains; and the peer group to which he belongs, rather than serving as an opposition group to the parents, tends to encourage and reinforce many values and patterns of the adult world.

This picture is quite at variance with the picture given by the authors cited above. While these findings must necessarily be restricted to the community under study and are closely related to its social and geographical isolation, they should have wider relevance for the study of adolescence. The findings not only challenge the popular characterization of adolescence but also suggest the need for important conditioning data in reports on particular studies and in the presentation of generalizations. Specifically we would suggest that in any particular study, the adolescent pattern be seen as part of its community context, that data on discontinuities be balanced by data on continuities, and that any generalizations specify the extent of social insulation and control provided by the community.

Theoretical aspects of this problem have been discussed elsewhere (Elkin and Westley, 1955); it is the purpose of this paper to present some of the research case material which demonstrates the continuity of adolescent socialization in the suburban community and the process by which such socialization occurs.

Community and Method

Suburban Town is a suburb of Montreal with a population in 1951 of less than 12,000. The commu-

* From *Social Forces*, 1957, **35**, 243–249.

nity has its own municipal government, police and fire departments, schools, churches, and recreational facilities. The average family size in 1951 was 3.5 persons. The family heads, over two-thirds of whom have managerial or professional positions, work in the City of Montreal and commute via a direct railroad line. Their median earnings in 1951 were over $5,700.

Twenty adolescents and their families were intensively studied. The adolescent sample, selected from lists provided by various residents of the community and community organizations, comprises approximately 15 percent of those in the community who met the criteria of selection. All were ages 14 or 15, of English origin, Protestant, and members of families of professional or managerial status.

The average interview time per family was approximately 10 hours. Following a preliminary interview with parents and child together, each adolescent was interviewed two or more times. These interviews were partially directed, the adolescent being asked to prepare a diary of day-to-day activities and to discuss certain activities, interests, and ideas. Finally, each mother and child separately was given an interview covering the same general subjects. These interviews were held on the same day, in succession, in order to prevent collusion. Supplementary data were also obtained from the life histories of approximately 20 post-adolescent college students who came from Suburban Town.[1]

The materials which follow may suggest that the children and parents of Suburban Town are paragons of adolescence and parenthood and have no serious psychological or interpersonal problems. No such implication is intended. The data presented focus on the behavior and more conscious attitudes of the respondents and do not directly concern the psychological health or ill health of either adolescents or parents.

The Protective Environment

For the adolescent in Suburban Town, the environment is integrated and protective. Usually, we stress the heterogeneity of modern society, the alternative

norms, conflicting patterns of behavior, and institutional complexity. However in Suburban Town there is a generally consistent and stable set of norms and expectations and we find that the adolescent is protected in various ways from contact with alternative patterns of behavior. This protectiveness may be seen in the effective isolation and social organization of the community.

Effective Isolation. The adolescent in Suburban Town has little opportunity to participate in, or become meaningfully familiar with, ways of life which differ greatly from his own. Within the community he has his school, community services, recreational facilities, and friends. Parental interest likewise functions as an effective control device since the parents, at any particular time, are likely to know what their children are doing and where and with whom they are. One mother says:

> I make it a point of knowing what he is doing. If he can't be home one afternoon when he's expected, he'll leave a note telling me what he's up to. I like to know where he is. If, for any reason, he's going to be late, he calls and lets us know.

From the parents' point of view, isolated Suburban Town is a "good" environment for their children, one with "positive advantages" and without danger of contact with impolite language and behavior, improper sex play, or delinquent activity. One mother expresses this as follows:

> You're lucky in an area like Suburban Town. All the activities have a religious bias and are under competent people. You don't have to worry about the children getting into trouble. All of John's friends are just impeccable.

The isolation of the effective environment is encouraged by the model of the parents themselves whose social life likewise tends to be circumscribed within the community. Through participation in local associations and activities, the parents implicitly define the community as a desirable area of delimitation.

Social Organization. The protective qualities of Suburban Town are further reinforced through the community's social organization. This is especially evident in the structuring of time of adolescents, the joint activities of adolescents and parents, and the collusive actions of parents in supervising adolescent behavior.

[1] We cannot be certain that the sample is representative of adolescents in the community. However, the relative size of the sample, the consistency of the findings, the support of case-history material of college students reared in Suburban Town, and the agreement with the description of adolescents in Elmtown (Hollingshead, 1949; Warner, 1949), temper the significance of this methodological deficiency.

The adolescent has little unstructured time. Typically, on school days, he spends his out-of-school hours doing about two hours of homework, helping in household activities, and participating in school organizations, directed sports, or church or "Y" activities. On weekends, he does have more free time, but even then he participates in some family projects, has certain household tasks, and often attends gatherings at which adults are present. In summers, he either works, attends camp, or vacations with his family at a summer cottage. Thus, much of the adolescent's activity has a productive or educative orientation, and he has little opportunity to "hang around" or devise "inappropriate" amusements. The following remarks illustrate this structuring of time.

> *Girl:* In the fall, sometimes we would visit each other's houses. Right now there is a keen interest in senior basketball and we stay and watch that. When I get home I practice the piano for about half to three quarters of an hour. Then I go upstairs and do my homework. After supper, I'll do the dishes so they don't pile up too much. After that I'll finish my homework. Then, if there is nothing else, I'll listen to the radio.

> *Boy:* On Saturday morning I help my father around the house. We've been building the recreation room downstairs. We cemented the walls, fixed up a place for cold storage, and now we've just started on the furnace room. We're going to do the garage next and we're building a patio, too. We both get a kick out of it.

In many areas no sharp distinction is made in the family between parental and adolescent activity. The adolescents, for example, participate with their parents in visiting relatives, team curling, work around the house, entertaining guests and other such activities, while the parents participate in many of the activities of the adolescents—they discuss their school courses and activities with them, attend the school's dramatic and athletic events, welcome their children's guests into their homes, and assist in their social gatherings.

The protectiveness of the setting is perhaps most evident in the joint actions of parents regarding the social activities of their adolescent children. Many instances were reported in which the parents, in collusion, decided how much allowances should be, the number of dates permitted per week, and the required hour of return from dates. In some instances, when a boy and a girl began dating each other steadily, the parents of the two conferred to discuss whether or not the relationship should be encouraged. The following statement of a 15-year-old girl cites one instance of such joint action.

> I never go out on a week night. Last year our parents thought we were going out too much. They got together and they all decided that we were. Then they said we could go out one night every weekend and we had to be in by twelve.

The protective environment is effective in Suburban Town because it has become the accepted pattern of life and because it is so completely accepted by the adolescents themselves. The adolescents accept the parents' prerogative of supervising their activities, willingly report the details of their lives,[2] and express little desire to participate in activities that take place outside the community. Such an internalization of controls on the part of the adolescents precludes any overt rebellion or any negative contrast with other patterns.

Continuity of Socialization

This protective environment is of significance primarily because it encourages a continuity in socialization between adolescence and adulthood, a continuity which is especially evidenced in our research in the congruence of attitudes of adolescents and parents towards heterosexual relationships and economic matters.

Heterosexual Relationships. In such situations as party behavior, discussions of marriage partner ideals, and dating, adolescents are being continually socialized for their adult roles and are internalizing the norms of the community. In giving parties, for example, the girls learn their proper hostess roles: they go over the guest list with their mothers and include those they *should* invite as well as those they *want* to invite; they are careful to have the same number of boys and girls; they send out formal invitations; and they make certain that the party guests mix. And the boys at these parties are so aware of their escort responsibilities that they may draw straws to decide who walks home with the less popular girls. The following statements illustrate

---

[2] Preliminary results of a comparative study in a working-class section of Montreal suggest sharp class difference in this regard. In the working-class section children report few details of their behavior to their parents and are not expected to do so.

how party behavior is so functional to the roles the adolescents are expected to play in later life.

Mother: In his own parties he knows that he has to see each of his guests to the door and to make sure that every girl has an escort home. I've told him that when he's the host it's his duty to make sure that the boys take the girls home.

Boy: Well, the girls always ask their friends to come to the party. But some of the girls' friends are not popular. Sometimes nobody wants to take them home. Usually what happens is that the boys draw straws. The hostess tries to arrange it so that everybody is taken home. It always gets worked out at parties.

Girl: Mom and I plan the parties. For balloons or anything like that, I buy them myself out of my savings. Mom encourages me to give parties because she wants me to be a good hostess. When you're married it's always better to be a perfect hostess. I find that I'm always a little bit afraid. Once everything gets going it's not too bad because you've got a chance to relax.

Continuity is also evident in the ideas of the girls about marriage. Both mothers and daughters believe that the girls should have careers, since marriage involves risks and a girl should be prepared for whatever contingency may arise. Also, in describing the ideal marriage mate, the girls, in all but one instance, stressed not his physical attractiveness, athletic ability, and popularity, but rather his occupation, class status, religion, and character. The daughters are not so absorbed in "adolescent culture" that they lose sight of their long-run goals. The following statements are typical of the comments about marriage.

Mother: I know Jane wants to get married, but she is not awfully definite just when. My own view is that she should finish her education before taking such a step. If she ever needed it in the future, she would have something to fall back on. . . . I would hate to see her marry anyone who is not on her own level, or who didn't have the same outlook. The only equipment I've given Jane is some sort of ability to discriminate. The rest is up to her.

Girl: The girls talk about it quite a bit. I don't care what he looks like. He must have the same interests as I do. He should also be able to support a family, though I don't care what he does. I wouldn't want a drunkard of course, and I don't want anybody with dirty fingernails, for instance.

Girl: I want to get married and go into journalism. It's the type of career that you can work at and still run a home. I wouldn't want to marry until I'm 21. By that time I would be educated enough to take that responsibility. . . . He could be a teacher. Not a ditch digger or somebody like that. He would have to be doing something constructive; I'd prefer a professional.

Dating patterns, although obviously an adolescent activity, likewise evidence such continuity. "Going steady," for example, is not uncommon among the adolescents of Suburban Town. However, "going steady" is under parental supervision and the adolescents themselves are quite sophisticated about it. The following statements are typical.

Boy: I figure this is the time to play the field. I think I'll stay this way until the middle of next year. Then it's a good idea to start going steady so you can be sure to go to all the important dances, like the graduation dance. It's important to go to that; so it's a good idea if you have a steady.

Girl: Well, going steady is all right, but it's silly to think of marriage at our age. You just stay clear of the subject. You might talk about getting married, you never talk about it as if you meant yourself. You know that you have to break up one day, but you just hope that that day will never come.

Mother: Norman went steady with Barbara Sloan. I didn't think it was a good idea. Mrs. Sloan and I had a talk about it. We were both against it. Then all the kids in the group stopped going steady and he stopped, too. Mind you, I suppose the boys and girls feel more secure when they go steady.

Economic Life. A continuity of socialization is also particularly evident in the parental training devices, attitudes, and aspirations associated with jobs, careers, and finances. The parents are ambitious for their children; however, since the husbands are salaried personnel and the families have high expenses in maintaining their way of life, they cannot leave their children either independent businesses or large sums of money. The children, therefore, must be trained to attain social and economic success through their own capabilities and characteristics. Thus, the parents feel it is important to inculcate in their children the "proper" economic attitudes: that work and saving are virtues; that given occupations are associated with given social statuses; and that money is to be used not for conspicuous display, immediate gratification, or speculation, but to achieve one's economic and social goals. The continuity of socialization is evidenced in that the adolescents by the ages of 14 or 15, have already well internalized these values and ideals. Note, for example, the following comments of parents and children regarding career aspirations, part-time work, allowances, savings, and discussions of family finances.

Career Aspirations

It is assumed by all members of the family that the sons will attend college and attain upper middle class positions. Although specific occupations may not yet be chosen, a concern with careers is evident.

Mother: I want him to go to college but I don't see the point in his just going for a B.A. I was hoping that he might be interested in becoming a chartered accountant. You know, I have been nothing but confused at the high school meetings. They advise that you put off any decision until they're in college. That seems a little late to me. I know that the whole business worries us and it worries Johnnie.

Boy: Around here, university helps in business. If you don't have a university education you don't get the jobs. I like to play sports and lead a gay life but I'll have to settle down to work soon. Mom doesn't want me just to be having fun all the time.

Boy: I haven't really considered it yet. I am hoping to go to college, but I haven't considered what course. I've been thinking about engineering and commerce.

Part-Time Work

Part-time work has become the norm for the adolescent boys in the community and is not uncommon for the girls. To the parents, such work is a significant training device for character development. Work, it is said, teaches the children the necessity of labor, the value of money, and a sense of responsibility.

Mother: I've always encouraged the boys to take any stray jobs—cutting the grass of neighbors, putting up storm windows, or even baby-sitting. If I hear anyone say that he needs somebody to do this or that I immediately suggest the boys. It's not the money. They should learn that you just don't get money, you work for it. It develops a sense of responsibility.

Mother: I have encouraged baby-sitting jobs. I feel that it's good for Jill to take on responsibility and to feel that she is earning money herself. We've talked about it and she agrees to it.

Boy: It was my idea to take a paper route to help along with my pocket money. I wanted to take some sort of a job this summer. I even tried applying for farm work. Before taking the camp job I wrote to the C.N.R. through my father's friend. But they had a full staff. A lot of my friends have paper routes so I got one, too. I didn't really need the extra; I don't spend that much money.

Allowances

All but one of the adolescents in our sample were given allowances, the allowances averaging $1.00 per week.[3] The allowance, to the parents, is a device for teaching the child that money is to be used carefully and wisely. The allowance "teaches" the child to save, to know the "value of money," and to distinguish important from unimportant expenditures. There are variations in the degree to which the adolescents themselves have internalized these attitudes, but they all recognize that these are the "proper" attitudes.

Mother: Their father has given each of them three times the amount of their age. At 15 Louise is getting 45 cents a week. Now she supplements that with her baby-sitting. She has done very well with her baby-sitting money. She has paid for her band lessons out of her savings. My husband has taught them not to waste money. Any jaunts that Louise takes she pays for herself. She even buys clothing for herself that she considers necessities.

Girl: Well, I get $1.00 a week. I don't buy lunches or anything like that out of my money; that all comes extra. If I go to a movie alone or with the girls I spend my own money. But most of the time, if I go, it's with a boy, and he pays the fare and for the movie. I can save most of my money. I'm not loaded or anything, but by this week end I should have $7.00 saved. I buy useful articles with it. Two weeks ago I bought a sweater, and now I want to get a cotton blouse.

Boy: I get $5.00 a month, but I have to pay for everything out of that. I have to buy my own bus and train fares, get a haircut, and all that. I have to get everything except my clothes out of that money. They are trying to get me trained. They give it to me all at once so I'll learn how to keep a budget. If I run short I'm just short. I have gone for over two weeks without bus money.

---

[3] The average allowance among a comparable age group in a working-class section of Montreal is $2.00 per week.

Savings

The puritanical attitudes of the parents toward money are also evidenced by their statements about saving. The parents wish to inculcate in their children the belief that money is not to be spent recklessly and, if not immediately necessary, should be put away for future use. The children are thus encouraged, and apparently successfully so, to view their economic lives as lives of continuity (see A. Davis and Dollard, 1940).

Mother: She gets a dollar a week. I started her off with fifty cents, then she graduated to seventy-five and now it's a dollar. I want her to save some of this, but I don't feel that she saves enough. She just uses it for pocket money. The thing I object to is that she doesn't save enough to buy things for herself.

Mother: We've always encouraged them to save. When they were little they had bank accounts opened for them. Whatever money they banked they got half again as much from us. Now Murray is going to Quebec, Ottawa, and Burlington with the school band. We'll pay for one of the trips, but he's got to have enough saved to pay for the rest himself.

Boy: I like to save money. I had about $25.00 saved up a little while ago. I don't know where it all went to. All of a sudden there was nothing left. My parents have encouraged me to save. They always say that if you learn how to save you have money when you need it. You realize it yourself when you see how fast $25.00 can disappear.

Discussion of Family Finances

Although the parents in our sample are most concerned about the expenditures of their children, they—with only one exception—strongly feel that the children should not know the family's financial position; consequently, they carefully avoid open discussions of family finances. This has two important implications for the socialization of the adolescents. First, by keeping the children from knowing the true financial position of the family, the parents are better able to rationalize the limited allowances they give and their demands for work and saving. Secondly, in their sensitivity to the subject, they undoubtedly suggest to their children that money is somehow important, mysterious and sacred.

Mother: No, that is something we never talk to the children about. My husband feels that the finances of the family shouldn't be open to criticism from the family. For instance, he wants to be able to say that they can't have this or that without feeling that the children would be able to say, but why not? From my point of view the only danger is that they might talk outside the home about it. I don't know why it is, but that's the type of thing you don't even tell your best friends.

Boy: Mother wouldn't even tell me my father's salary, or how much the car is worth, or even what her fur coat is worth. If I asked her how much it's worth she would think I'm only a kid and be embarrassed. I'm never allowed to ask my father what his salary is. I couldn't do that. He never discusses money with me like that. I don't mind. I sort of think it's a good thing.

Girl: I don't know how much Daddy gets a year or anything like that. Dad feels that we shouldn't know things like that. They sometimes talk about it, but it's not really meant for me to hear.

Socialization and the Peer Group

We noted that the peer group occupies an important place in the popular explanation of adolescence, serving the function of emancipating the child from the family while giving him psychological support. The peer group is here described as an opposition group to the parents with a unique and immature set of interests and values. In Suburban Town, we find no such peer groups.[4] On the contrary, the peer groups in Suburban Town generally are committed to the values of the parents and further a continuity in socialization. The peer group, for example, views part-time jobs and allowances as the norm for its members; it encourages participation in school organizations; it rates its members in terms of school grades; and the girls, in their groups, discuss the proprieties of entertaining and the desirable characteristics of husbands.

Boy: A guy should know how to dance and be in on the sports. Sports is very important. And something else: school work is very important too. You would be surprised just how much that counts for boys. I was at a party last year after I came first in the class. I could just stand there and not say a word all evening. Everybody came up to me and all that kind of stuff. Just because I came first in the class, I was the "brain" for the evening.

[4] There are a few "wild" individuals; however they represent a very limited proportion of the adolescents in the community. It is possible that, in many communities, a few "wild" individuals receive so much attention that others mistake them for typical residents.

Nor is the peer group isolated from the world of the adults. In fact, as we have observed, the peer group is almost completely under the observation of the community at large; and the family, in various ways, literally participates in its activities.

There are, of course, certain behavior patterns distinctive of the peer group—the adolescents have their own dress and language styles; they have characteristic dating patterns; they "kid around"; they explore in the area of heterosexual relations; some collect popular records. However, it is evident that the adolescents are quite sophisticated about such peer group behavior, and the parents, by tolerantly and flexibly accepting such activities, often manage to guide and relate them to the very goals they have for their children. Thus, in the context of Suburban Town, the youth culture of the peer group neither indicates discontinuity nor the rejection of the adult world.

Conclusion

Current writers continue to view adolescence of the middle-class child as a period of tension, distinct from childhood and adulthood. They likewise see a link between the needs of the adolescent for emancipation and the youth culture of the peer group. The adolescent, in becoming emancipated from the family, is said to participate in a conformity-demanding group of his peers, and this participation serves to balance his needs for independence and security.

The reported research asks to what extent this picture is true of adolescents in an upper-middle-class suburb of Montreal. The data suggest that it is not true. In Suburban Town, the adolescent does not manifestly experience much storm and stress, and the peer group serves to reinforce rather than oppose parental values.

In summary, the adolescents live in a protective environment: their lives are in full view of the adults; their world is relatively consistent and integrated; and they have little direct acquaintance with other patterns of thought and behaviour. In this environment, the adolescents, by the ages of 14 and 15, have already well internalized the ideals and values of the surrounding adult society. The adolescents appreciate the keen interest of the parents in their activities and feel that their parents are working in their behalf; they are in close agreement with their parents on general career and marriage goals and the manner in which these goals are to be achieved; they recognize the value of the parental attitudes towards financial matters and the specfic training they receive in saving and handling allowances; they do not reject adult values or participate in an anti-adult "youth culture"; and they tend to look at their distinctive adolescent activities from a relatively sophisticated and integrated point of view.

Thus, the life of the adolescents in such an environment is both objectively and subjectively a period in continuity with the succeeding phase of life; it is the patterns of continuity in socialization which are dominant and striking rather than the patterns of discontinuity.

21

The Interaction of Family Variables and Gang Variables in the Aetiology of Delinquency*

Robert Everett Stanfield

A sociologist has recently written that "[w]herever one can develop a rationale for predicting interaction, one should make a conscious effort to construct and test theories that explicitly take advantage of interactive effects" (Blalock, 1965b, p. 374). In empirical research on opportunity theory in delinquency, some evidence has been presented showing interactive relationships between variables representing availability of both legitimate and illegitimate opportunities (Palmore and Hammond, 1964). This article is a further effort to press for theory building and testing through the use of statistical interaction in empirical studies.

Over the past decades, two major traditions have emerged in the aetiology of delinquency. These have been variously called the psychogenic and the sociogenic (Cohen, 1955, pp. 11–19), the psychiatric-psychoanalytic and the sociological (Clinard, 1957a) the individual and the collective (Weinberg, 1954). The first has traced delinquency to the development of a personality with a disposition toward the violation of law. The second has regarded delinquency as a phenomenon of cultural areas that lack social controls over the violation of law or that have positive supports for delinquent behavior.

Proponents of these traditions have argued whether the family or the gang has the greater importance in determining delinquent behavior. Supporters of the psychogenic tradition have tended to emphasize the association between juvenile crime and certain aspects of family life: rejection or lack of affection by a parent; the laxity, inconsistency, or severity of discipline; the absence or inappropriateness of a parent as a role model (e.g. Glueck and Glueck, 1950; McCord and McCord, with Zola, 1959). Those that hold the sociogenic view have maintained that delinquent behavior is learned in a

gang as a system of preferred behavior that is either a consequence of a dissociation in the social structure between culturally prescribed goals and culturally approved means (e.g. Cohen, 1955; Cloward and Ohlin, 1960) or a result of a conflict of values and norms among the social classes of society (W. B. Miller, 1958).

Theory and research in delinquency have benefitted from activity along independent lines of development within these two traditions, but further progress in the field might be achieved by investigating the relationship between the family and the gang in the aetiology of delinquency.

Theory Building with Expectations of Statistical Interaction

Some efforts at integrating the two traditions already exist in the literature of social science. C. R. Shaw and McKay (1931, esp. pp. 383–393) asserted that delinquent behavior occurs when an individual, disposed toward delinquency by a particular family situation, learns such behavior from a group of peers in a neighborhood that has traditional and positive influences acting in support of such behavior. F. Tannenbaum (1951, pp. 12–13) described delinquency as the consequence of the gang replacing the family as an individual's primary reference group due to the "inadequacy" of the family. Weinberg (1954) proposed that boys become delinquent "when, for individualized purposes of emotional security, self-enhancement, or conflict-resolution, they seek and select accessible associates from whom they learn, accept, and express criminal attitudes." He suggested an empirical test that would utilize, as independent variables, certain aspects of family relations, the capacity for peer relations, and the accessibility of delinquent or nondelinquent peers. Haskell (1960)

* From *Social Problems*, 1966, **13**, 411–417.

identified the family as a reference group aligned with the dominant cultural system and the peer group as a reference group aligned with a deviant subcultural system. The delinquent boy was an individual who had taken the gang as his primary reference group. Haskell explained the negative case of the nondelinquent gang boy by arguing that satisfying experiences in the family as a normative reference group could overcome the effect of the gang as a delinquent reference group.

There seems implicit in all these attempts at integration an extension of Sutherland's theory of differential association (1955, pp. 74–81), with the family and the gang regarded as competing groups within which the individual may encounter definitions favorable or unfavorable to the violation of law. The differential frequency, duration, priority, and intensity of interpersonal associations within these groups affect the extent to which the values of the group are accepted by the individual. All these views seem to assume that the family is on the side of conformity with law, that the gang favors violation of law, and that a breakdown of associations within the family virtually assures the victory of a gang.

These assumptions, however, may be questioned. It might be appropriate to leave the culture of the family and the culture of the gang (that is, the values and norms regarding conformity to or violation of law) to be determined empirically. Not all families may favor conformity to law; not all gangs may support violation of law. Further, the consequences of a breakdown of interpersonal associations within the family should be more precisely conceptualized.

Although satisfying experiences may increase receptivity to the culture of the group, dissatisfying experiences do not necessarily result in the adoption of an opposing or conflicting culture. Nonacceptance of the family culture renders an individual more receptive to the culture of other groups within his experience. It is possible that dissatisfying experiences in the home will make a boy more receptive to a gang culture that is not greatly different from his family culture. An encounter with a variant cultural pattern is most likely to occur when the socioeconomic status of the family differs from the socioeconomic status of the area in which it resides.

Satisfying experiences in the home do not diminish to a zero point the influence of the gang, but the boy is likely to select a peer group that has a culture compatible with that of the family. In contrast to Tannenbaum's view of the gang as a substitute for the family, one may see the gang as a group reinforcing the cultural pattern learned from the family. Thus, one may say that satisfying or pleasant experiences in a family increase the intensity of relationships within the family, leading to a greater probability of accepting the cultural pattern of the family. Acceptance of the family culture then tends to produce greater selectivity toward peers, leading toward the choice of a gang that supports the cultural pattern of the family. Unsatisfying or unpleasant experiences in a family, however, reduce the intensity of family relationships, leading to reduced receptivity toward family cultural patterns and susceptibility to outside (though not necessarily conflicting or opposing) cultural influences such as a gang.

These considerations suggest that explanation only in terms of direct causal relationships oversimplifies the situation. Family experiences and gang activity are related to delinquency only when such experiences and such activity occur in a cultural context that supports delinquent behavior. Unsatisfying family experiences are likely to result in delinquency to the degree that there exist in the neighborhood environment cultural definitions favorable to the violation of law. Gang activity is less likely to produce delinquent behavior when the gang does not have a culture providing support for criminal activity.

Confirmation of this view would depend on the empirical demonstration of interactive effects that can be adequately accounted for by these considerations. One may approach data with certain expectations of interactive effects. The effect of family experiences may vary according to the socioeconomic status of the family. Similarly, gang activity may be more strongly related to delinquency at one level of socioeconomic status than at another. Further, the impact of frequent peer activity may depend on the nature of family experiences.

Theory Testing with Observations of Statistical Interaction

Appearances in a court for one or more juvenile offenses as a dependent variable show in the Cambridge-Somerville Youth Study[1] a direct relationship with each of the three independent variables being examined here. (See Table 32.) The lower the

[1] For background on this study, see Powers and Witmer, 1951; McCord and McCord, 1958.

TABLE 32. DIRECT RELATIONSHIPS BETWEEN DELINQUENCY AND DISCIPLINE, SOCIOECONOMIC STATUS, AND PEER INVOLVEMENT

Father's occupational status	*Percentage convicted of delinquency*
Low	29% (n = 154)
High	18% (n = 99)
	Diff. = 11% $\chi^2 = 3.52$ p < .10
Father's discipline	
Erratic or lax	33% (n = 120)
Consistent	15% (n = 86)
	Diff. = 18% $\chi^2 = 7.13$ p < .01
Peer activity	
Frequent	30% (n = 132)
Occasional	19% (n = 118)
	Diff. = 11% $\chi^2 = 3.94$ p < .05

occupational status[2] of the father, the greater the percentage of boys appearing in court as juveniles for theft, assault, or sex offenses. A greater percentage of delinquent boys had fathers who were erratic or lax in discipline rather than consistent in discipline. A greater percentage of those active in gangs were delinquent than were those not active in gangs. In addition to these three direct relationships, one can find three meaningful instances of interaction among these variables.

First, the impact of paternal discipline seems clearly to be stronger among families of low socio-

low status families as among those from high status families.

Among families of low socioeconomic status, there is probably greater opportunity for a boy to encounter a cultural pattern outside the family that supports behavior that violates law. If family experiences are of the kind that reduce receptivity to the family culture, the boy from a low status family is more likely to come into contact with a delinquency-supporting culture than is a boy from a high status family. Unpleasant family experiences are more likely to produce delinquency in circumstances where there is an alternative cultural pattern that is favorable to the violation of law.

Second, delinquency is more strongly related to the frequency of peer activity among boys from high status families than among those from low status families. (See Table 34.) Frequent peer activity produces about the same delinquent proportion at both status levels in this study, but infrequent peer activity produces a much smaller proportion of juvenile offenders among those from high status families. The frequency of peer activity makes less difference in low status families.

The opportunities for learning delinquent behavior are less common for boys from high status families unless they spend a considerable amount of time on the street with friends. An individual from a low status family who associates rarely or only occasionally with peers still manages to learn delinquent behavior. The family itself may be the source of such learning. On the other hand, support for delinquency may so pervade the lower status levels that

TABLE 33. DELINQUENCY, SOCIOECONOMIC STATUS, AND DISCIPLINE

	Percentage with convictions for delinquency	
	Father's occupation	
	Low status	*High status*
Father's discipline		
Erratic or lax	39% (n = 77)	21% (n = 43)
Consistent	17% (n = 46)	13% (n = 40)
	Diff. = 22% $\chi^2 = 5.31$ p < .05	Diff. = 7% $\chi^2 = 0.54$ p > .60

economic status. (See Table 33.) The difference in the delinquent proportion between those with erratic or lax fathers, and those with consistent fathers, is about twice as great among those from

[2] Measured by a scale of occupational status described in A. J. Reiss, with Duncan, Hatt, and North.

learning such a cultural pattern can be accomplished without frequent interaction with peers.

Third, the difference in the proportion of juvenile offenders between those active with peers and those not active with peers is greater among those with erratic or lax paternal discipline than among those

TABLE 34. DELINQUENCY, SOCIOECONOMIC STATUS, AND PEER INVOLVEMENT

| | Percentage with convictions for delinquency | |
| | Father's occupation | |
	Low status	High status
Peer activity		
Frequent	31% (n = 83)	28% (n = 47)
Occasional	27% (n = 67)	8% (n = 51)
	Diff. = 4% $\chi^2 = 0.17$ p > .60	Diff. = 20% $\chi^2 = 5.39$ p < .05

TABLE 35. DELINQUENCY, DISCIPLINE, AND PEER INVOLVEMENT

| | Percentage with convictions for delinquency | |
| | Father's discipline | |
	Erratic or lax	Consistent
Peer activity		
Frequent	43% (n = 60)	16% (n = 44)
Occasional	23% (n = 57)	14% (n = 42)
	Diff. = 20% $\chi^2 = 4.66$ p < .05	Diff. = 2% $\chi^2 = 0.01$ p > .80

with consistent paternal discipline. (See Table 35.) Where paternal supervision is weak, frequent activity with peers tends to be associated with delinquency. Consistent discipline by the father keeps the probability of delinquency low, whether or not the boy is actively involved in a gang. Similarly, frequency of peer activity has a stronger effect when the father rejects the son.

The evidence in regard to the father's discipline suggests that the influence of the gang in producing delinquency is stronger when experiences within the family limit the degree to which an individual learns the family's cultural pattern. Lax or erratic discipline by the father obscures the distinction between approved and disapproved behavior. Paternal rejection leads a boy to seek warmer interpersonal relation-

TABLE 36. DELINQUENCY, DISCIPLINE, SOCIOECONOMIC STATUS, AND PEER INVOLVEMENT INVOLVEMENT

Father's discipline	Father's occupation	Peer activity	Expectation of delinquent outcome based on additive effects	Percentage convicted of delinquency
Erratic or lax (1)	Low status (1)	Frequent (1)	3 Very high	46% (n = 41)
		Occasional (0)	2 High	32% (n = 34)
	High status (0)	Frequent (1)	2 High	37% (n = 19)
		Occasional (0)	1 Low	9% (n = 23)
Consistent (0)	Low status (1)	Frequent (1)	2 High	14% (n = 22)
		Occasional (0)	1 Low	21% (n = 24)
	High status (0)	Frequent (1)	1 Low	18% (n = 22)
		Occasional (0)	0 Very low	6% (n = 18)

ships in another context, and, thereby, increases the boy's susceptibility to learning a cultural pattern that supports violation of law.

Although the number of cases in each cell drops rather low, some interesting findings consistent with expectations of interaction emerge when one examines the interrelationships among the dependent variables and the three independent variables. (See Table 36.) Assuming only additive effects, one would expect outcomes of the sort suggested by the column headed "Expectation of Delinquent Outcome Based on Additive Effects." The actual outcomes are somewhat consistent with those expected outcomes, but two of the outcomes seem somewhat lower than might have been anticipated. The combination of consistent discipline, low socioeconomic status, and active gang participation might have been expected to produce a proportion of delinquents in the thirty to forty percent range, consistent with the other combinations that have two of the three variables tending toward delinquency; it is, however, only fourteen percent. Similarly, the combination of erratic or lax discipline, high socioeconomic status, and lack of active gang participation might have been expected to have a percentage greater than nine percent. These low percentages are consistent with expectations based on the idea of interactive effects.

The low percentage of delinquents among those with consistent discipline, low father's occupational status, and gang activity may demonstrate the efficacy of consistent discipline in forestalling delinquency when the surrounding culture and the extent of peer group participation would suggest a high likelihood of delinquent behavior. The low percentage among those with erratic or lax paternal discipline, high father's occupational status, and infrequent gang activity, similarly, would demonstrate the efficacy of higher socioeconomic status and lack of peer group participation in forestalling delinquency despite the influence of bad discipline.

Conclusions

Evidence from the Cambridge-Somerville Youth Study gives support to a theoretical formulation of delinquency causation proposed in this paper. The findings of interactive effects demonstrate that explanation in terms of direct causal relationships is inadequate. Delinquent behavior is the consequence of *learning* a pattern of *culture* that supports the violation of law, and there is variation in outcome according to the content of the culture learned, the context in which the culture is learned, and the nature of experiences by which the culture is learned.

The demonstration of interactive effects indicates that the effects of experiences in the family and the gang on the learning of delinquent behavior are contingent upon the socioeconomic status of the group. Culture specifies the conditions under which family and gang experiences have a delinquency-producing impact. Socioeconomic status intensifies the relationship of delinquency to parental rejection and discipline at *lower* status levels. It intensifies the relationship of delinquency with the frequency of peer activity at *higher* status levels.

Further, the nature of family experiences performs a similar function of intensifying the effect of peer activity when discipline is low. Lack of parental supervision increases the influence of companions on the street.

Certain shortcomings of the data from the Cambridge-Somerville Youth Study (the nonrandom basis of selecting the study group, the incompleteness of records in some cases, and the small size and homogeneity of the study group) require that the findings reported here be treated as suggestive rather than conclusive.

Further, caution must be exercised in evaluating these data because perceived interaction among variables may actually be due to random error in one or more of the variables. Blalock (1965a, esp. pp. 44–45) points to this problem in developing a theory involving three or more variables.

This demonstration suggests, nevertheless, that deeper understanding of causation and greater accuracy in prediction may be achieved through the investigation of the interaction among independent variables that are statistically associated with a dependent variable. In the identification of the predelinquent, techniques of prediction based on an additive model of the joint effects of related factors may have some success, but prediction might be improved by combining predictive factors in both an additive and an interactive way.

These theoretical considerations have focused on the transmission through the family and the gang of an orientation toward delinquent or nondelinquent behavior rather than on the origin of such an orientation in the culture of the family or the gang (Cohen, 1955, pp. 18–19). Subsequent studies might attempt to use a similar kind of approach to relate theories of transmission to such theories of origin as that of differential opportunity structures (Cloward and Ohlin, 1960; Palmore and Hammond, 1964) or conflict of independently developed class cultures (W. B. Miller, 1958).

V

Friend and Peer

The adolescent is propelled into friendship by the psychic conflicts of his age and by the ego task he faces. He must detach his impulse life from the family; he needs a new authority to substitute for parental authority as he works through individuated inner controls; he needs to establish an identity and inner definition of self that is legitimized and corroborated by the responses of some relevant public. He needs friends desperately, and the character of the adolescent's need gives friendship at this period its peculiar cast. Theoretically at least, adolescents cleave to peer-group norms as though any deviation—in dress or attitude or behavior—somehow threatened the inner integrity. Adolescent girls are notorious for both the intensity and evanescence of their alliances (Hurlock and Klein, 1934; M. C. Jones, 1948).

Children have friendships before adolescence. Sullivan and other writers have, indeed, emphasized the preadolescent years as the critical period for friendship development. Before adolescence the child practices friendship skills, learns the rules of inclusion and exclusion, and builds peer-group allegiance. But during these years the child can come and go between friendship and family relationships with no critical emotional distinctions marking the shift. He may be more dependent in the family and more controlled outside the family, but his emotional energy is distributed among his relationships. The critical developments at adolescence disallow the family as the scene of much of the child's emotional life. Regressive dangers in the family force him to relocate his love. The child is driven to friendship.

The role of friend is described most easily in contrast to family roles. Family relationships, in a sense irrevocable, are actively maintained by a mixed pot of motives that can include love, guilt, and love of combat. Friendships are assumed freely on the basis of mutual attraction between individuals. Guilt induction is not a central control mechanism in friendship as it often is in family interaction. This does not, however, mean that friendship carries no obligations. A friend is expected to be reliable, to invest himself and give of himself in the relationship, to be both tolerant and loyal, to respond to his partner as a whole person, and to respect his friend and his friend's vulnerabilities. These obligations (and the right to expect the same of the partner) allow and insure the interaction that characterizes friendship: an interaction in which each partner can reveal or expose the self without fear of loss or humiliation.

Friendship is enlarging in a way that family relationships are not likely to be. It is not based on old myths and it does not encourage the continuation of old, comfortable, regressive patterns. It demands sensitivity and allows experimentation with new behaviors and new self-images. It is a relationship peculiarly suited to the intrapsychic conditions of adolescence.

The difference between adolescent friendship and earlier ties can be seen clearly in developmental data on conceptions of and attitudes toward friendships. Between 11 and 18 there are clear and continuous changes: from a concept of friendship as a parallel partnership focused on a common activity to a concept of mutuality in which the interaction itself claims focal interest; from no or relatively little emotional exchange to intense emotional interaction; from a relationship that cannot tolerate conflict to one that can contain and potentially resolve conflict. Among girls certain discontinuous changes are notable and point to the 14–16 year range as a particularly crucial time in like-sexed friendship: girls in this group are distinctive in their demand for loyalty and absolute security in friendship, in the strength of their need for similarity (or identity) between friends, and in their reluctance to exclude anyone from friendship (Douvan and Adelson, 1966).

Sex differences reported by Douvan and Adelson (1966) bear on the centrality of object ties in feminine development. Girls are advanced in interpersonal development compared to boys; they respond to questions about friendship with more articulate answers and more mature conceptions than boys do. An index of interpersonal maturity related significantly to other measures of ego development in girls; maturity in friendship was not significantly related to general ego development in boys.

Friendship Behavior

Research on adolescent friendship has concentrated heavily in the area of friendship choice, and the findings here are similar to findings on marriage-mate selection. Friends tend to be of similar social-class background (Hollingshead, 1949) and from the same neighborhood (E. A. Smith, 1962). Within limits set by social background, similarity in certain personal characteristics has been found in mutual friends as compared to nonmutual pairs. Mussen and Conger (1956), reviewing the field, report the following factors to be important in the formation of mutual friendships: similarity in mental age, interests, moral knowledge and standards; and similarity in the degree of social maturity, sociability, and social intelligence; criticalness of self or others, neuroticism, and extroversion. These authors also comment on changes in bases of friendship formation during the adolescent period: "In early adolescence, students appear to be strongly influenced by similar preferences in games and sports, by ability to think of and to do exciting things, and by duration of acquaintance. In later adolescence, such factors as acceptability of friends to members of the opposite sex (particularly among girls) become important" (p. 504).

Analyses of the stability of adolescent friendship present an incomplete and somewhat confusing picture. Horrocks and his co-workers (Horrocks and Buker, 1951; Horrocks and Thompson, 1946; Thompson and Horrocks, 1947) have reported increasingly stable friendships throughout childhood and adolescence. Their measure of stability consists of requesting children to name their three closest friends and repeating the question two weeks later. With regard to two-week friendships, adolescents are measurably more constant than younger children. But even at eighteen only 73 per cent of them name the same person as best friend after as short an interval as two weeks.

Not only is a measure of stability which spans only two weeks narrowly limited, but also this measure leaves ambiguous the nature of the relationship that is being judged stable or unstable. The ambiguity is pointed up by the sex difference found in these data and in a similar study by M. C. Jones (1948). Girls' relationships were found to be less enduring than those of boys. We know from other research that girls' friendships are both more intimate (Ausubel, 1954; Douvan and Adelson, 1966) and more often reciprocal (Ausubel, 1954; Flemming, 1932) than boys'. Since it is considerably less demanding to maintain casual relationships than it is an intimate friendship, the sex difference in stability may be simply an artifact of boys' less intense friendships. More precise measures of the nature of relationships seem crucial to a meaningful assessment of friendship stability. This work remains to be done.

The area that has received least attention in research on adolescent friendship is the daily interaction, the content and concerns of the relationship. A few excellent focused observational studies have produced insights about atypical adolescent groups like slum dwellers and Harvard men (Friedenberg, 1959; Goodman, 1960; Keniston, 1965). But the normal adolescent population has not been subjected to the same close and detailed observation. The studies by Becker, Geer, and Hughes (1963, 1965) on older adolescent groups and young adults combine insight and system and offer a model for the kind of theoretically relevant description so badly needed in this area. Unfortunately, no comparable description of the high school age group has appeared since Hollingshead observed the youth of Elmtown (1949).

Winch's model (1955) of similarity and complementarity in need structures, developed for analyzing marital patterns, also seems a promising approach for analysis of friendship patterns. One unfinished study of roommate stability among student nurses (D. R. Miller and Berman, 1965) has produced some provocative early findings. It seems that compatibility in roommate pairs depends on similarity in certain specific behavioral and attitudinal characteristics like heterosexual popularity and attitudes toward work and dating, and on complementarity in regard to certain less conscious and broader needs like passivity, dominance, and dependency.

Cliques, Peer Groups

Douvan and Adelson's findings indicate that the peer group assumes an important life of its own for boys—asserting influence through norms and claims on members' loyalty. The group as such supports boys in their move toward independence; they depend on this source of strength and reciprocate with fraternal loyalty. Girls, less provoked by inner striving for freedom, have less need for group support and tend rather to conceive a group as a setting in which to find close dyadic relationships. The whole area is marked by the crucial difference in the adolescent tasks of boys and girls: boys are dominated by needs for achievement and independence; girls' concerns center on developing interpersonal skills and on the need for love. The two sex groups use social relationships differently to support and express these central concerns.

We have indicated that in important decisions and choices, most adolescents are likely to seek parents' advice and opinions rather than to turn to their peers (Douvan and Adelson, 1966; Solomon, 1961). But important decisions and choices represent a small proportion of the behavior of adolescents, and there are obviously less deliberate and less dramatic behaviors—the stuff of daily life—in which the values and norms of a peer group make their force felt.

The adolescent is vulnerable to evaluation by others and his perception of their evaluation sharpens as he grows older. Studies by Ausubel, Schiff, and Gasser (1952) and DeJung and Gardner (1962) both document the increasing accuracy with which youngsters perceive their sociometric status among their peers as they increase in age from nine through 17. Ausubel and his associates detect an interesting disruption in this development which DeJung and Gardner do not find: a temporary reversal at about the onset of puberty.

J. S. Coleman (1961) has demonstrated the force of peer values in determining sociometric ratings of students. He found that high school students develop value systems, outside the official academic values, centering on athletic skills, student activity, and social leadership. He has shown that students who do not meet the student-peer criteria and are not members of "the leading crowd" are generally aware that they are not, and sometimes wish they were. Under these circumstances, the nonelite have lower self-esteem than either members of the elite group or nonmembers who say they don't want to be members. Since adolescence is a time of matching inner continuities against the social reality of others' responses to the self, evaluation by any relevant group is bound to have an impact on this process. Studies of cliques suggest that the game of inclusion and exclusion is both fevered and deadly at adolescence. Younger children form groups and practice exclusion, but at adolescence the force of the identity quest invests these ritual forms with greater significance.

Clique formation at adolescence is based on similarity in background (e.g., social class, race), skills, and values. A number of studies have revealed the force of social class in defining clique lines (J. S. Coleman, 1961; Havighurst *et al.*, 1962; Hollingshead, 1949). Friendships may transcend class lines, and individuals may be included in cliques outside their own class, but the clique itself is always predominantly made up within class lines.

Inclusion in a dominant clique depends also on possession of skills valued by the peer group (which values, in turn, may be urged on the society of peers by the dominant clique that personifies them). For boys, this means athletic skills and for girls, social-leadership abilities (J. S. Coleman, 1961). Horowitz's findings (1967) corroborate Coleman's conclusions about factors leading to popularity with peers and add some information about factors that may lead to specific rejection by peers.

A curious and provocative finding reported by Iscoe and Carden (1961) indicates that popularity among peers is related to conformity to sex-role expectations. Using experimental measures of field dependence (i.e., the degree to which an individual's perceptions are dependent on background factors as compared to focal stimuli) which had previously yielded stable sex differences in early adulthood (but not at younger ages), these investigators found that the popular boys tended to be field independent and most popular girls field dependent, compared to their less popular peers. Sociometric choices cluster around those children and adolescents who have incorporated the sex-appropriate behavior that will presumably distinguish the males and females in their group in adulthood. Tuddenham (1952) reported a similar finding based on ratings and questionnaire data. Viewing these studies in combination with Coleman's analysis, one is impressed with the imposing force of sex-role issues in forming dominant peer values during adolescence.

The dominant peer-value system in American high schools and colleges is anti-intellectual in content. Studies of high schools reveal the low value high school students attach to the scholar image and the difficulty bright and competent students face in accepting the image as their own. Scholarly boys do accept it increasingly as they progress through high school, but bright girls do not (J. S. Coleman, 1961; A. J. Tannenbaum, 1962).

At the college level, peer-group values are less exclusively and less strongly anti-intellectual, but they are nonetheless a far cry from the liberal and humanistic ideals that make up institutional goals as professed in college catalogues. Competitive athletics and social leadership hold their own as competing values. Even at an intellectually select school like Vassar, the values of the peer culture have been described as predominantly nonacademic (Freedman, 1956). It is tempting to see this as an anti-adult system rather than primarily anti-intellectual. According to this view, the peer culture says in effect, "We have needs and interests other than the ones that the established adult authorities recognize." We hesitate before this kind of generalization for two reasons. First, the adult culture is not demonstrably different from youth culture in value orientation. Hollingshead (1949) and others (Friedenberg, 1959; Havighurst *et al.*, 1962), observing the American high school, note that parents and even teachers, principals, and superintendents value athletics and extracurricular events at least as highly as they do the school's academic standing.

Our other reason for hesitating has to do with the enormous variation in social science generalizations about youth culture over the past thirty years (Grinder, 1964). Social scientists have moved from the view that the dominant function of youth culture is anti-adult expression, to the more popular current view that youth culture is a benign apprentice system that socializes children to responsible adult patterns. It may be that the youth culture has changed, but it seems equally possible that social scientists have mellowed. That the change is not entirely a function of new empirical findings is indicated by the fact that both views are represented among researchers who have current data in hand (Grinder, 1964; Keniston, 1965; E. A. Smith, 1962).

The peer culture—or primary groups that form within it—often mediate demands from the adult world, and cushion the adolescent against the values and demands of that world. Sometimes the peer society functions as a demand sorter, cueing the adolescent as to which demands he must meet, and which he can ignore. An example of this in an older group comes from a study of medical students (Becker *et al.*, 1963). The authors note that medical students could probably not survive the uncoordinated and extravagant demands of the medical faculty if this programming of priorities did not develop.

Heterosexual Friendship and Dating

The preadolescent child spends his social hours largely in sex-segregated friendship and play groups. Around adolescence he begins his encounters and experiments with heterosexual social life. Just how and when the transition from unisexual to heterosexual socializing occurs remain somewhat obscure; the data are not consistent. *Dunphy* (1963) describes the transition for Australian youth as one in which the like-sexed groups of preadolescence begin to join into loose combines that offer a setting for heterosexual interaction while maintaining the support of the earlier like-sexed friendship groups. This coalescing of intact like-sexed groups also occurred in Elmtown (Hollingshead, 1949) and River City (Havighurst *et al.*, 1962). Only after a period of heterosexual group life did adolescents begin to pair off in dating.

Douvan and Adelson (1966) report critical changes in the nature of boy-girl interaction occurring in girls at fourteen. Girls under fourteen share active team sports with boys and make no very sharp distinction between activities appropriate for like-sexed and co-ed clubs. Beyond fourteen, girls share individual sports (swimming, golf, tennis) and social activities with boys, but not team sports, and they distinguish more sharply between all-girl and co-ed activities.

Broderick and Fowler (1961) report that children in one middle-class southern city have extensive cross-sex social interaction as early as the fifth grade. They interpret this as a new pattern based on greater understanding and sharing of values across sex groups, and see in this development some danger of a reduction in the clarity of sex-role definitions. Burchinal (1964), however, has pointed out that the data reported by Broderick and Fowler on beginning dating are so at variance with findings from other studies that their sample, or the meaning of dating to these southern children, or both, must be regarded as deviant.

The normal age for beginning dating is fourteen for girls, fifteen for boys (Douvan and Adelson, 1966; Lowrie, 1951). Most observers agree that American children are dating earlier today (Broderick and Fowler, 1961; *Burchinal,* 1964) compared to twenty years ago, and the data available, though unsatisfactory from the point of view of sampling, support this conclusion

(E. A. Smith, 1962). Claims that children begin dating in grade school are not, however, supported by most current data (*Burchinal*, 1964; Douvan and Adelson, 1966).

The function of the American dating system, often misconstrued by Europeans as courting behavior, is to reintroduce the child to the forms of heterosexual social life while to some extent protecting him from damaging failure or loss of self-esteem through a highly prescribed system of roles. Dating behavior is as ritualized as medieval courtly love, but has, at least in its early stages, much less to do with sex. The obligations of a good date include cheerfulness, the capacity to control moods and impulses, and good manners. Both high school and college students see dating primarily as a social relationship rather than a courtship pattern tied to mate selection and marriage (Lowrie, 1951). Even "steady dating" seems often to be unrelated to courtship. *Burchinal* (1964), reviewing research, concludes that steady dating for social reasons is probably as important and as common as steady dating that is marriage-oriented. Most adolescents who report steady dating in high school have no thought of marrying during high school; most of them have at least two steady relationships during high school; and most of the relationships break up, usually without serious harm to the partners.

What are the social gains to be had from dating? Among the most important is increased status and acceptance in the peer group. Both dating and steady dating are associated with extracurricular activity and higher prestige ratings. Steady dating, often thought to be the refuge of insecure adolescents, is, in fact, more commonly the pattern of particularly active and popular students (*Burchinal*, 1964; Douvan and Adelson, 1966).

Among girls, progress in dating is related to increasing maturity in conceptions of both heterosexual and like-sexed relationships. Girls who are just beginning to date are defensive and suspicious in their attitudes toward boys, and they demand security and loyalty from their girl friends. As girls gain greater experience in dating (and presumably greater security), they show greater awareness of boys as people and more appreciation for the individuality of girl friends. Some examples may clarify these changes. In direct and projective questions, girls in the early dating phase emphasize the importance of the dating personality. They attribute popularity to specific skills like conversation and dancing, while older girls more often see popularity with boys as the result of sensitivity, understanding, and interest in the boy. The early daters stress the importance of "face" in a projective situation in which a girl's date shows an interest in another girl (i.e., they think the girl should "not let the boy think she cares, or is jealous"). They tend to manipulate the boy (e.g., they suggest that the girl might talk the situation over with the other girl). Older girls are less defensive and more likely to talk to the boy about their feelings (Douvan and Adelson, 1966).

By seventeen, virtually all American girls date, and some 30 per cent have formed a relatively steady relationship with one boy. The greater ease of their relationships with boys is reflected in reduced defensiveness, and it carries over to their relationships with other girls by reducing the intensity of their need for sameness and security in their like-sexed relationships (Douvan and Adelson, 1966).

A persistent popular concern in our society centers on the long-range effects of early dating and steady dating. Specifically, the question asked is whether acceleration in heterosexual development will lead to earlier marriages. *Burchinal* (1964) offers a tentative answer in his review of the field:

> The relationship between young marriage and younger-than-average ages for initial dating offers a basis for . . . these apprehensions. On the other hand, although ages for initial dating have declined greatly since World War II, and going steady has become a more common experience, young marriage rates, after a sharp increase between 1940 and 1950, have remained relatively stable for the last decade (p. 632).

I. L. Reiss (1961) concludes on the basis of his extensive research and knowledge of the literature that "in the area of sexual codes and behavior, the evidence shows more conservatism and responsibility [among teen-agers] than one might otherwise suspect" (p. 61). Despite great popular concern about adolescents' initiation into heterosexual patterns, and despite the relatively extensive research in the area, a great deal of ambiguity and obscurity remains. *Burchinal* suggests that more comprehensive and particularly more longitudinal studies are needed "to determine the various outcomes of different dating histories and patterns" (p. 632).

22

A Study of the Friendship
Fluctuations of Preadolescents*

John E. Horrocks
Mae E. Buker

Introduction

In a previous study Horrocks and Thompson (1946; Thompson and Horrocks, 1947) investigated the degree of friendship fluctuation among 1874 adolescent boys and girls. It was the purpose of the present study to investigate the degree of fluctuation in preadolescent friendships and to compare the results with those obtained by Horrocks and Thompson in their earlier study. The development of acceptable social behavior has frequently been stressed as one of the more important aims of education. An inquiry into the stability of friendship among children in the various years of school, particularly as it changes or remains constant from year to year should serve as a further step toward an understanding of the development of social behavior. Many of the early studies of interpersonal relationships were concerned with the development of methods of observing the social behavior of the child. Recently the emphasis has shifted to the observation and measurement of the child's acceptance by his contemporaries and to interaction in social groups. Friendship is one form of acceptance and plays an important rôle in group interaction.

Subjects

The 366 subjects originally selected for participation in this study were obtained from a suburban community near Columbus, Ohio, and consisted of all the children in one of that community's two elementary schools enrolled in grades one through five, and those in one session of the kindergarten. Ages ranged from five through 10 years and the sample consisted of 179 girls and 187 boys. The children

* From *The Journal of Genetic Psychology*, 1951, 78, 131–144.

came from families whose socioeconomic status was considerably above that of the average American family. Intelligence quotients ranged from 75 to 128 with the median well above 100.

As is almost inevitable in a school situation, the sample of the testing periods varied somewhat due to absence, the admission of new students moving into the community, withdrawals, and classroom changes. About 90 per cent of the sample was common to all testing periods, or 327 out of 366 individuals. Table 37 presents the number of subjects,

TABLE 37. NUMBER OF SUBJECTS PRESENT AT BOTH TESTING PERIODS

Chronological age		Boys	Girls	Boys and girls
5		16	20	36
6		19	25	44
7		36	25	61
8		35	31	66
9		30	33	63
10		28	29	57
	Total	164	163	327

classified by chronological age, who were present at all testing periods. After the collection of data the names of those absent at one or both of the testing periods were eliminated as *selectors* of best friends, although this did not affect their status as *selectees*.

Procedure

All of the children selected for this study were given a slip of paper upon which the following request was mimeographed:

Please write below the names of your three best friends, or the children you like best in your classroom. List the one you like the best first; second best, second; and third best, third.

Three numbered lines were provided for the subjects to write down the names of their three best friends. Each classroom in the study was self-contained, and so each classroom teacher explained verbally what the students were to do, emphasizing that the best friend's name was to be placed first and that friends outside the classroom were not to be named. With the kindergarten children it was necessary for the teacher to interview each child privately and also to record his response. In the first and second grades and in some of the other rooms, a list of the names of the children in the room was placed on the board. This served to help the children in spelling the names of their friends and called to mind the names of the children who were absent at the time the test was given.

Two weeks later the children were again asked to list their three best friends in order of preference. Slips of paper were supplied upon which the same directions used the first time were mimeographed. The following sentences were added:

> Your best friends now may or may not be the same as your best friends two weeks ago. Write the names of the ones you like best now.

Special help was again given to the younger children.

Four weeks later another measure of friendship fluctuation was determined in the same manner as the first and was in turn followed by a retest after two weeks. Thus, two two-week testing periods, four weeks apart, were employed in this study, making a total time span of eight weeks. The study was made during March and April in order to have allowed the children to have been in the same classroom together since September.

The two-week interval was selected (*a*) because it was believed that it gave the children a short enough time so that they would have some opportunity to remember whom they had chosen in the first choosing situation, yet it was considered a long enough time to allow the presence or absence of characteristic trends in fluctuation to be shown through a comparison of the data on both tests; and (*b*) because it was desired for the purpose of the research that the results of the present study be comparable with the previous one made by Horrocks and Thompson.

A two-week testing period four weeks after the first two-week period was given to determine whether or not what is true of a given two-week period is also true of a later two-week period.

The method used in determining friendship fluctuation was the same as that devised by Horrocks and Thompson for their study. Their method of computing the friendship fluctuation indices was as follows:

> The three friends chosen by each subject during the second choice situation were compared with the three friends chosen two weeks previously.
>
> If the friends chosen the second time duplicated in personage and rank over the friends chosen two weeks previously, the index of friendship fluctuation was considered to be zero.
>
> If the friends chosen the second time duplicated in personage but differed in rank order from the friends chosen two weeks previously, an index of friendship fluctuation was computed by assigning a numerical value of one to each rank that a friend of the second choice situation was separated from the rank initially assigned to him; e.g., if the original rankings were: like best, John; second best, Bill; third best, Carl; and the second rankings were: like best, Carl; second best, John; third best, Bill; the fluctuation index as computed by this procedure would be four; since Carl is removed two ranks, Bill one rank, and John one rank from the original rankings.
>
> If the subject during the second choice situation chose among his three best friends boys or girls whom he had not previously chosen, the following numerical values were assigned to these new friends; two for a person not previously mentioned who became the subject's third-best friend during the second choice situation, three for a person not previously mentioned who became the subject's second-best friend, and four for a person not previously mentioned who became the subject's best friend.

Table 38 may help to clarify the procedure employed to obtain this over-all index of friendship fluctuation.

TABLE 38. SUBJECT y, FEMALE, AGE 10

	First choice situation	*Second choice situation*
Best friend	Mary	Mary
Second-best friend	Patricia	Jane
Third-best friend	Jane	Doris
Friendship Fluctuation Index: 3		

Results

The results of the first two-week testing period have been reported first. Unless otherwise designated, reference is to the results of this period.

The means and standard deviations of the distributions of friendship fluctuation for the various chronological age levels are presented in Table 39.

TABLE 39. Sex Differences by Age in Indices of Friendship Fluctuation

Chronological age	Girls		Boys		
	Mean	SD	Mean	SD	t
5	5.80	2.87	4.75	2.20	1.21
6	5.20	2.65	5.42	2.66	0.27
7	5.44	2.17	4.86	2.38	0.98
8	4.65	2.66	4.23	2.35	0.67
9	3.79	1.87	4.27	3.10	0.73
10	3.55	2.53	3.21	2.12	0.54

These data are based on an analysis of 163 girls and 164 boys. In this table are also presented the results of statistical comparisons of the distributions of friendship fluctuation of boys and girls at the various age levels. Table 40 presents the means and standard

TABLE 40. Sex Differences by Grade in Indices of Friendship Fluctuation

Chronological age	Girls		Boys		
	Mean	SD	Mean	SD	t
Kindergarten	5.59	2.86	4.89	2.13	.86
1	5.04	2.63	5.25	2.47	.29
2	5.45	2.41	4.91	2.58	.84
3	4.57	2.53	3.89	2.27	1.05
4	4.08	2.13	4.31	3.08	.34
5	3.08	2.31	3.27	2.21	.28

deviations of the distribution of friendship fluctuation for the various grade levels.

The *t*'s obtained in the statistical analyses presented in Tables 39 and 40 indicate that the small differences in friendship fluctuation between the boys and girls at each of the chronological-age and grade levels can reasonably be attributed to random errors of sampling. From these statistical analyses one cannot reject with a reasonable degree of confidence the null hypothesis that there are no differ-ences in friendship fluctuation between the boys and girls at the various age and grade levels.

The magnitude of the standard deviations for both sexes demonstrates that there are considerable individual differences in the stability of friendships at all of the chronological-age and grade levels studied.

As shown in Tables 39 and 40 there appears to be for both boys and girls a trend toward greater stability in friendship with increasing age or grade level, but with about the same amount of individual variation within each age and grade level.

TABLE 41. Boy-Girl Composite Indices of Friendship Fluctuation by Age

Chronological age	N	Mean	SD
5	36	5.33	2.65
6	44	5.30	2.65
7	61	5.10	2.31
8	66	4.42	2.52
9	63	4.02	2.54
10	57	3.39	2.33

TABLE 42. Boy-Girl Composite Indices of Friendship Fluctuation by Grade

Grade	N	Mean	SD
Kindergarten	40	5.28	2.57
1	51	5.14	2.55
2	64	5.17	2.52
3	61	4.15	2.38
4	65	4.18	2.60
5	46	3.17	2.26

The results of the statistical analyses comparing the fluctuation index of each chronological age group of girls with that of every other age group of girls are presented in Table 43. The obtained *t*'s indicate that, comparatively, the mean fluctuation indices of the nine- and 10-year-old girls are significantly lower than the means of the five-, six-, and seven-year-old girls. The differences between the means of the other age groups of girls are not statistically significant at acceptable levels of confidence.

Statistical analyses, presented in Table 44, indicate that the mean fluctuation index of the 10-year-old boys is significantly lower than the means of the five-, six-, and seven-year-old boys. The differences between the means of the other age groups of boys are not statistically significant at acceptable levels of confidence.

The statistical analyses of the combined data for boys and girls are presented in Table 45. The results indicate that the mean fluctuation indices of the nine- and 10-year-old elementary school children are significantly lower than the means of the five-, and six-, and seven-year-olds. The mean of the 10-year-old group is also significantly lower than the mean of the eight-year-old group.

From the foregoing analysis it would appear that there is a trend toward greater stability with increasing chronological age, and that the onset of such stability tends to begin somewhat earlier with girls than it does with boys.

TABLE 43. RESULTS OF STATISTICAL COMPARISONS OF THE DISTRIBUTION OF FRIENDSHIP FLUCTUATION INDICES OF THE SIX CHRONOLOGICAL AGE GROUPS OF GIRLS

Chronological age	5	6	7	8	9	10
10						—
9					—	.41 (60)
8				—	1.48 (62)	1.62 (58)
7			—	1.22 (54)	3.00** (56)	2.91** (52)
6		—	.34 (48)	.76 (54)	2.24* (56)	2.29* (52)
5	—	.71 (43)	.46 (43)	1.40 (49)	2.72** (51)	2.74** (47)

Chronological age

* In tables 43–46 the italicized numbers are the *t*'s for the various chronological age group comparisons. The numbers in the parentheses represent the numbers of degrees of freedom for the various *t* values. Those *t* values statistically significant at the 5 percent level of confidence are indicated by a single asterisk; while those significant at the 1 percent level of confidence are designated by two asterisks.

TABLE 44. RESULTS OF STATISTICAL COMPARISONS OF THE DISTRIBUTION OF FRIENDSHIP FLUCTUATION INDICES OF THE SIX CHRONOLOGICAL AGE GROUPS OF BOYS

Chronological age	5	6	7	8	9	10
10						—
9					—	1.51 (56)
8				—	.06 (63)	1.79 (61)
7			—	1.11 (69)	.84 (64)	2.89** (62)
6		—	.75 (53)	1.59 (52)	1.35 (47)	2.95** (45)
5	—	.79 (33)	.16 (50)	.74 (49)	.59 (44)	3.85** (42)

Chronological age

TABLE 45. RESULTS OF STATISTICAL COMPARISONS OF THE DISTRIBUTION OF FRIENDSHIP FLUCTUATION INDICES OF THE SIX CHRONOLOGICAL AGE GROUPS OF GIRLS AND BOYS COMBINED

Chronological age	5	6	7	8	9	10
10						—
9					—	1.40 (118)
8				—	.89 (127)	2.34* (121)
7			—	1.58 (125)	2.45* (122)	3.98** (116)
6		—	.40 (103)	1.73 (108)	2.51* (105)	3.75** (99)
5	—	.05 (78)	.43 (95)	1.65 (100)	2.38* (97)	3.53** (91)

Chronological age

Comparison with the Previous Adolescent Study

Since the procedures and techniques used in the present study were identical with those used by Thompson and Horrocks (1947) in their study of friendship fluctuations among urban adolescents, it is possible, to some extent, to compare the friendship stability of urban youth at the various age levels included in these two studies. However, it should be noted that there are differences in the school samples included in these two studies. An attempt was made in the Thompson and Horrocks study to select schools enrolling pupils from average socio-economic status families, while in the present study the subjects are drawn from a single school system enrolling a large number of children from families of above average socio-economic status. While the populations of the communities utilized in both studies were approximately the same, the communities in

TABLE 46. RESULTS OF STATISTICAL COMPARISONS OF THE DISTRIBUTION OF FRIENDSHIP FLUCTUATION INDICES OF THE FOURTEEN CHRONOLOGICAL AGE GROUPS*

Chronological age (rows, right-hand labels) vs. Chronological age (columns, bottom labels)

Age	6	7	8	9	10	11	12	13	14	15	16	17	18
17												—	.79 (177)
16											—	1.72 (309)	1.81 (196)
15										—	2.46 (339)	4.12** (320)	3.31** (207)
14									—	.71 (288)	3.03** (277)	4.59** (258)	3.64** (145)
13								—	.26 (296)	.52 (358)	3.07** (347)	4.78** (328)	3.70** (215)
12							—	.73 (296)	.90 (226)	.23 (288)	2.07* (277)	3.63** (258)	3.09** (145)
11						—	1.01 (149)	.54 (219)	.35 (149)	.86 (211)	2.48* (200)	3.56** (181)	3.32** (68)
10					—	.75 (92)	.21 (169)	.38 (239)	.56 (169)	.03 (231)	2.03* (220)	3.38** (201)	2.96** (88)
9				—	1.40 (118)	.45 (98)	1.78 (175)	1.29 (245)	1.03 (175)	1.64 (237)	3.63** (226)	4.95** (207)	4.11** (94)
8			—	.89 (127)	2.34** (121)	1.23 (101)	2.85** (178)	2.41* (248)	2.08* (178)	2.74** (240)	4.81** (229)	6.16** (210)	4.84** (97)
7		—	1.58 (125)	2.45* (122)	3.98** (116)	2.54* (96)	4.71** (173)	4.36** (243)	3.92** (173)	4.65** (235)	6.65** (226)	8.00** (205)	6.19** (92)
6	—	.40 (103)	1.73 (108)	2.51* (105)	3.75** (99)	2.62* (79)	4.23** (156)	3.93** (226)	3.60** (156)	4.17** (218)	5.90** (207)	7.02** (188)	5.90** (75)
5	.05 (78)	.43 (95)	1.65 (100)	2.38* (97)	3.53** (91)	2.50* (71)	3.96** (148)	3.67** (218)	3.37** (148)	3.90** (210)	5.38** (199)	6.38** (180)	5.58** (67)

Chronological age

the earlier studies were self-contained cities located some distance from the nearest large population center, while the community used in the present study was a suburb immediately adjoining a comparatively large metropolitan center, although it did possess an independent business and shopping district of its own. Under the circumstances the communities involved are not directly comparable, although they have many things in common; and this fact should be kept in mind in interpreting the comparative results cited.

The results of the statistical analysis comparing the fluctuation index of each chronological age group from year five to age 18 are presented in Table 46. In this table the data from the Thompson and Horrocks study have been combined with those of the present study. The obtained *t*'s indicate that, comparatively, the mean fluctuation of the nine- through 18-year-old groups are significantly lower than the mean fluctuation indices of the five-, six-, and seven-year-olds. The mean fluctuation indices of the 12- through 18-year-old children are also significantly lower than the means of the eight-year-old group. In addition the means of the 16-, 17-, and 18-year-old groups are significantly lower than those of the nine- through 15-year-old group. The differences between the means of the other age groups are not statistically significant at acceptable levels of confidence.

This statistical comparison indicated that there is a significant trend toward greater stability in friendship with increasing chronological age from year five through year 18 on the basis of the index used.

The means of the friendship fluctuation indices for the boy-girl composite population are also presented graphically in Figure 25. The combined data for these 1232 urban boys and girls show a consistent downward trend in friendship fluctuation from year five to 17.

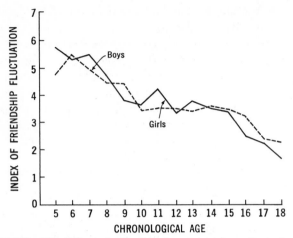

FIG. 25. The relationship between chronological age and friendship fluctuation for an urban sample of 585 boys and 647 girls.

Relation Between Friendship Fluctuation and Social Acceptability

Under the assumption that low social acceptance by one's age mates might serve to increase a child's fluctuation status, it was decided to compare the friendship fluctuation index with a social acceptance index.

In setting up a social acceptance index two criteria had to be met. First, since several groups were involved the social acceptance index had to be of such a nature that it would have uniform significance regardless of the size of the group. Second, the index would be most efficiently stated in numerical terms to facilitate the computation of a coefficient of correlation between the two indices. To meet these criteria the following scoring system was devised: first choice, 3 points; second choice, 2 points; third choice, 1 point. Thus, if a child in the first testing or choosing situation received one first place choice, three second place choices, and two third place choices, he would have a score of 3 plus 6 plus 2, or a total of 11 as his social acceptability rating.

A product-moment coefficient of .065 was obtained between friendship fluctuation index and the social acceptability index. Thus, there is practically no relationship between a person's friendship fluctuation and his acceptance by his group as determined by this study. The individual who is well accepted by his group and the one who is poorly accepted by his group will each tend to fluctuate in his friendships to about the same degree.

Comparison of the First and Second Testing Periods

The results obtained at the second testing period are not dissimilar to those secured at the first testing period. However, the t's obtained in the statistical comparison of the distribution of friendship fluctuation of boys and girls at the various age levels at the second testing period are on the whole higher than those obtained at the first testing period. There is a significant difference in friendship fluctuation between boys and girls at age eight. However, in view of the lack of significant differences revealed in both testing periods one is led to conclude that there are probably no reliable differences in friendship fluctuation at the age levels included in this study. It is true, however, that both testing periods showed a tendency toward greater stability of friendship with increasing age.

Discussion

The results of the present study apply, of course, only to the sample used in the study. Different results might well be obtained with other representative samples. The study does seem indicative, however, of the general trend in friendship development of the child as he progresses throughout the public schools from kindergarten through grade twelve. However, in view of the large individual variations it is apparent that here as in other phases of the child's development there are individual growth patterns.

From previous sociometric studies it is also true that results depend upon the nature of the question asked. In this study the question was asked, "who is your best friend?" The person responding might well ask, best friend for what, and in the absence of any definition by the testor, make his own definition. In an unpublished study made at Ohio State University, the senior author found low correlations among persons nominated when best friends for various specific purposes were asked for. Further, each subject was compelled to confine his nominations to his grade group. It is possible that a number of the subjects would have preferred to nominate someone outside the grade group, and a somewhat different pattern of fluctuation might have ensued. Still, confining the selection to the immediate group did furnish a picture of the friendship situation *within* that particular group.

The method of computing the index might also be called into question particularly since there was no accurate quantitative way of indicating the values of given positions on the list of best friends. For the purpose of the index it was assumed that a second choice position was as far removed, in comparative selection strength, from a first choice position as a third choice position was removed from a second choice position. It may well have been that for many subjects first and second choice were equal and which person they listed in first as compared to second position was purely a chance matter.

Summary

The purpose of this study was to investigate the degree of friendship fluctuation among elementary school children and to compare the degree of fluctuations with that of urban adolescents as determined by Thompson and Horrocks (1947). All of the children from grade one through grade five in a suburban public school, and one of the two kindergarten groups coöperated in this study. The children ranged in age from five to 10 years of age. There were 163 girls and 164 boys in the group.

Friendship fluctuation was determined by pupil choices through the use of a sociometric test. The procedure and techniques used by Thompson and Horrocks were used in the present study. The subjects were asked to list their three best friends on two occasions, 14 days apart. Four weeks later another measure of friendship fluctuation was determined in the same manner. Analyses which included an index of friendship fluctuation were made of their responses.

The data showed a trend toward greater stability in friendship with increasing chronological age and a corresponding higher grade placement. These findings support the results of the previous adolescent study. The means of the friendship fluctuation indices for the various chronological age groups included in the two studies tended to form a continuous curve, showing a consistent downward trend in friendship fluctuation from year five to year 18.

Analysis revealed practically no relationship between a person's friendship fluctuation and his acceptance by his group.

The results of the first and second two-week testing periods were similar. Both showed a trend toward greater stability in friendship with increasing chronological age.

23

Predictions of Adolescent
Popularity and Rejection from
Achievement and Interest Tests*

Herbert Horowitz

In the 35 years since its introduction by Moreno, the technique of sociometric measurement has come to be used widely for studying interpersonal choice. A major trend in this research has been the effort to isolate factors associated with popularity and rejection among children and adolescents. Summaries of the research finding in this area, as well as in other areas of sociometric measurement, are contained in the reviews of Lindzey and Borgatta (1954) and in *The Sociometry Reader* (Moreno *et al.*, 1960). To cite but a few of the large body of related findings, it has been found, for example, that popularity is positively associated with athletic ability and interest (Feinberg, 1953; Feinberg, Smith, & Schmidt, 1958; Krumboltz, Christal, & Ward, 1959; McGraw & Tolbert, 1953), positively associated with sociability and social adjustment (Bonney, 1946; Feinberg, 1953; Feinberg *et al.*, 1958; Kuhlen & Bretsch, 1960), and negatively associated with school newspaper activity (Krumboltz *et al.*, 1959).

The present study sought to extend these findings using multiple rather than single criteria typical of previous work in the area and using a larger and more representative sample of adolescents than has been used previously.

Method

Description of the Sample

The sociometric data for the present study were collected in conjunction with the high school testing program constituting Project TALENT (Flanagan, Davis, Dailey, Shaycoft, Gorham, Orr, & Goldberg, 1964). The sociometric data came from a subsample of eight schools selected from the 1,353 schools

* From *Journal of Educational Psychology*, 1967, 58, 170–174.

constituting the TALENT sample. The eight schools were chosen to maximize generalizability to the national high school age group. Each school in the sample was representative of one of the eight (continental) regional areas defined by the United States Office of Education. In selecting schools for the subsample, however, an attempt was made to limit the variability of the size of the schools. Thus, the number of students in each grade ranged only from 57 to 161. Summing across all grades and all schools, the sample contained 1,437 males and 1,505 females. For all of these individuals sociometric data as well as regular Project TALENT testing data were available.

The Sociometric Criterion Scores

Within each of the four grades, each male and female student was asked to list the three boys within their own grade they most "like to be with" and, in addition, the three boys they least "like to be with." Each student was then required to give the same six nominations (three positive and three negative) for the female students in his or her class. Thus, four kinds of sociometric scores were obtained for each student.

1. Same-Sex Attraction Score (SS-A): the number of times the individual was nominated as liked by members of his (her) own sex, weighted by dividing by the number of same-sex students in that grade.
2. Opposite-Sex Attraction Score (OS-A): the number of times the individual was nominated as liked by members of the opposite sex, weighted by dividing by the number of opposite-sex students in that grade.
3. Same-Sex Rejection Score (SS-R): the number of times the individual was nominated as disliked by members of the same sex, weighted by dividing by the number of same-sex students in that grade.

4. Opposite-Sex Rejection Score (OS-R): the number of times the individual was nominated as disliked by members of the opposite sex weighted by dividing by the number of opposite-sex students in that grade.

The actual weights used in computing these scores varied from the low 20's to the upper 80's. From this it can be seen that the social groups in which these scores were taken, while variable, were not very large.

Product-moment correlations among these criteria in each sex showed the two kinds of attraction scores (SS-A and OS-A) to be highly positively correlated, as were the two kinds of rejection scores (SS-R and OS-R). Furthermore, correlations between attraction and rejection scores, while significantly different from zero, were much lower and negative. Factor analyses of these criteria in each sex (reported in Horowitz, 1966) yielded two independent factors, readily identified as "attraction" (same-sex and opposite-sex) and "rejection" (same-sex and opposite-sex). These factors accounted for approximately 80% of the total variance in the criterion scores. Nevertheless, it was decided to use the four criterion scores *separately* in the present analyses since it was possible to obtain variations between the two kinds

of attraction criteria or between the rejection criteria in their relationships to the predictors.

The Predictors

In all, 15 Project TALENT variables were used as predictors.[1] These variables (listed in Table 47) were the ones remaining after preliminary analyses with a larger group of predictor variables resulted in elimination of variables whose relations to the criteria had been shown to be weak or inconsistent. Although such variable-selection procedures have been employed previously (e.g., Krumboltz, Christal, & Ward, 1959), there is always the danger of inadvertently capitalizing on chance relationships in the data. However, this does not appear to be the case here. In the original matrices of correlation of 56 predictors and four criteria (sexes combined in these matrices), 158 (70%) of the 224 correlations were significant at the $p = .05$ level, as compared with 11 correlations which would be significant if only chance conditions were operating.[2] Thus, it is clear

[1] Standardization and other normative data about all 15 predictors (except the socioeconomic index) are contained in Flanagan *et al.*, 1964.
[2] With samples of this size, rs as small as $\pm.06$ are significantly different from zero at the $p = .05$ level.

TABLE 47. PRODUCT-MOMENT AND MULTIPLE CORRELATIONS AMONG FIFTEEN PROJECT TALENT PREDICTOR VARIABLES AND FOUR SOCIOMETRIC CRITERIA BY SEX

	Intercorrelations							
	Males				Females			
	Attractiveness		Rejection		Attractiveness		Rejection	
Predictors	SS-A	OS-A	SS-R	OS-R	SS-A	OS-A	SS-R	OS-R
Literature information	.12	.14	−.01	−.06	.06	.08	−.09	−.07
Music information	.08	.19	−.01	−.08	.11	.12	−.12	−.12
Scientific attitude information	.12	.14	−.02	−.06	.11	.16	−.14	−.14
Sports information	.22	.27	−.11	−.15	.09	.13	−.09	−.10
Sociability scale	.17	.22	−.04	−.06	.15	.18	.03	−.03
Impulsiveness scale	.01	.00	.09	.07	−.00	.04	.10	.06
Leadership scale	.16	.20	.02	−.01	.15	.22	.03	−.01
Literary-linguist interest	.06	.14	.06	.02	.04	.11	−.02	−.03
Social service interest	.04	.12	−.01	−.06	.10	.10	−.08	−.08
Musical interest	.02	.11	.09	.03	.04	.04	−.01	.01
Sports interest	.18	.17	−.15	−.19	.12	.15	−.04	−.09
Outdoors interest	.01	−.03	−.06	−.12	.03	.07	−.00	−.02
Labor interest	−.08	−.13	.01	.01	−.05	−.07	.02	.04
English test total	.16	.21	−.09	−.12	.18	.16	−.18	−.18
Socioeconomic level index	.11	.17	.03	−.04	.12	.19	−.08	−.12
Corrected R$_{mult}$	.31*	.39*	.25*	.27*	.29*	.34*	.26*	.26*

Note.—For samples of this size to be significant at the $p = .01$ level, r must be greater than or equal to .08. For males, $N = 1,437$; for females, $N = 1,505$.

* $p < .01$.

that many variables other than the 15 selected were related to the criteria. Although the original analyses were done with combined sexes, the analyses to be reported here were done separately for each sex. In this way, it was possible to study the replicability of the findings across sex.

In the analysis each of the 15 predictors was correlated individually with the four criteria. In addition, multiple correlations were performed with composite sets of the 15 predictors.

Results

The upper portion of Table 47 shows the intercorrelations among 15 predictors and four criteria. It can be observed that, in absolute terms, the correlations are small, none of them exceeding ± .30, and many do not exceed ± .10. Second, the criteria of attractiveness (SS-A and OS-A) are generally more strongly correlated with the predictors than the corresponding criteria of rejection. This is particularly true for the males. A third point to note is that the correlations show a reflection in sign from those in the attractiveness columns (usually positive) to those in the rejection columns (usually negative).

The bottom row of Table 47 shows the eight multiple correlations between each of the criteria and the 15 predictors. All of these correlations are statistically significant and account for at least twice as much variance as the largest bivariate correlations between that criterion and any of the predictors. That is, there is considerable enhancement of predictability of both popularity and rejection criteria through multiple correlation technique.

The following variables were the best predictors of popularity in both sexes: the English test total, interest in sports, and the self-rating personality scales of sociability and leadership. A particularly important additional variable for predicting males' popularity is their *knowledge* of sports (sports information test).

The results for rejection are, in some respects, the reverse of those for popularity. For both males and females, English test total and information about and interest in sports are negatively related to rejection; and, for females, the socioeconomic variable predicts both popularity (positive association) and rejection (negative association). From these results it is clear that some overlap exists between factors associated with popularity and those accounting for rejection. To see *how much* overlap exists, the obtained correlations for attractiveness were correlated with each other and with those for rejection. In doing this, the algebraic sums of the two product-moment correlations for each predictor in each adjacent pair of columns were obtained (SS-A + OS-A and SS-R + OS-R). Then these four sets of 15 sums of correlations were themselves correlated. These *r*s are shown in Table 48. The table shows that, within a given kind of affect, cross-sex correla-

TABLE 48. INTERCORRELATIONS OF FOUR SETS OF FIFTEEN CORRELATION COEFFICIENTS BETWEEN FIFTEEN PROJECT TALENT PREDICTORS AND SOCIOMETRIC CRITERIA

	Attractiveness		Rejection	
	Males	*Females*	*Males*	*Females*
ATTRACTIVENESS				
Males	—	+.87	−.70	−.62
Females	—	—	−.53	−.56
REJECTION				
Males	—	—	—	+.64

Note.—All correlations in this table are significantly different from zero at or beyond the $p = .05$ level. See text for explanation of derivation of correlations reported in this table.

tions of the sums of original correlations are positive and high (particularly for attractiveness). In this way, these results provide some proof of replicability of the findings for independent subsamples. However, more importantly, the correlations between attractiveness and rejection (both within and across sexes) are also high and, predictably, negative. Thus, these data show clearly that the *patterns of association* among predictors and criteria are quite consistent, that is, that the *relative* power of different predictors remains quite stable with variations in sex of *S* and nature of affect.

Discussion

The present data delineate a pattern of interpersonal values in the adolescent world of American high schools which is similar to the one described by Coleman in his extensive study of *The Adolescent Society* (J. S. Coleman, 1961). One of the major findings of that report was that, although athletes were chosen more frequently (by several criteria of interpersonal popularity) than scholars, the "athlete-scholars" were the most popular of all, suggesting positive valuation of both academic and athletic achievements. The present results support that finding in showing strong relationships between, on the one hand, popularity and rejection criteria and, on the other hand, interest and achievement predictors from both the intellectual and athletic domains.

While the present study supports previous investigations in showing a multiplicity of associations between sociometric choices and other factors, clearly the variables were not equally successful as predictors of popularity and rejection. While some overlap exists among variables associated with popularity and those associated with rejection, these variables (English test total, sports information, sports interest, socioeconomic index) are a minority of the complete set of 15. The finding that relatively few variables relate to both popularity *and* rejection is meaningful in light of the results obtained with the criterion score analyses (Horowitz, 1966). The fact that the criteria separated into two factors, "attraction" and "rejection," suggests that predictors related to attractiveness might be different from those related to rejection. Support for this expectation was found in the present data, in spite of the significantly consistent patterns of prediction which were also found (Table 48). For instance, leadership and

sociability personality scales have fairly strong positive associations with popularity, but, with one exception, statistically nonsignificant relationships to rejection. Similarly, while labor interest was negatively related to attractiveness, it had only nonsignificant correlations with rejection. Finally, at least one of the 15 variables, the impulsiveness scale, seemed to be associated only with rejection.

Thus, the present data, when considered alongside the results of the criterion analysis, suggest that there may be three clusters of psychometric variables which predict popularity and rejection: those associated only with popularity, those associated only with rejection, and those associated (to a lesser degree) with both popularity and rejection. The ultimate test of this hypothesis would require a multivariate analytic procedure with a different, and probably much larger, set of predictors which had previously been shown to be related to popularity and/or rejection. Such a procedure would not only increase the total variance which multiple correlations could explain; it would also reveal the particular constellations of variables which are associated, in the first place, with popularity; second, with rejection; and, finally, with both popularity and rejection.

24

The Social Structure of

*Urban Adolescent Peer Groups**

Dexter C. Dunphy

Most writers on adolescence emphasize the influence of peer groups on the course of adolescent social maturation. Indeed some regard the peer group as of comparable significance to the family and the school in the socialization of urban adolescents. Parsons, for example, states: "The family offers a wide enough range of role participations only for the young child. He must learn, by actual participation, progressively more roles than his family of orientation can offer him. It is at this point that the peer group and school assume paramount importance (Parsons and Bales, 1956, p. 38)." Existing research has established that a major difference in sex composition exists between typical preadolescent and adolescent groups. Preadolescent groups are almost universally unisexual in composition, with play centering around sex-categorized activities and role models (Ausubel, 1954; Bossard, 1948). The "gang age" thus appears to consolidate the oedipal crisis by reinforcing the child's learning of his basic sex role, such learning taking place mainly at this stage through identification with the parent of the child's own sex. Adolescence by contrast is marked by an increasing volume of heterosexual choices of preferred associates. During adolescence most persons achieve membership in a heterosexual group and acquire a heterosexual role (Connel *et al.*, 1957; Hollingshead, 1949).

With some notable exceptions, field studies of adolescent peer groups have been few and inadequate and most studies of adolescent groups have aimed to assess the importance of isolated factors rather than to study groups as functioning entities. With the exception of studies of delinquent gangs, the literature is practically devoid of thorough analyses of particular groups and their dynamics. Consequently documented information on the forms and functions of adolescent peer groups is limited. Many writers distinguish two types of adolescent groups, usually referred to as "cliques" and "crowds." The

most obvious difference between these two groups is their size. Hurlock, for instance, refers to the crowd as "the largest of the social units formed by adolescents (1949, p. 173)." The clique is usually regarded as smaller, more clearly defined and more cohesive than the crowd. Hollingshead states: "When there is a lack of homogeneity the peer group may be a clique, which is smaller and more purposefully organized than is the crowd. Exclusion of those who do not belong is the express purpose of the clique (p. 448)." A wide survey of the use of these two terms in the literature on adolescence reveals no clear indication of the relative size limits of the two types of group nor agreement on what different functions, if any, these two groups perform for their members. While Hurlock (1949, p. 173) suggests that cliques are the basic elements in a crowd, Cole states that the clique "prevents many social contacts from taking place and reduces the effectiveness of those that do occur (Cole, 1948, p. 264)." Similarly no clear picture exists of the internal structural properties of adolescent peer groups (e.g., leadership) nor of the dynamics by which groups function to induce the learning of a mature heterosexual role. The study reported here was therefore undertaken to provide some detailed information on the types, sizes, structure, and dynamics of adolescent peer groups in non-institutionalized urban settings.

The Research Design

This article summarizes some of the results of a field study undertaken in Sydney, Australia, between February, 1958, and December, 1960. Informal peer associations of adolescents were located in the community and studied in their natural settings. The research methods were developed in a pilot project with 60 adolescents. The subjects of the investigation itself were 303 adolescents amongst whom boys

* From *Sociometry*, 1963, 26, 230–246.

and girls were included in approximately equal numbers.[1] Ages ranged from 13 to 21 years. The groups were scattered throughout the Sydney Metropolitan area, were from differing socioeconomic backgrounds (although predominantly middle class) and were in most cases connected in some way with sponsored youth organizations. These clubs were used as points of departure for an exploration of the natural groups to which their members belonged, each group being studied for a period of from four to six months. Two natural associations of "unattached" youth were included to check a possible bias arising from the method of choosing subjects; no important differences were found between the structure and dynamics of these groups and the other groups in the study.[2]

The main problem in investigating the structural properties of adolescent groups is to find an appropriate method of research. Because of their informal nature, the most satisfactory method is participant observation. However, since these are adolescent peer groups, the adult observer is denied membership and full participation in them. A modified version of the participant observer approach was developed in a pilot study. This consisted in making initial contacts with youth through institutional settings, establishing rapport, and subsequently moving out into non-institutional settings. The author spent many hours on streetcorners, in milkbars and homes, at parties and on Sydney beaches with the groups being studied. All groups were informed of the nature of the study and agreed to cooperate. Other more formal methods were used in conjunction with informal observation and participation. Questionnaires were administered to all subjects, diaries were kept concurrently by the members of each group in which interaction with peers for a period of a week was recorded in detail; the majority of the subjects were interviewed at length, their answers to questions being recorded on tape. The result was a flexible method of observation designed to gather a large amount of detailed information with as little interference as possible to the normal functioning of the groups under study.

[1] In natural groups such as these, there are some membership changes over time. The numbers refer to the total membership of the groups at the time the sociometric questionnaire was administered.

[2] However, the extent to which this sample of Sydney youth is "typical" is not known. Of the "natural associations," one was a hierarchy consisting of two crowds, the other, a lower-class gang at Stage 1 (see Figure 26).

Results

Group types. An initial attempt to locate group boundaries through sociometric means proved confusing because of a considerable lack of correspondence between individual subjects' responses when asked to list those who belonged to their "crowd." However, observation of interaction, and interviewing, revealed a high level of consensus on the boundaries of membership groups. Groups were clearly recognized as definite entities, and high status members of these groups could give accurate (i.e., verifiable by observation of interaction) descriptions of group boundaries and could also list members in status terms. In fact, while many members could not accurately describe their own positions in the group structure, they could usually describe the positions of others with some precision.

Two kinds of groups were located by participant observation, by interview, and by analysis of the diaries. These corresponded fairly closely with those referred to as cliques and crowds in the literature, and this terminology will be applied to them here. Both types of groups are true peer groups since group members are of similar age and regard each other as acceptable associates.

The first and most obvious basis of differentiation between the group types was size, the clique being smaller than the crowd. Forty-four cliques were located varying in size from three to nine members and having an average membership of 6.2. Crowds were considerably larger. Twelve crowds were located having a range of membership from 15 to 30 and an average size of 20.2. On the average then, the clique is only about one-third the size of a crowd. No group was observed with a membership in the range 10 to 14. Therefore, if these groups are typical, cliques and crowds are not two ends on a continuum of size but two distinct groups on a numerical basis alone. An examination of the two types of groups shows why this is so. *The crowd is essentially an association of cliques.* There was little variation in the number of cliques within the twelve crowds. No crowd had more than four or less than two component cliques. The average number of cliques forming a crowd was 3.1.

The distinct upper limit of nine members for the clique suggests the intimacy of the relationships between members. The limited membership makes possible the strong cohesion which is a marked characteristic of these groups. Their similarity in size to the family possibly facilitates the transference of the individual's allegiance to them and allows them to provide an alternative center of security. The larger number in the crowd obviously precludes such close relationships between members. Interviews showed that from the point of view of a member within one clique within a crowd, members of other cliques are acceptable associates but not "real buddies" like the members of his own clique.

While the cliques are the basic units in crowd structure, not all cliques were associated in crowds. This held for five of the 44 cliques in the study whose members either were not accorded or did not seek, status in a crowd. They were outside the crowd structure as some individuals (isolates) were outside the clique structure. Clique membership appears to be a prerequisite of crowd membership, since no case was found of an individual possessing crowd membership without at the same time being a member of a clique. On the other hand, one could be a clique member without being a crowd member. The members of cliques normally lived in close residential proximity and this appeared to be the main ascriptive requirement for clique membership. The cliques associated in a crowd were from adjacent residential localities and their members were of similar age and level of social development. Contrary to Cole's view, quoted above, cliques do not limit social contacts, but, on the contrary, the acquirement of clique membership is virtually the only way in which such contacts can be established and expanded.

Within localities, crowds were differentiated on an age basis, with two or three crowds associated in a status hierarchy. Five of these hierarchies, each in a different suburb, were objects of investigation in the study. Invariably the mean age of members of a crowd higher in the hierarchy was higher than the mean age of members of a crowd lower in the hierarchy. All but one of the crowds in the study formed part of a hierarchy of two or three crowds, and in some hierarchies, upper status members of one crowd occupied low status positions in the crowd above. The difference between age means of crowds adjacent in such hierarchies varied from seven months to three years and seven months, but averaged about two years.

Since age was a major factor underlying crowd differentiation, it is not surprising that where two crowds were adjacent in a crowd hierarchy, the social distance between them (as measured by relative frequency of interaction) varied with the difference between the mean ages of their members. When there was a large gap between the mean ages of adjacent crowds, interaction between the members of the two crowds was extremely limited. Where the gap was small, interaction was far more frequent and the upper status members of the lower crowd tended to hold low status positions in the crowd above.

All crowds were heterosexual, and within crowds there was a consistent difference between the ages of boys and girls. In all crowds boys were older on the average than the girls with whom they associated. Differences between the mean ages of boys and girls in the same crowd ranged from three months to one year and ten months but averaged ten months. Many of the cliques of later adolescents were heterosexual and in all these the same age relationship between the sexes was apparent. The differentiation of the sexes along age lines parallels the typical age relationship between spouses in marriage.

Cliques and crowds perform different functions for their members. The clique centers mainly around talking. The members of one hierarchy, for example, recorded 69 clique settings and 25 crowd settings in their diaries. Of the 69 clique settings, the predominant activity in 56 of them was talking, while it was the main activity in only five of the 25 crowd settings. A similar trend was found in all groups. Analysis of the content of conversation in the clique shows that it performs an important instrumental function in that it is the center for the preparation of crowd activities, for dissemination of information about them, and for their evaluation after they are over. The crowd, on the other hand, is the center of larger and more organized social activities, such as parties and dances, which provide for interaction between the sexes. It acts as a reservoir of acceptable associates who can be drawn on to the extent required by any social activity. Thus cliques and crowds are not only different in size; they are also different in function.

There is a tendency for clique and crowd settings to be distributed differently throughout the week. In the hierarchy mentioned above, 16 of the 25 crowd settings took place at the weekend and only nine during the week. Of the clique settings, however, 47 occurred during the week and only 22 at the weekend. In all hierarchies the majority of crowd settings occurred at weekends, while the majority of clique settings occurred on weekdays.

Structural change. In considering the hierarchical arrangement of crowds, certain general trends in the structural development of peer groups through the

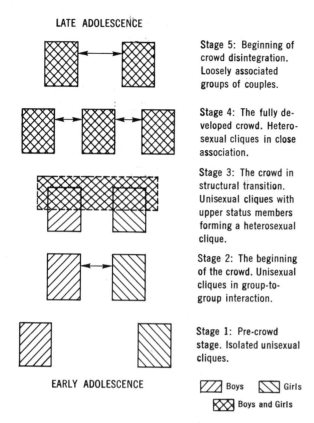

LATE ADOLESCENCE

Stage 5: Beginning of crowd disintegration. Loosely associated groups of couples.

Stage 4: The fully developed crowd. Heterosexual cliques in close association.

Stage 3: The crowd in structural transition. Unisexual cliques with upper status members forming a heterosexual clique.

Stage 2: The beginning of the crowd. Unisexual cliques in group-to-group interaction.

Stage 1: Pre-crowd stage. Isolated unisexual cliques.

EARLY ADOLESCENCE

Boys   Girls

Boys and Girls

FIG. 26. Stages of group development in adolescence.

adolescent period became apparent. Some structural characteristics consistently appear before others in all hierarchies. An abstract ideal-typical outline of structural development is portrayed in Figure 26.

The initial stage of adolescent group development appears to be that of the isolated unisexual clique: i.e., isolated in terms of any relationship with corresponding groups of the opposite sex. This primary stage represents the persistence of the preadolescent "gang" into the adolescent period. Stage 2 introduces the first movement towards heterosexuality in group structure.[3] Unisexual cliques previously unrelated to cliques of the opposite sex now participate in heterosexual interaction. At this stage however, interaction is considered daring and is only undertaken in the security of a group setting where the

individual is supported by the presence of his own sex associates. Interaction at this stage is often superficially antagonistic. Stage 3 sees the formation of the heterosexual clique for the first time. Upper status members of unisexual cliques initiate individual-to-individual heterosexual interaction and the first dating occurs. Those adolescents who belong to these emergent heterosexual groups still maintain a membership role in their unisexual clique, so that they possess dual membership in two intersecting cliques. This initiates an extensive transformation of group structure by which there takes place a reorganization of unisexual cliques and the reformation of their membership into heterosexual cliques (stage 4). While the cliques persist as small intimate groups, their membership now comprises both sexes. Stage 5 sees the slow disintegration of the crowd and the formation of cliques consisting of couples who are going steady or engaged. Thus there is a progressive development of group structure from predominantly unisexual to heterosexual groups. In this transition, the crowd—an extended heterosexual peer group—occupies a strategic position. Membership in a crowd offers opportunities for establishing a heterosexual role. The crowd is therefore the most significant group for the individual, but crowd membership is dependent upon prior membership in a clique. In fact, the crowd is basically an interrelationship of cliques, and appears to consolidate the heterosexual learning appropriate to each stage of development. The majority of clique members, therefore, possess a determinate position in an extended hierarchical arrangement of cliques and crowds, in which high status is accorded to groups most developed in heterosexual structure. The course of the individual's social development appears to be strongly influenced by his position within this structure.

Internal properties. Boundaries of peer groups were clearly defined and boundary definition operated as a form of social control. Crowd boundaries were most rigidly defined. When peer group members were asked to choose associates to join them in a number of situations, only four to eight percent of choices were directed outside the crowd. On the other hand 37 to 47 percent of choices were directed

---

[3] I have deliberately not specified modal ages for the onset of the stages outlined in Figure 26. The variation in the ages at which these phases of group development are encountered is so great that measures of central tendency, by themselves, would be misleading; and any useful estimate of standard deviations would require a much more comprehensive study than that described here. The average age of members in one isolated clique of girls (stage 1), for example, was 16 years

0 months. On the other hand, stage 3 had been reached by another clique of girls with an average age of only 13 years ten months, and the average age of the interacting clique of boys was 14 years six months. The figure suggests the order of structural changes in the adolescent peer group but the differing rates, and conditions affecting these rates, need further, more extensive investigations.

outside the members' own cliques to members of cliques within the same crowd. The majority of choices were made within the respondent's own clique. Clique boundaries were less sharply defined than crowd boundaries since some individuals were willing to choose members of other cliques in the same crowd. Very few were prepared to choose outside their own crowd.

Boundary definition was a constant process which could be observed in recurring decisions such as who would be invited to parties or on swimming excursions. The meaning of boundary definition in practice can be illustrated by describing a party in which members of two crowds from the same hierarchy were involved. The hierarchy consisted of three crowds, the upper and middle crowds being fairly narrowly differentiated by age and therefore having two "marginal" members in common. At the instigation of the author, members of these two crowds were invited to a party held by one of the members of the upper crowd. Clique boundaries were most obvious at the beginning and the end of the evening. Members arrived and left in cliques. At the party itself, however, the cliques within each crowd showed a tendency to merge and members interacted across clique boundaries. The crowds were strongly differentiated. Although everyone was initially in the lounge room, the younger crowd gradually relegated itself to the kitchen, leaving the upper crowd in possession of the lounge room. This arrangement persisted throughout the rest of the evening. The two marginal members were clique leaders in the middle crowd, low status followers in the upper. Their behavior reflected their position in the hierarchy, for they oscillated from one room to the other throughout the evening. Two isolates, whom the author had arranged to be invited, showed contrasting ways of adjusting to the situation. The girl made no attempt to relate herself to either group, remained seated in one corner of the lounge room all evening, rarely spoke, and was left to make her own way home, unaccompanied. The boy attempted to relate himself to the upper crowd leader, was ignored, and remained on the fringe of those who gathered around this status figure. Thus both cliques and crowds are boundary maintaining systems in certain situations. When together, cliques in the same crowd tend to merge. However, only boundaries between cliques are relaxed. Those who did not possess membership in a component clique were not accepted into the crowd, whether or not they attempted to relate themselves to it.

In order to acquire a membership role, an individual has to pass from outside through the boundary into the group. This is definitely a matter of achievement. Members of groups reported that they had to "push themselves forward" to enter a group. A typical statement was: "Someone who gets in and pushes, gets into a group easiest. You just have to get in and push. People who stand back just don't make the grade." Acceptance into a group was not just a matter of achievement but also of conformity. It was reported by those who had achieved membership that a new member had to "fit in," "be the same to us." Or, as one boy put it: "All groups have a certain temperament of their own. Anyone new has to fit in; he must have similar aspects and outlooks and like similar things." By demanding initial conformity to peer group standards, members ensured that the group would be a cohesive entity capable of controlling the behavior of those in it in the interests of the dominant majority. The basic consensus of values which results is a major factor in the strong *esprit de corps* of most adolescent peer groups.

It is possible to lose a membership role and to pass through the group boundary out of the group. This was due to one of two causes, as was shown by an examination of a number of concrete cases. Firstly, ostracism was sometimes the result of a member's rejection of the authority of the group. A member who regarded himself as superior to others in the group, or his judgment as superior to the judgment of the group, was quickly cut down to size. Persistence in such an attitude involved exclusion from the group and the redefinition of the boundary to exclude the offender. Loss of a membership role could also occur where an individual failed to maintain achievement, especially heterosexual achievement, at the level of his peers. This involved at first a loss of status. Continued failure to achieve meant that the member was simply dropped from the group with a consequent readjustment of the group boundary.

Entrance to a peer group depends on conformity, and failure to continue to conform at any stage means exclusion from the group. Thus the definition of the group boundary is an important means of social control which ensures the maintenance of a high level of achievement in social development.

Role differentiation: Leader and sociocenter. Most adolescents claimed that their groups did not possess leaders. ("We don't like to think that there's a boss over us.") However, cliques were normally referred to by the name of one person in the group, e.g., "John Palmer's group." Other statements showed that while adolescents strongly denied that they had leaders, they did in fact implicitly recognize one person in the group as the incumbent of a leadership position. The following statement is typical of many made when adolescents discussed the groups they knew. "Rod has a group at Waverton, Joanne down there at North Sydney, and Julia up at Crows Nest. The groups revolve around them." In each peer group in the study there was one individual who occupied the major leadership position and who played an important and distinctive role in relating the group to its environment.

The structure of the external system of the cliques was basically composed of the relationship of the clique leaders' positions to each other, and these positions were integrated primarily through a common relationship with a crowd leader. In fact, the clique leaders assumed group representative roles in the external system of the clique. They were better known outside their group than any of their followers—a finding consistent with Whyte's account (1943) of gang structures. Thus there were two types of leadership position differentiated, corresponding with the two main types of adolescent groups. There were both clique and crowd leaders. Clique leaders were more socially mobile than their followers and were in more frequent contact with others outside the clique. The communication structure of the crowd consisted in the interrelationship of the clique and crowd leadership positions. Consequently clique leaders were better informed than their followers about what was going on in the crowd, and played a decisive part in decision making. The high status accorded the crowd leader's position is reflected in verbal and written comments about those who occupied these positions. The crowd leader appeared to be a coordinating and integrating figure in the social structure of the crowd whose presence set the seal of success on a crowd event. The incumbent of this position was always a male, and usually the leader of the largest and most heterosexually advanced clique in the crowd. Thus he had already shown his organizational capacity in a clique setting. Each clique leader was also the focus of intra-clique interaction. He was thus not only the best informed person in his clique about events and people in the crowd but also the best informed person about what was going on in his own clique. As such, he occupied a strategic position between

the external and the internal systems of his own group. His followers realized this and relied on the leader for information about others in the clique and in the crowd and about clique and crowd activities. While the clique leader's position is subordinate to that of the crowd leader, it is also invested with power and high status.

The clique leader's role in the coordination of his clique with others in the crowd exposes him to two sources of role expectations. In his position as leader of the clique he is expected by members of the clique to perform essential leadership functions. As a key figure in the crowd structure, he is subject to the expectations of the other clique leaders in the crowd. His subordinate position in relation to the crowd leader means that he is particularly susceptible to influence from that source. He is thus in a position where he relays the general wishes and attitudes of his followers to others in the crowd and the influence of others, particularly status superiors, to his followers. The leader role consists of organizational skills required for the coordination of clique activities with the activities of other cliques in the crowd. It also consists of personality traits allowing the leader to mix freely with others outside his clique and maintain friendly relations within the clique. *Most importantly he has to play an advanced heterosexual role since the crowd is essentially a heterosexual association.* Leaders dated more often, were more likely to be going steady, and had achieved this relationship earlier than other members of their cliques. Where a follower attained a superior level of heterosexual achievement than the leader, there was a change of leadership or a splitting of the group structure. The admired form of heterosexual role varies with the stage of structural development of the group. For instance, an aggressive role towards the opposite sex is admired at stage 2 (see Figure 26), but results in loss of a leadership position if maintained by the leader at stage 3.

Leaders were not only superior in heterosexual development but were responsible for maintaining the general level of heterosexual development in their cliques. They acted as confidants and advisors in matters of heterosexual behavior and even organized "partners" for "slow learners." They thus brought about a progressive development in heterosexual relationships on the part of those in their groups. The clique leaders, one of whom is also the crowd leader, form an elite within the extended peer group or crowd. An elite is a small proportion of the population who together exercise a degree of control over persons and resources disproportionate to their number. The leaders are an elite in this sense in that, together, they strongly influence the behavior of those in their cliques by consistently maintaining the pressure to achieve higher levels of social development. They do this through their centrality in the communication structure and their possession of the most valued "resources" of their groups: organizational skills, desired personality traits, and the ability to play an advanced sex role.

Within the crowd, role differentiation occurred also along the expressive dimension. Just as there was a central instrumental role in the crowd (the crowd leader), so there was a major expressive role referred to here as a "sociocenter." The sociocenter was a specialist in humor. While the status accorded this position varied from one crowd to another, the position was well established in all crowds. The incumbent was always popular, well-liked and the most extraverted member of the crowd. When the crowd gathered he usually dominated the center of the groups's attention with a continual flow of witticisms and practical jokes. Because of the attention paid him in crowd settings, adults frequently regarded the sociocenter as the leader and inferred that the group was therefore essentially frivolous in character.

The degree to which the sociocenter role was differentiated varied considerably from one crowd to another, and the extent of the differentiation appeared to be influenced by the character of the crowd leader's role. In crowds where the crowd leader was seen by the members as playing an authoritarian, directive role, the sociocenter was highly differentiated. Where the crowd leader was seen as non-directive, as leading simply by virtue of superior social skills, the role was less differentiated. The more the crowd leader directly or indirectly forced the pace of social achievement in the crowd, the more highly differentiated the role of the sociocenter appeared.

This bears a similiarity to R. F. Bales' finding (Parsons and Bales, 1956) that differentiation in small problem-solving laboratory groups occurred along two axes, instrumental and expressive, and resulted in the emergence of a "task specialist" and a "best-liked man." These types appear to correspond to the "crowd leader" and the "sociocenter" reported above. Bales suggested that

> a certain amount of ambivalence tends to center on the task specialist. He tends to be liked be-

cause he is satisfying needs in relation to the task area. But he also tends to arouse a certain amount of hostility because his prestige is rising relative to the other members, because he talks a large proportion of the time, and because his suggestions constitute proposed new elements to be added to the common culture, to which all members will be committed if they agree. Whatever readjustments the members have to make in order to feel themselves committed will tend to produce minor frustrations, anxieties and hostilities. These are centered to some degree on the object most active in provoking the disturbance—the task specialist (p. 297).

In the adolescent peer group, the leader is the person who plays the most advanced heterosexual role. He moves the group to participate in heterosexual activities and encourages members to develop more mature heterosexual roles. While the members are generally motivated to achievement, this still implies new levels of conformity and commitment. The crowd leader's role is therefore particularly analogous to that of the task specialist who is similarly concerned with increased performance and similarly induces culture change. Like the task specialist, also, the peer group leader is the center of the communication pattern and high in status relative to the other members. It seems likely that the sociocenter performs the system function of relieving the tension created in the group by the leader, tension which is at its highest in the heterosexual crowd situation. His specialization in humor, a form of tension release, supports this interpretation. The more the leader dominates, the more tension is created and the more differentiated the sociocenter role becomes. If this did not occur, the tension would tend to destroy the cohesion of the group and thus impede progress toward higher goals. Bales has noted the interdependence of these two roles in his groups and this was apparent in the peer groups. They are by nature high consensus groups since only members who conform to the culture of the group are admitted. The crowd leader and the sociocenter play mutually supportive roles in the crowd structure, the complementarity of the two roles preserving the equilibrium of the crowd.

Socialization process in the adolescent peer group. The primary stage of socialization, which occurs in the family, is largely achieved through the identification of the child with his parents and his consequent incorporation of their norms. This stage has a strong effect on the acquisition of a basic sex role. The peer group at adolescence assumes many of the functions previously performed for the individual by the family and is thus of considerable significance in promoting his increasing independence from the family. If there is an internal consistency in the whole process of socialization through childhood and adolescence, we would expect socialization to take place through an identification with the peer group leaders similar to that with the parents. At the beginning of this article it was mentioned that discrepancies were observed when subjects were asked to name those in their crowd. The list given by an individual usually did not match very well the group others named as his associates and which could actually be observed in concrete situations. However, in the social structure of these membership groups as identified by participant observation, through interviews, and through analysis of diary records, these discrepancies showed up as a highly consistent and meaningful trend. When clique members were asked to name those in their crowd, they tended to name those in their own clique and the leadership elite of their crowd. The leadership elite was in fact highly "overchosen" in the sense that they received many more choices than they themselves made. There was a consistent discrepancy in the direction of high status between the groups in which the individuals actually participated and the groups to which they referred themselves.

By using a chi square technique, the probability of this trend occurring by chance could be tested. However, the test could be applied only to hierarchies where there were proportionately few inter-crowd choices so that the crowds could be treated as if they were independent entities. Four of the five hierarchies met this criterion. Two hypotheses were tested. (a) Leaders, when choosing outside their own clique and within the same crowd, choose other clique leaders significantly more than they choose followers, when allowance is made for the relative proportion of leaders to followers. (b) Followers, when choosing outside their own clique and within the same crowd, choose clique leaders significantly more than they choose followers, when allowance is made for the relative proportion of leaders to followers. Hypothesis (a) was supported in three of the four hierarchies at the 0.1%, 1%, and 2% levels respectively, but the chi square was not significant in the fourth. Inspection of the fifth hierarchy shows that those choices made within the crowd boundaries show the same trend. Hypothesis (b) was supported in all four hierarchies at the .1%, 1%, .01%, and 5% levels respectively. Inspection of those

choices made within crowd boundaries in the fifth hierarchy shows the same trend.

In some cases, choices were made of members of other crowds in the same hierarchy. These were usually choices between high status members of one crowd and low status members of another older crowd. Fifty-three choices of this kind were made in all the hierarchies. Forty-nine of these were directed upwards to members of crowds higher in status than the ones to which the choosers belong. The remaining four were directed downwards to members of crowds lower in status. Thus an examination of all extra-clique choices reveals a strong and highly significant tendency to list clique leaders in the same crowd and members of a crowd higher in the status hierarchy when naming associates. In particular, those lower in status than the chooser tend to be omitted. Members of the leadership elite within crowds were particularly overchosen. These results can be interpreted as showing a general upward trend in status terms in the pattern of identification in these groups. In naming those who belong to their "crowd," therefore, these adolescents apparently listed their *reference* rather than their *membership* groups, suggesting that the social structure is stabilized by the ego-involvement of clique members with the clique and crowd leaders.

These data lend support to S. Freud's notion, advanced particularly in his *Group Psychology and the Analysis of the Ego* (1922), that a primary group is a number of individuals who have taken the same person, the leader, as their ego-ideal. "We already begin to divine that the mutual tie between members of a group is in the nature of an identification of this kind, based upon an important emotional, common quality; and we suspect that this common quality lies in the nature of the tie with the leader" (p. 108). Thus Freud's view emphasizes that the bond with the leader is of more importance to group stability than are the ties between the members and that, in fact, it is the former which confers significance on the latter. "A primary group of this kind is a number of individuals who have put one and the same object in the place of their ego-ideal and have consequently identified themselves with each other in their ego" (p. 120). Freud regarded the family as the prototype of every human group and the leader as a parent substitute. Certainly the position of the leader in the peer group is analogous in some ways with that of the parent and a similar identification appears to occur. However, the evidence above does suggest that there is identification not only with the leader of one's clique, but beyond that an identification with a number of status figures in the wider peer group—the crowd. The interviews suggested that there is a progressive differentiation of this object system. Generally speaking, the lower a member's status in the social structure, the less differentiated the mental picture he possessed of the positions of others and their relationships with each other. It seems reasonable to deduce from this that the first stage of socialization into a group of peers, the clique, is dependent on the differentiation by the initiate of the leader, and his identification with him. From this stage the pattern of identification suggests that there is a progressive differentiation of the whole object system and a single reference idol (the clique leader) is replaced by a system of social objects which consists basically in the pattern of crowd leadership positions and roles in their interrelationships.

Discussion

In the socialization of the individual his transition from the nuclear family to wider adult society can take place in many ways. In western urban society, the peer group is one important avenue through which this can occur. In Sydney, for instance, where this study was undertaken, it appears that about 70 percent of boys and 80 percent of girls at ages 14 and 15 belong to peer groups similar to those dealt with here (Connell *et al.*, 1957). If the groups reported are typical, socialization within the peer group system is an extension of socialization within the family system and shows important resemblances in pattern. There is, for instance, a similar differentiation of structure along instrumental and expressive lines with both high status instrumental and expressive roles functioning to preserve the equilibrium of the peer group system. As in the family, the individual

proceeds through a series of successively more complex systems of relationships and in the process identifies with status figures, internalizing their roles. Thus his personality continues to expand through the progressive differentiation of his object system.

It appears of some significance that socialization within the adolescent peer group system begins as the stable state the individual enjoyed as latency child in the family is upset by new social expectations at puberty, leading him to establish an increased dependence on the peer group. Initially this group is the unisexual clique, which represents the continuation of the preadolescent "gang" and at this stage is a group comparable in size to the family. In order to achieve and maintain membership in this group, the individual must show his readiness to conform to the group's authority. This is made easier through his identification with the clique leader who embodies many of the social skills and personality traits admired in the group. The clique establishes and reinforces the individual's drive to achieve heterosexuality, since it is, or becomes, a subsystem of the crowd; the crowd in its turn is only a subsystem of a hierarchy of crowds. Thus through clique membership the individual is inducted into an extended peer group system markedly different from the family in size. About middle adolescence there is a major transformation of the clique system which has persisted in a relatively stable form. A new clique system evolves from this structurally unstable stage. Groups become heterosexual, members having established a significant relationship with a member of the opposite sex. The crowd persists long enough to ensure that the basic role characteristics underlying this relationship are thoroughly acquired. It then breaks up into cliques of loosely associated couples as members move towards marriage. The social structure of urban adolescent peer groups has the effect of maintaining a high level of achievement which ensures that most adolescents progressively acquire an increasingly mature heterosexual role.

25

Adolescent Dating

*Attitudes and Behavior**

Lee G. Burchinal

The conceptual relationships between dating and courtship have never been fully agreed upon by most American students of the phenomena.

Following the lead of Waller (1937), some students of family behavior have maintained a distinction between dating and courtship. One set of norms supposedly applied to dating roles, whereas another applied to courtship roles. More recent students of dating and courtship have abandoned this distinction and, instead, speak of a courtship continuum. The crux of the problem is that dating is a social relationship capable of wide variation in its meaning and functions, not only to family sociologists, but also to participants in the dating system, even between two persons who comprise a dating dyad. As more knowledge has become available, previous conceptual differences over "aim-inhibited" dating versus courtship have lost their meaning. Instead, the impressive features of American dating patterns have been their diversity and versatility in coping with changes in sex roles. Terms such as "playing the field," "favorite date," "competitive dating," "noncommitment steady dating," or "committed steady dating" (E. A. Smith, 1962) are used to describe the varied patterns.

Although sociologists have written much about courtship and mate selection, careful study of dating began only after World War II. Prior to this time, much of the thinking about dating was dominated by the conceptions of Waller (1937). As recently as 1948, for instance, Lowrie (1948) could publish a paper rightly entitled. "Dating: A Neglected Field of Study." Since then, at least several dozen studies of high school dating patterns have appeared. Still more studies on the dating and courtship of college students are available, but there is little direct research on the dating and courtship behavior of post-high school and noncollege youth.

Dating, as an American innovation, developed in the urban areas and among college students in the 1920's in response to the emancipation of women, increased leisure time, greater emancipation of youth, higher real incomes, commercialized recreation, and the extension of coeducational institutions. During the late 1930's and the 1940's, dating moved to the high school level. In these few decades, norms have been evolving to guide dating behavior. To some extent, these norms are perceived differently by adults and by adolescents, although they are not shared equally by all persons in either age group.

Some of the important norms and related generalizations pertaining to the earlier phases of dating in the United States are summarized in seven major areas.

Initial Ages at Dating

Contrary to popular opinion, boys and girls begin to date and go steady at approximately the same ages. Girls may begin and attain physical maturity earlier than boys, but recognized sex differences in physical development appear to have little relation to ages at initial dating. Dating is a social relationship which is defined by cultural norms, not by biological developments per se. Apparently, only a minimum level of physical development is necessary for initiating dating.

Lowrie (1952) provides the most conclusive evidence for the similarity of mean or median ages for first dates or first steady dating among boys and girls. Bardis (1958), W. J. Cameron and Kenkel (1960), and Bock and Burchinal (1962) provide supplemental support for Lowrie's generalization.

Median ages for initial dating among the high school males and females in Lowrie's samples ranged between 14.1 and 14.9 years; medians for the college samples ranged between 14.7 and 15.7 years. On the average, these students began dating in the ninth and tenth grades. The averages reported by Bardis (1958), W. J. Cameron and Kenkel (1960), and Bock and Burchinal (1962) were toward the lower

* From "The Premarital Dyad and Love Involvement" in H. T. Christensen, ed., *Handbook of Marriage and the Family* (Chicago: Rand, McNally, 1964), pp. 624–628.

end of the ranges reported by Lowrie. These data for beginning ages at dating do not support the cries of alarm, especially in the press, about preteen dating. Some preteen dating undoubtedly occurs. Cameron and Kenkel, for instance, reported that the range in ages at first dates was from 11 to 18 in their population of high school seniors in Mason City, Iowa. But it appears that most students are not dating, in the usual sense of the word, during elementary school years or the first years of junior high school.

Although boys and girls begin to date at the same ages and generally date classmates initially (Crist, 1953; Lowrie, 1952), both sexes recognize female social precocity. For instance, Bardis (1958) found that females would like males to begin dating at older ages, and males would like females to begin dating at younger ages.

These attitudinal differences probably are reflected in behavior. Long-established differences in ages at marriage and in various levels of courtship suggest that, while girls are first interested in boys their own ages, they soon turn to older boys for attention and dates, and older boys, in turn, interest themselves in younger girls.

Transition to Dating

The transition from single-sex associations to association in heterosexual groups or paired-heterosexual association probably is less abrupt and less traumatic today than previously. Casual and friendly relations between the sexes in later adolescence and adulthood appear to have drifted downward into late childhood and early adolescence, periods which generally are assumed to be characterized by mutual antagonism between boys and girls. Broderick and Fowler (1961), for instance, found norms which encourage and sustain cross-sex interaction among children in the fifth through seventh grades. A majority of the children claimed to have a sweetheart, and most expected reciprocation. Their claims did not seem to be wishful thinking, nor were they kept as hidden loves from afar; most of their classmates knew of and were able to identify various pairs.

Data reported by Broderick and Fowler for dating in these grades are not in agreement with data reported by Lowrie and others. About 45 percent of the boys and 36 percent of the girls in the Broderick and Fowler sample who were 10 and 11 years old claimed to have had at least one date. Still higher percentages were reported among the 12 and 13 year

olds: 70 percent of the boys and 53 percent of the girls claimed they had dated. These percentages require means or medians well below the levels reported in other studies. It is possible that the youth from the middle class, southern, urban community studied by Broderick and Fowler began dating earlier than other youth in the northern or midwestern urban centers included in the studies previously discussed. Other data by Lowrie (1961) indicated that Texas youth begin dating earlier than youth in Ohio or California, which may suggest regional differences in ages at initial date. On the other hand, the sizes of the differences between the Broderick and Fowler results and other research on ages at initial dating suggest that the respondents in the sample they studied probably defined or interpreted dating in a less restrictive sense than respondents in other studies.

Insecurity in Dating

Although the transition to dating may be easier today than before, many youth still report considerable anxiety and unhappiness about their dating relationships. A national sample of high school students reported common feelings of inadequacy in dating and feelings of shyness, self-consciousness, or being ill at ease (Christensen, 1952; Christensen, 1958, pp. 231–245). Furthermore, large percentages of each sex were anxious for the other sex to assume more initiative in making dates. In another study, one-half of the high school students reported fears and anxiety over their first dates (Crist, 1953). The anxiety of the youth may be related to the fact that most of these ninth-grade students said they dated primarily because the group expected it, not because they wanted to. Breed (1956) found that two-thirds of the boys and girls in two social status levels, from business and working-class families, agreed they were "pretty scared" that they would do "something wrong" on their first dates.

Frustration is not limited to initial dating experience. Williams (1949) surveyed approximately 1,500 high school students in comparable urban and rural communities in Michigan and Georgia. One-fourth of the males and one-third of the females felt that they were failures in dating and courtship. Over half wanted to date more frequently, and one-third reported they did not know how to act on dates. One-third reported that dating was not a pleasurable experience and that they experienced fear while on dates. Their personal insecurity was reflected in their need for material possessions to give them status in dating, particularly among boys.

Dating Norms

The normative structures that control dating have not been described clearly. Norms emanate from different and sometimes conflicting reference groups, particularly the parent-adult and the peer group; and, for individuals, dating norms change over time with greater dating experience and progressive commitment leading toward marriage. Changes in dating norms also occur from one generation to another, as reflected in the decline of ages for initial and more serious dating relationships and marriage. Not only do gaps exist in our understanding of the dating norms, but there are inconsistencies among some of our present findings as well.

Broadly speaking, dating behavior among youth at any given time represents the dynamic synthesis of previous experiences and the interplay of the influences of parental and other adult reference groups and peer reference groups. In some areas, the two sets of influences appear to reinforce one another; in other areas, adult and peer influences are less harmonious or are in conflict. But peer reference groups also show wide variations in permitted, desirable, or disapproved behavior.

Several areas in which general agreement is found among adult and peer reference groups include the desirable characteristics sought in a date and in male-female status and role relationships. Considerable agreement has been found for the ratings of boys and girls for seveal kinds of characteristics desired in a date. Christensen (1952) reported a correlation of .73 between the rankings of boys and girls for the importance of things looked for in a date, a correlation of .93 for ratings of conduct patterns characteristic of each sex, and a correlation of .83 for the degree of self-criticism applied to dating situations by boys and girls. The characteristics judged to be important in a date reflected evaluations congruent with adult values for dating and mate selection. These included being physically and mentally fit, being dependable, taking pride in manners and personal appearance, being clean in speech and action, having a pleasant disposition and a sense of humor, being considerate of one's date and others, acting one's age, and not being childish. (Cf. Christensen, 1958, pp. 231–264.)

Sex reference groups differed, however, in the fact that boys gave greater emphasis to the domestic skills of the female and her attractiveness, whereas girls attached greater importance to the man's financial position and his attitudes toward intimacy. Additional differences between the sexes occurred in the degree to which boys and girls accepted criticism or projected blame for things which went wrong on dates. Boys assigned about two-thirds of the blame to females. Projection of blame on boys was less true of females; they attributed more to their own sex (Christensen, 1952; Christensen, 1958, pp. 231–243).

Family and adult reference groups appear to be stronger for girls than for boys and seem to influence the behavior of the former more than the latter. Crist (1953) reported that parents influenced the behavior of girls more than boys, younger children more than older children, and farm students were influenced more by their parents than rural nonfarm or urban students. Mothers had closer relationships than fathers with both boys and girls, but the relationship was more intimate between mothers and daughters than between mothers and sons. P. H. Landis (1960) also observed that girls felt closer to their parents and felt that they could discuss their dates more with their parents than could boys.

Crist (1953) noted that most of the parents of the youth he interviewed used democratic control techniques; only a few were authoritarian. As parents became better acquainted with dating and other practices of their adolescents and friends, they became more lenient, and family dominance gave way to peer-group norms. Where conflicts occurred between parental and peer norms, though, farm children more frequently continued to accept family norms, whereas rural nonfarm and urban children tended to accept peer norms.

Other data indicate that rural youth begin to date later and have more doubts and fears about dating than urban youth (W. M. Smith, 1952). Smith found that 73 percent of the urban females in his university sample had their first date before 15 years of age, whereas 67 percent of the rural females had their first date when they were 15 years of age or older. Fifty-eight percent of the rural men first dated when they were 16 or younger, in contrast to 70 percent of the urban men.

Adult and peer reference-group norms continue to provide more freedom for boys and to maintain greater control over girls. P. H. Landis (1960) reported that boys less frequently sought parental permission for first dates, had greater freedom in their time limits, were allowed to date more frequently than girls, and were subject to parental vetoes regarding dating partners less frequently than girls. These normative differences are reflections of the double sexual standard, one of the basic norms that structures dating behavior from the most casual to the most intimate sexual relationships.

Sexual behavior is not discussed at any length in this paper. However, data from two studies relevant to the operation of the double sex standard in high school dating patterns are presented to provide a more complete description of high school dating. First, Breed (1956) observed that chivalry as well as prowess was institutionalized in male reference groups. A larger percentage of girls than boys agreed that boys should stop further sexual advances if a female said no, whether the boy thought she meant it or not. But the percentage of boys agreeing that boys should stop increased from 41 percent for the situation where the boy thought she didn't mean it to 89 percent when the boy knew she meant him to stop. This difference in attitude reflects the value of respect for the female—especially a female of whom the male is fond and from whom he also wants affection—and represents the institutionalized basis for idealization in love.

Second, the results of the national sample reported by Christensen indicated that females more frequently favor the double sexual standard for dating behavior than males. The females were more critical of their own sex than were men. Females apparently accept male-dominated dating, courtship, and marriage norms and recognize that masculine values have priority (Christensen, 1952). Yet, while accepting these conditions, females function effectively in the male-dominated heterosexual milieu.

Among those who were not going steady or were not engaged, females from 16 to 21 years of age dated more frequently than males. And, as might be expected, with those who were going steady or were engaged, differences in the frequency of dating between males and females were nonsignificant (Lowrie, 1956).

Some of the influences of the adolescent peer reference groups on dating and other adolescent behavior are well known. However, it is easy to overemphasize the influence of peer groups in contrast to family or adult reference groups in establishing dating norms. It was observed that student values in dating generally reflected accepted adult values for interpersonal relationships. And, with a few additional years beyond high school, young persons seem to conform to some of the endogamous norms.

Positive attitudes toward religiously endogamous dating can be used to represent internalization of adult mate-selection norms of religious endogamy. Burchinal (1960) found that positive attitudes toward religiously endogamous dating increased from the high school to the university level, even after the socioeconomic status of the youth was controlled. This finding suggests that as youth became older and approached marriage, they internalized adult mate-selection norms more strongly.

The Burchinal investigation also showed that farm students were more favorably disposed toward religiously endogamous dating than nonfarm students. This observation reinforces the earlier finding that farm students adhered more strongly than nonfarm students to family or adult norms when these conflicted with peer norms. Higher-status students and those who were frequent church attenders held more positive attitudes toward religiously endogamous dating, and girls favored religiously endogamous dating more than boys. Age, farm-nonfarm residence, sex, family status, and degree of church attendance each were related to the religiously endogamous norm independent of the other four variables. Data also have been presented by Burchinal and Chancellor (1962a; 1962b) for relationships between the ages of spouses, farm-nonfarm occupations of husbands, and the occupational status of husbands and interreligious marriage rates. Where analyses were comparable, the results based on the attitudes of high school and college students were consistent with the marriage results: interreligious marriage rates were inversely related to status and age and were greater among couples that included grooms employed in nonfarm in contrast to farm occupations.

Other data reveal an interesting variation from the generalization that youth probably grow into conventional dating and marriage norms as they enter young adulthood. Leslie and Richardson (1956) and Coombs (1962) found that adherence to the status and religious endogamous norms occurred more frequently among college youth who lived at home during courtship, or who courted their spouses prior to coming to college, as compared with college youth who did not live at home or who met or courted after coming to campus. In these studies, campus norms, in contrast to family or hometown norms, appeared to provide less support for endogamous mate selection.

26

*Sexual Codes in Teen-Age Culture**

Ira L. Reiss

Teen-age sexual codes reflect quite clearly the bold outlines of adult sexual codes. The high degree of conformity in teen-age culture increases the observability of teen-age beliefs and adds to our understanding of adult beliefs. The teen-ager exists in a world somewhere between youthful idealism and adult realism, and his sexual codes reflect this state of being. In a very real sense, he is a marginal man with one foot in the world of the child and the other foot in the world of the adult (A. J. Reiss, 1960).

The teen-ager is at the stage at which it is vitally important for him to learn how to exist in society independent of his parents. For this reason, he transfers his dependence to his peers and strives to learn from them the secrets of entrance into the adult world. One would think that this vaguely defined status of "almost adult" would lead to confusion and weak statements of belief. To a large extent, this is the case, but, nevertheless, it is equally true that it leads to dogmatic statements of belief and a search for conviction through conformity. Teen-agers translate and adapt the sexual codes of adults to fit their particular circumstance and state of mind.[1]

Going Steady

When unchaperoned dating gained prevalence in the early part of this century, it involved a much more rapid change of dating partners than occurs today. Nevertheless, by the time of World War II, going steady had taken root, and, today, it seems that slightly more than half of the high school students have some going-steady experience. Even among the early teen-agers, possibly one quarter go steady.[2]

Class differences are important in examining the going-steady complex. It seems that those high school people who go steady and plan to go to college are not likely to marry their high school steadies, and those who are from lower economic classes and who do not plan to go to college are much more likely to marry their high school steadies (Herman, 1955). Thus, in looking at the custom of going steady, one must realize that there are different subtypes and that the consequences differ for each type.

Although a psychologist may point to the security of going steady as its chief reason for being, as a sociologist, I would point out how Western society has, for centuries, been developing an association of sexual behavior with mutual affection. This association is hard to achieve in casual dating; but, in steady dating, sex and affection can quite easily be combined, and, in this way, a potential strain in the social system is reduced. Another area of strain which is reduced by going steady is the conflict a girl may feel between her desire for sexual experience and her desire to maintain her reputation. For many, sexual behavior is made respectable by going steady (Ehrmann, 1959, p. 14). In these ways, one may say that no other dating custom is quite as central to the understanding of teen-age sexual codes as going steady.

---

* From *The Annals of the American Academy of Political and Social Sciences*, 1961, 338, 53–62.

[1] Of course, there is a biological basis for sexual behavior, but social scientists seem generally agreed that the specific way the sexual drive expresses itself is learned. The wide variety of sexual codes throughout the world testifies to the fact that whatever differences exist biologically between men and women can be compensated for by cultural training. The best source for cross-cultural information is Ford and Beach (1951). For a discussion of this entire issue, see I. L. Reiss (1960, Chap. 1).

[2] For evidence, see Daly (1951, p. 30). It may be well to note here that the author has conducted a pilot study to test the hypothesis that the advent of the junior high school has spread heterosexual knowledge and behavior to younger age groups and thus encouraged earlier dating. In support of this, one may cite Dr. J. B. Conant's belief that the junior high imitates the high school in its social characteristics. In addition, the anticipatory socialization of sex games like "spin the bottle," "post office," and "flashlight" begin today prior to junior high levels and thus prepare students for dating in junior high. The author's evidence indicates a connection between junior high school and early dating patterns.

Girls' Sexual Codes

One of the most popular sexual codes among teen-age girls is petting-with-affection. This code is a modern day subtype of our formal abstinence standard. This subtype of abstinence seems extremely popular among high school couples who are going steady. Such couples feel it is proper to engage in heavy petting if they are going steady, the justification being that they are in love or at least extremely fond of each other. The petting-with-affection sex code probably grew along with the going-steady custom; they both illustrate adaptations of our dating institution to the newer unchaperoned dating circumstances.

What evidence do we have for such petting behavior among teen-agers? Though surely not perfect, the most extensive study of sexual behavior is that done by the Institute for Sex Research, formerly headed by Alfred C. Kinsey and now run by Paul H. Gebhard. It should be noted that the Kinsey studies are most valid for urban, white, northeastern, college-educated people, and, thus, great care must be taken when applying the results to other groups. The reader should keep in mind the tenuousness of any such generalizations made in this paper.

Kinsey's data show that, of the females who were twenty years old or older when interviewed, about one fifth to one fourth admitted they had petted to orgasm while still in their teens. Most of this behavior occurred between the ages of sixteen and twenty. About three-quarters of all the girls twenty years old or more admitted being aroused by some form of petting or kissing in their teens, and approximately 90 percent stated they had at least been kissed during their teens (Kinsey *et al.*, 1953, Chap. 7).

Those girls who marry in their teens start their petting and kissing behavior earlier than those who marry later. In general, the few years previous to marriage are by far the most sexually active for girls. Lower class females marry earlier, and, thus, they are more active in their teens and are more likely to marry their teen-age steadies.

The above rates are averages for Kinsey's entire sample of several thousand females; were we to take only the females born in more recent decades, the rates would be considerably higher. For example, of those females born before 1900, only 10 percent ever petted to orgasm in their teens, whereas, of those girls born in the 1920's almost 30 percent, or three times the proportion, petted to orgasm in their teens (Kinsey *et al.*, 1953, p. 244).

It seems clear that we have developed not only new dating forms such as going steady but also, as we have seen, new sexual codes to go with them. These new codes allow females much more freedom in heavy petting, provided affection is involved. Of course, other girls, particularly in the early teens, adhere to standards which only permit kissing, and a few others adhere to standards which allow full sexual relations, but, by and large, petting-with-affection seems the increasingly popular sex code for high school girls.

The most recent evidence of the nature of teen-age sex codes comes from the author's study and also supports these contentions (I. L. Reiss, 1967). The study involves 1,000 high school and college students, most of whom are teen-agers. It is clear that petting-with-affection is an extremely popular code with teen-age girls, particularly with the teen-agers who are high school juniors and seniors.

Finally, one should note that, in my own study and in the Kinsey study, religion was another key factor affecting girls' sexual beliefs and behaviors. Those girls who were devout in their religion were much more conservative in their sexual behavior and belief. Religion was not as strong a factor for boys and did not control their behavior as much. As we shall see, amount of education was the key determinant for male sexual behavior.

Boys' Sexual Codes

Among the teen-age boys, we find a quite different code dominant. Abstinence is given some form of lip service, particularly among the more highly educated classes, but, by and large, it is not an operational code; it is not adhered to in the behavior of the majority of the teen-age boys. Even among the males destined for college, about half have coitus in their teens; among those who stop their education in high school, about three-quarters have coitus in their teens, and, among those whose education stops before high school, about eight-tenths have coitus in their teens. Thus, it is clear that the majority of all males, in this sample of Kinsey's, at least, experienced full sexual relations before reaching twenty years of age (Kinsey *et al.*, 1948, p. 550).

For teen-age girls, the rate of nonvirginity appears to be considerably lower. Kinsey reports approximately 20 per cent nonvirginity for females by age twenty. Of course, the greater liberality of the boys does not involve a single standard; that is, they are predominantly adherents of the double standard which allows boys to have coitus but condemns girls for the same thing. This is an ancient standard reaching back many thousands of years in Western culture. It is by no means a universal standard, however, for we do find many cultures where the sexes are treated equally (I. L. Reiss, 1960, Chap. 4).

Although in recent generations, due to our greater equalitarianism and the evolving nature of the dating institution, the double standard seems to have been weakened sharply, it is still quite dominant among teen-age boys. The greater freedom allowed the male child in almost all areas of life constantly buttresses this standard and makes it seem obvious to teen-agers. Teen-agers are not sufficiently objective or sophisticated to be bothered by the contradictions in this or any other sexual code. For example, if all women abided fully by the double standard, then no men could, for the men would have no partners! Thus, this code operates only to the extent that someone violates it.

Some of these double standard teen-age boys will condemn a girl who accepts petting-with-affection, for they believe heavy petting is improper for girls. However, my own data indicate that most of these teen-age males will accept heavy petting in a going-steady relationship. They, of course, allow themselves to go further and may try to have coitus with a steady in order to see if she is a "good" girl. It is not unusual to find a relationship either broken up or its affectionate nature altered if a girl gives in to her double standard steady. Such condemnatory behavior on the part of double standard males keeps many girls from going as far sexually as they might want to. Thus, the double standard male eliminates many potential sex partners because of the attitude he takes toward such sex partners.

Teen-age double standard males are often stricter than their older brothers who accept coitus for a girl when she is in love and/or engaged. These teen-age males are supported in this rigidity by the conformity of their peer group. Double standard males typically view the act of coitus as a conquest, as a source of peer group prestige. Thus, they are quite prone to tell their friends all of the details of any affair. This characteristic tends further to discourage females from yielding to double standard males. Instead, the girl is encouraged to be, in part at least, a tease, that is, to show just enough sexual activity to keep the male interested but not enough to arouse his condemnation. Sexual behavior in this sense involves a great deal of the aspect of a game. Sex comes to be used as a power leverage to control the relationship.

Under such circumstances, sexual desire is developed so sharply in the male and so differently in the female that the male wants the female to be both sexually active and sexually pure. Under such conditions, sexual behavior can only with great difficulty relate directly to feelings of affection. This is particularly true for the act of coitus. In fact, one finds very often an inverse relation, in that boys prefer to have coitus with girls they do not care for, because they regard the girls they do care for as "too good" for such behavior. Girls, too, may control their sexual reactions, particularly with someone they care for, until they are sure they will not be condemned for their sexual response.

Thus, in the area of coitus among teen-agers, the double standard does seem to block the association of sex and affection. However, one should quickly add that, on the level of petting, sex and affection can more easily be combined, for this behavior is much more likely to be accepted for both sexes by both males and females.

Minor Standards

There are minor teen-age standards which are more permissive than petting-with-affection or the double standard. For the older teen-ager, the most popular minor standard is what I shall call permissiveness-with-affection (I. L. Reiss, 1960, Chap. 6). This standard accepts full sexual intercourse for both boys and girls, provided they are involved in a stable, affectionate relationship. The degree of stability and affection required varies among adherents from feeling strong affection to being in love and engaged. Some teen-age couples who are going steady have coitus in accord with this standard. The situation here is quite different from that of the double standard boy and his girl friend, for, in permissiveness-with-affection, both the boy and girl accept for each other what they are doing. They combine sex with affection and use affection as one of the key justifications of the sexual act.

There is a class difference in sexual standards among boys. My evidence indicates that the lower classes are more likely to be strong supporters of the double standard, while the upper classes, though still mostly double standard, contain a large proportion of boys who are not so dogmatic in their beliefs and a minority who accept permissiveness-with-affection. In general, the upper classes seem to stress equality of the sexes and the importance of affection more than the lower classes. A permissiveness-without-affection code seems more widespread at the lower levels.

Age is a crucial factor among teen-agers. Teen-agers under sixteen are much more likely to accept only kissing than are older teen-agers, who may accept petting or coitus. As noted earlier, religion does not restrict sexual behavior as much among boys as it does among girls. Education is a more important factor, with the more highly educated groups being the most conservative.

Promiscuity

The newspapers from time to time pick up stories of high school "sex clubs" and other forms of promiscuous teen-age sexual behavior (Lawton and Archer, 1951). The available evidence indicates that promiscuous coitus is common predominantly for double standard males and a few females. Promiscuous coitus is not common on an equalitarian basis, that is, where both male and female accept the behavior as right for each other. Our culture has stressed the association of sex-with-affection to such an extent that it is difficult, at least for many females, to violate this association in coitus. In the case of petting, one finds more likelihood of violation of this norm by both men and women, but, in the case of coitus, it is much more often violated by males. Ehrmann's study of 1,000 college students supports this difference between male and female sexual activity and attitudes (1959, pp. 263–266). Females, in addition to associating love with sexual behavior more than males, also have more nonsexual motives for sexual behavior, such as the desire to please the boy or to cement a relationship (Kirkendall and Gravatt, 1961).

During the teens, the sexual outlets of boys and girls differ considerably. The chief outlet for girls seems to be masturbation and petting, whereas for boys the chief outlets include coitus at the fore. In Kinsey's sample, about one third of the girls masturbated to orgasm in their teens, while over 90 percent of the boys have so masturbated in their teens (Kinsey *et al.*, 1953, p. 173; Reevy, 1961). Despite their high rate of masturbation, males also have a high rate of coitus. The lower class boys rely less on masturbation and petting and more on coitus for their sexual outlets than do those boys who go to college.

The teen-age girl today is still typically the much more conservative partner and the guardian of sexual limits. However, she appears increasingly to be a half-willing guardian who more and more seeks her self-satisfaction and strives to achieve sexual equality (McKee and Sherriffs, 1960).

There is a general trend in American society toward more equalitarian and more permissive sexual codes in all areas (I. L. Reiss, 1960, Chap. 10). This is true for teen-age sexual codes, too. The growth within abstinence of petting-with-affection is one sign of this increasing equalitarian and permissive force. Also, within the double standard, one finds increased willingness by males to accept some coitus on the part of females, especially if it occurs when the girl is in love and/or engaged. Finally, in the minor standard of permissiveness-with-affection, one sees this trend in the increased strength of this standard among teen-agers, particularly among older, college teen-agers. And these trends toward equalitarianism and permissiveness seem even stronger among older dating couples in their twenties. The teen-agers are relatively new at sexual behavior, and they, at first, grab the basic outlines of the older couples' codes. With the passage of time, they come to behave in a somewhat more equalitarian and permissive manner.

In my current research, there is evidence that the real change-over in a teen-ager's sexual code is more one of integrating attitudes and changing overt behavior than of changing basic attitudes. In short, it seems that a person holds his basic sexual attitudes in rudimentary form in his teens, but he is not fully ready to act upon them and has not fully learned how to combine these values into a coherent code of living. As he learns to do this, his behavior changes and so does his awareness of his beliefs and their unity, but his basic beliefs may well remain the same. This entire area of how our sexual beliefs are formed and how they change is in need of more careful study. My own research is aimed at probing some aspects of this problem.

Parents are prone to be most aware of what they consider excessive sexual behavior, for they are concerned about the consequences of such behavior as they may affect their children. Thus, parents complain about sexual acts of which they become aware, and they often believe teen-agers are sexually promiscuous. Actually, according to our best estimates, the real increases in teen-age sexual behavior over the last generation are not in the area of sexual intercourse but rather in the area of petting and in the public nature of some petting behavior (Kinsey *et al.*, 1953, pp. 275, 339 *passim*). Thus, these parents of today have probably had similar rates of coitus but perhaps lower rates of petting. In addition, one should note that the petting behavior today very often is not promiscuous but occurs in a stable affectionate relationship.

Youth Culture: Tame or Wild?

About twenty years ago, Kingsley Davis and Talcott Parsons wrote of a youth culture and of a parent-youth conflict and, in doing so, implied in part that youth culture was largely irresponsible, impulsive, and antiadult (K. Davis, 1940; Parsons, 1942). Many people have come to share this view and to expect rather extreme sexual behavior from teen-agers. I myself formerly accepted this view of the teen-ager as valid. However, after examining the evidence in the key areas of teen-age sexual behavior, I must admit that I can no longer accept such a conception of youth culture without serious modification and qualification. I would submit that the vast majority of our approximately twenty million teen-agers are not only not extreme but are quite conservative and restrained in the area of premarital sexual codes and behavior when we compare them to their older brothers and sisters.

There is evidence to show that teen-agers are unsure of how far to go sexually, that they feel ill at ease on dates, and that they are concerned with such "tame" issues as whether one should kiss good night on a first date (Remmers and Radler, 1957, pp. 83, 225–236). A recent study showed that teen-agers rate themselves lower in comparison to adults than adults rate them. Teen-agers in this study rated adults considerably higher than themselves on most all "good" qualities (Hess and Goldblatt, 1960). These are hardly the attitudes of an arrogant or antiadult youth. They seem more those of a group desirous of becoming like adults and striving toward that goal.

Further, when we look at the rates of female petting to orgasm in the Kinsey studies, we find considerably more of this behavior among girls in their twenties than among girls in their teens. The coitus rate for females doubles between the ages of twenty and twenty-five. Masturbation rates also increase considerably after the teens (Kinsey *et al.*, 1953, Chaps. 5, 7, 8). In all these ways, the teen-agers seem more conservative than those individuals who are in their twenties.

August Hollingshead's excellent study of a midwest community also gives evidence on the con-

servatism of youth. He found a very close correspondence between social class of parents and social class of teen-agers' dating partners. In this study, too, we are given a picture of youth culture that is very much like adult culture in its status consciousness. Hollingshead and others have also noted the fact that a large proportion of the teen-age population is virtually not involved in any dating. A good estimate for the high school age group would be that about one third of the boys and one fifth of the girls are not involved in dating (Hollingshead, 1949, p. 227; M. Davis, 1958, p. 136).

Venereal Disease and Pregnancy

Let us now examine two key indices, venereal disease and pregnancy, which should give us additional insights into the behavior of teen-agers. Teen-agers do have significant rates of venereal disease and illegitimacy. However, the press has largely exaggerated such rates. The teen-age rate of veneral disease for ages 15 to 19 is only about a third of the rate for the 20 to 24 age group and is also lower than that of the 25 to 29 age group (Richman, 1960, p. 7; 1961, pp. 36–43).

There has been a slight rise in the number of teen-age venereal disease cases in recent years, and this has received much publicity. It is quite likely that the actual rates for teen-agers are not higher and that this slight increase is due to the greater number of teen-agers today. More than 80 percent of the venereal disease reported is from older groups of people. Finally, the rate of venereal disease among teen-agers is not evenly distributed in the teen-age group. As far as we can tell from reported cases, it is highly concentrated in the lower social classes (Richman, 1960, pp. 6, 20).

When one examines the national figures for unwed mothers, one finds that 40 percent are teen-agers. Here, too, several qualifications are needed. First, most of these reported cases are Negro, and class status in general is low. The upper classes, according to Paul Gebhard's recent study, are much more willing to resort to abortion (Gebhard *et al.*, 1958, pp. 45, 160). The upper classes, also, have a greater ability to stay out of public statistics and may, thus, show lower rates. According to Clark Vincent's study, when upper class females become pregnant before marriage, it is more likely to be the result of a love affair, whereas, when lower class females become pregnant, it is more likely to be a result of a casual affair (Vincent, 1961, p. 143). Thus, there are important class differences here, too.

When we compare teen-age unwed motherhood with that for girls in their twenties, we find that the older girls have about the same proportion of the illegitimate children. We also find that the teen-age rates are not increasing as much as the rates for older groups. For example, in 1940 teen-age mothers were 46 percent of the total; in 1957 they were 40 percent.

Thus, from the evidence of national figures, it seems reasonable to conclude that it is a small and specific segment of the teen-age population that becomes involved with venereal disease or premarital pregnancy. Furthermore, the people in their twenties seem somewhat more likely to be involved in such circumstances. Also, these older couples are much more involved in adult culture in terms of their occupations and their nearness to marriage, and yet their sexual behavior is less conservative.

A warning must be added at this point concerning the venereal disease rates and unwed motherhood rates. They are far from perfect indices and, as mentioned, many higher class people manage to be excluded from them because they can afford more private means of coping with their problems. However, to the extent that we use these rates, we fail to find support for the charges made about teen-agers. It is no doubt true that teen-agers are irresponsible in the sense that they seek "to have a good time," but I would suggest that, in the area of sexual codes and behavior, the evidence shows more conservatism and responsibility than one might otherwise suspect. It may be well to avoid the over-all impressions given by a general use of the term "youth culture" as described by Parsons. Here, as elsewhere, qualification and specific research is a step toward better theoretical formulation and better understanding.

A Final Overview

What has occurred in teen-age sexual codes in recent generations is a working out of sexual practices acceptable to teen-agers. Many of these practices are at the level of petting. In short, as unchaperoned dating came into vogue and as adolescence became more prolonged due to our specialized industrial culture, young people worked out additional sexual codes to supplement and modify the older codes of abstinence and the double standard. There always were people who engaged in coitus; today there are more, but, for girls in their teens, it is still a minor activity. When we look at petting, we note something different, for here we see a much more continuous and current change among teen-agers—it is here in this middle ground that teen-agers have come to accept a petting-with-affection standard. The equalitarian and permissive aspects of this standard in many cases lead at later ages to acceptance of the more radical permissiveness-with-affection standard. However, during the teens, petting-with-affection is probably the major standard involved in stable affectionate relationships at middle and upper class levels.

At the present time, it is impossible to predict precise changes in sexual codes. This is especially true because, as we have seen, there are differences according to social class, religion, educational level, and so forth. But one can say that all the signs indicate a continued trend toward equalitarian and permissive codes. The trend seems to be toward that which now obtains in the Scandinavian countries, with the inclusion of sex education in the schools and with permissive attitudes on the formal as well as covert levels. This does not forebode the end of the double standard, for the double standard is still deeply rooted in our male dominant culture, but it does mean a continued weakening of the double standard and more qualifications of its mandates.

Teen-agers are a paradoxical group. They are not as wild as their parents or they themselves sometimes think. Teen-agers do want independence. But, judging by their sexual codes, they want independence from their parents, not from the total adult culture.

VI

Student

From the day that he enters his first classroom, a youngster finds that the role of student is one of the two or three most important roles which he is called upon to play. Not only does school occupy about as much of his waking hours as his home life does, but it is primarily as a student that the grown-up world outside of his family comes to know and evaluate him, and as a student that he meets many of his peers.

Important as it is from the very first, the most significant change in the student role at adolescence is in the degree to which it becomes a more serious, even urgent matter, especially for boys. Its shadow falls more definitely over the future and colors plans for further education and vocational choice. It is apparent to parents and youngsters alike that school provides the main path for social mobility in contemporary America. To hold your own and forge ahead requires first of all adequate or outstanding achievement; mediocrity as a student is a major obstacle to success. The adolescent school years are the time for decisions, and the junior and senior high schools are the proving grounds.

Youngsters are keenly aware of the importance of education for future success (Gold, 1963), and Adams (1964) has recorded increasing concern with school problems in the adolescent years especially on the part of boys, who mention school more often than any other place as the site of their biggest problems.

Parents also recognize the importance of academic achievement by their adolescent sons and daughters. Especially noteworthy is the mounting evidence that parents from lower social statuses regard education as important for their children, as do parents from higher statuses (Gold, 1963; A. J. Reiss and Rhodes, 1961; Sears, Maccoby, and Levin, 1957). Glenn (1963) has found that amount of education is the primary criterion for prestige among predominantly lower-status Negroes. Lower-status parents may not be very confident that their youngsters will achieve higher education and better jobs, but they earnestly aspire to these goals.

Unfortunately, for all their aspirations, lower-status parents do not nourish so well the motives and skills necessary to enable their youngsters to compete successfully with their higher-status peers. Research on the achievement motive reveals this, both directly and by implication. Working-class adolescents respond less consistently than middle-class adolescents to achievement cues, abstract standards, and verbal rewards (Douvan, 1956; Rosen, 1956). Findings on the antecedents of the achievement motive point to the importance of a family pattern in which the father is respected as head of the family (McClelland *et al.*, 1953), and in which the child by adolescence is allowed some power to govern his own affairs and is guided in the use of this power by warm, permissive parents (Douvan and Adelson, 1966; G. H. Elder, 1962; McClelland *et al.*, 1953; Morrow and Wilson, 1961). Moderate concentration of power in the hands of fathers is associated with teachers' estimates that boys are responsible, that is well-behaved, students (Bronfenbrenner, 1961). These child-rearing patterns are known to be less common in the lower class (Douvan and Adelson, 1966; G. H. Elder, 1962; Rosen, 1956, 1961).

Central, then, to adolescents is the role of student with its demands for satisfactory academic performance and a polite kind of deportment. This is the student role from the point of view of educators, parents, and grown-ups in general, and as it is understood by essentially all adolescents (Witryol, 1950): an intelligent, diligent, and compliant application to adult-prescribed educational tasks.

However, the school is not only an adolescent's place of work; it is also his club, where he goes to meet friends and to engage in a range of formal and informal extracurricular activities. The adolescent faces divergent demands as a student because he is at the same time expected to act like one of the gang by his schoolmates. Several studies (J. S. Coleman, 1961; Gordon, 1957; Remmers and Radler, 1957) indicate that while adolescents will not necessarily punish academic achievement, they favor a kind of application to the job of student which is neither too diligent nor too compliant. Coleman reports that most of the boys in his high school sample would rather be remembered as good athletes, and most of the girls, as social leaders, than as brilliant students. Remmers and Radler found that about one-third of the polled students thought that "learning how to get along with people" is the most important thing to learn in high school, compared to the 14 percent who valued the acquisition of basic knowledge and skills.

All of the studies mentioned above agree about the relationship of sex and social status to adolescents' values. For example, Coleman's data indicate that higher-status adolescents admire the brilliant student not much more than their lower-status peers do. Boys value scholarship more than girls do, and their respect for it grows as they approach high school graduation; but even among senior boys, scholarship is not valued by as many as value athletic ability. One unfortunate reflection of boys' more intense interest in academic success can be seen in the increased incidence of cheating among boys in the 12th grade, compared to those in grade 7. Girls show no comparable increase in cheating, reflecting very likely their involvement in social values (*Feldman and Feldman*, 1967).

The non-academic values of the peer group may affect actual academic performance in some cases. In an analysis of factors contributing to a decline in academic performance at the junior high school level, *Finger and Silverman, (1966)* found academic motivation, academic plans, and self-control-deliberateness to be highly related to maintaining high level performance in the transition from elementary to junior high school. They found that "the extent to which a student remains uninvolved in the youth culture is strongly related to the fate of his grades on entering junior high school," and speculate that "the junior high school years may represent an incubation period during which low academic plans and high youth-culture involvement nurture the development of those attitudes that constitute low academic motivation."

Adolescents' feelings about school come mainly from two sources, then, corresponding to the dual roles they play in the school setting: (a) from their friendships and the status they achieve among their schoolmates; (b) from their achievement as students. For some adolescents, their relationships with teachers are also an important determinant of their relationship to school in general, and probably teachers condition most of their students' attitudes toward school to some degree. But relationships with teachers are not likely to be a major factor in determining school orientations. On the one hand, teachers are not named so often as the source of problems in school (Meissner, 1961; Remmers, 1962); and on the other hand, fewer than 10 per cent of adolescents choose a teacher as their adult model (Douvan and Adelson, 1966; Havighurst, Robinson, and Dorr, 1946).

Some adolescents certainly use a close relationship with a teacher to satisfy a specifically adolescent need. Feeling a growing danger in a total investment in their parents and sensing a wider world than their homes, some adolescents choose teachers as primary figures from whom to learn and after whom to model themselves. Teachers, along with grown-up relatives and close family friends, make up the limited set of adults with whom American adolescents consistently interact and who are thus available as adult models in addition to their parents.

Since their social life, their academic achievement, and occasionally their teachers provide the main sources of satisfaction with school, then it follows that more higher-status adolescents will be happier about their school experiences than will their lower-status peers. For lower-status youngsters as a group receive lower grades and fewer academic honors (Abrahamson, 1952; Coster, 1959; Gold, 1963); are less popular and participate less in extracurricular activities (*Abrahamson*, 1952; Coster, 1959; Langworthy, 1959); and are regarded more negatively by teachers (Becker, 1952). Students and teachers alike, regardless of their own social origins, seem to share middle-class values about the ideal student and schoolmate (Havighurst and Neubauer, 1949; Weckler, 1949), although some researchers have found that lower-status adolescents are more tolerant of interpersonal aggression among boys (Maas, 1954; Pope, 1953).

Of the high school students polled in the Purdue Opinion Poll (Remmers and Hackett, 1950), 79 percent said that they liked school. This figure may be somewhat exaggerated, since it does not include school dropouts and students who were absent when the questionnaires were administered and includes only students in those high schools which subscribe to the Purdue service, but it is likely that most adolescents do like school. Although they complain about their teachers (grouchy, unclear, or unfair) or about the subject matter (boring, difficult, useless), most of them believe that most of their teachers are at least adequate and some exceptionally good; and most of them say that at least a few of their courses are fun, interesting, or even stimulating. Since satisfaction is generally lower among lower-status youngsters, it is no surprise to find that they are most likely to reject the student role altogether and drop out.

The holding power of American high schools has been increasing steadily over the past decade, so that about 64 percent of the students who had entered fifth grade in 1954 graduated from high school in 1962, compared to only 51 percent who graduated in 1950. The dropouts are disproportionately boys from lower-status families (Bledsoe, 1959; Sofokidis and Sullivan, 1964). The majority of dropouts leave school officially as soon as they reach the legal age, 16 in most states. Their attendance records suggest that many of them have all but officially dropped out before they turned 16.

If one asks the youngsters themselves why they dropped out, most of them say simply that they didn't like school (E. S. Johnson and Legg, 1944; Sofokidis and Sullivan, 1964), and they often cite difficulty with the work, or with teachers, or they mention financial reasons. On the other hand, data describing dropouts reveal that they are characteristically poor students (*Cervantes*, 1965a; Cook, 1956; Kuhlen, 1952; Sofokidis and Sullivan, 1964); they do not usually participate in extracurricular activities (*Cervantes*, 1965a; Sofokidis and Sullivan, 1964); and they are relatively unpopular with their schoolmates (*Cervantes*, 1965a; Kuhlen, 1952). That is, the reason many adolescents dislike school enough to leave, knowing that leaving jeopardizes their future, seems to be that they do not meet any of the demands of the student role, neither the performance demands of adults nor the social demands of their schoolmates. They are especially likely to drop out if their relationship with their parents is so poor that their parents' aspirations and insistence cannot hold them in the face of pressures to flee from the classroom. Boys are especially vulnerable to pressures to drop out, since the student role is more central to their image of themselves now and in the future; and they are more autonomous from their parents. To continue to commit themselves to the role of student under these conditions would be to identify themselves as failures.

Even for many of the dropouts, however, the school-club retains some of its attraction as a place to be. It is not uncommon to find the jobless dropouts hanging around the schoolyard, still "going to school" but not enough to hurt.

27

Changes in Academic

Performance in the Junior High School*

John A. Finger, Jr.
Morton Silverman

One does not have to undertake a scientific study to discover that academic underachievement constitutes a significant problem at all levels of the educational process. However, it is not clear whether academic failure is the same sort of phenomenon in both older and younger students. Conceivably, academic achievement could be a developmental process that starts in the early grades and follows its course through to college graduation or beyond. It is equally possible, however, to view an academic career as a series of events that entail varying demands upon a student's academic assets and liabilities. In an earlier study (Finger and Schlesser, 1965), it was shown that a preliminary edition of the Personal Values Inventory (PVI) (Schlesser and Finger, 1962) could identify the academic motivation factor as early as the seventh grade. The characteristics of academic motivation at the junior high school level are quite similar to those identified in secondary and college students. It would seem, then, that starting at levels as low as the seventh grade, academic motivation bears a continuous and significant relationship to academic success.

Things are less clear, however, with elementary school students. Some preliminary explorations with the PVI have suggested that academic motivation cannot be identified in elementary school students, that, at best, it bears but a weak relationship to elementary school grades. Whether these tentative findings are attributable to differences between older and younger students, the differing demands of their teachers or problems in test construction, they raise the question of discontinuity in academic motivation and performance.

In reviewing the school histories of a large number of students in the schools of New York State, Armstrong (1964) has demonstrated that the junior high school era is one of two periods in educational

careers where abrupt changes in school performance occur. While some children earned good grades in junior high school after a history of poor elementary school marks, approximately 45 percent of the boys and girls with good elementary school records went on to do only fair or poor work in junior high school. The indications of a significant discontinuity in educational career at the junior high school level were underscored by Armstrong's report of the frequent irreversibility of these changes. Relatively few of the students whose school grades deteriorated in junior high school went on to do good or even fair work at the high school level.

The influences shaping an academic career at the start of the junior high school period are obviously numerous and complex. This study was designed to explore one aspect of this complex period, the relationship between academic motivation as measured by the PVI, and changes in grades between elementary school and junior high school.

Procedure

In the spring of 1964, the State of Rhode Island tested all sixth grade students on a battery of intelligence and achievement tests. The students' scores on the California Test of Mental Maturity, the California Achievement Test in Reading, Language and Arithmetic and the Scholastic Testing Service Work-Study Skills Test were made available for this study. All available seventh grade students in five junior high schools of two Rhode Island cities who had attended selected elementary schools were tested with the PVI in November, 1964. The PVI is an objective self-administered test that inquires into students' values and interests through frank questions. The test yields 11 scores, in the areas of home, persistence, self-control—deliberateness, self-views, school defenses, planning, school attitudes, non-

* From *Personnel and Guidance Journal*, 1966, 45, 157–164.

academic activities, student's academic plans, peer academic plans, and parental academic plans.

One section of the PVI asks students to report their school marks in academic subjects for both the current and preceding years. These self-reported marks were used to classify students as to their levels of performance in elementary school and junior high school. There was a large attrition in the data in that only students with complete state testing records to whom the PVI was administered were included. There was no reason to expect, however, that the way in which the sample was selected biased the results.

Results

Because of the oft-reported sex difference in elementary school performance, correlation matrices were calculated separately for boys and girls, utilizing the seven PVI variables, the self-reported grades, the California Mental Maturity Test scores, and the various achievement test scores. Factor analyses of the correlation matrices identified an intelligence factor that involved both achievement test scores and the mental maturity test scores, and three factors defined from the PVI scores—academic moti-

vation, academic plans, and youth-culture involvement. The factor patterns for boys presented in Table 48 and for girls presented in Table 49 were essentially the same.

The factor analytic findings are consistent with the results of an earlier study (Finger & Schlesser, 1965) that employed a preliminary edition of the PVI and found the two factors of intelligence and academic motivation to have loadings on school marks. While the preliminary and revised edition used in the current study identified the same factors, the academic motivation factor in the revised edition is much more clearly delineated. The academic motivation factor summarized contributions from seven of the 11 PVI areas. The test items involved tended to concern themselves with ambition and work, the value that students placed on school success. The academic plans factor summarized the value the student and the significant people in his life placed on higher education. The youth-culture factor was derived from student reports of the importance they attached to pleasurable activities and thrill-seeking.

Students were classified according to marks they had received in elementary school and then cross-classified in terms of the grades they had received in junior high school. The procedure identified students who had earned junior high school marks that

TABLE 48. FACTOR ANALYSIS OF ACADEMIC CREDENTIALS (VARIMAX ROTATION)
BOYS—GRADE 7, N = 233

| | | *Factors* | | |
	Intelligence	Academic Motivation	Academic Plans	Youth Culture Involvement
Personal Values Inventory Scores				
Home	—	.70	—	—
Persistence	—	.78	—	—
Self-control—deliberateness	—	.44	—	−.72
Self views	—	.77	—	—
School defenses	.31	.64	—	—
Planning	—	.57	.32	—
School attitudes	—	.63	—	−.46
Non-academic activities	—	.37	.27	.47
Student's academic plans	.32	—	.66	—
Peer academic plans	—	—	.44	—
Parental academic plans	—	—	.75	—
California Mental Maturity				
Language	.72	—	—	—
Non-language	.77	—	—	—
California Achievement				
Reading vocabulary	.80	—	—	—
Reading comprehension	.86	—	—	—
Spelling	.71	—	—	—
Arithmetic reasoning	.56	—	—	—
Arithmetic fundamentals	.67	—	—	—
Scholastic Work Study Skills	.84	—	—	—
Marks—Junior High School	.57	.48	—	—
Elementary school	.64	.37	—	—

TABLE 49. FACTOR ANALYSIS OF ACADEMIC CREDENTIALS (VARIMAX ROTATION)
GIRLS—GRADE 7, N = 256

| | | *Factors* | | |
	Intelligence	Academic Motivation	Academic Plans	Youth Culture Involvement
Personal Values Inventory Scores				
Home	—	.71	—	—
Persistence	—	.83	—	—
Self-control—deliberateness	—	.25	—	−.82
Self views	—	.74	—	—
School defenses	—	.65	—	−.45
Planning	—	.66	—	—
School attitudes	—	.55	—	−.63
Non-academic activities	—	—	.54	—
Student's academic plans	.40	—	.66	—
Peer academic plans	—	—	—	—
Parental academic plans	—	—	.78	—
California Mental Maturity				
Language	.72	—	—	—
Non-language	.78	—	—	—
California Achievement				
Reading vocabulary	.78	—	—	—
Reading comprehension	.85	—	—	—
Spelling	.67	—	—	—
Arithmetic reasoning	.51	—	—	—
Arithmetic fundamentals	.63	—	—	—
Scholastic-Work Study Skills	.82	—	—	—
Marks—Junior High School	.62	.52	—	—
Elementary school	.69	.33	—	—

were "higher" than, the "same" as, "lower" than, and "much lower" than their elementary school grades. A difficulty with the classification procedure was that students who had earned very high elementary school marks could not earn higher ones in junior high school nor could the students who had earned very low marks in elementary school go on to earn still lower ones. The students who had earned A in elementary school and continued to earn A in junior high school were classified in the gain group even though their marks remained the same. A scatter diagram was plotted at each level of elementary school performance. The percent of students assigned to a category of junior high school marks was kept approximately equal for the various levels of elementary school marks. These procedures corrected in part for statistical regression.

Analyses of variance were calculated for all of the variables. However, only the results of four of these analyses are presented. One variable has been selected to represent each of the four factors shown in Tables 48 and 49.

Intelligence and the Change in Performance

When the California Mental Maturity Language scores are tabulated for the various groups, there are significant differences among the categories. The differences shown in Table 50 were primarily related to elementary school marks rather than to change in performance at the junior high school level. Those students who earned higher marks in junior high school than elementary school had a mean mental maturity language score of 112, whereas those who earned much lower marks had a mean score of 110. In contrast those students who had earned A in elementary school were 21 IQ points higher than those who had earned C. The overall trend of Table 50 seems to indicate that while intelligence was largely unrelated to the change in performance at the junior high school level, it was highly related to the marks earned in elementary school. Only among the students who earned the highest marks in elementary school was there any indication that intelligence was involved in this shift in marks. Those who had earned A and were classified as higher had an average intelligence score of 126 whereas those classified as much lower had an average score of 116.

Academic Motivation and the Change in Performance

In contrast to the results found with intelligence, academic motivation appeared to be highly related

TABLE 50. MENTAL MATURITY LANGUAGE SCORES OF SEVENTH GRADE STUDENTS CROSS-CLASSIFIED BY JUNIOR HIGH SCHOOL AND ELEMENTARY SCHOOL MARKS

Elementary Marks	Mental Maturity Language Scores				
	Junior High School Marks Compared with Elementary School Marks				
	Higher	Same	Lower	Much Lower	Total
A	126 N = 8	121 N = 11	119 N = 15	116 N = 8	120
A–B+	115 N = 15	117 N = 27	120 N = 28	117 N = 16	117
B	111 N = 18	115 N = 37	111 N = 59	110 N = 22	112
B–C+	111 N = 18	108 N = 34	104 N = 42	106 N = 18	107
C	102 N = 16	101 N = 31	98 N = 36	101 N = 12	100
Under C	—	—	—	—	95
Total	111	111	109	110	
	$F_{468}^{20} = 6.47$		$P < .01$	$\sigma = 14.3$	

NOTE: Mean Intelligence all Rhode Island 6th grade pupils = 108.

TABLE 51. PERSISTENCE SCORES OF SEVENTH GRADE STUDENTS CROSS-CLASSIFIED BY JUNIOR HIGH AND ELEMENTARY SCHOOL MARKS

Elementary School Marks	Persistence Scores				
	Junior High School Marks Compared with Elementary School Marks				
	Higher	Same	Lower	Much Lower	Total
A	16.9 N = 8	18.6 N = 11	15.0 N = 15	16.4 N = 8	16.6
A–B+	17.7 N = 15	15.7 N = 27	15.3 N = 28	11.1 N = 16	15.1
B	19.3 N = 18	15.2 N = 37	15.1 N = 59	11.9 N = 22	15.2
B–C+	15.9 N = 18	14.4 N = 34	12.8 N = 42	10.6 N = 18	13.4
C	17.2 N = 16	12.8 N = 31	12.1 N = 36	12.4 N = 12	13.2
Under C	—	—	—	—	10.7
Total	17.4	14.9	14.0	12.0	
	$F_{468}^{20} = 5.86$		$P < .01$	$\sigma = 4.5$	

to the change in performance at the junior high school level. The findings presented in Table 51 indicate that those students who were classified as earning higher grades had a persistence score of 17.4 while those classified as earning much lower grades had an average persistence score of 12. These scores are more than seven standard errors apart. There are also differences in the persistence scores among those who received the highest marks in elementary school and those who received the lowest. While the possible cause-and-effect relationships involved will be considered later, it is of interest to note that academic motivation bears a significant relationship to school performance by the sixth grade. Furthermore, the persistence scores are very uniform in their downward trend with the change in performance at the junior high school level. The discrepancies in this trend, particularly apparent in those who had earned elementary school marks of A, are probably due to interactions with intelligence. (The actual influence of the persistence score can only be seen when the groups compared are equal in intelligence, for both intelligence and persistence are highly correlated with grades.)

Academic Plans and the Change in Performance

The academic plans that students have for their own future education were selected to represent the academic plan factor. The findings presented in Table 52 indicate that students who show a large drop in performance at the junior high school level had lower academic plans than those who went on to earn the same or higher grades. Whereas those students who earned higher grades in junior high school had a mean academic plan score of 25.3, students who experienced much lower junior high school grades had a mean score of 21.3. It is rather interesting to find academic plans to be strongly related to elementary school marks. While possible

cause-and-effect relationships continue to invite speculation, it is apparent that a student's educational plan bears a pronounced relationship to his performance in elementary school. As with persistence, the academic plan scores seem very uniform in their downward trend except for those students who had earned A in elementary school. It is not possible to say whether this reversal is related to the unequal intelligence of the groups or whether the performance of these students is related to different characteristics because of their higher intelligence and superior elementary school performance.

Self-Control—Deliberateness and the Change in Performance

The extent to which a student remains uninvolved in the youth-culture is strongly related to the fate of his grades on entering junior high school. The findings presented in Table 53 indicate that while "self-control—deliberateness" bears but a weak relationship, if any, to elementary school marks it is significantly related to the change in performance at the junior high school level. Those classified as earning higher marks had "self-control—deliberateness" scores approximately five standard errors higher than those classified as earning much lower grades.

TABLE 52. ACADEMIC PLAN SCORES OF SEVENTH GRADE STUDENTS CROSS-CLASSIFIED BY JUNIOR HIGH SCHOOL AND ELEMENTARY SCHOOL MARKS

| | *Student's Academic Plan Scores* | | | | |
| | *Junior High School Marks Compared with Elementary School Marks* | | | | |
Elementary School Marks	*Higher*	*Same*	*Lower*	*Much Lower*	*Total*
A	26.9 N = 8	30.2 N = 11	27.1 N = 15	27.1 N = 8	27.9
A–B+	31.1 N = 15	28.6 N = 27	26.4 N = 28	24.5 N = 16	27.5
B	25.4 N = 18	25.1 N = 37	23.8 N = 59	20.5 N = 22	23.8
B–C+	23.5 N = 18	21.4 N = 34	18.2 N = 42	21.2 N = 18	20.5
C	20.9 N = 16	15.4 N = 31	15.6 N = 36	14.9 N = 12	16.3
Under C	—	—	—	—	17.6
Total	25.3 $F^{20}_{488} = 5.16$	23.1	21.5 $P < .01$	21.3 $\sigma = 9.7$	

TABLE 53. SELF-CONTROL—DELIBERATENESS SCORES OF SEVENTH GRADE STUDENTS CROSS-CLASSIFIED BY JUNIOR HIGH SCHOOL AND ELEMENTARY SCHOOL MARKS

| | *Self-Control—Deliberateness Scores* | | | | |
| | *Junior High School Marks Compared with Elementary School Marks* | | | | |
Elementary School Marks	Higher	Same	Lower	Much Lower	Total
A	11.6	12.5	11.4	9.4	11.3
	N = 8	N = 11	N = 15	N = 8	
A–B+	12.3	12.4	11.0	9.6	11.4
	N = 15	N = 27	N = 28	N = 16	
B	12.4	11.8	11.1	9.1	11.1
	N = 18	N = 37	N = 59	N = 22	
B–C+	12.4	11.3	11.2	9.6	11.1
	N = 18	N = 34	N = 42	N = 18	
C	12.0	10.7	10.0	10.6	10.6
	N = 16	N = 31	N = 36	N = 12	
Under C	—	—	—	—	10.4
Total	12.2	11.6	10.9	9.6	
	$F^{20}_{468} = 2.12$		P < .01	$\sigma = 3.2$	

Discussion

With previous research indicating that academic motivation is highly related to grades earned in college (Finger & Schlesser, 1963), prognosis for the student experiencing a decline in academic performance may be viewed as a poor one. Whatever characteristics of the student are summarized in the "academic motivation" measure, they are not only vital to his success in school as of junior high school but thereafter as well. The findings presented by Armstrong (1964) argue similarly. Students who experienced a drop in performance at the junior high school level were rarely able to improve at a later point in their educational careers. It would appear to be possible to make rather accurate predictions of eventual academic performance as early as the beginning of the seventh grade.

The question of what causes the student to drop in performance is obviously an important one. The persistence section of the PVI is largely a self-report of the students' attitudes toward studying and the effort expended in school work. While this no doubt accounts for the predictive efficacy of the PVI, questions remain both as to the nature and etiology of these attitudes. One might view the decline in school performance as symptomatic of a syndrome of difficulties, as reflecting the influences of low academic plans and high involvement in youth-culture. The factor analytic data, however, suggest that these are unrelated characteristics. In an earlier report

(Finger & Schlesser, 1965), it was indicated that while the youth-culture involvement factor could not always be identified, it emerged in a sufficient number of factor anlyses (Finger, 1966) to indicate that those with low academic motivation were not always youth-culture oriented. While low academic plans may contribute to the development of low academic motivation, unsuccessful college students present obvious examples of the independence of academic plans and academic motivation. Possibly, however, the junior high school years may represent an incubation period during which low academic plans and high youth-culture involvement nurture the development of those attitudes that constitute low academic motivation.

Understanding the causes of the development of low academic motivation is an intriguing and vital issue. It would seem that at least by the sixth grade, academic motivation and academic plans bear important relationships to school marks. One might argue that the two had their origins in the early elementary school years and at some point, either in the sixth grade or earlier, helped determine the student's grades. In terms of this speculation, deficiencies in motivation and plans would cause poor school marks. It may also be conjectured, however, that poor school marks result in a diminished concern for school. This is to say that students' attitudes may be a result of a history of academic achievement rather than its cause.

While one hypothesis for the development of low

academic motivation could emphasize the lack of satisfaction derived from school experience and direct attention to the influence of lack of success in creating attitudes unfavorable toward school, such a hypothesis would be inadequate to account for the drop in performance of those whose previous school performance has been high, nor would such a hypothesis account for the fact that some students who have done average or below-average work continue to strive and in many cases improve their performance.

Our assumption is that performance levels are stabilized by the development of ego defenses that enable the student to justify school performance. This repertoire of rationalizations takes many forms, such as lowering of self-expectations, changing the conceptions of what one can do ("I just can't do math"), and failing to recognize the self as responsible for low performance ("The test wasn't fair"). The rationalization system comes into being in response to school performance that is below a student's own expectations or that is below expectations of the peer group or the home. Thus, rationalizations develop as a reaction to the school performance. As they become increasingly effective in dissipating feelings of inadequacy and in fending off adult criticism, they become internalized, and stabilized, and increasingly difficult to change. Our hypothesis is that it is these ego defenses that make striving unnecessary. The data presented give evidence to support the hypothesis that these defenses have developed in some students prior to entering the seventh grade.

The question of the cause of low or lowered school performance remains. Leaving aside considerations of the function of intelligence on school performance, which has been shown to be highly related to elementary school marks, one can concentrate on the lowered performance at the junior high school level. For some students lowered performance can be attributed to the pre-existent ego defenses. The drop in performance may be wholly accounted for because in the departmentalized junior high school more demands are placed upon the student to work and strive outside of school than was the case in elementary school. However, this explanation does not account for the drop in performance of those students who had previously done well. Their lowered performance may be attributable to a wide variety of influences: the peer group norm, the learning of the rationalization system from peers and parents who developed it in response to their school experiences, the increased independence striving where school success may be interpreted as conforming to adult norms or where the self can only exert itself by standing in opposition to the imposition of parental demands.

It is apparent that many students do well in elementary school despite all of the reasons, intellectual and other, that would lead one to believe that they should not do so. These students seem to bring to school an array of abilities and capacities that satisfy demands made of them in the self-contained classroom. Their success would seem to be a function of their ability to meet demands made by the school situation. In the course of an educational career, however, demands made by the educational process and the school situation change and with these changes comes the possibility of incompatibility—the possibility of a student no longer being able to meet the demands made of him. This is to suggest that the educational process consists of a number of crisis points, points at which the compatibility of the student's abilities and the school's demands are at issue. Success or failure encountered at such crisis points would no doubt influence the student's motivation and plans for the future.

In her classic study, Ruth Benedict (1938) has described adolescence in our society as a period of developmental discontinuity. The adolescent in our culture emerges with a disquieting abruptness from the childhood period of minimal demands to the huge array of requirements thrust upon the young adult. The junior high school years would seem to be an educational period of disquieting discontinuity for many students, a period of painful crisis and important consequences. This perspective would suggest that if students are to survive these periods of crisis the demands made of them by the school must be consistent with their abilities and capacities, both intellectual and non-intellectual.

28

*Scholastic Effects of the Social System**

James S. Coleman

Important as psychological effects are, they are not the only important effects of a high-school experience. Schools are intended to do more than watch over their students' psyches.

Some of the most explicit goals of high schools are those having to do with matters of the mind: transmission of knowledge, development of mental skills, and inculcation of positive attitudes toward learning. Effects of the adolescent system on some of these matters are the concern of this paper.

Effects upon the Image of Intellectual Activity

We have seen that the leading crowds of boys want more to be remembered as a star athlete, less as a brilliant student, than do the student bodies as a whole. Similarly, the leading crowds of girls were oriented away from thinking of themselves as a brilliant student, and were oriented toward, in some schools, the image of activities leader, and in others, the image of most popular.

This means that the social elites of these high schools are less willing to see themselves as engaging in intellectual activity, and find the idea of being seen as "intellectuals" more repugnant, than do those who are outside the leading crowds. By extrapolation to adulthood, these same social elites will be similarly oriented away from anything with a strong stamp of intellectual activity upon it. Such extrapolation is perhaps not too far-fetched, because this research includes not only small-town schools, part of whose leading crowds will remain in the town, and not only working-class schools, whose leading crowds will be a social elite only to their working-class constituency, but also urban middle-class schools—and, with Executive Heights, an upper-middle-class school that trains the children of some of the larger society's social elite. The leading crowds in this last school are even more oriented away from the "brilliant student" image than are the

leading crowds of other schools, with less than 10 percent of the boys and one percent of the girls in the leading crowd wanting to be remembered as a brilliant student.[1]

Even if this study included only leading crowds that would never become the social elite of the larger society, the matter would still be important. For they nevertheless come to be the elites of the towns and cities in which they remain, and thus become the "grassroots" leaders of attitudes toward intellectual activities.

Most of the post–high-school consequences of the leading crowd's wanting to be remembered as a brilliant student can only be conjectured, but from one outside source has come evidence of an important consequence. In a study of graduate students in American universities a question was asked of each graduate student in the sample: "Were you a member of the leading crowd when you were in high school?" He could classify himself as a member of a leading crowd, as a member of another crowd but not a leading crowd, as a member of no crowd, or as an "outsider." These students were also asked whether they regarded themselves as intellectuals. Table 54 below shows the proportion who considered themselves intellectuals as a function of the crowd they were in—or not in.

The result is clear: even among the highly select group of high-school students who end up in graduate school studying for an advanced degree, those who were in the leading crowd in high school are

* In *The Adolescent Society* (New York: Free Press, 1961), pp. 244–278.

[1] This almost complete absence of wanting to be remembered as a brilliant student is both more surprising and more disconcerting than in the other schools. For this leading crowd is about 50 percent Jewish (56 percent for boys, 62 percent for girls, if only those with 10 or more choices are included; 41 percent for boys, 49 percent for girls if all with two or more choices are included); in view of the traditional Jewish cultural emphasis on education and learning, one would not expect this. These results strongly suggest the decay of this tradition, and its replacement by the values of the dominant Protestant social elite, among those Jews whose mobility brings them into this elite. It is very likely that the parents of these Jewish children, many of whom had lower-middle-class origins, themselves wanted to be thought of as a brilliant student when in school, rather than as star athletes or activities leaders, as their sons and daughters now do.

TABLE 54. SELF-IMAGE AS AN INTELLECTUAL AMONG AMERICAN GRADUATE STUDENTS, IN RELATION TO THEIR SOCIAL LOCATION IN HIGH SCHOOL

	Members of leading crowd	Members of other crowd	Not members of any crowd, or outsider
Percent who consider themselves definitely or in many ways an intellectual	43	48	49
Number of cases	(859)	(725)	(570)

slightly less likely to consider themselves intellectuals, although, by any definition, they are surely engaging in intellectual activity.

One might dismiss this result with the notion that anyone in a leading crowd, whatever the school's values, will less likely think of himself as an intellectual than someone on the outside. However, foreign students, who had attended high school in Europe or somewhere else outside this country, were included in this same graduate-student study. Table 55 below shows their self-images as a function of whether or not they were in the leading crowd.

TABLE 55. SELF-IMAGE AS AN INTELLECTUAL AMONG FOREIGN GRADUATE STUDENTS IN AMERICAN UNIVERSITIES, IN RELATION TO THEIR SOCIAL LOCATION IN HIGH SCHOOL

	Members of leading crowd	Members of other crowd	Not members of any crowd, or outsider
Percent who consider themselves definitely or in many ways an intellectual	63	42	59
Number of cases	(126)	(114)	(125)

Among students who had attended foreign high schools, there are two differences from the Americans: the average level of considering themselves intellectuals is higher; but most crucial to our analysis, those who were members of the leading crowd in their high school were slightly *more* likely to consider themselves intellectuals than those who were not members of the leading crowd—exactly opposite to the result for graduates of American high schools.

To go back to the high-school level, are there any differences in the intellectual images—wanting to be remembered as a brilliant student—among those schools where the adolescent culture rewards such activity and those where it does not? Table 56 shows,

TABLE 56. PERCENT OF BOYS AND GIRLS WANTING TO BE REMEMBERED AS A BRILLIANT STUDENT, IN SCHOOLS WHERE THE REWARDS FOR ACADEMIC ACHIEVEMENT ARE HIGHER AND IN THOSE WHERE THESE REWARDS ARE LOWER

BOYS	All boys	Those mentioned 10 times or more as members of leading crowd
"High" schools (1, 2, 3, 5, 7, 8)	35.1%	24.0%
Number of cases	(2,781)	(108)
"Low" schools (0, 4, 6, 9)	27.2	9.5
Number of cases	(1,578)	(74)
GIRLS	All girls	
"High" schools (1, 6, 8, 9)	24.6%	12.0%
Number of cases	(2,414)	(142)
"Low" schools (0, 2, 3, 4, 7)	34.6	19.7
Number of cases	(1,555)	(117)

for boys and girls, the proportions wanting to be remembered as a brilliant student among all students, and among those mentioned ten or more times as members of the leading crowd; in the schools where scholarship is more rewarded and in those where it is less rewarded.

The boys as a whole more often want to be remembered as brilliant students in "high" schools; and the boys in the leading crowds in these schools do also. Although, in both sets of schools, the members of the leading crowd less often want to be remembered as brilliant students than the school as a whole, this decrease is far less for the schools where there are more rewards for academic achievement.[2]

For the girls, the matter is somewhat different. In

[2] The difference still exists, though it is attenuated, when the most upper-middle-class school, Executive Heights, where so few in the leading crowd want to be remembered as brilliant students, is excluded. Excluding Executive Heights, the percentages are 29.7 and 15.8 for the student bodies, and leading crowd groups, respectively, in the "low" group of schools.

the schools where there are more social rewards for academic achievement, the level of wanting to be remembered as a brilliant student is *lower* in the total student bodies and among the members of the leading crowd than it is in the other schools. As will become evident shortly, this apparently derives from the fact that the "high" schools include three of the four most middle-class schools. As the analysis will show, the relation between boys and girls in a middle-class school operates to make the label of "brilliant student" something for a girl to shy away from, although lesser scholastic accomplishments may be desired. This is most evident in the most upper-middle-class school, Executive Heights, where not one of the 49 girls in the top leading crowd re-

sponded that she wanted to be remembered as a brilliant student.

Impact of the System upon Self-Image of Boy Scholars and Girl Scholars

To examine further the matter of "intellectualism," and the degree to which it is dampened or encouraged in these systems, another question may be asked: what about those named as best scholar? Do these systems "allow" a scholar to desire to be remembered as a brilliant student as much as they allow a star athlete to want to be remembered as an athletic star, or do they make him shy away from such an image of himself? And what about the self-

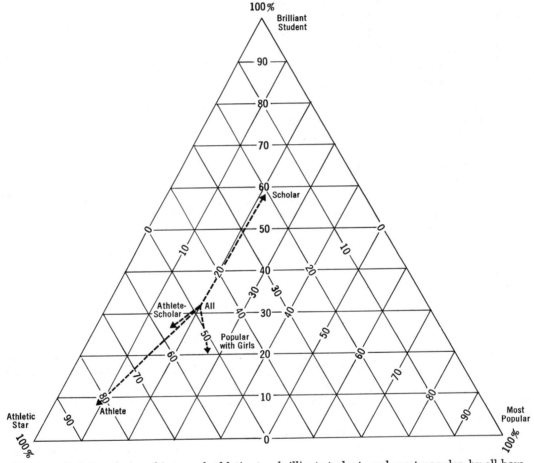

FIG. 27. Relative choice of image of athletic star, brilliant student, and most popular, by all boys, and by boys named as athletes, scholars, and popular with girls.*

* Number of cases:

scholar only	214
athlete-scholar	50
athlete only	192
most popular	154

image of the girl who is seen as best scholar, whom we have seen to be in such a disadvantaged social position in most of these cultures? How would she like to be remembered? Figures 27 and 28 show, for the boys and the girls, how the people who were considered as best scholars by others wanted to be remembered. The boys' chart, Figure 27, includes as well all students, those named as athlete-scholars, those named as athlete only, and those named as most popular with girls. The athletes and the scholars go very far toward 100 percent in wanting to be athletic star or brilliant student respectively. But the athlete goes much nearer the 100 percent point than does the scholar—presumably because the culture "allows" him to think of himself as an athletic star by giving very positive evaluations to this image,

more so than to the image of brilliant student. This is reflected as well by the athlete-scholar, whose self-image is shifted in the athletic direction rather than the academic one. Given both achievements, so that he can think of himself in either way, he more often chooses to think of himself as an athletic star.

The picture is somewhat different for the girl scholars. They are "pulled" only about 14 percent in the direction of the brilliant-student image, only up to 43 percent (compared to 58 percent for the boy scholars). (There were no "leaders in activities" identified by the questionnaire, so that there is no such comparison possible, as there was with athletes for the boys.) The girl who is named as best dressed and best scholar is no more likely to want to be remembered as best scholar than the average girl.

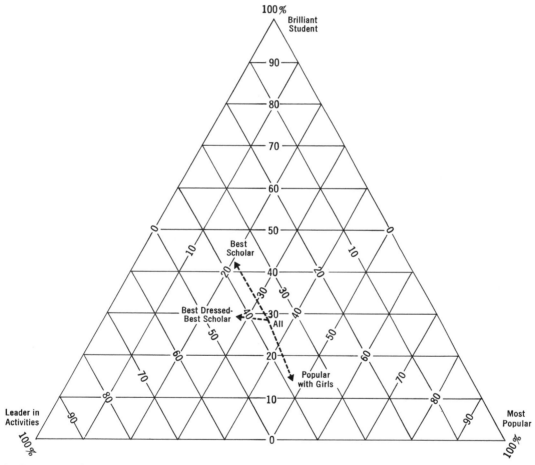

FIG. 28. Relative choice of image of leader in activities, brilliant student, and most popular, by girls named as best scholar and most popular with boys.*

* Number of cases:
 students only   260
 best dressed student   89
 most popular   114

These results, then, show several things: first, the boy who is named as best scholar does not want to think of himself as a brilliant student nearly so much as the best athlete wants to think of himself as an athletic star. The culture has failed to encourage such a self-image among those who are entitled to it by their achievement. The boy scholar, however, is far more likely to want to see himself as a scholar than is the girl scholar, who is presumably repelled by the culture's negative evaluation of this image. The lack of social rewards for the girl who is thought of as best scholar makes it understandable that these girls, good students though they might be, would not flock to this image in great numbers.

This different response on the part of girl scholar and boy scholar to their role in the school leads to the question: what happens over time? Are the girls discouraged from holding an image of themselves that is not rewarded and, therefore, move away from it? Do the high school years move them away from a brilliant student image, or were they away to begin with?

The comparison between boys and girls, shown in Figure 29, is striking: boys and girls start very close to the same point, but then diverge, the best girl students becoming *less* likely over the four years to want to be remembered for their scholastic achievements, and the best boy students becoming *more* likely to want to be remembered in this way.[3] This shows the differential impact of the culture upon girls who achieve highly scholastically, and boys who

[3] There is a reversal in the senior year among boys; the small number of cases makes it difficult to know whether this is a general result.

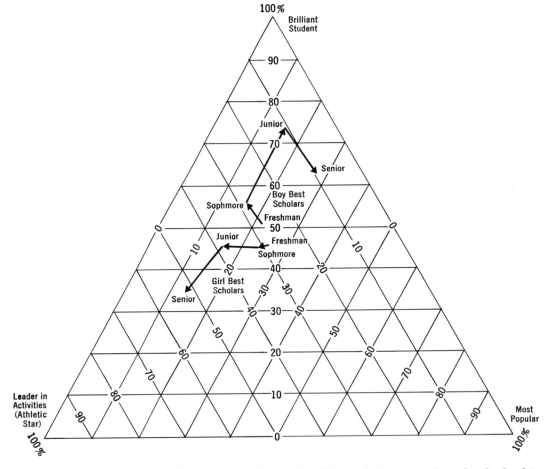

FIG. 29.   Relative choice of three images by boy and girl best scholars in each grade of school.*

* Number of cases:	girls	boys
freshman	66	55
sophomore	80	72
junior	57	45
senior	53	42

do so. It shows also the greater strain placed on girls, for they make considerably better grades, and they are more motivated to conform to parental and teacher's expectations. Yet they are under a constraint from the culture not to be "brilliant students."

This examination of budding intellectualism in the high schools—and, as a cynic might put it, the way in which it can be nipped in the bud by the values of the adolescent culture—suggests the powerful impact that the adolescent culture can have on the larger society. People who can and do achieve scholastically are a nation's intellectual resource; if the social system within which their education takes place undercuts any desire to think of themselves, and be thought of, as intellectuals, then these resources stand a good chance of being wasted or ill-used. Some of the ways in which these resources are affected by the forces of the adolescent culture will be examined in the next section.

Boys' and Girls' Grades in School

The results above, showing girl scholars shrinking away from the "brilliant-student" image, suggest a constraint against a girl's appearing too bright. But this constraint is not the only one under which a girl labors. She is also constrained to "be a good girl," to "do well in school," to conform to adult demands—much more than a boy. One consequence of this has always been that girls work harder in school and get better grades.

The higher grades of girls are no less evident in these schools than in others. Table 57 below shows the average grades of boys and girls in each of these schools.

TABLE 57. AVERAGE GRADES OF BOYS AND GIRLS IN THE TEN SCHOOLS OF THE STUDY*

GRADES

School	Boys	Girls	Difference
Farmdale	4.10†	4.71	.61
Marketville	3.65	4.58	.93
Elmtown	4.20	4.76	.56
Maple Grove	4.27	4.84	.57
Green Junction	3.96	4.38	.42
St. John's	3.66		
Newlawn	3.45	4.36	.91
Millburg	3.66	4.57	.91
Midcity	3.62	4.07	.45
Executive Heights	4.01	4.53	.52

* Average grades for each class were found; then these were averaged, weighting each class equally.
† A = 8, B = 6, C = 4, D = 2, F = 0.

The double constraints upon girls—to do well, but not to be brilliant—are evident in other ways as well. For many a girl, the solution to the dilemma of "good, but not aggressively brilliant" is an ingenious one: she gets good grades, but she is never extremely outstanding. She is neither better than the best boy student nor poorer than the worst. Her grades are "compressed" by the double constraints of conforming to the two norms. As a result, the grades of a girl are more nearly alike from course to course than those of a boy, and the within-girl variance in grades is less than for boys. If a girl has a B average, she has more B's and fewer A's and C's than does a boy with a B average.

Table 58 below shows the average variance among the various grades received by each girl, and the

TABLE 58. THE WITHIN-PERSON VARIANCES OF PRESENT GRADES FOR BOYS AND GIRLS IN TEN SCHOOLS*

VARIANCE

School	Boys	Girls	Difference
Farmdale	1.46	1.43	.03
Marketville	2.26	1.48	.78
Elmtown	2.19	1.94	.25
Maple Grove	2.02	1.65	.37
Green Junction	1.45	1.48	−.03
St. John's	2.65		
Newlawn	2.33	1.92	.41
Millburg	2.55	1.94	.61
Midcity	2.18	1.65	.55
Executive Heights	2.28	2.13	.15

* Variances were computed by calculating the variance of each student's grades, then averaging for each of the four classes in school. These averages were then averaged, with each class equally weighted. For those unfamiliar with the use of variances, this is the square of the standard deviation. One standard deviation from the mean in both directions will include about 70 per cent of the cases. Thus, to use the example of boys in Midcity, the variance is 2.18 and the standard deviation is 1.47. For a boy whose grade average was 4.0, about 70 per cent of his grades are within the range 4.00 ± 1.47, that is, from 2.53 to 5.47.

average variance for each boy's grades. In every school but Green Junction, the average girl's grades cluster together more closely than do those of the average boy. This suggests strongly that the girls are motivated to "do well" in everything, whether it is something at which they excel or not, while boys are less constrained by parents' demands and the demands of the adolescent culture to be "good" in those things they care less about. At the same time, the boys are free to excel in the things they do care about.

The results shown in Table 58 do not seem to relate to the value systems of the different schools. In general, the variances are larger in the larger schools than in the smaller ones. The average variance for girls in small schools is 1.60 compared to an average of 1.93 in the large schools; for boys, the small-school average if 1.88, compared to 2.33 for the four large schools, and 2.40 if St. John's is included. This suggests the possibility that low variances from course to course are partly a function of the greater consensus about a student that develops among teachers in the small schools. In the large schools, teachers will less often know a boy's or girl's reputation regarding schoolwork, and might therefore give a grade that is more independent of those given by other teachers. If this were so, the variance among a student's grades in different subjects should decrease from freshman to senior, as he is in school longer, and teachers know him better. But this is not so. The variance among each person's grades as a freshman was calculated, and this compared with the present variance from course to course, for the sophomores, juniors, and seniors. In all but two of the nineteen cases—ten schools for boys, nine for girls—the variance *increased* from year to year. Only for the girls of Marketville and the boys of Green Junction is there an average decrease in variation. In all other school-sex groups, a boy's or girl's grades have become more and more heterogeneous through his high-school career. Thus, the teachers' consensus about a boy or girl seems not to be manifest in the grades.

Consistent with the generally lower variation in a girl's grades, the *increase* in variation of a girl's grades over the years of school is less than that of a boy's grades in most of the schools. A girl's grades are not only more tightly clustered, but the clustering is less likely to "loosen up" than is a boy's in the upper grades of high school. The girl apparently stays subject to constraints to be good but not aggressively brilliant, while a boy's grades in later years come more and more to be a function of his own variable interest.

I.Q.'s of Best Scholars among Boys and Girls

The lower variance among a girl's grades can be interpreted as a result of simply the one norm to "do well in school." By working at her capacity in all subjects, a girl would achieve roughly similar grades in all subjects, while a boy, working only in those which interest him, will have a wider range of grades. Girls would thus achieve higher average grades (as Table 57 showed that they do), along with a lower variance from one course to another. Is it simply that girls work harder in response to the pressures from parents and teachers, or do they respond also to the second constraint, the constraint not to be a "brain"?

The evidence suggests strongly that they are responding to this second pressure as well. In an earlier section, the tendency of girls named as best scholars to shy away from the image—or stigma, as it may sometimes be—of being a brilliant student indicates that they feel it best not to be seen as *too* bright. In other words, at the top levels of scholarship, the second norm, holding down effort, seems to operate. Further evidence in this direction is provided by looking at the I.Q.'s of best scholars. If there is a constraint against being too bright, then many of the girls who could be top scholars will be constrained not to work so hard. Those girls whom others see as "best scholars" in their grade will not be brightest. If, as suggested, there is less constraint upon a boy not to be aggressively bright, the boys named as best scholars should be, on the average, brighter than the girls so named.

This is in fact true, as Table 59 indicates. Even though the average I.Q. of boys is lower than that of girls, the average I.Q. of boys named as "best scholars" is *higher* than that of girls named as best scholars.[4] Furthermore, this result is consistent from school to school. The best boy scholars have higher

[4] The I.Q. tests differed from school to school, but since the number of boys and girls in each school was approximately equal, this difference has no effect on the result in Table 59.

TABLE 59. AVERAGE I.Q.'S OF BEST BOY SCHOLARS AND BEST GIRL SCHOLARS (NAMED TWO OR MORE TIMES), COMPARED WITH OVER-ALL SEX MEANS

	Boys	*Girls*	*Boys minus Girls*
Best scholars	116.5 (N = 295)	114.0 (N = 348)	2.5
All students	101.3 (N = 3,688)	105.0 (N = 3,746)	−3.7
Scholars minus others	15.2	9.0	6.2

absolute I.Q.'s than best girl scholars in every school but two; and in every school but Marketville is the relative I.Q. (measured in terms of standard deviations above the school-sex mean) higher for girls than boys. Throughout the analysis, Marketville has shown especially high rewards for girl scholars.

These results, together with the earlier ones showing the girls' grades to be better than boys', suggest the peculiar dilemma of the girl—she is pushed toward doing well in school by her allegiance to parents and teachers; but if she wants dates and popularity, she is constrained from working to her scholastic capacity. Consequently, many of the brightest girls manage to hide their intelligence, leaving somewhat less bright girls to be named as best scholars.

The Different Role of Girls in Different Social Contexts

It was evident in visiting the schools that a girl's role varies somewhat in different adolescent communities. One of the major differences seemed to be a class difference. In working class schools, there seemed a greater role-differentiation between boys and girls—boys more masculine, more aggressive, girls more feminine, more passive. Upper-middle class boys and girls seemed to be more *alike*. One way this difference manifests itself is in dating behavior. In working class groups, girls tend to date boys *older* than themselves; in the modern middle class, where role-differentiation is at a minimum, boys date girls about the same age.

The age-discrepancy in dating, however, is only one manifestation of the role-differentiation of boys and girls in working class groups, and the lack of such differentiation in upper middle class. There are other manifestations more directly relevant to scholastic matters. One of these is the criteria boys use to evaluate girls. All girls were asked:

Which of these items is most important in making a girl popular with the boys around here? That is, among the boys who really rate, which of these things count most? (Rank from 1 to 6.)

     Coming from the right family
     Leader in activities
     Clothes
     High grades, honor roll
     Being cheerleader
     Being in the leading crowd

The categories of this question are identical to those of an immediately preceding question, which asked about a girl's popularity with *other girls*. Our present concern is with the way in which girls feel that good grades affect popularity with boys, compared to the way they affect popularity with other girls. Do they see good grades as helping their popularity with boys *more* or *less* than it does their popularity with other girls?

The answer is *less*, in every school. In every school, the average rank of "high grades, honor roll" is considerably lower as an aid to a girl's popularity with boys than as an aid to her popularity with other girls. But the degree to which it is lower varies sharply from school to school, as Table 60 shows.

TABLE 60. DIFFERENCES IN RANK OF "HIGH GRADES, HONOR ROLL" FOR A GIRL'S POPULARITY WITH OTHER GIRLS AND HER POPULARITY WITH BOYS

School	Difference in rank
Farmdale	.38
Marketville	.87
Elmtown	.53
Maple Grove	.69
Green Junction	.53
Newlawn	.53
Millburg	.39
Midcity	.64
Executive Heights	.88

One might have expected this difference to be greatest in the predominantly working-class schools, where boys are presumably less interested in middle-class propriety and conformity. Yet exactly the reverse is true: the decrease is greatest in Executive Heights, then in Marketville, Maple Grove, and Midcity—all four of these the more middle-class, white-collar schools, with Executive Heights the most white-collar of all.

Why do the girls in the more middle-class schools feel that boys care nothing for their grades? The boys are themselves interested in grades, for many will need them for college entrance; one would suppose that they, far more than the boys from working-class backgrounds, would put a premium on a girl's scholastic achievement.

It seems, however, that matters work differently. In a working-class milieu, the greater role differentiation between the sexes affects the way boys evaluate girls. Schoolwork and good grades are a girl's achievement, something to make a boy look up to a girl, but not something for him to achieve himself. In contrast, academic success is not a girl's province in a middle-class milieu, but something with which a boy must be concerned as well. Conversely, a girl's grades are not something to make her more attractive to him as someone to date.

That this difference does exist is evident by an inspection of boys' and girls' grades, in Table 57, presented earlier. In three schools, the average girls' grades are at least .9 points higher than the average boys' grades, a difference far greater than in the other schools; these are Marketville, Newlawn, and Millburg. Two of the three—Newlawn and Millburg—have the smallest proportion of boys with white-collar backgrounds of any of the nine schools. At the other extreme, the three schools with the *least* difference between boys' and girls' grades are Green Junction, Midcity, and Executive Heights—and the latter two have the highest proportion of boys with white-collar backgrounds.

These comparisons suggest that there is a greater role differentiation in the working-class milieu with respect to academic work: girls outdistance boys further in these schools than in schools that are more nearly white-collar. However, this still does not imply that working-class boys give more status to a girl scholar than do middle-class boys. There is some evidence to indicate that among the white-collar, middle-class boys, the "activities girl"—the clubwoman of the high school—has preempted the place held by the outstanding girl scholar in the working-class schools. One question in particular in the questionnaire indicates this. Boys were asked, in the supplementary questionnaire:

> At the left, below, are some descriptions which we have taken from the yearbook of "M" high school, listing the activities in which . . . girls have taken part during the year in high school. Can you guess what these girls were like? On the line following each description put the number of the words that would fit each girl from those listed at the right.

A. FHA; Yearbook editor; Octet; Class Secretary; Prom Committee.

B. National Honor Society; Spanish Club; Student Council; Dramatics Club.

1—a good example
2—a square
3—a scholar
4—a grind or bookworm
5—an active leader
6—a joiner
7—prom queen
8—beautiful but dumb
9—popular with boys
10—ambitious

Of these two hypothetical girls, the first is more active, the "clubwoman" of the school. The second is more nearly the student, less busily active, conforming to the school's standards and being rewarded by honors for her conformity.

Of the descriptive words at the right, 1, 5, 7, and 9 may be assumed to have positive implications. We can then ask how many of these positive descriptions are given to each of these two hypothetical girls by boys in the extreme schools—the working-class suburb, Newlawn, and the well-to-do suburb, Executive Heights. In Newlawn, the sum of positive mentions, computed as a percentage of the total boys who answered the question, was 68.9 percent for the activities girl and 77 percent for the scholar. In Executive Heights, the activities girl received 85.2 percent positive mentions and the scholar only 75.7 percent. The boys in Newlawn felt more positively about the scholar, while those in Executive Heights felt more positively about the activities leader.

The same difference exists for the other schools. The four schools that are most middle-class—the same schools in which the girls felt boys most devalued good grades in judging a girl—have an average ratio of 1.03 positive mentions for the activities girl to the scholar. For the five more nearly working-class schools, the ratio is 0.93.

It is true, then, that in the eyes of the boys in a white-collar school, a girl's good grades are not as much of an asset as among the boys in more nearly a working-class school. This result, out of accord with initial expectations, suggests that as society becomes more and more white-collar, the kind of image that girls will be striving for in school is only obliquely related to academic achievement, and is more nearly that of the activities girl, the teen-age replica of the adult clubwoman. That this is more than mere speculation is indicated by the Executive Heights girls' response to wanting to be remembered as a brilliant student: they were by far *lowest* in the proportion choosing the brilliant student image, by far highest in the proportion choosing the "leader in activities" image. Even the girls named as best scholars in this school were exceptionally low in wanting to be remembered as a brilliant student. Only 19 percent of them—fewer than in any other school—wanted to be remembered as a brilliant student.

Thus, the lack of role differentiation in a white-collar milieu does more than pull up the average boy's grades. It draws the achievement-oriented girl away from scholastic achievement, toward achievement in "activities." In part, this is a shift from a rather passive role, conforming to adult demands, to a more active role as a "big wheel" in the activities of student life. This kind of girl responds less to the demands of parents, more to the demands of the adolescent community; she strives to be a leader in those activities the adolescent culture holds important rather than striving to achieve in what parents and teachers hold important.

Relation between Ability and Achievement in School

In every social context, certain activities are highly rewarded, while others are not. The activities that are rewarded are those for which there is strong competition—the activities in which everyone with some relevant ability will compete. In such activities, the persons who achieve most should be those with most potential ability. In contrast, in unrewarded activities, those who have most ability may not be motivated to compete; consequently, the persons who achieve most will be persons of lesser ability. Thus, in a high school where basketball is important, nearly every boy who might be a good basketball player will go out for the sport, and the resulting basketball stars will likely be those boys with most ability. If, in the same school, volleyball does not bring the same status to those who star in it, few boys will go out for the sport, and those who end up as members of the team will not necessarily be the boys with most potential ability.

Similarly with academic achievement: where such achievement brings few social rewards, those who are motivated to "go out" for scholarly achievement will be few. The high performers, those who receive good grades, will not be the boys whose ability is greatest, but will be a more mediocre few. The "intellectuals" of such a society, the best students, will not in fact be those with most intellectual ability. The latter, knowing where the social rewards lie, will be off in the directions that bring social rewards.

Based on these ideas, the original research design included the hypothesis that in those systems where academic achievement was rewarded by the adolescent culture, the correlation between I.Q. and grades in school would be higher. In carrying out the analysis, it became evident that this correlation (within a given class) changed over the course of the years in school—most often decreasing, but sometimes increasing. With such data on changes, it was possible

to add a supplementary hypothesis: in those social systems where scholastic achievement is rewarded, the correlations either increase over time, or decrease less than in the other schools. The data that allow examination of these hypotheses are presented in Table 61. For boys and girls separately, the correla-

TABLE 61. CORRELATION WITHIN A CLASS BETWEEN FRESHMAN GRADES AND I.Q., AVERAGED OVER THE FOUR CLASSES IN SCHOOLS; AND THE AVERAGE YEARLY CHANGE IN THE CORRELATION BETWEEN GRADES AND I.Q.

	BOYS		GIRLS	
School	Correlation	Change	Correlation	Change
Farmdale	.603	+.029	.607	−.131
Marketville	.591	+.097	.504	+.024
Elmtown	.516	+.007	.645	+.054
Maple Grove	.620	−.012	.579	−.017
Green Junction	.559	+.043	.583	−.029
St. John's	.404	−.046		
Newlawn	.615	−.053	.603	−.020
Millburg	.493	+.007	.446	+.080
Midcity	.611	−.026	.571	−.014
Executive Heights	.540	−.030	.682	−.112

tion between I.Q. (ordinarily given in the eighth or ninth grade in all these school systems; in Elmtown, I.Q.'s were not available for the present freshmen) and average freshmen grades are given. The correlation is averaged over the four classes, but in each case using freshman grades of that class.[5] Along with the correlation is the average yearly increase or decrease in the correlation. This is based on changes in the correlation for a given class, that is, the correlation between I.Q. and present grades received, minus the correlation between I.Q. and freshmen grades. There were three such differences, one for each of the three upper grades, and an average yearly change was computed from these.

Perhaps these data show some relationship to the variations in importance of scholastic achievement in the different schools. If they do, the relationship is an obscure or complex one. The schools where scholastic activity is more highly rewarded by the culture are not distinguishable from those where it is

[5] This correlation was generally lower for seniors than for freshmen, very likely due to (a) the fact that dropouts were eliminated from the computation for later grades, making the population more homogeneous in both grades and I.Q., and thus tending to lower the correlation; and (b) the grades and I.Q's were farther apart in time for seniors than for freshmen.

not. There do not even appear *general* differences between boys and girls. In short, it appears that the original hypothesis is not at all validated.

Upon reflection, however, one might question the original hypothesis in that the reasoning on which it was based related only to those at the top, those with highest ability. Thus, at the intermediate and low levels of ability one would have no reason to expect a higher correlation in those climates that rewarded scholastic activity than in those that did not. The question is, are the *high* achievers the ones with the most ability?

To examine this, the I.Q.'s of all boys whose average grades were 7 or 8 (A or A−) were examined relative to the I.Q. of the student body as a whole. The variations are quite great: in Marketville, the boys who made an A or A− average have I.Q.'s 1.53 standard deviations above the school average; in Farmdale, their I.Q.'s are only about a third this distance above the mean, .59. Given this variation, the question may be asked: do these variations in ability of the high performers correspond to variations in the social rewards for, or constraints against, being a good student?

Figure 30 shows, for the boys, the relation between

the social rewards for academic excellence—that is, the frequency with which "good grades" was mentioned as a criterion for being in the leading crowd—and the ability of the high performers, measured in terms of the number of standard deviations their average I.Q. exceeds that of the rest of the boys in the school.

For the boys, the relation is extremely strong. Only St. John's deviates. In this school, many boys have their most important associations outside, rather than within, the school, so that the student body constitutes far less of a social system, able to dispense social rewards and punishments, than in other schools.

Similarly for the girls, Figure 30 shows the I.Q. of high performers as a function of the proportion of girls saying that it takes "good grades" to get into the leading crowd.[6] Unfortunately, most of the schools are closely bunched in the degree to which good grades are important among the girls, so that

[6] For the girls, only girls with a grade of 8 (that is, a straight A average) were included. Since girls get better grades than boys, this device is necessary in order to make the sizes of the "high performer" group roughly comparable for boys and for girls. Schools differed somewhat in the proportion of A's, constituting about 6 percent of the students in the small

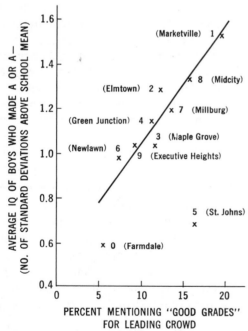

FIG. 30.   Relation between importance of good grades for membership in school's leading crowd and I.Q. level of those who made best grades in school, for boys.

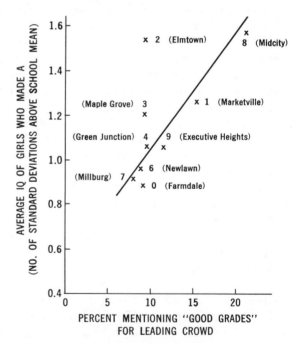

FIG. 31.   Relation between importance of good grades for membership in school's leading crowd and I.Q. level of those who made best grades in school, for girls.

there is too little variation among them to examine this effect as fully as would be desirable. Elmtown is the one school that, among the girls, deviates most from the general relationship.[7]

The effect of these value systems in letting academic ability express itself in high achievement is evident among the girls as it is among the boys. It is important to realize that these effects are not merely due to the school facilities or its social composition. The two schools highest in the importance of scholastic achievement for both boys and girls are Marketville and Midcity, the first a small-town school of 350 students and the second a city school of 2,000 students. In both, there are fewer students with white-collar backgrounds than in Executive Heights, which is somewhere in the low middle in terms of the values its students place on academic achievement, but more than in Millburg or Green Junction, which are also somewhere in the low middle. The highest expenditure per student was $695 per year in Executive Heights, and the lowest was little more than half that, in Green Junction. These two schools are close together on the graphs of Figures 30 and 31.

These results are consistent with a recent (1956–57) extensive unpublished study through Connecticut using standard tests of achievement and ability, sponsored by the Connecticut Citizens for the Public Schools. The study found no correlation between

per pupil expenditure in a school and the achievement of its 10th grade students relative to their ability. The effects shown in Figures 30 and 31 suggest why: that students with ability are led to achieve only when there are social rewards, primarily from their peers, for doing so.

As has been evident throughout this research, the variation among schools in the status of scholastic achievement is not nearly so striking as the fact that in all of them, academic achievement did not "count" for as much as did other activities in the school. Many other attributes were more important. In every school the boys named as best athletes and those named as most popular with girls were far more often mentioned as members of the leading crowd, and as someone to "be like" than were the boys named as best students. And the girls who were named as best dressed, and those named as most popular with boys, were in every school far more often mentioned as being in the leading crowd and as someone to be like, than were the girls named as best students.

The relative unimportance of academic achievement, together with the effects shown above, suggest that the adolescent subcultures in these schools exert a rather strong deterrent to academic achievement. In other words, in these adolescent societies, those who are seen as the "intellectuals," and who come to think of themselves in this way, are not really those of highest intelligence, but are only the ones who are willing to work hard at a relatively unrewarded activity.

The implications for American society as a whole are clear. Because high schools allow adolescent societies to divert energies into athletics, social activities, and the like, they recruit into adult intellectual activities many people with a rather mediocre level of ability, and fail to attract many with high levels of ability.

Consequences of the Social Climate for Homework and College Attendance

Two factors that might at first seem highly dependent upon the social climate of the school are the amount of homework that a teen-ager does and his intentions about attending college. Yet both of these matters apparently have their primary sources elsewhere. The amount of homework done depends

---

schools, only about 3 percent in Newlawn and Millburg, 1 percent in Midcity, and 2 percent in Executive Heights. In Midcity and Executive Heights, enough girls were added and assigned the average grade of the 7 (A−) group to bring the proportion to 3 percent, comparable with the other large schools. The difference, however, between the large and small schools, remains. Newlawn is located, according to the leading-crowd question used for this graph, near the bottom, rather than in the upper group where it has been classified throughout the analysis. Because the proportion of girls getting A's is somewhat smaller than the proportion of boys getting A's and A−'s the relative I.Q.'s of the girls in Figure 31 cannot be directly compared with those of boys in Figure 30.

[7] The I.Q.'s among the girls in Elmtown show a peculiar distribution. There were six girls whose I.Q. was listed in the office records as exactly 140, although no other girl in the school had an I.Q. listed above 130. Five of these six "140-I.Q." girls had a grade average of 8. Of the 18 other girls whose I.Q. was listed as 120 or above, the grade average was far less: 5.9. It is hardly likely that this school contains 24 girls in the sophomore to senior classes with I.Q.'s of 120 or greater; the I.Q. test given undoubtedly overestimated the actual I.Q.'s in this school. The test used in this school is SRA Primary Mental Abilities, which has a top score of 140; six girls in the school had a raw score above this point and were given the top score.

TABLE 62. ESTIMATED EDUCATIONAL ATTAINMENT OF BOYS AND GIRLS WITH AGCT SCORES OF 130 OR HIGHER*

	BOYS		GIRLS		BOTH SEXES	
	Annual no.	*Per cent*	*Annual no.*	*Per cent*	*Annual no.*	*Per cent*
In age group of 2,200,000	76,000	100	76,000	100	152,000	100
Finish high school	74,000	97	74,000	97	148,000	97
Enter college	48,000	63	32,000	42	80,000	53
Graduate from college	42,000	55	28,000	37	70,000	46
Receive Ph.D.	2,350	3.1	250	0.3	2,600	1.7

* From Wolfle (1954, p. 183).

largely on two things: upon the amount of home-work assigned by the teachers, and upon family background. College-going apparently depends more upon the aspiration a student's family has for him to attend college, and upon their interest in seeing him dependent upon them for four more years. However, the climate apparently has some effect—a peculiarly selective one—upon studying and upon college intentions.

Although father's education or occupation is only a rough indication of family constraints and desires for the child, it will be used here as a partial indicator of them. To be sure, in a community like Executive Heights, a boy or girl whose father has only a high-school diploma is likely to be of far higher status and have far greater aspirations for his child, than a father who has the same education but lives in Newlawn. Such differences should be kept in mind in interpreting the graphs below.

In Figures 32 and 33 the proportion of boys and of girls who spend two hours or more per day on homework is given for four groups, classed according to father's education. Because the various educational groups are not large in some schools, some fluctuations are undoubtedly due to chance, so that no interpretation should be attempted for separate educational groups, but only for the school as a whole and for general trends.

There is some over-all increase in studying with increase in father's education—although not nearly so much as one might expect. Among the small schools the major deviations for the boys are Farm-dale and Green Junction—two schools similar in two respects: little value attached to good grades, and much less homework is assigned than in the other schools. It is not possible to say which of these two factors is responsible for their difference from the other three small schools. A glance at the large

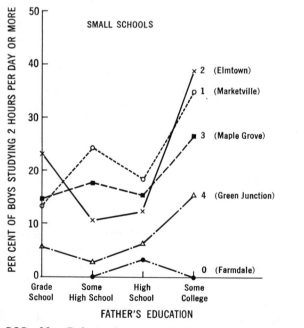
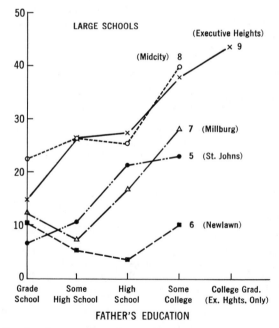

FIG. 32.   Relation between a boy's father's education and the time he spends studying at home, for each school.

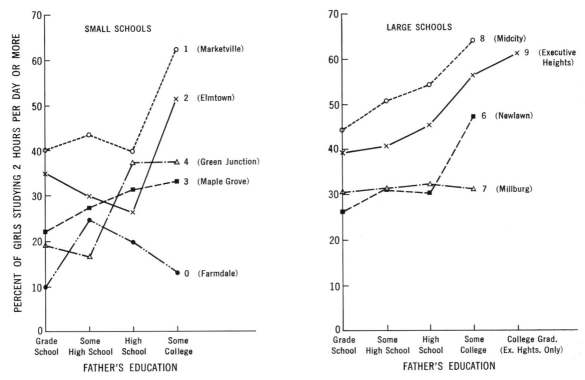

FIG. 33. Relation between a girl's father's education and the time she spends studying at home, for each school.

schools, however, suggests that it is more nearly the teacher's assignments than the value system; for in St. John's and Millburg, where good grades are more important for status than in Executive Heights, studying is nevertheless lower. Executive Heights and Midcity, where most is expected of students by their teachers, are highest of the large schools.

It seems that the value system has an impact upon studying for all girls, and not only for those with high educational backgrounds (Figure 33). Girls in Marketville and Midcity, with the two most scholastically oriented value climates, are highest and about equal in studying for all educational groups. The value systems among the girls in these two schools differed sharply from the others. In general, it appears that the value climate has more effect upon girls' studying than upon boys'.

There is a much higher correlation of father's education with college-going than with studying. The students from higher educational backgrounds study slightly more than the others; but they plan far more to go to college than do the others.

The proportion of Executive Heights girls and boys who say they are going to college is higher than in any of the other large schools—especially among the girls, although as Figure 33 showed, their study-

ing was *less* in each educational group than among the girls in Midcity or Marketville. This apparently reflects parental expectations, and the fact that college going is the "thing to do" in this school. That is, the adolescent value system probably affects a boy's or girl's tendency to go to college in this school, *not* because the values emphasize scholastic achievement, but because they emphasize college-going.

Among the small-school girls, those in Elmtown are the only ones who radically deviate, in every educational group, by their low college-going. One might be tempted to attribute this to the non-academic status system of the school, were it not for the fact that college-going in Farmdale, Maple Grove, and Green Junction—where scholastic achievement is as unimportant as in Elmtown—is so much higher. It is more probable that this is, again, a value of the larger culture, as in Executive Heights but in reverse: that for a girl, going to college is not a highly valued matter in the community. This perspective is traditionally held to be a "working-class value"; but this community is not so working-class as Newlawn or Millburg, and little more so than Green Junction. Even when father's education is held constant, there is less college-going among the Elmtown girls than among the girls in those schools. In the white-collar occupational groups, the difference is 30 to 40 percent compared to the other small schools—a difference that cannot be attributed to social class of parents. Thus, somewhat inexplicably, college-going is particularly low among Elmtown girls.

An interesting large school-small school difference also appeared. In the large schools, the college-going of *boys* is generally higher than in the small schools (when father's education is held constant). The reverse is true for the girls: college-going tends to be higher in the small schools (with the exception of Elmtown) than in the large ones, for each educational group. Furthermore, the boys in these small towns are less likely—at least according to intentions expressed—to go to college than are the girls in these communities from the same backgrounds. In the city and suburban schools, the boys are *more* likely to go than the girls from the same educational backgrounds.

These differences may be due to a different relationship of girls and boys to the community in large and small towns. In the small town, boys were far more likely than girls to say they would take a job in the same town rather than in a different one, if the jobs were equal. The girls far more often want to leave town. The dynamics of the process are unclear, but it is clear that girls want far more to leave town than do the boys. It is likely that many boys can follow into their father's occupation, business, or farm. In the city or suburb, following in parental footsteps is not so easy, since the father works away from home, often outside the community. Thus, the city or suburb has little to offer a boy unless he has formal training, and can get a job by virtue of training through bureaucratic channels. In contrast, the girls' "career chances," that is, their chances of making a good marriage, are more augmented by college for the small-town girl than for the city girl. For a small-town girl, college expands the range of boys from whom she can find a mate more than it does for the large-school girl, who already has a larger selection in her school and community.

These interpretations are only suggestive, for the evidence to test them is not available. The present evidence does suggest, however, that there are important differences in the relation of boys and girls to a small town, and that these differences vanish or reverse in the city.[8]

Altogether, the effects of the climates on college-going and studying seem less than one might a priori expect. When there *are* effects, they seem most pronounced for the girls—e.g., the high studying of Midcity and Marketville girls, the low college-going of Elmtown girls.

Consequences of Different Structures: The All-Around Boy vs. the Specialist

The different structures among elites have consequences for the ways in which boys will expend their energies. In a school where it is important to be *both* an athlete and a scholar, and perhaps a ladies' man as well, many boys will spread their energies over all these areas. In a school where it is important to be an athlete *or* a scholar, boys will tend to specialize. Some boys will concentrate on doing well scholastically, while others will concentrate on being good athletes.

The different structures also have consequences on how the high achievers are perceived in the system. In a system that rewards the athlete-scholar, when a boy is thinking of someone to model himself after, he thinks of this all-around boy, leaving the specialist aside. In particular, when thinking of a good student to be like, his thoughts will quickly turn to the boy who is a "good all-around guy" as well—a boy who is not a grind, but who makes the football team and is popular with girls.

In the schools where athletics and scholastics are rewarded separately, they are seen as distinct activities. A good student who is regarded as a model is looked up to *because* he is a good student, not because this makes him a good all-around boy. If an athlete is looked up to as a model, it is *as* an athlete, not as an all-around boy who achieves in everything.

Is it better to create all-around boys or specialists? Is it better for the social system to push an athlete toward studying and a scholar toward athletics, or to push them further in their present directions? Is it better for the system to be pluralistic by giving rewards for various activities independently, or to be pluralistic in a more restricted sense, by giving rewards only for a certain combination of activities?

These questions cannot be answered here, but a few consequences of the two different systems may be examined. First, certain schools especially reward the "all-around boy." This is most pronounced in Executive Heights, but, among the large schools,

---

[8] The oppressive norms of a small town seem partly responsible for this result. Girls are more constrained by these norms, and if they stay in town are expected to become the upholders and transmitters of the norms. No such burden is imposed on the boys.

Midcity and St. John's show the same tendency. Millburg and Newlawn do not. Among the small schools, Maple Grove and Elmtown reward the all-around boy, as does Green Junction to a lesser degree. Marketville and Farmdale keep the two roles separate, and Marketville rewards them both highly.

Consequences for Grades of Top Athletes and Top Scholars

One consequence of this structural difference is in the grades of the star athletes and star scholars. In a school where the two roles are rewarded only in combination, the star athletes will tend to work harder in school. Their grades should be higher than their counterparts in schools where the athlete is rewarded for athletic excellence alone.

Conversely, the boys seem as star scholars will not be extreme scholars. Both because the best students will have their energies diverted to other activities, such as athletics, and because the boys seem as best students will sometimes be good athletes who merely stand out somewhat in studies, the grades of "best students" will not be exceedingly high.

Where the roles are separate, and a boy receives no special rewards for being an all-around boy, the star athlete will not worry about good grades, and the star student will concentrate on them. And because scholastic success is a distinct arena of achievement, the boys named as best students will be the best students, not just athletes who do well in studies.

Table 62 below shows, for each of the small

schools, the average grades of boys named seven times or more as best students and those named seven times or more as best athletes. The schools are grouped according to whether they offer rewards for the all-around boy or for the specialist. Grades are on an 8-point scale (8 = A, 6 = B, . . . , O = F).

Table 62 shows strikingly the effect of this structural difference: in Maple Grove, where there are a number of "all-around boys" and they are highly rewarded, the grade difference between the top students and top athletes is only 1.2 points—less than one letter grade. In Marketville, where the two roles are separately rewarded, and Farmdale, where neither is highly rewarded but there is no attention to the all-around boy, the grade difference is 4.2 and 4.5 respectively—more than *two* letter grades. The top scholars in these two schools make nearly straight A averages, and the top athletes C−; while in Maple Grove, the difference is between B+ and B−; in Elmtown, A− and B−; and in Green Junction, B+ and straight C.

The structural differences among these schools thus have a very powerful influence on the way top scholars and top athletes distribute their energies—whether they concentrate on their strengths or distribute their efforts.

The top scholars and athletes in the large schools are shown in Table 63. The top scholars and top

TABLE 62. AVERAGE GRADES OF TOP STUDENTS (7 OR MORE CHOICES) AND TOP ATHLETES (7 OR MORE CHOICES) IN THE FIVE SMALL SCHOOLS

GRADES

	Top scholars	Top athletes	Differ-ence
REWARDS FOR "ALL-AROUND BOY"			
Maple Grove	6.8	5.6	1.2
Elmtown	7.0	5.0	2.1
Green Junction	6.9	4.0	2.9
REWARDS FOR "SPECIALIST"			
Marketville	7.4	3.2	4.5
Farmdale	7.5	3.0	4.5
NUMBER OF CASES			
Maple Grove	(6)	(5)	
Elmtown	(6)	(7)	
Green Junction	(6)	(6)	
Marketville	(5)	(6)	
Farmdale	(2)	(1)	

TABLE 63. AVERAGE GRADES OF TOP STUDENTS (7 OR MORE CHOICES) AND TOP ATHLETES (7 OR MORE CHOICES) IN THE FIVE SMALL SCHOOLS

GRADES

	Top scholars	Top athletes	Differ-ence
REWARDS FOR "ALL-AROUND BOY"			
Executive Heights	6.8	4.8	2.0
Midcity	7.1	4.5	2.6
St. John's	7.6	4.1	3.5
REWARDS FOR "SPECIALIST"			
Newlawn	7.4	4.3	3.1
Millburg	7.9	3.3	4.6
NUMBER OF CASES			
Executive Heights	(17)	(17)	
Midcity	(11)	(20)	
St. John's	(11)	(20)	
Newlawn	(9)	(9)	
Millburg	(8)	(12)	

athletes in the one school with greatest rewards for the all-around boy have the least grade difference. The school is Executive Heights, and the difference is between B+ and C+, one letter grade. At the opposite extreme is Millburg, the school where the all-around boy gets least rewards, beyond those of the pure athlete and pure scholar. The difference is between straight A and C−, more than two letter grades difference.

The other schools are in between. The only one where the grade difference seems inconsistent with the structure of rewards is St. John's. Here the grades of the two groups are rather far apart (A− and C), although, as Chapter V showed, there are rewards for the all-around boy. This is the only school among the ten in which the grades of the top athletes and scholars fail to reflect the structure of social rewards.

There are, then, definite consequences of the specialization of roles of athlete and student, or the pressure toward all-around achievement. In both small and large schools, grade differences of top athletes and top scholars correspond to the extra social rewards given to the athlete-scholar. Where there is little extra social encouragement of the athlete-scholar, the two roles diverge, with the athlete and scholar becoming "specialists." In schools like Maple Grove and Executive Heights, where there is much social encouragement of the combined roles, the boys seen as best students are not really such good students, while the athletes are less specialized as athletes and get better grades.

Such specialization, surprisingly enough, does not increase markedly as the size of the school increases. In the large schools, there is as much overlap of choice between the best scholars and best athletes as in the smaller ones, and the grades of top athletes and top scholars are no further apart in the large schools. The variation within each size group is far greater than the variation between groups. The two largest schools, for example, Executive Heights and Midcity, show *less* specialization among athletes and scholars than do the two smallest ones, Marketville and Farmdale.

Consequences for the Stability of the System: Marketville as an Example

The status system among the boys in Marketville is a particularly interesting one, because its structure is different from that of the other small schools. The status systems of Elmtown and Maple Grove encourage a combination of athlete and scholar in the same boy; the status system of Green Junction re-

wards only the athlete, regardless of his interest and capabilities in scholastic matters; the status system of Farmdale has few rewards for either athlete or scholar; but the status system of Marketville gives rewards to the athlete and the scholar, viewed as separate roles.

Here scholars and athletes are more nearly "specialists"—the first concentrating on doing well scholastically, and the second achieving little in scholastic matters. The best students think of themselves more as scholars in this school, and want to be remembered as a "brilliant student," more than is true in the other small schools. On the basis of both quantitative and qualitative evidence, it appears that the boys named as best scholars in Marketville had more interest in intellectual pursuits than their counterparts in the other small schools.

Yet there is some evidence for another consequence of this system of "separate but equal" roles for the student and athlete, a consequence for the value climate itself.

In Marketville, there is a great difference between the senior class and the other three in the importance of scholastic achievement for the status system. The seniors were almost the lowest of all the ten schools, while the other classes were at or near the top of the list. No other school showed such a striking difference between classes. In another way as well, the boys in Marketville appeared to deviate from the general image of a scholastically oriented status system. Over the school year, the proportion choosing the image of brilliant student as the way to be remembered decreased greatly (over 6 percent decrease, while no other school decreased more than 2 percent). Thus, just as there was a great difference between classes in the value climate of Marketville boys, there was a great change over the period of the year. What accounts for these peculiarities in a system that otherwise rewards scholastic achievement highly?

Marketville had a remarkably successful athletic season, both in basketball and in football. As small as this school is, two senior boys were offered athletic scholarships by state universities, one for his football prowess and the other for his basketball ability. In this senior class, no boys were really outstanding scholastically—in contrast to the junior class, where the boy most often named as best student was the center of the leading group, a boy with aspirations to study political science at Harvard.

In Marketville, the absence of an outstanding senior scholar and the presence of outstanding athletes seem to be responsible for the very great difference between the senior class and the others. Similarly, the extreme success in athletics may have been responsible for the changes in the value system that occurred over the year. It appears that this success in athletics "swamped" the value system of the school for 1957–58, and the presence of outstanding athletes in the senior class swamped the value system in that class.

How did athletics swamp the value system? Paradoxically, colleges had a hand in the matter—three respectable universities. One of the two star athletes in the senior class is a likable farm boy whose real interest was exhibited in an interview. When asked about his interests, he said, "I fight chickens." He and his older brother and father staged cockfights in the country. He had made the acquaintance of a racing man who offered him a job in Florida racing greyhounds. By springtime, matters had changed. When asked, "How long have you planned to go to college?" he replied, "Last semester—since I got this football recognition and track recognition, colleges became interested in me right away." They were colleges that most students in school might aspire to: the Universities of Indiana, Illinois, and Tennessee. Meanwhile, the brilliant junior boy, interested in studying political science and then law, was not being sought out by any college, and would doubtless need to ferret out information about college admission as best he could when time came for him to attend college.

Thus, not just the student body and the community, but colleges as well gave the laurels of success to the star athlete. Possibly as a result, the values of the school shifted sharply toward athletics.

It seems reasonable to assume that these radical shifts that occurred in Marketville were partially due to the structure of the status system, that is, the differentiation of roles between scholar and athlete. It seems likely that such a status system is in a balance far more delicate than one in which the roles of athlete and student are combined. Students differ from year to year; good athletes who are personally popular will turn up during some years, while other years will cast up good scholars with similarly likable personalities. If the good athletes are also induced to pass off as good scholars, and the good scholars induced to achieve in athletics, the value system cannot be radically altered by this varying supply from year to year, and by the variable success in athletics. If, however, as in Marketville, the roles are specialized, then it seems likely that the value system will fluctuate widely as the supply of scholars and athletes fluctuates from year to year.

In one sense, then, a value system that combines these two roles includes a "safety device" which the other does not. It will never become highly academically oriented, but neither will it become primarily focused on athletics. Which is the more desirable system from the point of view of these schools' aims is not easy to tell. Is dilution worse than swamping? Given the context in which these schools operate, they must decide this question, consciously or not. But the context, in which colleges play their part, as exemplified above, forces the alternatives upon them.

This instability should of course be less and less with increase in the size of the school, for the supply of boys is large enough not to be affected so much by chance factors. It is in the small schools where this structural difference in the status system may be expected to have its greatest impact.

29

Our Status System

and Scholastic Rewards*

Stephen Abrahamson

Cultural anthropologists and sociologists alike seem agreed today on the idea that wherever man lives with man in sufficient numbers, there will arise a social status system based on specific criteria for each culture. Although many Americans have denied and often still deny that there is a social status system in our society, a more general acceptance of the concept has evolved. The idea of a status system need not be antithetical to democratic principles if the keys to mobility—no matter what the criteria of status—are available to all in such a manner that each man may achieve the status which he is desirous and capable of achieving.

In our society, the evidence seems to point to five ways of "improving" social status:

1. *Marriage.* It is possible for a man or woman to choose a mate from a social class higher in the social scale . . . and thus be in a position to gain acceptance by that class . . .
2. *Personality.* Sometimes it is possible for a person with a pleasing "personality" and the ability to adapt to new behavior patterns easily and gracefully to gain acceptance into a "higher" social class by using his "personality," "charm," and "manners". . .
3. *Special Talent.* Some very talented persons are able to gain acceptance to "higher" social classes because they are "gifted" in one way or another . . .
4. *Sheer Perseverance.* Some persons by possessing a double quality of capacity and ability can "work their way up." These people have the capacity to apply themselves to their work up to 16 hours a day and the ability to do a creditable job . . .
5. *Education.* Some people are able to train themselves for "better" occupations and greater earning power. Occupation is the greatest single factor in determining social class and money is necessary for the symbols of status. Thus education is of great impor-

tance to the average person of lower class standing when it comes to mobility . . . (Raths and Abrahamson, 1951, p. 1).

The first four of these "keys" to mobility are available to limited numbers of persons. Only the key supplied by education can be said to be available to almost everyone. However, to what extent do we in America make education available to all? It is true that in most states there are laws making attendance in school compulsory at least between the ages of eight and 16. But from extensive evidence Warner (Warner, 1949) points out that a "myth is built around compulsory school attendance. It is believed the authorities 'make the children go to school' until they are 16 years of age" (pp. 205). He further indicates that his Jonesville study indicated that "74% of the 345 adolescents out of school in the spring of 1942 had withdrawn from school before they were 16 years of age" (Warner, 1949, p. 205).

There are questions to be considered about the children who are in school. Is the treatment they receive such as to offer tham real equality of educational opportunity? Does a child's social status (his family's status, that is) help determine what success he might achieve in school? The following data were compiled in an effort to test the hypothesis: there is a relationship between the social class status positions of students in a community and the rewards and punishments received by students.

Six different communities were chosen as a "proving ground." Two of them were urban; two were suburban; and the other two were away from large urban centers. At least three home room groups from each school were included—one seventh, one eighth, and one ninth-grade group. Warner's Index of Status Characteristics (Warner, Meeker, and Eells, 1949) was employed to determine the social status of these students. Table 64 shows the distribution in the six schools according to social class status of the students. School No. 1 and School No. 2 are the suburban schools; School No. 3 and School No.

* From *The Journal of Educational Sociology*, 1952, **25**, 441–450.

TABLE 64. PERCENTAGE OF STUDENTS IN EACH SOCIAL CLASS BY SCHOOLS

| Social Class | Schools | | | | | | |
	No. 1	No. 2	No. 3	No. 4	No. 5	No. 6	Total
Upper-Middle	26.00	21.05	20.29	10.00	5.15	1.03	13.19
Lower-Middle	40.00	51.88	28.99	33.53	35.29	16.49	35.46
Upper-Lower	29.00	19.55	39.13	46.47	52.94	54.64	40.57
Lower-Lower	5.00	7.52	11.59	10.00	6.62	27.83	10.78
Total	100.00	100.00	100.00	100.00	100.00	99.99	100.00
	N = 100	N = 133	N = 69	N = 170	N = 136	N = 97	N = 705

4 are those away from a large urban center; School No. 5 and School No. 6 are the urban schools. It is interesting to note that the schools are arranged in order of decreasing upper-middle class population. In other words, the two suburban schools had the highest percentage of upper-middle class students; the two urban schools had the lowest percentage of upper-middle class students.

Once the social class status of the students was determined, the next step of the work was to examine the distributions of rewards and punishments. The following six reward and punishment factors were studied:

1. Academic grades on report cards and/or permanent records.
2. Favors and punishments by the teachers as measured by two scales appearing in *Student Status and Social Class* (Raths and Abrahamson, 1951).
3. Social acceptance of the students by their peers.
4. Offices held by the students in school and/or classroom government.
5. Participation by the students in extracurricular activities.
6. Prizes and awards made by the school.

A proportionate distribution of each of the six reward factors was drawn up. This proportionate distribution was based on the population distribution according to social class. In other words, where 26 percent of the population sample was upper-middle class, they would be expected to receive 26 percent of the A's, 26 percent of the B's, etc; they would be expected to hold 26 percent of the offices; they would be expected to receive 26 percent of the high social acceptance scores, etc. These proportionate distributions were then compared to the actual

distributions. Although this procedure is purely a statistical device, it is discussed more fully later.

The grades assigned to the students by the teachers were tallied according to the social class status backgrounds of the students. The evidence was overwhelming. The students in the upper-middle and lower-middle classes received much more than their proportionate share of the high grades and much less than their proportionate share of the low grades. The students in the upper-lower and lower-lower classes received just the opposite: that is, less than their proportionate share of the high grades and more than their proportionate share of the low grades. Table 65 indicates that upper-middle class students received 343 A's and B's compared to their share of 216 while they also received only 19 D's and E's compared to their share of 75. At the other end

TABLE 65. DISTRIBUTION OF ACADEMIC GRADES BY SOCIAL CLASS

| Social Class | Grades | |
	A and B	D and E
Upper-Middle	343	19
	(216)	(75)
Lower-Lower	48	136
	(147)	(51)

of the scale, the lower-lower class students received 48 A's and B's compared to their share of 147 while they received 136 D's and E's compared to their share of 51.

In addition, there was a marked tendency for the schools with the greater percentage of upper-middle class students to give out more high grades and fewer low grades than the schools with the smallest percentages of upper-middle class students.

According to the teachers themselves, there was a tendency to favor the students from higher social class backgrounds. The teachers indicated that the students of higher social class backgrounds were chosen more often for the little favors—running errands, monitoring, committee chairman, and the like—than were the other children. Obversely, when it came to handing out disciplinary measures, there was a tendency for the students of lower social class backgrounds to receive much more than their share according to the ratings of the teachers.

Participation in extra-curricular activities in a school program acts as a reward in that the students involved in the activities develop a deeper sense of appreciation for school, a higher level of morale, and a keen feeling of sharing in the school program. Again, the evidence was obvious. The higher the social class background of the students, the more they tended to participate in extra-curricular activities. The lower the social class background, the more the students tended to participate in no extra-curricular activities.

In three of the six schools the social class status backgrounds of the students winning the much-coveted American Legion Award for the last three years were investigated. Of 18 winners, 14 were of upper-middle class background and the other four of lower-middle class background. *No upper-lower and lower-lower class students were among the winners.* The social class distribution of the winners comes into sharper focus when examined against the fact that one-third of the sample populations from the three schools were in the two lower classes.

How about the rewards distributed by the students themselves? The information about the early adolescent indicates that a powerful motivating force in the lives of this age group is social acceptance. Here, again, the evidence is clear. The students from the higher social class backgrounds tended to receive higher social acceptance scores while the students from lower social class backgrounds tended to receive lower social acceptance scores.

TABLE 66. DISTRIBUTION OF SOCIAL ACCEPTANCE SCORES BY SOCIAL CLASS

Social Class	Scores	
	High	Low
Upper-Middle	45 (22)	27 (48)
Lower-Lower	3 (19)	62 (40)

Table 66 indicates that 45 upper-middle class students received high social acceptance scores compared to their share of those scores of 22. Only 27 upper-middle class students received low scores compared to their share of 48. The reverse relationship is true of the lower-lower class students.

The nature of the Ohio Social Acceptance Scale brought out a piece of incidental information that is very interesting. The scoring of the test yields two scores for each student: one, his acceptance rating by members of the opposite sex; the other, his acceptance rating by members of the same sex. In all the schools, both same sex and opposite sex distributions were significantly related to social class backgrounds of the students. It is interesting to note, however, that in every school except one, the opposite sex scores were not so closely class-bound as were the same sex scores.

Almost all secondary schools have some provision for student participation in government. The six schools included here were no exceptions. There was a great variety of offices—from the usual class presidents, student representatives and bankers to unusual town meeting sergeants-at-arms and panel discussion moderators.

In all of the six schools, almost all of the offices were held by upper-middle and lower-middle class students. *No lower-lower class student held an office.* The upper-middle class students held approximately three times their share of offices while the upper-lower class students held less than one-third of their share of offices.

It is interesting to note that in the schools where there was a higher percentage of upper-middle class students there were more offices for the students to hold. It is almost as if the provision of opportunity for participation in student government activities were proportional to the percentage of upper-middle class students in the school population.

Just how important are these rewards and punishments? An integral part of the educative process is motivation of learning. It is generally accepted today that rewards provide the strongest motivation in a learning situation. In summarizing research on the use of rewards and punishments, Bird points out that ". . . learning should be attended by reward and directed by instruction whenever maximum efficiency and adjustment to social demands are desired" (1940, pp. 61–96). Karen Horney (1937) indicates that success is one of the greatest encouragements to further success. Finally, W. H. Burton (1929) has this to say about punishments:

Our Status System and Scholastic Reward

Is punishment ever effective in building good habits? At first glance it would seem that punishment, being attended by annoyance, would be effective in stamping out undesirable habits. However, the annoyance is apt in many cases to be attached, not to the act, but *to the agent of punishment* or to the "getting found out" (p. 306).

Teachers in the public school have an obligation in the interest of the furthering of democratic goals to provide learning incentives for *all* children. Since rewards provide motivation and punishments often induce "giving up," equality of opportunity through education carries with it a need for equality in the distribution of rewards and punishments.

In carrying out this study the investigator made use of a theory of proportionate distribution—described earlier in the discussion. Strenuous objection to the use of this device stems from the application of a rival hypothesis to the distribution of rewards and punishments, namely: that the distribution of rewards is related to *intelligence* and that through the relationship of intelligence to social class, a relationship between rewards and social class appears. The work of Allison Davis (Eells *et al.*, 1951) indicates that such a hypothesis is really begging the question. His studies of intelligence and intelligence testing show that present measures of intelligence for the most part have been derived from testing situations that favor children of higher social class backgrounds and that lower class children have essentially the same average intelligence as higher class children. His findings are supplemented by the UNESCO *Statement on Race* (Montagu, 1952)—a statement endorsed by the world's leading authorities in anthropology, sociology, biology, and psychology. The statement says in part:

It is now generally recognized that intelligence tests do not in themselves enable us to differentiate between what is due to innate capacity and what is the result of environmental influences, training and education. Wherever it has been possible to make allowances for differences in environmental opportunities, the tests have shown essential similarity in mental characteristics among all human groups (Montagu, 1952).

While admittedly students of greater native intelligence should be able to reap the rewards of a competitive situation, the indications are, at present, that these junior high school students of higher social class background are gathering the fruits of our public education system in competition with students of lower social class background who probably possess equal intelligence. Students "earn" rewards in schools today usually on the basis of academic achievement, "correct" social behavior, and personality and leadership qualities. Children from higher social class background homes probably begin school with an advantage in the first two of those factors. The early advantage may obtain for them more praise and recognition from the teachers and more rewards than for their equally capable classmates who enter school at a disadvantage because of their social class background. The advantage for the students from the higher social classes probably grows, bringing about personality and leadership quality gains for these people, while an attitude of general discouragement is probably fostered in the hearts of the children from lower social class backgrounds.

By the time the children are in the junior high schools, the pattern is overwhelmingly noticeable. It is not just coincidence that children of higher social class background seem to have cornered the market in rewards. It is not coincidence that the basis for rewards in the junior high schools corresponds to the advantages with which the children of higher social class backgrounds come to school. The reward and penalty systems of junior high schools reflect the values and standards of the higher social class groups. Furthermore, teachers, being largely of middle class background themselves, are probably operating in a way that reflects the values of our status system and—albeit unconsciously—are treating the students of higher social class backgrounds with extra rewards, the students of lower social class backgrounds with extra punishments, and the "middle" group of students quite fairly, in general.

In a world torn by strife between the adherents of rival ideologies, the future of our democratic way of life may well depend on how well we live our democracy at home. A glaring discrepancy between what is said about equality of opportunity in education and what actually exists has been pointed up. The situation thus described presents a great challenge to education today. The acceleration of living and the evergrowing crescendo of crisis give us cause to wonder how much time is left to tackle the problem.

30

Family Relations of

Bright High-Achieving and

Under-Achieving High School Boys*

William R. Morrow
Robert C. Wilson

The present article reports data on the family relations of bright high school boys making good grades as compared with bright high school boys making mediocre or poor grades.

Of numerous studies of school achievement, few have obtained data regarding family relations correlates. These few have indicated a positive association between student achievement and emotionally supportive home situations. This general finding applies to elementary school pupils, high school students, and college students.

More specifically, parents of high-achievers have been found to give their children more praise and approval (Rickard, 1954), to show more interest and understanding (Tibbets, 1955), to be closer to their children (Kimball, 1953), to make their children feel more family "belongingness" (Walsh, 1956) and identification with parents (Tibbets, 1955). On the other hand, parents of under-achievers have been reported to be more domineering (E. S. Jones, 1955; Kimball, 1953) and overrestrictive (Rickard, 1954) and to use more severe and frequent punishment (Conklin, 1940; Kimball, 1953), which is at the same time less effectual (Conklin, 1940). Parents of under-achievers have also been found more likely either to baby their youngsters *or* to push them excessively (Hattwick and Stowell, 1936) and to present to their youngsters either low *or* extremely high (pressuring) demands for achievement (Rickard, 1954). Finally, homes of under-achievers are reported to show more tension (E. S. Jones, 1955) and more parental disagreement as to standards of behavior expected of their youngsters (Tibbets, 1955).

Most of these studies have been based on quali-

tative data such as interviews. Many had sampling limitations such as a very small sample and questionable equation of groups. No previous study seems to have dealt with family relations correlates of school achievement among high school students of superior intelligence.

In the present research the groups compared were carefully equated, the sample was relatively homogeneous in intelligence, all subjects being of superior intelligence, and the data were obtained by structured measuring instruments.

Before the present study was initiated, exploratory interviews covering various topics including family relations were held with a few bright high- and under-achieving high school boys. On the basis of these interviews as well as the studies cited, it was hypothesized that the reported family relations of high-achievers, as contrasted with those of under-achievers, are characterized by: (a) more emotionally supportive home environments; and, more specifically, (b) greater family sharing in recreation, decision-making, and exchange of confidences and ideas; (c) greater mutual parent-child affection, acceptance, trust, and approval; (d) less parental domination, severity, and restrictiveness; (e) more sympathetic parental encouragement of achievement, but less overinsistence on achievement; (f) greater harmony between parents and more regularity of home routines.

It was hypothesized further that students' family relations influence their school achievement via certain mediating variables. Specifically, it was hypothesized that supportive home environments are associated with positive student attitudes toward (a) teachers, (b) school, and (c) intellectual activities, as representing the adult world of parents, and that each of these mediating attitude variables would be associated with school achievement.

* From *Child Development*, 1961, **32**, 501–510.

Method

Sample

The sample included two equated groups each containing 48 high school boys of superior intelligence (120 IQ or above). The groups were equated for grade in school, socioeconomic status,[1] and intelligence. Each group contained 19 ninth-graders, 14 tenth-graders, and 15 eleventh-graders. Each group likewise contained one upper class, 15 upper-middle class, 23 lower-middle class, and 9 lower class boys. The mean IQ of the high-achieving group was 126.0; that of the under-achievers, 125.3, the difference being nonsignificant.

The groups differed in grade-point average in academic courses (with a minimum of three academic courses for each student). The high-achievers maintained an average of 1.00 to 1.67 (1 being the best grade possible, 5 the poorest) during the school year 1955–1956. The under-achievers maintained an average of 2.75 to 5.00, 2.75 being regarded as under-achievement for students of superior intelligence.

Data Collection

Several types of information about family relations were obtained from the students through group-administered questionnaires. The students were not asked to sign their names, but birthdates and other data were used to identify questionnaires for the purpose of selecting the sample. Otherwise, anonymity was maintained and information on individuals kept confidential.

The students' family relations as seen by themselves were evaluated primarily by 16 self-report Family Relations Scales. Each scale consisted of six questions about the student's relations with his parents (or foster parents). The scales were presented in consecutive order, but without scale titles or breaks in spacing. Each student was asked to

indicate to what extent each item described his own home situation, using the following four response categories:

1. Not at all   or   Almost Never
2. A Little   or   Sometimes
3. Considerably or   Often
4. Very Much   or   Very Often (or Almost Always)

The student was assigned a score on each scale by summing his scores on the six items in the scale. A score was also obtained on the total of all scales (except Harmony of Parents),[2] conceived as an index of Over-all Family Morale.

Following are the scale titles and a sample item for each scale:

1. *Family Sharing of Recreation.* "Do you and your family go on picnics or outings or trips together?"
2. *Family Sharing of Confidences and Ideas:* "Do your parents discuss their work and activities with you?"
3. *Family Sharing in Making Decisions.* "Do your parents let you help decide everyday family policies, rules, and ways of living?"
4. *Parental Approval.* "Does either parent ever seem to wish that you were a different sort of person?" (Negative item, scored in reverse.)
5. *Parental Affection.* "Do your parents openly show affection for you by word or action?"
6. *Parental Trust.* "How confident do your parents seem to be that you will behave properly away from home?"
7. *Parental Approval of Peer Activities.* "Do your parents object to some of your activities with your friends and acquaintances?" (Negative item.)
8. *Student Acceptance of Parental Standards.* "Do you agree with your parents' ideas about life?"
9. *Student Affection and Respect for Parents.* "Would you like to be the same kind of parent that your parents have been?"
10. *Lack of Parental Overrestrictiveness.* "Do your parents try to direct your activities?" (Negative item.)
11. *Lack of Parental Severity of Discipline.* "How often do your parents punish you?" (Negative item.)

[1] After all other criteria had been met except equating the groups for socioeconomic status and IQ, the high-achieving group included five more upper class boys than did the under-achieving group, 12 more upper-middle class boys, and nine more lower-middle class boys. The under-achievers included 12 more lower class boys than did the high-achieving group. This imbalance is consistent with previous findings of a positive association between academic achievement and family socioeconomic status for elementary and high school students (H. A. Coleman, 1940; Collins and Douglas, 1937; Gough, 1946; Lewis, 1941; Musselman, 1942), though not for college students, for whom findings on this point have been inconsistent (*see*, for example, Harris, 1940).

[2] The Harmony of Parents Scale was scored only for students with two parents living together. The N for this scale was 40 in each achievement group, re-equated for grade in school, socioeconomic status, and intelligence.

12. *Lack of Parental Overprotection.* "Do your
    parents try to protect you too much against
    difficulties or dangers?" (Negative item.)
13. *Lack of Parental Overinsistence on Achieve-
    ment.* "Are your parents always after you
    to work hard to become a success?" (Nega-
    tive item.)
14. *Sympathetic Encouragement of Achieve-
    ment.* "Do your parents inspire you to want
    to develop your abilities?"
15. *Regularity of Home Routine.* "Are your
    meals served at regular hours?"
16. *Harmony of Parents.* "Do your parents
    openly show affection or consideration for
    each other?"

The students were also asked to provide sociological data on parents' marital status, occupation, and
education and on the ages and sexes of their siblings.
In addition, each student was asked to respond to
three checklists: (a) a list of activities (e.g., "music,"
"insects or beach life," "fish or hunt," "billiards")
to be checked as to which ones his parents had
taught him or developed his interest in, yielding an
"intellectual," a "nonintellectual," and a total score;
(b) a list of 11 high school goals or values (in the
areas of academic achievement, athletics, social relations and status, general adjustment, morals, and
religion) to be checked as to which his parents
considered "most" and "least" important (three
each to be checked) for him to attain; (c) a similar
list of 11 adult goals (e.g., "be outstanding in your
occupation," "live a happy life," etc.) to be checked
the same way.

The questionnaire also included four open-ended
questions: "What sort of person is your mother?"
"What sort of person is your father?" "What do you
like most about your home and family?" "What
would you like to change about your home and
family?"

The following measures of *hypothesized mediating variables* (between family relations and school
achievement) were obtained: (a) a six-item attitude
scale (with a five-point scale for each item) designed
to measure Negative Attitudes to Teachers, which
yielded a corrected odd-even reliability of .69; (b) a
similar six-item attitude scale designed to measure
Negative Attitudes to School, which yielded a corrected odd-even reliability of .85; (c) a 72-item
interest-inventory scale (with dichotomous items)
designed to measure Interest in Intellectual Activities (esthetic activities, social problems, natural science, and formal symbol manipulation such as
mathematics and puzzles), which yielded a corrected
odd-even reliability of .77.

Analysis of Data

The internal consistency *reliability* of each Family
Relations Scale and of the Over-all Family Morale
Scale was evaluated by computing an odd-even
product-moment reliability coefficient. Differences
between high- and under-achievers on each scale and
on the over-all scale were tested for significance by a
median test.

Group differences in checklist responses were
tested for significance by a median test for scale
scores and by a chi square test for single items.

As for the open-ended questions, response categories potentially differentiating between the two
achievement groups were determined by studying an
inspection sample. These categories were cross-
validated by being scored[3] "blind" on another sample of 66 boys in each group with groups equated for
grade in school, socioeconomic status, and intelligence. Differences between groups were tested for
significance by chi square and median tests.

Pearson product-moment correlations were obtained between the Over-all Family Morale scale and
the several measures of mediating variables concerned with attitudes toward teachers, school, and
intellectual activities. These correlations were computed separately for the total sample, for high-
achievers only, and for under-achievers only. In addition, differences between achievement groups on
these mediating variables were tested for significance
by a median test.

All tests of significance used were two-tailed.

Results

Family Relations Scales

Results on the Family Relations Scales are presented in Table 67. The internal consistency reliability of the 16 six-item scales appeared to be sufficiently satisfactory for purposes of group comparison: all but three of the corrected odd-even
coefficients were above .70. The 90-item Over-all
Family Morale Scale yielded a reliability of .97.

Nine of the 16 six-item scales differentiated between the high- and under-achieving groups in the
predicted direction beyond the .05 level, seven of
these nine beyond the .01 level. The Over-all Family
Morale Scale differentiated beyond the .001 level.

High-achievers more often than under-achievers

[3] In view of the low validity obtained in this cross-validation,
time was not invested in having a second judge score the
material to provide a measure of interjudge agreement.

TABLE 67. FAMILY RELATIONS SCALES: MEDIAN TESTS*

Scale Title	r†	Per Cent Above Median		p
		Highs (N = 48)	Lows (N = 48)	
Family Sharing of Recreation	.76	69	44	.02
Family Sharing of Confidence & Ideas	.84	63	35	.01
Family Sharing in Making Decisions	.88	60	44	ns
Parental Approval	.56	73	33	.001
Parental Affection	.88	60	42	ns
Parental Trust	.73	60	25	.001
Parental Approval of Peer Activities	.94	71	42	.01
Student Acceptance of Parental Standards	.69	52	25	.01
Student Affection & Respect toward Parents	.91	58	44	ns
Lack of Parental Overrestrictiveness	.63	56	29	.01
Lack of Parental Severity of Discipline	.70	69	42	.01
Lack of Parental Overprotection	.77	52	56	ns
Lack of Parental Overinsistence on Achievement	.75	63	46	ns
Parental Encouragement of Achievement	.74	60	40	.05
Harmony of Parents (N = 40)	.72	63	48	ns
Regularity of Home Routine	.76	52	46	ns
Over-all Family Morale	.97	67	33	.001

* Two-tailed tests.
† Odd-even reliability coefficient, corrected by Spearman-Brown formula.

(a) described their families as typically sharing recreation, ideas, and confidences; (b) described their parents as approving and trusting (the areas of sharpest difference between the two groups), affectionate, encouraging (but not pressuring) with respect to achievement, and relatively nonrestrictive and nonsevere; and (c) described themselves as accepting their parents' standards.

An equal majority of both groups described their parents as having a relatively harmonious relationship, portrayed their homes as having a fairly regular routine, denied that they were either seriously overprotected or excessively pressured to achieve, and said they felt considerable respect and affection for their parents.

Even in the areas of greatest difference, however, there was considerable overlap between the two groups. On the Over-all Family Morale Scale nearly a third of the high-achievers scored below the median, and nearly a third of the under-achievers scored above the median.

Sociological Data

The two groups did not differ significantly in any of the sociological factors on which data was obtained. The data contradict the stereotyped notion that a mother's working outside the home inevitably leads to neglect which conduces to poor school performance (and other dire consequences). Actually 47 percent of the high-achievers (as against 37 percent of the under-achievers) reported that their mothers were working outside the home!

Check Lists

The two groups showed essentially no significant differences in their responses to the check lists.

Open-Ended Questions

In the inspection sample 34 potentially differentiating response categories were noted, of which 25 were grouped in five "high" combined categories and nine were grouped in three "low" combined categories. In the cross-validation only two "high" combined categories (out of eight combined categories) and four single "high" categories differentiated significantly (in the predicted direction).

Fifty-one percent of the high-achievers as against 33 percent of the under-achievers ($p < .05$) were scored in the combined category, "Positive references to intrafamily relationships." Two single categories in this grouping also differentiated significantly: "References to parental interest in family or student" (29 percent to 12 percent, $p < .01$); and "References to parents' outgoing, positive shaping of student's development" (12 percent to 0 percent, $p < .02$).

The combined category, "References to 'Golden Rule' virtues of parents" was scored significantly more often for high-achievers (56 percent to 29 percent, $p < .01$). Two single categories in this group also differentiated significantly: "Parents described as 'considerate' or 'thoughtful' " (17 percent to 4 percent, $p < .05$); and "Parents described as 'understanding' " (36 percent to 17 percent, $p < .02$).

These results are consistent with those on the Family Relations Scales.

Mediating Variables

The correlation between Over-all Family Morale and Negative Attitudes to Teachers was $-.67$ for the total sample, $-.46$ for high-achievers only, and $-.60$ for under-achievers only. The corresponding correlations between Family Morale and Negative Attitudes to School were $-.69$, $-.32$, and $-.65$. The correlations between Family Morale and Intellectual Interests were $.57$, $.31$, and $.49$. All of the obtained correlations are significant at the $.05$ level or better. On each of the three measures of mediating variables the two achievement groups differed at the $.001$ level in the expected direction.

These results are consistent with the hypothesis that supportive family relations foster academic achievement *via* promoting positive attitudes toward teachers, school, and intellectual activities, as symbols of the adult world of parents. However, other interpretations of the direction of causality are not excluded.

Summary

The reported family relations of 48 high school boys of superior intelligence making high grades were compared with those of a group making mediocre or poor grades, equated for grade in school, socioeconomic status, and intelligence. The main measuring instrument was a set of 16 six-item questionnaire scales (with a four-point scale for each item), on which each subject was asked to describe his family relations. The students also provided sociological data, check-list data on parental goals for the student, and open-ended question data on conceptions of parents. In addition, attitude scale data were obtained on variables hypothesized to mediate the influence of family morale on student achievement.

The results supported the hypotheses that bright high-achievers' parents reportedly engage in more sharing of activities, ideas, and confidences; are more approving and trusting, affectionate, and encouraging (but not pressuring) with respect to achievement; are less restrictive and severe; and enjoy more acceptance of parental standards by their youngsters. Not supported were hypotheses that under-achievers' families show more over-protectiveness, more high-pressure for achievement, more parental disharmony, more irregularity of home routine; differences in goals for their youngsters; or differences in sociological factors such as parents' marital status, current occupation of either parent, or number and ages of siblings.

The results also supported the hypothesis that family morale fosters academic achievement among bright high school boys *via* fostering positive attitudes toward teachers and toward school and interest in intellectual activities, as mediating variables. However, other hypotheses as to the direction of causality are not ruled out.

31

Family Background,

Primary Relationships,

and the High School Dropout*

Lucius F. Cervantes

During the next decade, an estimated 8,000,000 United States youths will terminate their education before completing high school. Most studies that deal with this vast personal and social wastage conclude that the family of the dropout is in some way deficient. What has not been specified, however, is in exactly what ways this family differs from that of the graduate. It is to this question of the specific differences between the family backgrounds of the dropout and the high school graduate that this article addresses itself.

School authorities in Boston, St. Louis, New Orleans, Omaha, Denver, and Los Angeles each cooperated in providing 25 "matched" pairs of white youths. In all pairs, one had dropped out of school and the other was successfully completing the last semester of his high school education. The youths were matched on the variables of sex, age, I.Q., high school attended, and general socioeconomic background. The youth originated in lower-class families (70 percent blue-collar; 30 percent lower white-collar); the median income was slightly less than $5,000 per year. The 300 respondents, with but 14 exceptions, were either 17 or 18 years of age.

The three instruments of research which were utilized in processing the teen-age sample were a questionnaire, a taped interview of approximately 40 minutes, and a Thematic Apperception Test.

Assumptions and Hypothesis

This article works within the framework of two assumptions:

(1) In our automated, industrial society, the completion of a high school education is

* From *Journal of Marriage and the Family*, 1965, **27**, 218–223.

a minimum requirement for civilizational adequacy.

(2) The enduring core of the "school personality" is primarily fashioned within the home and to a great extent mirrors the domestic subculture existent there.

The guiding hypothesis tested in this segment of the research was that the family background of the dropout is less characterized by primary relationships than is the family background of the high school graduate.

The Primary Group as a Conceptual Framework

Central to the theoretical field of this study is the concept of primary group. Cooley originated this concept to refer to "the nursery of human nature." The importance of primary relations is that they provide the experiences which are basic to the formation of personality (Cooley, 1956). Broom and Selznick present three testable characteristics of the primary group relationship: (1) it is *personal*, (2) it involves *a depth of intercommunication*, and (3) it gives *personal satisfactions* (Broom and Selznick, 1964).

Acceptance of a total person. The first criterion of the primary group tested was whether the members accept each other as persons. "To feel understood and accepted," "to be a real member of the team," "to feel that you belong" are ways of expressing the resulting psychic state, or, in the words of Cooley (1956), "Perhaps the simplest way of describing this wholeness is by saying that it is a 'we'; it involves the sort of sympathy and mutual identification for which 'we' is the natural expression" (p. 23).

Four questions were asked of each of the teen-age respondents concerning this mode of acceptance:

(1) "Would you say that your whole family both understands and accepts each other?" tapped the general milieu of family common understanding and acceptance.

(2) "Would you say that your family both understands and accepts *you*?" established whether the respondent felt that he personally was understood and accepted by his family.

(3) "And would you say that you both understand and accept them?" ascertained whether this pattern was reciprocal.

(4) "Did your family encourage and help you in your plans for a good job or in your school plans?" assayed the "we-ness" or solidarity-feeling of the family as seen by the teen-ager.

Case histories. In response to the first question, "Would you say that your *whole* family both understands and accepts each other?" the following replies may be cited as typical.

Dropout Edward, I.Q. 93, of New Orleans:

> Very little. Like before you all came. We was having a big argument. My sister keeps dogging me. When I come in she tells me to get out or go to work or something like that. She is stupid. She don't understand me. And my mother doesn't understand me. She just don't have time to understand me. She's got to be worried with my brothers and sisters and I can take care of myself. I can look after myself and make my own decisions and all. . . .

Graduate José, Spanish-American, I.Q. 111, of Denver:

> Yes, my mother and father both go to work in the morning and my brother and sisters and I have our certain jobs to do in the morning to clean the house up.

The responses that the 300 youths gave to the question, "Would you say that your *whole* family both understands and accepts each other?" were scored by a panel of three social scientists on a five-point scale of "Intrafamily Understanding and Acceptance." The results, in percentage distributions, are presented in Table 68.[1]

The first approach in ascertaining the depth of "primariness" in the families of the dropouts and the graduates was decisive in its results. Of the dropouts, four out of five (43% + 41%) perceive

[1] In testing the hypotheses of this report for statistical significance, the Kolmogorov-Smirnov two-sample, one-tailed test is used (Siegel, 1956).

TABLE 68. INTRAFAMILY UNDERSTANDING AND ACCEPTANCE

	Very Little	Little	Moderate	Much	Very Much
Dropouts	43	41	9	5	2
Graduates	3	15	20	24	38[a]

[a] N = 300 (150 dropouts, 150 graduates). Hypothesis: Families of dropouts manifest less intrafamily understanding and acceptance than families of high school graduates. D = .439; χ^2 (2df) = 130.28, p < .001.

their families as understanding and accepting each other either "very little" or "little." Of the graduates, four out of five (20% + 24% + 38%) perceive their family's understanding and acceptance of each other as "moderate," "much," or "very much." The overwhelming majority of the dropouts see their families as failing to accept each other; the overwhelming majority of the graduates see their families as accepting each other as complete persons.

How do you fit into the picture? The first question does not adequately test the linkage between the family's pattern of personal acceptance and the teen-ager himself. Is the youth, in replying about the emotional interrelationships that exist within his family, likewise describing the types of relationship that exist between him and his family? When he states that his family accepts each other very well, is he implying that they accept him too? It is quite possible to conceive of cases where all the other members of the family understand and accept one another but the teen-ager feels that he is completely misunderstood and rejected. For this reason, the next question was more specific: "How do you fit into the picture? Would you say that your family both understands and accepts *you*?"

The replies to the second question mirrored those to the first question. Four out of five (79%) of the dropouts replied in terms approximating those of Dropout Dan Y. of Denver (age 17, I.Q. 123), who confessed that he had never felt understood or accepted:

> I always felt left out. But really I think I need the time that the others got. . . . It's just that I felt left out. It seems when I was little I was always left out. I wasn't one of the family, really.

Far different were the reports of the graduates. Four out of five (84%) judged that they were both understood and accepted by their families.[2]

[2] Hypothesis: Dropouts perceive themselves as less understood and accepted by their families than do graduates. D = .633; χ^2(2df) = 120.2, p < .001.

And would you say that you both understand and accept them? This next question unintentionally served as a jolt to the standard egocentric adolescent belief that it is always the teen-age self that is misunderstood and never misunderstanding.

The statistical summary of responses to this third question yielded results identical to the previous two: four out of five (79%) of the dropouts judged themselves as understanding and accepting their families "very little" or "little" while four out of five (82%) of the graduates judged themselves as understanding and accepting their families "moderately," "much," or "very much."[3]

Did your family encourage and help you in your plans for a good job or in your school plans? A person engaged in a social system characterized by the "we" feeling of integration and solidarity demanded by the ideal primary group will subordinate to some significant extent his own interests to those of the other members of the group and will in turn feel supported by their encouragement and assistance. Group integration has been defined in operational terms as "the degree to which units of a social system are oriented toward optimizing rewards for other units of the system (Hamblin, 1958; see also E. M. Rogers and Sebald, 1962).

It was hypothesized that the dropouts would perceive themselves as receiving less encouragement from their families in their educational and occupational plans than the graduates would perceive. As

Less surprising was the finding that nine times as many dropouts as graduates (18% vs. 2%) felt that their parents pushed "too much" by pressuring and nagging them. When a teen-ager is doing poorly in his school work, both he and his parents become sensitized and vulnerable, and adjust to the situation by various defensive and offensive techniques that prove exacerbating to all parties involved.

The youths' responses to the four questions concerning the first criterion of a primary group—personal acceptance—lead to the conclusion that in four out of five cases, the climates of the families of dropouts and stay-ins are at opposite poles of the acceptance-rejection continuum.

Depth of intercommunication. Questioning respondents concerning their families' verbal communication patterns within their homes proved to be a fruitful source of affect-laden responses that sharply discriminated the perceived milieu of the family of the dropout from that of the graduate.

Does your family talk things over with each other very often? Dropout Carole H., I.Q. 102, of Denver, replied,

> No. Never! We all go our own ways. It's a family but I can't sit down and talk to my father about what I should do. And my brother and I don't even speak. There is no real companionship.

TABLE 69. FAMILY ENCOURAGEMENT OF THEIR TEEN-AGERS' EDUCATIONAL AND OCCUPATIONAL PLANS (IN PERCENTAGES)

	Very Little	Little	Moderate	Much	Very Much	Too Much
Dropouts	31	18	16	16	1	18
Graduates	30	11	14	43	1	2[a]

[a] N = 300 (150 dropouts, 150 graduates). Hypothesis: Dropouts perceive themselves as receiving less encouragement from their families in their educational and occupational plans than graduates perceive. D = .268; χ^2 (2df) = 23.08; p < .001.

indicated in Table 69, this hypothesis was validated, but there were some surprises. Four out of ten of the graduates (30% + 11%) felt that their families had given them "very little" or "little" encouragement in their educational plans. As they perceived the situation, their academic success was due all but completely to their own efforts and not to their family's assistance.

[3] D = .614; X^2(2df) = 113.09, p < .001.

Graduate John D., I.Q. 93, of New Orleans, said,

> Yes. . . . Lately my father talks with me and tells me why he wants me to go to college—why he and my mother definitely want me to try. And explains how it was for him. He quit when he was young and he works for the city—sanitation department. He had a heart attack about three years ago and now he is a watchman for them and I believe he makes only about $65.00 a week. He says there is no advancement for him. He wants

me to get a good job . . . and there is one boy I run around with and he wants to go to college with me, and my girl wants me to go to college too.

The differences of family background between the dropout and graduate in intrafamily communication can be seen from the percentage distribution on a five-point scale (Table 70).

The results of Table 70 are decisive: 81 percent

such data. The interest was rather in the frequency of intrafamilial recreational activities presumably indicative of the pleasure that the family experienced in being with each other under a variety of circumstances. Here are two typical replies:

Vivian M., I.Q. 100, of Omaha:

We were all never together at one time. . . . My parents left at six in the morning and didn't get home until four. I just played hookey. . . .

TABLE 70. COMMUNICATION WITHIN THE HOME (IN PERCENTAGES)

	Very Infrequent	Infrequent	Moderate	Frequent	Very Frequent
Dropouts	43	38	11	6	2
Graduates	3	17	20	24	36[a]

[a] N = 300 (150 dropouts, 150 graduates). Hypothesis: There is less intrafamily communication in the families of dropouts than in the family of graduates. D = 633; χ^2 (2df) = 87.48, p < .001.

(43% + 38%) of the dropouts receive their life's basic orientation in a nuclear family of inadequate intercommunication, and 80 percent (20% + 24% + 36%) of the graduates receive their life's basic orientation in a nuclear family of at least adequate intercommunication.

III. *Pleasurable experiences.* Closely allied to the level of verbal intercommunication within a family is its level of shared recreational activities. Enjoyment of each other's company in a variety of circumstances is the third characteristic of the primary group. A family that chooses to spend its leisure hours in each other's company manifests that antagonism and tension are not a staple of their relationships but rather that harmony and mutual enjoyment are.

Family and leisure. In asking respondents, "If your *whole* family had some free time, how would they usually spend it?" the interest was not primarily in the type of leisure-time activities in which they indulged. General research has already established

When I finally told them, they were sick about it but I had already signed myself out.

Patricia S., I.Q. 98, of New Orleans:

We would all have dinner together and then maybe we would all go for a ride in the afternoon and maybe we would all go to a show that night or visit some of the relatives.

The over-all statistical picture of the 300 replies is perfectly clear in Table 71.

According to the perceptions of the youths, four out of five (79%) of the dropouts' families participate in leisure activities together either "very infrequently" or "infrequently." Three out of four (75%) of the graduates' families reportedly are accustomed to participation in such family activities.

IV. *Happiness within the home.* As a resume of the differences between the family backgrounds of the dropouts and the graduates, all interviews were reviewed, and each was scored on the one variable of

TABLE 71. FAMILY JOINT LEISURE SCALE (IN PERCENTAGES)

	Very Infrequently	Infrequently	Occasionally	Frequently	Frequently Very
Dropouts	53	26	13	6	2
Graduates	8	17	25	25	25[a]

[a] N = 300 (150 dropouts, 150 graduates). Hypothesis: Dropouts manifest less family joint leisure activity than graduates. D = .540; χ^2 (2df) = 87.48, p < .001.

life-long family "happiness" as reported by the respondent.

To continue one's education beyond the obligatory date, which in all large U.S. cities is one's sixteenth birthday, means to retain one's dependent role upon one's parents at the very time that the

tion, and if there has been continued pleasure accruing from being with each other under a variety of circumstances, this family, in accord with the criteria of modern formulations, is considered to be both an ideal primary group and characterized by "happiness." Table 72 has been obtained by the three-

TABLE 72. HAPPINESS WITHIN THE HOME (IN PERCENTAGES)

	Very Unhappy	Unhappy	Indifferent	Happy	Very Happy
Dropouts	35	27	25	10	3
Graduates	17	5	14	16	48[a]

[a] N = 300 (150 dropouts, 150 graduates). Hypothesis: The dropouts report their homes as being less happy than do the graduates. D = 4.2; $\chi^2 = 59.9$, p < .001.

teen-ager is striving to establish his identity as an independent agent. A youth in a less than pleasant home will have a bias to discontinue his abrasive dependence upon his family which the student role requires of him. A lower-class youth who does not experience in the domestic milieu that "state of well-being and pleasurable satisfaction" (the dictionary definition of "happiness") is not as likely to continue in his subordinate role as a domestic dependent but will more likely seek to terminate the dependence by making himself economically independent. A youth who is not having his basic needs of personal recognition, friendly intercommunication, and various pleasurable experiences realized within the family system will have to seek the satisfaction of these needs outside the family system. This will usually mean that he turns to the peer group. To the extent that this occurs, his commitment to the family is minimized and to the peer group is maximized. That the family system is, within American culture, more characteristically pro-academic while the independent peer group culture is more characteristically anti-academic seems probable. A youth who is having long-term interpersonal problems in his home quite probably mirrors his troubled home situation in a troubled school situation. A seriously unhappy youth is more probably unable to be an academic achiever. This was the thinking behind summarizing the primary relations material in terms of "happiness."

To measure happiness within the home throughout the total life history of the respondent, this study uses the criterion of an ideal primary group. If the family has accepted each other as "total persons," if there has been a depth of intercommunica-

member panel's evaluation of each of the 300 interviews and the registering of these evaluations on a standard five-point scale.

The typical home of the dropout (35% + 27%) is reported as having been characteristically unhappy; the typical home of the graduate (16% + 48%) is reported as having been characteristically happy.

The homes of the youths interviewed were either in similar or identical neighborhoods. Externally, the homes appeared identical. Internally, there were on an average the same number of children, and by matched pairs the respondents were of the same age, the same sex, the same native ability, and had attended the same high schools. Yet the different climate of happiness in the homes of the dropouts as contrasted with the graduates is startling. Unhappiness is the characteristic of the one group, happiness that of the other.

Summary and Interpretation

Each of the interview questions that reflected the climate of primary relations in the home distinguished the dropout from the graduate at the highest level of significance (.001). In the semantics of statistical tests, this means that the difference found between the two groups could have happened but once in a thousand times by chance.

Previous studies have noted that the family backgrounds of dropouts generally differ from those of graduates. The present study reconfirms this common observation but has gone a step further by specifying exactly how the domestic environment of the lower-class academic achievers differs from that of the nonachievers. It remains to point out the link between socialization in a home where primary relationships are dominant and success in the school context.

Every successful student needs three prerequisites. First, he needs a strong self-image that is the product of being accepted as a worthwhile person and of various success experiences. This self-image of personal worth insures the child that he is wanted and induces a feeling that he can succeed in a task undertaken. Secondly, the successful pupil needs the intellectual alertness, the vocabulary, and the reading potentials that only extensive intercommunication with sympathetic confidants can readily supply. Third, the advantaged young scholar needs to derive pleasure from team work, competition, and the discipline inherent in orderly social interaction. The import of this study is that these academic prerequisites are more readily acquired by the child who has been brought up in a family that is a primary group.

Registration on the first day of school does not bring these school readiness patterns to the six-year-old. The Gluecks (E. Glueck, 1956; S. Glueck, 1960) maintain that the potential delinquent can be spotted with a 90 percent predictive reliability when he is six years old by an analysis of his family's patterns of affection, discipline, and solidarity. The present conclusion suggests that the same predictive reliability of school success or failure could be made of a child of average I.Q. on the first day of school by an analysis of the prevalance or absence of primary relations in his family background.

Many variables in addition to family background are highly significant in their impact upon premature withdrawal from the school process. I.Q., income, class affiliation, peer pressures, school experiences, and occupational orientations are but a few that can be mentioned. But no matter what other variables are at work, the nuclear family is of critical import. A law of polarization is evidence in the teen-age world today. The dropout is generally the product of a family deficient in primary relations. This study of a matched lower-class population indicates that the family which nurtured the youth who did not continue his education is of a different caliber than that which produced the teen-ager who continues his education at least to high school graduation.

32

Transition

*of Sex Differences in Cheating**

Solomon E. Feldman
Martin T. Feldman

In their study of college cheating, Hetherington and Feldman (1965) found that males were more likely to cheat on academic examinations than females, a finding that reverses the incidence rates for children (R. V. Burton, 1963; Hartshorne and May, 1928). The authors speculate that by the time of college entrance, males have become more motivated to succeed academically and thus will take greater risks, including cheating, to do so. The current study tests the hypothesis that this shift in incidence of cheating occurs during the high school years, a time paralleled by an increased interest by the male in academic mastery.

Method.—A total of 81 seventh grade (45 male and 36 female) and 73 twelfth grade (40 male and 33 female) students unwittingly served as Ss. These students represented a seventh grade Social Studies class and a twelfth grade English class drawn from a school serving a basically suburban and well-to-do community.

The class teachers administered a difficult 30-item objective "creative achievement" test under task-oriented instructions, i.e., that the test itself was of prime interest to the researcher. On the following school day Ss were told that the teacher had not had an opportunity to score the test, and their help was enlisted. Each student received his own paper and was asked to score the questions according to the key placed on the blackboard. Shortly, the teacher was called from the room but prior to her departure attempted to increase ego orientation by mentioning that upon her return students might compare grades. As the tests had been previously scored, the criterion of two or more changed answers could be used to classify a student as having cheated. It should be noted that among the various styles of cheating elucidated by Hetherington and Feldman (1965) this situation only taps unplanned cheating that is done individually.

Results.—The distribution of cheating behavior as a function of school year and sex is presented in Table 73. In order to assess the interaction of those two variables with cheating incidence a multiple contingency analysis (Sutcliffe, 1957) was performed.

Although the incidence of cheating among twelfth graders surpassed that of seventh graders (42.5% vs 28.4%), the difference is not statistically significant ($\chi^2_c = 2.64$, $.20 > p > .10$). Closer examination reveals that this increase reflects primarily an increased incident of cheating among males. While only 22.2% of seventh grade males cheated, 50% of twelfth grade males cheated. For females there was some decrease in cheating comparing seventh vs twelfth graders, 36.1% vs 33.3%. This differential change in cheating is reflected by the lack of a significant over-all difference in sex rate for cheating ($\chi^2_c = 0$) and by the significant three-way interaction of sex, year, and cheating ($\chi^2_c = 6.03$, $.02 > p > .01$). Over and above the sex differences, incidence of cheating under what could be considered as mildly ego-involving conditions speaks

TABLE 73. INCIDENCE OF CHEATING AS A FUNCTION OF GRADE AND SEX

| | 7th Graders | | 12th Graders | |
	Cheaters	*Non-cheaters*	*Cheaters*	*Non-cheaters*
Males	10	35	20	20
Females	13	23	11	22

* From *Psychological Reports*, 1967, **20**, 957–958.

to the pull of this type of behavior and suggests parametric studies of the degree of ego-involvement as it relates to cheating.

A comparison of the incidence figures of this type of cheating by twelfth graders with the college students in Hetherington and Feldman's (1965) sample, suggest predictable cheating rates. In the previous study the over-all incidence was 41 percent, while for males the rate was 46.2 percent and for females the rate was 35.9 percent; the corresponding figures

in this study were 42.5 percent, 50 percent, and 33.3 percent.

The present results suggest that during the high school years males exhibit an increased propensity to engage in cheating. The extent to which this change reflects the hypothesized increase in pressures for academic attainment, changes in "moral character traits," or changes in risk-taking behaviors awaits future clarification.

VII

Worker

The choice of an occupation is the task traditionally assigned to adolescence. During this era the child presumably becomes critically aware of the work life—of the need to choose a vocation toward which he can gear education and other instrumental activities, of the variety of work roles, of the relationships that bind adulthood, economic independence, and vocational responsibility into a tight value nexus. In fact, the extended preparation required for many jobs in our society has created a situation—at least in privileged sectors of the society—in which young men may enjoy most prerequisites of adult status long before they are qualified to practice their chosen professions or are economically independent. Yet in socializing children, we still equate adulthood with adult work functions; and we urge children, particularly in adolescence, to see adult freedom and economic independence as synonymous and as tied to the acquisition of a job. Before high school and increasingly through the high school period, children are urged to choose a future work role and to begin preparing for it.

Douvan and Adelson's data from the national sample studies (1966) indicate that adolescents, particularly boys, have absorbed the culture's training. They think of job choice and job preparation as presenting the most crucial decisions they face. The vocational area mobilizes and focuses a great deal of adolescent concern.

In this section we will look at work experience during adolescence, and at the development of job choice, aspirations, and expectations and some of the factors that influence the nature and process of choice. Work-relevant motives and values have been discussed in the section on the student role and will be discussed again later in the section dealing with self and identity.

Job Experience During Adolescence

Direct and successful work experience can be a highly significant support to adolescents through this period of accelerated change. It serves as a base for observing at least one aspect of the occupational world and helps to focus occupational interests for middle-class youngsters who face broad, and sometimes ambiguous, choices. One study (Slocum and Empey, 1956) of the occupational plans of high school seniors and college students found that relevant work experience was cited as a source of influence in occupational choice more than any other factor (from 20 percent to 50 percent of all

students in the various groups). Positive job experiences facilitate rehabilita-
tion of delinquent boys (Haskell, 1960). One fifth of the 14–16-year-old
boys and girls in a national study (Douvan and Adelson, 1966) list work
experiences and success in work as a source of self-esteem, and the proportion increases to 35 percent for girls seventeen and eighteen. The
question that elicited these answers ("What do you do—at home, or at
school, or with your friends—that makes you feel important or useful?") did
not refer specifically to work, yet the job setting accounts for as high a percentage of responses as do either home-tied or school-related activities.

While their final commitment to a work role occurs in most individuals
when adolescence proper is ending or has ended, the vocational issue assumes
a central position in the life and concerns of youngsters during this stage.
A large proportion of adolescent boys and girls commit some part of their
out-of-school time to jobs. And evidence indicates that this job experience
provides one important expression for the adolescent's need to establish his
autonomy and competence. The occupational identity is especially crucial
to the boy, and the processes of vocational development in adolescent boys
have attracted a considerable research interest.

Vocational Plans

Several theorists have offered schemes for charting the course of vocational
development. Influenced by general theories of development like Erikson's
and Piaget's, the several schemes are remarkably consistent. In his review
of the field, Borow (1966) uses Ginzburg's theory (1951) to represent work
in this field. Its richness of detail and fruitfulness in research commend it for
this purpose.

Ginzburg has broken the process of job selection into three developmental stages: the *fantasy* period (up to age 11 or so), the *tentative* period
(11 to 17 years of age) in which the adolescent develops greater awareness of
the differentiated occupational spectrum and of the necessary qualifications
for various jobs. Near the close of this stage adolescents begin to consider and
amalgamate interests, abilities, and values in their job choices, and to recognize external reality as a factor in the choice as well. The *realistic* period of
choice, begun around the end of the seventeenth year, sees the development
of a plan that integrates personal and external factors into a relatively firm
vocational goal.

Ginzburg's theory derived from his own extensive research, and it is therefore not surprising that most large studies of occupational development
report findings that are consistent with the theory. Douvan and Adelson
(1966), Bachman (1967), and others working with large samples find the
same movement from less to greater refinement and realism as boys progress
through adolescence. *Gribbons and Lohnes* (1965) report the same trend
in their analysis of the values implicit in boys' thought about work at different ages.

The large studies also agree that the occupational area is less salient for
girls during adolescence. Douvan and Adelson report that although girls are

just as ready to talk about future work, their plans reveal gaps and discrepancies which take on pattern and meaning only if one abandons a male concept of work and assumes that future work is conceived by the girl primarily as a means to express feminine needs (e.g., nurturing, helping) and to attain the feminine goals of marriage and motherhood (so that, for example, a central feature girls seek in a job is "nice people to work with" or "meeting new people").

When a girl says that she will be a doctor *or* a nurse, the status-skill discrepancy between her alternatives may seem a mark of immaturity. When, however, we recognize that work is not as heavily invested with achievement for her and that the two jobs share the expression of nurturance, we see that our categories for deriving a maturity measure may simply not be suited to the realities of girls' development. As Ginzburg has phrased it, the young woman's movement through the substages of the reality period is complicated by the contingencies of marriage and the economic status of her future husband, if she should marry. Since both contingencies are uncertain at the end of the tentative choice period, she has no clear picture of how they will affect her life and therefore cannot make a decisive vocational choice.

O'Hara's findings (1962) indicate that girls may advance through the early stages of vocational development more rapidly than boys do, and Ginzburg has noted that girls in our culture have more direct experience with aspects of traditional feminine work roles than boys have with masculine work. At any rate it seems clear that the process of choice is quite different in boys and girls because of the girls' overriding concern about marriage, which is both a sex role and an occupational role for her. *Rezler's* study (1967) demonstrates the unique qualities of girls whose occupational choice and posture are similar to the choices of achievement oriented boys. And the older boys, in justifying their choices, make fewer demands for personal gratification and fulfillment from the job. They more often choose jobs because they are available or because they offer security. It is as though they decrease investment in the work role as they approach the occupational world and assess their chances. *Caro and Pihlblad* (1965) found that lower class boys made a rather sharp distinction between what job they would *like* to have and what they think they will actually do.

Adolescent boys' vocational plans are associated with their families' current social status. Early adolescent sons of unskilled and semi-skilled workers aspire on the whole to the same professional positions as the sons of professionals do. It is clear that lower status boys are about as aware of the prerequisites and perquisites of the professions and accord them the same status as their higher status age mates do. But as they grow older and closer to entering the world of work, their experiences with themselves as students and the realities of gaining further education lead lower status boys to plan for employment of lesser prestige and actually to cut back their aspirations.

We know from their attitudes and plans for education that both lower class children and their parents know the goals of the culture and want them. But the parents do not know or cannot transmit the instrumental attitudes and behaviors necessary to achieve them and the children, lacking the means, abandon or reduce their goals.

For the boy in our culture, occupational planning serves to bridge the adolescent present and the adult future. The future job determines many present choices and activities and lends meaning and pattern to them. Vocationally-relevant activities in the present reaffirm the reality of his future adulthood and his growing competence to handle adult status and responsibilities. Douvan and Adelson (1966) found that the degree to which a boy was handling this aspect of his future was also the best available indicator of his overall adolescent ego integration.

33

Shifts in Adolescents' Vocational Values[*]

Warren D. Gribbons
Paul R. Lohnes

Career psychology has attended closely to the emerging vocational interests and aspirations of youth, but little is known about the reasons for the preference patterns which have been described. It has been suggested repeatedly that family press shapes the occupational concepts of youth (e.g., Tiedeman and O'Hara, 1963, p. 83), but the available empirical evidence fails to support this view (Brunkan & Crites, 1964). It seems more reasonable to emphasize, as Super has all along (e.g., Super, et al., 1963b), that a system of self-concepts provides the matrix for specific occupational concepts, censoring and molding them to a comfortable fit in the matrix, and that the self-concept system itself is a product of a vast congeries of determinants. In this melange of causes, family-related variables contribute to the fomentation of self-concepts, but so do such factors as neighborhood, community and regional influences, educational and religious factors, mass media exposures, and friendships. Taking the system of self-concepts as the immediate control over occupational preferences, then, it seems likely that some hierarchy of values embedded in the system dominates the preference-building process. One career psychologist has expressed this hypothesis as follows:

> If there is a single synthesizing element that orders, arranges, and unifies such interactions, that ties together an individual's perceptions of cultural promptings, motivating needs, mediating symbols, differentiating characteristics, and sense of resolution, that relates perception to self-concepts, and that accounts most directly for a particular decision or for a mode of choosing, it is here suggested that that element is the individual's value system (M. Katz, 1963, p. 16).

The authors are involved in a longitudinal study of the career development of 111 boys and girls which was begun in 1958, when the senior author interviewed the subjects first. At that time they were beginning the eighth grade in several junior high schools in metropolitan Boston's outlying cities. They were interviewed again in the last months of the tenth grade (1961), and again late in the senior year of high school (1963). No subjects were lost during the five-year period. Agreeing with Katz, the authors report in this paper on the inferred value hierarchies of these boys and girls, as they have been judged from the interview protocols, and on the changes observed in these value hierarchies over five years of development. Other aspects of the longitudinal study data have been reported in Gribbons (1964) and Gribbons and Lohnes (1964a, 1964b, 1965a). Answers were sought to two questions about values for this study:

1. Is there an important shift in the typal hierarchy of vocational values over five years of adolescence?

2. Is there an important difference between the developed typal hierarchy of vocational values for boys and that for girls?

Method

Before attempting to answer these questions from the data, an account of the interview questions that elicited the responses from which the values of the subjects were judged and ranked is in order. Precisely the same interview form was employed in 1958 and in 1961. Of its 43 questions, the following provided the stimuli for expression of values:

1. What made you decide to take X curriculum?
2. What made you decide not to take Y or Z curriculum?
3. Is there any advantage to taking the college curriculum?
4. Why would you like to become an X (occupation)?
5. What particular interests would X occupation satisfy?

[*] From *Personnel and Guidance Journal*, 1965, **44**, 248–252.

6. What interests do you have that will not be satisfied by X?

7. As you know, things that are important to us are called values. Tell me about some of your values.

8. What values of yours would working as an X satisfy?

9. What values of yours would not be satisfied in your occupation as an X?

10. Which of your values will conflict with one another in your choice of an occupation?

The 1963 interview was conducted on the basis of a somewhat different set of questions, from among which the following served to elicit vocational values responses:

1. What is the most important factor to consider in making an occupational choice?

2. Why do you consider this factor important?

3. In the eighth grade you were considering the possibility of becoming an X, and in the tenth grade an X', and now you plan to be an X". Will you tell me what has strengthened this decision (or caused you to change your mind)?

4. Do you feel that the occupation you will enter is a matter of chance or choice? Can you tell me why?

5. What would you like to get out of life? What do you think would make you happy and satisfied?

6. What would you like to get out of work?

7. Can you tell me something of how you feel about going to work?

8. When you think about work, is there anything you feel to be especially disagreeable about it?

Those responses were classified as values that seemed to provide broad guideposts to action or that entailed a commitment to long-range goals. Because of the high degree of specificity of the instructions for coding protocol materials, this judge had no difficulty in reaching an unambiguous categorization of each response unit. Although no formal reliability study was done, the authors feel that the reliability of categorization must have been very high. It was found that 12 general categories accommodated the responses tallied as value indicators, as follows, with some examples of indicators:

Advancement: opportunity to get ahead; good future in it; can become a manager; can work from bottom up.

Demand: good job for later on; it's in demand; teachers are needed.

Geographic Location, Travel: like to fly; able to travel; learning from travel; raises transportation problems.

Interest: like to work with my hands; really enjoy it.

Marriage and Family: get married eventually; be happy with husband and children; want a nice home and kids.

Social Service: help others; to further society; giving something to humanity; making people happy; like to help children.

Personal Contact: chance to meet new friends; like to meet people; working with others; get to know people better.

Preparation, Ability: where abilities lie; what I'm good at; suited to it.

Prestige: people look up to you; earn recognition, respectability.

Salary: earn enough to support family; good income; bank account.

Satisfaction: happy at work; fulfill myself; doing something worthwhile.

Personal Goals: improve self; get to know myself better.

Typal value hierarchies were created for each age and sex by ranking the 12 values according to the number of subjects mentioning each. The authors are aware that this procedure involves the popularity of a value category rather than the intensity with which it is employed by those who use it. Table 74 reports the resulting ranking of the values for each age and sex, and the frequencies on which the rankings are based. It should be noted that some values were employed by almost all the subjects (the maximum possible frequency for any age-sex combination is 55), and others were very seldom employed.

Time Shifts in the Typal Hierarchies

Satisfaction and *interest* were far and away the most popular types of values put forward in the eighth grade, and remained so for both sexes in the other interviews. So heavily saturated are these two categories that the authors wish they knew how to break them down into smaller units, but no workable scheme has suggested itself. Our generalization is that the vocational values which were uppermost in the thoughts of our subjects early in adolescence remained uppermost throughout the five-year period.

Marriage and family is always employed by more girls than boys, and becomes consistently more popular with both sexes as they advance in years. The boys are persistently interested in *salary* and

TABLE 74. TYPAL HIERARCHIES OF VOCATIONAL VALUES FOR EACH SEX AND AGE

	8th Grade				10th Grade				12th Grade			
	Girls (N = 57)		Boys (N = 54)		Girls (N = 57)		Boys (N = 54)		Girls (N = 57)		Boys (N = 54)	
Values	Rank	f	Rank	f	Rank	f	Rank	f	Rank	f	Rank	f
Satisfaction	1	48	1	47	2	50	1	51	1	51	2	50
Interest	2	47	2	44	1	51	2	47	2	49	1	51
Marriage and Family	7.5	9	11	4	7	14	12	4	3	30	4	22
Personal Contact	3.5	24	6	11	3	35	5	16	4	25	6.5	14
Social Service	3.5	24	5	12	4	26	8	13	5	23	8	10
Preparation, Ability	9	5	7.5	10	9	7	6	16	6	15	6.5	14
Advancement	12	0	10	7	12	4	11	7	7	14	9	7
Salary	11	3	3	19	9	7	3	25	8	13	3	41
Personal Goals	5	14	7.5	10	6	13	4	20	9.5	8	10	6
Demand	10	4	12	3	11	6	10	9	9.5	8	11	4
Location, Travel	6	12	9	8	5	15	9	12	11.5	3	12	2
Prestige	7.5	9	4	13	9	7	7	15	11.5	3	5	16
Girls vs. Boys:			Rho = .50				Rho = .52				Rho = .62	

For Girls: 8th vs. 10th, Rho = .95; 8th vs. 12th, Rho = .46; 10th vs. 12th, Rho = .52

For Boys: 8th vs. 10th, Rho = .84; 8th vs. 12th, Rho = .68; 10th vs. 12th, Rho = .50

prestige; the girls not so. The girls are persistently interested in *personal contact* and *social service;* the boys less so and decreasingly so over time. There is a decreasing concern with *personal goals, geographic location,* and *travel,* and corresponding increase in concern with *preparation, ability,* and *advancement* on the part of both sexes. There is little or no concern with *demand* at any time. Apart from the sex differences noted, to be discussed below, perhaps the most noticeable trend is from "idealism" in the eighth grade (*social service, personal goals, location and travel*) to "realism" in the twelfth (*marriage and family, preparation and ability, advancement*), which is probably to be applauded. This evidence for the emergence of more mature values somewhat contradicts the finding of Dipboye and Anderson that "little change takes place [in occupational values] during [his] high school career" (1959, p. 124). However, as noted, there are important constancies over the five years in our data also.

Sex Differences in Developed Typal Hierarchies

Super included only boys in his Career Pattern Study (1957), and it has been suggested by friends that the sex mix in the small sample of this research may have been rash. Consideration of the developed (i.e., twelfth grade) typal hierarchies of vocational values for the two sexes does reveal an important contrast. Where the boys have given high rank to *salary* and *prestige* values, the girls have given high rank to *personal contact* and *social service* values. This finding lends some support to the theoretical notion of Harrod and Griswold (1960) that girls are people-oriented, in that they like to meet people and help them, whereas boys are career- or extrinsic-reward-oriented in that they are most concerned with salary, security, and prestige.

The comparison of the final hierarchies for the two sexes is dominated by the similarities rather than by the differences, however. There is over-whelming concern with *satisfaction* to be found in vocation and the opportunity to satisfy *interest* particularly. Both groups have arrived at very high concern for *marriage and family.* In line with the result of Astin and Nichols that "men are more likely to give a response with vocational content, whereas women are much more likely to give a response with family or marriage content" (1964, p. 56), it is true that our girls spoke of marriage in terms of husband and children, while our boys spoke of it in terms of providing basic necessities and some luxuries for the family. The two hierarchies are also in near agreement on the position given to *preparation and ability,* and the low positions given in *advancement, personal goals, demand,* and *location and travel.*

Conclusions

It has been said that "students make choices in terms of the kind of person they believe themselves to be" (Holland, 1963–1964, p. 97). We have argued that the value categories favored by adolescents in their discussion of vocational issues reveal aspects of their self-concept systems which are crucial in determining occcpational preferences. Enough early maturity and constancy in the typal hierarchies of vocation values over five years of adolescence has been shown to warrant challenging Ginzberg's theoretical position that values do not play an important part in early vocational development. Even the eighth-grade value statements of our sample of youth are relatively free of "fantasy" elements, although we do discern a shift from "idealism" to "realism" over the five years. Our interpretation of our data is that the constancy it shows bespeaks a maturity of self-concepts early in the eighth grade sufficient to justify close attention from counselors at that time, while the shifts testify to a healthy maturation during adolescence.

Although theoreticians emphasize that career development differs for boys and girls (e.g., Matthews, 1963), and we have noted a bit of a people-oriented (girls) versus career-oriented (boys) differentiation in our developed typal hierarchies, it is our contention that the similarities in our data outweigh the differences, and that our boys and girls appear to be rather alike in their employment of vocational value categories.

It has been shown that school counselors can interfere successfully in the vocational development process (Gribbons, 1960; Shimberg, 1962). It would seem that counselors should assist young people at an early age to an increased awareness of their personal value hierarchies, to the improvement of their values, and to the integration of their values and their aspirations and plans.

34

Aspirations and Expectations:

A Reexamination of the Bases

for Social Class Differences in the

Occupational Orientations

*of Male High School Students**

Francis G. Caro
C. Terence Pihlblad

That there is a strong relationship between a person's social class background and his own occupational achievement is well established (e.g. Lipset and Bendix, 1959, pp. 11 ff). A young man from a lower class family is far less likely to move into a professional, technical, or managerial position than is his middle or upper class counterpart. These eventual social class differences in occupational achievement are anticipated by differences in the occupational orientations of male adolescents. Research on high school students consistently shows that lower class boys see themselves moving towards occupations which, in terms of general societal standards, are more modest than those pursued by boys from higher social class backgrounds (e.g. Caro and Pihlblad, 1964; Empey, 1956; Hollingshead, 1949, p. 285; Hyman, 1953, p. 435; Sewell, Haller, and Straus, 1957; R. Stephenson, 1957).

The purpose of the present paper is to examine possible sources of social class differences in the occupational orientations of male youths. Based on a general consideration of possible reasons for the development of commitment to limited objectives, an attempt will be made to account for the relatively modest occupational orientations of lower class young persons.

Goal setting. It is assumed here that persons can and do rate possible goals on a desirability dimension. Some goals are judged to be desirable while others are thought to be undesirable. It is conceiv-

* From *Sociology and Social Research*, 1965, **49**, 464–475.

able that in some cases there is a societal agreement on the preference ordering of some category of goals. Where such an agreement on the ranking of goals exists, it might be anticipated that everyone would strive for the highest possible objective. In reality, however, it may usually be observed that orientation towards the most desirable goal is far from universal. Many if not most persons direct themselves toward more modest objectives.

A distinction may be made between two general sources of limited goal orientations. First, it is possible that an individual's preference hierarchy may be at odds with the general consensus. His notion of what is most desirable may be inconsistent with the majority view. From his perspective, he may be pursuing the highest conceivable objective; but from the societal perspective, he has his sights set somewhat lower.

Limitations in perceived accessibility to desired objectives represent a second general source of departure from high goal orientations. If a person sees that it would be difficult or impossible for him to realize the objective he most desires, he may redirect his energies toward a goal which he believes to be more attainable. He may share general societal notions about what constitutes the most desirable goals, but for practical reasons may direct his behavior toward a more modest objective.

In the first case, the process by which the individual sets his goal is independently different from the general consensus. In the second case, the individual operates within the general preference structure, making adjustments to fit the obstacles which he sees to be standing in his way.

These two general sets of explanations may be posed to account for the less ambitious occupational objectives of lower class youths. On the one hand, there may be class differences in evaluation of the occupational structure; persons with a lower class background may have different ideas about what constitutes desirable work. While the general societal tendency is to prefer white collar work, persons with a lower class background may tend to consider blue collar work more desirable.

On the other hand, lower class youths may share general occupational preferences but perceive preferred occupations to be less accessible than do middle and upper class boys. A belief that admission to high prestige fields is difficult or impossible may discourage development of ambitious occupational objectives. A boy with an interest in a particular white collar job but with limited financial resources, for example, may conclude that he cannot afford the necessary education. He may compromise his ambition by setting his sights on a career in some blue collar field.[1]

Aspirations and expectations. Operationally, the distinction between an occupational aspiration and expectation may be used to attempt to locate the source of limitations in a person's occupational goal orientation. An occupational preference or aspiration (the occupation a person would like to have) may be taken to represent a pure occupational value—uncontaminated by perceived limitations in accessibility. An occupational expectation (the occupation a person thinks he actually will have) may be interpreted as a reality-based compromise with an aspiration. Using a general societal ranking of occupations as a referent, the size of the disparity between level of aspiration and level of expectation may be interpreted as a reflection of a person's perception of access limitations. If there is no difference between level of aspiration and level of expectation, it may be concluded that there is no perception of access

restrictions. In other words, the person believes that what he wants is within reach. But to the extent that the level of expectation is lower than the level of aspiration, it may be concluded that the person perceives access limitations.

Occupational aspirations and expectations, then, should indicate whether class differences in occupational orientation result from differences in occupational values and/or from differences in perception of the accessibility of occupational objectives. A social class comparison of aspirations would test the value hypothesis. A comparison of the relative size of the aspiration-expectation disparity would show differences in perception of accessibility.

An earlier inquiry. Working with the North-Hatt occupational prestige scale, Empey (1956) attempted a social class comparison of the occupational aspirations and expectations of male high school seniors. He reports a positive relationship between the level of the boys' socioeconomic backgrounds and the prestige level of their occupational preferences. Occupational expectations tended to run below aspirations, but a statistically significant difference between aspirations and expectations was found only in the case of *middle* class boys. The size of the aspiration-expectation disparity was not specifically considered.

In showing class differences in occupational aspirations, Empey's data may be interpreted as support for the hypothesis that these are class differences in the manner in which the occupational structure is evaluated. With respect to the possibility of class differences in the perception of accessibility of desired occupations, the data are ambiguous. Support for that hypothesis would have required a larger disparity between level of aspiration and level of expectation for lower than middle and upper class youth. It is possible that Empey's finding of an aspiration-expectation difference only in the case of middle class youths is an artifact stemming from the concentration of his respondents in middle class categories. With more cases in his lower class categories, he might also have found statistically significant differences there.

Current procedures. A recent survey of high school seniors in a metropolitan area provides an opportunity to reexamine the source of class differences in the occupational goals of male students.[2]

---

[1] The two general explanations employed here of possible sources of class differences in the occupational orientations of male high school students have their parallels in contemporary delinquency theory. The possibility of differences in the evaluation of the occupational structure is consistent with Miller's notion of an autonomous lower class culture. See, for example, Kvaraceus and Miller, 1959. The hypothesis that the modest occupational orientations of lower class youngsters stems from the perceived inaccessibility of more highly desired objectives parallels the arguments of a group, which includes Cohen (1955) and Cloward and Ohlin (1960), that members of all classes share common values.

[2] The study was conducted in Jackson County, Missouri, one of six counties in the Kansas City Metropolitan Area, including the central business district, most of the population of the central city, several suburbs, a satellite city, and a rural fringe area.

TABLE 75. MEAN OCCUPATIONAL ASPIRATIONS, OCCUPATIONAL
EXPECTATION, AND ASPIRATION-EXPECTATION DISPARITY FOR
MALE STUDENTS BY SOCIAL CLASS*

9 = highest prestige			1 = lowest prestige	
Social Class	*Number*	*Occupational Aspiration*	*Occupational Expectation*	*Aspiration Expectation Disparity*
Upper	149	7.79	7.58	.21
Middle	447	7.17	6.87	.30
Lower	82	6.26	5.57	.69
Overall Comparisons (analysis of variance)		$a < .01$		$a < .01$
Individual Comparisons (Scheffe) $P < .05$		Upper > Middle Middle > Lower		Upper < Middle Middle < Lower

* Includes only those listing both an occupational aspiration and expectation. The assumption of an interval scale is implicit in the parametric statistics employed here. Strictly speaking, the occupational prestige scale provides ordinal data only. On the basis of generous assumptions, the present occupational aspiration-expectation rankings are treated as if they approximated an interval scale.

Structured questionnaires were administered to all male public high school seniors. In an attempt to measure their occupational preferences or aspirations, students were asked, "What occupation would you *like to have* when you are 25 to 30 years old?" This was followed by an item designed to elicit more realistic information on the students' anticipated or expected occupational positions: "What job or occupation do you think you *actually will have* when you are 25 to 30 years old?" Responses to both items were categorized on the basis of a nine-point scale adapted from the North-Hatt scale of occupational prestige (Reissman, 1959, pp. 401–404). Two criteria were utilized for social class designations: father's occupation (according to North-Hatt rating) and father's education (according to number of years of school completed). Three social class levels were employed in the present analysis:

Upper   Students whose fathers were in high prestige occupations and had at least completed high school;

Middle   Students whose fathers had medium prestige occupations and who had completed at least grade school but no more than two years of college;

Lower   Students whose fathers had low prestige occupations and who had not completed high school.[3]

[3] The terms "upper," "middle," "lower" employed here in connection with social class are intended to designate levels or groupings arbitrarily specified for comparative purposes. They are not necessarily identical to any "real" social class groups.

Only those students whose background characteristics were such that they fell into one of the three "pure" social class categories were included in the present analysis.

Basic findings. The current findings are consistent with previous studies in showing that those from the upper social strata tended to aspire to higher level occupations than did those from lower social class levels (Table 75). Predictably, expectations tended to run somewhat below aspirations. What is of particular interest here is the fact that the present data show a relationship between a student's social class background and the size of the disparity between his occupational aspirations and expectations. The aspiration-expectation disparity for lower class boys are .69 compared to .30 and .21 for middle and upper class boys respectively. Lower class students did not anticipate being able to come as close to realizing desired occupational objectives as did middle and upper class students.

Interpretation. The present data show, then, that differential perception of the accessibility of various occupations contributes to social class differences in the occupational orientations of male high school students. The replication of earlier findings of social class differences in level of occupational aspiration may also be interpreted as support for the differential evaluation hypothesis. The data are consistent with the hypothesis that class differences both in evaluation of the occupational structure and in perception of access to desired occupations contribute to the class differences in occupational orientations.

Balance theory and the present finding of firm evidence for class differences in perceived occupational accessibility, however, suggest an alternate explanation of the observed class differences in occupational aspiration (Heider, 1958). It may be argued that announced aspirations and expectations are not independent. Serious commitment to an occupational goal which is perceived to be unattainable may be a source of considerable personal frustration. Balance theory suggests that an attempt would be made to reduce the disquieting discrepancy. An adolescent considering his occupational future could reduce the imbalance between what he wants and what he thinks he can get by scaling down his aspirations. This process of balancing preferences and anticipations can be cultural as well as individual. A child growing up in a lower class setting may be discouraged by parents and teachers from fostering occupational objectives which are thought to be unattainable. By encouraging development of modest occupational goals, "responsible" adults try to save the young person from eventual occupational disappointment. An attempt is made to deflate aspirations so that they will correspond to what are thought to be realistic expectations.

It may be argued that there are no basic class differences in evaluation of the occupational structure. Observed class differences in occupational aspirations may be attributed, rather, to "expectation drag." Prior to the present inquiry, there may have been a class-based, artificial lowering of aspirations to lessen uncomfortable imbalances between high aspirations and modest expectations.[4]

To establish firm evidence of actual preference for

---

[4] The balance theory argument could also be used to refute the present contention that there are class differences in perceived access to desired occupations. It may be that class differences in occupational values are basic. Because of the strength of their commitment to high occupational achievement, those from high social backgrounds may artificially raise their announced expectations to match their aspirations. Reported aspirations may, then, reflect goal commitment more than they do perception of reality limitations. On the other hand, it can be argued that strong commitment to a goal may itself be instrumental to realization of that goal. The strongly committed person many surmount obstacles which might stymie someone who cared less.

a limited occupational goal, it would be necessary to show that a respondent is committed to a modest goal despite awareness of the accessibility of occupational objectives which, with respect to general societal standards, are preferable. A respondent, for example, may claim to aspire to a particular blue collar job despite a general consensus that white collar jobs are more desirable. To show that he actually prefers the blue collar occupation, it would be necessary to show that although the person recognizes the white collar occupations to be within his reach, he retains a preference for the blue collar job.

Educational achievement and occupational orientation. That in a technologically advanced society success in the occupational sphere is generally linked to educational achievement need not be documented here (e.g. Halsey, Floud, and Anderson, 1961). Data collected as part of the current inquiry are consistent with findings of previous studies in showing that social class and educational achievement are strongly related.[5] On a standardized test of academic achievement, the test performance of young persons from a low social class background was greatly inferior to that of young persons from middle and high social class backgrounds (Table 76). Of those from low social class backgrounds, 55

---

[5] Performance on a standardized test of academic aptitude was used to measure achievement. Information on test score performance was provided by school officials. In the Kansas City school district, a School and College Ability Test was used. Students in other Jackson County high schools took the Ohio Psychological Examination. For the S.C.A.T., individual scores were given a percentile value according to national norms. In the case of the Ohio Psychological, state norms were utilized since no national norms were available. On the assumption that percentile positions on the two instruments are roughly comparable, data from the two tests were combined on a percentile basis. Respondents were divided into three test score groupings of roughly equal size:

High	80th to 100th percentiles,
Medium	50th to 80th percentiles,
Low	1st to 50th percentiles.

TABLE 76. SOCIAL CLASS AND ACADEMIC APTITUDE OF MALE STUDENTS

Social Class	Number	Total Percent	Academic Aptitude Percent		
			High	Medium	Low
Upper	243	100.0	58.0	24.7	17.3
Middle	807	100.0	38.4	34.5	27.1
Lower	170	100.0	15.9	28.8	55.3

$\chi^2 (4) = 103.91$ $P < .001$

TABLE 77. MEAN OCCUPATIONAL ASPIRATION, OCCUPATIONAL
EXPECTATION, AND ASPIRATION-EXPECTATION DISPARITY FOR
MALE STUDENTS BY ACADEMIC APTITUDE*

9 = highest prestige   1 = lowest prestige

Academic Aptitude	Number	Occupational Aspiration	Occupational Expectation	Aspiration Expectation Disparity
High	401	7.79	7.58	.21
Medium	262	7.05	6.50	.55
Low	185	6.12	5.64	.48
Overall Comparisons (analysis of variance)		$\propto < .01$		$\propto < .01$
Individual Comparisons (Scheffe)		H > M		H < M + L
($\propto < .05$)		M > L		M > L

* Includes only those listing both an occupational aspiration and expectation.

percent fell in the low aptitude category. Only 27 percent and 17 percent of the middle and high social class males respectively scored in the low aptitude range. It can be anticipated that these performance differences would affect qualification of students for admission to college and their chances for success there if they should attend. It is likely, then, that inferior academic achievement is an important factor in the low occupational achievement of persons from the lower social strata.

Of immediate interest is the question whether youths see ability as a factor effecting their access to desired occupations. It might be expected that those who do well academically see themselves coming closer to realizing their occupational objectives than those who are scholastically less successful. The relationship between academic aptitude and the size of the disparity between occupational aspirations and expectations is a potential source of evidence.

As shown by Table 77, academic aptitude is related to announced occupational orientation. Those with high aptitude ratings indicated that they aspired to more prestigious occupations than did those with medium aptitude ratings. Those with medium ratings, in turn, claimed to want and expect more prestigious occupations than did those from lower class backgrounds. Of greater interest here is the fact that the size of the aspiration-expectation disparity was related to academic aptitude. Those in the high aptitude grouping saw themselves coming closer to desired occupational objectives than did those in the middle and low aptitude groupings.

Somewhat surprising is the slight suggestion that low aptitude students saw themselves as more successful in realizing desired occupational objectives than medium aptitude students. A possible explanation of the unanticipated optimism of those with low aptitude ratings is that they aspire to occupations for which academic achievement is irrelevant. Lack of academic ability may be perceived as a barrier to desired occupations primarily among those who aspire to high prestige occupations.

In an attempt to determine whether academic aptitude is related to occupational orientation apart from the more basic relationship between social class and occupational orientation, the aptitude comparison was repeated with social class held constant. Mean occupational aspirations for each class and aptitude level are reported in Table 78. At each

TABLE 78. MEAN OCCUPATIONAL ASPIRATION BY
SOCIAL CLASS AND ACADEMIC APTITUDE*

9 = highest prestige   1 = lowest prestige

Social Class	Academic Aptitude			Overall Comparisons (analysis of variance)
	High	Medium	Low	
High	7.96	7.96	5.73	$\alpha < .01$
Middle	6.86	5.88	5.09	$\alpha < .01$
Low	6.75	5.17	4.91	$\alpha < .01$

* Includes only those listing both an occupational aspiration and expectation.

social class level, aptitude was positively associated with announced occupational aspiration; those with high aptitude ratings indicated that they aspired to more prestigious occupations than did those with medium and low aptitude ratings. In the case of aspiration-expectation disparities, the data are powerful enough to show a statistically significant difference among the aptitude levels only in the case of those from high social class backgrounds (Table 79). In the middle and low social class groups, the

TABLE 79. MEAN OCCUPATIONAL ASPIRATION-EXPECTATION DISPARITY BY SOCIAL CLASS AND ACADEMIC APTITUDE*

Social Class	Academic Aptitude			Overall Comparisons (analysis of variance)
	High	Medium	Low	
High	.11	.44	.20	$\alpha < .05$
Middle	.18	.32	.39	Not Sig.
Low	.50	.83	.52	Not Sig.

* Includes only those listing both an occupational aspiration and expectation.

data are only suggestive of a complex relationship between academic aptitude and perceived access to desired occupations. It does appear that high academic achievement tends to encourage confidence in a high occupational orientation. A possible explanation of the responses of those with less ability is that they tend to adopt one of two patterns: (1) they

retain a high occupational-goal orientation and perceive academic weakness as a potential barrier to realization of objectives and (2) they revise occupational aspirations downward to a point where academic deficiencies seem less relevant.

Summary

To account for social class differences in the occupational orientations of male students, two possible sources were considered: (1) independent differences in evaluation of the occupational structure and (2) differences in perception of the accessibility of desired occupations. Observed class differences in the size of the disparity between reported occupational aspirations and expectations were interpreted as firm support for the perceived accessibility hypothesis. Two interpretations were offered for observed social differences in occupational aspirations: (1) in addition to class differences in the perception of access to desired occupations, there are class differences in the evaluation of the occupational structure; and (2) there are no basic class differences in occupational values, but prior to the investigation there had been a class-related, artificial lowering of aspirations to balance realistic expectations. The current data provide no basis for discrimination between these interpretations.

Academic aptitude was considered as an important factor mediating social class differences in occupational orientations. The data suggest that students perceive their academic ability as a factor affecting their access at least to high prestige occupations.

35

Characteristics of

High School Girls Choosing Traditional

or Pioneer Vocations*

Agnes G. Rezler

In spite of the fact that every third worker in the labor force is a woman and that professional employment increased 41 percent from 1950 to 1960, the participation of women in the professions is greatly lagging behind (U.S. Dept. of Labor, 1963, p. 28). Many able girls graduating from high school do not go on to college, and those who do major predominantly in education, nursing, the social sciences, or English. It is particularly in the natural sciences, medicine, engineering, and mathematics that women are outnumbered by men. In 1960 only seven percent of the physicians employed in the United States were women, nine percent of the natural scientists, including mathematicians, and less than one percent of the engineers (U.S. Census, 1960).

This state of affairs can be easily explained by the cultural stereotype according to which a girl may go to college and work for a few years, in a "feminine" occupation, such as teaching, nursing, or secretarial work, until her first child is born. As early as grades 4, 5, and 6, four occupations account for two-thirds of all choices made by girls: teacher, nurse, secretary, and mother (O'Hara, 1962). The primary interest of most girls is a factor called "male association" by Crissy and Daniel (1939) in their study of senior high school girls' replies to the Strong Vocational Interest Blank. Steinmann, Levi, and Fox (1964) showed that while college girls feel that they could combine a career with being a wife and mother, they also feel that men do not want to marry career girls who will continue to work. Hewer and Neubeck (1964) also came to the conclusion that most entering college freshmen accept the traditional role of women and believe that the home will satisfy all of their needs. Consequently, very few girls seek out long and rigorous professional training.

* From *Personnel and Guidance Journal*, 1967, **45**, 659–665.

In view of this fact it seems particularly important to encourage those few girls who are intellectually able, and also motivated, to major in mathematics or the sciences. Since their choice deviates from the cultural stereotype, they are likely to experience doubts and discouragement from parents, teachers, and peers. It is the function of the counselor "to be on the side of the angels": to help those girls to realize their potential. The purpose of this study is to describe the characteristics of the atypical pioneer girl and thus enable the counselor to recognize her early in high school and to support her in her chosen goal.

Within this frame of reference the study will seek answers to the following specific questions:

1. What are the characteristics of the "pioneers" —high school juniors and seniors who wish to be physicians, mathematicians, or natural scientists? Can they be differentiated from the "traditionals"—girls who wish to be nurses or elementary school teachers—on measures of intelligence, achievement, interest, and personality?
2. Besides measures of intelligence, achievement, interest, and personality, can the counselor make use of such additional informaas best- and least-liked subjects, hobbies, and stability of vocational goal, to separate the pioneers from the traditionals?
3. Among the pioneers, can those preferring to be physicians be differentiated from those wishing to be mathematicians or scientists?
4. Among the traditionals, can those preferring to be nurses be differentiated from those wishing to be teachers?

Previous Research

Rossi (1965) has already investigated this problem among college graduates three years after graduation.

She divided these young women into three groups: (1) the homemakers, who had no career goal other than to be housewives; (2) the traditionals, whose long-range career goals were in fields in which women predominate; (3) the pioneers, whose long-range goals were in heavily masculine-dominated fields, such as the natural sciences, medicine, engineering, or business administration. Rossi's first finding was that traditional women were very similar to homemakers: family and social life represented the major arenas in their lives. Traditionals characterized themselves as "dependent" and "socially competitive," while pioneers saw themselves as "dominant" and "occupationally competitive." Pioneers also had less interest in the family, wanted fewer children, were more oriented to ideas, and approved of maternal employment to a greater extent. Being less predisposed to dependence, they were less apt to marry young and were prepared to establish more egalitarian relationships with men and with people older than themselves.

From Roe's studies of male physical scientists and biologists (1951), it appears that what various scientists have in common is superior intellectual, spatial, and mathematical ability and low interest in social activities. They are not antisocial; they are just not interested in other persons to any great extent. Rational controls are important to them and they tend to be persistent rather than aggressive.

All the interest data regarding nurses and teachers agree that nurses are high on social service and scientific interests (M. H. Anderson & McManus, 1942). Hosinski (1965) in a recent study suggests that the nursing role seems to be broad enough to accommodate a range of personality structures and levels of intelligence.

A large number of studies have focused on teachers, who seem to have several characteristics in common with nurses. Since ministering to people is part of both occupations, it is not surprising to find that teachers, as well as nurses, have high social service interest. This pronounced interest in people is particularly strong in elementary teachers and overshadows their interest in the subject matter (J. Shaw, Klausmeier, Luker, & Reid, 1952; Klausmeier, Luker, & Stromswold, 1951). Jackson and Guba (1957) investigated the need structure of female in-service teachers and found the following occupational "syndrome": they were high on deference, order, and endurance, and low on heterosexuality and exhibitionism. M. S. MacLean, Gowan, & Gowan (1955) found elevated K scores on the Minnesota Multiphasic Personality Inventory for all kinds of education students, an indication of the conscientious, responsible, conforming, controlled, and friendly personality.

Method

Subjects. The locale of the study was a suburban Catholic girls' high school in the midwest. The average IQ in that school on the California Test of Mental Maturity is 112 and most of the girls come from middle-class homes. The sample was drawn from the junior and senior classes. Every girl whose current vocational goal was medicine, mathematics, or a natural science was considered a pioneer. Out of 515 juniors and seniors, 14 wanted to go into medicine, 11 into mathematics, and 8 into science. Traditionals were chosen at random from the large group of juniors and seniors who wanted to be nurses or elementary teachers. Fourteen prospective nurses and 19 prospective teachers were selected.

Sources of data. California Test of Mental Maturity (CTMM) scores were used as a measure of intelligence. Cumulative grade-point averages served as the measure of overall achievement in high school. Scores on the Preliminary Scholastic Aptitude Test (PSAT) were used to measure academic aptitude for college.

The Kuder Vocational Preference Record, which yields scores on outdoor, mechanical, computational, scientific, persuasive, artistic, literary, musical, social service, and clerical interests, was administered to juniors and seniors. The Holland Vocational Preference Inventory (VPI) was administered concurrently with the Kuder. The VPI consists of 160 occupational titles and yields 12 scores: 10 personality and two response-set scores. The 10 personality scales are as follows: realistic, intellectual, social, conventional, enterprising, artistic, self-control, aggression, masculinity, and status. The two response-set scores stand for acquiescence and infrequency.

The students' personnel record cards were reviewed to obtain information on their subject matter preferences, hobbies, and stability of vocational goals, based on records from the freshman through the senior year. These recordings served to indicate degree of persistence in vocational goals. Best- and least-liked subjects for elementary school and hobbies were also recorded upon entering high school. Finally, students were interviewed in groups of four to discuss their post-high school plans.

TABLE 80. COMPARISON OF TEST SCORES FOR PIONEERS AND
TRADITIONALS

Tests	Pioneers ($N = 33$)		Traditionals ($N = 33$)		t	p
	Mean	S.D.	Mean	S.D.		
KUDER						
Computational	32.09	8.98	23.42	14.33	3.14	.005
Scientific	48.36	12.28	34.06	13.05	4.60	.005
Social Service	51.33	11.89	61.54	13.23	3.30	.005
HOLLAND						
Infrequency	5.00	2.91	6.61	3.02	2.20	.05
Intellectual	6.93	4.28	3.12	3.28	4.05	.005
Social	5.45	3.16	8.06	3.83	3.00	.005
Self-control	8.96	4.23	10.93	3.12	2.14	.05
Masculinity	6.39	2.27	4.39	3.36	3.51	.005
Status	8.09	3.12	9.39	2.22	1.94	.05
Grade-point average	3.05	.17	2.30	.48	6.50	.005
CTMM IQ	119.03	9.91	110.81	12.09	2.98	.005
PSAT						
Verbal	56.27	6.14	41.42	9.87	6.65	.005
Math.	56.03	9.97	40.96	8.07	7.73	.005

Results

Comparison of pioneers with traditionals. In Table 80 the mean scores of the pioneers are compared with those of the traditionals. Inspection of the table shows highly significant differences on several scales. The pioneers have higher computational and scientific interests and are more intellectual and masculine than the traditionals. They also score higher on the CTMM and on both parts of the PSAT, and receive higher grades. The traditionals outscore the pioneers in social service interest and on the infrequency, social, self-control, and status scales of the Holland VPI. In view of these data, the answer to the first question is a definite affirmative: the pioneers can be differentiated from the traditionals on measures of interest, personality, and academic ability.

In order to answer the second question, changes in vocational choices were considered. Ten out of 33 pioneers had chosen their present vocational goal when freshmen and nine out of these 10 wanted to be physicians. The would-be mathematicians and scientists showed a great deal of fluctuation between the freshman and senior years. Several of these girls remarked somewhat whimsically during their interviews that they probably would end up teaching mathematics or science in high school, because that is a "safe" field for women, although they would not like to teach.

Fourteen out of 33 traditionals had chosen nurs-

ing or teaching when they were freshmen. The nurses were more stable in their vocational goals than the teachers. Several would-be teachers started out with nursing and changed their goals to teaching later. Office work was also a popular early choice for those who later chose teaching.

Since only about one-third of the girls did stick to their freshman vocational goals, one can only conclude that two out of three pioneers, as well as traditionals, are likely to change their goals between the freshman and senior years. Girls who intend to be physicians or nurses are more likely to stay with their early choices than girls who are drawn to mathematics, the sciences, or teaching.

Likes and dislikes for elementary school subjects proved to be unrelated to vocational goals. Mathematics and science are the two most frequently preferred subjects by pioneers as well as by traditionals. Geography elicits only negative votes in both groups. English is disliked by three times as many pioneers as traditionals, but since pioneers named reading as a hobby this may be due to a dislike for grammar and writing compositions. Their hobbies do not help to distinguish pioneers from traditionals, either. The favorite pastime for most of these girls is sports, regardless of their vocational aspirations. About one-fourth of both groups enjoy cooking and sewing; they also like music and reading equally.

In view of these findings, neither hobbies nor preferences for elementary school subjects can serve as guideposts to differentiating pioneers from tradi-

tionals. Persistence of vocational choice is more typical of girls who wish to be physicians, and perhaps
also of nurses. The other girls change their goals
several times during the high school years. Mathematicians and scientists are quite doubtful even in
their senior year, while elementary teachers have
made a firm choice by then.

Comparisons of pioneer subgroups. The next step
is to see whether pioneer subgroups can be established on the basis of test scores. For this reason the
scores of girls preferring medicine were compared
with the scores of girls preferring mathematics and
science. (The latter two groups were combined to
increase the number of cases in this subgroup.)
These comparison are presented in Table 81.

Significant differences between the two pioneer
groups are present on two Kuder and six Holland
scales. Those girls who desire to enter medicine have
higher social service and scientific interests as well as
higher scores on the acquiescence, infrequency, intellectual, social, self-control, and aggressive scales of
the VPI. It has been shown elsewhere that there is a
significant correlation between scientific interest and
intellectual orientation, and between social service
interest and social personality (Rezler, 1967b). The
fact that future physicians are more interested in
helping people than are mathematicians or scientists
is not surprising, but their more pronounced intellectual outlook does come as a surprise. Perhaps the
fact that the medical group has been more steadily
committed to its vocational goal while the mathematicians and scientists are still hesitant about entering a masculine, competitive career produces this
difference. This hesitancy is also reflected in the
significant differences of the two response-set scales.

The higher acquiescence and the lower infrequency
score of the medical group may be interpreted as an
expression of a more determined, positive vocational
outlook with high aspirations and confidence in their
ability to achieve their goals. The higher scientific
interest of the medical group may be attributed
partly to their goal-directness and partly to the
mathematicians' lack of interest in the natural
sciences.

It is noteworthy that these two pioneer groups do
not differ in academic ability or performance: both
are considerably above average. Hence, intelligence
and achievement test scores will not be helpful in
differentiating the future physician from the future
chemist or mathematician. These differentiations
will have to be made on the basis of interest and
personality test scores.

Comparison of traditional subgroups. Finally, the
scores of elementary school teachers and nurses were
compared to obtain an answer to the fourth question: Can traditionals be separated into subgroups?
The results are presented in Table 82.

According to the Kuder scores, prospective
teachers are more interested in literary, computational, and clerical activities than are nurses, while
the latter prefer scientific and outdoor activities
more than do teachers. Since elementary teachers are
responsible for teaching reading, as well as arithmetic, while nurses do not get involved in either
literary or computational tasks in their daily tour of
duty, differences in literary and computational interests fit in well with occupational requirements. But
clerical duties are part and parcel of both professions
and have become increasingly emphasized in nursing, with extensive charting. Perhaps the lack of

TABLE 81. COMPARISON OF TEST SCORES FOR PROSPECTIVE PHYSICIANS WITH
MATHEMATICIANS AND SCIENTISTS

Tests	Medical (N = 14)		Math & Science (N = 19)		t	p
	Mean	S.D.	Mean	S.D.		
KUDER						
Scientific	54.71	7.65	43.68	13.10	3.03	.005
Social Service	55.29	7.54	48.42	13.76	1.83	.05
HOLLAND						
Acquiescence	12.07	4.16	9.11	4.69	2.71	.01
Infrequency	4.14	2.74	5.63	2.95	2.01	.05
Intellectual	9.07	2.70	5.37	4.61	2.89	.005
Social	7.00	3.09	4.32	2.79	2.58	.005
Self-control	7.36	3.97	10.16	4.11	1.78	.05
Aggressive	6.21	3.40	3.63	3.76	2.06	.05

TABLE 82. COMPARISON OF TEST SCORES FOR PROSPECTIVE ELEMENTARY SCHOOL TEACHERS AND NURSES

Tests	Nurses (N = 14)		Elementary Teachers (N = 19)		*t*	*p*
	Mean	S.D.	Mean	S.D.		
KUDER						
Outdoor	36.50	11.73	27.32	10.47	2.32	.05
Computational	18.07	8.14	27.37	16.69	2.11	.05
Scientific	40.14	11.07	29.58	12.85	2.53	.01
Literary	16.71	7.82	22.26	9.60	1.83	.05
Clerical	42.57	14.63	52.58	14.45	1.95	.05
HOLLAND						
Intellectual	5.14	3.84	1.63	1.74	3.19	.005

clerical interest on the part of prospective nurses explains the complaints of many new nurses who find themselves spending more time charting than providing bedside care. The future nurses' preference for scientific activities is further underlined by their significantly higher scores on the Holland intellectual scale. While there is no difference in the measured intelligence and academic achievement of these two traditional groups, the nurses prefer intellectual and scientific tasks. Differentiation between these two groups of traditionals should be based primarily upon interest measures.

Implications for Counseling

From these results it seems clear that prospective pioneers can be separated from traditionals by the time of the junior year in high school. Pioneers have significantly higher academic aptitudes and achievements, accompanied by more-pronounced intellectual and masculine personalities and higher scientific and computational interests. Among the pioneers, physicians are more people-oriented than are mathematicians or scientists, which is reflected in their interest as well as in their personality test scores. Consequently, counselors should watch for these cues to recognize pioneers in general and physicians in particular. The latter group are likely to have made an earlier vocational choice and will have a clearer picture of their professional goal than the former.

Because high school girls are fighting against their own fears as well as against cultural standards when they consider pursuing a pioneer vocation, they need more help from the counselor than just occupational information. Super *et al.* (1963a) emphasized the intimate relationship between the self-concept and vocational development. He emphasized also that "reality factors—the reality of personal characteristics and the reality of society—play an increasingly important part in occupational choice with increasing age, from early adolescence to adulthood." Pioneers need the counselor's help to integrate their self-concepts with reality factors. This is a crucial and difficult task that many adolescents cannot complete successfully on their own and, therefore, many of them decide to subjugate their "personal reality" to "social reality." In the case of pioneers, this may take the form of settling for a teaching career instead of pursuing their real vocational interests.

The counselor's role is more limited with traditional girls. These girls are basically social- and status-oriented in a feminine way; their main goal is marriage and a family. Their needs will be best met by accepting the role of housewife and mother, and they consider teaching or nursing mainly as a stopgap until marriage or as an insurance policy against future emergencies. Since their interests and personality characteristics resemble very closely the population averages, their vocational choice depends chiefly upon the relevant sex stereotypes. As suggested by Roe (1956), personality and interest factors have much smaller differentiating effects on occupational choice in persons who fall within the middle ranges of the population.

36

Social Class, Social Mobility

and Delinquent Behavior*

Gerald J. Pine

Most studies reporting on the relationship between social class status and delinquency denote the greater number of delinquents come from the lower status groups (Burgess, 1952; Dirksen, 1948; Kvaraceus, 1944–45; Maller, 1937; Neumeyer, 1949). Delinquency is usually considered a lower class phenomenon. However, the research reporting a significant relationship between delinquent behavior and lower socioeconomic status has been characterized by a built-in bias, i.e., the use of official delinquency statistics that do not reflect a considerable amount of delinquent behavior. Official delinquency data is biased in favor of upper- and middle-class youth. Middle- and upper-class children are less likely to become official delinquency statistics since their behavior is more frequently handled outside the sphere of formal legal institutions. The middle and the upper classes control various means of preventing detection, influencing official authority, and generally "taking care of their own" through psychiatrists, clinics, and private institutions, thus avoiding the police and the courts—the official agencies (Bloch and Flynn, 1956; Clinard, 1957b; Cohen, 1955; Glaser, 1960; Kvaraceus and Miller, 1959; Nye, 1958; Porterfield, 1946; Wallerstein and Wyle, 1946; Wattenberg and Balistrieri, 1952).

In addition to the built-in bias of official delinquency data, studies reporting on the relationship between social class status and delinquent behavior are characterized by another critical shortcoming: a paucity of empirical material on a significant dynamic of social class—social mobility. What bearing does movement from one social class to another class have on delinquent behavior? What are the implications of vertical movement between classes in regard to norm-violations? The question of social mobility has an important place in the study of social class and its impact on delinquent behavior for two reasons: (1) Social mobility introduces a dynamic feature of possible change into a class system, and (2)

it can alter the structure and patterns of class relationships as the consequences of mobility introduce changes into those close relationships.

It is the purpose of this paper to present the results of a study designed to determine the significance of the relationships between social class status, social mobility status, and delinquent behavior as these relationships exist in a general population of adolescents selected without known delinquency histories.

Study Design

The study was conducted in Old Colony, an urban community located in New England. The sample population included 683 pupils in grades nine through twelve. To avoid the bias of official delinquency statistics, a general population of adolescents was selected. The population of adolescents in a community is not entirely "non-delinquent" even though they are not committed to institutions or treatment agencies. Therefore, in order to determine the distribution and form of delinquent behavior among the social classes it was necessary to start, not with known delinquents, but with a representative sample of boys and girls.

The sample population was stratified into three social class status groups (upper-middle, lower-middle, and lower), three social mobility status groups (up, down, stable), six occupational aspiration groups, and three educational aspiration groups. To accomplish the stratification of the sample, the following instruments were used: Warner's Index of Status Characteristics, a multi-factor mobility scale consisting of eight different factors (the pupil's parental socioeconomic status, his course membership in school, his plans for high school and college education, the plans of his peers for further education after high school, his occupational aspirations, his occupational mobility status, and his academic

* From *Personnel and Guidance Journal*, 1965, **43**, 770–774.

grades), and a questionnaire entitled "Vocational and Educational Data Sheet."

Warner's Index of Status Characteristics includes four factors, each weighted according to their predictive power of social class participation. Ratings are made on the factors of: parental occupation, source of income, type of house lived in, and neighborhood area. The sum of the ratings is placed on a scale and a social class equivalent obtained.

The eight-factor mobility scale was employed in the following manner, e.g., a pupil whose parents belonged to class II (lower-middle), who was enrolled in the college preparatory course, definitely planned to graduate from high school, planned to attend college, whose friends planned on further education after high school, who aspired to enter a profession, had above average grades, and whose occupational mobility direction was up—would be categorized as moving upward. Again, a pupil whose parents belonged to class I (upper-middle), was enrolled in a general course, planned to graduate from high school, wasn't sure about attending college, whose friends definitely did not plan on continuing education after high school, had average grades, aspired to enter a skilled trade, and whose occupational mobility direction was down—this pupil would be categorized as mobile in a downward direction. A pupil whose parents belonged to class III (lower), was enrolled in a commercial course, planned to finish high school but definitely did not plan to go on to college nor did his friends plan on further education, and who aspired to enter a skilled job, whose occupational mobility was stable, and whose grades were average—would be classified as stalled or stable.

The examples above provide neat and clean illustrations of how the mobility scale was used. However, for many pupils not all criteria indicated movement in a single direction—some criteria showed upward movement, other criteria reflected downward or stable placement. In such cases, since the factor of social status position served as the reference point in deciding mobility status, if four of the remaining seven factors pointed in one direction, i.e., upward or downward, the pupil was so classified. Where there was no clear evidence of a definite mobility trend in one of the three possible directions, then a student was classified as being stable.

Information regarding delinquent behavior was collected through the use of an anonymous questionnaire consisting of 120 items designed to obtain a measure of an individual's degree of involvement in several categories of delinquent behavior. From the delinquency inventory 15 scores were obtained for each individual: gross delinquency score, delinquency treatment score, alcohol offenses score, physical assault, property damage, theft, school offenses, familial offenses, motor vehicle offenses, truancy score, narcotics offenses, felonies, misdemeanors, number of offenses, and a group delinquent activity score.

The delinquency inventory was validated by comparing the scores of contrasted groups, a validation procedure used by Nye (1958) in a similar study. Gross delinquency scores[1] were computed for the 320 non-institutionalized adolescent boys who comprised the male population of the study sample. Gross delinquency scores were also computed for a sample of institutionalized adolescents consisting of 108 boys who were in grades seven, eight, and nine at the Lyman School for Boys, Westboro, Massachusetts. The distribution of delinquency scores in two groups "known to be different" shows discrimination between these two groups.

When a gross delinquency score of 110 is used as a cutting point it places 22 institutionalized adolescents below that point and 86 above. The 22 or 20 percent are "misplaced" whereas 80 percent are correctly placed. In the non-institutionalized population 74 boys scored at or above the cutting point, and 246 scored below. Seventy-seven percent are placed correctly and 23 percent incorrectly. Therefore, the delinquency inventory can be said to adequately distinguish between groups known to be different.

Each subject's score on each of the 15 delinquency variables was located on a five-point continuum ranging from "least or no involvement" to "maximum or most involvement." The relationships between social class status, social mobility, and each of the delinquency variables were analyzed by the use of the chi-square technique. The .05 level of probability was used as the criterion of significance.

Results

The following results were evident:

1. No significant relationships were found to exist between social class status and 12 of the 15 delinquency variables (Table 83). Significant relationships were found to exist between social class status and alcohol offenses, felonies, and group delinquent

---

[1] Gross delinquency score is the total sum of weighted responses given for all inventory items.

TABLE 83. A SUMMARY OF CHI-SQUARE TESTS OF SIG-
NIFICANCE BETWEEN SOCIO-ECONOMIC STATUS AND
DELINQUENT BEHAVIOR (WITH 8 DEGREES
OF FREEDOM)

Delinquency Variable	χ^2	*P*
Group Delinquent Activity	109.711	.001
Felonies	27.665	.001
Alcohol Offenses	16.246	.05
Property Damage	15.210	.10
Familial Offenses	14.398	.10
Narcotics Offenses	12.863	.20
Physical Assault	8.389	.50
Delinquency Treatment	7.335	.50
Theft	5.748	.70
Truancy	5.609	.70
School Offenses	5.423	.80
Gross Delinquency Score	4.855	.80
Motor Vehicle Offenses	3.569	.90
Number of Offenses	3.449	.95
Misdemeanors	2.489	.98

activity. Upper-middle class students were found to
be more involved in alcohol offenses and were also
found to participate more in delinquent behavior as
a collective activity than were students from the
other two classes. Proportionately more members of
the lower-middle class and lower class were involved
in felonies than were members of the upper-middle
group.

Among the groups controlled by grade and sex
two relationships were found to be significant. In the
freshman-sophomore sample and the junior-senior
sample upper-middle class members were more involved in alcohol offenses than members from the
other two classes.

TABLE 84. A SUMMARY OF CHI-SQUARE TESTS OF SIG-
NIFICANCE BETWEEN SOCIAL MOBILITY STATUS AND
DELINQUENT BEHAVIOR (WITH 8 DEGREES
OF FREEDOM)

Delinquency Variable	χ^2	*P*
Number of Offenses	167.616	.001
School Offenses	57.700	.001
Delinquency Treatment	51.535	.001
Gross Delinquency Score	43.115	.001
Property Damage	34.431	.001
Misdemeanors	31.660	.001
Theft	30.982	.001
Truancy	30.131	.001
Familial Offenses	27.767	.001
Alcohol Offenses	27.280	.001
Group Delinquent Activity	26.187	.001
Felonies	24.477	.01
Physical Assault	22.308	.01
Motor Vehicle Offenses	16.586	.05
Narcotics Offenses	10.107	.30

2. Surprisingly, no significant relationship was
found to exist between social class status and delinquency treatment scores indicating no preferential
treatment was accorded the offenders of higher
status.

3. Significant relationships were found to exist
between social mobility status and all but one delinquency variable (narcotics offenses)—Table 84. Students moving downwardly in the social structure
were more involved in physical assault offenses,
theft, felonies, school offenses, property damage,
misdeameanors, truancies, motor vehicle offenses,
and alcohol offenses. Proportionately, they had
higher gross delinquency scores and delinquency
treatment scores; they participated in more norm
violations, and their norm violations were more collective type activities than individual. Students
moving upwardly in the social structure were least
involved in the offenses cited and had lower delinquency treatment scores and lower gross delinquency
scores. Students in the stable mobility position were
more heavily involved in familial offenses than
members of the other two classes. Fifty-one of the 60
relationships among the groups controlled by grade
and sex were found to be statistically significant. In
the freshman-sophomore and junior-senior samples,
and in the subgroups of boys and girls, the downwardly moving student is more involved in delinquent behavior than the upwardly moving student
or the student in the stable mobility position.

4. Significant relationships were found to exist
between educational aspirations and 10 of the 15
delinquency variables: misdemeanors, school
offenses, alcohol offenses, motor vehicle offenses,
narcotics offenses, physical assault, truancy, group
delinquent activity, delinquency treatment, and
familial offenses. Students planning to enter college
were least or moderately involved in the delinquency
offenses; adolescents definitely not planning to enter
college were most heavily involved in the delinquency offenses.

5. Significant relationships were found to exist
between occupational aspirations and four of the
delinquency variables. Students who aspired to professional and managerial occupations were more involved in alcohol and familial offenses than students
aspiring to other occupations; they also participated
in more norm violations among the students planning
to become skilled tradesmen, foremen, etc. Narcotics
offenses were participated in by proportionately more
students who had formulated no definite occupational plans and those students who aspired to enter
the professions and management positions.

Conclusions and Implications

The primary conclusion made in this study is that delinquent behavior is less a function of the class an individual is in at the moment and much more a function of the class to which he aspires or toward which he is moving. In examining the relationship between social class and delinquent behavior it is not only important to know what class an individual is in but perhaps more important to know if he is securely located in the class, if he has just managed a toe-hold in the class, or if he has just moved down from a class.

The findings indicate delinquent behavior is not a lower-class phenomenon. However, one aspect of the question of class differential in delinquent behavior which invites further investigation is the relationship between value system and delinquency. Social-class status may be more accurately measured in terms of value systems than in terms of economic factors such as occupation, housing, residence, and income. The lower-class boy moving upward into the middle class may be guided in his behavior by a middle-class value system and, therefore, might be more accurately described as a member of the middle class.

The behavior of the middle-class boy moving downward in the social structure may be influenced primarily by lower-class concerns and he might be more accurately described as lower class. It is quite possible for a child to live in a lower-class neighborhood and in the midst of a lower-class culture and still be considered middle class.

An explanation of the strong relationship between downward mobility and delinquent behavior may be found in Reissman's (1959) hypothesis regarding the psychological consequences of "downward mobility." He suggests that the psychological consequences of "downward mobility" can be channeled away from the individual to avoid injury to self-conceptions and self-repect. The individual imputes to others the blame for his or his family's descent in the social structure. His frustration and his failure are poured into an explanation that implicates society or society's institutions as the cause of it all. Hostile and negative attitudes toward others and toward authority develop.

If the intensity of the psychological consequences of "mobility failure" is in proportion to the degree of failure, then it is not difficult to understand the strength of the relationship between downward mobility and delinquent behavior. Certainly, downward mobility represents the greatest failure in the mobility process. For, in a culture which highly esteems the success value, what constitutes a greater failure than the failure to at least maintain one's status quo in the social structure?

VIII
Citizen

One of the roles an individual is called upon to play is "citizen" of his society. He is expected to feel loyal and patriotic and to obey his society's laws. In a democratic society, he is supposed to participate actively and knowledgeably in politics, at the very least by voting when given the opportunity. Ideally, he also devotes some portion of his time, effort, and resources to the common good.

Training children as citizens is one of the primary functions of American schools. The process begins in the earliest grades and continues through the high school years and beyond. The family is expected to support the school's efforts by bringing up good citizens; and as children grow toward adolescence, formal organizations like the Boys Club and the Campfire Girls contribute to the training in citizenship. By the time a youngster is an adolescent, he has had years of training and is expected to approximate adult citizenship behavior. Indeed, the data on political socialization which we review in this section reveal that for better or worse adolescents do resemble their elders in the role of citizen perhaps more than in any other role. For this reason, we introduce this review of adolescents as citizens with some data on adult Americans.

Political Socialization

The context of the political behavior of American adolescents includes such facts as these: less than two-thirds of adult Americans of voting age turn out for presidential elections; only around 10 percent contribute any money to political campaigns; only around three percent work at all actively in a campaign (Campbell *et al.*, 1960). About three-quarters of American teen-agers' parents consider themselves partisans of the Democrats or the Republicans, and their party identification is decisive for their voting behavior and for their political opinions. Only about one-third of adult Americans approach important political issues with even a guess about the current Administration's stand on that issue; some notion, however, inaccurate, about party differences on these issues; and opinions of their own.

So while the ideology of "good citizen" prescribes political awareness and regular voting, adult behavior differs widely from the ideal. It seems that politics is either not central to an important citizen role or the citizen role itself is not central to American society.

Not that American youngsters are unpatriotic. In a sample of American high school students, 80 percent agreed in 1952 that "there is hardly any-thing lower than a person who does not feel a great love, gratitude and respect for our flag" (Mainer, 1963). Indeed, development of pride in being Ameri-cans and of a firm allegiance to our country precedes adolescence. This al-legiance is infused with and, in part, maintained by a religious affirmation (*Easton and Hess*, 1962).

But few teenagers take interest in political affairs, if their reading habits are any index of their interests. Less than five percent of boys aged 14 to 16 reported reading material having to do with politics outside of their school work, and less than 14 percent of the boys read newspapers. The figures among the 14–16-year-old girls are about the same, but about 25 percent of girls aged 17 and 18 read newspapers and about eight percent read about politics outside of school (Douvan and Adelson, 1966). While the survey of boys did not extend to boys over 16, we may assume that at least as great a proportion of older boys as girls develop interests in reading about politics, because Remmers and Radler (1957) find that, among the high school students sampled in the Purdue Opinion Poll, boys are more politically aware than girls at every level.

A different measure of interest in politics shows a much greater proportion of interested teenagers. Remmers found that 65 percent of ninth-graders, and 78 percent of twelfth-graders said they followed the 1952 political cam-paign to some degree. (Neither the Purdue Opinion Polls nor the Institute for Social Research studies include school dropouts. It seems reasonable to assume that their interest in politics would be lower than the interest of those still in school.)

In general, data on American adolescents' interest in politics suggest that something under 10 percent show a continuing interest in political affairs but about 80 percent, like their parents, are caught up every four years in a presidential campaign which draws their attention to politics.

Lack of interest in political affairs is reflected in adolescents' lack of knowl-edge about current affairs and about government in general. Studies by Dimond (1953), from 1945 to 1949, and by Greenstein (1965) in 1958 permit us to gauge the level of political knowledge among adolescents in Detroit and New Haven, respectively. Dimond found that Detroit youngsters could correctly answer an average of 30 items on a 60-item recognition test of im-portant current national, state, and local figures and events. For example, virtually all the students could identify Harry S Truman as the (then) Presi-dent of the United States, but only 38 percent of the high school boys and 35 percent of the high school girls knew that the legislation recently defeated by a United States Senate filibuster was a civil rights bill. Junior high school students were less knowledgeable than high school students. Dimond con-cludes, "The knowledge of current affairs possessed by the pupils tested by the study was meager" (p. 169). Dimond attributes a marked decline in knowl-edge among adolescents from 1945 to 1949 to a slackening of interest in news generally after the end of World War II.

Greenstein reports that in New Haven 66 percent of the eighth-graders have "a reasonably accurate understanding" of what the President and their Mayor do; 63 percent of what Congress does; 43 percent of what their

Governor does; and 37 percent of what their State Legislature does. Many more eighth-graders are knowledgeable than younger children, and we may presume that political knowledge grows somewhat more widespread as youngsters progress through adolescence. However, the data on knowledge among adults (Campbell *et al.*, 1960) suggest that the ceiling is not far above these eighth-graders.

The combination of a high level of patriotism with low levels of political interest and political knowledge seems to make American adolescents confused and inconsistent on political matters. For example, Mainer (1963) reports that 62 percent of a Purdue Opinion Poll sample felt that "some politicians place too much emphasis upon the principle 'America for Americans' " while 73 percent of these same teenagers opposed any relaxation in the limitations on foreign immigration into this country. A series of studies of teenagers' views on civil liberties (Heath, Maier, and Remmers, 1958; Remmers, 1963) reveal strong libertarian tendencies in some respects (78 percent deny police the right to hold persons in jail without telling them of any formal charges against them) and anti-libertarian tendencies in others (74 percent assert that the police or FBI may sometimes be right in giving a man the "third degree" to make him talk). Although there is evidence that more politically knowledgeable adolescents hold more firm and consistent beliefs in the Bill of Rights, there is no evidence that twelfth-graders are either more knowledgeable or more consistent than ninth-graders (Horton, 1963).

Knowledge about political parties, or even a clear concept of what a party is, does not seem to be necessary for a youngster to declare his allegiance to a party. Most American children declare their allegiance to their parents' party by the time they are 10 years old (*Easton and Hess*, 1962; Greenstein, 1965). The proportion increases through adolescence, Nogee and Levin (1958) finding that about 70 percent of Boston University students who cast their first vote in the 1956 election adhered to their parents' party. Havemann and West (1952) report that 58 percent of a national sample of college graduates identified with the same political party as their fathers; among those who reported that their fathers identified with a party, 85 percent followed their fathers' preference. From 70 percent to 80 percent of a national sample of adults reported that they follow their parents' political party preferences (Campbell *et al.*, 1960).

Changes in party preference do occur, however, and we consider now the conditions under which changes occur among adolescents—although we suspect that most of the changes take place after individuals have left adolescence and have directly experienced changes in their social environment independently from their parents. Middleton and Putney (1963) found that, when college students perceive their parents as not interested in politics, their emotional closeness to the parents bears no relationship to their agreement with the parents' political views. When students believe that their parents are interested in politics, on the other hand, their closeness is directly related to the degree of agreement with their parents' politics. Two related interpretations of these data may be made: when young adults know their parents are interested in politics, they can use this sphere to express their filial loyalty or hostility; or, when they themselves have become interested in politics through their parents' influence, then the partisan role becomes an important part of their statement about their relationship to their origins.

Various researchers have reported that geographic or social mobility leads to shifts in political orientation among adults. However, relatively few adolescents experience such changes independently from their parents. The experience which most nearly approximates such a change is moving from home to residence on a college campus. We have already seen that this change does not generally produce a change in party preference. Sometimes, however, students find themselves on a campus where political affairs are of central concern. Newcomb (1943) describes such a situation in his study at Bennington College. We may conclude from his findings that when students are drawn into associations with students and faculty for whom politics is of major concern, and when their home environment offers little resistance because of lack of concern or closeness, many students will shift in their political orientation and party preference.

Maccoby, Matthews, and Morton (1954) contribute data on the effects of both social mobility and relationships to parents as they affect new voters' allegiance to their parents' party and political values. New voters who report that their parents controlled them rather strictly when they were younger were more likely to desert their parents' party than those who report a moderate degree of parental control. When new voters held occupations of higher status than their fathers, they were more likely to shift from their parents' Democratic allegiance to the Republicans, the dominant party in the social stratum which they were entering. Downwardly mobile or static new voters did not shift so much. In general, however, Maccoby and her associates found that most new voters allied themselves with their parents' party and accepted what they perceived were their parents' political values.

Whether adolescent shifts in political orientation are predominantly shifts to the political left or right is in doubt. Among students at Boston University who shifted in party loyalties, changes occur about equally in both directions (Nogee and Levin, 1958). At Bennington, shifts in political orientation were mainly to the left (Newcomb, 1943). In their survey of students on 16 different campuses, Middleton and Putney (1963) found that students "are far more likely to move to the left of their parents than to the right." We suspect that movement one way or another depends heavily on the political climate in which the shift occurs, indeed, which generates the shift. If college students who shift from their parents' views move largely toward the left, it is probably because the political climate on college campuses is left of the political views held in most of the homes from which students come.

Where comparisons of males with females can be made (Greenstein, 1965; Hyman, 1959; Remmers and Radler, 1957), the following generalizations are possible: males are more knowledgeable and interested in political matters than females, and they are more likely to shift from the parents' party preference and political orientation.

Where age comparisons are possible (Douvan and Adelson, 1966; Greenstein, 1965; Hyman, 1959; Remmers and Radler, 1957), it seems clear that political interest, knowledge, and initiative increase with age, more so among males than females, and that greater increments occur prior to and in early adolescence.

Another aspect of political consciousness develops during adolescence along with increasing political interest, knowledge, and party affiliation, namely, a consciousness of a *political community*. *Adelson and O'Neil* (1966) interviewed 120 suburban Michigan youngsters, aged 11 to 17, asking them to participate in the formation of a hypothetical government. They conclude:

> With advancing age there is an increasing grasp of the *nature and needs of the community*. As the youngster begins to understand the structure and functioning of the social order as a whole, he begins to understand too the specific institutions within it and their relations to the whole. He comes to comprehend the autonomy of institutions, their need to remain viable to sustain and enhance themselves. Thus the demands of the social order and its constituent institutions, as well as the needs of the public, become matters to be appraised in formulating political choices.

37

*The Child's Political World**

David Easton
Robert D. Hess

Framework of Analysis

Most research with regard to adult perceptions of and attitudes towards political reality has been directed to factors operating on adults as such. The underlying assumption is that what adults see and the way in which they feel and behave in politics are outcomes of variables that act upon them as full-fledged members of a political system. This paper adopts what, but for Freud, we might identify as a Platonic or Rousseauan point of view. It assumes that the range of alternative behaviors open to the adult is also intimately related to his experiences as a child and that the kind of political reality the adult perceives and his attitudes about it are restricted by what he has learned during his early years.

Not that these early influences on behavior are absolute in character; under appropriate circumstances the adult is able to escape, transcend or modify his early political inheritance. In politics as in other areas of experience, so-called reality testing continues throughout life. The significance of early impressions is that those values and attitudes acquired in childhood are likely to change much more slowly than those developed through later experience, especially in maturity. If this is so, unless we know something about the values and attitudes with which a person is armed in childhood, we cannot fully understand the matrix within which he interprets and responds to the ongoing stream of political events in adulthood.

The content that is transmitted from older to younger generations in the area of politics we shall call political orientations. They consist of political knowledge, attitudes, and standards of evaluation. The processes through which a young person acquires his basic political orientations from others in his environment we shall call political socialization. Our problem is: With regard to what subjects and through what processes of socialization are basic

* From *Midwest Journal of Political Science*, 1962, **6**, 229–246.

political orientations transmitted from generation to generation in the American political system?

Socialization joins a multiplicity of other factors that contribute to the stability or change of political systems. A political system may establish itself in many ways, as through agreement or force, fission or fusion. But having done so, every system is confronted with the task of coping with the stresses imposed upon it from internal factors, from its social environment such as the economy, culture, or social structure, or from other political systems. To maintain its integrity as a system, even while it is in process of change, it must be able to mobilize support on its own behalf continuously, or at the very least keep the members of the system in a state of indifference. Typical procedures for stimulating support include coercion, perceived satisfaction of the needs and demands of the members, generation of positive motivation and identification through manipulation of symbols, verbal and otherwise, regulation of communications, and the like.

From the point of view of factors contributing to the maintenance or change of a system, there are three major objects with respect to which the extent of consensus or cleavage may prove to be significant. We shall call these the government, the regime, and the political community (Easton, 1957; Easton and Hess, 1961). *Government* refers to the occupants of those roles through which the day-to-day formulation and administration of binding decisions for a society are undertaken. *Regime* is used to identify the slower changing formal and informal structures through which these decisions are taken and administered, together with the rules of the game or codes of behavior that legitimate the actions of political authorities and specify what is expected of citizens or subjects. The *political community* represents the members of a society looked upon as a group of persons who seek to solve their problems in common through shared political structures.

These objects or subject-matters towards which political orientations may be directed constitute three different analytic levels of a political system with respect to which consensus or cleavage may occur. Given the type of political system, it makes a profound difference whether consensus prevails with respect to any or each of the levels. In a democratic system, dispute concerning the occupants of governmental roles and their policies is common and expected; only under very special circumstances will such differences undermine the system as a whole. In a totalitarian system, however, governmental differences typically threaten the regime, although they may have little effect on the political community. But in numerous political systems, such as those characterized by segmentary lineage structures, it is common for sharp cleavage over governmental authorities to leave the regime undisturbed but to lead to the fission of the community and the hiving off of one or more of the antagonists to form independent political systems (see Easton, 1959).

The identification of these analytically separate levels of a political system together with the three types of political orientations provides a way of conceptualizing research with regard to political socialization. When presented in tabular form, this classification offers us a set of nine cells each of which represents a type of orientation acquired by each succeeding generation in a political system. Consensus and cleavage in the area of each cell is postulated as significant for the maintenance and change of a political system, depending upon the specific kind of system being examined and the circumstances under which we find it.[1]

In this theoretical context, the current overemphasis in socialization research on attitudes and behavior related to party position, political ideology, and voting choices tends to freeze inquiry at the governmental level. It thereby serves to distract attention from other important aspects of socialization, if it does not conceal them entirely. In favor of

---

[1] A final point about our theoretical underpinnings. "Maintenance of a system" as used here is not a static concept. We view political life as an ultrastable system of behavior. Unlike conventional interpretations suggested by equilibrium analysis, political systems normally do not respond supinely to the factors operating on them by tending to return to old or move to new positions of equilibrium. Rather, a political system is here interpreted as capable of purposively and selectively acting upon its internal and external social environment, thereby modifying itself, its environment or both in an effort to achieve its goals. Hence we can describe its behavior as ultrastable. It has built-in ways of changing its course of action and may even go so far as to transform its characteristic modes of behavior. In this positive and creative way it may be able to maintain its continuity at one or another of the three levels.

Types of Political Orientations

Levels of a Political System	Basic Political Orientations		
	Knowledge	Values	Attitudes
Community			
Regime			
Government			

problems at the governmental level, we are prone to neglect the need to understand the varying kinds of basic orientations members of a system acquire with regard to the regime and political community.

For example, one vital determinant affecting the probability of a system persisting over time consists of the kinds of attachments or sentiments (attitudes) towards the regime and community induced in young people through the processes of socialization. We have little understanding of the nature of this attachment, its variations, and its developmental pattern as the child matures. Although this is only one among a multitude of new perspectives suggested by this theoretical formulation, it is critical in the functioning of a political system. We shall now turn to an examination of the light that some empirical research we have under way can shed on the nature of these attachments and the underlying socializing processes.

The Formative Years in Politics

The following analysis is based on extensive pre-testing data collected over the last five years and most recently in connection with a national study of over 12,000 elementary school children in selected areas of political socialization. The results of the pre-testing reported here involve certain limitations. For example, they do not take into account important variations due to ethnicity, religion, region, educational systems, family political background, and the like, characteristics that will receive considerable attention in our final study. But our preliminary data do yield some important impressions worth opening up for discussion at this early stage in our research, especially with regard to trends and possible relationships among significant variables.

Existing research on young people has put its main emphasis on the adolescent during his high school years (ages 14–17), perhaps on the assumptions that it is only the older child who displays the first glimmerings of an interest in politics and that this is where political development is likely to occur. Our preliminary investigations bear out neither of these premises. Every piece of evidence indicates that the child's political world begins to take shape well before he even enters elementary school and that it undergoes the most rapid change during these years.

A little-recognized fact is that political learning gets a good start in the family during the pre-school period. When the child first asks his parents a question typical in our society: "Daddy, who pays the policeman?" or "Why can't you park your car there?" and when the father replies: "The city or mayor pays him," or "It is against the law to park there," the child has here received from a trusted source an early and important introduction to politics broadly conceived. In effect he is being gently exposed to the notions that in the given regime there is a difference between public and private sectors of life, that there is a need to obey rules and regulations regardless of individual whim or desire, and that there exists some higher authority outside the family to which even all-powerful parents are subject. Through indirect and casual ways like these, the child at a tender age begins to build up his conception of political life. This is so even though, according to our preliminary data, the words *politics* and *politician* usually do not become part of his vocabulary until he is 11 or 12 years old and even though politics has a relatively low salience compared to school, sports, and other play activities and interests.

Our pre-testing also suggests that by the time the child has completed elementary school, many basic political attitudes and values have become firmly established. What is even more important, and dramatically contrary to expectations and implications of existing literature, it appears that by the time the child enters high school at the age of 14, his basic political orientations to regime and community have become quite firmly entrenched so that at least during the four years of high school little substantive change is visible. In that period his own interest in politics may be stimulated—although our data indicate that the high-point in reported political interest may occur in 7th and 8th grades—and, as we would expect, he learns much more about the structure and practices of government and politics. Formal education bolstered by the mass media is likely to be the source of such knowledge. But for most young people, there is little evidence that fundamental attitudes and values with respect to the regime and political community are any different when they leave high school than they were upon entrance.

The truly formative years of the maturing member of a political system would seem to be the years between the ages of three and 13. It is this period when rapid growth and development in political orientations take place, as in many areas of non-political socialization.

Attachment to the Political Community

By the time children have reached second grade (age seven) most of them have become firmly attached to their political community. Imperceptibly they have learned that they are Americans and that, in a way they find difficult to define and articulate, they are different from members of other systems. As we find in most other aspects of the child's political world, and as we would expect, the responses are highly colored with emotion and occur long before rational understanding or even the capacity to rationalize political orientations are evident.

Thus the sentiments of most children with respect to their political community are uniformly warm and positive throughout all grades, with scarcely a hint of criticism or note of dissatisfaction. When interviewed about where they would like to live for one week, a year or the rest of their lives, some children favor travel for a shorter or longer time. But in most cases it is beyond their capacity to imagine themselves living anywhere other than the United States for the rest of their lives. And a high proportion would not even like to take permanent leave of the immediate places where they happen to live.

One of the processes contributing to this outcome we could easily have anticipated. The feelings initially aroused by immediate but diffuse social objects are extended to include specifically political ones. It would appear that national sentiment, loyalty, patriotism or love of country—all ingredients of attachment to political community—may rest on such unpretentious foundations as these.

In the development of this attachment, the child early learns to admire and cherish those things and persons that are local and close, that form part of his personal experience and are therefore meaningful to him, and that in most cases represent undifferentiated social objects. Thus when the political context of the question is not concealed from the child, and he is asked to list the three best things about

America, children in the lower grades (ages 7–9) consistently speak about such general social objects as their schools, the beauty of their country, its animals and flowers, and the goodness and cleanliness of its people. Very few politically differentiated items appear. Those that do, convey pride in the President, the policeman, the flag, and freedom.[2] The President and policeman are two authority figures with which the child is quite familiar and, at the early grades, just about the only two for most children. Only one impersonal abstract symbol, that of freedom, regularly appears at this age level. The meaning attributed to it is quite non-political and diffuse, however. A person is conceived to be free when he can do whatever he wishes, an appealing thought to the adult dominated child.

Only as the child grows older do the warm feelings already generated with respect to these things of personal significance spread to impersonal political symbols, to differentiated political objects, and to the broader and more inclusive aspects of the political community. Thus although in the higher grades (ages 12–13) children continue to mention schools, the moral worth of people in the United States, and the like, by that time reference to items such as these declines sharply. The majority of responses to the same question now include such specifically political items of an abstract or impersonal character as democracy, government, voting, and elaborations of freedom to mean freedom of speech, press, religion, and choice of occupation. The same pride and positive feelings that were displayed more diffusely at an earlier age are now also invested in a distinctively political direction. The feelings stimulated by the concrete, personally experienced part of the child's immediate world seem to be transferred, as the child grows older, to abstract political symbols. "America" itself as a symbol of the political community now becomes laden with specifically political content, and an early non-political attachment to general social aspects of the community is transformed into a highly political one.

A second process joining forces with fondness for the immediate concrete environment quite unexpectedly proved to be religious in nature. In a secular society that adults have frequently described as essentially materialistic and where adults have sought to maintain a clear separation between church and state, there was little reason for suspecting that in the early grades religious sentiments would be instrumental in generating support for the political community. As it turns out, however, not only do many children associate the sanctity and awe of religion with the political community, but to ages nine or 10 they sometimes have considerable difficulty in disentangling God and country.

In many schools it is customary to pledge allegiance to the flag each morning as classes begin or at other regular intervals.[3] The pledge is brief but it is said in a formal, solemn atmosphere. Levity brings down sanctions from the school authorities and sincerity is approved. The exact procedures associated with the pledge may vary. In some cases the flag is saluted; in others, the right hand is held over the heart. But the repetition of the pledge assumes the character of a ritual.

When the children in grades two and three were interviewed around the question, "To whom do you take the pledge of allegiance?" the answers were distributed among flag, country, and for the single largest minority, God. Not only do we find the explicit statement that God is the object of the pledge, but when probed with regard to its functions, many children interpreted the pledge as a prayer. They saw it as a request either to God or to some unidentified but infinite power for aid and protection. At times it is even understood as an expression of gratitude, again to some unspecified being, for the benefits already received. Only when we reach the fourth or fifth grade in our pretest interviews, and more rapidly thereafter, do we find a tendency for children to stress the pledge as an expression of loyalty to country, solidarity with one's fellows, and an assertion of the need to perform one's duties as a citizen. The religious theme does not disappear entirely, but over the sample it becomes subordinate to the political.

Although our limited data do not permit full interpretation of the processes at work here in linking the child to the political community and its symbols such as the flag, in all likelihood there is an association in the child's mind of the form and feeling tone of religious ritual with the political ceremony of pledging allegiance. Specific invocation of God in the pledge itself would clinch the point for the child.

Religious affect, it appears, is being displaced

[2] Even though children in grade 2 are already able to associate themselves with the label Republican or Democrat, this touches on the regime rather than the community level and will be discussed later.

[3] "I pledge allegiance to the flag of the United States of America and to the Republic for which it stands, one nation under God, indivisible, with liberty and justice for all."

upon political object, less by design than by the natural assimilation of political with religious piety and ritual. We might infer that the depth and peculiar strength of religious sentiments, if only because of their early introduction to the child and numerous social sanctions enlisted in their aid, become subtly transferred to the bond with the political community. The fact that as the child grows older he may be able to sort out the religious from the political setting much more clearly and restrict the pledge to a political meaning, need not thereby weaken this bond. The initial and early intermingling of potent religious sentiment with political community has by that time probably created a tie difficult to dissolve.[4]

Attachment to the Structure and Norms of the Regime

Our pre-testing suggests that, as with regard to the political community, in a relatively stable system such as the United States firm bonds are welded to the structure of the regime quite early in childhood. By the time children reach the 7th and 8th grades, most of them have developed highly favorable opinions about such aspects of the political structure as the Presidency, Congress, or "our government" in general. The Constitution has become something of the order of a taboo that ought not be tampered with in its basic prescriptions. Yet children know very little about the formal aspects of the regime and much less, if anything, about its informal components. How then do they acquire and develop ties to the structure of a regime about which they have negligible and blurred information and equally little understanding?

Our data indicate several things. First, what is most apparent to most children in the realm of politics is the existence of an authority outside the family and school. Second, initially and continuously through the elementary school years, this external authority is specifically represented in the Presidency and the policeman, a local appointed official. Although as the child grows older he becomes increasingly aware of other institutions of authority, such as

the courts, Congress, and local elected officials, the President and the policeman remain extremely visible. And third, emotional rather than rational processes are at work on these cognitions. They enable children to develop favorable feelings for the presidential form of authority in the United States long before they know very much of a concrete nature about it.

Interviews and questionnaires reveal that the first point of contact children are likely to have with the overall structure of authority is through their awareness of the President (see also Greenstein, 1960). When children at a young age are asked in separate items about who makes the laws, runs the country, helps the country most, best represents the government, or, in a political context, who helps you most, the responses consistently favor the President. Authority figures at the lower reaches of the regime, such as the policeman or mayor, will be very familiar to most younger children. On occasion the Senate, Congress or the courts will cross their cognitive horizon. But in general, between the polar extremes of the policeman and the President, it is the rare child in the early grades who sees anything but a truly blooming, buzzing political confusion. For most children at this stage the President *is* the political structure. Even where the child knows about the Vice-President, he is frequently seen as an aid to the President; and the Senate and House of Representatives as well are considered to be subordinate and subject to the orders of the President.

In the acquisition of attachments to the regime as a whole, it turns out to be critical that there is this well defined point in the political structure that is highly visible and important for the children, whether young or old. Without it or some comparable institution we might have difficulty in understanding how the child would be able to formulate some introductory, if crude conception of political authority and some early feelings with regard to its worth. It provides the child with a means for "seeing" the structure in a clear and simple way and possibly identifying with it. Although in the United States the Presidency may be the vehicle for these purposes, in other systems of course we might suspect it to be a king, a chief or a great leader.

In an earlier paper (Hess and Easton, 1960) we have shown that it is likely that the child's attachment to the structure of the regime is mediated through the attitudes he acquires towards this focal point, the Presidency. From grade 2, the earliest grade it was feasible to test, most children in a group

[4] For such political systems as we find in the USSR where religious sentiment is discouraged or in many African societies where religion is not so clearly associated with newly developing political systems, it would be interesting to search for substitute mechanisms that come into play in the early years of the child to mold his sentiments with respect to the political community.

of approximately 350 reported highly positive feelings about the President. When children through grade 8 were asked to compare the President to most men with regard to such personal and moral characteristics as honesty, friendliness, overall goodness, and liking for others, and such performance qualities as his knowledge and application to work, the vast preponderance see him as measuring up to most men or surpassing them. And even when father was compared to the President with regard to these characteristics, few rate father higher, and in some role performance qualities they rank him even lower. In subsequent tests of other children, they uniformly see the President possessed of all the virtures: benign, wise, helpful, concerned for the welfare of others, protective, powerful, good, and honest.

It is not surprising to find that a high percentage of children hold as strongly positive feelings about their father as they do about the President. What is unexpected is that even though the President is subject to intense partisan dispute, children should have at least as high an opinion of the President, and an even higher one with regard to some qualities. As we have shown (Hess and Easton, 1960), part of this can be explained by the increasing capacity of the child, as he grows older, to differentiate the role of President from that of father. But part is probably a function of other socializing processes at work.

These varied processes concern what we have found to be typical ways in which children may respond to all figures of authority. In the first place, children display a strong tendency to generalize attitudes developed in connection with authority in their immediate experience to perceived authority beyond their knowledge and direct contact. The authority figures with which they have earliest and most intimate contact are of course their parents, and it is this image of authority that they subsequently seem to transfer to political figures that cross their vision. The child not only learns to respect and admire political authorities, but with regard to many characteristics sees them as parents writ large.

But more than that is involved. As noted already, maturing children develop the capacity to discriminate between qualities that are appropriate to the role of the President, and they see the latter as quite different from father in these respects. But with regard to those qualities of moral and personal worth already mentioned, even though there is a linear decline for children in successively higher grades, the absolute level of response remains quite high—at or above 50 percent.

These data suggest that in attributing so much personal and moral worth to both parental and political authority the child is responding not to what the authority figures are, but in terms of what he would expect them to be. Parents and President together are reported less in the image of any real parent than of one strongly reflecting the ideal expectations of our culture. Indeed additional testing that had the child compare teacher, father, President, and policeman bears out the broader hypothesis that children tend to view all significant and approved authority, political or otherwise, as similar to an ideal parental model.

The probable consequences of this idealization are apparent. In the first place, it should contribute to the ease with which maturing members of the American political system develop a strong attachment to the structure of the regime. The part that is initially visible and salient for the child represents everything that is good, beneficial, and worth cherishing. In the second place, in so far as feelings generated with respect to the Presidency as a focal point are subsequently extended to include other parts of the political structure—an area that still needs to be investigated—this may well be the path through which members of the system come to value the whole structure. If so, it would be a vital determinant contributing to the stability of the regime.

What still needs to be explained, however, is the origin of this impetus towards idealization. Here our preliminary data permit us to speculate broadly about the nature of the socializing processes.

In part, the high idealization of approved authority may reflect important psychological needs of the child. Confronted with the pervasive and inescapable authority of adults, and realistically aware of his own helplessness and vulnerability, the child must seek some congenial form of accommodation. For a small minority, rebellion, aggression, and mistrust may be the chosen avenues. But for most, adaptation is more likely to take the form of imputing to authority qualities that would permit the child to construe the authority in a most favorable light. By idealizing authority and by actually seeing it as benign, solicitous, and wise, the child is able to allay the fears and anxieties awakened by his own dependent state. A potentially threatening figure is conveniently transformed into a protector. Hence in spite of what he may learn about authority figures, about their foibles and shortcomings, he has a strong incentive to continue to idealize. As our data show, even though as they grow older fewer children hold the same high opinion of the President, the absolute level remains high. The security needs of the child in this way become an important ingredient in the socializing process.

In addition, however, the impetus to idealize authority also has its origin in the learning process itself, that is, in the attitudes children learn from adults. However little it may have been recognized, adults in the United States show a strong tendency to shelter young children from the realities of political life. In many ways it is comparable perhaps to the prudery of a Victorian era that sought to protect the child from what were thought to be the sordid facts of sex and parental conflict. In our society politics remains at the Victorian stage as far as children are concerned. Some adults—and there is reason to believe they are numerous—feel it is inappropriate to let the child know about what is often felt to be the seamy and contentious side of politics. He is too young, he will not understand, it will disillusion him too soon, awareness of conflict among adults will be disturbing, are some of the arguments raised against telling the whole truth. The child has to learn as best he can that in politics the stakes are high, passions are strong, motivations may be less than pure and altruistic, conflict is endemic, and men have the capacity to place self, party or occupation above country. Adults tend to paint politics for the child in rosier hues. And the younger the child the more pronounced is this protective tendency.

What this means is that in addition to learning political ideals from adults the child may also learn to idealize or romanticize politics. For example, some testing at the high school level (ages 14–17) indicates that romantic notions about politics are not fully or largely dissipated even by that stage. The child's inner need to create a benevolent image of authority coincides with and is thereby strongly reinforced by the partial, idealized, and idealizing view of political life communicated to him by protective adults.

But in spite of these forces working in the direction of idealization, our data do suggest that, contradictory as it may seem, at least in some areas the child is quite capable of facing up to the passions and conflict in political life and that he is equally capable of tolerating such stress without succumbing either to cynicism or to disenchantment with political authority. The area of conflict to which the child is particularly exposed at the youngest age is the presidential electoral campaign. In an age of tele-

vision, it is an area which cannot be concealed from him. He is aware of the acrimony of debate over the merits of alternative candidates, and more important, he easily learns that people align themselves on different sides and that it is proper for people so to commit themselves. The child even goes further. Simultaneous with the emergence of high positive affect with regard to the President, it is quite revealing to discover that young as they are, children in the early grades learn to tolerate partisan commitment on their own part and to accept alternative partisanship on the part of others as one of the rules of the game. Partisan differences—and at times even conflict—so generated are not interpreted as hampering the acceptance of the outcome of electoral campaigns, esteem for the victor, or the legitimacy of the authority so established. This constitutes the beginning of what later in life becomes a rather complex set of attitudes and represents an introduction to a major norm of democratic society.

Most children do not become familiar with the term political party until the fourth and fifth grade at the earliest. But before this, as early as the second grade, large numbers are nevertheless able to assert a party identification. In a pre-test sample of about 700 children, a strong majority in each grade from 2 through 8 state that if they could vote they would align themselves with either of the two major parties in the United States. Interviews around responses such as these indicate that in the early grades—the point at which party preference becomes well established—the children may be adopting party identification in much the same way that they appropriate the family's religious beliefs, family name, neighborhood location or other basic characteristics of life.

Nor do most children display partisan feelings in a purely formal way. They seem to be aware of the implications of party preferences as an expression of explicit commitment to a point of view, however superficial their understanding of this point of view may be. Thus of a pre-test sample of over 300 children, a large majority reported that they participated in a partisan spirit in the last presidential campaign by wearing candidate buttons. Most of these children who were in grades 4 through 8 responded that they did so as a way of taking sides or for purposes of helping their candidate win. A minority were less sensitive to the expression of partisan commitment involved, but said they took sides because they thought it was fun to do so, or because they were simply imitating their friends or parents. But they did feel the pressure to adopt a partisan posture, however apolitical its meaning was for them.

But partisanship does not seem to interfere with what we may interpret as the early origins of a belief in the legitimacy of political authority. When some 200 pre-test children were asked whether the candidate who loses an election should ask his followers to help the winner, an overwhelming majority beginning in the early grades and increasing with age responded in the affirmative. The dissenting minority here is of course interesting and needs to be explored.

Thus even though the child idealizes political authority as the result of the socializing processes to which he is exposed, at the same time he acquires regime norms that make it possible for him to tolerate comfortably the campaign conflict surrounding the choice of these authorities. As a result, the attachment to authority achieved through the mechanism of idealization is not disturbed or displaced by electoral passions and cleavage. The importance of this type of socialization for the stability of a democratic regime needs no elaboration.

Conclusion

We have touched on only a few selected topics of socialization of knowledge and attitudes with respect to two major objects, the political community and the regime. We have reported only from tentative and limited preliminary data. But what this theoretically determined approach does reveal is that processes of attachment to the political community and the regime begin at a considerably earlier age than one would expect. The political content that is socialized shows signs of being buttressed by powerful sentiments linked to religion, family, and internal needs of the dependent child. If what is learned early in life is hard to displace in later years, we have here an important increment to our understanding of the sources of stability in the American political system. Comparative research in systems experiencing considerable change and in those developing nations moving toward a unified entity for the first time should help us in better understanding the contribution of socialization to political instability and change.

38

Growth of

Political Ideas in Adolescence:

The Sense of Community*

Joseph Adelson
Robert P. O'Neil

During adolescence the youngster gropes, stumbles, and leaps towards political understanding. Prior to these years the child's sense of the political order is erratic and incomplete—a curious array of sentiments and dogmas, personalized ideas, randomly remembered names and party labels, half-understood platitudes. By the time adolescence has come to an end, the child's mind, much of the time, moves easily within and among the categories of political discourse. The aim of our research was to achieve some grasp of how this transition is made.

We were interested in political ideas or concepts —in political philosophy—rather than political loyalties per se. Only during the last few years has research begun to appear on this topic. Earlier research on political socialization, so ably summarized by Hyman (1959), concentrated on the acquisition of affiliations and attitudes. More recently, political scientists and some psychologists have explored developmental trends in political knowledge and concepts, especially during childhood and the early years of adolescence; the studies of Greenstein (1965) and of Easton and Hess (1961, 1962) are particularly apposite.

Our early, informal conversations with adolescents suggested the importance of keeping our inquiry at some distance from current political issues; otherwise the underlying structure of the political is obscured by the clichés and catchphrases of partisan politics. To this end, we devised an interview schedule springing from the following premise: Imagine that a thousand men and women, dissatisfied with the way things are going in their country, decide to purchase and move to an island in the Pacific; once there, they must devise laws and modes of government.

* From *Journal of Personality and Social Psychology*, 1966, **4**, 295–306.

Having established this premise, the interview schedule continued by offering questions on a number of hypothetical issues. For example, the subject was asked to choose among several forms of government and to argue the merits and difficulties of each. Proposed laws were suggested to him; he was asked to weigh their advantages and liabilities and answer arguments from opposing positions. The interview leaned heavily on dilemma items, wherein traditional issues in political theory are actualized in specific instances of political conflict, with the subject asked to choose and justify a solution. The content of our inquiry ranged widely to include, among others, the following topics: the scope and limits of political authority, the reciprocal obligations of citizens and state, utopian views of man and society, conceptions of law and justice, the nature of the political process.

This paper reports our findings on the development, in adolescence, of *the sense of community*. The term is deliberately comprehensive, for we mean to encompass not only government in its organized forms, but also the social and political collectivity more generally, as in "society" or "the people." This concept is of course central to the structure of political thought; few if any issues in political theory do not advert, however tacitly, to some conception of the community. Hence the quality of that conception, whether dim, incomplete, and primitive, or clear, complex, and articulated, cannot fail to dominate or temper the child's formulation of all things political.

The very ubiquity of the concept determined our strategy in exploring it. We felt that the dimensions of community would emerge indirectly, in the course of inquiry focused elsewhere. Our pretesting had taught us that direct questions on such large and solemn issues, though at times very useful, tended to evoke simple incoherence from the cognitively un-ready, and schoolboy stock responses from the facile. We also learned that (whatever the ostensible topic) most of our questions informed us of the child's view of the social order, not only through what he is prepared to tell us, but also through what he does not know, knows falsely, cannot state, fumbles in stating, or takes for granted. Conse-quently we approached this topic through a survey of questions from several different areas of the schedule, chosen to illuminate different sides of the sense of community.

Method

Sample

The sample was comprised of 120 youngsters, equally divided by sex, with 30 subjects at each of four age-grade levels—5th grade (average age, 10.9), 7th (12.6), 9th (14.7), and 12th (17.7). The sample was further divided by intelligence: At each grade level, two-thirds of the subjects were of average in-telligence (95–110) and one-third of superior intelli-gence (125 and over), as measured by the California Test of Mental Maturity.

This paper will report findings by age alone (to the next nearest age) and without regard to sex or intelligence. We were unable to discover sex differ-ences nor—to our continuing surprise—differences associated with intelligence. The brighter children were certainly more fluent, and there is some reason to feel that they use a drier, more impersonal, more intellectualized approach in dealing with certain questions, but up to this time we have not found that they attain political concepts earlier than sub-jects of average intelligence.

The interviews were taken in Ann Arbor, Michi-gan. We were able to use schools representative of the community, in the sense that they do not draw students from socioeconomically extreme neighbor-hoods. The children of average IQ were prepon-derantly lower-middle and working class in back-ground; those of high intelligence were largely from professional and managerial families. Academic families made up 13 percent of the sample, concen-trated in the high IQ group; 5 percent of the "aver-age" children and somewhat over one quarter of the "brights" had fathers with a professional connection to The University of Michigan. In these respects—socioeconomic status and parental education—the

sample, which combined both IQ groups, was by no means representative of the American adolescent population at large. Yet our inability to find differ-ences between the IQ groups, who derive from sharply different social milieux, makes us hesitate to assume that social status is closely associated with the growth of political ideas as we have measured them, or that the findings deviate markedly from what we would find in other middle-class suburbs.

Reliability

In order to appraise the lower limits of reliabil-ity, only the more difficult items were examined, those in which responses were complex or ambigu-ous. For five items of this type, intercoder reliabili-ties ranged from .79 to .84.

Results

When we examine the interviews of 11-year-olds, we are immediately struck by the common, pervasive incapacity to speak from a coherent view of the political order. Looking more closely, we find that this failure has two clear sources: First, these chil-dren are, in Piaget's sense, egocentric, in that they cannot transcend a purely personal approach to matters which require a sociocentric perspective. Second, they treat political issues in a concrete fash-ion and cannot manage the requisite abstractness of attitude. These tendencies, singly and together, dominate the discourse of the interview, so much so that a few sample sentences can often distinguish 11-year-old protocols from those given by only slightly older children.

The following are some interview excerpts to illustrate the differences: These are chosen randomly from the interviews of 11- and 13-year-old boys of average intelligence. They have been asked: "What is the purpose of government?"

11A. To handle the state or whatever it is so it won't get out of hand, because if it gets out of hand you might have to . . . people might get mad or something.
11B. Well . . . buildings, they have to look over buildings that would be . . . um, that wouldn't be any use of the land if they had crops on it or something like that. And when they have high-ways the government would have to inspect it, certain details. I guess that's about all.
11C. So everything won't go wrong in the coun-try. They want to have a government because they respect him and they think he's a good man.

Now the 13-year-olds:

> 13A. So the people have rights and freedom of speech. Also so the civilization will balance.
>
> 13B. To keep law and order and talk to the people to make new ideas.
>
> 13C. Well, I think it is to keep the country happy or keep it going properly. If you didn't have it, then it would just be chaos with stealing and things like this. It runs the country better and more efficiently.

These extracts are sufficiently representative to direct us to some of the major developmental patterns in adolescent thinking on politics.

Personalism

Under *personalism* we include two related tendencies: first, the child's disposition to treat institutions and social processes upon the model of persons and personal relationships; second, his inability to achieve a sociocentric orientation, that is, his failure to understand that political decisions have social as well as personal consequences, and that the political realm encompasses not merely the individual citizen, but the community as a whole.

1. "Government," "community," "society" are abstract ideas; they connote those invisible networks of obligation and purpose which link people to each other in organized social interaction. These concepts are beyond the effective reach of 11-year-olds; in failing to grasp them they fall back to persons and actions of persons, which are the nearest equivalent of the intangible agencies and ephemeral processes they are trying to imagine. Hence, Subject 11A seems to glimpse that an abstract answer is needed, tries to find it, then despairs and retreats to the personalized "people might get mad or something." A more extreme example is found in 11C's statement, which refers to government as a "he," apparently confusing it with "governor." Gross personalizations of "government" and similar terms are not uncommon at 11 and diminish markedly after that. We counted the number of times the personal pronouns "he" and "she" were used in three questions dealing with government. There were instances involving six subjects among the 11-year-olds (or 20 percent of the sample) and none among 13-year-olds. (The most striking example is the following sentence by an 11: "Well, I don't think she should forbid it, but if they, if he did, well most people would want to put up an argument about it.")

Although personalizations as bald as these diminish sharply after 11, more subtle or tacit ones continue well into adolescence (and in all likelihood, into adulthood)—the use of "they," for example, when "it" is appropriate. It is our impression that we see a revival of personalization among older subjects under two conditions: when the topic being discussed is too advanced or difficult for the youngster to follow or when it exposes an area of ignorance or uncertainty, and when the subject's beliefs and resentments are engaged to the point of passion or bitterness. In both these cases the emergence of affects (anxiety, anger) seems to produce a momentary cognitive regression, expressing itself in a loss of abstractness and a reversion to personalized modes of discourse.

2. The second side of personalism is the failure to attain a sociocentric perspective. The preadolescent subject does not usually appraise political events in the light of their collective consequences. Since he finds it hard to conceive the social order as a whole, he is frequently unable to understand those actions which aim to serve communal ends and so tends to interpret them parochially, as serving only the needs of individuals. We have an illustration of this in the data given in Table 85. Table 85 reports the answers

TABLE 85. PURPOSE OF VACCINATION

	Age			
	11	*13*	*15*	*18*
Social consequences (prevention of epidemics, etc.)	.23	.67	1.00	.90
Individual consequences (prevention of individual illness)	.70	.33	.00	.10

Note.—$\chi^2(3) = 46.53$, $p < .001$. In this table and all that follow $N = 30$ for each age group. When proportions in a column do not total 1.00, certain responses are not included in the response categories shown. When proportions total more than 1.00, responses have been included in more than one category of the table. The p level refers to the total table except when asterisks indicate significance levels for a designated row.

to the following item: "Another law was suggested which required all children to be vaccinated against smallpox and polio. What would be the purpose of that law?"

A substantial majority—about three quarters—of the 11-year-olds see the law serving an individual end—personal protection from disease. By 13 there has been a decisive shift in emphasis, these children stressing the protection of the community. At 15 and after, an understanding of the wider purposes of vaccination has become nearly universal.

Parts and Wholes

Another reflection of the concreteness of younger adolescents can be found in their tendency to treat the total functioning of institutions in terms of specific, discrete activities. If we return to the interview excerpts, we find a good example in the answer given by Subject 11B on the purpose of government. He can do no more than mention some specific governmental functions, in this case, the inspecting of buildings and highways. This answer exemplifies a pattern we find frequently among our younger subjects, one which appears in many content areas. Adolescents only gradually perceive institutions (and their processes) as wholes; until they can imagine the institution abstractly, as a total idea, they are limited to the concrete and the visible.

Table 86 is one of several which demonstrates this. The subjects were asked the purpose of the

TABLE 86. PURPOSE OF INCOME TAX

	Age			
	11	13	15	18
General support of government	.23	.33	.47	1.00*
Specific services only	.23	.17	.23	.00
Do not know	.53	.50	.30	.00

Note.—p level refers to row designated by asterisk.
* $\chi^2(3) = 9.54$, $p < .05$.

income tax. The responses were coded to distinguish those who answered in terms of general government support from those who mentioned only specific government services. (In most cases the services referred to are both local and visible—police, firefighting, etc.) We observe that the percentage of those referring to the government in a general sense rises slowly and steadily; all of the high school seniors do so.

Negatives and Positives

Before we leave this set of interview excerpts, we want to note one more important difference between the 11- and 13-year-olds. Two of the former emphasize the negative or coercive functions of government ("To handle the state . . . so it won't get out of hand"; "So everything won't go wrong . . .").

The 13-year-olds, on the other hand, stress the positive functions of the government—keeping the country happy or working properly. This difference is so important and extensive that we will treat it in depth in a later publication, but it should be discussed at least briefly here. Younger subjects adhere to a Hobbesian view of political man. The citizenry is seen as willful and potentially dangerous, and society, therefore, as rightfully, needfully coercive and authoritarian. Although this view of the political never quite loses its appeal for a certain proportion of individuals at all ages, it nevertheless diminishes both in frequency and centrality, to be replaced, in time, by more complex views of political arrangements, views which stress the administrative sides of government (keeping the machinery oiled and in repair) or which emphasize melioristic ends (enhancing the human condition).

The Future

The adolescent years see a considerable extension of time perspective. On the one hand, a sense of history emerges, as the youngster is able to link past and present and to understand the present as having been influenced or determined by the past. On the other, the child begins to imagine the future and, what may be more important, to ponder alternative futures. Thus the present is connected to the future not merely because the future unfolds from the present, but also because the future is *tractable*; its shape depends upon choices made in the present.

This idea of the future asserts itself with increasing effect as the child advances through adolescence. In making political judgments, the youngster can anticipate the consequences of a choice taken here and now for the long-range future of the community and can weigh the probable effects of alternative choices on the future. The community is now seen to be temporal, that is, as an organism which persists beyond the life of its current members; thus judgments in the present must take into account the needs of the young and of the unborn. Further, the adolescent becomes able to envision not only the communal future, but himself (and others) in possible statuses in that future as well.

The item which most clearly expose the changing meaning of the future are those dealing with education. When we reflect on it, this is not surprising: Education is the public enterprise which most directly links the generations to each other; it is the communal activity through which one generation orients another toward the future. Several questions of public policy toward education were asked; in the answers to each the needs of the communal future weigh more heavily with increasing age. One item runs: "Some people suggested a law which would require children to go to school until they were sixteen years old. What would be the purpose of such a law?" One type of answer to this question was coded "Continuity of community"; these responses stress the community's need to sustain and perpetuate itself by educating a new generation of citizens and leaders. Typical answers were: "So children will grow up to be leaders," and "To educate people so they can carry on the government." Looking at this answer alone (analysis of the entire table would carry us beyond this topic), we find the following distribution by age (see Table 87).

TABLE 87. PURPOSE OF MINIMUM EDUCATION LAW

	Age			
	11	13	15	18
Continuity of community	.00	.27	.33	.43

Note.—$\chi^2(3) = 11.95, p < .01$.

Another item later in the interview poses this problem: "The people who did not have children thought it was unfair they would have to pay taxes to support the school system. What do you think of that argument?" Again the same category, which stresses the community's continuity and its future needs, rises sharply with age as shown in Table 88.

TABLE 88. SHOULD PEOPLE WITHOUT CHILDREN PAY SCHOOL TAXES?

	Age			
	11	13	15	18
Continuity of community	.10	.10	.47	.60

Note.—$\chi^2(3) = 18.61, p < .001$.

Finally, we want to examine another education item in some detail, since it offers a more complex view of the sense of the future in adolescent political thought, allowing us to observe changes in the child's view of the personal future. The question was the last of a series on the minimum education law. After the subject was asked to discuss its purpose (see above), he was asked whether he supports it. Almost all of our subjects did. He was then asked: "Suppose you have a parent who says 'My son is going to go into my business anyway and he doesn't need much schooling for that.' Do you think his son should be required to go to school anyway? Why?"

Table 89 shows that as children advance into adolescence, they stress increasingly the communal

TABLE 89. SHOULD SON BE REQUIRED TO ATTEND SCHOOL THOUGH FATHER WANTS HIM TO ENTER BUSINESS?

	Age			
	11	13	15	18
Yes, education needed to function in community	.00	.23	.43	.77***
Yes, education good in itself	.03	.23	.20	.27
Yes, education needed in business	.40	.47	.23	.13
Yes, prevents parental coercion	.57	.47	.43	.23

Note.—p level refers to row designated by asterisk.
*** $\chi^2(3) = 25.54, p < .001$.

function of education. Younger subjects respond more to the father's arbitrariness or to the economic consequences of the father's position. They are less likely to grasp the more remote, more general effects of a curtailed education—that it hinders the attainment of citizenship. Representative answers by 11-year-olds were: "Well, maybe he wants some other desire and if he does maybe his father is forcing him"; and ". . . let's say he doesn't like the business and maybe he'd want to start something new." These children stress the practical and familial aspects of the issue.

Older subjects, those 15 and 18, all but ignored both the struggle with the father and the purely pragmatic advantages of remaining in school. They discoursed, sometimes eloquently, on the child's need to know about society as a whole, to function as a citizen, and to understand the perspectives of others. Here is how one 18-year-old put it:

> . . . a person should have a perspective and know a little bit about as much as he can rather than just one thing throughout his whole life and anything of others, because he'd have to know different things about different aspects of life and education and just how things are in order to get along with them, because if not then they'd be prejudiced toward their own feelings and what *they* wanted and they wouldn't be able to understand any people's needs.

Older subjects see education as the opportunity to become *cosmopolitan*, to transcend the insularities of job and kinship. For the older adolescent, leaving school early endangers the future in two ways. On the personal side, it threatens one's capacity to assume the perspective of the other and to attain an adequate breadth of outlook; thus, it imperils one's future place in the community. On the societal side, it endangers the integrity of the social order itself, by depriving the community of a cosmopolitan citizenry.

Claims of the Community

We have already seen that as adolescence advances the youngster is increasingly sensitive to the fact of community and its claims upon the citizen. What are the limits of these claims, the limits of political authority? To what point, and under what conditions can the state, acting in the common good, trespass upon the autonomy of the citizen? When do the community's demands violate the privacy and liberty of the individual? The clash of these principles—individual freedom versus the public welfare and safety—is one of the enduring themes of Western political theory. Many, perhaps most, discussions in political life in one way or another turn on this issue; indeed, the fact that these principles are so often used purely rhetorically (as when the cant of liberty or of the public good is employed to mask pecuniary and other motives) testifies to their salience in our political thinking.

A number of questions in the interview touched upon this topic tangentially, and some were designed to approach it directly. In these latter we asked the subject to adjudicate and comment upon a conflict between public and private interests, each of these supported by a general political principle—usually the individual's right to be free of compulsion, on the one hand, and the common good, on the other. We tried to find issues which would be tangled enough to engage the most complex modes of political reasoning. A major effort in this direction was made through a series of three connected questions on eminent domain. The series began with this question:

> Here is another problem the Council faced. They decided to build a road to connect one side of the island to the other. For the most part they had no trouble buying the land on which to build the road, but one man refused to sell his land to the government. He was offered a fair price for his land but he refused, saying that he didn't want to move, that he was attached to his land, and that the Council could buy another piece of land and change the direction of the road. Many people thought he was selfish, but others thought he was in the right. What do you think?

Somewhat to our surprise, there are no strong developmental patterns visible, though we do see a moderate tendency (not significant statistically, however) for the younger subjects to side with the landowner (see Table 90). The next question in the

TABLE 90. WHICH PARTY IS RIGHT IN EMINENT-DOMAIN CONFLICT?

	Age			
	11	13	15	18
Individual should sell; community needs come first	.30	.20	.30	.40
Detour should be made; individual rights come first	.60	.47	.27	.37
Emphasis on social responsibility; individual should be appealed to, but not forced	.10	.17	.17	.07
Ambivalence; individual is right in some ways, wrong in others	.00	.13	.27	.17

series sharpened the issue somewhat between the Council and the reluctant landowner:

> The Council met and after long discussion voted that if the landowner would not agree to give up his land for the road, he should be forced to, because the rights of all the people on the island were more important than his. Do you think this was a fair decision?

The phrasing of the second question does **not** alter the objective facts of the conflict; yet Table 91

TABLE 91. SHOULD LANDOWNER BE FORCED TO SELL HIS LAND?

	Age			
	11	13	15	18
Yes, rights of others come first	.40	.37	.63	.70
No, individual rights come first	.57	.50	.33	.07**
No, social responsibility should suffice	.03	.10	.00	.23

Note.—p level refers to row designated by asterisk.
** $\chi^2(3) = 12.17, p < .01$.

shows decisive shifts in position. It is hard to be sure why: perhaps because the second question states that the Council has considered the matter at length, perhaps because the Council's decision is justified by advancing the idea of "the people's rights." Whatever the reason, we now see a marked polarization of attitude. The younger subjects—those 11 and 13—continue to side with the landowner; those 15 and 18 almost completely abandon him, although about one quarter of the latter want to avoid coercion and suggest an appeal to his sense of social responsibility.

The final question in the series tightened the screws:

> The landowner was very sure that he was right. He said that the law was unjust and he would not obey it. He had a shotgun and would shoot anyone who tried to make him get off his land. He seemed to mean business. What should the government do?

The landowner's threat startled some of the subjects, though in very different ways depending on age, as Table 92 shows: The younger subjects in

TABLE 92. WHAT SHOULD GOVERNMENT DO IF LAND-OWNER THREATENS VIOLENCE?

	Age			
	11	13	15	18
Detour	.60	.63	.37	.10
Government coercion justified	.23	.27	.57	.83

Note.—$\chi^2(3) = 29.21$, $p < .001$.

these cases did not quite know what to do about it and suggested that he be mollified at all costs; the older subjects, if they were taken aback, were amused or disdainful, saw him as a lunatic or a hothead, and rather matter-of-factly suggested force or guile to deal with him. Nevertheless, this question did not produce any essential change in position for the sample as a whole. Those older subjects who had hoped to appeal to the landowner's social conscience despaired of this and sided with the Council. Otherwise, the earlier pattern persisted, the two younger groups continuing to support the citizen, the older ones favoring the government, and overwhelmingly so among the oldest subjects.

These findings seem to confirm the idea that older adolescents are more responsive to communal than to individual needs. Yet it would be incorrect to infer that these subjects favor the community willy-nilly. A close look at the interview protocols suggests that older adolescents choose differently because they reason differently.

Most younger children—those 13 and below—can offer no justification for their choices. Either they are content with a simple statement of preference, for example: "I think he was in the right"; or they do no more than paraphrase the question: "Well, there is really two sides to it. One is that he is attached and he shouldn't give it up, but again he should give it up for the country." These youngsters do not or cannot rationalize their decisions, neither through appeal to a determining principle, nor through a comparative analysis of each side's position. If there is an internal argument going on within the mind of the 11- or 13-year-old, he is unable to make it public; instead, he seems to choose by an intuitive ethical leap, averring that one or the other position is "fair," "in the right," or "selfish." He usually favors the landowner, because his side of the matter is concrete, personal, psychologically immediate, while the Council's position hinges on an idea of the public welfare which is too remote and abstract for these youngsters to absorb. Even those few children who try to reason from knowledge or experience more often than not flounder and end in confusion. A 13-year-old:

> Like this girl in my class. Her uncle had a huge house in _____, and they tore it down and they put the new city hall there. I think they should have moved it to another place. I think they should have torn it down like they did, because they had a law that if there was something paid for, then they should give that man a different price. But then I would force him out, but I don't know how I'd do it.

What we miss in these interviews are two styles of reasoning which begin to make their appearance in 15-year-olds: first, the capacity to reason consequentially, to trace out the long-range implications of various courses of action; second, a readiness to deduce specific choices from general principles. The following excerpt from a 15-year-old's interview illustrates both of these approaches:

> Well, maybe he owned only a little land if he was a farmer and even if they did give him a fair price maybe all the land was already bought on the island that was good for farming or something and

he couldn't get another start in life if he did buy it. Then maybe in a sense he was selfish because if they had to buy other land and change the direction of the road why of course then maybe they'd raise taxes on things so they could get more money cause it would cost more to change directions from what they already have planned. [Fair to force him off?] Yes, really, just because one person doesn't want to sell his land that don't mean that, well the other 999 or the rest of the people on the island should go without this road because of one.

In the first part of the statement, the subject utilizes a cost-effectiveness approach; he estimates the costs (economic, social, moral) of one decision against another. He begins by examining the effects on the landowner. Can he obtain equivalent land elsewhere? He then considers the long-range economic consequences for the community. Will the purchase of other land be more expensive and thus entail a tax increase? Though he does not go on to solve these implicit equations—he could hardly do so, since he does not have sufficient information—he does state the variables he deems necessary to solve them.

The second common strategy at this age, seen in the last part of the statement, is to imply or formulate a general principle, usually ethico-political in nature, which subsumes the instance. Most adolescents using this approach will for this item advert to the community's total welfare, but some of our older adolescents suggest some other governing principle—the sanctity of property rights or the individual's right to privacy and autonomy. In either instance, the style of reasoning is the same; a general principle is sought which contains the specific issue.

Once a principle is accepted, the youngster attempts to apply it consistently. If the principle is valid, it should fall with equal weight on all; consequently, exceptions are resisted:

> I think that the man should be forced to move with a good sum of money because I imagine it would be the people, it said the rights of the whole, the whole government and the whole community, why should one man change the whole idea?

And to the question of the landowner's threatening violence: "They shouldn't let him have his own way, because he would be an example. Other people would think that if they used his way, they could do what they wanted to." Even a child who bitterly opposes the Council's position on this issue agrees that once a policy has been established, exceptions should be resisted:

> Well, if the government is going to back down when he offers armed resistance, it will offer ideas to people who don't like, say, the medical idea [see below]. They'll just haul out a shotgun if you come to study them. The government should go through with the action.

The Force of Principle

Once principles and ideals are firmly established, the child's approach to political discourse is decisively altered. When he ponders a political choice, he takes into account not only *personal* consequences (What will this mean, practically speaking, for the individuals involved?) and pragmatic *social* consequences (What effect will this have on the community at large?), but also its consequences in the realm of *value* (Does this law or decision enhance or endanger such ideals as liberty, justice, and so on?). There is of course no sharp distinction among these types of consequences; values are contained, however tacitly, in the most "practical" of decisions. Nevertheless, these ideals, once they develop, have a life, an autonomy of their own. We reasoned that as the adolescent grew older, political principles and ideals would be increasingly significant, and indeed would loom large enough to overcome the appeal of personal and social utility in the narrow sense.

To test this belief we wanted an item which would pit a "good" against a "value." We devised a question proposing a law which, while achieving a personal and communal good, would at the same time violate a political ideal—in this case, the value of personal autonomy. The item ran: "One [proposed law] was a suggestion that men over 45 be required to have a yearly medical checkup. What do you think of that suggestion?" The answer was to be probed if necessary: "Would you be in favor of that? Why (or why not)?" Table 93 shows the distribution of responses.

The findings are interesting on several counts, aside from offering testimony on the degree to which good health is viewed as a *summum bonum*. The 11-year-olds, here as elsewhere, interpret the issue along familial and authoritarian lines. The government is seen *in loco parentis*; its function is to make its citizens do the sensible things they would otherwise neglect to do. But our primary interest is in the steady growth of opposition to the proposal. The

TABLE 93. SHOULD MEN OVER 45 BE REQUIRED TO HAVE A YEARLY MEDICAL CHECKUP?

	Age			
	11	13	15	18
Yes, otherwise they would not do it	.50	.07	.00	.03***
Yes, good for person and/or community	.50	.80	.70	.60
No, infringement on liberties	.00	.13	.27	.37**

Note.—p level refers to row designated by asterisk.
** $\chi^2(3) = 11.95$, $p < .01$.
*** $\chi^2(3) = 33.10$, $p < .001$.

basis for opposition, though it is phrased variously, is that the government has no business exercising compulsion in this domain. These youngsters look past the utilitarian appeal of the law and sense its conflict with a value that the question itself does not state. These data, then, offer some support to our suggestion that older adolescents can more easily bring abstract principles to bear in the appraisal of political issues. Strictly speaking, the findings are not definitive, for we cannot infer that all of those supporting the law do so without respect to principles. Some of the older adolescents do, in fact, recognize the conflict implicit in the question, but argue that the public and personal benefits are so clear as to override the issue of personal liberties. But there are very few signs of this among the younger subjects. Even when pressed, as they were in a following question, they cannot grasp the meaning and significance of the conflict; they see only the tangible good.

Discussion

These findings suggest that the adolescent's sense of community is determined not by a single factor, but by the interaction of several related developmental parameters. We should now be in a position to consider what some of these are.

1. *The decline of authoritarianism.* Younger subjects are more likely to approve of coercion in public affairs. Themselves subject to the authority of adults, they more readily accept the fact of hierarchy. They find it hard to imagine that authority may be irrational, presumptuous, or whimsical; thus they bend easily to the collective will.

2. With advancing age there is an increasing

grasp of the *nature and needs of the community.* As the youngster begins to understand the structure and functioning of the social order as a whole, he begins to understand too the specific social institutions within it and their relations to the whole. He comes to comprehend the autonomy of institutions, their need to remain viable, to sustain and enhance themselves. Thus the demands of the social order and its constituent institutions, as well as the needs of the public, become matters to be appraised in formulating political choices.

3. *The absorption of knowledge and consensus.* This paper has taken for granted, and hence neglected, the adolescent's increasing knowingness. The adolescent years see a vast growth in the acquisition of political information, in which we include not only knowledge in the ordinary substantive sense, but also the apprehension of consensus, a feeling for the common and prevailing ways of looking at political issues. The child acquires these from formal teaching, as well as through a heightened cathexis of the political, which in turn reflects the generally amplified interest in the adult world. Thus, quite apart from the growth of cognitive capacity, the older adolescent's views are more "mature" in that they reflect internalization of adult perspectives.

4. We must remember that it is not enough to be exposed to mature knowledge and opinion; their absorption in turn depends on the growth of *cognitive capacities.* Some of the younger subjects knew the fact of eminent domain, knew it to be an accepted practice, yet, unable to grasp the principles involved, could not apply their knowledge effectively to the question. This paper has stressed the growth of those cognitive capacities which underlie the particular intellectual achievements of the period: the adolescent's increasing ability to weigh the relative consequences of actions, the attainment of deductive reasoning. The achievement of these capacities—the leap to "formal operations," in Piaget's term—allows him to escape that compulsion toward the immediate, the tangible, the narrowly pragmatic which so limits the political discourse of younger adolescents.

5. In turn the growth of cognitive capacity allows *the birth of ideology.* Ideology may not be quite the right word here, for it suggests a degree of coherence and articulation that few of our subjects, even the oldest and brightest, come close to achieving. Nevertheless there is an impressive difference between the younger and older adolescents in the orderliness and internal consistency of their political perspectives. What passes for ideology in the younger respondents

is a raggle-taggle array of sentiments: "People ought to be nice to each other"; "There are a lot of wise guys around, so you have to have strict laws." In time these sentiments may mature (or harden) into ideologies or ideological dispositions, but they are still too erratic, too inconsistent. They are not yet principled or generalized and so tend to be self-contradictory, or loosely held and hence easily abandoned. When younger subjects are cross-questioned, however gently, they are ready to reverse themselves even on issues they seem to feel strongly about. When older subjects are challenged, however sharply, they refute, debate, and counterchallenge. In some part their resistance to easy change reflects a greater degree of poise and their greater experience in colloquy and argument, but it also bespeaks the fact that their views are more firmly founded. The older adolescents, most conspicuously those at 18, aim for an inner concordance of political belief.

These then are the variables our study has suggested as directing the growth of political concepts. We must not lean too heavily on any one of them: The development of political thought is not simply or even largely a function of cognitive maturation or of increased knowledge or of the growth of ideology when these are taken alone. This paper has stressed the cognitive parameters because they seem to be so influential at the younger ages. The early adolescent's political thought is constrained by personalized, concrete, present-oriented modes of approach. Once these limits are transcended, the adolescent is open to influence by knowledge, by the absorption of consensus, and by the principles he adopts from others or develops on his own.

A Developmental Synopsis

We are now in a position to summarize the developmental patterns which have emerged in this study. It is our impression that the most substantial advance is to be found in the period between 11 and

13 years, where we discern a marked shift in the cognitive basis of political discourse. Our observations support the Inhelder and Piaget (1958) findings on a change from concrete to formal operations at this stage. To overstate the case somewhat, we might say that the *11-year-old* has not achieved the capacity for formal operations. His thinking is concrete, egocentric, tied to the present; he is unable to envision long-range social consequences; he cannot comfortably reason from premises; he has not attained hypothetico-deductive modes of analysis. The 13-year-old has achieved these capacities some (much?) of the time, but is unable to display them with any consistent effectiveness. The *13-year-olds* seem to be the most labile of our subjects. Depending on the item, they may respond like those older or younger than themselves. In a sense they are on the threshold of mature modes of reasoning, just holding on, and capable of slipping back easily. Their answers are the most difficult to code, since they often involve an uneasy mixture of the concrete and the formal.

The *15-year-old* has an assured grasp of formal thought. He neither hesitates nor falters in dealing with the abstract; when he seems to falter, it is more likely due to a lack of information or from a weakness in knowing and using general principles. His failures are likely to be in content and in fluency, rather than in abstract quality per se. Taking our data as a whole we usually find only moderate differences between 15 and 18. We do find concepts that appear suddenly between 11 and 13, and between 13 and 15, but only rarely do we find an idea substantially represented at 18 which is not also available to a fair number of 15-year-olds.

The *18-year-old* is, in other words, the 15-year-old, only more so. He knows more; he speaks from a more extended apperceptive mass; he is more facile; he can elaborate his ideas more fluently. Above all, he is more philosophical, more ideological in his perspective on the political order. At times he is consciously, deliberately an ideologue. He holds forth.

39

Age and Sex Patterns of Social Attitudes*

A. C. Rosander

The Maryland youth survey, the final report of which is now available (Bell, 1938), was concerned not only with the social and economic characteristics of youth 16 to 25 years of age, but with their attitudes toward important social and economic questions.

One of the most significant aspects of these data on attitudes is how the latter changed as the youth increased in age. The data are extensive, since for each of the nine age-groups between 1300 and 1600 youth were interviewed, about equally divided between the sexes. While age is the major factor under consideration, the effect of sex will be included in all but a few questions. How the attitudes of youth from different types of home and educational backgrounds change as they grow older is a question of basic significance for which data are available, but a treatment of it is beyond the scope of this discussion.

Some of the attitudes which we shall discuss will represent overt behavior, while others will represent what are commonly called beliefs or opinions. In the former category are included drinking intoxicating beverages to any degree, voting at the last opportunity, and attending church. In the latter group are attitudes toward war, child labor, government relief for the unemployed, government regulation of minimum wages and maximum hours in business and industry, the election of capable men to public office, and sex education in the schools. The attitude of all youth toward the economic value of his schooling, and the attitude of employed youth toward the wages which he was receiving at the time of the interview, which was during the Summer or Fall of 1936, were also investigated.

[*Author's note:* The data in this survey were obtained from personal interviews of a judgment sample of 13,528 youths chosen by interviewers using a controlled selection method. It is not a probability sample (which we would use today), and hence the data cannot be interpreted by means of the theory of probability and mathematical statistics, which requires certain conditions be met such as random and independent selection of individuals. This does not invalidate the data, but it does mean we cannot get as much out of the data as we otherwise could. However, the judgment sample yields satisfactory data in cases where frequency of an attitude is about the same in all age and sex groups. Furthermore, some bias in this sampling method is reduced (but not entirely eliminated) by tabulating proportions by age-sex groups. Sampling, however, is only one source of variation in the data. Major sources of nonsampling variation in the data are: (1) the phrasing of the question since changing only one word may greatly influence responses; (2) the variation within and between interviewers requiring careful training in a standard procedure; and (3) nonresponse from those who have no attitudes or refuse to reveal their attitudes. In this survey these sources were given careful consideration and considerable effort made to minimize their influence.]

Kind and Level of Government Relief

The youth were questioned with regard to the kind and level of relief, if any, that the government should provide the needy unemployed. By health and decency level was meant something more than that necessary for food, housing, and clothing such as money to maintain health and provide for an occasional movie. The data indicate that among male youth, eight percent were opposed to any form of government relief, 89 percent favored government work relief, while 81 percent believed relief should be on a health and decency level. The corresponding percentages among female youth were nine, 88, and 83, respectively.

Minimum Wages and Maximum Hours

The responses to the question "In reference to the fixing of minimum wages and maximum hours, to what degree should the government participate?" showed that 54 percent of each sex was in favor of such a measure applied to all business and industry. The proportion of youth who indicated the four

* From *The Journal of Educational Psychology*, 1939, **30**, 481–496.

TABLE 94. ATTITUDE TOWARD GOVERNMENT REGULATION OF MINIMUM WAGES AND MAXIMUM HOURS IN BUSINESS AND INDUSTRY—MARYLAND, 1936

	Percent with specified attitude[1]									Percentage base	
	Yes, in all business		Yes, in some business		No regulation at all		No opinion				
Age	Male	Female	Male	Female	Male	Female	Male	Female		Male	Female
16	51.7	55.4	23.7	18.0	16.0	13.0	8.6	13.6		776	724
17	53.3	48.8	23.4	23.6	16.5	13.1	6.8	14.5		722	686
18	56.0	55.5	22.1	19.6	15.7	14.3	6.2	10.6		712	761
19	50.4	50.8	21.4	20.8	17.0	11.3	11.2	17.1		863	771
20	53.8	57.2	22.6	16.8	15.7	12.1	7.9	13.9		810	820
21	50.8	57.2	23.0	14.6	18.1	14.5	8.1	13.7		817	785
22	56.3	54.8	20.7	19.7	15.0	13.1	8.0	12.4		695	681
23	58.2	56.0	17.2	18.9	14.7	12.2	9.9	12.9		639	588
24	57.7	54.2	18.1	18.9	13.4	12.9	10.8	14.0		789	731
Total	54.1	54.5	21.4	18.9	15.8	13.0	8.7	13.6		6823	6547

[1] Within each age group the four percentages for each sex add to 100.0.

major responses to the question, and the number of youth on which these percentages are based, are shown in Table 94. The favorable attitude of these youth relative to government regulation of minimum wages and maximum hours is almost as prevalent in one age-sex group as in another.

An eight percent absolute range in variability of proportions occurs in each sex group; this is about twice as great as that observed for the relief questions, and at a lower magnitude. In addition it appears that the older male youth (22 to 24 years), probably because a greater proportion is employed, to the extent of four percent are more in favor of this type of government regulation than are the younger male youth.

It is significant to note that more than half the youth in all the groups of voting age were in favor of a more far-reaching law than the one passed by Congress in June, 1938.

Child Labor

By child labor is meant the gainful employment of children under 16 years of age. The question used by the interviewers was as follows: "Under what circumstances, if any, should government permit the gainful labor of children under 16 years of age?" The total number of male and female youth answering this question in each age group, and the proportions indicating the responses specified in the column headings are shown in Table 95.

TABLE 95. ATTITUDE TOWARD THE GAINFUL EMPLOYMENT OF CHILDREN UNDER SIXTEEN YEARS OF AGE—MARYLAND, 1936

	Percent of each age-sex group[1]									Percentage base	
	No child labor		If family needs financial aid		Under other permissive circumstances		Under any circumstance				
Age	Male	Female	Male	Female	Male	Female	Male	Female		Male	Female
16	44.2	52.0	37.7	37.3	12.7	7.5	5.4	3.2		764	713
17	47.8	46.5	35.4	39.9	12.8	9.6	4.0	4.0		718	676
18	49.6	52.6	35.0	34.7	11.6	9.9	3.8	2.8		708	755
19	43.1	47.6	40.6	39.3	11.4	10.4	4.9	2.7		854	760
20	51.0	48.1	32.7	38.1	12.3	11.0	4.0	2.8		798	804
21	49.5	49.0	34.3	36.6	11.9	11.5	4.3	2.9		810	787
22	47.4	45.8	37.2	38.0	12.0	13.3	3.4	2.9		685	677
23	47.0	47.7	32.9	35.4	14.9	14.8	5.2	2.1		630	579
24	44.5	51.7	34.9	31.7	17.6	13.9	3.0	2.7		774	725
Total	47.1	49.1	35.7	36.8	13.0	11.2	4.2	2.9		6741	6476

[1] Within each age group the four percentages for each sex add to 100.0.

While the fluctuation of percentages by age covers an eight percent band, and a slightly higher proportion of the female youth is opposed to child labor, still no age bias exists among the female youth, although there probably is some bias in the male youth from 20 to 24 years of age. This may be due to the fact that a greater proportion of farm workers was included in ages 23 and 24 than in the younger age groups.

Sex Education in Schools

The question as to whether sex information should be offered in the school was answered in the affirmative by approximately three-fourths of all the youth. Several points are to be observed from the data given in Table 96.

The first two ages for the male youth are on a slightly lower level than the average of the remaining seven ages. For the female youth the 16-year-old group is definitely lower than the average and gives evidence of an upward trend, while the 23- and 24-year-old groups tend to be somewhat higher than the other groups. The difference of 11 percent between the 16-year-olds and the 23-year-olds is real, and cannot be explained by sampling fluctuations. However, between the ages of 17 and 22, there is no trend, but only an attitude plateau.

Another characteristic is the widening gap between the sexes beyond 20 years of age which may be explained to some degree by the larger proportion of married female youth than married male youth in these upper age groups, who as a result of marriage may have become conscious of the need for definite sex education.

Opinion Toward War

Youth were asked their opinion toward war and, on the basis of the responses, were classified by the interviewers according to their principal reaction. One of these categories was the statement or its equivalent that "war is needless and preventable." With regard to this specific response the data in Table 96 show some very interesting relationships.

The approximately constant difference of 12 percent between the two sexes shows that sex and not age is the significant factor in this case. Even so, more than half of the male youth expressed this attitude toward war. Whether the downward trend observable in both sexes beyond the age of 21 continues into the late twenties and thirties is an interesting but unanswered conjecture. The narrow range of proportions for the female youth in contrast with the greater fluctuations in those of male youth, shows that the former, regardless of age, represent a more homogeneous attitude group than the latter. It is interesting to compare this question which does not show an age trend with the other war question in which youth were asked what they would *do* in

TABLE 96. ATTITUDES TOWARD HOW CANDIDATES FOR PUBLIC OFFICE ARE ELECTED, TOWARD WAR, AND TOWARD SEX EDUCATION IN THE SCHOOLS—MARYLAND, 1936

Percent and number of each age-sex group with specified attitude

| Age | "Candidates are not elected by merit" | | "War is needless and preventable" | | | | "Yes, have sex education in the schools" | | | |
| | Percent | Percentage base | Percent | | Percentage base | | Percent | | Percentage base | |
			Male	Female	Male	Female	Male	Female	Male	Female
16	28.5	1514	52.9	67.0	781	730	71.7	70.6	782	732
17	31.5	1423	57.0	67.6	723	691	69.9	73.7	727	696
18	30.6	1483	57.0	66.1	711	762	76.7	78.3	717	766
19	29.6	1656	54.3	67.7	867	780	72.9	73.4	873	783
20	31.4	1643	54.9	66.8	810	826	77.6	77.7	814	829
21	34.1	1620	56.6	68.8	818	794	73.3	75.5	824	796
22	31.3	1401	55.4	67.8	702	695	71.3	75.3	704	697
23	32.3	1242	51.9	65.4	642	595	75.7	81.9	646	596
24	31.7	1546	52.2	64.5	797	743	74.3	78.2	802	744
Total	31.1	13528	54.7	66.9	6851	6616	73.6	76.0	6889	6639

case war was declared, in which an age variation was discovered. (See Table 99.)

Candidates for Public Office

The last of the questions which illustrated a constant trend of proportions by age is that in which youth stated his attitude as to how candidates were elected to public office. We report here that group of youth who thought that candidates were elected not on the basis of personal merit to fill the office competently, but by such means as "pull," money, false promises, political machines. The various proportions for each age, both sexes combined, are shown in Table 96. With the exception of the 16-year-olds who are slightly low (two and six-tenths percent below the mean), and the 21-year-olds who are slightly high (three percent above the mean) no age group deviates very much from 31 percent.

Attitudes Showing Changing Proportions by Age

Drinking.—Drinking as defined in the survey meant taking intoxicating beverages to whatever degree however slight; no attempt was made to distinguish drinking on special occasions, moderate drinking, or extreme drinking. Data were obtained not only with regard to those who drank and those

who did not, but also the division of the latter group into those who were not opposed to drinking in contrast to those who were opposed. The proportion of each sex at each age group who answered in one of these three specified ways is shown in Table 97.

The trend of the proportions indicates that opposition to drinking as here defined decreases as age increases, among female youth as well as among male youth. The former group never becomes as predominately tolerant as the latter group, but the general trend is the same.

Since the drinking group among female youth make a net absolute gain of 26.5 percent between the ages of 16 and 24, this means that the group opposed to drinking lost members to the drinking group as age increased. The same trend is also true of the percentages for male youth. This inference as well as the others made elsewhere in this discussion obviously are based upon the assumption that an age group is representative of any preceding age group when the latter reaches the age in question.

Most of the absolute gain in drinking among male youth occurred between the ages of 16 and 21; among female youth between 17 and 20. With the two sexes combined, 32 percent of the 16-year-olds stated they drank, while 64 percent of the 24-year-olds gave a similar answer. The fact that both curves of percentages are flattening out after the age of twenty is reached suggests that this type of behavior is a development of the late teens; it is possible, of course, that additional gains are made during ages beyond 24.

TABLE 97. ATTITUDE OF YOUTH TOWARD DRINKING INTOXICATING BEVERAGES (PERCENT OF EACH AGE-SEX GROUP)[1]—MARYLAND, 1936

| | Drinks[2] | | Does not drink | | | | Percentage base | |
| | | | Not opposed | | Opposed | | | |
Age	Male, percent	Female, percent	Male, percent	Female, percent	Male, percent	Female, percent	Male	Female
16	37.6	26.1	41.3	41.7	21.1	32.2	777	723
17	44.6	27.7	34.9	39.5	20.5	32.8	716	693
18	53.3	39.0	28.2	33.6	18.5	27.4	709	758
19	61.5	43.4	23.1	28.5	15.4	28.1	864	771
20	63.8	51.4	21.9	25.4	14.3	23.2	805	820
21	70.1	53.5	19.6	26.6	10.3	19.9	818	779
22	71.6	54.1	17.7	26.6	10.7	19.3	700	684
23	68.3	55.2	20.6	26.1	11.1	18.7	637	587
24	74.8	52.6	17.5	29.8	7.7	17.6	795	732
Total	60.7	44.7	24.9	30.8	14.4	24.5	6821	6547

[1] The three sex groups within each age add horizontally to 100.0 per cent.

[2] This means drinking to any extent or degree however slight.

Table 98. Frequency of Church Attendance—Maryland, 1936

Percent of each age-sex group[1]

Age	Never		Holidays only		Once a month		Once a week		Percentage base	
	Male	Female	Male	Female	Male	Female	Male	Female	Male	Female
16	10.7	8.6	12.9	11.8	16.1	14.1	60.3	65.5	782	730
17	12.7	11.2	14.0	11.4	22.3	20.0	51.0	57.4	726	695
18	14.8	10.3	16.6	14.8	19.3	18.7	49.3	56.2	716	765
19	17.6	13.8	17.9	15.6	22.1	23.5	42.4	47.1	871	783
20	17.7	13.9	20.7	18.0	24.2	22.7	37.4	45.4	811	828
21	18.0	18.4	22.1	18.9	25.2	22.0	34.7	40.7	822	793
22	21.2	16.1	22.2	19.8	23.6	23.1	33.0	41.0	703	696
23	20.3	15.3	23.7	18.8	24.0	24.1	32.0	41.8	645	596
24	22.0	17.9	26.3	21.4	25.1	22.9	26.6	37.8	801	742
Total	17.2	14.0	19.6	16.7	22.5	21.2	40.7	48.1	6877	6628

[1] Within each age group the four percentages for each sex add to 100.0.

Voting.—Information relative to whether or not the youth eligible to vote had voted at the last opportunity, and the reasons why the non-voters did not vote were obtained from 4184 youth, 22, 23, and 24 years of age. In most cases the last opportunity was a Spring or Fall election prior to the presidential election of 1936. Of these youth 37 percent of the 22-year-olds, 60 percent of the 23-year-olds, and 67 percent of the 24-year-olds had voted at the last opportunity. Of the entire group 55 percent voted while 45 percent did not.

Of those who did not vote 44 percent gave lack of interest as the reason. This class increased from 35 percent for the 22-year-olds, to 51 percent for the 23-year-olds, and to 52 percent for the oldest group. On the other hand, 24 percent of the youth gave no reason at all for not voting, but this class decreased from 35 percent to 16 percent to 11 percent for the three age groups, respectively.

Church Attendance.—Youth were asked to indicate how often during the preceding 12 months they had attended church. These responses were classified into four groups: (1) Those who did not attend once, (2) those who attended on holidays only, (3) those who attended on the average once a month, and (4) those who attended on the average once per week. The proportions at each age for each sex that fell into each of these groups are shown in Table 98.

The most marked change—and this appears to be true for each sex—is the steady decrease in the percentage of youth attending church once a week, and the increase in the proportions attending church less

often or never. At age 24 male youth are almost equally divided among the four classes; while at this same age female youth show a leveling-off tendency relative to the early ages, but it is not so marked as that for the male youth. For both male and female youth about half of the absolute loss in the percentage of those going to church weekly took place between the ages of 16 and 19.

War Action.—Youth were asked not only to express their opinions toward war, but also to state what action they believed they would take in case war were declared by this country. The age and sex proportions for each category of response are given in Table 99.

That both age and sex are factors influencing expressed war action is clearly evident from the data. Not only is there a steady decline in proportions of "volunteers" for each sex, but at every age the sex difference is pronounced, the female youth having the smaller proportions of war enthusiasts. The opposite position of refusing to go, or trying not to go, shows the reverse trend, the proportions by age increasing for each sex, with the female youth having the larger proportions of refusals.

With regard to the attitude "go if drafted" some, but not much, age difference is observable; sex is apparently a factor, with the female youth somewhat less inclined toward this view. Obviously, there is a correlation between proportions of responses, since if they are high for one response they must be low for other responses.

The diverging trend of the sex lines as age increase for both volunteers and refusals, indicates that

TABLE 99. WAR ACTION YOUTH INDICATED HE WOULD TAKE IN CASE WAR WERE DECLARED[1]—
MARYLAND, 1936

Percent in each age-sex group[4]

Age	Volunteer		Go if drafted[2]		Refuse to go[3]		Other action		Does not know		Percentage base	
	Male	Female	Male	Female	Male	Female	Male	Female	Male	Female	Male	Female
16	46.5	34.5	38.3	40.8	10.3	14.8	1.2	1.6	3.7	8.3	780	731
17	39.6	29.5	46.7	44.9	8.9	17.9	1.5	0.9	3.3	6.8	723	692
18	37.4	29.7	47.8	41.4	9.9	19.6	0.6	2.0	4.3	7.3	715	765
19	36.7	28.2	47.9	42.0	10.0	18.4	0.8	1.9	4.6	9.5	869	781
20	33.0	23.5	47.9	45.6	13.4	20.1	1.9	1.2	3.8	9.6	812	826
21	34.4	21.4	46.7	42.3	12.4	23.8	1.1	2.6	5.4	9.9	815	791
22	31.1	20.6	50.5	41.6	13.8	24.3	1.2	2.9	3.4	10.6	701	690
23	32.3	18.2	49.5	47.9	13.1	25.6	1.1	1.5	4.0	6.8	644	593
24	28.4	16.9	51.6	45.8	15.1	26.5	1.5	2.0	3.4	8.8	800	739
Total	35.5	24.8	47.4	43.5	11.9	21.1	1.2	1.9	4.0	8.7	6859	6608

[1] Girls answered with regard to what they believed their sweethearts, brothers, or husbands should do.

[2] Or if invasion threatened.

[3] Includes those who would seek exemption, or perform only non-combatant service.

[4] Within each age the percentages for each sex add to 100.0.

as age increases female youth become more rapidly anti-war than do the male youth.

While the female youth show the most pronounced attitudes relative to this question, they also show regularly for each age about twice the proportion of uncertain action as do the male youth.

[*Author's note:* Table 99 illustrates the difficulty of getting a valid behavioristic statement of attitude toward war when the circumstances surrounding a specific war are missing. There appears to be no generalized attitude toward war as such since the refusal rates in 1936 in Maryland clearly did not exist five years later when World War II began. This is even more clearly brought out by the refusal rates of religious groups: 29 percent of Jewish youth declared that they would refuse to go to war compared to 14 percent of Catholic youth (Bell, 1938, p. 246); yet, far from refusing to fight in World War II, Jewish youth had turned strongly pro-war by the time the United States joined the battle.]

Wages Received.—The attitude of the employed youth toward their own weekly wages indicated the general extent of dissatisfaction among youth relative to the wages they received. The evidence is clear that as age increased the proportion who believe that they are paid what they are worth declined from 57 percent at age 16 to 37 percent at age 24. Correlatively the proportions who stated they were under-

paid increased from 31 percent to 49 percent for the same age range.

The trend by age for a particular occupation or field would throw further light on this question, but in the absence of that the following occupational differences will be cited: Among the female employed youth the groups showing the greatest amount of wage dissatisfaction were the teachers and the textile factory machine workers, 60 percent of each stating that they were underpaid. Beauticians and bookkeepers showed the lowest proportions: 27 and 25 percent, respectively. Among the skilled or semi-skilled male employed youth the textile factory machine workers showed the greatest dissatisfaction (71 percent) while the clothing factory machine workers and truck drivers ranked lowest (39 percent).

Economic Value of Schooling.—The effect of experience on youth's attitude toward the economic value of his own schooling is clearly shown by the data. While the proportion who saw little or no economic value in his schooling increased by age from 20 to 30 percent, those who thought it was of great or considerable value dropped from 63 to 48 percent, most of which took place between the ages of 16 and 19. This suggests the disillusioning effect of experience in the employment market.

Sex Education in the Elementary Grades.—The answers to the question "If sex education should be given in the school at what level should it begin?" showed a fair proportion of both male and female youth in favor of beginning it somewhere in the elementary-school grades. The percentages of youth in favor increased from 15 to 23 for the male group, and from 18 to 32 for the female group, as age increased from 16 to 24 years. At every age the proportion in favor was from three to 10 percent higher among the female youth than among the male youth, revealing a sex as well as an age difference with regard to this question.

Interpretation

Approximately constant proportions appear to be associated with certain verbal opinions and beliefs which can be taken on at a relatively youthful age. This can be done because no direct personal behavior is involved in holding the belief. It may be that many social and economic opinions and beliefs acquire adult proportions of acceptance even before the teen age is reached. Opinions which are widely discussed and deliberately taught in the home and elsewhere are likely to be of this type.

The fact that certain verbal attitudes are held as commonly among 16-year-olds as among 24-year-olds suggests the need of determining the trend of the line beyond these limits. The formation of social attitudes of national and international importance is not limited to the older or to the so-called "mature" ages over 21. They are as prominently held by those in their early teens. If it can be shown that certain basic social and economic attitudes are formed in the four, six, or eight years prior to the age of 16, then the challenge to parents and to teachers is indeed great.

The attitudes whose proportions change with age are not the verbal opinions but the more behavioristic patterns which, obviously, involve overt behavior relative to that of others. Possibly this difference reflects the growing change in values which youth acquire as they compare social and economic realities which they meet with childhood teachings and taboos. The attitudes toward drinking and sex education in the elementary grades appear to be reactions against mores of long standing. The decline in church attendance may grow out of increasing social and economic obligations and the corresponding change in interests arising therefrom. To what extent it represents a breaking away from parental control, to what extent it means that youth formerly received social and emotional benefits from the church which they are now obtaining in other ways, we cannot say.

One possible explanation of the change in attitude toward war, slight as it is, may be that the older youth are more conscious of something to live for. It is well known that recruiting appeals draw the younger unemployed and otherwise footloose male much easier than his older married and employed brother. While there appears to be an appreciable increase in the opposition to war as the age of youth increases, still this group is relatively small, accounting for no more than one-quarter of the whole.

Economic security increasingly becomes a problem of major concern to these youth as they grow older. Their attitude toward the economic value of their schooling, and that of employed youth toward their own wages, presumably show the effects of experience in the economic world. In any case, it appears that as age increases the tendency is to put a higher evaluation on oneself and a lower rating on schooling.

40

Peer Group and School
and the Political Socialization Process*

Kenneth P. Langton

The role of education as a significant political socialization process is widely accepted among social scientists and educators. Numerous studies point to positive correlations between education level and political cognition and participation. But beyond this point agreement ends. While many studies have demonstrated with varying degrees of certitude the formal role of curriculum and the teacher in the socialization process, the inconclusive and contradictory nature of the findings has led many students of socialization to a closer examination of the less formal environment of the school. (For a concise summary of this problem and related bibliography, see J. S. Coleman, 1965, pp. 18–25). Yet only a few studies have examined the influence of the informal school environment upon political socialization (Levin, 1961; Ziblatt, 1965).

The purpose of this paper is to examine empirically the impact of the class climate in peer groups and schools upon the reinforcement or resocialization of political attitudes and behavior patterns.

The major questions are as follows:

1. What is the relationship between the class homogeneity-heterogeneity of peer groups and schools and the isolation of lower class students from the political and economic norms of higher class students? For example, do homogeneous class peer groups and schools reinforce the political culture of the working class while heterogeneous class environments tend to resocialize lower class students in the direction of norms held by students of higher classes?

2. Does the heterogeneous class climate of both the peer group and school have a cumulative effect upon the resocialization of working class political attitudes and behavior patterns?

3. What are the cross-cultural implications of these findings for the conscious manipulation of the school environment?

* From *The American Political Science Review*, 1967, **61**, 751–758.

While these questions are of sufficiently broad scope to be amenable to empirical testing in any political culture in which class cleavages exist, the primary source of data for this study is a national sample of 1287 students in government aided secondary schools in Jamaica, W. I. In addition, tangential comparative data on the influence of the class climate of the school is available from a survey of 1349 primary and secondary school students in Detroit, Michigan.[1]

The Peer Group

The influence of the group upon the perceptions and expressed opinions of an individual is one of the better documented generalizations in the small group literature. James S. Coleman (1961) has shown in a striking manner the power of a particular group—the student peer group—in setting the values of its members. When we turn to more manifestly political orientations, Theodore Newcomb (1943) has demonstrated that college peer or prestige groups may play an important role in the political resocialization process.[2]

Yet perhaps one of the foremost functions of the peer group is to transmit the culture of the wider society of which it is a part. While student peer groups may have a subculture of their own, they also teach the adult subculture of which they are a part and reinforce the norms and social patterns held by adult society (Havighurst and Neugarten, 1962, Ch. 5). Social class, religious and ethnic subcultures may

[1] I wish to thank Drs. Roberta S. Sigel and Irving S. Sigel for the use of their data, which was gathered from selected Detroit secondary and primary schools in 1964 during their study of school children's reactions to the assassination of President Kennedy. See Sigel, 1965.

[2] Unfortunately, peer group is a term frequently used without definition. It does not always refer to a primary or face-to-face group, but is often applied to age, grade, and social class cohorts. In this study peer group refers to a face-to-face group of "best friends."

be transmitted through the peer group. A child who grows up in a working class family learns the working class way of life. If he enters a school peer group composed of students from the same social class, this may act to reinforce as well as elaborate the class attitudes and expectations learned in the family. Certainly one of the first points to emerge in Hyman's summary of the literature (1959) is the relative lack of discontinuity in the socialization process in the United States. While there are some discontinuities, more impressive is the general acceptance of the political orientations of one's parents.

In addition to its function of transmitting or reinforcing the political culture of the society, the peer group may provide a social system in which the individual learns new attitudes and behavior. For example, while the peer group with a homogeneous class composition may operate to reinforce the class way of life and associated political orientations of its members, a lower class boy or girl entering a heterogeneous class peer group where he interacts with individuals of higher social status may learn from them new ways of behaving and believing. The literature suggests that these higher status peers become especially significant as models for identification. For they are in a position to reward peer group members of lesser status by bestowing approval, attention, leadership, or by giving permission to participate in peer activities or to employ certain symbols. Harvey and Rutherford (1960) found that American students in heterogeneous class peer groups tended to change their opinions in the direction of those held by high status peers. However, this shift was greater in higher (6th–11th grades) than in lower grades. The development of status consciousness may be in corollary of the maturation process. Remmers and Radler (1957) found in their national sample of high school students that respondents from low income homes were more likely to defer to the opinions of their peers on racial questions than were students from medium and high income homes. Low income students were also much more likely than respondents from higher income families to follow the dictates of their peers, rather than to suggest new group activity (1957, pp. 234–237).

Interestingly enough, C. Stendler (1949) found that in Brasstown out-of-school peer groups were generally more class-homogeneous, while there was a greater tendency for peer groups within the school to cross class lines. This suggests that the environment of the school peer group may be more conductive to

resocialization than informal cohort groups outside the school.

From the preceding discussion we might hypothesize that the primary function of homogeneous class peer groups in the political socialization process is to reinforce the way of life and associated political orientations of the lower classes, and thus, to maintain the political and cultural cleavages which may exist between the classes. On the other hand, we hypothesize that heterogeneous class peer groups function in an important way to resocialize the attitudes of working class members in the direction of those held by higher class peers.

Class Differences

A consistent pattern of political cleavages exists among the different social stata in Jamaican society.[3] In light of the research findings in the United States on the relationship between objective class and political attitudes, we are not surprised to find that working class students in Jamaica are less committed to the values of a "democratic" order, less supportive of the civil liberties of Jamaican minority groups, less positively oriented toward voting, and less politicized than the middle and upper classes.[4] The relationships are linear in all cases with the working and upper classes occupying opposite ends of the various dependent indices.[5]

[3] The respondent's social class is determined by his position on an index composed of two items: the occupation of his father and the education of his mother or father—whichever is higher.

[4] It has generally been found that working class Americans have a lesser sense of citizenship duty and disposition to vote than those of higher social class (Lane, 1959, pp. 157–160). H. H. Remmers found that American high school students from the lower classes were less tolerant of civil liberties and less disposed toward the norms of a "democratic" order than were higher class students (*Purdue Opinion Poll*, 1951; Remmers and Radler, 1957, ch. 8).
Both Remmers and Radler (1957) and Herbert Hyman (1959, pp. 34–35) found that students from low income and less educated families were less politicized than their counterparts from higher classes. The reader should note that the degree of class polarization on comparable political attitudes and issues can be expected to vary between countries. Moreover, it has been demonstrated that the degree of class polarization within a country is likely to vary over time (Converse, 1958).

[5] Respondents were asked to express their opinions on the following:
General "democratic" orientation: "Economic security is more important than political freedom."
Attitude toward voting: "It won't matter much to me if I vote or not when I become an adult."
Civil Liberties: "Rastafarians (Jamaican minority group) should not be allowed to hold public meetings even if they gather peacefully and only make speeches."
Politicization: Respondents' placement on this index was

We also attempted to ascertain the respondents' general orientation toward the political system as a whole. This diffuse system affect is likely to vary between political cultures and, more important for the purposes of this study, negative and positive affect may vary between social classes. Almond and Verba found, for example, that in the United States, Great Britain, and Mexico, the better educated respondents and those with higher status occupations were more likely to express general pride in their respective political systems than those from lesser statuses (Almond and Verba, 1963, p. 105).

In contrast, we find in Jamaica a linear increase in positive affect or "support" and a decrease in ambivalence as social class decreases.[6] There appears to be no relationship between class and negative affect or "opposition" to the political system (Table 100).

TABLE 100. RELATION OF SOCIAL CLASS TO SYSTEM LEGITIMACY

Social Class	System Legitimacy			
	Support	Ambivalent	Oppose	N
	%	%	%	
Working Class	40	46	14	462
Middle Class	33	53	14	272
Upper Class	28	55	17	338

The relatively stronger support and less political cynicism found among the working class may be explained in terms of the class appeals and charismatic nature of Jamaican politics. Both political parties in Jamaica have attempted to project the charisma of their respective leaders before the working class Jamaican. Most successful political campaigns combined charisma with "bread and butter" trade union issues and directed these appeals primarily at the working class. While the lower classes may have found these appeals and the tone of Jamaican politics particularly appealing it has only tended to make the more educated classes increasingly suspicious of "mob appeal" and intolerant of alleged corruption and waste.

Students were also asked to give their opinions on certain economic issues. Some of these issues impinge directly upon class prerogatives.[7] Generally the findings conform to the well documented proposition that the lower class is less economically "conservative" than the higher classes.

Although class polarization on the preceding political and economic issues is not as dramatic in Jamaica as it might be in other societies, given the consistent pattern of political cleavages that exist among the different social strata, we hypothesized that peer groups and schools play an important role in reinforcing or resocializing the political and economic attitudes of the working class.

*Peer Class Environment
and Political Socialization*

The class homogeneity-heterogeneity of the respondent's peer group was based on his perception of the peer environment. We asked respondents if their best friends in school were in the same social class as they or a different social class. House and money criteria were given as class indices. Students who responded "the same social class" were categorized as being members of homogeneous class peer groups. Those who responded that their best school friends were from "higher, lower as well as the same social class" as theirs were categorized as being members of heterogeneous class peer groups. If, for example, a respondent had an objective working class status and he said that his best friends in school were members of the same social class as he, then for the purposes of this study, that school peer group will be considered to be of a generally homogeneous working class nature.

It is possible that there may be some systematic distortion in the respondent's perception of group homogeneity. However, research findings reported later in this paper appear to minimize the problem. We found, for example, that when we use a more objective indicator of class homogeneity in the school, the effects of the class atmosphere were similar to those reported for the peer group.

When we examine the relationship between class homogeneity-heterogeneity of peer groups and the attitude of working class respondents on the political

---

determined by the frequency in which they discussed politics with members of the family, school friends, teacher or politicians; and the frequency in which political articles were read in the national newspaper.

The differences between the position of the working class and the upper class on each of these four variables was 15, 12, 13, and 13 percent, respectively.

[6] Respondents were asked: "Do you feel politics and the government have been honest, dishonest, neither honest nor dishonest?" This question might also be considered a measure of general political cynicism.

[7] The questions were as follows:

"Do you think the rich should give up their privileges?"

"Should there be some upper limit, such as 10,000 pounds a year, on how much any one person can earn?"

variables discussed above, we find that homogeneous peer groups function to reinforce working class political norms and the existent political cleavage between the working class and other social classes.[8] On the other hand, working class students in heterogeneous class peer groups (hetpeers) appear to be resocialized in the direction of higher class political norms.[9] For hetpeers are less committed to economic aggrandizement at the expense of political liberty (Gamma: +.37), more disposed towards fulfilling their voting obligation (+.40), and less intolerant of minority groups (+.44) than their classmates in homogeneous class peer groups (hompeers).[10]

TABLE 101. RELATION OF PEER CLASS ENVIRONMENT TO POLITICAL ATTITUDES AMONG WORKING CLASS STUDENTS

Peer Class Environment	Dependent Variable			
	Student Politicization*			
	% Low	% Medium	% High	N
Homogeneous	44	26	30	215
Heterogeneous	34	36	30	205
	System Legitimacy*			
	Support	Ambivalence	Opposition	N
	%	%	%	
Homogeneous	45	42	13	206
Heterogeneous	33	51	16	193

* See footnotes 13 and 15 for the items included in these tables.

[8] In each case working class students in homogeneous class peer groups assume an attitudinal position which is farther from that of the middle and upper classes than is the attitudinal position of the working class in general.

[9] The political differences found between working class students in homogeneous and heterogeneous peer groups is explained primarily as a function of the resocialization process in heterogeneous class peer groups. This difference might also be explained by a process of selection. Heterogeneous class peer groups may only select working class members who have the same values as they do or high I.Q. students may select or be co-opted into heterogeneous groups. However, this alternative explanation appears doubtful when the analogous influence of *school* class atmosphere is examined later in this paper. When using controlled selection, objective criteria of class atmosphere, and the same dependent variables, effects similar to those reported for the peer group are also found in the school.

[10] All references to hompeers and hetpeers are for working class students only. Middle-class hompeers and hetpeers are not discussed in this paper but will be subjects for later analysis.

Peer heterogeneity appears to have no effect upon the development of highly politicized students (Table 101). They are found in equal percentages both in homogeneous and heterogeneous peer groups. While the class environment of such intermediary socialization agencies as the peer group adds explanatory power to the movement from low to medium politicization among working class students, other variables must be sought—such as family and peer group politicization—to explain the development of high politicization.

Apparently interaction with higher class peers, who tend to be more suspicious of the charismatic tone of Jamaican politics and of alleged political corruption, has a "rationalizing" influence upon working class students. Working class hetpeers are less supportive and more ambivalent toward the political system than are hompeers (Table 101). This influence of the heterogeneous class peer group upon the legitimacy attitudes of the working class is effective despite the fact that it is contrary to the message in Jamaican "civics" textbooks which emphasize support. It suggests that the political information the respondent hears informally which represents "real" political attitudes is more significant in the socialization process than the formal education he receives. Wylie (1964) makes the same observation regarding informal vs. formal political socialization of French school children (pp. 207–209).

Peer group class environment also has an effect on the economic attitudes of working class students. Students in heterogeneous class peer groups appear to move away from the more liberal attitudinal positions held by their classmates in homogeneous groups toward the more conservative economic orientations of the middle and upper classes. They are less inclined to respond that the rich should give up their privileges (+.48) or that earning limits should be established (+.37) than are hompeers.

Thus, we see throughout that heterogeneous class peer groups consistently function to resocialize the working class toward the level of politicization and political outlook of the higher social classes. On the other hand, the net effect of homogeneous class peer groups is to reinforce the political and economic culture of the working class.

The School

The school (like the peer group) may reinforce social and political class differences by the virtue of the fact that it is composed of students of the same social class. On the other hand, if students from various classes are assigned to a school, the resulting environment may promote the resocialization of working class students by grouping them with adolescents of higher social status.

In her study of selected midwestern schools in the United States, B. Neugarten (1946) found that lower class children and adolescents generally deferred to the higher status students in heterogeneous class schools by ascribing more favorable personality traits to them than to students of their own class.[11] Other research indicates that students from the lower socioeconomic classes who attend heterogeneous class schools have higher educational aspirations than those in more homogeneous school climates. The authors attribute the difference in aspirations at least in part to the dominant class character of the high school or grade cohort (Wilson, 1959; Michael, 1961).

In order to test our hypothesis, we ordered the schools in the Jamaican sample by their class environment. Schools categorized as "homogeneous" have a dominant working class environment and, for working class students, are the closest analog to homogeneous class peer groups. The school with the most balanced distribution of classes can be considered the closest analog to the environment of the heterogeneous class peer group.

In the determination of the class environment of the school the individual student is treated as a respondent whose class attributes (objective class of his parents) constitute a part of the total school class climate. This differs from the method used to determine peer class environment. In the latter case the respondent was used as an informant about the class homogeneity of the peer group.

When we examine the relationship between school class climate and the same political variables, a familiar pattern develops. Homogeneous class

schools reinforce working class political norms and maintain the political cleavage between the working class and the other social classes. On the other hand, working class students in heterogeneous class schools appear to be resocialized in the direction of higher class political norms.[12] They are less inclined to forsake political liberty for personal gain (+.51); more disposed toward fulfilling their voting obligation (+.38); more tolerant of minority groups (+.40); more politicized (+.32); and less supportive and more ambivalent toward the political system than their counterparts in homogeneous schools (+.30).

School class environment appears to have little effect upon economic attitudes. It is possible that among the working class economic attitudes may be more "hard core" and resistant to change than the more esoteric political attitudes. This may be particularly true within the wider school environment where the pressures to conform and defer to higher class norms may not be as great as in the small face-to-face heterogeneous peer group. The rigidity with which these attitudes are held may vary between cultures. We might find adherence to economic aggrandizement less a part of the working class culture in more affluent societies. This will also depend, of course, on the visibility of class differences in the society.

The Peer Group and School Environment

The interaction between the wider school environment and the socializing process within the peer group pose intriguing questions and manifest the need for further research. To what degree, for example, has the school class environment outside the peer group contributed to the reported differential influence of peer class environment upon political socialization? Do we still find the reported effect of different peer class environments within schools with relatively homogeneous class environments?

---

[11] In her study in Jonesville, Neugarten (1949) found students in heterogeneous class environments continued to defer to the perceived "favorable characteristics" of upper class students from elementary school through high school. While in the higher grades in secondary school there was no tendency to defer to lower class students and deference to higher status students was still clearly operative, adolescents were increasingly disposed to defer horizontally in more complex ways. In other words, being the student council president or the captain of the football team might make one equally if not more subject to deference as being from an upper class family. However, as Mary C. Jones (1958) has so cogently observed, higher social status is strongly associated with access to prestigious student offices in the high school.

[12] It is possible, of course, that differences found between working class students in homogeneous and heterogeneous class schools could be due to selection rather than the operation of different school environments. In other words, working class students with the attitudinal syndrome found among working class students in heterogeneous class schools may actually seek out the more heterogeneous class schools to matriculate. Fortunately, the Jamaican Ministry of Education was able to provide information on this matter. Because of its local school policy, there is no evidence that differences in political attitudes between working class students in homogeneous-heterogeneous class schools is due to any significant degree to selection rather than the socializing influences of the school class environment. For an expanded discussion of this point see Langton, 1965, p. 198.

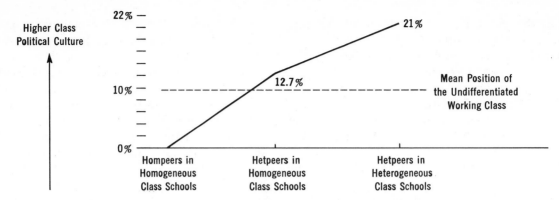

FIG. 34. The cumulative effect of heterogeneous class environment in peer groups and schools among working class students.*

* This figure represents the mean difference between the positions taken by hompeers in homogeneous class schools and hetpeers in homogeneous and heterogeneous class schools on the seven previously discussed variables. The position of hompeers on homogeneous class schools provides the base line.

Does the heterogeneous class environment of both the peer group and school have a cumulative effect upon the resocialization of the working class? Based on previous findings, we might predict that working class hetpeers in heterogeneous class schools will be the farthest removed from the political culture of their class.

In Figure 34 we see evidence that the heterogeneous class climate of the peer group and school is indeed cumulative. There is a mean linear change in the predicted direction between the positions taken by hompeers in homogeneous class schools and hetpeers in homogeneous and heterogeneous class schools on all seven of the previously discussed variables. The cumulative direction of change is consistently toward the political culture of the higher classes. The mean difference between the position of hompeers in homogeneous class schools and hetpeers in heterogeneous class schools is 21 percent.

It is also evident that the impact of the peer group appears to be independent of the broader class environment within the school. When school class homogeneity is controlled, heterogeneous class peer groups still appear to play a significant role in resocializing working class students in the direction of higher class political norms.

Finally, it seems obvious that to compare the political culture of an undifferentiated working class with that of higher classes tends to underestimate the political cleavages in the society. For the cleavage between the political culture of hompeers in homogeneous class schools and the higher classes is

much greater.[13] It is also very likely that this differentiation will increase as the respondents pass into the early years of adulthood.

School Class Climate and the Political Socialization Process in the United States

Other than the suggestive literature discussed above, there appear to be no empirical studies of the effect of peer group or school class climate upon the political socialization process in the United States. However, in 1964 a study was conducted in Detroit, Michigan, of school children's reaction to the assassination of President Kennedy. Secondary analysis of the data from this sample of 1349 students may illuminate the potential influence of school class environment upon politically relevant variables. Two questions in the survey dealt with the denial of Oswald's civil rights, another attempted to ascertain children's idealization of the President. An analysis of the data reveals an inverse correlation between social class and propensity to deny Oswald his civil rights (Gamma: −.44).[14] Working class students are more likely than middle or upper class students to be "glad" that Oswald was killed by Ruby and to want to see President Kennedy's murderer "shot or beat

[13] The mean difference between the positions taken by the undifferentiated working class and working class hompeers in homogeneous class schools on the seven variables is 9.7 percent, with the latter group consistently taking a position farthest removed from that of the higher classes.
[14] Respondents' social class is based upon their father's occupation.

up." Working class students are also more likely to idealize the role of the President and to feel that all American Presidents have "done their job well" than are middle or upper class students (+.38).

In order to examine the impact of school class environment upon these attitudes among working class students, the schools in the Detroit study were ordered by their objective class environment as were the schools in the Jamaican study.[15]

When we examine the relationship between school class climate and these three variables in Detroit we see what is becoming a consistent pattern. Heterogeneous class schools appear to be re-socializing working class students in the direction of higher class political norms: working class students in heterogeneous class schools are less inclined to deny Oswald his civil rights (+.44, +.37) than are those in more homogeneous environments. Interestingly enough, they also take a less benevolent view of the Presidency (+.36)—a finding not incompatible with the greater political cynicism found among working class Jamaicans in heterogeneous class schools.

Conclusion

Throughout this paper we have seen that working class students in heterogeneous class schools and peer groups consistently differ in the same direction from their counterparts in homogeneous class environments. If, as seems to be the case, peer groups and schools are important agencies of change, then the question many educators and students of politics may ask is as follows: How can we take advantage of students' potentialities for change—and of the power of peer and school environment to induce change—in such ways that change will most probably occur in the direction of our educational, social, and political objectives?

[15] Because of the reduced N resulting from the class control, it was necessary to include both primary and secondary schools in the index (i.e., grades 4, 6, 8, 10, 12). This may diminish the reported effect of school class climate to the extent that status consciousness is a corollary of the maturation process (see Harvey and Rutherford, 1960).

The social scientist would suggest on the basis of the preceding discussion and findings that there is a potential for introducing "modernizing" norms to the lower classes via heterogeneous class environments. He might also point out that the organization of vocational and technical schools for the working class, as is being done in many less industrialized countries, may reinforce existent political-culture cleavages within the society. However, the results of this study indicate that any manipulation of peer grouping or class environment within schools should be preceded by a careful survey of one's objectives and an analysis of the political culture of the different social classes. For we found that working class students in a heterogeneous class environment not only are more politicized, have more "democratic" attitudes, give greater support to civil liberties, and have more positive orientations toward voting; they are also more economically conservative. Equally, if not more important, in a culture where the higher classes tend to be more politically alienated (Jamaica), working class students in heterogeneous class environments are more ambivalent and less supportive of the political system than those in more homogeneous class climates.

This means that the existence of potential system "pathologies" in the form of political class cleavages may be less threatening to long run stability than the resocializing effect of heterogeneous class school and peer environments. For while this process may reduce class cleavages, it creates an enlarged category of students who are not only more politicized but also less supportive of the political system—certainly a potentially dangerous output in national political systems in their early stages of development.

However, the problems which the socializing function of different peer group and school environments may create for the political system does not mean that the planner must seek to enable the lower classes to live comfortably with their "inferior" social and cultural status à la Huxley. What it does mean is that the creation of heterogeneous class socializing environments to promote the stability of democratic political systems will be maximized when the higher classes are generally supportive of the political system.

IX

Believer

It is appropriate to follow the section on adolescents as citizens with one on adolescents as believers. First, most Americans probably feel that a belief in God and adherence to some faith is a characteristic of a good citizen. Atheism smacks of Communism. Second, the church is the institution through which many Americans enact their citizenship and by which they are integrated into their communities. Third, the development of adolescents as believers seems strikingly parallel to their development as citizens in several important respects. How adolescents acquire the faith of their parents or discard it, and what part this faith plays in their lives, resembles closely their acquisition and enactment of the citizen role.

Here we review the literature on the extent, nature, and functions of religious belief in adolescence and suggest some of the conditions for change.

The great majority of adolescents believe in God. *Kuhlen and Arnold* (1944) found that about 84 percent of youngsters aged 12 to 18 "know there is a God," while another 11 percent "wonder about it," and 5 percent do not believe in God. Remmers and Radler (1957) report that 83 percent of their sample of youngsters in grades 9 through 12 believe that "God knows our every thought and movement."

Whether there is any real desertion of religion with growing maturity during adolescence is in doubt. For example, Kuhlen and Arnold's data show a decline in the proportion of firm believers, from 94 percent at age 12 to 79 percent at age 18, more of the 18-year-olds becoming agnostic rather than atheistic—but Remmers and Radler find no such shift.

Somewhere between 60 percent and 70 percent of adolescents go to church at least once a week, and two studies agree that there is a slight decline in regular church attendance among older adolescents (Remmers and Radler, 1957; *Rosander*, 1939). The Remmers and Radler data suggest that while fewer older adolescents attend worship service regularly, more of them participate in church affairs through youth groups.

M. C. Jones (1960) has found a marked increase from 1935 to 1959 in church-going and interest in religion among adolescent girls, and some small increase among boys.

The church which adolescents attend is overwhelmingly the church of their parents, especially their mothers. Bell (1938) and Remmers and Radler set the proportion between 80 percent and 90 percent.

While substantial proportions of adolescents believe in God and attend church services and church affairs regularly, and while there is little change in these proportions over the course of adolescence, older adolescents may hold a different concept of religion from the one they held when they were just entering adolescence. Data on this point are, however, contradictory. Kuhlen and Arnold record an increase of 11 percent from age 12 to age 18 in the proportion of youngsters who believe that "God is a strange power working for good, rather than a person." On the other hand, neither Dimock (1937) nor Remmers and Radler detect a decline in the personification of God. Kuhlen and Arnold also report sharp declines over ages twelve to eighteen in the proportions who believe in God as rewarding good and punishing evil, in hell as the eternal abode of the sinner, and in the literalness of the Bible. These data suggest that if there are any changes at all in the nature of religious beliefs or religious practices during adolescence, the trend is slight. Hollingsworth (1933) suggests that such changes are not related specifically to adolescence but rather to intellectual maturity, pointing out that they occur as often among intellectually gifted eight-year-olds as among average 12-year-olds. Supporting this, Goldman (1965) reports a positive relationship between the abstractness of adolescents' God-concepts and their capacity for formal operations in the Piagetian sense.

Youngsters grow more tolerant toward the religious beliefs of others as they grow into adolescence. According to both the Remmers and Radler and the Kuhlen and Arnold data, fewer late adolescents equate goodness with believing in God or adhering to a specific religion. Here, too, as in the case of changes in the concept of God, it is likely that intellectual maturity and perhaps increasing appreciation of the diversity in the world around them account for these changes.

Those adolescents who attend church more frequently and who have firmer religious beliefs make more rigid moral judgments than their less religious peers. Middleton and Putney (1962) in the United States, and *Wright and Cox* (1967b) in England found the former were likely to declare a series of misbehaviors "always wrong" than the latter despite extenuating circumstances and without mitigating considerations. These two studies suggest a function which religious belief may serve in impulse control at adolescence; for both demonstrate that religious adolescents more severely condemn private indulgence like smoking and sexual behavior than violations of the social compact such as lying and stealing. We cannot be confident, however, that this pattern is more prevalent at adolescence than during other developmental phases because neither study has a developmental design.

There are almost no systematic data on the relationship between moral and ethical behavior and religiosity, and no data we have found trace this relationship through adolescent development. Hartshorne, May, and their associates report no relationship between religious behavior and cheating behavior among children 11 to 14 years old in their *Studies in Deceit* (1928). Middleton and Putney (1962) detect no relationship between their measures of adolescents' religiosity and their self-reported misbehavior. Similarly, Ross (1950) concludes that his sample of postadolescent YMCA members did not seem to relate their religion very much to other aspects of their lives. On the other hand, regular church attendance is negatively related to juvenile delinquency (Wattenberg, 1950). Church attendance may, however, be symptomatic of a kind of relationship between an adolescent and his family and his community which inhibits delinquency, rather than an inhibitor in itself, and it may be a background factor which persuades juvenile authorities to release youngsters without record.

Some observers conclude from the data on increasing church attendance and interest in religion in recent years that adolescents are growing more committed to religion. In our opinion, however, data like Hartshorne and May's and Ross's suggest that most adolescents' relationships to their religion are similar to most of their relationships with their grandmothers: both come with the family and are supposed to be respected on account of their age, but neither is really stimulating or relevant.

There are exceptions to this general picture, youngsters for whom the role of believer is central to their identities. Studies of religious conversion provide the best data available for understanding the place religion plays in their lives. The data on conversion—the sudden, highly emotional commitment to believing—agree that conversion is almost exclusively an adolescent phenomenon (Clark, 1929; Starbuck, 1899). Neither of the two classic studies indicates what proportion of adolescents experienced conversion when the studies were made, because in both studies subjects were largely limited to those who had experienced a distinct religious awakening which resulted in a sustained religious commitment. The peak years for sudden conversion among these individuals were 13 or 14 for the girls and 15 or 16 for the boys.

Gradual "religious awakening" is also most likely to occur during adolescence. People have a more difficult time fixing the date of the beginning of this experience because it is not so striking an event as conversion. When Starbuck collected his data at the close of the last century, the age curves for religious awakening corresponded closely to those for conversion. However, Clark's study thirty years after produced curves which peaked sharply at a younger age, at about 12 years old. Both Clark and Starbuck found few subjects who reported making their strong commitments to the role of believer before or after the adolescent years.

It is not difficult to find problems of adolescence reflected in the emotions immediately preceding conversion. Most of Starbuck's subjects recalled feeling depressed and anxious and overwhelmed by a sense of sin. The researcher was so struck by the frequency with which his respondents wrote of feeling unintegrated and at odds with themselves, he concluded that the central psychological function of conversion (and religious awakening as well) was to restore a sense of wholeness to the individual. Some of Clark's subjects thirty years later reported similar feelings but the incidence of strong emotions of any kind was under 30 percent.

We find the theme of identity running through Starbuck's and Clark's data on conversion. At a time 35 to 65 years ago when the role of the believer was more central to the ideology of our society, it offered itself as a possible focal point for the individual adolescent. Were he to choose to become a Christian, in a sense in which the very words "become a Christian" are seldom understood nowadays, the adolescent would find his family, other adults, and his friends reflecting his new role to him positively; he would also find in his new role a fairly clear set of guides for his thought and behavior which would provide strong external support for impulse control. He could be an identifiable someone who was comfortable.

Since the turn of the century, the role of the believer seems to have lost its power as a unifying alternative for adolescent identity. Clark's data from the 1920's suggest that this decline had begun by then. More of his subjects seem to have become committed as a matter of conformity rather than through a choice made in crises. As we have noted, more of them committed themselves at a younger age, at the beginning of puberty, and fewer of them in an emotional turmoil.

In our day, the role of believer is like the role of the citizen in that both enjoy widespread public legitimacy but lack the potency to command commitment and serve as an integrating part of personality. The role of believer seems to be more potent to regulate surface behavior when we compare the regularity of church-going to poll-going, but the evidence suggests that it seldom goes deeper.

It is likely that adolescents abandon belief under conditions similar to those which we have detected for political estrangement. That is, believing is an important issue to their parents; their relationship with their parents is poor; and they find support for abandoning belief, especially among their peers (Putney and Middleton, 1961).

If this is true, then we should find in counter-conversion, or militant abandonment of belief, conditions which more closely match political conversion. One study (*Vetter and Green*, 1932) suggests that this is so among a sample of male members of the American Association for the Advancement of Atheism questioned in 1931. This study found that atheists perceived their parents to be of more than ordinary piety: "College students (compared to Association members) rating their parents . . . described far fewer of them as being 'rigid' in their religious observances." No data are presented which allow us to assess the atheists' relations with their parents. The evidence is clear, however, that the sample contains a high percentage of political rebels: 42 percent of the atheists deserted the party as well as the religion of their parents.

The role of the believer is relevant to our understanding of adolescents even today. It probably continues to serve an important integrating function for some adolescents. Even where it does not serve such a function among most adolescents, their relationship to religion in a society which prescribes it may be symptomatic of their personality organization. *Strunk* (1958c) reports a moderately high correlation between a positive self-image and an index of religious behavior among 136 high school juniors. The index of religious behavior is by no means a measure of piety or religious morality; it is more likely an index to feeling at one with the mainstream of society.

41

Age Differences

in Religious Beliefs and Problems

During Adolescence*

Raymond G. Kuhlen
Martha Arnold

Problems in the realm of values, philosophy of life, and religion have long been considered a major area of adjustment confronting adolescents. Marked changes in religious views are assumed to occur and many crucial problems to arise. At the college level it has been fairly well demonstrated that, on the average, profound change does not occur. That seniors are only slightly more liberal in outlook than freshmen has been demonstrated in studies by D. Katz and Allport (1931), Dudycha (1933), and others. However, adequate evidence indicating age differences in beliefs held and problems faced during the adolescent period is not available for ages below college. Dimock, who has reported one study of younger adolescents, concludes that his data reveal "the relatively static nature of religious ideas of the adolescent during the four-year period (12–16) encompassed by this study," thus apparently contradicting popular opinion (Dimock, 1936; 1937, p. 168). It is probable, however, that the type of analysis followed by Dimock in his research has obscured a number of trends,[1] and his data can hardly be accepted as evidence demonstrating that religious ideas do not change during adolescence.

The research summarized in the present paper was an attempt to explore the nature of religious beliefs held during the adolescent period, and to test by at least one type of evidence the hypothesis that adolescence is a period of increasing religious problems. It differs from other investigations in that the results have been analyzed both with respect to specific problems faced and beliefs held, and with respect to relative age periods during adolescence, thus providing an age perspective in which to view such specific changes as might occur.

Procedure

A questionnaire was prepared which listed 52 statements representing various religious beliefs (sample statements are contained in Table 103) which were to be marked according to whether the subject "believed" the statement, did "not believe" the statement, or did not know whether he believed it or not but had "wondered about" it. A second part of the questionnaire listed 18 problems of a religious sort with directions asking the subject to circle an "N," an "S," or an "O" depending upon whether he felt that a particular problem troubled or bothered him "never," "sometimes," or "often."

Responses from 547 sixth, ninth, and twelfth graders were obtained. The exact number of subjects and the mean age of each grade group are contained in Table 102. The significance of the use of these three grade groups in the study of adolescence lies in the fact that the sixth grade group is largely pre-pubescent, the ninth grade group pubescent (at least for boys; girls mature somewhat earlier), and twelfth grade group post-pubescent. The sampling of these three phases of development during the age range in which adolescence normally occurs should be sufficient to provide evidence of any marked trend occurring during this period. During the discussion to follow, these groups will be referred to as 12, 15, and 18 year-olds. As might be expected, the groups were

* From *The Journal of Genetic Psychology*, 1944, **65**, 291–300.
[1] See the "Discussion" section of this paper for a further elaboration of this point. Franzblau (1934) has shown that beliefs of Jewish adolescents become more liberal with increased age, and A. N. MacLean (1930) has presented data indicating the percentage of children of adolescent years who hold certain specific beliefs.

TABLE 102. Number of Cases, Mean Age, and Standard Deviation in Years of Groups Studied

Grade	N	Boys Mn. Age	SD	N	Girls Mn. Age	SD	Total No.
6	80	12.4	1.2	94	12.0	0.9	174
9	128	15.2	1.0	115	14.9	1.0	243
12	49	18.1	0.8	81	17.8	1.0	130

quite heterogeneous with respect to church membership. Among the 12, 15, and 18 year-old groups respectively there were 19, 33, and 10 Catholic boys and 26, 19, and 18 Catholic girls. The rest were scatted among Protestant denominations, with an occasional child of Jewish faith, or who indicated no church attendance.

Changes in Religious Beliefs

The findings were analyzed first by ascertaining what proportion of each age group checked each statement indicating belief, disbelief, or uncertainty regarding that statement. Certain results of this analysis are summarized in Table 103. An examination of

TABLE 103. Changes in Specific Religious Beliefs During Adolescence as Shown by the Percentage of 12, 15, and 18 Year-Old Children Who Checked Various Statements Indicating (a) Belief, (b) Disbelief, or (c) Uncertainty (Wonder)*

Statement	"Believe" 12	15	18	"Not Believe" 12	15	18	"Wonder About" 12	15	18
God is a strange power working for good, rather than a person.	46	49	57	31	33	21	20	14	15
God is someone who watches you to see that you behave yourself, and who punishes you if you are not good.	70	49	33	18	37	48	11	13	18
I know there is a God.	94	80	79	3	5	2	2	14	16
Catholics, Jews and Protestants are equally good.	67	79	86	9	9	7	24	11	7
There is a heaven.	82	78	74	4	5	5	13	16	20
Only good people go to heaven.	72	45	33	15	27	32	13	27	34
Hell is a place where you are punished for your sins on earth.	70	49	35	16	21	30	13	27	34
Heaven is here on earth.	12	13	14	69	57	52	18	28	32
People who go to church are better than people who do not go to church.	46	26	15	37	53	74	17	21	11
Young people should belong to the same church as their parents.	77	56	43	13	33	46	10	11	11
The main reason for going to church is to worship God.	88	80	79	6	12	15	4	7	6
It is not necessary to attend church to be a Christian.	42	62	67	38	23	24	18	15	8
Only our soul lives after death.	72	63	61	9	11	6	18	25	31
Good people say prayers regularly.	78	57	47	9	29	26	13	13	27
Prayers are answered.	76	69	65	3	5	8	21	25	27
Prayers are a source of help in times of trouble.	74	80	83	11	8	7	15	10	9
Prayers are to make up for something that you have done that is wrong.	47	24	21	35	58	69	18	17	9
Every word in the Bible is true.	79	51	34	6	16	23	15	31	43
It is sinful to doubt the Bible.	62	42	27	18	31	44	20	26	28

* Discrepancies between the totals of "Believe," "Not Believe," and "Wonder About," and 100 per cent represent the percentages who did not respond to the statements. Differences of 8 or 9 will ordinarily yield a CR of 2.0, depending upon the magnitude of the percentages involved.

these findings indicates clearly that a number of rather significant changes have occurred. First to be noted is the fairly marked discarding of such beliefs as "Every word in the Bible is true," "It is sinful to doubt the Bible," "God is someone who watches you to see that you behave yourself, and who punishes you if you are not good." Roughly two-thirds (close to 70 percent) of the 12-year olds believed these statements to be true; only a third or less of the 18-year olds would agree. Other statements which were notably less frequently believed by 18- than 12-year-olds are "Only good people go to heaven," "Hell is a place where you are punished for your sins on earth," and "Prayers are to make up for something wrong you have done." Thus many rather specific beliefs taught to, or picked up by, young children are no longer held by most of those in the late teens.

Second, a greater tolerance with respect to religious beliefs and practices is apparent with development into adolescence. Thus *more* 18- than 12-year olds agree that "Catholics, Jews, and Protestants are equally good," that "It is not necessary to attend church to be a Christian." Fewer 18- than 12-year olds believe that "People who go to church are better than people who do not go to church," that "Young people should belong to the same church as their parents," and that "Good people say prayers regularly."

Third, it will be noted that drops in the proportion "believing" a statement are not necessarily compensated for by increases in the proportion "not believing" that statement. With respect to certain beliefs, at least, the issues are far from settled even by 18 years of age. More of the 18-year-old group, for example, "wonder about" the statement "Every word in the Bible is true," than who agree with the statement or who disbelieve it. In the case of 12 of the 19 statements contained in Table 103, there is a trend toward increased "wondering." Such is true of beliefs involving the hereafter (death, heaven, and hell), certain concepts of God, certain beliefs with respect to prayer and belief in the Bible.

It is evident from these data that the religious views of adolescents in the late teens differ from those of 12-year-old children in a number of very significant ways. In fact, of the 52 statements included in this study, changes were great enough in 36 statements to be two or more times their standard errors.[2] That even the 18-year-old group have not

yet reached a satisfactory religious philosophy is suggested by the amount of uncertainty that exists with respect to various beliefs and concepts. However, it must be admitted that many a person with a "satisfactory" set of religious beliefs would check "wonder about" when asked to react in one of three stated ways to statements such as those of this study.

Religious Doubts and Problems

It might be expected in view of the data thus far presented that there would be a general increase during development in adolescence in the proportion of statements "wondered about" and probably also in the number of problems faced. Both expectations are in line with the beliefs apparently held by many writers in the field of adolescent psychology. Two lines of evidences are presented regarding this question. First a "wonder score" was obtained for each subject by counting the number of items he checked as "wondering about." Second, a "problem score" was obtained by an analysis of the responses of each subject to the second portion of the questionnaire. Responses to the problems there listed were summarized by giving weights of zero, one, and two respectively to responses of "never," "sometimes," and "often," and summing the 18 responses. The results of such analyses are summarized in Table 104.

TABLE 104. TRENDS DURING ADOLESCENCE IN THE GENERAL EXTENT OF DOUBT AND CONCERN REGARDING RELIGIOUS ISSUES AS SHOWN BY MEAN "WONDER" AND "PROBLEM" SCORES OF THE THREE AGE GROUPS

| | Age | | | $CR_{Diff.}$ |
	12	15	18	12–18
Wonder scores	7.9	8.1	8.7	1.1
Problem scores	9.7	9.9	9.9	0.3
No. of cases	174	243	130	

A slight trend is noticeable in the case of the average number of statements wondered about, but the difference between the 12-year-old and the 18-year-old groups is so small compared to the amount of sampling error probably present that it cannot safely be considered more than a chance difference. In the case of the "problem scores" no difference

[2] It would have been desirable to study age changes for particular groups, especially Catholic and Non-Catholic, but

there were too few cases in any particular category to make such analysis significant.

TABLE 105. FREQUENCY WITH WHICH PARTICULAR RELIGIOUS PROBLEMS EXIST AT
VARIOUS AGES THROUGH ADOLESCENCE AS SHOWN BY PERCENTAGE OF DIFFERENT AGE
GROUPS WHO CHECK EACH PROBLEM AS SOMETIMES OR OFTEN PRESENT

| | | Age | | $CR_{Diff.}$ |
Problem	12	15	18	12–18
Having a different religion from other people	34	25	27	1.3
Disliking church service	33	47	60	4.9
Being forced to go to church	30	31	27	0.6
Disliking parents' religion	11	8	12	0.7
Failing to go to church	67	67	67	0.0
Changing my idea of God	29	25	31	0.4
Losing faith in religion	27	32	31	0.8
Doubting prayer will bring good	37	44	35	0.4
Getting help on religious problems	53	54	56	0.6
Choosing a religion	21	20	15	1.5
Parents objection to church membership	23	14	11	2.6
Wanting to know the meaning of religion	53	48	60	1.2
Wanting communion with God	59	47	57	0.3
Heaven and hell	53	53	66	2.3
Sin	71	62	72	0.2
Conflicts of science and religion	42	50	57	2.6
Being teased about my religious feelings	26	22	18	1.5
Wondering what becomes of people when they died	67	56	80	2.3
Number of cases	174	243	130	

appeared in the means for the three age groups. Thus insofar as these findings are concerned, the hypothesis that adolescence is a period of *generally* increased religious doubts and problems is clearly not substantiated. Since age trends here (and also sex differences) are slight, it was decided to compare Catholics with non-Catholics by grouping sixth, ninth, and twelfth grades and both sexes together. When this was done, it became apparent that Catholics had lower scores in both "wonders" and "problems" than did the non-Catholics. In the case of "wonder scores" the mean difference was 3.0 (CR 4.9); in the case of "problem scores" the mean difference was 1.2 (CR 2.2).

That age trends exist with respect to the particular problem faced is to be expected, and appropriate data revealing such trends are presented in Table 105. Over half of the 18-year-old group of subjects indicate that the following problems trouble them sometimes or often: Disliking church service, Failing to go to church, Getting help on religious problems, Wanting communion with God, Wanting to know the meaning of religion, Heaven and Hell, Sin, Conflicts of science and religion, Wondering what becomes of people when they die. It would seem as though adolescents do have certain religious problems regarding which they would like help, but apparently find conventional religious programs unsatisfying. Three of the problems listed—Disliking

church services, Heaven and Hell, and Wondering what becomes of people when they die—become more prevalent with increased age, the critical ratios of the 12- to 18-year-old differences in these cases being over 2.0. One problem—Parents' objection to church membership—decreases sufficiently to show fair statistical reliability. Just what is meant by this response is not clear. It may be that parents of 12-year olds consider them too young to join a church.

Discussion

It is not implied by the selection of age groups of varying statuses with respect to pubescence, that the differences shown are a function of pubescence. Rather, it would seem more reasonable to assume that they are the result of accumulated experience in combination with increasing intellectual maturity which makes the adolescent more capable of interpreting the environment of ideas and facts in which he is becoming increasingly immersed. Greater intellectual maturity might be expected to increase sensitivity to inconsistencies either among the beliefs and views an individual contacts, or between his already established beliefs and new learnings. Also with greater maturity the adolescent is more capable of abstract generalizations which might result in discarding some specific beliefs in favor of more general ones.

Do such findings have any practical value? To the psychologist and others interested in human development such data are of interest as descriptions of how development proceeds. But are there any implications for those interested in religious education? Two obvious implications may be mentioned. First, those issues represented by statements which are increasingly "wondered about" as age increases may give clues as to appropriate topics for consideration in the teen years in both Sunday School classes and young people's groups. Second, beliefs discarded by children as they grow older may well be studied for their implications for teaching at earlier ages. Children's concepts regarding religion are more concrete and specific than are those of adults, the latter tending to be abstract and general. This change represents the normal growth of concepts. It would seem desirable that the specific and concrete beliefs taught to children be beliefs compatible with the more abstract adult views, and not beliefs later to be discarded because of incompatibility.

It is worthwhile to point out that in research of this sort, average scores may very well obscure more facts than they reveal. This is the writer's criticism of Dimock's study. In contrast to his conclusion of the relatively static nature of religious ideas in adolescence, the present findings reveal rather significant shifts during the ages considered. The need for detailed analysis is revealed even within the present study. Average "wonder scores" and "problem scores" showed little change. Yet analysis of responses to specific beliefs and problems indicated changes of high statistical reliability. The meaning of any "score" rests to a considerable extent upon the particular questions or items which that score summarizes. When items showing increasing frequency of checking are added in with other items of a decreasing trend, the differences cancel and a fairly stable over-all score may conceal the actual change.

It is probable that the use of a questionnaire dealing exclusively with religious issues has momentarily focused the subjects' attention upon a rather narrow range of human experience, and by taking these experiences out of the context of everyday living may give a biased picture of the importance of such issues and problems in the lives of adolescents. Three of the problem items used in the present study were included in a modified form of the Mooney *Problem Check List* (Junior High Level) used by the senior writer in another study. Although 22, 48, and 25 percent of ninth graders in the present study checked these items as bothering them sometimes or often, only nine, 18, and 20 percent of a group of 100 ninth graders so checked the same items when they were included among a great variety of other kinds of problems. This is simply another illustration of the part the instrument used plays in determining the "facts" discovered, and warns agains too literal an interpretation of the absolute figures presented in this paper. The differences noted and trends revealed, however, may more safely be depended upon.[3]

Summary

Five hundred forty-seven children and adolescents, in three groups which averaged 12, 15, and 18 years of age, responded to a questionnaire which listed 52 statements representing various religious beliefs and 18 problems dealing with religious issues. Many significant differences appeared in religious beliefs when 12-year olds and 18-year olds were compared. A greater tolerance with respect to religious beliefs and practice, a discarding of a number of specific beliefs and increased "wondering about" statements regarding the hereafter (death, heaven, hell) constituted the major trends. An analysis of responses of "wondering about" particular beliefs and "problems" did not substantiate the commonly accepted hypothesis that adolescence is a period of generally increased religious doubts and problems. Catholics "wondered about" fewer beliefs and checked fewer problems than did non-Catholics. However, the specific problems checked by the subjects indicated that many do have problems of a religious sort, want help (in fact, one of the greatest problems seemed to be getting such help), but are dissatisfied with conventional church services.

[3] One report by Mooney (1942) suggests that religious and moral problems are relatively minor in importance in adolescence when compared with other types of problems.

42

Personality and Group

Factors in the Making of Atheists*

Geo. B. Vetter
Martin Green

Arm-chair generalizations regarding the personality traits or characteristics of individuals of particular opinion or attitude groups are slowly giving way to some form or other of systematic inquiry. Thus we have seen no less than a half dozen separately reported attempts at identifying and characterizing such groups as "radicals," "liberals," "conservatives" or "atypicals" (Vetter, 1930a, 1930b). Unfortunately, the work to date has been largely done on groups of docile college students; and, while these are excellent subjects from the standpoint of reliability and intelligence of results, there is no denying that the American college student is by and large, a rather standardized product. One will not find, in a college group, many of the most ardent Fundamentalists, atheists, or Communists. College, and the process of getting into it, allows but scant opportunity for the development of such enthusiasms. Extremes of social, political and religious outlook will have to be sought for outside of college walls. But there's the rub! The very groups that would undoubtedly show the most interesting results are perhaps hardest to apprehend.

The human subject exacts experimental limitations unheard of in dealing with animal behavior, particularly when the subject of inquiry is one heavily buttressed with emotional habits. It requires no great ingenuity to point out the limitations and shortcomings of the various questionnaire methods of gathering data. And yet, the matter is not so simply dismissed. There is a large segment of social behavior that is mainly verbal, and there are many attitudes and sets in an individual that are accurately discoverable by a simple question. If I ask a man "Are you a Methodist?" I can be reasonably certain that he is ready enough to answer truthfully unless I

have given him some hint or reason for falsifying. The condition of "being a Methodist" rather than something else is largely a question of a few distinctive serial verbal response habits. So too with "being a Single Taxer," or holding other opinions or attitudes. These exist largely as a lip allegiance to certain phrases or shibboleths. They have hardly any other objective manifestations. How else would one apprehend them but by the simple question? There are many other attitudes, facts and factors that one can uncover by simply questioning the subject.

We have no intention here, however, of going lengthily into the question of the merits of the questionnaire method of study. We aim merely to set forth briefly the results of 600 questionnaires sent out by mail to a random sample of the members of the American Association for the Advancement of Atheism. These questionnaires were distributed with the cooperation of the officials of the organization and 350 replies were received.

Results

1. *Age distribution.*—The ages were grouped in five-year classes and compared for distribution with similar groupings for the male sex in the census data for the United States of 1920. In general, the atheists include less than a chance quota of the age groups below 50 years of age. Between 50 and 60 the ratios are about even. Above 60 the atheist age groups are larger. The only exception is that the age group of 30 to 34 years inclusive has about four percent more than its chance quota. This age includes a large number of men who served in World War One and many of them gave the war as the cause of their becoming atheists. Perhaps the older age groups are a result of the period of freethinking agitation of Ingersoll's day. Many of them point to this influence in their own estimate of the factors that made them atheists.

* From *Journal of Abnormal and Social Psychology*, 1932, **27**, 179–194. The contemporary reader will find this early article clearly dated in some respects. The reference to "docile college students" must be seen in the context of the thirties to avoid an irony that the authors did not intend.

2. *Place of Birth.*—For purposes of regional comparison the states were grouped into five divisions, Northeast, Middle West, South, Great Lakes, and Far West. The percentages of Atheist distribution were then compared with the total populations of these groups in the United States census of 1900. All these groups of states with the exception of the Southern group contributed more than their proportional quota to the atheist sample, particularly the Northeast and Far West. The South alone ran far behind.

3. *Sex.*—Of the 350 questionnaires returned, 325 were from men. This is about the ratio of the sexes in the total membership roll of the organization. This difference becomes still more impressive when the comparison is extended to the sex ratios in American religious bodies, where the males contribute only 43 percent as against 57 percent females (Bureau of Census, 1916). The sex difference is not only one of passivity on the part of the males toward religion but it carries over into a definite antagonism. A study of the few returns obtained from women seems to indicate a preponderance of rather intense and unfortunate emotional experiences on the part of these women with organized religion. Typical of these are misplaced confidence in the integrity of church deacons, disappointments in the reputed efficacy of prayer, attempted rape by a travelling evangelist and other personal misdemeanors of the clergy. The one return showing abnormal symptoms was from a woman. To simplify the treatment of results, only the men are included in the following results.

4. *Race.*—With two exceptions, all returns were from members of the white race.

5. *Parental National Origins.*—The parents of 24 percent of these atheists were born in different countries. For the population as a whole this percentage is about 8 percent. Only 42 percent of the atheist's parents are native American born. In 1900, 76 percent of all persons over 21 years of age were native born. The percentage of native born in the United States changed but little between 1890 and 1910, hence but little error enters in this comparison by the arbitrary use of 1900 as the year for making comparisons.

Comparing the percentages of the atheists' parentage by nationality groups with the United States census report of 1900 on national origins we find that when corrections are made to eliminate the part played by Jewish immigrants,[1] almost without exception the countries of dominant Protestant stock

contribute more than their probable quota and dominantly Catholic countries contribute less. In fact, the only exceptions to this are to be found in the cases of countries from which the total immigration is very small.

6. *Religion of parents.*—The Protestant parents contribute more than their quota when compared to the number of them in the United States, the Catholics much less. The single exception is the case of Baptist parentage. But this again checks the previously observed item of distribution in the United States where we found the South was far behind in its quota. Baptists are probably the dominant group in this region. Jews and Methodists seem to make the largest proportional contribution to the ranks of the atheists. 82.5 percent of the parents were listed as being definitely affiliated with some religious creed. 17.5 percent were definitely classed as Freethinkers, agnostics, atheists or reported as affiliated with no religion. This is probably a somewhat higher percentage than would have been found in the country at large around the turn of the century, the childhood period of the average atheist of our group. Again, we have no means at present of estimating the probable percentage of atheists in the country at that time. An interesting figure but again hard to evaluate is the fact that 30 percent of the parents were of different religious faith. Inasmuch as the total percentage of freethinking parents is only about one-half the mixed marriages and as no particular tendency for the freethinkers to make mixed marriages could be noted, there remains an interesting question as to the possible causal role played by such mixed matings. It is to be remembered that religious organizations have always been generally suspicious and disapproving of matings outside the fold. Careful examination of the reports of these cases shows that if the religious difference between the parents is as great as between Protestant and Catholic there is a marked tendency to less rigid religious observances in the home. Where one of the members of the family is a Freethinker there is a decided decline in the rigidity of observances.

7. *Changes in parental religious beliefs.*—This was explored to discover if there is any evidence that there was any considerable vacillation or weakening in the family worship as a prelude to the atheism of the child. In only 30 cases was there a change reported. Thirteen were shifts from one Protestant sect to another, six of which were to Christian Sci-

[1] *I.e.*, when the total number of Russian immigrants is corrected by subtracting the number of Jews from the total.

ence. Three were from Protestant to Catholic and one from Catholic to Protestant. Five were described as losing interest in religion to the extent of ceasing to attend any church. Eight others reported far-reaching changes that involved a discontinuance of religious worship and belief and the adoption of agnostic or atheistic attitudes. Thus, while perhaps five percent of the atheists can be ascribed to direct home influence, there is no evidence that they come in general from homes of weakened religious observances.

8. *Intensity of religious activity and observance.*—These results can be shown in a simple table:

| | *Percentages* | | |
DEGREE OF RELIGIOUS DEVOTION	*Father*	*Mother*	*Average*
Rigid	33	40	37
Occasional	24	30	27
Lax	19	19	19
None at all	25	11	18

Here, in spite of the general tendency of children to agree with or make a defense of the attitudes or opinions of parents, is a marked tendency for the atheists to rate their parents as of more than ordinary piety. College students rating their parents today, describe far fewer of them as being "rigid" in their religious observances. Perhaps the last years have seen a general change in that direction. It may be that atheists are as much the product of overly pious parents as of freethinking background. Here the extremes include over 50 percent of the homes, which is probably high.

9. Twenty-seven percent report being more congenial with the father; 73 percent with the mother. This will probably please the Freudians until some one checks up on women and other groups. But it might be noted that this balance of congeniality with the mothers exists in spite of the higher percentages of mothers that were rated as "rigid" in religion. Compared to a college group, this ratio of congeniality with the mothers is not so impressive. A generous sample of New York University students confronted with the same question give a somewhat smaller percentage (66 percent) for the men but the women gave 75 percent as more congenial with the mother.

10. *Mortality of parents.*—This proved to be one of the most interesting findings. Taking the younger group of the atheists (those who had completely broken with the church by the time they were 20 years old), it was found that half of them had lost one or both parents before that time. This is at least twice the normal mortality rate for that age group. Not knowing the ages of the parents at the time of the births of these atheists, we took 28 years as the median age of the mothers. This is probably much too high for only 35 percent of all children are born to women over 30 years of age and the atheists comprise twice as many oldest children as youngest children. Also, to make certain that any difference which might appear would not be due to comparison with a favorable mortality rate, we took for comparison the highest sectional rates we could find. For the fathers we assumed an age of 30, but the difference would not be materially changed if we advanced the age of the fathers by several years. This is hardly warranted in view of the high percentage of oldest children in this group.

11. *Church attendance.*—Before age 15, about 90 percent report church or Sunday School attendance. This drops to 61 percent after 15. While 59 percent describe their attendance as "regular" before 15, only 27 percent do so for the period after 15. The percentages reporting no attendance at all change from 9 percent before 15 to 39 percent after fifteen. Thirty-five percent report attending because they were forced to, 25 percent went willingly and devoutly while the remaining 40 percent aimed only to please parents or to be with friends, more giving the former reason. It is of interest to note that those reporting a willing and devout attendance at church became atheists at later ages.

12. *Ages of leaving church and of becoming atheist.*—Because these values will want to be com-

Ages	Per Cent Leaving Church	Per Cent Becoming Atheist
Before 15	8.0	6.7
15–19	46.0	35.2
20–24	21.7	24.0
25–29	6.7	10.2
30–34	3.8	4.2
35–39	2.2	3.8
40–44	1.9	2.6
45—	3.2	4.2
Never attended	6.4	Never were religious 9.3

pared with each other and also with tables of religious conversion, they are here combined for convenience into a single table.

Two cases reported themselves as still attending church.

The comparison with Starbuck's figures (1899) for Christian conversion experiences is interesting. While there is a general similarity of distributions, the religious conversions exceed the atheistic before age 20 while at 20 and above the atheists lead. That is, a greater part or proportion of atheist "conversions" occur at age 20 or later than is the case with "religious" conversions. While in Starbuck's study, 90 percent of the conversions come between the ages of 10 and 20, only 54 percent of the atheists ceased attending church by that age and only 41 percent had become avowed atheists.

13. Fifty-six percent of those attending church at one time report their attendance as dwindling slowly. Forty-four percent report breaking off suddenly. In this connection, it might be interesting to note the factor of time relationship between the cessation of all devout observances and a definite discarding of all religious beliefs. Six percent report losing all religion before discontinuing church attendance. Thirty percent report both changes taking place during the same year. Twenty-five percent discarded all religion one to two years after ceasing church attendance; 17 percent, 3–5 years after; 13 percent, 6–10 years; 4 percent, 11–15 years; 2.5 percent, 16–20 years; 2 percent, 21–25 years after leaving the church. The two processes are thus, far from being simultaneous processes.

14. The questions asked are "Do you believe you had a happy childhood?", and the same for adolescence. These questions are among those few so far found to reveal apparently significant factors in the developmental background of atypical opinion groups. The following table gives the percentages of several atypical opinion groups reporting an unhappy childhood and adolescence:

The college opinion groups given above represent the extreme 10 percents of some 706 cases previously reported upon (Vetter, 1930a, 1930b).

These differences would seem to indicate that the roots of social opinions and attitudes are far deeper than is ordinarily suspected, that they are related perhaps to very early personality and experiential factors.

15. Ninety-three report having held at some time, a faith other than that of their parents. Of these, 19 were Catholics, six Jews and 68 Protestants. Of the 19 Catholics, 12 tried Protestantism, two tried Judaism and one Buddhism. Of the six Jews, two tried Catholicism. Of the Protestants, 42 tried Protestant sects other than their own. Seven were Catholics for a time.

16. Deism, Unitarianism, and agnosticism are the usual creeds tried, if any, before abandoning religious faith. Many also reply with names like "modernism," "skepticism" or even pantheism. In general, the creeds tried before a complete break from religion are those in which the hard and fast dogma of the older religions has already given way.

17. Another interesting finding is the apparent influence of belonging to a minority religious group. At the time they dropped their religion, twice as many were living in places where their own faith was a minority group, as were living where their own faith was the dominant one. Typical is the Catholic becoming an atheist while living in Salt Lake City. It is not without cause that the pious shepherd greets with apprehension the announcement that a member of his flock is removing to a place where there is no organization for his faith.

18. The answers to a question concerning political party affiliations throws interesting light on a question often asked, that of the relation between attitudes in one field of opinion with those in another. As it is commonly asked, "Is the religious radical likely to be the political radical and vice-versa?" Our results certainly show a high percentage

	Percentages "unhappy" in		
Opinion Group	Childhood	Adolescence	Number of Cases
Atheists (U.S.A.)	31.3	30.0	320
Communists (N.Y.)	21.5	35.7	40
College "Radicals"	25.0	50.0	60
College "Conservatives"	0.0	4.0	62
College "Reactionaries"	13.0	16.0	65

of change in political opinions toward the radical end of the spectrum. Before becoming atheists, 64 percent were Republicans or Democrats and 26 percent Socialists or Communists. Now only 29 percent are Republican or Democratic while 54 percent are Socialist or Communist. The non-partisan group also increased from 10 percent to 17 percent. It might well be pointed out that the original 26 percent of Socialists and Communists is already much higher than the average for the population as a whole and that the large increase in political radicalism following the embracing of Atheism is but the acceleration of a tendency already present. Certain it is at least that radicalism in one field does not tend to make one conservative in another, at least so far as politics and religion are concerned. The impression that radicalism in one field was often associated with extreme conservatism in another probably gained popular credence from certain overcorrections often practiced by individuals holding unpopular opinions. The village Socialist of twenty years ago who was popularly accused of wanting to "divide up" everything often compensated by paying cash and never owing anyone. So too the lone atheist; he often overcorrected in his morals what he lacked piety, in a day when the two were not too well distinguished by the average man.

19. *Order of birth in family.*—Here we find confirmation of the importance of the personality differences apparently fixed in early childhood (Goodenough and Leahy, 1927). No less than 36 percent of the atheists were oldest children while only 15 percent were "youngest" children, when sheer chance should make the numbers of each about equal. About 9 percent were "only" children. All these figures are really more impressive when it is seen that these people came from families averaging five children, and when the percentages are compared to like values for the radical opinion group in college students (Vetter, 1930a, 1930b). The effect of the family situation on the emotional life of the

child certainly seems to be worth extensive study, when its effects appear in situations as remote as this.

20. The "Foster-Child Fantasy." This question was added with the hope of turning up added evidence of the character of the early family situation of the child. Less than 3 percent reported childhood doubts of the authenticity of their parents, which is a far smaller percentage than will be found in a sample of college students.

Perhaps the most interesting part of the study is a comparison of the factors to which the individuals themselves ascribe their anti-religious attitudes and the type of causal factor suggested by the results of this study. The most common "causes" given by the subjects, in order of frequency were the following: wide reading of history, science and religion (mentioned 75 times); disgust with religious hypocrisy (60); influence of particular author or book (55); a by-product of Socialist materialism (30); effects of college education (25); effects of study of sciences (25). Less frequently does one find emotional factors mentioned, such as: illness and death in family, the horrors of war, the futility of prayer, the evils and unhappiness in the world. Yet, it is just such emotional factors as revealed in questions 16 and 28 that seem to bear a causal relation to the making of atypical opinion groups. While it is true that not all persons who lose their parents in their early life or all oldest children or all those who feel they had an unhappy childhood or adolescence or all urban people, become atheists, it is equally true that not everyone who reads history, religion, science or Socialism becomes an atheist. Probably both kinds of events play their causal role. That Ingersoll and Paine tend to make atheists will be conceded by everyone, but that rather innocent aspects of family life, excess piety in the parents, the Bible, or perhaps even parochial schools stand in a similar role will probably be hotly disputed—particularly by those who have failed to grasp the wholly pluralistic nature of the causal factors bearing on human behavior.

43

A Study of the Relationship

Between Moral Judgment

and Religious Belief in a Sample

of English Adolescents*

Derek Wright
Edwin Cox

Introduction

In a number of studies, both in England and in the United States, it has been found that severity of moral judgment is associated with various indices of religious belief and practice (Chesser, 1956; Dedman, 1959; Gorer, 1955; Klinger *et al.*, 1964; Lindenfeld, 1960; London *et al.*, 1964; Middleton and Putney, 1962; Social Surveys Ltd., 1964; Thornton *et al.*, 1964). Most of these studies have focussed upon various forms of sexual behavior, but they also provide evidence that the tendency for believers, as compared with unbelievers, to pass stricter judgments is to some extent general. Among English samples, believers have been found to be more likely than unbelievers to condemn litter dropping and tax evasion, and to say that they are worried about exceeding the speed limit.

Middleton and Putney (1962), however, offer grounds for thinking that the relationship between moral judgment and religion is not entirely general, but depends upon the nature of the behavior being judged. They distinguish between "ascetic" or "private" morality, where the consequences of actions are felt mainly by the wrongdoer, and "social" morality, where the consequences are felt in the first instance by others. The authors argue that, since social morality is a function of living in communities, it will be common to believers and unbelievers alike, whereas "ascetic" morality derives from religious traditions and will be less strongly supported by unbelievers than by believers. They do, of course, recognize fully the tentative nature of the

* From *The Journal of Social Psychology*, 1967, **72**, 135–144.

distinction. The examples of behavior falling within the concern of ascetic morality which they used in their study were various forms of sexual activity, gambling, smoking, and drinking; social actions were represented by stealing, cheating, and aggression toward others. With a sample of American students, they found significant relationships between indices of religiosity and the condemnation of antiascetic behavior, but no evidence of corresponding relationships for antisocial behavior.

A further result of the Middleton and Putney study, and one which has been found elsewhere, was that women tended to adopt a stricter moral tone than do men. This was true for both ascetic and social issues, but the difference was greater for the former than for the latter.

The main purposes of the present study are as follows: (*a*) To examine the degree of severity of moral judgment, on a number of behavioral items, of a socially defined segment of the population; to test for generality of moral judgment over different items; and to consider the relationship of severity of moral judgment to such factors as sex difference and experience of coeducation. (*b*) To analyze the relationship between moral judgment and various indices of religious belief and practice, and to discover whether this relationship is stronger for ascetic than for social aspects of morality.

Method

The Sample

The sample consisted of 2276 pupils, of whom 49.6 percent were boys and 50.4 percent girls, drawn from the sixth forms of 96 maintained grammar schools in England, excluding Wales and Scotland. For those unacquainted with the English system, this means pupils who are above average in intelligence, who are mostly pursuing courses of study designed to prepare them for various institutions of further education, and whose parents lack either the money or the desire to send them to schools that are independent, or semi-independent, of the State system. Thirty-five of the schools were coeducational, the remainder restricted to one sex. The ages of the pupils ranged from 16 to just over 18 years, with the majority falling between 17 and 18 years.

A list of 100 schools, drawn at random from the total number of maintained grammar schools in England, was obtained from the Ministry of Education, and the headmasters and headmistresses invited to cooperate. Sixteen schools declined. Of these, 12 gave fairly full reasons for refusing, all of which were of a practical nature and none of which suggested a relevant, systematic bias. However, the only two Catholic schools declined to cooperate. A further random sample of 16 schools was approached. All were prepared to cooperate, but the scripts from four arrived too late or were lost in the post. Within each school, 25 pupils were chosen from the second year of the sixth form according to a predetermined method. Not all schools had 25 in this class.

The Questionnaire

The questionnaire contained items on religious belief and practice, the Bible, the Church, religious education, and moral judgment, and took over an hour to complete. In the present context we shall be concerned only with the first and last sections.

In the moral judgment section, subjects were presented with a list of different forms of behavior and asked to rate them. The list contained the following: Gambling, Drunkenness, Smoking, Lying, Stealing, Premarital Sexual Intercourse, Suicide, and Color Bar. These were chosen because it was found that they were among the moral issues most discussed by boys and girls of the kind to be sampled. Subjects were asked to rate each of them on the following scale:

A—it is always wrong,
B—it is usually wrong but is excusable in certain circumstances,
C—it is usually excusable but is sometimes wrong,
D—it is never wrong, and
E—I have not made up my mind.

A space was provided below each item, and subjects were urged to give the reasons for their choice. These comments will be analyzed in detail elsewhere; in the present context only occasional reference will be made to them.

The indices of religiosity used were as follows: two five-point rating scales, one of confidence in the existence of God, and the other of confidence that Jesus was the Son of God; a four-step measure of frequency of church attendance, from weekly to never; a three-step measure of private prayer, from daily to never; and denomination.

The questionnaires were completed in school time and under supervision. Anonymity was guaranteed.

Results and Discussion

General

The percentages of the total numbers of boys and girls falling in each category of response for each moral judgment item are given in Table 106.

The meaningfulness of these results is limited both by the fact that subjects were required to make abstract, highly general judgments which were unrelated to concrete situations, and by the fact that judgments were not related to personal decisions and actions. The procedure could be defended, however, on the grounds that it was the only way to sample a variety of different sorts of behavior in a comparable fashion and in a short space of time, that the rating categories permitted subjects to give qualified responses, and that both in a pilot study and in the main survey it was plain that subjects found the operation a meaningful one. It can be added that less than 5 percent of the subjects made comments that were judged to be logically inconsistent with the rating category chosen.

A further caution needed when comparing items for severity of condemnation is that responses might have been influenced by the connotative associations of the labels used. To illustrate, the label "Premarital Sexual Intercourse" may have produced fewer negative responses than would have occurred if the term "Fornication" had been used. However, it was impossible to make the labels equally neutral in evaluative connotation without elaborate circumlocution, so instead the simplest and most direct terms were selected.

As can be seen from Table 106, the item which received the most uncompromising condemnation

TABLE 106. THE PERCENTAGES OF THE TOTAL SAMPLE ENDORSING THE DIFFERENT RATING CATEGORIES

Moral issue	Sex	Always wrong	Usually wrong	Sometimes wrong	Never wrong	Undecided
Gambling	Boys	10.7	16.9	57.0	8.3	7.1
	Girls	19.4	27.1	37.9	3.5	12.1
Drunkenness	Boys	30.6	46.5	17.9	2.0	3.0
	Girls	44.9	44.4	7.8	1.1	1.8
Smoking	Boys	14.9	10.2	32.4	31.6	10.9
	Girls	12.3	8.9	36.2	24.4	18.2
Lying	Boys	19.1	73.9	5.2	0.5	1.3
	Girls	23.8	72.8	2.2	0.3	0.9
Stealing	Boys	70.8	27.5	0.6	0.3	0.8
	Girls	71.2	27.8	0.5	0.1	0.4
Premarital Sexual Intercourse	Boys	28.6	27.6	20.5	10.2	13.1
	Girls	55.8	25.2	6.6	2.4	10.0
Suicide	Boys	32.0	28.7	13.0	15.2	11.1
	Girls	33.4	32.7	10.1	8.7	15.1
Color Bar	Boys	74.0	16.8	3.2	2.4	3.6
	Girls	85.3	8.9	1.6	1.5	2.7

was Color Bar, with Stealing a close second. These distributions, together with the comments made, suggest that property and social justice are important concerns of the subjects. At the other extreme, Smoking and Gambling received the least condemnation, with nearly a third of the boys and a quarter of the girls judging that the former was not really a moral issue at all.

In order to test whether severity of judgment is general or specific to each issue, the items were interrelated via the chi square test. For the boys, 23 out of the 28 tests were significant, and five were not significant; for the girls, 22 tests were significant and six were not significant. Of the 11 nonsignificant results, eight concerned Color Bar. Among boys, this item is independent of Gambling, Smoking, Stealing, and Premarital Sexual Intercourse, but related to Drunkenness and Lying ($p < .01$) and Suicide ($p < .001$); among girls it is independent of Gambling, Drunkenness, Smoking, and Stealing, and only weakly related to Lying, Premarital Sexual Intercourse, and Suicide ($p < .05$). The remaining nonsignificant results were less systematic. Among boys, Suicide and Lying—and among girls, Drunkenness and Lying, and Suicide and Stealing—were unrelated. A possible explanation is that these pairs each include a social and an ascetic item. However, other social and ascetic items are related, and the two most social items (as rated by independent judges)—namely, Stealing and Color Bar—are not related to each other for either sex.

In general, then, there is a strong tendency for those who adopt a strict moral attitude on one item to do so on the others, with the exception of Color Bar. It is not entirely clear why Color Bar should be an exception, but the comments written afford one clue. From the remarks of a minority of subjects, it seems that for some subjects Color Bar was conceived in logical rather than moral terms. These subjects stressed the complete irrelevance of skin color, comparing it with hair color or weight, rather than focussing upon those personal consequences of being the object of discrimination which make the issue a moral one. This may reflect the fact that many of the subjects had had no direct experience of colored people.

Nonreligious Factors

a. Sex difference. Girls were significantly more severe in their judgments than were boys on all issues with the exception of Stealing, where the difference was in the same direction but not significant, and Smoking, where the difference was significant but not in the same direction. On the latter item, girls were more undecided than were boys.

b. Age and subject studied. No relation could be found between moral judgment responses and type of subject studied at school for either sex. The same was true for age, except that among girls, age and Suicide were related ($p < .01$), with both the younger and the older girls being more condemnatory.

c. Coeducation. Within each sex, pupils in single-sex schools were compared with pupils in coeducational schools to see if there was any association between experience of coeducation and moral judgment. Among boys, no evidence of such an association could be found for any of the moral issues. Among girls, judgments were significantly related to type of school on only two issues, Smoking ($p <$ .02) and Premarital Sexual Intercourse ($p <$ .05). In each case, girls in coeducational schools were less condemnatory than girls in single-sex schools. This suggests that coeducation is not an important factor in moral judgment, in marked contrast to the relation between religious belief and coeducation (Wright and Cox, 1967a). However, if the differences in moral judgment between types of school were in the main not significant, such differences as did exist were consistently larger for girls than for boys. Contingency coefficients were calculated, and it was found that seven out of eight were larger for

girls than for boys ($p <$.03 on a Sign Test. Moreover, all the differences for the girls were in the direction of closer similarity to boys in coeducational schools, whereas boys in coeducational schools were more similar to girls on half the items only, as compared with boys in single-sex schools. The evidence, though slender, supports the finding for religious belief (Wright and Cox, 1967a) that girls in coeducational schools are more likely to be assimilated to the boys than the other way round.

Religious Factors

All moral judgment items were tested for association with the four indices of religious belief and practice using chi square. Among boys, all associations were significant, and most very highly, with the exception of that between belief in God and Smoking. Among girls also, all associations were highly significant except those between Color Bar and belief in God, churchgoing, and private prayer, which

TABLE 107. THE PERCENTAGES OF THOSE ENDORSING THE "ALWAYS WRONG" CATEGORY, WHO FALL IN THE EXTREME RELIGIOUS POSITIONS

Moral issue	Completely confident of the existence of God	Completely confident Jesus was the Son of God	Weekly churchgoing	Daily private prayer
Boys				
Gambling	37.0	44.2	59.5	42.1
Drunkenness	35.8	36.2	46.8	32.4
Smoking	21.9	21.9	35.7	25.3
Lying	32.7	33.6	41.4	32.6
Stealing	21.9	21.8	32.3	21.6
Premarital Sexual Intercourse	35.6	35.8	44.8	30.2
Suicide	30.1	30.6	40.3	31.9
Color Bar	22.0	22.5	32.7	23.4
Total sample	19.6	20.9	30.1	20.4
Subjects endorsing A or B on all items	48.6	50.7	61.4	44.3
Girls				
Gambling	59.6	63.4	76.7	55.1
Drunkenness	49.3	52.4	54.1	48.3
Smoking	46.7	47.0	54.5	50.4
Lying	51.0	50.6	56.9	48.6
Stealing	42.0	43.4	51.6	39.1
Premarital Sexual Intercourse	50.6	53.1	60.0	47.3
Suicide	56.2	54.3	62.8	48.0
Color Bar	42.8	42.5	51.8	39.1
Total Sample	39.1	39.4	49.7	37.7
Subjects endorsing A or B on all items	61.8	66.7	73.5	59.8

Note: "A" means the action is judged to be always wrong, and "B" means the action is judged to be usually wrong but excusable in certain circumstances.

were not significant; and that between belief in Christ and Color Bar, which was only weakly significant ($p < .05$). In all instances, the religious subjects were more likely to adopt the stricter moral position, though on one or two items the relationship was not entirely linear. Few denominational differences could be found, although there was a significant tendency for Baptist and members of smaller Christian sects to be more strict than others about Gambling and Drunkenness.

The extent to which the moral items were related to indices of religiosity is indicated by Table 107. This table is based only on those subjects who endorsed the "always wrong" category. For each moral item, the percentages of those in the "always wrong" category who adopt the extreme religious position on the several indices are given. For comparative purposes, the table also includes the percentages of the total sample who fall into the extreme religious categories, and the corresponding percentages of those subjects who endorse either A or B on every moral item. This last group was very small, consisting of 70 boys and 102 girls.

As can be seen, all percentages are higher than the corresponding ones for the whole sample. It is also clear that the moral items vary quite widely in the degree to which they are associated with religiosity.

In order to test whether the degree of association was related to the ascetic-social dimension, 14 male and 14 female undergraduates placed the eight moral items in rank order for this dimension using the method of paired comparison. Ascetic moral issues were defined as those in which the consequences of behavior are felt primarily by the individual, social moral issues as those in which the consequences are felt primarily by others. Coefficients of Concordance between judges were found to be .45 ($p < .001$) for males and .64 ($p < .001$) for females. Ranks were averaged and reranked, giving a final rank order for each sex. The correlations between asceticism and religiosity were then calculated for each sex, and are given in Table 108.

Although all correlations are in the predicted direction, only one is significant. The item which fitted the prediction least well was Smoking, since it was ranked the most ascetic by both male and female judges, and yet was not strongly related to religion, especially among boys. This item is, however, to some extent atypical, since over 40 percent of both boys and girls were undecided, or did not think it a moral issue at all. If this item is dropped,

TABLE 108. CORRELATIONS BETWEEN THE ASCETICISM OF MORAL ITEMS AND THEIR ASSOCIATION WITH RELIGIOUS BELIEF AND PRACTICE
($N = 8$)

Boys	%	Girls	%
Belief in God	.31 (n.s.)	Belief in God	.43 (n.s.)
Belief in Christ	.36 (n.s.)	Belief in Christ	.57 (n.s.)
Churchgoing	.53 (n.s.)	Churchgoing	.45 (n.s.)
Private prayer	.31 (n.s.)	Private prayer	.76 (.05)

five out of the eight correlations become significant.

We may conclude that, in general, these results do offer some support for the findings of Middleton and Putney (1962). The more ascetic the moral issue, the greater the difference between the responses of religious and nonreligious subjects. The results differ from those of Middleton and Putney; in that even for the most social item, religious subjects tend to be more severe than other subjects.

Analysis of the comments made by subjects on all items reveals a clear difference between the devout and the nonreligious. The nonreligious tend to argue that, if a form of behavior has no undesirable consequences for other people, it is not a legitimate matter for the moral evaluation of others; the devout claim that the individual's life is not his own, that all his behavior concerns God, and that hence there is no part of it which may not be the subject of moral evaluation on occasion. However, from the specific reasons given by the devout for their moral beliefs, it would seem that these beliefs may be serving more than one function. Some devout subjects express considerable disgust for antiascetic behavior, and offer as their reasons for condemning it the fact that they involve loss of self-control or self-respect, and the giving way to "animal" instincts of fear and lust. When such reasons, together with appeals to absolute authority, are given in support of an unqualified condemnation, we may suspect that the beliefs are serving a defensive function. On the other hand, some devout subjects are more concerned with future personal development, and see the ascetic moral rules as the necessary condition of growth into self-respect and responsibility. Such subjects, though they condemn astiascetic behavior, are likely to qualify their judgments with the recognition that under certain circumstances such behavior is not detrimental to personal integrity. These subjects do draw attention to the fact that religious belief, in addition to all its other functions, can serve to support a program of personal development.

Summary

A representative sample of 2276 boys and girls, drawn from the second year of the sixth forms of state maintained grammar schools in England, completed a questionnaire which included items on moral judgment and religious belief and practice. The main findings were as follows:

1. The subjects were most condemnatory of Color Bar and Stealing, and least condemnatory of Smoking and Gambling.

2. There was a general tendency for responses on one item to be associated with responses on the others, with a notable exception of Color Bar, which was largely independent.
3. On nearly all items, girls were more severe in their judgments than were boys.
4. Age, subject studied, and experience of coeducation were not found to be related to moral judgment.
5. Consistently, indices of religiosity were found to be related to severity of moral judgment.
6. The more ascetic the moral issue, the stronger the association with religious belief and practice.

44

Relationship Between Self-
*Reports and Adolescent Religiosity**

Orlo Strunk, Jr.

Recently, Cowen (1954) discovered a relationship between negative self-concept scores and religiosity, although, as he pointed out, cross checking was needed. Cowen's finding suggested a tendency for high negative self-concept Ss, as defined by scores made on the Brownfain Self-Rating Inventory (Brownfain, 1952), to hold less intense religious beliefs than low scorers. In light of early studies in the psychology of religion, this finding seems reasonable, since very often theologies have placed great emphasis on the sinfulness of man and the general depravity of all. However, Strunk (1958a), in conducting a correlational analysis on need for cognition and value schemata, found no relationship between self-concept and religious values (Strunk, 1958b).

In light of these observations, it was the purpose of the present study to test further the possible relationship between self-concept, or, more accurately, self-reports (Combs and Soper, 1957), and religiosity.

Procedure

Ss were 136 high school juniors, 55 males and 81 females. The mean age of the group was 16.4 years. Ss were given two inventories, the Brownfain Self-Rating Inventory, filling out the "private self" form only (Brownfain, 1952, p. 598), and the Religiosity Index, a seven-item questionnaire especially constructed for the present study.

The "private self" form of the Brownfain inventory merely instructs S to rate himself on an eight-point scale on 20 traits in terms of how he really thinks he is. The procedure here is unlike that described by Brownfain (1952) and Cowen (1954) where differences between ratings constitute a score indicating stability of the self-concept. In the present

* From *Psychological Reports*, 1958, **4**, 683–686.

study, scoring was done by adding all ratings made by each S, dividing the number of traits rated by 20, the results of this procedure yielding a mean self-rating score for each rater.

The Religiosity Index[1] was constructed with religiosity being operationally defined as fairly frequent attendance at church, regular contributions of money and time to the church, the reading of some type of religious literature, regular prayer activity, a belief that the person's own religious beliefs and needs were stronger than average when compared with those of peers, and the admittance of a feeling that some sort of religious belief is necessary for a mature outlook on life. The items measuring religiosity were drawn in part from several similar inventories and attitude scales (Allport *et al.*, 1948; Rhodes, 1948). It was possible to score as high as 25 on this index (high religiosity) and as low as one (low religiosity).

The instruments were administered in a classroom situation. Ss were instructed not to identify themselves on the forms. The instructions for both instruments were read so as to avoid misunderstanding. Any questions arising from unfamiliarity with vocabulary were answered by the administrators.

Results and Discussion

A correlational analysis between scores obtained on the Brownfain Self-Rating Inventory and the Religiosity Index produced a product moment correlation of .32, which is significant at better than the .01 level ($n = 136$).

The mean self-rating score was 6.04 ($SD = .78$), which, according to the Brownfain inventory, is

[1] The Religiosity Index contains the following items (weights of responses are in italics): 1. During the past six months I have attended church: *4*, regularly (at least once a week); *3*, fairly frequently; *2*, occasionally; *1*, rarely; *0*, never. 2. During the past six months I have given money to the church: *4*, by tithing (giving 10% of your personal income); *3*, regularly; *2*, occasionally; *1*, rarely; *0*, never. 3. During the past six months I have devoted time to the church, e.g., to act as a teacher, speaker, cutting the grass, serving for a supper, cleaning the church, choir, or by doing some other service for the church: *3*, regularly; *2*, occasionally; *1*, rarely; *0*, never. 4. During the past six months I have read some devotional literature, e.g., *Upper Room, Catholic Review, Bible, Torah*, etc.: *3*, daily; *2*, fairly frequently; *1*, rarely; *0*, never. 5. During the past six months I have prayed: *4*, daily; *3*, fairly frequently; *2*, occasionally; *1*, rarely; *0*, never. 6. How would you say that your own religious beliefs and religious needs compare with those of other young people your own age? *4*, stronger than average; *2*, about average; *0*, less than average. 7. Do you feel you need some sort of religious belief in order to have a mature outlook on life? *3*, yes; *0*, no; *1*, doubtful.

described as "distinctly above average but not outstanding." Scores on the self-report instrument ranged from 4.05 to 7.45. The mean of 6.04 is slightly lower than that obtained on a college population of similar size where the mean was 6.17 ($SD = .69$) (17).

In order to test further this relationship, Ss were divided into high and low scorers on the self-rating inventory. The mean religiosity score for the low self-rating group was 14.42 ($N = 26$) and for the high group, 18.06 ($N = 33$). The difference between these means is significant at well beyond the .01 level ($t = 3.59$).

Taken as a whole, these results seem to demonstrate a definite tendency for religiously-oriented adolescents to have a relatively affirmative self-concept, as compared with less religiously-oriented adolescents. This finding is contrary to some of the classical research and discussion of adolescent religion where guilt and negative feelings toward self have been emphasized.

Perhaps the historical and cultural elements may partially explain the trend manifested in the present study. Practically all of the classical studies on adolescent religious experience were conducted during the early part of the present century, when a theology of self-abasement and a negative emphasis were dominant. It may be that with the contemporary theological trend toward liberality has come, either directly or indirectly, a propensity toward enhancement of the self picture. To verify this possibility would require more extensive study. Another possibility is that specific denominational membership may be a significant factor. Except for the fact that a very large majority of the sample in the present study was Protestant, specific denominational affiliation was an unknown variable.

Certainly there is a rich field of hypotheses available here. As Strange has recently observed,

> Self-realization in the psychological realm is connected with religious faith. An adolescent who believes in God as a "very present help" not only in time of trouble but also as a daily source of guidance for his best development, has a certain resource of strength and courage. He is not alone. His concept of himself extends into infinity (1957, p. 123).

Are the data in this study a manifestation of Strange's assertion? Only additional research in the psychology of religion will answer such a question.

As we direct our research on the self-concept and

its formation through the internalization of value schemata, and, more specifically, as we attempt to understand the religious connotations of selfhood as compared with the psychotherapeutic ones (C. R. Rogers, 1958), we will have to deal with influence of religion and other value systems in the codification of the self-concept. Though the classical psychological studies of religion may prove helpful in this respect, it appears that new research will have to be initiated in view of the radical changes in religion itself.

Summary

136 high school students were given a modified form of the Brownfain Self-Rating Inventory and the Religiosity Index. By dividing the group into high ($N = 33$) and low ($N = 26$) scorers on the Brownfain instrument, it was possible to compare the responses of these two groups on religiosity. A significant difference was found between the high and low self-report scorers, those adolescents with a relatively affirmative self-report tending to score higher on religiosity than the less affirmative self-report scorers. A product-moment correlation of .32 between self-reports and religiosity scores also indicated this marked relationship. Since these relationships appear to contradict results of some classical studies in the psychology of religion, and interest in understanding the significance of value schemata in the formation of the self-concept is growing, further research in the psychology of religion is urged.

X

Self-Concept,
Self-Esteem
and
Identity

This concluding section concerns the processes by which the disparate aspects of adolescent personality may be integrated. These integrative processes themselves have important characteristics and raise crucial issues for youngsters. For from the process of integrating his component roles with one another, with his changing physiology, with his unique temperament and style, and with his unique life history, emerges the adolescent's concept of himself.

Self, then, is a configuration with characteristics of its own, more than the sum of its parts. For example, we will here distinguish the central from the peripheral components of self, and we will consider the forces that make some components of self more central than others. This will lead us quickly to a discussion of the sex role in adolescence, which up to this point has not been granted its own focus. We will also review the literature on the stability of adolescent self-concept, which is a way of questioning whether there is much of a self in adolescents at all. Finally, we will discuss adolescents' feelings about themselves, that part of the total configuration of self which is self-esteem.

Before moving ahead to integrating our materials in part around the concept of *identity*, we do well to invoke a cautionary note from Erik Erikson about the use of the term.

> . . . Usually the term is used without explanation as if it were obvious what it means; and, indeed, faddish as the word has become, it has also come to mean to many something both profound and unfathomable.
>
> Social scientists sometimes attempt to make it more concrete. However, if they do not quickly equate it with the strangely pat question, "Who am I?", they make such words as "identity crisis," "self-identity," or "sexual identity" fit whatever they are investigating. For the sake of logical or experimental maneuverability (and in order to keep in good academic company) they try to treat these terms as matters of social roles, personal traits, or conscious self-images, shunning the less manageable and the less obscure (and often more sinister) implications of the concept (Erikson, 1966, p. 146).

It is clear that the social scientists who edited this book are to no small degree guilty of the errors of which Erikson warns. We have attempted to make "identity" more concrete, and our treatment of the construct has been for the sake of logical and experimental maneuverability; and in the process we have not come to terms with that something both profound and unfathomable which we sense. Our objective, somehow to organize a portion of the systematic empirical work in adolescence, sets these unavoidable limits.

We have, however, been mindful of the essential dimensions of identity as Erikson uses the term: of the "subjective sense of an invigorating sameness and continuity"; of the "something which can be experienced as identical in the core of the individual and yet also identical in the core of a communal culture"; of a "complementarity of an inner synthesis in the individual and of role integration in his group." These dimensions of the construct have infused our choice and organization of materials throughout, and here they become more explicit.

Stability of Identity

In the midst of all the changes of adolescence—changes in the child's body and changes in the social demands and expectations he encounters—what happens to the individual's self-concept. We can expect change and instability—indeed, one can reasonably wonder whether there will be anything stable enough to be considered a self-concept. The self at this stage is highly vulnerable to the evaluations and opinions of others (Friedenberg, 1959; H. E. Jones, 1943) because of the unsteady, shifting internal grounds. The adolescent's concept of self is subject to radical and rapid alterations—in response to external social cues (Blos, 1962; A. Freud, 1946), physiological changes (W. D. Smith and Lebo, 1956), and internal mood shifts. It is a departure from earlier forms in at least two respects: the adolescent defines himself in psychological and social (rather than physical) terms more commonly than younger children do. And at adolescence, the child is often for the first time able to distinguish the self as subject from the self as object, to see the self as changeable, and to determine to make it over in accord with some ideal conception. These developments can be seen in responses to the question "What would you like to change about yourself if you could." Eighteen-year-old girls give many more responses than 11-year-old girls, and in particular they give more responses dealing with personality characteristics rather than physical or situational features. Boys also list more changes, especially internal personality changes, as age increases from 14 to 16 (Douvan and Adelson, 1966). The ideal concept to which they orient becomes both more seperated from the immediate family circle and more abstract in character as youngsters move through adolescence. Havighurst and his coworkers found that parents were most often chosen as personal models by pre-adolescent children, and that by the end of adolescence choices clustered around visible adults other than parents or had become abstract—a listing of ideal characteristics rather than an ideal individual (*Havighurst, Robinson, and Dorr*, 1946).

While adolescents more commonly think of the self as changeable compared to younger children, nevertheless their self-concepts hold fairly stable. *Engel* (1959) reports that the self-concepts of 172 middle-class junior high and high school students correlated .78 after an interval of two years. Self-concept in this study was measured by a rank-ordering of personal traits for relevance to the self. With only a fair degree of short-term test-retest reliability (.68) in this self-concept measure, the correlation over two years is even more impressive. How stable the self-concepts of Engel's adolescents are compared to the self-concepts of younger children or adults we do not know, for we have no comparable data. There are no differences in stability between the older and younger students in Engel's sample. E. V. Piers and Harris (1964) compared the stability of self-concept over a four-month interval among third, sixth, and tenth graders and found no age differences. Piers' and Harris' correlations at all three age levels were, like Engel's, in the .70's.

These data indicate that self-concept does not fluctuate widely through adolescence. Adolescents undergo drastic maturational changes, are subject to some sharp changes in their social roles, and many experiment with different personal styles; but all this change seems to fall short of touching the core of their self-descriptions.

Centrality in Self

A large number of studies have investigated the bases of adolescent self-concept, and we have some information on the nature of the core of their self-descriptions. An overview of the data suggests that the sex-role is likely to be at the core of an American adolescent's identity. Kagan and Moss (1962) have demonstrated the imposing effect of traditional sex-role definitions on the form of development from childhood to adulthood. Their findings indicate that the degree of stability of particular personality traits is highly contingent on their correspondence to traditional sex-role conceptions. Characteristics conceived as feminine (e.g., passivity, dependency) show a high degree of stability from childhood to adulthood in females but not in males. Similarly, aggression is highly continuous in males, not in females. Boys and girls who are equally dependent in childhood diverge at about adolescence in response to differential social pressures. The boy feels sex-specific pressure to become independent and manly; the girl, on the other hand, can (and preferably will) continue to be passive-dependent because of traditional concepts of femininity.

Two separate studies indicate the importance of an adequate sex-identity to adolescent health. Mussen (1961) found that high masculinity among adolescent boys is related to other indices of psychological health such as self-esteem and to positive and rewarding relations with fathers. In Douvan and Adelson's national study of adolescents (1966), a similar measure of traditional feminine interests among girls related strongly to other areas of ego functioning. Girls who score low on feminine orientation are less developed socially, less poised and graceful in interacting with adults; they have a lower level of social energy and a more restricted time perspective than the highly feminine girls. Analysis of girls' vocational plans and aspirations indicates that they are infused with feminine needs: to help others, meet people, find an attractive social setting in which to find potential husbands. However ambitious or modest a girl's job plans, they serve implicitly the same non-vocational agenda.

Sex-identity was found to relate to the conception of self as consistent from situation to situation among college undergraduates, although the nature of the relationship is different among males compared to females (Heilbrun, 1964). The relationship among the young men was straightforward; those who described themselves as more masculine felt more self-consistency. Among the young women, however, higher self-consistency was related either to strong feminine or strong masculine self-concepts; those who described themselves as moderately feminine tended to describe inconsistent selves. One interpretation of these data, in terms of the concepts guiding this review, is that the university environment offers essentially two salient roles to a co-ed: student or girl friend. A young woman can come down solidly on either of these and move about the campus acting consistently according to these role demands, the former more masculine and the latter more feminine. Or she can vacillate between the two and feel at odds with herself, for the role of woman-student has not been clearly defined.

Conscious concern about sex-role resolutions is clearly common among girls at least by college age (Goldsen *et al.*, 1960; Komarovsky, 1953). This great concern with feminine goals reflects the fact that identity for the girl is tied closely to the identity of the man she marries, but it also results from the fact that by college age girls are aware of the conflict between other more individual goals and the culture's definition of femininity. Add to all of this the fact that feminine resolution is not a matter of individual choice or action, that it depends on the girl's *being chosen*—and one wonders only that girls do not have greater anxiety about it. For boys, the case is somewhat different. Identity for them has at least two nuclei—the self-as-worker and the self-as-male. The culture requires the boy to settle both issues, and does not define them as conflicting goals.

Throughout the preceding sections, we have noted important sex differences in the centrality of various roles to adolescent identity. We have seen that their role as son/daughter is important to both boys and girls, but that girls remain more dependent on their parents and boys tend to establish a degree of autonomy more quickly. Data confirm the psychoanalytic hypothesis that it is more crucial to an adequate self-concept and psychological health for boys to establish a positive relationship with their fathers, and girls, with their mothers (Andry, 1960; Dignan, 1965; Gold, 1963; Mussen, 1961).

The relative centrality of the roles of peer-friend and student also differs between the two sexes. The centrality of personal achievement to self-concept in boys, and the importance of personal attractiveness and popularity to girls appear repeatedly in the findings of Douvan and Adelson (1966). When asked what makes them feel "important and useful," for example, the boys refer to work and achievement; girls more often to acceptance, popularity, and praise from others. Similarly, the achievement theme appears in the worries boys report, while girls more commonly worry about peer acceptance and popularity. When the chance to be a big success is pitted against security, most boys choose the opportunity to achieve. The achievement issue is not simply less important for girls, it is different. Girls are not without their golden dreams, but these dreams are not of personal achievement or success; their personal goals are to attract and to hold love.

We have already reviewed J. S. Coleman's data (1961). While the bright student image never becomes the most highly valued for either sex group, boys say they would like to be remembered as good students increasingly as they move through the high school years, and girls continue to undervalue the scholar image. Boys near the end of high school begin to tie school into a concept of the vocational future, and competence in school takes on greater significance for them. The athlete-scholar received more sociometric choices than any other group in Coleman's study. The girl nearing high school graduation focuses future planning on marriage, and popularity continues to hold a central position in her value structure. As she gets closer to marriage and feminine fulfillment, academic values decrease in relevance.

Social position interacts with sex to determine the relative salience of the student and peer-friend, probably not because of the social value of the position itself but because of the motives and skills learned in different social settings. Since middle-class adolescents are better equipped to perform as students, their success encourages them to think of themselves more as students.

Self-Esteem

As adolescents develop the capacity to regard themselves as objects, they increasingly evaluate themselves. This attitude toward themselves has both conscious and unconscious elements, as all attitudes do, but the study of unconscious elements of self-regarding attitudes has been limited by lack of instruments to measure them, although some beginnings have been made (Friedman, 1957; Shore, Massimo, and Ricks, 1965). So studies of adolescent self-esteem have focused on the conscious level.

The level of an individual's self-esteem depends most heavily upon the evaluation he makes of the central components of himself and their integration. His own evaluation, in turn, depends mainly upon the evaluation reflected to him by the people who matter to him, by the standards of his reference groups, and by the effectiveness of his self in helping him reach his goals. The continuing influence of adolescents' parents is evident here again. If an adolescent perceives that his parents are concerned for him, then his evaluation of himself is likely to be higher (Rosenberg, 1965).

An indication of the problems that may occur in the process of accurately sensing reflected evaluations comes from an analysis of the self ratings and ratings of others produced by a group of adolescents and their parents (*Hess & Goldblatt*, 1957). Both adolescents and parents rate adolescents positively on most qualities, but adolescents clearly misperceive the parents' evaluations, thinking them to be more negative than they in fact are. It seems clear that in their zeal to correct their children and keep them on the straight path, parents reflect to their adolescent children a more negative evaluation than they intend. This finding adds context to studies of family interaction which report that families in which communication is open and extensive encourage the development of more self-confident, integrated adolescents.

Since the core of self differs between boys and girls, it follows that their self-esteem depends upon different components. Most girls derive a sense of esteem through social, interpersonal adequacy. Boys can establish their sense of value in more varied ways—by direct sexual expression, by independence and autonomy, by asserting competence to achieve in any one of a number of competitive fields (athletics, a career-line, intellectual activity, leadership in school affairs, responsibility in a job). Girls' greater dependence on specific social validation of their femininity means that dating, acceptance, and popularity are more critical to them than to boys (Douvan and Adelson, 1966; Kagan, 1964; Phelps and Horrocks, 1958). Popularity becomes a proof of feminine worth, a guarantee of future marriageability.

Results of an analysis of mobility aspirations among adolescents bear on the relationship between competence and self-esteem in the boy. Boys who aspire to upward mobility—who appear from all available evidence to be a highly competent group—also show a strong sense of self-esteem. They are rated by interviewers as poised and self-confident. And they indicate a realistic, self-critical attitude in answer to the question about changing themselves. Downwardly mobile boys, who are by all available measures less competent and less achievement-oriented, more often wish for changes in the self that are so extensive or so central that they indicate self-rejection. Interviewers rate these boys much lower on poise and self-confidence (Douvan and Adelson, 1966).

In data for girls, there are no clear and simple ties between achievement-competence in the work sphere and self esteem. But interpersonal skill and a developing concept of feminine adulthood relate closely to measures of self-esteem (Douvan and Adelson, 1966).

Rosenberg's large study of adolescent self-esteem (1965) also high-lighted its ties to achievement and interpersonal skills, although his analysis did not separate boys from girls. Self-esteem was measured here by a 10-item scale and related closely to achievement in school and to occupational expectations. Subjects with low self-esteem much less often thought they had the qualities and characteristics required for success in the jobs of their choice. Low self-esteem is also strongly, though complexly, related to interpersonal competence. Adolescents with low self-esteem tend to describe themselves as withdrawn, excessively sensitive, and suspicious. They tend to provoke problems with peers and so to confirm their fears and suspicions about the social world.

A variant form of low self-esteem—a swaggering verbal self-confidence combined with low scores on measures of ego strength—characterizes boys from divorced families living with their mothers (Douvan and Adelson, 1966). The authors interpret such extreme self-assurance as a defense against anxiety about masculinity. These boys tend to reject adult masculine models and they are markedly rebellious toward adult authority.

Engel (1959) also identified adolescents with "defensive-positive" esteem and found that their psychological adjustment was as adequate, according to MMPI measures, as the adjustment of boys and girls with undefensive, positive esteem; both of these groups measured as better adjusted than youngsters with low self-esteem. Engel's data also demonstrate that low self-esteem is an uncomfortable attitude for adolescents to maintain toward themselves: more negatively than positively evaluated identities shifted after two years, and these shifts were characteristically to "defensive-positive."

Engel's data indicate that self-esteem increases as youngsters grow through adolescence. E. V. Piers and Harris' data (1964) illuminate the course of self-esteem from preadolescence: third-graders and tenth-graders have on the average equally high levels of self-esteem, but sixth-graders have significantly lower self-esteem than either the younger or older groups. These two studies suggest that the fairly sudden beginning of adolescent change is unsettling to youngsters, but that most of them manage to adapt to the change increasingly well as they mature, some only by a process of distortion that must be called defensive however successful it may be.

To summarize, self-esteem crystallizes at adolescence around respectable display of those characteristics which are most important, that is, those which lie at the core of self-definition. Centrality depends heavily on a society's prescriptions of what an adolescent should be, and American society conditions this prescription most heavily according to sex. Those youngsters who do not measure up may become anxious and show signs of disturbance. Most adolescents, however, learn to measure up, and many who are unable to, manage to conceal their shortcomings from themselves so that the modal level of self-esteem is comfortably high.

45

The Status of Adolescents

in American Society:

A Problem in Social Identity*

Robert D. Hess
Irene Goldblatt

Adolescents occupy an ambiguous position in American society. As a phase in personal and social development adolescence is a recognized period experienced by every American youth. As a status in the social structure, however, it is loosely defined at both entry and exit transition points and offers a set of vague and often conflicting roles. The age behaviors expected of adolescents by adults are viewed by society with ambivalence and anxiety. With the possible exception of old age, no other phase of individual development is so clearly marked by negative connotations and lack of positive sanctions.

It is obviously one of the central objectives of socialization to bring pre-adult members to equal status in the adult society. However, the difficulty of achieving this transition is affected by the subordinate individual's perception of the relative position of his status group in the structure of the society and by the attitudes of adults and their willingness to permit expressions of autonomy on the part of subordinate members.

Although there has been little systematic research on the status of adolescents in American society, as viewed by adults or by adolescents themselves, it is generally assumed that the attitudes of the society toward its teen-age members are characteristically depreciatory and often hostile. Our preliminary interviews with adolescents revealed their awareness of a presumed inferior reputation among adults. Adolescents frequently expressed the belief that they are, as a group, subject to condemnation, criticism and general devaluation by adults and that there exists among adults a stereotype of adolescents as sloppy, irresponsible, unreliable, inclined toward destructive and anti-social behavior. It was the objective of our research to explore the evaluation of

* From *Child Development*, 1957, **28**, 459–468.

adolescents by both teen-agers and parents and the relationship between opinions of parents and teen-agers within the same family.

Research Procedure

The Instrument

To obtain evaluations of adolescent and adult reputations, a set of rating scales of 20 pairs of adjectives was constructed. These pairs were selected from comments offered by teen-agers and adults in interviews about the problems of parent-teen-ager interaction. The adjectives represent socially desirable aspects of character and personality, and define in part the standards toward which the middle-class child is directed by his elders and, to a lesser extent, the terms in which the adolescent evaluates himself. The members of each pair can be viewed as positive and negative ends of a specific behavior continuum. Each pair of adjectives was set up on a seven-point scale, 7 representing the highest, or most desirable, rating, and 1 the lowest (*see* Table 109).

Testing Procedure

Each subject was asked to use the scales in making ratings on (a) the "average teen-ager," (b) the "average adult," (c) "teen-agers" from the viewpoint of an adult, and (d) "adults" from the viewpoint of an adult. This resulted for each adolescent in a set of ratings on teen-agers and adults and his prediction of the manner in which teen-agers would be rated by adults.[1] Similarly, each parent was in-

[1] The rating scales were administered twice over a three-week interval to a group of six adolescents. Ninety two per cent of the scores shifted only one scale step or less from the first to the second administration of the scales.

structed to rate (a) the average "teen-ager," (b) the "average adult," (c) "teen-agers" from the viewpoint of a teen-ager, and (d) "adults" from the viewpoint of a teen-ager.

The testing procedure gave rise to the following sets of data:

A. Actual evaluation of own status group, or "self-rating"
  1. adolescents' rating of teen-agers
  2. parents' rating of adults
B. Evaluation of the other status group, or "actual reputation"
  1. adolescents' ratings of adults
  2. parents' rating of teen-agers
C. Predictions of how the other status group would rate own status group, or "expected reputation"
  1. adolescents' predictions on how adults would rate teen-agers
  2. parents' predictions on how teen-agers would rate adults
D. Predictions of how members of the other status group would rate themselves, or "predicted self-rating"
  1. adolescents' predictions of how adults would rate adults
  2. parents' predictions of how teen-agers would rate teen-agers

Sample

Ratings were collected in conjunction with an interview study of 32 families, a study concerned with exploring beliefs and attitudes about teen-agers as these affect parent-child relationships during the adolescent period. The sample was composed of 32 adolescents, 16 boys and 16 girls, and 54 parents, 30 mothers and 24 fathers. In each family, interviews and rating scales were administered to the mother and her teen-age child. The father was interviewed in slightly more than one-half of the families. However, whenever possible, rating scales were obtained from fathers, even if they were not accessible for interviewing. All interviews were taken in the home and the rating instrument was administered in the course of the interview.

The families in the sample were upper-middle and middle class in a metropolitan area. Twenty-three of the families were Protestant, one was Catholic, and seven were Jewish. There was one mixed marriage, Protestant and Jewish.

Average age of the boys was 15.9 years; the average of the girls, 15.5 years. The average high school grade of both boys and girls was 2.8. Two of the adolescent subjects attended private, non-denomina-

TABLE 109. MEAN ITEM RESPONSE BY ADOLESCENTS

| | RATINGS OF | | PREDICTIONS OF ADULTS' RATINGS OF | |
Traits	Teen-Agers	Adults	Teen-Agers	Adults
1. Neat–untidy	4.81	5.88	3.17	5.68
2. Patient–impatient	2.94	4.72	2.23	5.06
3. Cooperative–uncooperative	4.59	5.38	3.37	5.86
4. Serious–frivolous	4.50	5.56	2.70	5.41
5. Responsible–irresponsible	4.62	6.22	2.76	6.07
6. Courteous–rude	4.81	5.81	3.17	5.83
7. Mature–immature	4.62	6.06	2.87	6.00
8. Cautious–impulsive	2.69	5.44	2.10	5.28
9. Consistent–inconsistent	3.56	5.44	2.37	5.76
10. Grateful–ungrateful	4.81	5.72	3.00	5.83
11. Reliable–unreliable	5.19	5.97	3.40	5.93
12. Stable–unstable	4.35	5.47	2.90	5.93
13. Moral–immoral	5.16	5.53	3.80	5.79
14. Self-directed–easily influenced	3.72	5.28	3.17	5.68
15. Respectful–disrespectful	4.78	5.75	3.37	5.79
16. Unspoiled–spoiled	3.97	5.03	2.67	5.72
17. Considerate–inconsiderate	4.44	5.62	3.07	5.83
18. Self-controlled–wild	4.59	5.88	2.80	6.11
19. Thoughtful–thoughtless	4.66	5.66	3.13	5.86
20. Loving–angry	4.81	5.69	3.60	5.72
Means	4.38	5.60	2.80	5.71

tional schools, one attended a parochial school, and the remaining 29 were enrolled in a public high school.

Findings

Perception of the Status Difference between the Two Groups
Ratings of the Two Groups on "The Average Teen-Ager"

Both adolescents and parents rated teen-agers in a mildly favorable manner. Fifteen of the ratings by adolescents fell above the scale mean (4.0) and five below (Table 109). The mean rating that adolescents gave to teen-agers, on all items, was 4.38. Parents rated teen-agers above the scale mean on 14 of the items and below on six (Table 110). Expected differences between the ratings of parents and those of adolescents did not emerge. Only three of the differences between adolescent and parent ratings were statistically significant at the .05 level of confidence (items 1, 7, 13). On one of these, the moral-immoral continuum, the parents gave teen-agers a significantly higher (more positive) rating than did the adolescents themselves.

Ratings by the Two Groups on "The Average Adult"

Both adolescents and parents believe that adults are superior to the teen-ager on all but one (item 13) of the 20 characteristics. Not only did both groups rate the adult more favorably than they rated the teen-ager, but the adolescent subjects gave much higher mean ratings to adults than did the parents. The mean rating on all items by adolescent subjects was 5.60; that of the parents was 4.86. Adolescents rated adults higher than did the parents on each of the 20 items. Sixteen of these item differences were statistically significant. Only items 4, 8, 13, and 19 showed insignificant differences.

The Extent of Perceived Differences between Teen-Agers and Adults

The difference between each group's rating of teen-agers and its rating of adults (Tables 109 and 110, col. 2 minus col. 1) can be considered an expression of the distance in status as it is differently perceived by the two groups. It has already been noted that teen-agers are rated in a mildly favorable manner by both groups, and that adults are believed to be superior to teen-agers. However, adolescents accentuate in their ratings the relative superiority of

TABLE 110. MEAN ITEM RESPONSE BY PARENTS

| | RATINGS OF | | PREDICTIONS OF TEEN-AGERS' RATINGS OF | |
Traits	Teen-Agers	Adults	Teen-Agers	Adults
1. Neat–untidy	3.98	5.00	4.93	5.00
2. Patient–impatient	2.48	3.69	5.14	2.58
3. Cooperative–uncooperative	4.45	4.84	5.96	3.84
4. Serious–frivolous	4.80	5.20	5.62	5.82
5. Responsible–irresponsible	4.87	5.24	6.02	6.09
6. Courteous–rude	4.44	4.86	5.48	4.30
7. Mature–immature	3.98	5.02	5.60	5.36
8. Cautious–impulsive	2.72	4.78	4.11	5.18
9. Consistent–inconsistent	3.57	4.18	5.53	3.18
10. Grateful–ungrateful	4.59	4.82	5.60	3.66
11. Reliable–unreliable	4.98	5.10	5.91	4.93
12. Stable–unstable	4.45	4.76	5.64	4.98
13. Moral–immoral	5.98	5.46	5.87	5.51
14. Self-directed–easily influenced	4.18	4.32	5.85	5.18
15. Respectful–disrespectful	4.50	5.22	5.56	4.70
16. Unspoiled–spoiled	3.70	4.31	5.54	4.22
17. Considerate–inconsiderate	4.22	4.78	5.66	3.77
18. Self-controlled–wild	4.62	5.34	5.32	5.16
19. Thoughtful–thoughtless	4.09	5.24	5.54	4.49
20. Loving–angry	4.83	5.14	5.32	4.57
Means	4.27	4.86	5.51	4.63

adults over teen-agers. In scale terms, the distance between adults and teen-agers is perceived by the adolescents to be almost twice as large as that seen by parents.

These differences apparently represent the different concerns of the two groups. Both groups share the opinion that teen-agers have a relatively long way to go before they reach the adult level of self control. However, the adolescent subjects seem to feel that they are much less "responsible" and less "self-directing" than adults, while the parents seem relatively unconcerned about these characteristics.

Expected Reputation

The Attempt to Predict the Ratings of the Other Group

The adolescent's view of his status in the social system is a function of the reputation he anticipates from adults as well as his own view of his age group. It is significant, then, that the adolescents of our sample predict that teen-agers will be evaluated in a generally unfavorable manner by the adult group.

All of the ratings which the adolescent subjects anticipate will be given to teen-agers by adults fall below the scale mean (Table 109, col. 3). Adolescents expect that the lowest ratings will describe them as impulsive, impatient, inconsistent, spoiled, frivolous, irresponsible, and wild. In contrast to the unfavorable reputation adolescents believe the teen-ager has, the parents in the sample believe that their own status group has a mildly favorable reputation among teen-agers.

Disparity between Expected Reputation and Self-Ratings

The difference between the adolescents' own rating of teen-agers and their predictions of the average adults' rating of teen-agers can be regarded as a measure of the extent to which teen-agers will feel underrated or depreciated. The data indicate that adolescents expect to be underrated on each of the items. On 18 of the items (all except 8 and 14) the difference between self-ratings and expected ratings is statistically significant (Table 109). By contrast, parents predict that teen-agers will significantly underrate adults on only six items (2, 3, 9, 10, 17, 19; Table 110, col. 2 minus col. 4).

The items on which the parents feel that adults will be underrated can be seen as relating to tension in interpersonal relationships. However, parents believe that qualities of maturity which are relatively independent of interpersonal relationships will either be accurately perceived by the teen-ager or even overrated. These ratings suggest that parents feel they will be seen as mature but unsympathetic or ill-intentioned in interpersonal affairs. They feel that they will be seen as more "uncooperative," "ungrateful," "impatient," and "thoughtless" than they really are.

Ratings Indicating Expected Perception of Status Differences

Predictions of the Self-Ratings of the Other Group

The disparities already mentioned are emphasized by the belief each group has about the ratings which they think members of the other group will give themselves. Two sets of predictions are involved: the adolescents' predictions of how adults will rate themselves, and the parents' predictions of the ratings teen-agers will give themselves (Table 109, col. 4; Table 2, col. 3). Both groups believe that members of the other status group will have very favorable opinions of themselves. Parents predict that teen-agers will rate themselves above the scale mean on all items. Adolescents believe that adults will rate themselves above the mean on all items. The difference between the two sets of predicted self-ratings is very small.

Disparity between Predicted Self-Ratings and Own Ratings

The parents' predictions of the teen-ager's favorable opinion of himself represents a belief that teen-agers will overestimate themselves on the traits in question, since the parents themselves give a generally lower rating to teen-agers. In contrast the adolescent expects that parents will see themselves in the same favorable light as he sees them. In effect, teen-agers are expressing confidence in the parents' judgment, even when the parents are evaluating themselves. By the same rationale, parents expect that teen-agers will be conceited, or, at best, unrealistic when judging themselves. This expectation is expressed by significant differences on 17 of the 20 items (exceptions are 13, 18, and 20; Table 110, col. 1 minus col. 3). There is only one reversal: parents say that teen-agers will underrate themselves on "moral" behavior.

Comparison of the rank ordering of items revealed that parents believe teen-agers will emphasize items having to do with readiness for emancipation from parental control. Such items as "responsible," "mature," "consistent," "stable," and "self-directed" rank higher in the predicted self-estimate than in the parents' ratings of adolescents. In complementary fashion, parents expect that adolescents will rate themselves *relatively* low on "self-controlled," "cautious," "neat," and "patient." This indicates that these parents believe that teen-agers think of themselves as ready to lead their own lives—but along rather hedonistic lines.

The Expected Perception of Status Difference

A measure of predicted status differential between the two groups may be obtained by a comparison between the view the adolescent has of his reputation with adults and the view he thinks adults will have of themselves. This is the teen-ager's prediction of his relative status in the eyes of the adults.

Considered in these terms, the data show that *adolescents think adults will see themselves as vastly superior to the average teen-ager* (Table 109, cols. 3 and 4). Further, adolescents predict that adults' opinion of the status difference will be much greater than adolescents believe it is (Table 109, cols. 1 and 2 compared with cols. 3 and 4).[2]

[2] An indication of the characteristic adolescent attitude toward their status in adult minds is seen in the relatively small range that appeared in the predicted ratings. In rating their own group and the adult group, the range between highest and lowest mean rating is three scale steps; in the predicted ratings this range is two scale steps. The adolescents, then, are predicting that the average adult will show little discrimination in evaluating teen-agers and will underrate them even on traits on which the teen-agers feel most competent and acceptable. The parents do not make a comparable assumption in the ratings they expect from teen-agers.

Parental Attitudes and the Ratings by Own Teen-Agers

It was assumed that the ratings given by adolescents to the "average adult" and to the "average teen-ager" were not unaffected by the attitudes encountered in their own family experience. The ratings of parent-child pairs were examined, therefore, to determine the degree of association between mother-child pairs and between father-child pairs.

The resulting coefficients offer evidence that the mother's attitudes are more influential than the father's in determining the attitudes of the teen-agers. The mother's perception of status difference (Table 110. col. 2 minus col. 1) correlates significantly with the extent to which her teen-agers feel underrated (Table 109, col. 1 minus col. 3). That is, the larger the status difference that the mother perceives between adults and teen-agers, the lower the reputation that her adolescent predicts teen-agers have. This relationship is highly significant and holds for both mother-daughter and mother-son pairs (Table 111). However, the father's perception of the adult–teen-ager status difference appears to have virtually no effect upon the attitudes of his children as indicated by insignificant coefficients with both sons and daughters.[3]

Although adolescents appear to be sensitive to their mothers' evaluations, their own ratings of teen-agers are relatively independent of parental opinion. The comparison between the ratings of parents and their children on the "average teen-ager" reveals no significant association between adolescents and either father or mother (Pearson r's of .062 and .067

[3] The attitudes of fathers about teen-agers are significantly related to those of the mothers in the sample (Pearson $r = .44$) but their perception of the status difference between the two groups is not (Pearson $r = .18$).

TABLE 111. COEFFICIENTS OF ASSOCIATION (TAU) BETWEEN THE RATINGS OF PARENTS AND OWN CHILDREN

| | *Children Expectation of Underevaluation (Table 109, col. 1–col. 3)* | | | |
	Girls	N	Boys	N
Parents: Perception of Status Difference (Table 110, col. 4–col. 1)				
Mother	.55*	(13)	.59*	(13)
Father	.13	(11)	.00	(10)

* $p < .01$.

respectively). The teen-ager's feeling about his group's reputation among adults thus appears to be determined in part by the attitudes of his own mother toward teen-agers as a group but he resists her influence in making his evaluation of his own group.

Summary of Findings

1. Adolescents and parents agree in expressing mildly favorable opinions of teen-agers.

2. The adolescents tend to idealize adults, i.e., they have much higher opinions of adults than do the parents.

3. Adolescents see a relatively greater status difference between teen-agers and adults than do the parents.

4. Adolescents believe that the average adult has a generalized tendency to depreciate teen-agers. They feel that teen-agers have a uniformly low reputation among adults.

5. Parents anticipate that teen-agers will have a selective tendency to undervalue adults. They predict that adults will get lower ratings than they merit on items which refer to interpersonal relationships, but that they will be accurately evaluated on non-interpersonal maturity items.

6. Adolescents believe that the adults will evaluate themselves relatively accurately.

7. Parents believe that teen-agers have unrealistically high opinions of themselves.

8. Both adolescents and parents believe that the status difference between teen-agers and adults will be distorted to approximately the same extent by the other group.

9. The attitude of the adolescent about the relative status of teen-agers is significantly associated with the opinions of his mother about the adult–teen-age status difference. However, the opinion of his parents is not related statistically to his evaluation of the "average teen-ager."

10. The attitude of the father as expressed in the rating scales is not significantly associated with ratings of his own teen-age children.

Three trends in the data stand out as particularly relevant to parent-adolescent relationships and to theories of adolescent socialization: (a) the agreement between the two groups in their evaluation of teen-agers; (b) the perceptual distortions of both groups in predicting the response of the other group; and (c) the immense status difference between the groups that teen-agers believe exists in the minds of adults. The prominence of these trends emphasizes the difficulties faced by the adolescent in his effort to effect a transition from adolescence to adult roles and behavior.

From their own point of view, the adolescents credit themselves with an acceptable degree of achievement which, nevertheless, places their group in a subordinate position with respect to adults. This willingness to admit a differentiation between their own status and that of adults is in agreement with the views of adults, though it tends to exaggerate the status distance.

The assumption by parents that teen-agers have unrealistically high opinions of themselves is not corroborated by the data obtained from adolescents themselves. This parental belief may, to some extent, simply represent a response to, and acceptance at face value of, a protective bravado and air of competency which the adolescent assumes to protect himself, both from arousing parental anxieties and from his own feelings of inadequacy.

Our data suggest that one of the central problems in parent–teen-ager relations lies not so much in disparity between their respective evaluations of adolescents as in the fact that each group mistrusts or misunderstands the opinions of the other. Parents and adolescents thus interpret teen-age behavior and problems in different, and often contradictory, terms. For the adolescent, teen-age problems are expressed in terms of *ego functions*—autonomy, self-control and judgment based upon exploratory experience with adult roles. For the parent, the problems of teen-agers are primarily concerned with control of *id impulses* for which, they believe, parental supervision and control are essential. Both views, of course, are to a degree realistic and the families of our study which displayed a minimum of parent-child conflict were those in which parents and teen-agers were willing to recognize the importance of both viewpoints.

The status difference between the groups probably serves a positive socializing function for the teen-ager. A moderate overestimation of the attributes of adults offers a lever for the parent in the socializing process and provides motivation for the adolescent towards increased autonomy and maturity. However, the extreme idealization of the adult by the adolescent, when it is joined with a belief that personal achievements he has made are not recognized by adults, may retard ego development and encourage behaviors which defeat the objectives of both parents and adolescents themselves.

46

The Stability

*of the Self-Concept in Adolescence**

Mary Engel

Recent theory and research point to the importance of the self-concept in understanding and predicting constancies as well as changes in behavior (Brownfain, 1952; C. R. Rogers and Dymond, 1954; Taylor, 1955). It is generally believed that an individual's concept of himself achieves a rather high degree of organization during the course of development and comes to resist change once self-differentiation and self-definition have taken place (Lecky, 1945). As yet it is not known by what age the process of self-definition reaches stability. While we know that the concept of self remains relatively stable, even over extended periods of time, in young adults (Taylor, 1955), and while there are a number of theoretical and partially supported statements in the literature about the storms and stresses of certain aspects of adolescent development (Hall, 1904; Kuhlen, 1948), the fate of the self-concept in adolescence is still a matter for speculation. The studies that examine individual differences in the self-concepts of adolescents from a number of vantage points and in several settings (Balester, 1955; Blodgett, 1953; De Lisle, 1953), represent an inroad into the area of self-concept development. However, it is the longitudinal approach that is most appropriate when seeking answers to questions of development.

The primary purpose of the present study was to investigate the stability of the self-concept in adolescence over a two-year period. It was also its purpose to examine the relationship between whatever stability is found and the quality of the self-concept. The interrelationship between self-concept stability, quality of the self-concept, and several indices of adjustment was also examined.

Method

The data were obtained by testing and retesting 172 public school students, 104 of whom were in the

* From *Journal of Abnormal and Social Psychology*, 1959, **58**, 211–215.

eighth grade and 68 of whom were in the tenth grade at the time of the first testing. The same students served as subjects in 1954 and in 1956.[1] Table 112 presents the grade and sex distribution of Ss in the two-year study. An analysis of the fathers'

TABLE 112. SEX DISTRIBUTION OF SUBJECTS

	8th–10th Grade	10th–12th Grade
Boys	48	28
Girls	56	40
Total	104	68
Grand Total	172	

occupations revealed that the Ss were mostly of lower-middle and middle-class background.

The hypotheses were formulated in 1954. Their testing required the use of the following measures:

1. Self concept Q sort, paper and pencil form, consisting of items relevant to adolescent concerns.
2. Verbal Subscale of the Differential Aptitude Test, as an estimate of intelligence.
3. Scales D, Pd, and K of the MMPI, as measures of adjustment and "defensiveness."
4. Peer Rating Scale, as a sociometric assessment of adjustment, based on the model provided by Tuddenham (1952).
5. Teachers' Forced Choice Test as another independent measure of adjustment, developed by Ullman (1952).

The set of Q-sort items for the assessment of the self-concept in adolescents was developed along lines largely in conformity with the principles put forth by W. Stephenson (1935). Briefly, a large pool of items

[1] There were 243 Ss in 1954; the discrepancy between the 1954 and 1956 N can be accounted for by attrition during the two-year period. Whereas the over-all N of the longitudinal sample was 172, an N of approximately 149 was available for the testing of certain hypotheses, due to the absence of some Ss on some of the testing days in 1956.

was gathered covering areas of adolescent self-concern as empirically defined by Jersild (1952). The pooled judgments of psychologists, nonprofessional adults, and adolescents were used to reduce and refine the original set, 100 Q-sort items being retained. Judges could agree with demonstrable certainty that these items represent either positively or negatively toned self-referent attitudes. Examples are: "I can take criticism without resentment." "I see little about myself that's outstanding."

In responding, Ss had to distribute the 50 positively and 50 negatively toned items into 11 categories, ranging from "most like me" to "least like me." The frequency distribution of items was as follows:

Number of items
4 7 9 11 12 14 12 11 9 7 4
Category
1 2 3 4 5 6 7 8 9 10 11

Paper and pencil administration incurs some errors of measurement, probably not pertaining to item-sampling, that are not involved when the usual card sorting procedure is used. The test-retest reliability of the instrument was .68 over a ten-day period with an N of 23 (tenth grade students). This reliability figure was obtained by correlating the values assigned to each item, by each S, on two occasions and represents the mean of 23 correlations (z transformations were used in computing the mean r). It is slightly lower than similar statistics obtained by others, using the card sort (Taylor, 1955).

The maximum positiveness score that can be obtained on the Q sort used in this study is 600. A score of this magnitude would result from placing every one of the 50 positive items in the "most like me" end of the continuum. Placing an equal number of positive and negative items on the upper and the lower end of the continuum would give rise to a score of 300, the point of ambivalence. Customarily, the negative self-concept is defined as a positiveness score falling below the point of ambivalence, whereas the positive self-concept is usually defined as a positiveness score above the point of ambivalence.

In responding to the Peer Rating Scale, each member of a class writes down one to three names of others who seem to suit some brief behavioral descriptions, for example: "Who is the good sport, the person who always plays fair?" "Who gets mad easily and loses his or her temper often?" These descriptions can be roughly ordered along an adjustment–maladjustment continuum. Each S receives a score that reflects the extent to which his peers see him as well functioning in the school situation. The reliability of the Peer Rating Scale was established by test-retest of 22 Ss (ninth graders) over a one-week interval. The resulting value of .96 indicates that the adjustment scores derived from ratings of any one subject by the group as a whole are highly reliable.

Results and Discussion

Stability of Self-Concept

Analysis of the data obtained in 1954 from Ss who subsequently dropped out of school indicates that certain important personality differences may have existed between those who left and those who remained in the school. Because of the strong possibility of selective attrition, caution is indicated when generalizing from the results of the present study.

It was expected that the Ss would form three groups with regard to the self-concept: those maintaining positive self-regarding attitudes, those with negative self-regarding attitudes, and those with defensively positive self-concepts. Hypotheses were formulated on the basis of this expectation. All predictions were made in 1954 and were tested in 1956.

It was hypothesized that the self-concept of adolescents would be relatively stable over the two-year period. This hypothesis implies that the stability, internal organization, and crystallization of the self-concept is achieved earlier in development. Stability was defined by relatively high correlations between self-concept Q sorts in 1954 and 1956. Relevant data are presented in Table 113. The over-all mean corre-

TABLE 113. THE STABILITY OF THE SELF-CONCEPT OVER A TWO-YEAR PERIOD ITEM-BY-ITEM CORRELATIONS OF Q SORTS IN 1954 AND 1956

Group	N	Mean t	Ss	r Corresponding to Mean z Scores
Girls				
8th–10th grade	45	.6107	.2059	.54
10th–12th grade	37	.6794	.2204	.59
Boys				
8th–10th grade	44	.4775	.2636	.45
10th–12th grade	23	.6004	.2222	.54
Mean		.5919		.53

lation of .53, for all *S*s, indicates the extent of stability of the self-concept of adolescents over a two-year period, between grades eight and ten, and ten and twelve. Corrected for attenuation, the over-all mean correlation between the self-concept in 1954 and 1956 is .78.

It was also predicted that the self-concept of *S*s with a positive attitude toward themselves in 1954 would be significantly more stable over the two-year period than the self-concept of *S*s with a negative or defensive-positive self-concept. Results bearing on this prediction are presented in Table 114, in which the negative self-concept is defined by

TABLE 114. COMPARISON OF SELF-CONCEPT STABILITY BETWEEN POSITIVE, NEGATIVE, AND DEFENSIVE-POSITIVE SELF-CONCEPT GROUPS OVER THE TWO-YEAR PERIOD

Groups	N^a	Per Cent of Total N (172)	Mean stability[b]	s	t
Positive Self-concept	106	62	.6928	.2060	7.61*
Negative Self-concept	34	20	.3383	.1977	6.99*
Defensive-Positive Self-concept	32	18	.6379	.2138	
Defensive-Positive Self-concept and Positive Self-concept	—	—	—		1.30

* Significant beyond the .05 level.
[a] Classification on basis of 1954 data.
[b] Based on 1954 and 1956 data, total N for this column 149.

scores falling in the lower 20% of the distribution of self-concept scores, and positive self-concept by scores in the upper 80%. Where the self-concept was positive, and *S* also obtained a *K* score greater than 17 (measure of "defensiveness" derived from the MMPI), *S* was classified as manifesting a defensive-positive self-concept.

To test the hypothesis, correlations between *Q* sorts were converted into *z* scores as measures of stability. An over-all *F* test of differences in stability between self-concept groups resulted in an *F* ratio of 28.12, greatly exceeding the ratio of 5.30 needed for significance at $p = .05$. Individual *t* tests between groups support the conclusions that (*a*) *S*s whose self-concept was positive in 1954 were significantly

more stable over the two-year period than *S*s who had negative self-concepts in 1954; (*b*) *S*s whose self-concept was defensive-positive in 1954 were significantly more stable than those who had negative self-concepts; (*c*) *S*s whose self-concept was positive in 1954 did not differ significantly in stability from those whose self-concept was defensive-positive in 1954.

The prediction that older and younger *S*s would not differ significantly in stability of self-concept over the two-year period was supported. Age group differences in magnitude of *Q* sort correlations (self-concept stability) resulted in a *t* ratio of .60.

It was also expected that stability of the self-concept would be statistically unrelated to intelligence. Testing this prediction required correlating verbal intelligence scores (DAT) with self-concept stability scores. Correlations were nonsignificant, lending support to the hypothesis, except in the case of the tenth–twelfth grade girls, where an *r* of .36 was found between these two variables, which, with an N of 35, was significant beyond the .05 level.

On the assumption that cultural ambiguities concerning sex roles should be more likely to affect girls than boys, it was hypothesized that the self-concept of boys would be significantly more stable, over the two-year period than that of girls. This hypothesis was not upheld. The comparison of the mean stability between boys and girls resulted in a *t* ratio of .76.

In comparing the mean positiveness scores of the *S*s in 1954 and in 1956 (Table 115) we found an

TABLE 115. POSITIVENESS OF THE SELF-CONCEPT IN 1954 AND IN 1956

	1954			1956		
	N	M	s	N	M	s
Girls						
8th–10th grade	56	359.98	32.01	45	362.76	29.41
10th–12th grade	40	358.40	36.82	37	365.59	38.44
Boys						
8th–10th grade	48	351.29	34.68	45	352.25	37.15
10th–12th grade	27	360.81	23.03	24	369.75	25.72

unpredicted increase in mean positiveness. With the sexes combined, both grades shifted in a positive direction, the mean shift being significant beyond the .05 level in case of the older group ($t = -2.44$).

Stability of Self-Concept and Adjustment

The relationship between the stability of the self-concept and three measures of adjustment (teacher ratings, peer ratings, and MMPI measures) was explored through the following prediction: Ss who persist in a positive self-regarding attitude should be better adjusted, in terms of the MMPI, teacher ratings, and peer ratings, than those who persist in negative or defensive-positive self-concepts. Table 116

TABLE 116. THE DISTRIBUTION OF ALL SUBJECTS IN THE LONGITUDINAL SAMPLE WITH REGARD TO THE CHANGES AND CONSTANCIES OF THE SELF-CONCEPT AS SEEN IN 1956

Changes and Constancies of the Self-Concept Between 1954 and 1956	Number	Per Cent of Total Number Subjects
Maintained positive self-concept	76	44
Maintained negative self-concept	14	8
Maintained defensive-positive self-concept	11	6
Was defensive-positive in 1954 but did not maintain either defensiveness or positiveness of self-concept	16	9
Was positive but shifted to negative self-concept by more than 20 points	15	9
Was negative but shifted to positive by more than 20 points	17	10
Absent on more than one testing session in 1956 (unclassified)	23	13
Total	172	99

summarizes the "fate" of the quality of the self-concept for all Ss over the two-year period. More detailed analysis revealed that most of the shift in

self-concept quality occurred in the negative self-concept group. Ss who were classified as having negative self-concepts in 1954 more closely approached the mean by 1956. Such shift could be attributed to regression, except that no such shifting toward the mean took place in the case of Ss originally giving evidence of a positive self-concept.

In applying analyses of variance to adjustment indices between groups, 1956 adjustment measures were used. Table 117 shows that F ratios on MMPI scores were significant, whereas F ratios based on other adjustment measures were not.

Differences in MMPI measures were further examined by individual t applied to the column means. MMPI adjustment measures showed the group maintaining negative self-concepts to be significantly less well adjusted (scoring higher on D and Pd) in 1956 than others, partially upholding the hypothesis.

Concomitance of Change in Self-Concept and in Adjustment

It was predicted that a change in self-concept in the positive direction would be related to improved adjustment, and a change in self-concept in the negative direction would be related to impaired adjustment. For the purpose of testing this hypothesis Ss were regrouped and considered either "positive shifters" or "negative shifters" depending on a change of 20 points away from their original positive self-concept score either in the positive or negative direction. Only Ss on whom full sets of adjustment scores were available were included in this analysis. Adjustment scores for 1956 were subtracted from 1954 adjustment scores and t tests were applied to the mean difference scores. Table 118 presents the results bearing on this hypothesis, and supports the

TABLE 117. COLUMN MEANS AND F RATIOS FOR THREE SELF-CONCEPT GROUPS ON MEASURES OF ADJUSTMENT (1956 MEASURES USED)

Measures	Maintaining Positive Self-Concept		Maintaining Negative Self-Concept		Maintaining Positive Defensive Self-Concept		F
	N	M	N	M	N	M	
Pd	73	13.51	12	20.17	11	13.64	15.27*
D	73	14.90	12	22.25	11	15.18	21.20*
Peer rating	71	232.62	12	175.17	10	268.70	2.77
Teacher rating	72	22.00	14	18.86	10	23.00	2.18

* Significant beyond the .05 level.

TABLE 118. CHANGES IN ADJUSTMENT MEASURES CONCOMITANT WITH SHIFTS IN SELF-CONCEPT (BASED ON DIFFERENCE SCORES; 1956 SCORES SUBTRACTED FROM 1954 MEASURES)

Adjustment Measures	"Positive Shifters"				"Negative Shifters"			
	N	M	s	t	N	M	s	t
Pd (MMPI)	30	−.47	3.83	.67	13	−3.15	3.53	−3.22**
D (MMPI)	35	−.60	4.89	.73	15	−3.80	4.75	−3.10**
K (MMPI)	35	−2.94	4.41	−3.95*	22	.23	4.85	.22
Teacher rating	40	.83	7.33	.02	22	.23	4.85	.23
Peer rating	37	−25.97	66.55	−2.37**	17	15.53	93.24	−.69

* Significant beyond the .05 level and in the direction opposite from the predicted one.

** Significant beyond the .05 level and in the predicted direction.

conclusion that "negative shifters" obtained significantly higher *Pd* and *D* scores in 1956 as predicted; however, "positive shifters" became more "defensive" in that they obtained significantly higher *K* scores in 1956 than in 1954; "positive shifters" were seen as significantly more well adjusted by their peers in 1956 than in 1954. Changes in teacher ratings did not differentiate between groups. Thus, this final hypothesis was only partially confirmed.

It should be borne in mind that this study explored mainly one aspect of the self-concept, the conscious self-concept. It may well be that in spite of the consistencies found in adolescents over a two-year period, considerable changes took place in aspects of the concept of self that are less readily admissible into awareness. The exploration of self-concept consistency and its concomitants on a deeper level of personality would require a clinical approach which was precluded by the use of a fairly large number of Ss in the present study.

Summary

A study of the stability of the self-concept over two years in adolescence resulted in the following conclusions:

1. Relative stability of the self-concept was demonstrated by an over-all item-by-item correlation of .53 between *Q* sorts obtained in 1954 and in 1956, with an instrument of which the ten-day test-retest reliability was .68.

2. Subjects whose self-concept was negative at the first testing were significantly less stable in self-concept than subjects whose self-concept was positive.

3. Subjects who persisted in a negative self-concept over the two-year period gave evidence of significantly more maladjustment than subjects who persisted in a positive self-concept, when maladjustment is measured by high scores of scales *Pd* and *D* of the MMPI.

4. Subjects who showed less regard for themselves on the *Q* sort on retest, also shifted toward significantly more maladjustment on scales *Pd* and *D* of the MMPI.

5. Subjects who showed more regard for themselves on the *Q* sort on retest, also shifted toward significantly more adjustment on peer ratings.

6. The positive self-concept scores increased significantly between the two testings for the tenth–twelfth grade subjects, an increase which could not be attributed entirely to the effect of regression.

47

Some Changing Aspects
*of the Self-Concept of Pubescent Males**

Walter D. Smith
Dell Lebo

Introduction

Current literature on psychological theory utilizes the term *self-concept* as one important aspect of personality. It was the purpose of this study to observe any change occurring in the "concept of the self" during the period of rapid physiological change in early adolescence. Physiological phase classifications determined by appraisal of pubic hair development in 12-, 13-, 14-, and 15-year-old males categorized the youth studied. These physiological phase classifications served as the indicator of growth with which aspects of the self-concept were compared in terms of developmental progress.

The importance of the physical changes accompanying the adolescent transition is rarely minimized, even by writers whose particular emphasis and training are in the social-psychological realm. George H. Mead (1934) described the development of the self-concept as emerging directly from the behavior of others toward the individual and indirectly from the physical and other attributes of the individual. Horrocks very aptly describes the importance of the physical changes of adolescence by stating that the changes of adolescence "are often startling and even disquieting . . . it is usually difficult to adjust to the new physical actuality as well as to the new physical self-concept which that actuality involves" (1962, p. 314).

A process of adjustment is implied by Horrocks which suggests personality changes occurring concomitantly with physical changes. Zachary (1940) referred to the body as the "symbol of the self." Anna Freud (1935) attributes many of the adolescent's anxieties and uncertainties to a resurging sexuality of adolescence implying a biological basis for personality changes; however, she fails to explain the exact nature of this relationship in terms of the psychological concepts of the times.

* From *The Journal of Genetic Psychology*, 1956, **88**, 61–75.

On examining the psychological mechanism of the self-concept in a perspective of total growth it would appear that the physical changes of adolescence, no less than the rapid changes of infancy, will be reflected in the individual's behavior as he becomes aware of new abilities and new possibilities within himself, particularly as he relates himself to others. It is this viewpoint around which the study was developed. Others have made methodologically similar approaches but with little emphasis on the adolescent's own feelings about himself (Dimock, 1937; Stone and Barker, 1939; M. C. Jones and Bayley, 1950; Sollenberger, 1940).

Use of the Term Self-Concept

The present discussion does not propose to eliminate the ambiguities prevalent in the use of the term self-concept but rather to elaborate on its use in this report. The responses made by the subjects were evaluated in terms of their projective qualities of the self. In making these appraisals it is to be realized that the facility of complete self-realization does not occur spontaneously in childhood, but according to most researchers on the topic, develops slowly, by gradual changes. Gardner Murphy (1947, p. 343) explains the genesis of selfhood by three developmental levels similar to the process of individuation evidenced in maturation and motor learning. Piaget (1932) has also postulated levels, or stages, of moral development suggesting that the perception of the relation of one's self to the whole society does not occur until early adolescence. Jersild's definition of the "self" is "a composite of thoughts and feelings which constitute a person's awareness of his individual existence, his conception of who and what he is" (1952, p. 9). Recognizing the dynamic nature of "these thoughts and feelings," their reflection or expression in one's responses to his stimulus world seems inevitable and therefore appears accessible to our commonly used projective techniques.

Two assumptions of major concern emerge from this discussion. First, the self-concept, existing as a part of the totality commonly termed personality, is mirrored or projected in the behavior or responses of the individual. Second, this self-concept changes, gradually taking on the characteristics of the adult rôle in our society as a result of growth processes and learning experiences with major changes taking place during the rapid growth period of puberty. A description of these changes in self-concept and their relationship to the pubertal growth processes constitutes the problem area of the present study.

The instruments for measuring aspects of the self-concept were developed from instruments and techniques commonly used in personality appraisal. These were: (*a*) an adaptation of the *Vineland Social Maturity Scale,* (*b*) human figure drawings, and (*c*) paragraph completion items relating to heterosexual development and emancipation from parents.

Choice of Growth Indicator

To determine the effects of the rapid physical changes of puberty on the adolescent's self-concept the writers were faced with the problem of selecting the areas of growth in which measures of physical changes of puberty would be made. Use of maximum increments of growth as described by Shuttleworth (1937) was not practical due to the spotty growth records available for the subjects. Measures of maturity indicated by bone growth, while excellent when used as an indicator of total growth, would not appear to be of psychological importance to the individual as bone growth has no particular cultural or social value. It seemed evident that the growth measures to be used would necessarily be those for which a definite end point (or maturity) was known and towards which progress could be readily estimated. At the same time it was realized that certain areas of growth (particularly sex development) were of vast importance in the prestige system of boys and girls.

The growth processes of most importance psychologically to the adolescent male would presumably be those of enormous cultural and social significance, such as genital changes. M. C. Jones and Bayley state that "it is doubtful if any single event in the maturing process for boys can be compared in psy-

chological importance to the menarche in girls" (1950, p. 146). The growth indicator employed by these writers, skeletal development, has "received no cultural value-assessments" (p. 146) and would therefore be expected to show only negligible relationships to behavior in contrast to the high positive relationship expected between the male's genital development and his behavior. This relationship, however, may well be a function of many variables which do not always channel the data in the expected direction. Bayley acknowledges the many variables involved in such relationships by saying that "we must assume that somatic androgony is only one of a multiplicity of factors which may influence the direction of a person's interests" (1951, p. 59).

It was then decided that pubic hair growth would be used as the growth indicator because of its probable psychological significance and because of its close relationship to other areas of sexual and physical development (Stolz and Stolz, 1951). The modified Davenport Scale, described and illustrated by Stolz and Stolz (p. 318), served as the instrument by which developmental status as indicated by pubic hair growth was determined.

Choice of Subjects

Forty-two boys, 20 seventh graders and 22 eighth graders, in the Leon County High School, Tallahassee, Florida, served as subjects for the study. The chronological age range extended from 12 years to 15 years; much age overlapping between grades occurred. Also much overlapping in developmental status occurred with many of the seventh graders being as mature (on the pubic hair scale) as the most mature eighth graders. These factors merit consideration in the analysis of the data.

Nature of the Data

Physical Growth Measures

The 42 subjects were examined in order to determine their physical growth status as indicated by pubic hair development. With the assistance of a local pediatrician the writers, using the Davenport Scale, appraised the maturity of pubic hair development of each of the boys. The scale, a seven-point device extending from "0" (extreme immaturity) to "6" (adult status), clearly separated the subjects,

TABLE 119. PUBIC HAIR MATURITY RATINGS OF FORTY-TWO SEVENTH AND EIGHTH GRADE BOYS

Pubic hair maturity ratings

Grade	CA	0	I	II	III	IV	V	VI	Totals
SEVEN	12 years	6	1	1	1	—	—	—	9
	13 years	2	1	—	1	—	—	—	5
	14 years	1	—	—	1	—	—	—	2
	15 years	—	—	—	—	—	3	—	3
EIGHT	12 years	—	—	—	—	—	—	—	0
	13 years	2	2	1	1	2	3	—	11
	14 years	—	—	—	3	4	1	1	9
	15 years	—	—	1	2	—	—	—	3
								Total N = 42	

showing a wide range from extreme immaturity to adult status. Extreme immaturity (ratings of "0") was characteristic of nine boys in the seventh grade and two boys in the eighth grade, and a rating of "6" (complete maturity) was characteristic of only one boy, an eighth grader. The wide distribution of the sample provided an adequate group for testing the hypothesis that the rapid physical changes of adolescence are of influence on the "self-concept" of the boy in the pubescent cycle of development. Table 119 shows the nature of the distribution of pubic hair maturity ratings according to age and grade. Having established this physiological classification of the subjects, the data relating to the self-concept were treated.

Social Maturity and Pubic Hair Ratings

One of the best known devices for appraising social maturity is Doll's *Vineland Social Maturity Scale* (1946) which evaluates social maturity in terms of overt expression rather than in terms of attitude or preference. Because it was desired to secure quantitative indications of the subject's "self-concept" of social abilities and limitations, rather than a detailed social performance record, some modification of Doll's scale was required. An adaptation of items in the Vineland was made between nine and 15 in the form of a five-alternative multiple choice test. This instrument has been called the *Self Concept of Social Maturity Scale*. A typical item to which the subject responded by checking one answer follows:

Year 10. I play games such as baseball, football, basketball, tennis, checkers, or other rather difficult games. I understand the rules and methods of scoring.

I do it regularly ——————
I do it sometimes ——————
I have never done it, but I could do it if I wanted to ——————
I do not do it ——————
I cannot do it ——————

All items between years nine and 15 were modified in this fashion. The total scale contained 20 items distributed over the seven-year period; to respond to any item the subject was instructed simply to check the alternative which best described him. Scoring on a five-point scale was then made possible with "I do it regularly" being scored as five points and each alternative counting one point less down to "I cannot do it" which was allotted one point. The possible scoring range for the entire series then extended from 20 to 100.

An examination of the relationship between Self Concept of Social Maturity scores and the pubic hair ratings yielded a Pearson-r of +.56. This value, significant at beyond the .01 level of confidence (Table 2), demonstrates a relationship between the

TABLE 120. CORRELATION COEFFICIENTS BETWEEN BOTH PUBIC HAIR MATURITY RATINGS AND SELF-CONCEPT OF SOCIAL MATURITY SCORES AND CHRONOLOGICAL AGE

Maturity measure	n	Pearson-r	p
Self-concept of social maturity	42	+.56	<.01
Chronological age	42	+.24	>.05

subjects' self-concepts of social maturity and their physical maturity which merits consideration by those who work with adolescents. The significance of this relationship may be further enhanced by observing the correlation coefficient of $+.24$ (Pearson-r) obtained between the Self Concept of Social Maturity scores and chronological age. These two values ($+.24$ and $+.56$) were found to differ significantly (beyond the .05 level of confidence). The self-concept of social maturity (perhaps to be described as the way one sees oneself meeting the normal developmental social tasks of childhood and youth) of these subjects showed a closer relationship to the measures derived by pubic hair ratings than to chronological age. The original hypothesis gains strong support by this finding and further work of this nature with the Self-Concept of Social Maturity scale is suggested.

Human Figure Drawings and Pubic Hair Ratings

Human figure drawings, particularly of children and adolescents, have been of interest to psychologists for the last 70 years. This interest has centered on both developmental trends (Hall, 1883) and on drawings as offering clues to aspects of the personality. Goodenough (1926) used the human figure drawing to measure intelligence while the human figure drawing as a projective technique has been studied extensively by Machover (1949) who has provided many stimulating hypotheses for interpretation. Various writers have suggested relationships between an individual's human figure drawings and his social adjustment (Fiedler and Siegel, 1949; Yepsen, 1929; Hinrichs, 1935; Ochs, 1950). S. Levy (1950) has been explicit in describing the projective aspects of the human figure drawing by writing: "I have concluded that a drawing may be a projection of self-concept . . . an expression of . . . attitudes toward life and society in general" (p. 266). Most investigators have agreed that objectification of the method is needed.

In this study an objective analysis of the human figure drawings was made by using a check list of 52 drawing characteristics determined by a survey of procedures reported in the literature (Anastasi and Foley, 1943, 1944; Brown and Goitein, 1943; Elkisch, 1945; England, 1943; Goodenough, 1926; Lebo, 1951; Machover, 1949, 1951; McCarty, 1924; Mott, 1945; Royal, 1949; and Wachner, 1946). In some instances parts of the procedures of two or more writers have been combined into one entity or classification. Several standards of comparison are original with the writers.

In the interest of brevity, these items have been reduced for presentation to the following 11 categories:

1. Hair on head and body.
2. Shading, nature of lines and strokes, erasures.
3. Proportion.
4. Male adornment: cigarettes, cigars, pipes, Adam's apple.
5. General adornment; clothing.
6. Body characteristics: bust, profile, hands and legs, chest.
7. Comparison of area of male and female figure.
8. Location of drawing on paper.
9. Sex drawn first.
10. Completeness of drawing; amount of detail.
11. Age of figure drawn.

These characteristics were examined in both the male and female figures of the pre- and post-pubescent subjects. In order to obtain cells sufficiently large to treat by chi-square analysis, it was necessary to place the cutting point on the pubic hair scale between ratings of 2 and 3. Pre-pubescent in this section of the paper refers to subjects with ratings of 0, 1, or 2 while post-pubescent refers to subjects with ratings of 3, 4, 5, or 6. The low correlations obtained between pubic hair maturity ratings and intelligence (an r of $+.11$ with Kent *EGY* (1942, 1943) scores) and personality scores (an r of $-.05$ with Part I, California Test of Personality (Thorpe, *et al.*, 1942)) give some assurance that an examination of the drawings on the basis of pubic hair maturity ratings will not include drawing characteristics immediately referable to either intellectual or emotional factors.

The analysis of these data was made by comparing the responses of the pre- and post-pubescent subjects on the 52-item check-list; a frequency count was made for each item. To test the significance of the difference between the responses of the 18 prepubescent and 23 post-pubescent youth who completed the drawings a chi-square was then run on each of these characteristics. The results of the human figure drawing analysis are summarized:

1. Twenty-five drawing characteristics as applied to either male or female figure on first inspection appeared large enough to warrant chi-square analysis.

2. All subjects drew the male figure first. Sexual identification evidenced by sex of drawings showed no disturbance in this group. To Machover (1951)

drawing a figure of the opposite sex first is "evidence of confusion of sexual identification" (p. 360). F. R. Smith (1953) has presented data on 1,401 boys and girls distributed throughout the 12 school grades; approximately 20 percent of her males drew the female figure first. The data of the present study suggest a clear and realistic sex-role identification based on the criterion of drawing *own sex first*.

3. The boys with higher pubic hair maturity ratings showed a tendency, however not rigorously verified by statistical treatment, to more frequently include on their drawings of male figures such characteristics as moustache, whiskers, long hair, and heavily shaded hair. The attention given to hair on the male figures yielded a chi-square value significant below the .06 level of confidence. To Machover (1951) hair plays an important role in the sphere of sexual symbolism. It would seem that the adolescent boys endowed with more mature development of pubic hair actively projected their stronger feelings of sexual virility and power into the males they drew. The body-image would appear to show some relationship to actual body changes.

4. The pre-pubescent males (as compared with the post-pubescents) demonstrated a marked tendency to give their male figure drawings such masculine objects as cigars, pipes, cigarettes, scars, masks, and accentuated Adam's apples. The chi-square value obtained here reached a significance level beyond .01 thus leading to the inference that adolescent boys with immature pubic hair development resort to a different manifestation of sexual symbol. The pre-pubescent group resorted to the use of masculine articles other than hair in asserting male sexuality. It may be here suggested that the pre-pubescent male has need of proving his masculinity and achieving the adult body image; the preponderance of the sample seem to project their needs and feelings of inadequacy into their drawings.

5. Another point of differentiation of the pre- and post-pubescent youth was the significantly stronger tendency of the latter (chi-square value significant beyond the .01 confidence level) to adorn their male figures with neckties. Machover (1951) noted that ". . . ties are generally regarded as symbols of sexual adequacy, expressed on a social and clothing level" (p. 359).

6. In comparing size of the male and female human figures it was found that the post-pubescent group, significantly more often than the pre-pubescent group, drew their male figures larger than their female drawings (chi-square significant beyond the .02 confidence level). It may be speculated that the recognition of adequacy in the male's body-image and its clear significance to the post-pubescent subjects resulted in their greater male-female ratio of drawing area.

7. Other characteristics of the human figure drawings failed to show differences between the pre- and post-pubescent youth which could not be reasonably attributed to chance factors.

In summary additional support for the original hypothesis has been obtained; the self-concept, defined in terms of projections in the human figure drawings, appears to reflect in many ways the physiological changes of adolescence.

Paragraph Completions and Pubic Hair Ratings

Some of the obvious tasks of the boy or girl moving through the adolescent period are those concerned with heterosexual adjustment and emancipation from parents. In order to elicit additional responses from the subjects on these topics in a manner revealing the individual's self-attitudes without his being aware of the purpose of the task, a free response situation was arranged in which incomplete paragraphs were presented to the subjects. Written responses in the form of completing two stories were obtained. The subjects were directed to complete the following stories:

a. Heterosexual development. "John, Ed, and Tom are at the lake for a swim on Saturday afternoon. The boys borrow a boat and oars and are preparing to row out into the lake when Mary and Jane (girls who are in their room at school) arrive at the lake and say 'hello' to the boys. Then, . . . (please continue the story)." It will be noted that the range of possible responses is practically unlimited in that signs of maturity or immaturity in one's self-concept can be demonstrated in his treatment of a social situation demanding some kind of response to girls. The fact that there are three boys and only two girls leaves the individual boy free to go along with the crowd as a passive member, to leave the crowd completely, or to ignore the numerical difference and have the boys as a group act either friendly, indifferent, or antagonistic toward the girls.

The analysis of the responses to this situation demanded some arbitrary decisions in assigning quantitative values to the several kinds of possible conclusions. A first step in determining these values was to examine all the stories and arrange categories or groups of responses in that many stories were similar in content; five categories resulted from this grouping.

These categories were then arranged on a continuum ranging from very mature to very immature by ratings in terms of maturity of behavior and feeling by six psychologists (teachers in the areas of child and clinical psychology). The categories, arranged on the five-point scale from maturity to immaturity and reaching an average agreement on each item of 87 percent between the raters, were of the following nature: (*a*) boys requesting girls' company in boats and later continuing their interests by suggesting dates for the evening; (*b*) boys requesting girls to accompany them and the male frequently becoming the hero in rescuing the girls from the lake; (*c*) permitting the girls to accompany the boys but no suggestion of interest in the girls; (*d*) greeting the girls but making no advances; and (*e*) ignoring or escaping the girls. The distribution of scores on the five-point scale appeared by inspection to be distributed normally with a massing of scores around the central point of the scale.

In first examining the data the relationship was obtained between measures of maturity (pubic hair ratings) and the self-concept (as defined by the heterosexual development item). This value ($r = +.17$) failed to reach the "acceptable" .05 level of confidence (Table 121). It will also be noted (Table

TABLE 121. CORRELATION COEFFICIENTS BETWEEN BOTH PUBIC HAIR MATURITY RATINGS AND CHRONOLOGICAL AGE AND SELF-CONCEPT OF HETEROSEXUAL DEVELOPMENT

Maturity measure	n	Self-concept of heterosexual development Pearson-r	p
Pubic hair maturity ratings	42	+.17	>.05
Chronological age	42	+.37	<.02

121) that chronological age correlated $+.37$ ($p = < .02$) with the self-concept of "heterosexual development" item, thus demonstrating a closer relationship than was exhibited by pubic hair ratings. Although the expected direction of relationship was found to exist between maturity of pubic hair development and maturity of self-concept of heterosexual development, the relationship ($r = +.17$) did not attain the expected significance level. An inspection of the

data suggested marked differences between pre- and post-pubescent youth which are not revealed by correlational procedures.

It must be concluded that these data fail to support convincingly the hypothesis that an index of physical maturity such as pubic hair development will be significantly related to the pubescent male's self-concept as he projects himself into heterosexual situations. However, these findings do emphasize the developmental or changing aspect of the individual's self-concept. The relationships he visualizes between himself and girls of his age group may well depend upon both physical maturity and increased opportunities (time) for experiences—learning which would occur with added years of home, school, and community experiences.

b. Emancipation from parents. "Tom is about grown and has left home and school to go to another town 300 miles away to work. However, when he arrives at the town, he finds that he must wait two days before he can begin his job. His parents would like to have him come home and stay. He will only have enough money to pay for his food for one of the two days he must wait before beginning his job. Tom decides . . . (please continue the story)."

The above paragraph was designed to determine the strength of home ties of the subjects. Again it will be noted that a wide range of possible solutions exists; it was expected that strength of home ties would be demonstrated by the boys' determination to "stick-it-out" or by the readiness with which they turned back to their homes for the solution to the problem. A continuing dependence on parents would be evidenced by a readiness to return home, to turn to parents for assistance. That a self-concept of unreadiness to enter the adult world will be demonstrated by the pre-pubescent boy and a self-concept of adequacy and self-confidence will be demonstrated by the post-pubescent boy is the hypothesis to be tested.

The responses to the "Emancipation from Parent" item were arranged in order of maturity value in the same fashion as were the "Heterosexual Development" items. Categories of responses ranging from extreme immaturity to maturity were developed and all responses then assigned a position on the five-point scale. The arrangement of responses (from mature to immature) by the six psychologists was of the following nature: (*a*) the decision was to wait-out the remaining time, to get by with limited funds; (*b*) borrow money from the prospective employer or get a temporary job; (*c*) stay at the town but wire or write home for money; (*d*) abandon the job, return and stay with parents; and (*e*) turn to luck or fantasy for solution of the problem. There was an average agreement of 75 percent by the six psychologist raters on the location of each item in the scale.

The obtained responses tended to be distributed normally along the five-point scale; both seventh and eighth graders appeared in each of the five categories. Early inspection of the data suggested a tendency for the more mature individuals to rank higher on the "emancipation from parent" item.

Correlational analysis of these data with pubic hair maturity ratings was made (Table 122); a coeffi-

TABLE 122. CORRELATION COEFFICIENTS BETWEEN BOTH PUBIC HAIR MATURITY RATINGS AND CHRONO-LOGICAL AGE AND SELF-CONCEPT OF EMANCIPATION STATUS

Maturity measure	*n*	Self-concept scores on emancipation status Pearson-r	*p*
Pubic hair maturity ratings	42	+.27	>.05
Chronological age	42	+.40	<.01

cient (Pearson-*r*) of +.27 (*p* = > .05) was obtained which fails to reach the commonly accepted .05 confidence level. Chronological age again showed the closer relationship to the self-concept item by correlating +.40 (*p* = < .01) with the "emancipation from parents" score. Again the expected direction of relationship was not found sufficiently strong to support the original hypothesis in any convincing manner. However, the evidence is suggestive of a relationship between physical status and the adolescent male's self-concept in regard to dependency on parents. The higher chronological age relationship shown again impresses the writers with the necessity of time and experiences which are important in structuring the male role with which the adolescent boy identifies. The younger, less mature male tends to see himself as a little boy able to assume only limited responsibility for his own well-being and still relying heavily on his parents' protective care. The older and more mature adolescent males appeared to think themselves capable of meeting the exigencies of unfamiliar and trying circumstances.

In summary it will be noted that while the relationships have not been consistently close and uni-

form between the pubic hair maturity ratings and the self-concept in areas of "heterosexual development" and "emancipation from parents," the relationships which do exist are of such nature as to suggest further investigation of the influence that the physical and physiological changes of puberty have upon the self-concept of the adolescent male. Both the experiences coming with increased age and sexual maturity with its obvious external evidence associated with the prestige system of adolescent youth appear to be reflected in the individual's self-concept in regard to these important social relations.

Summary

The problem investigated was the relationship between the self-concept of pubescent males between years 12 and 15 and physical maturity as evidenced by the maturity of pubic hair development. The 42 subjects were classified according to pubic hair maturity ratings. The self-concept, as revealed through projective material, was then examined in relation to the pubertal status (pubic hair ratings) of the subjects. The following findings were reported:

1. A wide range of pubertal status (pubic hair maturity ratings) was reported; many of the younger subjects were as mature as the older subjects.

2. The "self-concept of social maturity" as indicated by the subjects' responses to items of a modified version of the *Vineland Social Maturity Scale* showed a marked positive relationship to pubic hair maturity status (Pearson-*r* of +.56, *p* = < .01), while chronological age and pubic hair maturity ratings showed a less significant relationship (Pearson-*r* of +.24, *p* = > .05).

3. Pre- and post-pubescent males differed significantly (beyond the .05 confidence level) in certain projective aspects of their human figure drawings. Adequate sex-role identification in all subjects was assumed from the fact that all subjects drew the male figure first. Post-pubescent as compared with pre-pubescent males appeared to project their stronger feelings of sexual virility or masculinity into the males they drew by their excessive attention to hair. Pre-pubescent as compared with post-pubescent males appeared to express their need for proving masculinity and achieving the adult body-image by their excessive use of masculine objects as cigars, pipes, cigarettes, scars, masks, and Adam's apples. The post-pubescent as compared with the pre-pubescent males tended more often to adorn their

male figures with neckties, a characteristic described by some writers as evidence of a feeling of sexual adequacy. Finally, the post-pubescents differed from the pre-pubescents in their apparent recognition of adequacy in body-image in that their male drawings were consistently larger than their female drawings.

4. Measures of self-attitudes in the area of heterosexual development showed a closer relationship to chronological age (Pearson-r = +.37, p = < .02) than to pubic hair maturity ratings (Pearson-r of +.17, p = > .05) suggesting that the adolescent male's self-attitudes in relation to girls is more dependent upon experiences (age) than upon his degree of physical maturity.

Measures of self-attitudes in relation to parents (emancipation from parents) also showed a closer

relationship to chronological age (Pearson-r of +.40, p = < .01) than to pubic hair maturity ratings (Pearson-r of + .27, p = > .05). These findings also suggest that the adolescent male's self-concept in relation to his dependency on or independence of parents is more closely related to experiences (age) than to the degree of physical maturity attained.

5. Finally, the data reported are of some practical importance as they emphasize the self-concept as an important and productive area of investigation in studies of pubescent youth. Longitudinal investigations of the relationships between physical growth and personality development during the pubescent cycle may well add valuable interpretative material to the psychology of adolescence.

48

The Development

of the Ideal Self in Childhood

and Adolescence*

Robert J. Havighurst
Myra Z. Robinson
Mildred Dorr

The purpose of this article is to describe the development of the ideal self, or the ego-ideal, as this is revealed by self-reports during childhood and adolescence. The data were obtained by asking boys and girls to write a brief essay on the subject, "The Person I Would Like To Be Like."

The concept of an ego-ideal or an ideal self has been found useful by the Freudian psychologists and by the social psychologists in studying the development of personality and character. But there is very

* From *Journal of Educational Research*, 1946, **40**, 241–257.

little factual information on which to base an extensive use of this concept.

The Freudians explain the origin of the ego-ideal as due to *identification* with people whom the child loves or admires or fears. Through the process of identification the child comes to imitate the values and attitudes of other people. The parents are the first and most important objects of identification. It is not stated clearly by the Freudians how important the later objects of identification are—such as teachers, youth group leaders, heroes of adventure and romance, and attractive age-mates. However, these writers generally attribute some importance to the people who follow the parents as objects of identification, believing that the ego-ideal of the adult is a composite of all the identifications the individual has made, with the figures of the parents still holding the most prominent place.

The social psychologists think of the ideal self as a name for the integrated set of *roles* and *aspirations* which direct the individual's life. These roles and attitudes they believe are taken on by the individual from parents, and from a variety of others, such as siblings, playmates, teachers, preachers, and others with prestige, and historical and fictional heroes, and worked over into his own thought and action.

While it is generally agreed that the ideal self or ego-ideal is important in the development of character and personality, and much attention has been given to the problem of its origin in the early years of life, very little work has been done on its development during childhood and adolescence.

Procedure

The procedure in this study was to ask children to write a brief essay on the topic "The Person I Would Like To Be Like." Similar topics and a similar method have been used in studies of children's ideals by a number of people (see Phelan, 1936). However, the wording of the assignment has varied in various studies, and this seems to have caused a considerable variation in results. Moreover, none of the previous studies has been devoted explicitly to throwing light on the *development* of the ideal self. A comparison of our results with those of other studies will be given at a later place in this paper.

We have used the following directions with boys and girls in the age-range 8 to 18:

> Describe in a page or less the person you would most like to be like when you grow up. This may be a real person, or an imaginary person. He or she may be a combination of several people. Tell something about this person's age, character, appearance, occupation, and recreations. If he is a real person, say so. You need not give his real name if you do not want to.

These directions give some very definite leads to the subject. This seems desirable, for many children would not know how to begin unless they were given some suggestion. Furthermore, this insures a degree of comparability in the essays, which makes it possible to rate them for the quality of the ideals expressed, something that has proved useful, though it is not reported in this paper.

It will be noted that the directions prevent the child from telling about his own age-mates as sources of his ideals, for he is asked to tell about the person he would like to be like *when he grows up*. This is an important limitation on the procedure, and prevents us from getting data on the relative importance of age-mates and of adults in the formation of the ego-ideal. Yet some children ignore the directions and describe an age-mate. This happens most often with children aged about fourteen.

Other essay topics have also been tried, such as "My Heroes," "Five People I Admire," "Where Do I Get My Ideals?" But none of them proved as useful as "The Person I Would Like To Be Like."

Results

Analysis of the responses in several sets of papers led to the use of the following categories.

I P — Parents and other relatives of the parental or grand-parental generation.

II S — Parent-surrogates: teachers, neighbors of the parental generation.

III G — Glamorous adults: people with a romantic or ephemeral fame, due to the more superficial qualities of appearance and behavior; e.g. movie stars, military figures, athletes. *Note:* characters in comic strips or radio dramas are included here, though they may be imaginary; e.g. Superman, Dick Tracy.

IV H — Heroes, people with a substantial claim to fame, usually tested by time, e.g. Florence Nightingale and Abraham Lincoln. However, certain living persons are placed in this category; e.g. Madame Chiang Kai-shek, the President, General MacArthur.

V H — Attractive and successful young adults within the individual's range of observation: these are usually young people who live in the community, or go to a local college, or lead a scout group, or are related to the subject—elder siblings, cousins, young uncles and aunts.

They can be observed by the subject in three dimensions, as it were—going about their daily work, making moral decisions, getting along with family and friends, preparing for an occupation.

VI C   Composite or imaginary characters: These are abstractions of a number of people. Sometimes they appear to be wholly imaginary, other times they are clearly a coalescence of qualities of two or three real persons.

VII M   Age-mates or youths only two or three years older than the subject. While the directions sought to prevent the naming of these people, some were named.

VIII NC   Miscellaneous responses, not classifiable among those mentioned above. A fairly frequent response in this category is "myself."

Some typical essays will serve to illustrate the various categories:

A

I want to be like my dad. He is gooder than other people. He acts good. He don't spank me. He fixes my toys. He don't scold me. Sometimes he takes my part when I fight with my big brother. My dad is big and strong. I think I want to be a farmer because that is good work.

This essay was written down by the teacher in a rural school as a six-year-old boy told it.

B

The person I want to be like is my brother, Joe. He likes to go to a show but not bad ones. My brother is always clean in his speaking so far as I know. His work is to learn how to drive an airplane. His age is 19. He is mostly happy even if there is trouble. He tries to be good as he can. He is a pretty good christian.

This was written by an eight-year-old girl who wants to be like her soldier brother.

C

I would like to be twenty-one years old. I would like to be kind. I would like to be beautiful. I would like to work in a munition plant. If I had a baby, I would play with it. I would like to be

Veronica Lake. I would like to be hostess on an airplane. And I would like to know how to fly an airplane. Have my husband be an actor and act with me. I would like to have a large house.

This essay, written by a ten-year-old girl, shows a choice of a *glamorous person* as the ego ideal.

D

When I am grown up, I would be about 22 years old and I would be in the army. The man I am thinking of has dark hair, brown eyes and is about 5 feet 9 inches. He is a staff sergeant in the U.S. Air Corps. After he eats his supper he goes to his room and reads or something. I would like to be like my uncle in the U.S. Air Corps.

Written by a ten-year-old boy, this essay falls into the category of the *attractive, successful young adult*. The boy knows his young uncle, knows how he spends his leisure time, and is in a position to imitate much of the behavior and the values of the young man.

E

Tom Sawyer or Huckleberry Finn

Because they always skipped school and go fishing and investigate places like caves, and all different places. To get into a cave with a flash light and a little to eat and find a treasure. They would go to different neighborhoods and have fights with the kids living there. He wasn't very talent but if you want to have a lot of fun it wouldn't be right to be too talented. And he didn't have to dress up in clean clothes, but he could run around in overalls, shirt and straw hat. He would go swimming in mud holes have a lot of fun because no one would be around to bother you. You hardly would know what day it was in the week because you would wear the same clothes practically all the time. I think that's the life I would like to live.

This essay was written by a twelve-year-old orphan boy who lives in a children's home operated rather strictly by a religious group. The boy's rebellion against the routine of the home is manifest. Classification of the ego-ideal is rather difficult, but we placed it in the *glamorous person* category.

F

First of all I'll say my ideal, Robert Taylor. I don't know what I'd do first if I could become his twin brother right now. The main things I like about my ideal are his looks, occupation and his beautiful female surroundings. When I go to a picture played by Robert, I sit and envy him most of the time and don't get much meaning from the picture. The age, I am not sure of how old Robert Taylor is, but I'm sure he is over twenty-three, the age I would like to be this instant. In that case that would have to be Mr. Taylor's age also if we were to be twin brothers. When I am old enough I am going to try every means possible to improve my looks. I am going to wear a Taylor mustache, train my hair to be nice as to my liking. I have light hair, brown eyes. According to this it would be quite easy to make my hair darker.

This was written by a sixteen-year-old boy, a painfully shy and ineffectual person. His choice of a glamorous person indicates his own immaturity as well as his wish to compensate for his inferiority.

G

When I was small I had several idols. That is, people whom I would want to be like when I grew up. One was nurse, another a doctor, a movie star, one of my aunts, my brother and I suppose there were lots more. But now I have no desire to be like any person in particular at all. Maybe it's because I'm older and I know, now, that no one is perfect, that everyone has good and bad points or maybe I've just changed my mind. I think that you as an individual, should be individual. Not to the extent of disregarding the morals and laws of society. I don't mean that, but what I mean is be yourself. Everyone, I don't care who it is, has something that no one else has and he shouldn't try to hide it by imitating others.

My greatest ambition is to be a woman. It probably sounds silly, because I suppose in one sense of the word, physically, I'll have to be, but I don't mean just physically. There are so many things you have to be, and do it seems to me, before you really are a woman. I hope I've made myself clear, although I doubt it very much.

A sixteen-year-old girl wrote this mature essay on her *composite, imaginary* ego ideal.

H

I want to be energetic. Someone once told me, "genius is 99% perspiration, and 1% inspiration." I want to be philosophical, and plump. My ideal is someone who is always astride the situation. I want to be like an imaginary person. This person, as I have said, must be a worker, plump, and philosophical. But he must also be efficient, and have a good sense of humor. I may be asking too much, but I would not like any broken limbs, or crippled faculties.

I don't care what I look like, just so I'm not too repulsive. I can't think of any particular occupation I will be suited for, but since I want to be able to write, I may devote my time to that.

Then, as a parting favor, I should like to be able to play tennis, or at least play at tennis.

I want each of my qualities able to give way to my sense of humor. Humor, to me, is one of the most important qualities of my future self.

This was written by a highly verbal and intelligent sixteen-year-old boy, showing a very abstract, *imaginary* ego-ideal.

Essays from several groups of subjects have been classified, with results shown in Table 123. The age of the group increases from left to right in the table. Groups A and I came from the same community, as did groups C and E. Changes with age should show most clearly in a study of these two pairs of groups. From inspection of the table it is at once evident that there is much apparently random variation from group to group, which is not explainable as due to change with age. This kind of variability from group to group may be explained as due to any or all of the following possible causes: (1) unreliability of the instrument, either in the responses of the subjects or in the categorization of the responses; (2) accidents of sampling, since the numbers in several of the groups are small; (3) differences in the social environments of the various groups. No doubt some of the variability is due to the sampling factor, but a considerable part is due to the other two factors, as will be shown later.

Several general conclusions may be drawn from Table 123. One conclusion is that the responses fall mainly into four categories, those of parents, glamorous adults, attractive and visible young adults, and composite, imaginary characters. Parent-surrogates such as teachers and older adults are seldom named, and heroes are very seldom named.

A second conclusion is that an age sequence exists, moving outward from the family circle, becoming more abstract, and culminating in the composite, imaginary person. This is by no means a rigid sequence. Some steps are omitted by some children. Yet a comparison of groups A and I and C and E gives evidence of the reality of the age sequence when the subjects of different ages are drawn from the same social environment.

The following hypothesis appears to account for the observed age trends. The child from the age of six to about eight generally chooses a parent or some other family member. Most children then move on to a choice either of a glamorous person or an

TABLE 123. CLASSIFICATION OF PERSONS DESCRIBED AS THE IDEAL SELF PERCENTAGE
DISTRIBUTIONS

Boys

Group	A	B	C	D	E	F	G	H	I
No. of Papers	60	26	89		94	85	106	31	48
CATEGORY									
I P	7	23	11	......	16	7	16	3	6
II S	0	0	0	......	0	2	2	0	11
III G	12	32	47	......	23	37	40	22	6
IV H	3	6	11	......	10	5	3	13	2
V A	53	30	23	......	21	15	24	9	25
VI C	25	6	8	......	28	28	15	19	48
VII M	0	0	0	......	2	1	0	13	2
VIII NC	0	3	0	......	0	5	0	19	0

Girls

Group	A	B	C	D	E	F	G	H	I
No. of Papers	100	36	105	17	114	70	80		86
CATEGORY									
I P	6	32	14	6	11	7	20	......	3
II S	2	0	2	0	4	12	9	......	1
III G	16	17	27	23	21	37	21	......	1
IV H	2	3	3	6	1	7	7	......	4
V A	36	13	25	18	25	18	23	......	28
VI C	33	22	23	29	35	18	15	......	61
VII M	3	8	6	12	3	1	5	......	2
VIII NC	0	5	0	6	0	0	0	......	0

Description of groups:

  A. Ten, eleven, and twelve-year-olds in a typical small midwestern community.

  B. Sixth-graders (age 11–12) in an industrial section of Chicago.

  C. Fifth and sixth-graders (age 11–12) in a war industry community.

  D. Girls at a Chicago Settlement House (ages 11–14), mostly Italian.

  E. Seventh and eighth graders (age 13–14) in a war industry community.

  F. Middle-class Negro children (age 12–14) in Baltimore.

  G. Ninth-graders (age 14–15) in a lower-middle-class suburb of Chicago.

  H. Boys (age 16–17) in a Vocational High School in Chicago.

  I. Sixteen and seventeen-year-olds in a typical small midwestern community.

attractive, visible young adult. The age for choosing a glamorous person is about eight to sixteen. The choice of an attractive, visible young adult may start at eight or ten and continue all through adolescence, or it may give way to a more abstract ego-ideal in the form of a composite imaginary person. The final and mature stage of the ego-ideal is the composite of desirable characteristics, drawn from all of the persons with whom the individual has identified himself during his childhood and adolescence.

A third conclusion is that social environment affects the choice of the ideal self. This is to be expected, since different social environments expose children to different kinds of people who may serve as objects of identification, and teach different values and aspirations. The effect of social environment is seen by comparing the frequencies of response in the glamorous person and composite person categories for various groups. Children from families of lower socio-economic status name a higher proportion of glamorous persons. This is seen by comparing groups A, B, and C, in Table 123, the members of which are all about the same age. The average socio-economic status of the members of group A is higher than that of the members of groups B and C. Carroll (1945) compared a Negro middle-class with a Negro lower-class group (age 12–14) and found that three-quarters of the lower-class responses fell into the category of glamorous adults, while only about half as many of the middle-class responses fell into this category.

A further influence of the social setting is to be found in the occasional presence of one or more unusually attractive adults in the environment of the group that is being tested. For example, one fifth-grade group happened to have a very attractive teacher, and the children mentioned this teacher frequently in their essays, although teachers generally are not mentioned very often.

The school program also has an influence on the responses of children in their essays. Sister Mary Phelan (1936) reports that for children in Catholic parochial schools the frequency of mention of religious persons increased after several months of teaching about ideals. Even such an event as a Washington's Birthday celebration will stimulate more mentions than usual of George Washington.

Table 124 shows the age of the persons mentioned in the essays. While there is again a good deal

TABLE 124. AGES OF PERSONS DESCRIBED AS THE IDEAL
SELF PERCENTAGE DISTRIBUTION

Group Age of Persons Mentioned	A	B	C and E	F	G	I
Under 20	16	18	23	14	13	6
20–29	72	33	35	49	36	65
30–39	9	29	29	27	51	16
40–49	3	16	10	4	(30 and	9
Over 50	0	4	3	6	over)	4

Note: Ten to 40 percent of the papers did not give ages. The age was often omitted when parents were mentioned. For description of groups, see Table 123.

of variation among the groups, this variation does not appear to be related to the age of the children. Most of them think of their ideal selves as being in the twenties or thirties.

There is one difference between our results and those of earlier studies which stands out quite clearly. We found very few mentions of "heroes" or great people of history or literature, while in the earlier studies the frequency of such characters was high. Sister Mary Phelan (1936) found over 60 percent of the responses at age from 11 to 18 to be either religious or historical or contemporary public

figures. Hill (1930) got about the same over-all results from public school children, although the number of religious characters was much less than in the parochial school papers.

These figures are to be contrasted with our own finding of less than 10 percent of the responses in the category of "heroes." However, to make our data more nearly comparable with those of Hill and Phelan, we should add the "glamorous adults" to the "heroes"; for a movie star or a prizefighter, if mentioned in one of Hill's or Phelan's papers, was counted in the category of "historical and contemporary characters." The examples given by these writers show that the counterparts of present-day "glamorous adults" were mentioned in the earlier studies, including: Clara Bow, Billie Dove, Babe Ruth, Douglas Fairbanks, Mary Pickford, Dizzy Dean, Jack Oakie, Eddie Cantor, The Arkansas Woodchopper, Shirley Temple, and Jackie Coogan.

It appears, however, that the "glamorous adult" was mentioned somewhat less frequently and the "hero" somewhat more frequently in the studies made 10, 20, and 50 years ago.

Conclusions

This study shows a developmental trend in the ideal self of the following nature. The ideal self commences in childhood as an identification with a parental figure, moves during middle childhood and early adolescence through a stage of romanticism and glamour, and culminates in late adolescence as a composite of desirable characteristics which may be symbolized by an attractive, visible young adult, or may be simply an imaginary figure.

Parents or members of the parental generation play a declining role in the ideal self as it is described by children after the age of eight or 10. "Glamorous" adults have their day in the child's ego-ideal between the ages of 10 and 15. Anyone older than 15 who reports a "glamorous" person as his ego-ideal is probably immature, by standards of development as found in most young people. It is not certain whether the stage of greatest maturity is that represented by our category of the attractive, visible adult or that represented by our category of the composite, imaginary character. Evidence from adults might settle this point.

The environment of the child has a great effect on his ideal self. Children and young people from families of lower socio-economic status as a group lag behind those of middle socio-economic status in progressing through the stage of selection of a glamorous adult as the ideal. Individuals in the child's environment influence his ideal self, especially if they are young adults. Thus an especially attractive teacher or youth group leader may symbolize the ego-ideal during the age period usually dominated by the glamorous person. Furthermore, the teaching of the school, especially if it is aimed at inculcating ideals through teaching about the lives of great people, certainly influences the child's report concerning his ideal self.

The high susceptibility of the child's response about his ideal self to rather short-term and superficial teaching influences raises some doubts about the validity of our method of securing information. It seems probable that the individual's core values and attitudes do not change as rapidly and easily as might be suggested by his changing, for example, from a movie star to a solid, successful young man in the local community for the symbol of his ideal self. Probably very few children or adolescents have enough insight into their own personalities to give a full report on their ego-ideals. Some individuals may even have a good deal of unconscious resistance to recognizing the nature of the ideal self. This may be the case with a number of boys and a few girls who insist, in a defensive tone, that they want to be like themselves and no one else.

Nevertheless, we may be sure that an individual will not report an ideal which is repugnant to him, nor will he report a set of ideals which he has not thought about at all. There is nothing for the individual to gain in the essay-writing situation by giving false witness about himself. If there has been no coaching of the child to name certain kinds of people when asked questions about his ideal self, the results represent something genuine and deep down in his personality.

The set of categories we have used to classify the persons mentioned seems to us to be useful in testing hypotheses about *development* of the ideal self. However, it leaves something to be desired as a measure of increasing maturity of personality. We were forced to choose between categories of persons and categories of qualities of persons. Categories based upon qualities might serve as a better indicator of maturity.

There is a great deal of evidence that the ideal self is deeply influenced by association with people who are in positions of prestige because they are older, more powerful, and better able to get the desirable things of life than the child or adolescent who observes them. Our study adds to this evidence. A boy or girl combines qualities of parents with qualities of attractive, successful young adults into a composite ego-ideal. The inference is clear that schools, churches and youth-serving agencies influence the ideals of youth as much or more through the presence and behavior of teachers, clergy, and youth-group leaders as through their verbal teachings.

49

Delinquent and Non-Delinquent

Perceptions of Self, Values

*and Opportunity**

Frank R. Scarpitti

Sociologic theory generally rejects the proposition that most delinquent behavior is motivated by deep psychologic problems or that it can be transformed through psychotherapy into socially acceptable conduct. Traditionally, sociologic theory de-emphasizes psychologic interpretations of cause and stresses the delinquent's social milieu as the generating factor in his deviancy. To the sociologist, the juvenile delinquent is principally the product of an environment in which deviancy is a normal and acceptable mode of adjustment. Thus, it is asserted that delinquent youth in slums and high delinquency areas operate from the standpoint of a value orientation taken over from the delinquent groups that flourish in their neighborhoods. Cohen (1955) suggests that one reason for this is the great status frustration experienced by working class boys. Some of them find solutions to their status problems by rejecting middle class values and internalizing a malicious, non-utilitarian, negativistic value orientation. This permits them to lash out at the dominant middle class society and to find status satisfaction in delinquent groups which reward deviancy. A similar view of the role of the social structure in creating delinquency is held by Miller (Kvaraceus and Miller, 1959). Although he does not specify which boys in the working class gravitate to delinquency, he assumes that delinquent behavior reflects the "focal concerns" of the lower class, such as smartness (cleverness), toughness, excitement, autonomy, fate and trouble. Hence, the delinquent may be seen as attempting to adhere to standards that are valued in the lower class community. Cloward and Ohlin (1960) contend that slum boys in American cities are cut off from access to legitimate opportunity and that many consequently embrace and legitimize illegal ventures and activities as vehicles of upward

mobility. However, Cloward and Ohlin (1960) like Cohen (1955) and Miller (Kvaraceus and Miller, 1959), do not specify the individual slum boy who turns to delinquent modes of activity as a result of his awareness of limited access to opportunity. They assume that differential access to opportunity is an active principle in delinquent behavior among slum boys in America. (It is not clear what the operational assumption would be for boys in cities of the world that do not have an open class system and vertical mobility, such as Bombay, Cairo and Bangkok.) On the other hand, Cloward and Ohlin (1960) indicate that, according to the nature of the particular slum, the boys are enveloped in criminal gang pursuits (e.g., theft), fighting gang activities or retreatist behavior (drugs). Here again, this typology of offenses is related to the sociologic characteristics of the slum area and is not directly linked to the individual who does or does not identify with such deviant patterns.

Rioting by working class Negro youths and young adults lends weight to theoretical formulations which emphasize the role of value orientation and differential opportunity as factors in the etiology of deviant behavior. Nevertheless, little empirical evidence has been furnished to support these theoretical contentions and several crucial questions must yet be answered. Most of the working class youths of Harlem did *not* take part in the riots and looting. Most of the youths who live in any high delinquency area are *not* delinquents. If delinquency results from lower class status (which negatively influences one's values and view of life's opportunities) then a large proportion of lower class boys who experience normal social development should be delinquent. Since this is *not* the case, it is necessary for us to ask whether delinquents *are* different from lower class and middle class non-delinquents in their value orientations and in their awareness of limited access

* From *Mental Hygiene*, 1965, **49**, 399–404.

to opportunity. We must also try to explain the non-delinquency that exists in the lower class.

A youth's value orientation and feelings about opportunity are a result of the social experiences that have impinged upon him and have become part of his mental picture of himself, i.e., his self-concept. They are two of the many factors which have molded him into a personality and which determine his behavior. If we assume that values and awareness of opportunity are a part of the self, then it is also legitimate to assume that they will vary with other measurable aspects of the self. For example, if the rejection of middle class values in American society is the result of unfavorable social experiences, then these experiences would also have negatively influenced other components of the individual's image of himself. If, on the other hand, the other components of the self are positive rather than negative, the positive elements of the self-concept may be strong enough to determine the individual's behavior despite his perceptions of values. The same thing may be said regarding feelings of blocked opportunity.

On the basis of this discussion, three important questions emerge:

1. Are delinquents actually different from non-delinquents in their perceptions of values and opportunity?
2. Are negative perceptions of middle class values and access to opportunity powerful enough to cause juvenile delinquency among lower class boys?
3. Are negative perceptions of values and opportunity indicators of a totally unhealthy self-concept, or can they be seen as operating somewhat independently of other self-image factors?

This paper will attempt to furnish a partial answer to these questions, which grow out of the contemporary sociologic explanations of juvenile delinquency.

We started with three sample populations. We had the responses to a structured questionnaire by 515 inmates of the Boys' Industrial School (BIS), Lancaster, Ohio, all of whom had been committed for delinquency, by 61 ninth-grade boys of a junior high school in a lower class area of Columbus, Ohio, and by 68 ninth-grade boys of a junior high school in a middle class area of Columbus, Ohio. The 515 delinquent boys from BIS represented practically the entire population of this state-supported training school for juvenile court commitments. The boys in the two junior high schools represented those who

were available during a scheduled period on the day of the administration of the questionnaire.

The BIS group was made up of 285 white boys and 230 Negro boys. Median age of the BIS sample was 16 years, 8 months. The BIS boys came overwhelmingly from the big cities of Ohio and from the lower social and economic areas in these cities. The North-Hatt Scale of Occupations (North and Hatt, 1947) was used to measure "social class position" as assessed from the father's occupation. The average occupational status score of the fathers of the BIS boys was 53, which is well below that recommended as the dividing line (Kahl, 1957, pp. 76–77) between lower class and middle class on the North-Hatt instrument (Clarke, 1956, p. 302).

Median age of the 61 ninth-grade boys from the junior high school in a lower economic and social area of Columbus was 15 years, 3 months. Since there were only a few Negro boys in the entire junior high school, they were eliminated from the ninth-grade sample. Consequently, all of the 61 lower-class ninth-grade boys were white. The average occupational status score on the North-Hatt Scale, according to father's occupation, was 60, which was significantly higher than the average score of the father's occupation among delinquent boys.

All 68 ninth-grade boys from the middle class area were white. Their median age was 14 years, 11 months (probably, less retardation in this group caused them to be younger). Average score of the father's occupation for this group was 76, significantly higher than the cutting point between lower and middle class, and much higher than the father's occupational score for both the lower class boys and the delinquent boys.

The Questionnaire

A team of one principal investigator and two assistants administered a structured questionnaire to the boys in the BIS and in the two ninth grades. The same introductory statement (eliciting cooperation) was made at all administrations. The principal investigator read the questions aloud, the boys who did not understand could raise their hands, and one of the circulating assistants quickly responded with help. Out of 522 boys originally tested at the BIS, only seven questionnaires had to be discarded because of unwillingness to cooperate fully.

The questionnaire consisted of four parts: (1) a

series of 46 items, taken from the Soc (socialization) scale of the California Personality Inventory (Gough and Peterson, 1952, p. 207). This measures a "veering" toward or away from delinquency; (2) 11 items developed by Rothstein (1961) to assess interpersonal competence or feelings of personal worth; (3) a value orientation scale (Landis, 1963, p. 408), consisting of 13 items, and (4) an awareness of limited opportunity scale (Landis, 1963), consisting of 14 items.

The two instruments under parts 3 and 4 (above) were especially designed to test a social class bias in value orientation and awareness of limited opportunity. The value orientation scale, entitled *How I Look at Things* and answered on a five-point response basis from "strongly agree" to "strongly disagree," sought to obtain the degree of acceptance or rejection of statements having a definite lower class orientation. For example: *Good manners are for sissies* or *Money is meant to be spent.* The awareness of limited access to opportunity scale, entitled "How the Future Looks to Me" and also scored on a five-point response pattern, attempted to assess the boys' perceptions of their life chances. For example: *A guy like me has a pretty good chance of going to college* or *There is a good chance that some of my friends will have a lot of money.* These items were chosen to test Cohen's (1955) and Cloward and Ohlin's (1960) contentions that some lower class children reject middle class values and that lower class children feel cut off from access to legitimate opportunity. If these contentions are valid, then the middle class group should respond to these items quite differently than the two lower class groups.

Findings

The contention is that value orientation and awareness of limited access to opportunity should vary from less to more favorable. This would occur as we move from delinquent to lower class to middle class adolescents. Average scores were computed for the three groups on the test instruments. In addition, the total BIS group was broken down into subgroups and studied on the basis of age, grade and race to determine differences which might lie within the heterogeneous delinquent population. Table 125 gives the average scores on the value and awareness instruments.

The scores for value orientation and awareness of limited access to opportunity move from delinquent through lower class to middle class in the expected direction. Descending average scores on these instruments indicate the favorable direction, based upon American middle class standards. The differences in the average scores of the 515 delinquents and the two non-delinquent groups are great enough to ensure that they are not due merely to chance variation, but reflect a true difference in the boys' feelings. However, the differences in the average scores of the various delinquent subgroups are too small to distinguish between these categories of the incarcerated group. Delinquents (despite age, race and grade) are similar in their rejection of middle class values and their awareness of having only limited access to opportunity. On the other hand, the two non-delinquent groups feel quite differently about these factors. The lower class boys reflect a position

TABLE 125. AVERAGE SCORES ON SELF-PERCEPTION INSTRUMENTS FOR DELINQUENTS AND LOWER AND MIDDLE CLASS NINTH-GRADE WHITE BOYS

Groups	Socialization Scale[a]	Interpersonal Competence[a]	Value Orientation[b]	Awareness of Limited Opportunity[b]
515 BIS boys	25.15	14.81	38.80	37.06
285 White BIS boys	24.24	14.80	37.29	37.17
140 Ninth-grade BIS boys	25.41	14.76	39.86	36.73
82 White, ninth-grade BIS boys	24.75	14.71	37.52	36.87
61 White, ninth-grade lower class boys	32.05	15.80	31.43	32.28
68 White, ninth-grade middle class boys	33.62	16.81	28.00	26.18

[a] High scores most favorable.

[b] Low scores most favorable.

half-way between those of the delinquent and the middle class groups.

The average scores on the other two measures of the questionnaire (the socialization scale and the interpersonal competence items) also show the expected gradient: unfavorable for the delinquents, less favorable for the lower class, ninth-grade white boys, and more favorable for the middle class, ninth-grade white boys. On these measures, the differences between the delinquent and non-delinquent groups are large enough to reflect true personality distinctions. The differences between the two non-delinquent groups, however, are not. In other words, the differences in average scores on the various tests which measure self-image are relatively small between the ninth-grade, lower and middle class boys and are much greater between the delinquents and the two groups of non-delinquents. Again, the strikingly similar scores achieved by the various subgroups of the delinquent population indicate that the subgroups cannot be differentiated on the basis of the self-perception scales used in this research.

Summary

These findings appear to substantiate the claim that delinquents and non-delinquents perceive middle class values and access to opportunity differently. Delinquents tend to reject middle class values and feel that they have very limited opportunity to achieve the rewards that are available to middle class children. Perhaps this is a consequence of the delinquents' incarceration. More likely, however, it is a precursor and predictor of their deviant behavior. Lower class, non-delinquent boys feel the same way, but to a lesser degree. Although they do not reject the dominant society's values as much as delinquents do, lower class non-delinquents are certainly less accepting of these values than are middle class boys. The same is true for the lower class non-delinquents' feelings of limited access to opportunity.

Two scales purport to give a more general picture of the individual: socialization (to what degree normative conformity has been internalized as a part of the personality) and interpersonal competence (feeling of personal worth). Here we see practically no difference between "good" lower class boys and "good" middle class boys. Despite their relative rejection of middle class values and their feeling of having limited access to opportunity, the lower class non-delinquents reflect self-concepts quite unlike the

delinquents'. Although their lower class status has resulted in their sharing many attitudes with the delinquent population (also lower class), the lower class non-delinquent boys' self-conceptions (primarily the products of family life) are more like those of the middle class boys. It would appear that the lower class boy's concept of self may be the factor which ultimately influences his social behavior.

To answer the questions posed earlier, these data permit us to say three things:

1. Delinquents are actually different from non-delinquents in being more negative in their perceptions of values and opportunity.

2. Negative perceptions of middle class values and a feeling of having blocked opportunity are not powerful enough to cause delinquency among lower class boys if other aspects of the personality permit the boys to see themselves as non-delinquent.

3. Relatively negative perceptions of values and opportunity are quite compatible with an otherwise positive or healthy picture of the self.

Conclusions

From these data, three types of boys seem to emerge. These types are what have been called the "delinquent," the "corner boy" and the "college boy" (Cohen, 1955). The "delinquent" is negatively predisposed toward middle class values and is acutely aware of his limited opportunities in life. His socialization has been inadequate and this has given him a poor image of himself and others. The "corner boy" (our lower class non-delinquent) is also negatively predisposed toward middle class values, although he is not as extreme in his rejection as is the delinquent. He too is aware that he has only limited access to opportunity, but this feeling is not as intense. His socialization has been more adequate, probably because he has experienced a more wholesome family life, and as a result he has a relatively positive concept of self. Lastly, the "college boy" accepts middle class values and feels that he has unlimited access to opportunity. His socialization has been effective, and his self-concept, in turn, is positive and healthy. This type of boy is most characteristic of the middle class non-delinquent described in this paper.

The crucial factor differentiating these three types is the self-concept. The boy who, as a result of favorable experiences with others in the family, peer group or school, comes to see himself as a "good boy" or as a "non-delinquent," has developed an inner containment, a buffer or insulation against delinquency (Reckless, 1961, Ch. 18). The good self-concept acts as a shield which protects him from the adversities of the environment. The more urban, industrialized, mobile and individualized American society becomes, the greater the reliance that must be placed on a self that is strong enough to make effective choices among alternatives, to steer away from danger and to manage daily living. The problem now is to find what produces a favorable set of self-perceptions that can act as an insulator against the pulls and pressures of a bad environment. What is it within the socialization process which enables some children, even in the slums, to hold the line against deviation? What are the specific components in the personality development of children that determine a favorable or unfavorable image of self? Finding answers to these questions is something in which sociologists, psychologists and psychiatrists can find a mutually beneficial area of study.

Index

Bibliography

Ackerman, M. W. "Social role" and total personality. Amer. J. Orthopsychiat., 1951, 21, 1-17.

Acord. L. D. Sexual symbolism as a correlate of age. J. Consult. Psychol., 1962, 26, 279-281.

Adams, J. F. Adolescent personal problems as a function of age and sex. J. Genet. Psychol., 1964. 104, 207-214.

Adelson, J., and O'Neil, R. P. Growth of political ideas in adolescdnce : The sense of community. J. Pers. Soc. Psychol., 1966, 4, 295-306.

Allen, R. M. Elements of Rorschach interpretation. New York: International Universities Press. 1954.

Allport, G. W., Gillespie, J. M., & Young, J. The religion of the post-war college student. J. Psychol., 1948, 25, 3-33.

Almond, G., and Verba, S. The civic culture. Princeton: Princeton Univ. Press, 1963.

Ames, L. B., and Ilg, F. Sex differences in test performance of matched girl-boy pairs in the five-to-nine-year-old age range. J. Genet. Psychol., 1964, 104, 25-34.

Ames, L. B., Metraux, R. W., & Walker, R. N. Adolescent Rorschach responses. New York: P. B. Hoeber, 1959,

Anastasi, A., and Foley, J. P. An experimental study of the drawing behavior of adult psychotics in comparison with that of a normal control group. J. Exp. Psychol, 1944, 34, 169-194.

Anastasi, A., and Foley, J. P. An analysis of spontaneous artistic productions by the abnormal. J. Gen. Psychol., 1943, 28, 297-313.

Anastasi, A., and Foley, J. P. Differential psychology. New York: Macmillan, 1953.

Anderson, J. E. The prediction of terminal intelligence from infant and preschool tests. In National Society for the Study of Education, Intelligence: its nature and nurture, 1940. Pp. 385-403.

Anderson, M. H., and McManus, R. L. Interests of nursing candidates: The pattern of interest and activities of 800 prenursing students. Amer. J. Nurs., 1942, 42 555-563.

Andry, R. G. Delinquency and parental pathology. London: Methuen, 1960.

Armstrong, C. M. Patterns of achievement in selected New York state schools. Albany: New York State Educ. Dep., 1964. (Mimeographed)

Asayama, S. Sexual behavior of the present-day Japanese students. Kyoto: Usui-Shobo, 1949.

Asayama, S. Comparison of sexual development of American and Japanese adolescents. Psychologia, 1957, 1, 129-131. (a)

Asayama, A. Records of sex. Osaka: Rokugatsusha, 1957. (b)

Astin, A. W., and Nichols, R. C. Life goals and vocational choice. J. Appl. Psychol., 1964, 48, 50-58.

Atherton, K. An exploratory analysis of some indices of socioeconomic status. Unpublished manuscript, Institute of Human Develpm. Univ. of California, Berkeley, 1958.

Ausubel, D. P. *Theory and problems of adolescent development.* New York: Grune and Stratton, 1954.

Ausubel, D. P., Balthazar, E. E., Rosenthal, I., Blackman, L. S., Schpoont, S. H., & Welkowitz, J. Perceived parent attitudes as determinates of children's ego structure. *Child Develpm.,* 1954, *25,* 173-183.

Ausubel, D. P., Schiff, H. M., and Gasser, E. B. A preliminary study of developmental trends in socio-empathy: Accuracy of perception of own and others' sociometric status. *Child Develpm.* 1952, *23.* 111-128.

Baldwin, A. L., *Behavior and development in childhood.* New York: Dryden Press, 1955.

Balester, R. S. The self-concept and juvenile delinquency. Unpublished doctoral dissertation, Vanderbilt Univ., 1955.

Balint, M. Der Onaniebgewohnungskampf in der Pubertat. *Z. psychoanal. Padag.,* 1934, 8, 374-391.

Bandura, A., and Walters, R. H. Agression. In H. Stevenson (Ed.), *Child psychology. 62nd Yearb. nat. Soc. Stud. Educ.* Chicago: Univ. Chicago Press, 1963, Part I, 364-415.

Bardis, P. D. Attitudes toward dating among students of a Michigan high school. *Sociol. Soc. Res.,* 1958, *42,* 274-277.

Barker, R. G., Wright, B. A., & Gonick, M. R. *Adjustment to physical handicap and illness.* Social Science Research Bulletin 55. New York, 1946.

Bayer, L. M. Build in relation to menstrual disorders and obesity. *Endocrinology,* 1939, *24,* 260-268.

Bayer, L. M. Build variations in adolescent girls. *J. Pediat.,* 1940, *17,* 331-344. (a)

Bayer, L. M. Weight and menses in adolescent girls with special reference to build. *J. Pediat.,* 1940, *17,* 345-354. (b)

Bayley, N. Some psychological correlates of somatic androgeny. *Child Develpm.,* 1951, *22,* 47-60.

Bayley, N. and Bayer, L. M. The assessment of somatic androgeny. *Am. J. Phys. Anthropol.,* 1946, *4,* 433-461.

Becker, H. S. Social-class variations in the teacher-pupil relationship. *J. Educ. Sociol.,* 1952, *25,* 451-465.

Becker, H. S., Geer, B., and Hughes, E. *Boys in white.* Glencoe, Ill.: Free Press, 1963.

Becker, H. S., Geer, B., and Hughes, E. *A Study of undergraduate student culture.* Unpublished manuscript, 1965. (Mimeographed)

Behrens, W. U. Ein Beitrag zur Fehlerberechnung bei wenigen Beobachtungen. *Landw. Jb.,* 1929, *86,* 807-837.

Bell, H. M. *Youth tell their story.* Washington, D. C.: American Council on Education, 1938.

Benedict, R. Continuities and discontinuities in cultural conditioning. *Psychiatry,* 1938, *1,* 161-167.

Beres, D., Gale, C., and Oppenheimer, L. Disturbances of identity function in childhood: Psychiatric and Psychological observations. *Amer. J. Orthopsychiat.,* 1960, *30,* 369-381.

Bernfeld, S. Uber eine typische Form der mannlichen Pubertat. *Imago,* 1923, *9,* 169-188.

Bernfeld, S. *Vom Dichterischen Schaffen der Jugend.* Wien: Int. Psychoanal. Verlag, 1924.

Bernfeld, S. Uber die einfache mannliche Pubertat. *Z. psychoanal. Padag.,* 1935, *9,* 360-379.

Bernfeld, S. Types of adoleseence. *Psychoanal. Quart.,* 1938, 7, 243-253.

Bernreuter, R. G. *The Personality Inventory.* Stanford, Calif.: Stanford Univ. Press, 1931.

Bibring, E. The mechanism of depression. In P. Greenacre (Ed.), *Affective disorders.* New York: International Universities Press, 1953, Pp. 13-48.

Bird, C. *Social psychology.* New York: D. Appleton-Century, 1940.

Birkness, V., and Johnson, H. C. Comparative study of delinquent and non-delinquent adolescents. *J. educ. Res.,* 1949, *42,* 561-572.

Blalock, H. M., Jr. Some implications of random measurement error for causal inferences. *Amer. J. Sociol.,* 1965, *71,* 37-47. (a)

Blalock, H. M., Jr. Theory building and the statistical concept of interaction. *Amer. Sociol. Rev.,* 1965, *30,* 374-380. (b).

Bledsoe, J. C. An investigation of six correlates of student withdrawal from high school. *J. Educ. Res.,* 1959, *53,* 3-6.

Bloch, H. A., and Flynn, F. T. *Delinquency: The juvenile offender in America today.* New York: Random House, 1956.

Blodgett, H. E. An experimental approach to the measurement of self-evaluation among adolescent girls. Unpublished doctoral dissertation, Univ. of Minnesota, 1953.

Blos, P. The contribution of psychoanalysis to the treatment of adolescents. In M. Heiman (Ed.), *Psychoanalysis and social work.* New York: International Universities Press, 1953, Pp. 210-241.

Blos, P. *On adolescence: A psychoanalytic interpretation.* New York: Free Press, 1962.

Bock, E. W., and Burchinal, L. G. Social status, heterosexual relations and expected ages of marriage. *J. Gen. Psychol.,* 1962, *101,* 43-51.

Bonney, M. E. A sociometric study of the relationship of some factors to mutual friendships on the elementary, secondary, and college levels. *Sociometry,* 1946, *9,* 21-47.

Bornstein, B. In discussion following the presentation of P. Greenacre's paper. "The Prepuberty Trauma in Girls," at the New York Psychoanalytic Society, March 1, 1949.

Borow, H. Development of occupational motives and roles. In Hoffman, M. L. and Hoffman, L. W. (Eds.) *Review of Child Development Research Vol. 2,* New York: Russell Sage Foundation, 1966.

Bossard, J. H. S. *The sociology of child development.* (rev. ed.) New York: Harper, 1954.

Bowen, M., Dysinger, R. H., and Basamanis, B. The role of the father in families with a schizophrenic patient. *Amer. J. Psychiat.,* 1959, *115,* 117-120.

Bowerman, C. E., and Elder, G. H., Jr. The adolescent and his family. Unpublished manuscript, 1962.

Bowerman, C. E., and Kinch, J. W. Changes in family and peer orientation of children between the fourth and tenth grades. *Soc. Forces,* 1959, *37,* 206-211.

Boyne, A. W., and Clark, J. R. Secular change in the intelligence of 11-year-old Aberdeen school children. *Human Biol.,* 1959, *31,* 325-333.

Bradway, K. P. I. Q. constancy in the Revised Stanford-Binet from the preschool to the junior high school level. *J. Genet. Psychol.*, 1944, *65*, 197-217.

Breed, W. Sex, class and socialization in dating. *Marr. Fam. Living*, 1956, *18*, 137-144.

Brenman, M. On teasing and being teased: and the problem of "moral masochism." *Psychoanal. Stud. Child*, 1952, *7*, 264-285.

Brim, O. G., Jr. Adolescent personality as self-other systems. *J. Marr. Fam.*, 1965, *27*, 156-162.

Broderick, C. B., and Fowler, S. E. New patterns of relationships between the sexes among preadolescents. *Marr. Fam. Living*, 1961, *23*, 27-30.

Bronfenbrenner, U. Socialization and social class through time and space. In E. E. Maccoby *et al.* (Eds.), *Readings in social psychology*. New York: Holt, 1958.

Bronfenbrenner, U. Some familial antecedents of responsibility and leadership in adolescent. In L. Petrullo and B. Bass (Eds.), *Leadership and interpersonal behavior*. New York: Holt, Rinehart, and Winston, 1961. Pp. 239-271.

Broom, L., and Selznick, P. *Sociology.* (3rd ed.) New York: Harper and Row, 1964.

Brown, E. A., and Goitein, P. L. The significance of body image for personality assay. *J. Nerv. Ment. Dis.*, 1943, *97*, 401-408.

Brownfain, J. J. Stability of the self-concept as a dimension of personality. *J. Abnorm. Soc. Psychol.*, 1952, *47*, 597-606.

Brunkan, R. J., and Crites, J. O. An inventory to measure the parental attitude variables in Roe's theory of vocational choice. *J. Counsel. Psychol.*, 1964, *11*, 3-12.

Bullen, A. K., and Hardy, H. L. Analysis of body build photographs of one hundred seventy-five college women. *Amer. J. Phys. Anthropol.*, 1946, *4*, 37-68.

Burchinal, L. G. Membership groups and attitudes toward cross-religious dating and marriage. *Marr. Fam. Living*, 1960, *22*, 248-253.

Burchinal, L. G. The premarital dyad and love involvement. In H. T. Christensen (Ed.), *Handbook of marriage and the family*. Chicago: Rand McNally, 1964. Pp. 623-674.

Burchinal, L. G., and Chancellor, L. E. Ages at marriage, occupations of grooms and interreligious marriage rates. *Soc. Forces*, 1962, *40*, 348-354. (a)

Burchinal, L. G., and Chancellor, L. E. Factors related to interreligious marriages in Iowa, 1953-1957. *Iowa Agr. & Home Econ. Exp. Sta. Res. Bull. No. 510*, 1962. (b)

Bureau of Census, Department of Commerce. *Religious bodies*. Washington, D. C.: U. S. Government Printing Office, 1916.

Burgess, E. W. The economic factor in juvenile delinquency. *J. Crim. Law Criminol. Police Sci.*, 1952, *43*, 29-38.

Burlingham, D. *Twins.* New York: International Universities Press, 1952.

Burton, R. V. Generality of honesty reconsidered. *Psychol. Rev.*, 1963, *70*, 481-499.

Burton, W. H. *The nature and direction of learning.* New York: D. Appleton, 1929.

Busia, K. A. Agni. *Encyclopedia Britannica.* Vol. 1. Chicago: Benton, 1963. P. 330. (a)

Busia, K. A. Ashanti. *Encyclopedia Britannica.* Vol. 2. Chicago: Benton, 1963. P. 567. (b)

Buxbaum, E. Angstäusserungen von Schulmädchen im Pubertätsalter. *Z. psychoanal. Pädag.*, 7, 401-409.

Buxbaum, E. Transference and group formation in children and adolescents. *Psychoanal. Study Child*, 1945, *1*, 351-365.

Cameron, N. *Personality development and psychopathology.* Boston: Houghton Mifflin, 1963.

Cameron, P. Confirmation of the Freudian psychosexual stages utilizing sexual symbolism. *Psychol. Rep.*, 1967, *21*, 33-39.

Cameron, W. J., & Kenkel, W. F. High school dating: a study in variation. *Marr. Fam. Living*, 1960, *22*, 74-76.

Campbell, A., Converse, P. E., Miller, W. E. and Stokes, D. E. *The American Voter.* New York: John Wiley, 1960.

Campisi, P. J. The Italian family in the United States. In R. F. Winch and R. McGinnis, *Selected studies in marriage and the family.* New York: Holt, 1953. Pp. 126-137.

Caro, F. G., and Pihlblad, C. T. Social class, formal education, and social mobility. *Sociol. soc. Res.*, 1964, *48*, 428-439.

Caro, F. G., and **Pihlblad, C. T.** Aspirations and expectations: A reexamination of the bases for social class differences in the occupational orientations of male high school students. *Sociol. Soc. Res.*, 1965, *49*, 464-475.

Carroll, R. E. Relation of social environment to the moral ideology and the personal aspirations of Negro boys and girls. *Sch. Rev.*, 1945, *53*, 30-38.

Cervantes, L. F. *The dropout.* Ann Arbor: Univ. Michigan Press, 1965. (a)

Cervantes, L. F. Family background, primary relationships, and the high school dropout. *J. Marr. Fam.*, 1965, *27*, 218-223. (b)

Chesser, E. *The sexual, marital, and family relationships of the English* woman. London: Hutchison Medical Publishers, 1956.

Christensen, H. T. Dating behavior as evaluated by high school students *Amer. J. Sociol.*, 1952, *57*, 580-586.

Christensen, H. T. *Marriage analysis: foundations for successful family life.* (2nd ed.) New York: Ronald Press, 1958.

Clark, E. T. *The psychology of religious awakening.* New York: Macmillan, 1929.

Clarke, A. C. The use of leisure and its relation to levels of occupational prestige. *Amer. Sociol. Rev.*, 1956, *21*, 301-307

Clinard, M. B. The sociology of delinquency and crime. In J. B. Gittler (Ed.), *Review of sociology: analysis of a decade.* New York: John Wiley, 1957. Pp. 465-499. (a)

Clinard, M. B. *Sociology of deviant behavior.* New York: Rinehart, 1957. (b)

Cloward, R. A. and Ohlin, L. E. *Delinquency and opportunity: A theory of delinquent gangs.* Glencoe, Ill.: Free Press, 1960.

Cohen, A. K. *Delinquent boys: The culture of the gang.* Glencoe, Ill.: Free Press, 1955.

Cole, L. *Psychology of adolescence*. New York: Rinehart, 1948.

Coleman, H. A. The relationship of socio-economic status to the performance of junior high school students. *J. Exp. Educ.*, 1940, *9*, 61-63.

Coleman, J. S. *The adolescent society*. New York: Free Press of Glencoe, 1961.

Coleman, J. S. *Education and political development*. Princeton: Princeton Univ. Press, 1965.

Collins, J. H., and Douglas, H. R. The socio-economic status of the home as a factor in success in the junior high school. *Elem. Sch. J.*, 1937, *38*, 107-113.

Combs, A. W., and Soper, D. W. The self, its derivative terms, and research. *J. Indiv. Psychol.*, 1957, *13*, 134-145.

Conklin, A. M. Failures of highly intelligent pupils. *Teach. Coll. Contrib. Educ.*, 1940, No. 792.

Connell, W. F., Francis, E. P., and Skilbeck, E. E. *Growing up in an Australian city*. Melbourne: Australian Council for Educational Research, 1957.

Connor, R., Greene, H. F., and Walters, J. Agreement of family member conceptions of "good" parent and child roles. *Soc. Forces*, 1958, *36*, 353-358.

Connor, R., Johannis, T. B., Jr., and Walters, J. Parent-adolescent relationships. II. Intra-familial conceptions of the good father, good mother, and good child. *J. Home Econ.*, 1954, *46*, 187-191.

Converse, P. E. The shifting role of class. In E. Hartley, *Readings in social psychology*. (3rd ed.) New York: Holt, 1958. Pp. 388-399.

Cook, E. S., Jr. An analysis of factors related to withdrawal from high school prior to graduation. *J. Educ. Res.*, 1956, *50*, 191-196.

Cooley, C. H. *The two major works of* . . . . Glencoe, Ill.: Free Press, 1956.

Coombs, R. H. Reinforcement of values in the parental home as a factor in mate selection. *Marr. Fam. Living*, 1962, *24*, 155-157.

Coster, J. K. Some characteristics of high school pupils from three income levels. *J. Educ. Psychol.*, 1959, *50*, 55-62.

Cowen, E. L. The 'Negative self concept' as a personality measure. *J. Consult. Psychol.*, 1954, *18*, 138-142.

Crissy, W. J. E., and Daniel, W. J. Vocational interest factors in women. *J. Appl. Psychol.*, 1939, *23*, 488-494.

Crist, J. R. High school dating as a behavior system. *Marr. Fam. Living*, 1953, *15*, 23-28.

Daly, M. *Profile of youth*. Philadelphia: Lippincott, 1951.

Davidson, H. H. A measure of adjustment obtained from the Rorschach protocol. *J. Prop. Tech.*, 1950, *14*, 31-38.

Davidson, H. H., and Gottlieb, L. S. The emotional maturity of pre- and post-menarcheal girls. *J. Genet. Psychol.*, 1955, *86*, 261-266.

Davis, A., and Dollard, J. *Children of Bondage*. Washington, D. C.: American Council of Education, 1940.

Davis, K. The sociology of parent-youth conflict. *Amer. Sociol. Rev.*, 1940. *5*, 523-535.

Davis, M. *Sex and the adolescent*. New York: Dial Press, 1958.

Dedman, J. The relationship between religious attitude and attitude towards premarital sex relations. *Marr. Fam. Living*, 1959, *21*, 171-176.

Dejung, J. E., & Gardner, E. F. The accuracy of self-role perception: A developmental study. *J. Exp. Educ.*, 1962, *31*, 27-41.

De Lisle, F. H. A study of the relationship of the self-concept to adjustment in a selected group of college women. Unpublished doctoral dissertation, Michigan State College, 1953.

Dennis, W. The adolescent. In L. Carmichael (Ed.), Manual of child psychology., New York: Wiley, 1946, 633-666.

Deutsch, H. *The psychology of women*. Vol. 1. New York: Gruen and Stratton, 1944.

Dignan, M. H. Ego identity and maternal identification. *J. Pers. Soc. Psychol.*, 1965, *1*, 476-483.

Dimock, H. S. New light on adolescent religion. *Relig. Educ.*, 1936, *31*, 273-279.

Dimock, H. S. *Rediscovering the adolescent*. New York: Association Press, 1937.

Dimond, S. E. *Schools and the development of good citizenship*. Detroit: Wayne Univ. Press, 1953.

Dipboye, W. J., & Anderson, W. F. The ordering of occupational values by high school freshmen and seniors. *Personnel Guid. J.*, 1959, *38*, 121-124.

Dirksen, C. *Economic factors in delinquency*. Milwaukee: Bruce, 1948.

Doll, E. A. *Vineland social maturity scale*. Minneapolis: Educational Test Bureau, 1946.

Douvan, E. Social status and success in striving. *J. abnorm. Soc. Psychol.*, 1956, *52*, 219-223.

Douvan, E., and Adelson, J. *The adolescent experience*. New York: John Wiley, 1966.

Dudycha, G. J. Religious beliefs of college students. *J. Appl. Psychol.*, 1933, *17*, 585-603.

Dunphy, D. C. The social structure of urban adolescent peer groups. *Sociometry*, 1963, *26*, 230-246.

Dupertuis, C. W., Atkinson, W. B., and Elftman, H. Sex differences in pubic hair distribution. *Human Biol.*, 1945, *17*, 137-142.

Duvall, E. M. Conceptions of parenthood. *Amer. J. Sociol.*, 1946, *52*, 193-203.

Easton, D. An approach to the analysis of political systems. *World Polit.*, 1957, *9*, 383-400.

Easton, D. Political anthropology. In B. J. Siegel (Ed.), *Biennial Review of Anthropology*. Stanford: Stanford Univ. Press, 1959.

Easton, D., and Hess, R. D. Youth and the political system. In S. M. Lipset and L. Lowenthal (Eds.), *Culture and social character*. New York: Free Press of Glencoe, 1961. Pp. 226-251.

Easton, D., & Hess, R. D. The child's political world. *Midwest J. polit. Sci.*, 1962, *6*, 229-246.

Eells, K. W., et al., under the chairmanship of A. Davis. *Intelligence and cultural differences*. Chicago: Univ. of Chicago Press, 1951.

Ehrmann, W. W. *Premarital dating behavior*. New York: Holt, 1959.

Elder, G. H., Jr. Structural variations in the child rearing relationship. *Sociometry*, 1962, *25*, 241-262.

Elder, G. H., Jr. Parental power legitimation and its effect on the adolescent. *Sociometry*, 1963, *26*, 50-65.

Elder, G. H., Jr. Adolescent socialization and personality development. 1965. (Mimeographed)

Elder, R. L. Traditional and developmental conceptions of fatherhood. *Marr. Fam. Liv.*, 1949, *11*, 98-100, 106.

Elkin, F., and Westley, W. A. The myth of adolescent culture. *Amer. Sociol. Rev.*, 1955, *20*, 680-684.

Elkisch, P. Children's drawings in a projective technique. *Psychol. Monogr.*, 1945, *58*, No. 1.

Ellis, R. W. B. Puberty growth of boys. *Arch. Dis. Childhood*, 1948, *23*, 17-26.

Empey, L. Social class and occupational aspiration: A comparison of absolute and relative measurement. *Amer. Sociol. Rev.*, 1956, *21*, 703-709.

Engel, M. The stability of the self-concept in adolescence. *J. Abnorm. Soc. Psychol.*, 1959, *58*, 211-215.

England, A. O. A psychological study of children's drawings. *Amer. J. Ortho-psychiat.*, 1943, *13*, 525-530.

English, O. S., and Pearson, G. H. J. *Emotional problems of living*. New York: Norton, 1945.

Erikson, E. H. Ego development and historical change. *Psychoanal. Study Child*, 1946, *2*, 359-396.

Erikson, E. H. *Childhood and society*. New York: W. W. Norton, 1950. (a)

Erikson, E. H. Growth and crises of the "Healthy personality." In M. J. E. Senn (Ed.), *Symposium on the healthy personality.* Supplement II: Problems of infancy and childhood, Transactions of Fourth Conference, March, 1950. New York: Josiah Macy Jr. Foundation, 1950. (b)

Erikson, E. H. The dream specimen of psychoanalysis. *J. Amer. Psychoanal. Ass.*, 1954, *2*, 5-56, (a)

Erikson, E. H. Wholeness and totality. In C. J. Friedrich (Ed.) Totalitarianism. Proceedings of a conference held at the American Academy of Arts and Sciences, March, 1953. Cambridge: Harvard Univ. Press, 1954. (b)

Erikson, E. H. Ego identity and the psychosocial moratorium. In H. L. Witmer and R. Kosinsky (Eds.), *New perspectives for research in juvenile delinquency.* U. S. Children's Bureau: Publication #356, 1956. Pp. 1-23.

Erikson, E. H. *Young man Luther: A study in psychoanalysis and history.* New York: Norton, 1958.

Erikson, E. H. *Identity and the life cycle.* New York: Internat. Univ. Press, 1959.

Erikson, E. H. The problem of ego identity. In *Identity and the life cycle.* New York: International Universities Press, 1959. (Psychol. Issues, 1959, I, no. 1) Pp. 110-164.

Erikson, E. H. The problem of ego identity. *J. Amer. Psychoanalytic Ass.*, 1956, *4*, 56-121.

Erikson, E. H. The concept of identity in race relations: Notes and queries. *Daedalus*, 1966 (Winter), 145-171.

Erikson, E. H., and Erikson, K. The confirmation of the delinquent. *Chicago Rev.*, 1957, Winter, 15123.

Federn, P. In *Die Onanie, Vierzehn Beiträge zu einer Diskussion der Wiener Psychoanalytischen Vereinigung.* Wiesbaden: J. F. Bergmann, 1912. Pp. 68-82.

Federn, P. *Ego psychology and the psychoses.* New York: Basic Books, 1952.

Feidler, F. E., and Siegel, S. M. The free drawing test as a prediction of non-improvement in psychotherapy. *J. Clin. Psychol.*, 1949, *5*, 386-389.

Feinberg, M. R. Relation of background experience to social acceptance. *J. Abnorm. Soc. Psychol.*, 1953, *48*, 206-214.

Feinberg, M. R., Smith, M., and Schmidt, R. An analysis of expressions used by adolescents at verying economic levels to describe accepted and rejected peers. *J. Gen. Psychol.*, 1958, *93*, 133-148.

Feldman, S. E., & Feldman, M. T. Transition of sex differences in cheating. *Psychol. Rep.*, 1967, *20*, 957-958.

Fenichel, O. Review of "The ego and the mechanisms of defense." *Int. J. Psychoanal.*, 1938, *19*, 116-136.

Fenichel, O. *The psychoanalytic theory of neurosis.* New York: Norton, 1945.

Ferenczi, S. In *Die Onanie, Vierzehn Beiträge zu einer Diskussion der Wiener Psychoanalytischen Vereinigung.* Wiesbaden: J. F. Bergmann, 1912, Pp. 6-10.

Finger, J. A. Academic motivation and youth-culture involvement: Their relationships to school performance and career success. *Sch. Rev.*, 1966, *74*, 177-195.

Finger, J. A., and Schlesser, G. E. Academic performance of public and private school students. *J. Educ. Psychol.*, 1963, *54*, 118-122.

Finger, J. A., and Schlesser, G. E. Non-intellective predictors of academic success in school and college. *Sch. Rev.*, 1965, *73*, 14-29.

Finger, J. A., Jr., and **Silverman, M.** Changes in academic performance in the junior high school. *Personnel Guid. J.*, 1966, *45*, 157-164.

Fisher, R. A. The comparison of samples with possibly unequal variances. *Ann. Eugen.*, London, 1939, *9*, 174-180.

Fisher, R. A. *Statistical methods for research workers.* (12th ed.) London: Oliver and Boyd, 1954.

Flanagan, J. C., Dailey, J. T., Shaycoft, M. F., Gorham, W. A., Orr, D. B., and Goldberg, I. *Design for a study of American youth.* Boston: Houghton Mifflin, 1962.

Flanagan, J. C., Davis, F. B., Dailey, J. T., Shaycoft, M. F., Orr, D. B., Goldberg, I., and Newman, C. A., Jr. The American high school student. Office of Educ. Cooperative Res. Branch Technical Report No. 635. Pittsburgh: University of Pittsburgh, 1964.

Flavell, J. H. *The developmental psychology of Jean Piaget.* Princeton, N. J.: Van Nostrand, 1963.

Fleming, E. G. Best friends. *J. Soc. Psychol.*, 1932, *3*, 385-390.

Ford, C. S., and Beach, F. A. *Patterns of Sexual behavior.* New York: Harper, 1951.

Franzblau, A. N. Religious beliefs and character among Jewish adolescents. *Teach. Coll., Columbia Univ., Contrib. Educ.*, 1934, No. 634.

Freedman, M. B. The passage through college. *J. Soc. Issues*, 1956, *12*, 13-28.

Freeman, F. N. Intellectual growth of children as indicated by repeated tests. *Psychol. Monogr.*, 1936, *47*, 20-34.

Freud, A. Schlagephantasie and Tagtaum. *Imago*, 1922, *8*, 317-332.

Freud, A. *Introduction to the technique of child analysis.* New York: Nervous and Mental Disease Publ., 1928.

Freud, A. *Psychoanalysis for teachers and parents.* New York: Emerson Books, 1935.

Freud, A. *The ego and the mechanisms of defense.* New York: Internat. Univ. Press, 1946.

Freud, A. and Dann, S. An experiment in group upbringing. The *Psychoanal. Stud. Child,* 1951, *6,* 127-168.

Freud, S. In *Die Onanie, Vierzehn Beiträge zu einer Diskussion der Wiener Psychoanalytischen Vereinigung.* Wiesbaden: J. F. Bergmann, 1912. Pp. 132-140.

Freud, S. *The three contributions to a theory of sex.* Trans. A. A. Brill, (3rd. rev. ed.) New York: Nervous and Mental Disease, 1918.

Freud, S. *Group psychology and the analysis of the ego.* New York: Liveright, 1922.

Freud, S. *New Introductory lectures on psychoanalysis.* Lecture 31: The anatomy of the mental personality. New York: Norton, 1933.

Freud, S. *A general introduction to psychoanalysis.* New York: Garden City, 1943.

Freud, S. *The interpretation of dreams.* New York: Random House, 1950.

Freud, S. On narcissism: An introduction. *Standard Edition, 14,* 73-102. London: Hogarth, 1957.

Friedenberg, E. Z. *The vanishing adolescent.* Boston: Beacon, 1959.

Friedman, I. Characteristics of the thematic apperception test heroes of normal, psychoneurotic, and paranoid schizophrenic subjects. *J. Proj. Tech.,* 1957, *21,* 372-376.

Gates, A. I. Nature and educational significance of physical status and of mental, physiological, social and emotional maturity. *J. Educ. Psychol.,* 1924, *15,* 329-358.

Gebhard, P. H., *et al. Pregnancy, Birth, and abortion.* New York: Harper, 1958.

Giallombardo, R. (Edit.) *Juvenile delinquency: a book of readings.* New York: Wiley, 1966.

Ginsburg, S. W. The role of work. *Samiksa,* 1954, *8,* 1-13.

Ginzberg, E., *et al Occupational choice.* New York: Columbia Univ. Press, 1951.

Glaser, D., as quoted in R. A. Cloward and L. E. Ohlin, *Delinquency and opportunity.* Glencoe, Ill.: Free Press, 1960.

Glenn, N. D. Negro prestige criteria: A case study in the bases of prestige. *Amer. J. Sociol.,* 1963, *68,* 645-657.

Glueck, E. Spotting juvenile delinquents: Can it be done? *Fed. Probation,* 1956, *20,* 7-13.

Glueck, S. (Edit.) *The problem of delinquency.* Boston: Houghton-Mifflin Co., 1959.

Glueck, S. Defense of the Glueck social prediction table. In N. Johnson, L. Savitz, and M. E. Wolfgang, *The sociology of punishment and correction.* New York: John Wiley, 1960, Pp. 265-272.

Glueck, S., and Glueck, E. *Unraveling juvenile delinquency.* New York: Commonwealth Fund, 1950.

Gold, M. *Status forces in delinquent boys.* Ann Arbor, Mich.: Univ. of Michigan Inst. of Soc. Res., 1963.

Goldman, R. J. The application of Piaget's Schema of Operational Thinking to religious story data by means of the Guttman Scalogram. *Brit. J. Educ. Psychol.,* 1965, *35,* 158-170.

Goldsen, R. K., Rosenberg, M., Williams, R., Jr., and Suchman, E. A. *What college students think.* Princeton, N. J.: Van Nostrand, 1960.

Goodenough, F. L. *Measurement of intelligence by drawings.* New York: World, 1926.

Goodenough, F. L., and Leahy, A. M. The effect of certain family relationships upon the development of personality. *Pedag. Sem. B. J. Genet. Psychol.,* 1927, *34,* 44-71.

Goodman, P. *Growing up absurd.* New York: Random House, 1960.

Goodnow, J. J., and Bethon, G. Piaget's tasks: The effects of schooling and intelligence. *Child Develpm.,* 1966, *37,* 537-582.

Gordon, W. *The social systems of the high school.* New York: Free Press of Glencoe, 1957.

Gorer, G. *Exploring English character.* London: Cresset, 1955.

Gough, H. G. The relationship of socioeconomic status to personality inventory and achievement test scores. *J. Educ. Psychol.,* 1946, *37,* 527-540.

Gough, H. G., and Peterson, D. R. The identification and measurement of predispositional factors in crime and delinquency. *J. Consult. Psychol.,* 1952, *16,* 207-212.

Greenacre, P. The prepuberty trauma in girls. *Psychoanal. Quart.,* 1950, 19, 298-317.

Greenstein, F. I. The benevolent leader: Children's images of political authority. *Amer. Polit. Sci. Rev.,* 1960, *54,* 934-943.

Greenstein, F. I. *Children and politics.* New Haven: Yale Univ. Press, 1965.

Greulich, W. W. Some observations on the growth and development of adolescent children. *J. Pediat.,* 1941, *19,* 302-314.

Greulich, W. W. and Dorfman, R. I., *et al.* Somatic and endocrine studies of puberal and adolescent boys. *Monogr. Soc. Res. Child develop.,* 1942, 7, No. 3.

Greulich, W. W., and Thomas, H. The growth and development of the pelvis of individual girls before, during and after puberty. *Yale J. Biol. and Med.,* 1944, *17,* 91-98.

Greulich, W. W., et al. A handbook of methods for the study of adolescent children. *Monogr. Soc. Res. Child Develop.,* 1938, *3,* no. 2.

Gribbons, W. D. Evaluation of an eight grade group guidance program. *Personnel Guid. J.,* 1960, *38,* 740-745.

Gribbons, W. D. Changes in readiness for vocational planning from the eighth to the tenth grade. *Personnel Guid. J.,* 1964, *41,* 908-913.

Gribbons, W. D., and Lohnes, P. R. Relationships among measures of readiness for vocational planning. *J. Counsel. Psychol.,* 1964, *11,* 13-19.

Gribbons, W. D., and Lohnes, P. R. Validation of vocational planning interview scales. *J. Counsel. Psychol.,* 1964, *11,* 20-26. (b)

Gribbons, W. D., and Lohnes, P. R. Predicting five years of development in adolescents from readiness for vocational planning scales. *J. Educ. Psychol.,* 1965, *56,* 244-253. (a)

386

Gribbons, W. D., and Lohnes, P. R. Shifts in adolescents' vocational values. *Personnel Guid. J.*, 1965, *44*, 248-252.

Grinder, R. E. Fidelity or alienation in the youth culture today. A review of Ernest A. Smith, "American Youth Culture." *Merrill-Palmer Quart.*, 1964, *10*, 195-204.

Grotz, B. Erotische Symbole. *Z. f. Sex.-wiss. u. Sex.-pol.*, 1930, *17*, 226-232

Hall, G. S. The contents of children's minds on entering school. *Psychol. Rev.*, 1883, *2*, 249-272.

Hall, G. S. *Adolescence.* Vol. 1. New York: Appleton, 1904.

Halsey, A. H., Floud, J., & Anderson, C. A. (Eds.) *Education, economy and society.* New York: Free Press, 1961.

Hamblin, R. L. Group integration during a crisis. *Hum. Rel.*, 1958, *11*, 67-76.

Hamilton, G. V. *A research in marriage.* New York: Lear, 1929.

Harnik, J. The various developments undergone by narcissism in men and women. *Int. J. Psychoanal.*, 1924, *5*, 66-83.

Harris, D. Factors affecting college grades: a review of the literature, 1930-1937. *Psychol. Bull.*, 1940, *37*, 125-161.

Harrod, G., and Griswold, N. Occupational values and counseling. *Voc. Guid. Quart.*, 1960, *9*, 60-66.

Hartley, E. L., & Hartley, R. E. *Fundamentals of social psychology.* New York: Alfred A. Knopf, 1952.

Hartmann, H. Comments on the psychoanalytic theory of the ego. *Psychoanal. Stud. Child*, 1950, *5*, 74-96.

Hartmann, H. *Ego psychology and the problem of adaptation.* New York: International Universities Press, 1958.

Hartmann, H., Kris, E., and Loewenstein, R. M. Comments on the formation of psychic structure. *Psychoanal. Stud. Child*, 1946, *2*, 11-38.

Hartmann, H., Kris, E., and Loewenstein, R. M. Some psychoanalytic comments on "Culture and personality." In G. B. Wilbur and W. Muensterberger (Eds). *Psychoanalysis and culture.* New York: International Universities Press, 1951. Pp. 3-31.

Hartshorne, H., and May, M. A. *Studies in deceit.* New York: Macmillan, 1928.

Harvey, J., and Rutherford, J. M. Status in the informal group: influence and influencibility at different age levels. *Child Developm.*, 1960, *31*, 377-385.

Haskell, M. R. Toward a reference group theory of juvenile delinquency. *Soc. Prob.*, 1960, *8*, 219-230.

Hattwick, B. W., and Stowell, M. The relation of parental over-attentiveness to children's work habits and social adjustments in kindergarten and the first six grades of school. *J. Educ. Res.*, 1936, *30*, 169-176.

Havemann, E. and West, P. S. *They went to college.* New York: Harcourt, Brace, 1952.

Havighurst, R. J., Bowman, P. H., Liddle, G. P., Matthews, C. V., Pierce, J. V. *Growing up in River City.* New York: John Wiley, 1962.

Havighurst, R. J., and Neubauer, D. Community factors in relation to character formation. In R. J. Havighurst and H. Taba (Eds.), *Adolescent character and personality.* New York: Wiley, 1949. Pp. 27-46.

Havighurst, R. J. and Neugarten, B. L. *Society and education.* (2nd ed.) Boston: Allyn and Bacon, 1962.

Havighurst, R. J., Robinson, M. Z., & Dorr, M. The development of the ideal self in childhood and adolescence. *J. Educ. Res.*, 1946, *40*, 241-257.

Heath, R. W., Maier, M. H., and Remmers, H. H. *High school students' opinions about democratic values and engineering.* Lafayette, Ind.: Division of Educational Reference, Purdue Univ., April, 1958.

Heider, F. *The psychology of interpersonal relations.* New York: Wiley, 1958.

Heilbrun, A. B., Jr. Conformity to masculinity-femininity stereotypes and ego identity in adolescents. *Psychol. Rep.*, 1964, *14*, 351-357.

Hendrick, I. Work and the pleasure principle. *Psychoanal. Quart.*, 1943, *12*, 311-329.

Henry, N. B. (Ed.) *Adolescence. 43rd Yearb. nat. Soc. Stud. Educ.* Chicago: Univ. Chicago Press, 1944.

Herman, R. D. The going steady complex: A re-examination. *Marr. Fam. Living*, 1955, *17*, 36-40.

Hertz, M. R. Personality patterns in adolescence as portrayed by the Rorschach Ink-blot Method: I. The movement factors. *J. Gen. Psychol.*, 1942, *27*, 119-188.

Hertz, M. R. Personality patterns in adolescence as portrayed by the Rorschach Ink-blot Method: III. The "Erlebnistypus" (a normative study). *J. Gen. Psychol.*, 1943, *28*, 225-276. (a)

Hertz, M. R. Personality patterns in adolescence as portrayed by the Rorschach Ink-blot Method: IV. The "Erlebnistypus" (a typological study). *J. Gen. Psychol.*, 1943, *28*, 3-45. (b)

Hertz, M. R., and Baker, E. Personality patterns in adolescence as portrayed by the Rorschach Ink-blot Method: II. The color factors. *J. Gen. Psychol.*, 1943, *27*, 3-61.

Hess, R. D. Parents and teenagers: Differing perspectives. *Child Stud.*, 1959-1960, *37* (1), 21-23.

Hess, R. D., and Easton, D. The child's changing image of the President. *Public Opin. Quart.*, 1960, *24*, 632-644.

Hess, R. D., and Goldblatt, I. The status of adolescents in American society: A problem in social identity. *Child Developm.*, 1957, *28*, 459-468.

Hetherington, E., and Feldman, S. E. College cheating as a function of subject and situational variables. *J. Educ. Psychol.*, 1965, *55*, 212-218.

Hewer, V. H., and Neubeck, G. Attitudes of college students toward employment among married women. *Personnel Guid. J.*, 1964, *42*, 587-592.

Hill, D. S. Personification of ideals by urban children. *J. Soc. Psychol.*, 1930, *1*, 379-393.

Hinrichs, W. E. The Goodenough drawing test in relation to delinquency and problem behavior. *Arch. Psychol.*, 1935, No. 175, 1-82.

Hoffer, W. Diaries of adolescent schizophrenics. *Psychoanal. Stud. Child*, 1946, *2*, 293-312.

Holland, J. L. A theory of vocational choice; vocational daydreams. *Voc. Guid. Quart.*, 1963-1964, *12*, 93-97.

Hollingshead, A. B. *Elmtown's youth.* New York: John Wiley, 1949.

Hollingworth, L. S. The adolescent child. In C. Murchison (Ed.) *A handbook of child psychology.* Worcester, Mass.: Clark Univ. Press, 1933. Pp. 882-908.

Horney, K. *The neurotic personality of our time.* New York: W. W. Norton, 1937.

Horowitz, H. Interpersonal choice in American adolescents. *Psychol. Rep.*, 1966, *19*, 371-374.

Horowitz, H. Prediction of adolescent popularity and rejection from achievement and interest tests. *J. Educ. Psychol.*, 1967, *58*, 170-174.

Horrocks, J. E. *The psychology of adolescence.* (2nd ed.) Boston: Houghton Mifflin, 1962.

Horrocks, J. E., and Buker, M. E. A study of the friendship fluctuations of preadolescents. *J. Genet. Psychol.*, 1951, *78*, 181-144.

Horrocks, J. E., and Thompson, G. G. A study of friendship fluctuations of rural boys and girls. *J. Genet. Psychol.*, 1946, *69*, 189-198.

Horton, R. E., Jr. American freedom and the values of youth. In H. H. Remmers (Ed.), *Anti-democratic attitudes in American schools.* Evanston, Ill.: Northwestern Univ. Press, 1963, 18-60.

Hosinski, Sr. Marion. Self, ideal-self and occupational role: Perceptual congruence in vocationally committed college women. Paper read at American Personnel and Guidance Association, Minneapolis, April, 1965.

Hurlock, E. B. *Adolescent development.* New York: McGraw-Hill, 1949.

Hurlock, E. B., and Klein, E. R. Adolescent "crushes." *Child Develpm.*, 1934, *5*, 63-80.

Hyman, H. The value systems of different classes. In R. Bendix and S. M. Lipset (Eds.), *Class, status,* and power. New York: Free Press, 1953, Pp. 426-442.

Hyman, H. H. *Political socialization.* Glencoe, Ill.: Free Press, 1959.

Ianni, F. A. J. The Italo-American teenager. *Ann. Amer. Acad. Polit. Soc. Sci.*, 1961, *338*, 70-78.

Inhelder, B., and Piaget, J. *The growth of logical thinking from childhood to adolescence.* New York: Basic Books, 1958.

Iscoe, I, and Carden, J. A. Field dependence, manifest anxiety, and sociometric status in children. *J. Consult. Psychol.*, 1961, *25*, 184.

Jackson, P. W., and Guba, E. G. The need structure of in-service teachers: An occupational analysis. *Sch. Rev.*, 1957, *65*, 176-192.

Jahoda, G. Sex differences in preferences for shapes: A cross-cultural replication. *Brit. J. Psychol.*, 1956, *47*, 126-132.

James, W. The will to believe. *New World*, 1896, *5*, 327-347.

Jersild, A. T. *In search of self.* New York: Bureau of Publications, Teachers College, Columbia Univ., 1952.

Johnson, E. S., and Legg, C. E. Why young people leave school. *Bull. Nat. Assn. of Secondary School Principals*, 1944, *28*, 3-28.

Johnson, R. C., and Medinnus, G. R. *Child psychology: Behavior and development.* New York: John Wiley, 1965.

Jones, A. Sexual symbolism and the variables of sex and personality integration. *J. Abnorm. Soc. Psychol.*, 1956, *53*, 187-190.

Jones, E. Einige Probleme des jugendlichen Alters. *Imago*, 1923, *9*, 145-168.

Jones, E. *The life and work of Sigmund Freud.* New York: Basic Books, 1955.

Jones, E. S. The probation student: what he is like and what can be done about it. *J. Educ. Res.*, 1955, *49*, 93-102.

Jones, H. E. *Development in adolescence.* New York: Appleton-Century, 1943.

Jones, H. E. The sexual maturing of girls as related to growth in strength. *Res. Quart. Amer. Ass. Hlth. phys. Educ.*, 1947, *18*, 135-143.

Jones, H. E. *Motor performance and growth: A developmental study of static dynamometric strength.* Berkeley, Calif.: Univ. Calif. Press, 1949.

Jones, H. E., and Conrad, H. S. The growth and decline of intelligence: A study of a homogenous group between the ages of ten and sixty. *Genet. Psychol. Monogr.*, 1933, *13*, 223-298.

Jones, M. C. Adolescent friendships. *Amer. Psychologist.* 1948, *3*, 352. (Abstract)

Jones, M. C. A study of socialization patterns at the high school level. *J. Genet. Psychol.*, 1958, *93*, 87-111.

Jones, M. C. A comparison of the attitudes and interests of 9th-grade students over two decades. *J. Educ. Psychol.*, 1960, *51*, 175-186.

Jones, M. C., and Bayley, N. Physical maturing among boys as related to behavior. *J. Educ. Psychol.*, 1950, *41*, 129-148.

Jung, F. T. The physiological changs incident to puberty. *Illinois M. J.*, 1941, *80*, 477-484.

Kagan, J. Acquisition and significance of sex typing and sex role identity. In M. L. Hoffman and L. W. Hoffman (Eds.), *Review of child development research.* Vol. I. New York: Russell Sage Foundation, 1964. Pp. 137-167.

Kagan, J., and Moss, H. A. *Birth to maturity.* New York: John Wiley, 1962.

Kahl, J. *The American class structure.* New York, Holt, 1957.

Katan-Angel, A. Die Rolle der "Verschiebung" bei der Strassenangst. *Int. Z. Psychoanal.*, 1937, *23*, 376-392.

Katz, D., and Allport, F. H. *Students attitudes.* Syracuse: Craftsman Press, 1931.

Katz, M. *Decisions and values.* New York: College Entrance Examination Board, 1963.

Keniston, K. *The uncommitted: Alienated youth in American society.* New York: Harcourt, Brace, and World, 1965.

Kent, G. H. Emergency battery of one-minute tests. *J. Psychol.*, 1942, *13*, 141-164.

Kent, G. H. Tentative norms for emergency battery. *J. Psychol.*, 1943, *15*, 137-149.

Kimball, B. Case studies in educational failure during adolescence. *Amer. J. Orthopsychiat.*, 1953, *23*, 406-415.

Kinsey, A. C., Pomeroy, W. B., Martin, C. E., *et al. Sexual behavior in the human male.* Philadelphia: W. B. Saunders, 1948.

388

Kinsey, A. C., Pomeroy, W. B., Martin, C. E., *et al.* *Sexual behavior in the human female.* Philadelphia: W. B. Saunders, 1953.

Kirkendall, L. A., and Gravatt, A. E. Teen-agers' sex attitudes and behavior. In E. M. and S. M. Duvall (Eds.), *Sex-ways in fact and faith.* New York: Association Press, 1961, Pp. 115-129

Klausmeier, H. J., Luker, A., and Stromswold, S. Factors influencing choice of teaching career among college sophomores. *J. Educ. Res.*, 1951, *45*, 23-32.

Klein, M. *The psychoanalysis of children.* London: Hogarth Press, 1946.

Klinger, E., Albaum, A., and Hetherington, M. Factors influencing severity of moral judgment. *J. soc. Psychol.*, 1964, *63*, 319-326.

Kluckhohn, F., and Spiegel, J. P. Integration and conflict in family behavior. *Group for the Advancement of Psychiatry*, 1954, *2*, Report No. 27.

Knight, R. P. Management and psychotherapy of the borderline schizophrenic patient. *Bull. Menninger Clin.*, 1953, *17*, 139-150.

Kohlberg, L. The development of modes of moral think-
ublished
958.
Amer. J.

d. New

isms of de-
5-146.

1 early auto-
, 1951, *6*,

Jew York:

J. H., Jr.
chool activi-
0.

ng adult
mer.

develop-

Kuhlen, R. G., and Arnold, M. Age differences in religious beliefs and problems during adolescence. *J. Genet. Psychol.*, 1944, *65*, 291-300.

Kuhlen, R. G., and Bretsch, H. S. Sociometric status and personal problems of adolescents. In J. L. Moreno *et al.* (Eds.), *The sociometry reader.* Glenco, Ill.: Free Press, 1960. Pp. 406-416.

Kvaraceus, W. C. Juvenile delinquency and social class. *J. Educ. Sociol.*, 1944-45, *18*, 51-54.

Kvarceus, W. C., & Miller, W. B. *Delinquent behavior: Culture and the individual.* Washington, D. C.: National Education Association, 1959.

Lampl-De Groot, J. On masturbation and its influence on general development. *Psychoanal. Stud. Child*, 1950, *5*, 153-174.

Landauer, K. Die Ich-Organisation in der Pubertät. *Z. psychoanal. Pädag.*, 1935, *9*, 380-420.

Lander, J. The pubertal struggle against the instincts. *Amer. J. Orthopsychiat.*, 1942, *12*, 456-462.

Landis, J. R., Dinitz, S., and Reckless, W. C. Implementing two theories of delinquency: Value orientation and awareness of limited opportunity. *Sociol. Soc. Res.*, 1963, *47*, 408-416.

Landis, P. H. Research on teen-age marriage. *Marr. Fam. Living*, 1960, *22*, 266-267.

Lane, R. E. *Political life.* Glencoe, Ill.: Free Press, 1959.

Langton, K. P. *Civic attitudes of Jamaican high school students.* Cooperative Research Project, U. S. Department of Health, Education and Welfare, 1965.

Langton, K. P. Peer group and school and the political socialization process. *Amer. Polit. Sci. Rev.*, 1967, *61*, 751-758.

Langworthy, R. L. Community status and influence in a high school. *Amer. Sociol. Rev.*, 1959, *24*, 537-539.

Lawton, S. U., & Archer, J. *Sexual conduct of the teenager.* New York: Spectrolux Corp., 1951.

Lebo, D. A preliminary investigation of the Rorschach *Y* response and the use of shading in the drawing of the human figure. Unpublished paper, Florida State University, 1951.

Lecky, P. *Self-consistency: A theory of personality.* New York: Island Press, 1945.

Leslie, G. R., and Richardson, A. H. Family versus campus influences in relation to mate selection. *Soc. Probl.*, 1956, *4*, 117-121.

Lessler, K. Sexual symbols, structured and unstructured. *J. Consult. Psychol.*, 1962, *26*, 44-49.

Lessler, K. Cultural and Freudian dimensions of sexual symbols. *J. Consult. Psychol.*, 1964, *28*, 46-53.

Levin, M. L. Social climates and political socialization. *Publ. Opin. Quart.*, 1961, *25*, 596-606.

Levy, L. H. Sexual symbolism: A validity study. *J. Consult. Psychol.*, 1954, *18*, 43-46.

Levy, S. Figure drawing as a projective test. In L. E. Abt and L. Bellak (Eds.), *Projective psychology.* New York: Knopf, 1950.

Lewis, W. D. A comparative study of the personalities, interests, and home backgrounds of gifted children of superior and inferior educational achievement. *J. Genet. Psychol.*, 1941, *59*, 207-218.

Lidz, T., Cornelison, A. R., Fleck, S., and Terry, D. The intrafamilial environment of the schizophrenic patient. I. The father. *Psychiatry*, 1957, *20*, 329-342.

Lidz, T., Parker, B., and Cornelison, A. R. The role of the father in the family environment of the schizophrenic patient. *Amer. J. Psychiat.*, 1956, *113*, 126-132.

Lindenfeld, F. A note on social mobility, religiosity and students' attitudes towards premarital sexual relations. *Amer. Sociol. Rev.*, 1960, *25*, 81-84.

Lindesmith, A. R., and Strauss, A. L. *Social psychology.* (rev. ed.) New York: Dryden Press, 1956.

Lindzey, G., and Borgatta, E. F. Sociometric measurement. In G. Lindzey (Ed.), *Handbook of social psychology*, Vol. I. Reading, Massachusetts: Addison-Wesley, 1954.

Lipset, S. M., and Bendix, R. *Social mobility in industrial society.* Berkeley: Univ. California Press, 1959.

London, P., Schulman, R. E., and Black, M. S. Religion, guilt and ethical standards. *J. Soc. Psychol.*, 1964, *63*, 145-159.

Lowrie, S. H. Dating, Dating, a neglected field of study. *Marr. Fam. Living*, 1948, *10*, 90-91, 95.

Lowrie, S. H. Dating theories and student responses. *Amer. Sociol. Rev.*, 1951, *16*, 335-340.

Lowrie, S. H. Sex differences and age of initial dating. *Soc. Forces* 1952, *30*, 456-461.

Lowrie, S. H. Factors involved in the frequency of dating. *Marr. Fam. Living*, 1956, *18*, 46-51.

Lowrie, S. H. Early and late dating: some conditions associated with them. *Marr. Fam. Living*, 1961, *23*, 284-291.

Maas, H. S. The role of members in clubs of lower-class and middle-class adolescents. *Child Develpm.*, 1954, *25*, 241-251.

Maccoby, E., Matthews, R. E., and Morton, A. S. Youth and Political change. *Publ. Opin. Quart.*, 1954, *18*, 23-29.

MacFarlane, J. W. Studies in child guidance: I. Methodology of data collection and organization. *Monogr. Soc. Res. Child Develpm.*, 1938, *3*, No. 6.

Machover, K. *Personality projection in the drawing of the human figure.* Springfield: Thomas, 1949.

Machover, K. Drawing of the human figure: A method of personality investigation. In H. H. Anderson and G. L. Anderson (Eds.), *An introduction to projective techniques.* New York: Prentice-Hall, 1951.

MacLean, A. N. Idea of God in Protestant religious education. *Teach. Coll., Columbia Univ., Contrib. Educ.*, 1930, No. 410.

MacLean, M. S., Gowan, M. S., and Gowan, J. C. A teacher selection and counseling service. *J. Educ. Res.*, 1955, *48*, 669-677.

Mainer, R. E. Attitude change in intergroup education programs. In H. H. Remmers (Ed.) *Anti-democratic attitudes in American schools.* Evanston; Ill.: Northwestern Univ. Press, 1963, Pp. 122-154.

Maller, J. B. Juvenile delinquency in New York City. *J. Psychol.*, 1937, *3*, 1-25.

Mannheim, K. *Utopia and ideology.* New York: Harcourt, Brace, 1949.

Martin, J. M. *Juvenile vandalism: a study of its nature and prevention.* Springfield, Ill.: Charles C. Thomas, Blackwell Sci. Pubs., 1961.

Matthews, E. Career development of girls. *Voc. Guid. Quart.*, 1963, *11*, 273-278.

Maxwell, P. H., Connor, R., and Walters, J. Family member perceptions of parent role performance. *Merrill-Palmer Quart.*, 1961, *7*, 31-37.

McCarthy, S. M. (Ed.). *Children's drawings: A study of interests and abilities.* Baltimore: Williams and Wilkins, 1924.

McClelland, D. C., Atkinson, J. W., Clark, R., and Lowell, E. L. *The achievement motive.* New York: Appleton-Century-Crofts, 1953.

McCord, W., and McCord, J. with Zola, I. K. *Origins of crime: A new evaluation of the Cambridge-Somerville youth study.* New York: Columbia Univ. Press, 1959.

McGraw, L. W., and Tolbert, J. W. Sociometric status and athletic ability of junior high school boys. *Res. Quart. Amer. Ass. Hlth. Phys. Educ. Recreation*, 1953, *24*, 72-80.

McElroy, W. A. A sex difference in preference for shapes. *Brit. J. Psychol.*, 1954, *45*, 209-216.

McKee, J. P., and Sheriffs, A. C. The differential evaluation of males and females. *J. Person.*, 1957, *25*, 356-371.

McKee, J. P., and Sheriffs, A. C. Men's and women's beliefs, ideals and self concepts. In J. M. Seidman (Ed.), *The adolescent.* (rev. ed.) New York: Holt, Rinehart, and Winston, 1960. Pp. 282-294.

Mead, G. H. *Mind, self, and society.* Chicago: Univ. Chicago Press, 1934.

Mead, M. Our educational problems in the light of Samoan contrasts. In *Coming of age in Samoa.* New York: William Morrow, 1928.

Mead, M. *Male and female.* New York: Morrow, 1949.

Meissner, W. W., S. J. Comparison of anxiety patterns in adolescent boys: 1939-1959. *J. Genet. Psychol.*, 1961, *99*, 323-329. (a)

Meissner, W. W., S. J. Some indications of the sources of anxiety in adolescent boys. *J. Genet. Psychol.*, 1961, *99*, 65-73. (b)

Meissner, W. W., S. J. Parental interaction of the adolescent boy. *J. Genet. Psychol.*, 1965, *107*, 225-233.

Michael, J. High school climates and plans for entering college. *Publ. Opin. Quart.*, 1961, *25*, 583-595.

Middleton, R., and Putney, S. Religion, normative standards and behavior. *Sociometry*, 1962, *25*, 141-152.

Middleton, R., and Putney, S. Student rebellion against parental political beliefs. *Soc. Forces*, 1963, *41*, 337-383.

Miller, D. R., and Berman, E. Personal communication, 1965.

Miller, D. R., and Swanson, G. E. *The changing American parent.* New York: John Wiley, 1958.

Miller, W. B. Lower class culture as a generating milieu of gang delinquency. *J. Soc. Issues*, 1958, *14* (3), 5-18.

Montagu, A. *Statement on race.* New York: Schuman, 1952.

Montagu, A. *Reproductive development of the female: With especial reference to the period of adolescent sterility.* New York: Julian Press, 1957.

Mooney, R. Surveying high school students' problems by means of a problem check list. *Educ. Res. Bull.*, 1942, *21*, 57-69.

Moreno, J. L., *et al.* (Eds.), *The sociometry reader.* Glencoe, Ill.: Free Press, 1960.

Morrow, W. R., and Wilson, R. C. Family relations of bright high-achieving and under-achieving high school boys. *Child Develpm.*, 1961, *32*, 501-510.

Mott, S. M. Muscular activity as an aid in concept formation. *Child Develpm.*, 1945, *16*, 97-109.

Murdock, G. P. *Africa: Its people and their cultural history.* New York: McGraw-Hill, 1959.

Murdock, G. P., Tuden, A., and Hammond, P. B. Africa peoples. *Collier's Encyclopedia.* Vol. 1. New York: Crowell-Collier, 1962. Pp. 254-270.

Murphy, G. Personality: *A biosocial approach to origins and structure.* New York: Harper, 1947.

Musselman, J. W. Factors associated with the achievement of high school pupils of superior intelligence, *J. exp. Educ.*, 1942, *11*, 53-68.

Mussen, P. H. Some antecedents and consequents of masculine sex-typing in adolescent boys. *Psychol. Monogr.*, 1961, *75*, No. 2 (Whole No. 506).

Mussen, P. H., and Boutourline-Young, H. Relationships between rate of physical maturing and personality among boys of Italian descent. *Vita Humana*, 1964, 7, 186-200.

Mussen, P. H., and Conger, J. J. *Child development and personality.* New York: Harper, 1956.

Mussen, P. H., and Jones, M. C. Self-conceptions, motivations, and interpersonal attitudes of late- and early-maturing boys. *Child Develpm.*, 1957, 28, 243-256.

Mussen, P. H., and Jones, M. C. The behavior-inferred motivations of late- and early-maturing boys. *Child Develpm.*, 1958, 29, 61-67.

Neimark, E. D. Information-gathering in diagnostic problem-solving: A preliminary report. *Psychol. Record*, 1961, 11, 243-248.

Neimark, E. D., and Lewis N. The development of logical problem solving strategies. *Child Develpm.*, 1967, 38, 107-117.

Neugarten, B. L. Social class and friendship among school children. *Amer. sociol. Rev.*, 1946, 51, 305-313.

Neugarten, B. L. The democracy of childhood. In W. L. Warner *et al.* (Eds.) *Democracy in Jonesville.* New York: Harper, 1949. Pp. 77-88.

Neumeyer, M. H. *Juvenile delinquency in modern society.* New York: Nostrand, 1949.

Newcomb, T. M. *Personality and social change.* New York: Dryden Press, 1943.

Newcomb, T. M. *Social psychology.* New York: Dryden Press, 1955.

Nicholson, A. B., and Hanley, C. Indices of physiological maturity: derivation and interrelationships. *Child Develpm.*, 1953, 24, 3-38.

Nogee, P. and Levin, M. B. Some determinants of political attitudes among college voters. *Publ. Opin. Quart.*, 1958, 22, 449-463.

North, C. C., and Hatt, P. Jobs and occupations: a popular evaluation. *Opinion News*, 1947, 9 (4), 3-13.

Novak, E. The constitutional type of female precocious puberty with a report of nine cases. *Am. J. Obst. and Gynec.*, 1944, 47, 20-42.

Nye, I. *Family relationships and delinquent behavior.* New York: John Wiley, 1958.

Ochs, E. Changes in Goodenough drawings associated with changes in social adjustment. *J. Clin. Psychol.*, 1950, 6, 282-284.

O'Connor, N., and Franks, C. Childhood upbringing and other environmental factors. In H. J. Eysenck (Ed.), *Handbook of abnormal psychology.* New York: Basic Books, 1961. Pp. 393-416.

O'Hara, R. P. The roots of careers. *Elementary Sch. J.*, 1962, 62, 277-280.

Otis, A. S. Otis Self-Administering Tests of Mental Ability. Higher Examination, Form A; Intermediate Examination, Form A. New York: World, 1922.

Palmore, E., and Hammond, P. E. Interacting factors in juvenile delinquency. *Amer. Sociol. Rev.*, 1964, 29, 848-854.

Parsons, T. Age and sex in the social structure of the United States. *Amer. Sociol. Rev.*, 1942, 7, 604-616.

Parsons, T., and Bales, R. F. *Family, socialization and interaction process.* London: Routledge and Kegan Paul, 1956.

Peck, R. F., and Havighurst, R. J. *The psychology of character development.* New York: John Wiley, 1960.

Phelan, Sister Mary. *An empirical study of the ideals of adolescent boys and girls.* Monograph 193. Washington, D. C.: Catholic Univ. of America, 1936.

Phelps, H. R., and Horrocks, J. E. Factors influencing informal groups of adolescents. *Child Develpm.*, 1958, 29, 69-86.

Piaget, J. *The moral judgment of the child.* New York: Harcourt, Brace, 1932.

Piers, E. V., and Harris, D. B. Age and other correlates of self-concept in children. *J. educ. Psychol.*, 1964, 55, 91-95.

Piers, G., and Singer, M. B. *Shame and guilt.* Springfield, Ill.: Thomas, 1953.

Pikas, A. Children's attitudes toward rational versus inhibitory parental authority. *J. Abnorm. soc. Psychol.*, 1961, 62, 315-321.

Pine, G. J. Social class, social mobility and delinquent behavior. *Personnel Guid.*, 1965, 43, 770-774.

Pope, B. Socio-economic contrasts in children's peer culture prestige values. *Genet. Psychol. Monogr.*, 1953, 48, 157-220.

Porterfield, A. L. *Youth in trouble.* Fort Worth: Leo Potishman Foundation, 1946.

Powell, M. Age differences in degree of conflict within certain areas of psychological adjustment. Unpublished doctoral dissertation, Syracuse Univ., 1952.

Powell, M. Age and sex differences in degree of conflict within certain areas of psychological adjustment. *Psychol. Monogr.*, 1955, 69, (Whole No. 387).

Powers, E., & Witmer, H. *An experiment in the prevention of delinquency: The Cambridge-Somerville youth study.* New York: Columbia Univ. Press, 1951.

Pressey, S. L., and Pressey, L. C. Interest-Attitude Tests. New York: Psychological Corporation, 1933.

Priesel, R., and Wagner, R. Gesetzmassigkeiten im Auftreten der extragenitalen sekundaren Geschlechtsmerkmale bei Madchen. *Ztschr. f. menschl. Vererb.-u. Konstitutionslehre*, 1931, 15, 333-352.

Project TALENT Bulletin 6. *Cognitive growth during high school.* Pittsburgh: Project TALENT, 1967.

Pryor, H. B. Certain physical and physiological aspects of adolescent development. *J. Pediat.*, 1936, 8, 52-62.

Psathas, G. Ethnicity, social class, and adolescent independence. *Amer. Sociol. Rev.*, 1957, 22, 415-423.

Purdue Opinion Poll. No. 30. November, 1951.

Putney, S., and Middleton, R. Rebellion, conformity and parental religious ideologies. *Sociometry*, 1961, 24, 125-235.

Rapaport, D. Some metapsychological considerations concerning activity and passivity. Unpublished manuscript, 1953.

Raths, L. E., and Abrahamson, S. *Student status and social class.* (rev. ed.) Bronxville, N.Y.: Modern Education Service, 1951.

Reckless, W. C. *The crime problem.* New York: Appleton-Century-Crofts, 1961.

Reevy, W. R. Adolescent sexuality. In A. Ellis and A. Abarbanel, *The encycolpedia of sexual behavior.* New York: Hawthorne Books, 1961. Pp. 52-67.

Reich, A. The discussion of 1912 on masturbation, our present-day views. *Psychoanal. Stud. Child,* 1951, *6,* 80-94.

Reiss, A. J. Sex offenses: The marginal status of the adolescent. *Law and Contemp. Prob.,* 1960, *25,* 309-333.

Reiss, A. J., with Duncan, O. D., Hatt, P. K., and North, C. C. *Occupations and social status.* New York: Free Press of Glencoe, 1961.

Reiss, A. J., and Rhodes, A. L. The distribution of juvenile delinquency in the social class structure. *Amer. Social. Rev.,* 1961, *26,* 720-732.

Reiss, I. L. *Premarital sexual standards in America.* Glencoe, Ill. : Free Press, 1960.

Reiss, I. L. Sexual codes in teen-age culture. *Annals Amer. Acad. polit. soc. Sci.,* 1961, *338,* 53-62.

Reiss, I. L. *The social context of premarital sexual permissiveness.* New York, Rinehart, and Winston, 1967.

Reissman, L. *Class in American society.* New York: Free Press, 1959.

Remmers, H. H. Cross-cultural studies of teenagers' problems. *J. educ. Psychol.,* 1962, *53,* 254-261.

Remmers, H. H., and Hackett, C. G. *Let's listen to youth.* Chicago: Sci. Res. Assocs., 1950.

Remmers, H. H., and Radler, D. H. *The American Teenager.* Indianapolis: Bobbs-Merrill, 1957.

Reynolds, E. L. The appearance of adult patterns of body hair in man. *Ann. New York Acad. Sci.,* 1951, *53,* 576-584.

Reynolds, E. L, and Wines, J. V. Physical changes associated with adolescence in boys. *Amer. J. Dis. Child.,* 1951, *82,* 529-547.

Reynolds, E. L., and Wines, J. V. Individual differences in physical changes associated with adolescence in girls. *Amer. J. Dis. Child.,* 1948, *75,* 329-350.

Rezler, A. G. Characteristics of high school girls choosing traditional or pioneer vocations. *Personnel Guid. J.,* 1967, *45,* 659-665. (a)

Rezler, A. G. The joint use of the Kuder Preference Record and the Holland VPI in the vocational assessment of high school girls. *Psychol. Sch.,* 1967, *4,* 81-84. (b)

Rhodes, W. E. Psychoanalytic theory and transcendent religious involvement in thirty young men. Unpublished Honors thesis, Wesleyan Univ., 1948.

Richman, T. L. *Veneral disease: Old plague—new challenge.* Public Affairs Pamplet No. 292. New York: Public Affairs Committee, 1960.

Richman, T. L. (Ed.) *Today's venereal disease control problem.* New York: American Social Health Association, 1961.

Rickard, G. The relationship between parental behavior and children's achievement behavior. Unpublished doctoral dissertation, Harvard Univ., 1954.

Riesman, D. *The lonely crowd.* New Haven: Yale Univ. Press, 1950.

Rinsland, H. D. *A basic vocabulary of elementary school children.* New York: Macmillan, 1945.

Roe, A. A psychological study of eminent physical scientists. *Genet. Psychol. Monogr.,* 1951, *43,* 121-239.

Roe, A. *The psychology of occupations.* New York: John Wiley, 1956.

Rogers, C. R. Reinhold Niebuhr's *The self and the dramas of history: A criticism. Pastoral Psychol.,* 1958, *9* (85), 15-17.

Rogers, C. R., and Dymond, R. F. (Eds.) *Psychotherapy and personality change.* Chicago Press, 1954.

Rogers, E. M., and Sebald, H. A distinction between familism, family integration and kinship orientation. *Marr. Fam. Living,* 1962, *24,* 25-30.

Rosander, A. C. Age and sex patterns of social attitudes. *J. educ. Psychol.,* 1939, *30,* 481-496.

Rosen, B. C. The achievement syndrome: a psycho-cultural dimension of social stratification. *Amer. Sociol. Rev.,* 1956, *21,* 203-211.

Rosen, B. C. Family structure and achievement motivation. *Amer. Sociol. Rev.,* 1961, *26,* 574-585.

Rosenberg, M. *Society and the adolescent self-image.* Princeton, N. J. : Princeton Univ. Press, 1965.

Rosenthal, M. J., Finkelstein, M., NI, E., and Robertson, R. E. A study of mother-child relationships in the emotional disorders of children. *Genet. Psychol. Monogr.,* 1959, *60,* 65-116.

Rosenthal, M. J., NI, E., Finkelstein, M., and Berkwits, G. K. Father-child relationships and children's problems. *Amer. Arch. Gen. Psychiat.,* 1962, *7,* 360-373.

Ross, M. G. *Religious beliefs of youth.* New York: Association Press, 1950.

Rossi, A. S. Women in science: Why so few? *Science,* 1965, *148,* 1196-1201.

Rothstein, E. An analysis of status images as perception variables between delinquent and nondelinquent boys. Unpublished doctoral dissertation, New York Univ., 1961.

Royal, R. E. Drawing characteristics of neurotic patients using a drawing-of-a-man-and-woman technique. *J. Clin. Psychol.* 1949, *5,* 392-395.

Sanford, R. N., *et al.* Physique, personality, and scholarship. *Monogr. Soc. Res. Child Develpm.,* 1943, No. 1.

Scarpitti, F. R. Delinquent and non-delinquent perceptions of self, values and opportunity. *Ment. Hyg.,* 1965, *49,* 399-404.

Schilder, P. *The image and appearance of the human body.* New York: International Universities Press, 1951. (a)

Schilder, P. *Psychoanalysis, man and society.* New York: Norton, 1951. (b)

Schlesser, G. E., and Finger, J. A. Personal Values Inventory. Hamilton, N. Y. : Colgate Univ., 1962.

Schonfeld, W. A. Primary and secondary sexual characteristics. *Amer. J. Dis. Child.,* 1943, *65,* 535-549.

Sears, R. R., Maccoby, E., and Levin, H. *Patterns of child rearing.* New York: Row, Peterson, 1957.

Seckel, H. P. G. Precocious sexual development in

children. *M. Clin. North America,* 1946, *30,* 183-209.

Sewell, W., Haller, A., and Straus, M. Social status and educational and occupational aspirations. *Amer. Sociol. Rev.,* 1957, *22,* 67-73.

Shaw, C. R., and McKay, H. D. *Social factors in juvenile delinquency: A Study of the community, the family, and the gang in relation to delinquent behavior.* Washington, D. C.: U. S. Government Printing Office, 1931.

Shaw, G. B. *Selected prose.* New York: Dodd, Mead, 1952.

Shaw, J., Klausmeier, H. J., Luker, A. H. and Reid, H. T. Changes occurring in teacher-pupil attitudes during a two-week workshop. *J. Apply. Psychol.,* 1952, *36,* 304-306.

Shaycoft, M. F. *The high school years: growth in cognitive skills.* (Interim report 3 to the U. S. Office of Education, Cooperative Research Project No. 3051.) Pittsburgh: Project TALENT, 1967.

Shimberg, B., and Katz, M. Evaluation of a guidance text. *Personnel Guid. J.,* 1962, *41,* 126-132.

Shipley, T. E., and Veroff, J. A projective measure of need for affiliation. *J. Exp. Psychol.,* 1952, *43,* 349-356.

Shore, M. F., Massimo, J. L., and Ricks, D. A factor analytic study of psychotherapeutic change in adolescent delinquent boys. *J. Clin. Psychol.,* 1965, *21,* 208-212.

Shuttleworth, F. K. Sexual maturation and the physical growth of girls age six to nineteen, *Monogr. Soc. Res. Child Develop.,* 1939, *4,* no. 5.

Shuttleworth, F. K. Sexual maturation and the skeletal growth of girls age six to nineteen. *Monogr. Soc. Res. Child Develop.,* 1938, *3,* no. 5.

Shuttleworth, F. K. The physical and mental growth of girls and boys age six to nineteen in relation to age at maximum growth. *Monogr. Soc. Res. Child Develop.,* 1939, *4,* no. 3.

Siegel, S. *Nonparametric statistics.* New York: McGraw-Hill, 1956.

Sigel, R. S. An exploration into some aspects of political socialization: School children:s reaction to the death of a president. In M. Wolfenstein and G. Kliman (Eds.), *Children and the death of a president.* Garden City: Doubleday, 1965, Pp. 30-61.

Simmons, K., and Greulich, W. W. Menarcheal age and the height, weight, and skeletal age of girls, age 7 to 17 years. *J. Pediat.,* 1943, *22,* 513-548.

Slocum, W. L. and Empey, L. T. Occupational planning by young women. Pullman, Wash.: Bull. 568 Agri. Exper. Sta. State Coll. of Wash., 1956.

Smith, E. A. *American youth culture: Group life in teenage society.* New York: Free Press of Glencoe, 1962.

Smith, F. R. The projective nature of the "draw-a-person" technique in its relation to the sex of the figure drawn. Unpublished Masters Thesis, Florida State Univ., 1953.

Smith, W. M., Jr. Ratimg and dating: a re-study. *Marr. Fam. Living,* 1952, *14,* 312-317.

Smith, W. D., and Lebo, D.Some changing aspects of the self-concept of pubescent males. *J. Genet. Psychol.,* 1956, *88,* 61-75.

Social Surveys Ltd. *Television and religion.* London: London Univ. Press, 1964.

Sofokidis, J. H., and Sullivan, E. A new look at school dropouts. U. S. Dept. of Health, Education, and Welfare: *Indicators,* April, 1964.

Sollenberger, R. T. Some relationships between the urinary excretion of male hormone by maturing boys and their expressed interests and attitudes. *J. Psychol.,* 1940, *9,* 179-189.

Soloman, D. Adolescents' decisions: a comparison of influence from parents with that from other sources. *Marr. Fam. Living,* 1961, *23,* 393-395.

Sontag, L. W. Biolgoical and Medical Studies at the S. S. Fels Research Institute. *Ch. Devel.,* 1946, *17,* 81-84.

Spiegel, L. A. A review of contributions to a psychoanalytic theory of adolescence. *Psychoanal. Stud. Child,* 1951, *6,* 375-393.

Stanfield, R. E. The interaction of family variables and gang variables in the aetiology of delinquency. *Soc. Prob.,* 1966, *13,* 411-417.

Starbuck, E. D. *The Psychology of religion.* London: Walter Scott, Ltd., 1899.

Starer, E. Cultural symbolism: A validity study. *J. Consult. Psychol.,* 1955, *19,* 453-454.

Steinmann, A., Levi, J., and Fox, D. J. Self-concept of college women compared with their concept of ideal woman and men's ideal woman. *J. Counsel. Psychol.,* 1964, *11,* 370-374.

Stendler, C. B. *Children of Brasstown.* Urbana: Bureau of Research and Service of the College of Education, Univ. of Illinois, 1949.

Stennett, R. G., and Thurlow, M. Cultural symbolism: The age variable. *J. consult. Psychol.,* 1958, *22,* 496.

Stephenson, R. *Mobility orientation* and gratification of 1,000 ninth graders. *Amer. Sociol. Rev.,* 1957, *22,* 204-212.

Stephenson, W. Correlating persons instead of tests. *Charact. Pers.,* 1935, *6,* 17-24.

Stolz, H. R., and Stolz, L. M. Adolescent problems related to somatic variations. In N. B. Henry, (Ed.), *Forty-Third Yearbook,* National Society for the Study of Education, University of Chicago, 1944, pt. 1. Pp. 80-99.

Stolz, H. R., and Stolz, L. M. *Somatic development of adolescent boys.* New York: Macmillan, 1951.

Stone, C. P., and Barker, R. G. Aspects of personality and intelligence in post menarcheal and premenarcheal girls of the same chronological ages. *J. Comp. Psychol.,* 1937, *23,* 439-455.

Stone, C. P., and Barker, R. G. On the relationship between menarcheal age and certain measurements of physique in girls. *Hum. Biol.,* 1937, *9,* 1-28. (b)

Stone, C. P., and Barker, R. G. The attitudes and interests of premenarcheal and post-menarcheal girls. *J. Genet. Psychol.,* 1939, *54,* 27-71.

Strange, R. *The adolescent views himself: A psychology of adolescence.* New York: McGraw-Hill, 1957.

Stratz, C. H. *Der Körper des Kindes und seine Pflege* (ed.3). Stuttgart: Ferdinand Enke, 1909.

Strunk, O., Jr. Need for cognition and value schemata. *Psychol. Newsltr.* 1958, 9, 160-161. (a)

Strunk, O., Jr. Note on self-reports and religiosity. *Psychol. Rep.,* 1958, *4,* 29. (b)

Strunk, O., Jr. Relationship between self-reports and adolescent religiosity. ;*Psychol. Rep.*, 1958, *4*, 683-686. (c)

Stuart, H. C. Medical progress: Normal growth and development during adolescence. *New England J. Med.*, 1946, *234*, 666-672, 693-700, 732-738.

Stuart, H. C. Physical growth during adolescence. *Am. J. Dis. Child.*, 1947, *74*, 495-502.

Sullivan, C. A scale for measuring developmental age in girls. *Catholic Univ. of Amer. Studies in Psychol. and Psychiat.*, 1934, *3*, No. 4.

Sullivan, H. S. *The interpersonal theory of psychiatry.* New York: Norton, 1953.

Super, D. E., *et al. Vocational development: A framework for research.* New York: Bureau of Publications, Teachers College, Columbia Univ., 1957.

Super, D. E., Crites, J. O., Hummel, R. C., Moser, H. P., Overstreet, P. L., and Warnath, C. F. Some generalizations regarding vocational development. In R. G. Kuhlen and G. G. Thompson (Eds.), *Psychological studies of human development.* (2nd ed.) New York: Appleton-Century-Crofts, 1963. Pp. 527-533. (a)

Super, D. E., *et al. Career development: Self-concept theory.* New York: College Entrance Examination Board, 1963. (b)

Sutcliffe, J. P. A general method of analysis of frequency data for multiple classification designs. *Psychol. Bull.*, 1957, *54*, 134-137.

Sutherland, E. H. *Principles of criminology.* (5th ed., revised by D. R. Cressey) Philadelphia: J. B. Lippincott, 1955 (originally published in 1927).

Symonds, P. M. *Adolescent phantasy.* New York: Columbia Univ. Press, 1949.

Tannenbaum, A. J. *Adolescent attitudes toward academic brilliance.* New York: Columiba Univ. Bur. of Pub., 1962.

Tannenbaum, F. *Crime and the community.* New York: Columbia Univ. Press, 1951 (originally published in 1938).

Tanner, J. M. *Growth at adolwscence.* Oxford: Blackwell Scientific Publications, Ltd., 1962.

Taylor, D. M. Changes in the self concept without psychotherapy. *J. Consult. Psychol.*, 1955, *19*, 205-209.

Terman, L. M., and Miles, C. C. *Sex and personality.* New York: McGraw-Hill, 1936.

Thompson, G. G., and Horrocks, J. E. A study of the friendship fluctuations of urban boys and girls. *J. Genet. Psychol.*, 1947, *70*, 53-63.

Thornton, A., Webb, R., and Weir, K. Student views on morality and the law. Unpublished report, Oxford University, Oxford, 1964.

Thorpe, L. P., Clark, W. W., and Tiegs, E. W. California test of personality-elementary series. Los Angeles: California Test Bureau, 1942.

Thouless, R. H. *General and social psychology.* (2nd ed.) London: Univ. Tutorial Press, 1947.

Tibbets, J. R. The role of parent-child relationships in the achievement of high school pupils. *Dissert. Abstr.*, 1955, *15*, 232.

Tiedeman, D. V., and O'Hara, R. P. Career development: Choice and adjustment. New York: College Entrance Examination Board, 1963.

Tooley, K. Personal communication, 1966.

Tuddenham, R. D. Studies in reputation: I. Sex and grade differences in school children's evaluations of their peers. *Psychol. Monogr.*, 1952, *66*, (Whole No. 333).

Tuma, E., and Livson, N. Family socioeconomic status and adolescent attitudes to authority. *Child Develpm.*, 1960, *31*, 387-399.

Ullmann, C. A. Identification of maladjusted school children. *publ. Hlth. Monogr.*, 1952, No. 7.

U. S. Census of Population: 1960 Detailed characteristics. U. S. Summary. Final report PC (1)-1D. Washington, D. C. : U. S. Government Printing Office, 1963.

U. S. Dept. of Labor, Women's Bureau. *American women.* Report of the President's Commission on the Status of Women. Washington, D. C. : The Bureau, 1963.

Veroff, J. Development and validation of a projection measure of power motivation. *J. Abnorm Soc. Psychol.*, 1957, *54*, 1-8.

Vetter, G. B. The measurement of social and political attitudes and the related personality factors. *J. abnorm. Soc. Psychol.*, 1930, *25*, 149-189. (a)

Vetter, G. B. The study of social and political opinions. *J. Abnorm. Soc. Psychol.*, 1930, *25*, 26-39. (b)

Vetter, G. B., and Green, M. Personality and group factors in the making of atheists. *J. Abnorm. Soc. Psychol.*, 1932, *27*, 179-194.

Vincent, C. E. Illegitimacy in the United States. In E. M. and S. M. Duvall (Eds.), *Sexways in fact and faith.* New York: Association Press, 1961. Pp. 139-151.

Wachner, T. S. Interpretation of spontaneous drawings and paintings. *Genet. Psychol. Monogr.*, 1946, *33*, 3-70.

Waller, W. *The rating and dating complex.* Amer. Sociol. Rev., 1937, *2*, 727-734.

Wallerstein, J. S., and Wyle, C. J. Our law-abiding lawbreakers. *Probation*, 1946, *26*, 107-112.

Walsh, A. *Self-concepts of bright boys with learning difficulties.* Columbia Univ., Teachers College, Studies in Education, 1956.

Warner, W. L. (Ed.) *Democracy in Jonesville.* New York: Harper, 1949.

Warner, W. L., Meeker, M., and Eells, K. *Social class in America.* Chicago: Science Research Associates, 1949.

Wattenberg, W. W. Church attendance and juvenile misconduct. *Sociol. soc. Res.*, 1950, *34*, 195-202.

Wattenberg, W. W., and Balistrieri, J. Automobile theft: A favored-group delinquency. *Amer. J. Sociol.*, 1952, *57*, 575-579.

Wechsler, D. *The measurement and appraisal of adult intelligence.* (4th ed.) Baltimore: Williams and Wilkins, 1958.

Weckler, N. L. Social class and school adjustment in relation to character reputation. In R. J. Havighurst and H. Taba (Eds.), *Adolescent character and personality.* New York: John Wiley, 1949.

Weinberg, S. K. Theories of crimimality and problems of prediction. *J. Crim. Law Criminol. Police Sci.*, 1954, *45*, 412-424.

394

Westley, W. A., and Elkin, F. The protective environment and adolescent socialization. *Soc. Forces,* 1957, *35,* 243-249.

Whyte, W. F. *Street corner society.* Chicago: Chicago University Press, 1943.

Williams, M. J. Personal and family problems of high school youth and their bearing upon family education needs. *Soc. Forces,* 1949, *27,* 279-285.

Wilson, A. B. Residential segregation of social classes and aspirations of high school boys. *Amer. Sociol. Rev.,* 1959, *24,* 836-345.

Winch, R. F. The theory of complementary needs in mate selection: final results on the test of the general hypothesis. *Amer. Sociol. Rev.,* 1955, *20,* 552-555.

Winter, W. D., and Prescott, J. W. A cross-validation of Starer's test of cultural symbolism. *J. Consult. Psychol.,* 1957, *21,* 22.

Witryol, S. L. Age trends in children's evaluations of teacher-approved and teacher-disapproved behavior. *Genet. Psychol. Monogr.* 1950, *41,* 271-326.

Wittels, F. The ego of the adolescent. In. K. R. Eissler (Ed.), *Searchlights on delinquency.* New York: International Universities Press, 1949.

Wright, D., and Cox, E. Religious belief and coeducation in a sample of sixth form boys and girls. *Brit. J. Soc. Clin. Psychol.,* 1967, *6,* 23-31. (a)

Wolfie, D. *America's resources of specialized talent.* New York: Harper and Brothers: 1954.

Wright, D., and Cox, E. A study of the relationship between moral judgment and religious belief in a sample of English adolescents. *J. Soc. Psychol.,* 1967, *72,* 135-144. (b)

Wylie, L. *Village in the Vaucluse.* (2nd ed.) New York: Harper, 1964.

Yamamoto, S. Sexual life of young men. *Seirigaku Kenkyu* (Physiological Studies), 1924, No. 1 & 2.

Yepsen, L. N. The reliability of Goodenough drawing test with feebleminded subjects. *J. Educ. Psychol.,* 1929, *20,* 448-451.

Zachary, C. B., and Lighty, M. *Emotions and conduct in adolescence.* New York: Appleton-Century-Crofts, 1940.

Ziblatt, D. High school extra curricular activities and political socialization. *Annals Amer. Acad. Polit. Soc. Sci.,* 1956, *361,* 20-31.